The International Institute

GW00367459

The Military Balance

1999·2000

Published by **Oxford University Press** for
The International Institute for Strategic Studies
23 Tavistock Street, London WC2E 7NQ

OXFORD
UNIVERSITY PRESS

IISS

The Military Balance 1999•2000

Published by Oxford University Press for
The International Institute for Strategic Studies
23 Tavistock Street, London WC2E 7NQ
http://www.isn.ethz.ch/iiss

Director .... Dr John Chipman

Assistant Director and Editor .... Colonel Terence Taylor

Defence Analysts
    Ground Forces .... Phillip Mitchell
    Aerospace .... Wg Cdr Andrew Brookes
    Naval Forces .... Joanna Kidd
    Defence Economist .... Digby Waller

Editorial .... Susan Bevan

Project Manager, Design and Production .... Mark Taylor

Production Assistant .... Anna Clarke
Research Assistants .... Michael Hurle, Sandra Martinez,
                                           Thomas Papworth, Todd Sample, Isabelle Williams

This publication has been prepared by the Director of The Institute and his staff, who accept full responsibility for its contents.

First published .... October 1999
ISBN 0-19-922425-0
ISSN 0459-7222

The Military Balance (ISSN 0459-7222) is published annually in October by Oxford University Press, Great Clarendon Street, Oxford OX2 6DP, UK. The 1999 annual subscription rate is: UK£75; overseas US$126.

Payment is required with all orders and subscriptions are accepted and entered by the volume (one issue). Please add sales tax to the prices quoted. Prices include air-speeded delivery to Australia, Canada, India, Japan, New Zealand and the USA. Delivery elsewhere is by surface mail. Air-mail rates are available on request. Payment may be made by cheque or Eurocheque (payable to Oxford University Press), National Girobank (account 500 1056), credit card (Mastercard, Visa, American Express, Diners', JCB), direct debit (please send for details) or UNESCO coupons. Bankers: Barclays Bank plc, PO Box 333, Oxford, UK, code 20-65-18, account 00715654. Claims for non-receipt must be made within four months of dispatch/order (whichever is later).

Please send subscription orders to the Journals Subscription Department, Oxford University Press, Great Clarendon Street, Oxford, OX2 6DP, UK *tel* +44 (0) 1865 267907 *fax* +44 (0) 1865 267485 *e-mail* jnl.orders@oup.co.uk.

In North America, *The Military Balance* is distributed by Mercury International, 365 Blair Road, Avenel, NJ 07001, USA. Periodical postage paid at Rahway, NJ, and additional entry points.

US POSTMASTER: Send address corrections to *The Military Balance*, c/o Mercury International, 365 Blair Road, Avenel, NJ 07001, USA.

Printed in Great Britain by Bell & Bain Ltd, Glasgow.

Contents

4   Preface *and* Explanatory Notes

Part I   Countries

12   United States
30   NATO and Non-NATO Europe
104   Russia
119   Middle East and North Africa
151   Central and South Asia
171   East Asia and Australasia
210   Caribbean and Latin America
244   Sub-Saharan Africa

Part II   Analyses and Tables

Analyses
280   The International Arms Trade
284   NATO Defence Industries
288   Lessons from Kosovo: Military Operational Capabilities
291   Peacekeeping Operations

Tables
300   International Comparisons of Defence Expenditure and
       Military Manpower in 1985, 1997 and 1998
306   Conventional Armed Forces in Europe (CFE) Treaty
307   Armoured Reconnaissance Vehicles
309   Ballistic and Cruise Missiles
313   Designations of Aircraft and Helicopters

Map and Figure

299   NATO Force in Kosovo (KFOR)
Inside back   Membership of European Security Organisations

Reference

319   Index of Countries and Territories
320   Index of Country Abbreviations
Detachable   Index of Abbreviations

Wallchart

Loose-leaf   The 1999 Chart of Armed Conflict

United States

NATO *and*

Russia

Middle East *and*

Central *and*

East Asia *and*

Carribean *and*

Sub-Saharan

Analyses *and*

The Military Balance is updated each year to provide an accurate assessment of the military forces and defence expenditures of 170 countries. The data in the current edition is according to IISS assessments as at 1 August 1999.

GENERAL ARRANGEMENT

Part I of *The Military Balance* comprises country entries grouped by region. Regional groupings are preceded by a short introduction describing the military issues facing the region, and significant changes in the defence economics, weapons and other military equipment holdings and acquisitions of the countries concerned. Inclusion of a country or state in *The Military Balance* does not imply legal recognition or indicate support for a particular government.

Part II contains analyses and tables. New elements in this edition include an analysis of lessons from the military campaign in Yugoslavia, and tables on armoured reconnaissance vehicles and ballistic and cruise missiles. Also new is an analysis of developments in the transatlantic defence industry, complementing the usual data on the global arms trade.

The loose wall-map is updated from last year to show data on recent and current armed conflicts, including fatalities and costs.

USING THE MILITARY BALANCE

The country entries in *The Military Balance* are a quantitative assessment of the personnel strengths and equipment holdings of the world's armed forces. The strengths of forces and numbers of weapons held are based on the most accurate data available, or, failing that, on the best estimate that can be made with reasonable confidence. The data presented each year reflect judgements based on information available to the IISS at the time the book is compiled. Where information differs from previous editions, this is mainly because of substantive changes in national forces, but it is sometimes because the IISS has reassessed the evidence supporting past entries. An attempt is made to distinguish between these reasons for change in the text that introduces each regional section, but care must be taken in constructing time-series comparisons from information given in successive editions.

In order to interpret the data in the country entries correctly, it is essential to read the explanatory notes beginning on page 5.

The large quantity of data in *The Military Balance* has been compressed into a portable volume by extensive employment of abbreviations. An essential tool is therefore the alphabetical index of abbreviations, which has until this year occupied the final two pages of the book. For greater ease of reference, we have this year transferred the index onto a laminated card that may be detached and used as a bookmark. Also new this year, country abbreviations are shown at the head of each country entry in Part I.

ATTRIBUTION AND ACKNOWLEDGEMENTS

The International Institute for Strategic Studies owes no allegiance to any government, group of governments, or any political or other organisation. Its assessments are its own, based on the material available to it from a wide variety of sources. The cooperation of governments has been sought and, in many cases, received. However, some data in *The Military Balance* are estimates. Care is taken to ensure that these are as accurate and free from bias as possible. The Institute owes a considerable debt to a number of its own members, consultants and all those who helped compile and check material. The Director and staff of the Institute assume full responsibility for the data and judgements in this book. Comments and suggestions on the data presented are welcomed. Suggestions on the style and method of presentation are also much appreciated.

Readers may use data from *The Military Balance* without applying for permission from the Institute on condition that the IISS and *The Military Balance* are cited as the source in any published work. However, applications to reproduce portions of text, complete country entries or complete tables of *The Military Balance* must be referred to the publishers. Prior to publication, applications should be addressed to: Journals Rights and Permissions, Oxford University Press, Great Clarendon Street, Oxford OX2 6DP, UK, with a copy to the Editor of *The Military Balance.*

Explanatory Notes

ABBREVIATIONS AND DEFINITIONS

Abbreviations are used throughout to save space and avoid repetition. The abbreviations may have both singular or plural meanings; for example, 'elm' = 'element' or 'elements'. The qualification 'some' means *up to*, while 'about' means *the total could be higher than given*. In financial data, '$' refers to US dollars unless otherwise stated; billion (bn) signifies 1,000 million (m). Footnotes particular to a country entry or table are indicated by letters, while those that apply throughout the book are marked by symbols (* for training aircraft counted by the IISS as combat-capable, and † where serviceability of equipment is in doubt). A full list of abbreviations appears on the insert.

COUNTRY ENTRIES

Information on each country is shown in a standard format, although the differing availability of information results in some variations. Each entry includes economic, demographic and military data. Military data include manpower, length of conscript service, outline organisation, number of formations and units and an inventory of the major equipment of each service. This is followed, where applicable, by a description of the deployment of each service. Details of national forces stationed abroad and of foreign-stationed forces are also given.

GENERAL MILITARY DATA

Manpower

The 'Active' total comprises all servicemen and women on full-time duty (including conscripts and long-term assignments from the Reserves). Under the heading 'Terms of Service', only the length of conscript service is shown; where service is voluntary there is no entry. 'Reserve' describes formations and units not fully manned or operational in peacetime, but which can be mobilised by recalling reservists in an emergency. Unless otherwise indicated, the 'Reserves' entry includes all reservists committed to rejoining the armed forces in an emergency, except when national reserve service obligations following conscription last almost a lifetime. *The Military Balance* bases its estimates of effective reservist strengths on the numbers available within five years of completing full-time service, unless there is good evidence that obligations are enforced for longer. Some countries have more than one category of 'Reserves', often kept at varying degrees of readiness. Where possible, these differences are denoted using the national descriptive title, but always under the heading of 'Reserves' to distinguish them from full-time active forces.

Other Forces

Many countries maintain paramilitary forces whose training, organisation, equipment and control suggest they may be used to support, or replace, regular military forces. These are listed, and their roles described, after the military forces of each country. Their manpower is not normally included in the Armed Forces totals at the start of each entry. Home Guard units are counted as paramilitary. Where paramilitary groups are not on full-time active duty, '(R)' is added after the title to indicate that they have reserve status. When internal opposition forces are armed and appear to pose a significant threat to a state's security, their details are listed separately after national paramilitary forces.

Equipment

Quantities are shown by function and type, and represent what are believed to be total holdings, including active and reserve operational and training units and 'in store' stocks. Inventory totals for missile systems (such as surface-to-surface missiles (SSM), surface-to-air missiles (SAM) and anti-tank guided weapons (ATGW)) relate to launchers and not to missiles.

   Stocks of equipment held in reserve and not assigned to either active or reserve units are listed as 'in store'. However, aircraft in excess of unit establishment holdings, held to allow for repair and modification or immediate replacement, are not shown 'in store'. This accounts for apparent disparities between unit strengths and aircraft inventory strengths.

Operational Deployments

Where deployments are overseas, *The Military Balance* lists permanent bases and does not normally list short-term operational deployments, particularly where military operations are in progress. An exception is made in the case of peacekeeping operations. The contribution or deployment of forces to peacekeeping operations is shown on pp. 291–299. Recent developments are also described in the text for each regional section.

GROUND FORCES

The national designation is normally used for army formations. The term 'regiment' can be misleading. It can mean essentially a brigade of all arms; a grouping of battalions of a single arm; or (as in some instances in the UK) a battalion-sized unit. The sense intended is indicated in each case. Where there is no standard organisation, the intermediate levels of command are shown as headquarters (HQs), followed by the total numbers of units that could be allocated to them. Where a unit's title overstates its real capability, the title is given in inverted commas, with an estimate given in parentheses of the comparable unit size typical of countries with substantial armed forces. Guidelines for unit and formation strengths are: **Company** 100–200 • **Battalion** 500–800 • **Brigade (Regiment)** 3,000–5,000 • **Division** 15,000–20,000 • **Corps (Army)** 60,000–80,000.

Equipment

The Military Balance uses the following definitions of equipment:

Main Battle Tank (MBT) An armoured, tracked combat vehicle, weighing at least 16.5 metric tonnes unladen, that may be armed with a 360° traverse gun of at least 75mm calibre. Any new-wheeled combat vehicles that meet the latter two criteria will be considered MBTs.
Armoured Combat Vehicle (ACV) A self-propelled vehicle with armoured protection and cross-

country capability. ACVs include:

Heavy Armoured Combat Vehicle (HACV) An armoured combat vehicle weighing more than six metric tonnes unladen, with an integral/organic direct-fire gun of at least 75mm (which does not fall within the definitions of APC, AIFV or MBT). *The Military Balance* does not list HACVs separately, but under their equipment type (light tank, reconnaissance or assault gun), and where appropriate annotates them as HACV.

Armoured Infantry Fighting Vehicle (AIFV) An armoured combat vehicle designed and equipped to transport an infantry squad, armed with an integral/organic cannon of at least 20mm calibre. Variants of AIFVs are also included and indicated as such.

Armoured Personnel Carrier (APC) A lightly armoured combat vehicle, designed and equipped to transport an infantry squad and armed with integral/organic weapons of less than 20mm calibre. Variants of APCs converted for other uses (such as weapons platforms, command posts and communications vehicles) are included and indicated as such.

Artillery A weapon with a calibre of 100mm and above, capable of engaging ground targets by delivering primarily indirect fire. The definition covers guns, howitzers, gun/howitzers, multiple-rocket launchers and mortars.

Military Formation Strengths

The manpower strength, equipment holdings and organisation of formations such as brigades and divisions differ widely from country to country. Where possible, the normal composition of formations is given in parentheses. It should be noted that where both divisions and brigades are listed, only separate brigades are counted and not those included in divisions.

NAVAL FORCES

Categorisation is based on operational role, weapon fit and displacement. Ship classes are identified by the name of the first ship of that class, except where a class is recognised by another name (such as *Udalay, Petya*). Where the class is based on a foreign design or has been acquired from another country, the original class name is added in parentheses. Each class is given an acronym. All such designators are included in the list of abbreviations.

The term 'ship' refers to vessels with over 1,000 tonnes full-load displacement that are more than 60 metres in overall length; vessels of lesser displacement, but of 16m or more overall length, are termed 'craft'. Vessels of less than 16m overall length are not included. The term 'commissioning' of a ship is used to mean the ship has completed fitting out and initial sea trials, and has a naval crew; operational training may not have been completed, but otherwise the ship is available for service. 'Decommissioning' means that a ship has been removed from operational duty and the bulk of its naval crew transferred. Removing equipment and stores and dismantling weapons, however, may not have started. Where known, ships in long-term refit are shown as such.

Definitions

To aid comparison between fleets, the following definitions, which do not necessarily conform to national definitions, are used:

Submarines All vessels equipped for military operations and designed to operate primarily below the surface. Those vessels with submarine-launched ballistic missiles are listed separately under 'Strategic Nuclear Forces'.

Principal Surface Combatant This term includes all surface ships with both 1,000 tonnes full-load displacement and a weapons system for other than self-protection. All such ships are assumed to have an anti-surface ship capability. They comprise: aircraft carriers (defined below); cruisers (over 8,000 tonnes) and destroyers (less than 8,000 tonnes), both of which normally have an anti-air role and may also have an anti-submarine capability; and frigates (less than 8,000 tonnes) which normally have an anti-submarine role. Only ships with a flight deck that extends beyond two-thirds of the vessel's length are classified as aircraft carriers. Ships with shorter flight decks are shown as helicopter carriers.

Patrol and Coastal Combatants These are ships and craft whose primary role is protecting a state's sea approaches and coastline. Included are corvettes (600–1,000 tonnes carrying weapons systems for other than self-protection); missile craft (with permanently fitted missile-launcher ramps and control equipment); and torpedo craft (with an anti-surface ship capability). Ships and craft that fall outside these definitions are classified as 'patrol'.

Mine Warfare This term covers surface vessels configured primarily for mine laying or mine countermeasures (such as mine-hunters, minesweepers or dual-capable vessels). A further classification divides both coastal and patrol combatants and mine-warfare vessels into offshore (over 600 tonnes), coastal (300–600 tonnes) and inshore (less than 300 tonnes).

Amphibious This term includes ships specifically procured and employed to disembark troops and their equipment onto unprepared beachheads by means such as landing craft or helicopters, or directly supporting amphibious operations. The term 'Landing Ship' (as opposed to 'Landing Craft') refers to vessels capable of an ocean passage that can deliver their troops and equipment in a fit state to fight. Vessels with an amphibious capability but not assigned to amphibious duties are not included. Amphibious craft are listed at the end of each entry.

Support and Miscellaneous This term covers essentially non-military support, and the inclusion of these vessels provides an indication of the operational capability of naval forces in terms of range and the ability to sustain operations.

Weapons Systems Weapons are listed in the order in which they contribute to a ship's primary operational role. Significant weapons relating to the ship's secondary role are added after the word 'plus'. Short-range self-defence weapons are not listed. To merit inclusion, a surface-to-air missile system must have an anti-missile range of 10km or more and guns must be of 100mm bore or greater. Exceptions may be made in the case of some minor combatants with a primary gun armament of a lesser calibre.

Aircraft All armed aircraft, including anti-submarine warfare and maritime-reconnaissance aircraft, are included as combat aircraft in naval inventories.

Organisations Naval groupings such as fleets and squadrons frequently change and are often temporary; organisations are shown only where it is meaningful.

AIR FORCES

The term 'combat aircraft' refers to aircraft normally equipped to deliver air-to-air or air-to-surface ordnance. The 'combat' totals include aircraft in operational conversion units whose main role is weapons training, and training aircraft of the same type as those in front-line squadrons that are assumed to be available for operations at short notice. Training aircraft considered to be combat-capable are marked with an asterisk (*). Armed maritime aircraft are included in combat aircraft totals. Operational groupings of air forces are shown where known. Squadron aircraft strengths vary with aircraft types and from country to country.

Definitions

Different countries often use the same basic aircraft in different roles; the key to determining these roles lies mainly in aircrew training. In *The Military Balance* the following definitions are used as a guide:

Fixed Wing Aircraft

Fighter This term is used to describe aircraft with the weapons, avionics and performance capacity for aerial combat. Multi-role aircraft are shown as fighter ground attack (FGA), fighter, reconnaissance and so on, according to the role in which they are deployed.

Bombers These aircraft are categorised according to their designed range and payload as follows:

Long-range Capable of delivering a weapons payload of more than 10,000kg over an unrefuelled radius of action of over 5,000km;

Medium-range Capable of delivering weapons of more than 10,000kg over an unrefuelled radius of action of between 1,000km and 5,000km;

Short-range Capable of delivering a weapons payload of more than 10,000kg over an unrefuelled radius of action of less than 1,000km.

A few bombers with the radius of action described above, but designed to deliver a payload of less than 10,000kg, and which do not fall into the category of FGA, are described as **light bombers**.

Helicopters

Armed Helicopters This term is used to cover helicopters equipped to deliver ordnance, including for anti-submarine warfare. They may be further defined as:

Attack Helicopters with an integrated fire control and aiming system designed to deliver anti-armour, air-to-ground or air-to-air weapons;

Combat Support Helicopters equipped with area suppression or self-defence weapons, but without an integrated fire control and aiming system;

Assault Armed helicopters designed to deliver troops to the battlefield.

Transport Helicopters The term describes unarmed helicopters designed to transport personnel or cargo in support of military operations.

ARMS ORDERS AND DELIVERIES

Tables in the regional texts show arms orders and deliveries listed by country buyer for the past and current years, together with country supplier and delivery dates, if known. Every effort has been made to ensure accuracy, but some transactions may not be fulfilled or may differ from those reported.

DEFENCE ECONOMICS

Country entries in **Part I** show defence expenditure, selected economic performance indicators and demographic aggregates. **Part II**, *Analyses and Tables*, contains an international comparison of defence expenditure and military manpower giving expenditure figures for the last two years against a bench-mark year in constant US dollars. The aim is to provide an accurate measure of military expenditure and of the allocation of economic resources to defence. All country entries are subject to revision each year, as new information, particularly that regarding defence expenditure, becomes available. The information is necessarily selective. A wider range of statistics is available to IISS members on request.

In **Part I**, individual country entries typically show economic performance over the past two years, and current-year demographic data. Where these data are unavailable, information from the last available year is provided. Defence expenditure is generally shown for the past two years where official outlays are available, or sufficient data for reliable estimates exist. Current-year defence budgets and, where available, defence budgets for the following year are also listed. Foreign Military Assistance (FMA) data cover outlays for the past year, and budgetary estimates for the current and subsequent years. Unless otherwise indicated, the US is the donor country. All financial data in the country entries are shown both in national currency and US dollars at current-year, not constant, prices. US dollar conversions are generally, but not invariably, calculated from the exchange rates listed in the entry. In a few cases, notably Russia and China, purchasing-power-parity (PPP) rates are used in preference to official or market-exchange rates.

Definitions of terms

To avoid errors in interpretation, an understanding of the definition of defence expenditure is important. Both the UN and NATO have developed standardised definitions, but in many cases countries prefer to use their own definitions (which are not in the public domain). For consistency, the IISS uses the NATO definition (which is also the most comprehensive) throughout.

In *The Military Balance*, military expenditure is defined as the cash outlays of central or federal government to meet the costs of national armed forces. The term 'armed forces' includes strategic, land, naval, air, command, administration and support forces. It also includes paramilitary forces such as the *gendarmerie*, customs service and border guard if these are trained in military tactics, equipped as a military force and operate under military authority in the event of war. Defence expenditures are reported in four categories: Operating Costs; Procurement and Construction; Research and Development (R&D); and Other Expenditure. Operating Costs include: salaries and pensions for military and civilian personnel; the cost of maintaining and training units, service organisations, headquarters and support elements; and the cost of servicing and repairing military equipment and infrastructure. Procurement and Construction expenditure covers national equipment and infrastructure spending, as well as common infrastructure programmes. It also includes financial contributions to multinational military organisations, host-nation support in cash and in kind, and payments made to other countries under bilateral agreements. FMA counts as expenditure by the donor, and not the recipient, government. R&D is defence expenditure up to the point at which new equipment can be put in service, regardless of whether new equipment is actually procured. The fact that the IISS definitions of military expenditure are generally more inclusive than those applied by national governments and the standardised UN format means that our calculated expenditure figures may be higher than national and UN equivalents.

The issue of transparency in reporting military expenditures is a fundamental one. Only a minority of the governments of UN member-states report defence expenditures to their electorates, the UN, the International Monetary Fund (IMF) and other multilateral organisations. In the case of governments with a proven record of transparency, official figures generally conform to a standardised definition of defence expenditure, and consistency problems are not usually a major issue. Where these conditions of transparency and consistency are met, the IISS cites official defence budgets and outlays as reported by national governments, NATO, the UN, the Organisation for Security and Cooperation in Europe (OSCE) and the IMF. On the other hand, some governments do not report defence expenditures until several years have elapsed, while others understate these expenditures in their reports. Where these reporting conditions exist, *The Military Balance* gives IISS estimates of military expenditures for the country concerned. Official defence budgets are also shown, in order to provide a measure of the discrepancy between official figures and what the IISS estimates real defence outlays to be. In these cases *The Military Balance* does not cite official defence expenditures (actual outlays), as these rarely differ significantly from official budgetary data. The IISS defence-expenditure estimates are based on information from several sources, and are marked 'ε'. The most frequent instances of budgetary manipulation or falsification typically involve equipment procurement, R&D, defence industrial investment, covert weapons programmes, pensions for retired military and civilian personnel, paramilitary forces, and non-budgetary sources of revenue for the military arising from ownership of industrial, property and land assets.

The principal sources for economic statistics cited in the country entries are the IMF, the Organisation for Economic Cooperation and Development (OECD), the World Bank and three regional banks (the Inter-American, Asian and African Development Banks). For some countries basic economic data are difficult to obtain. This is the case in a few former command economies in transition and countries currently or recently involved in armed conflict. The Gross Domestic Product (GDP) figures are nominal (current) values at market prices, but GDP per capita figures are nominal values at PPP prices. GDP growth is real not nominal growth, and inflation is the year-on-year change in consumer prices. Two different measures of debt are used to distinguish between OECD and non-OECD countries: for OECD countries, debt is gross public debt (or, more exactly, general government gross financial liabilities) expressed as a proportion of GDP. For all other countries, debt is gross foreign debt denominated in current US dollars. Dollar exchange rates relate to the last two years plus the current year. Values for the past two years are annual averages, while current values are the latest monthly value.

Calculating exchange rates

Typically, but not invariably, the exchange rates shown in the country entries are also used to calculate GDP and defence-expenditure dollar conversions. Where they are not used, it is because the use of exchange rate dollar conversions can misrepresent both GDP and defence expenditure. This may arise when: the official exchange rate is overvalued (as with some Latin American and African countries); relatively large currency fluctuations occur over the short-to-medium term; or when a substantial medium-to-long-term discrepancy between the exchange rate and the dollar PPP exists. Where exchange rate fluctuations are the problem, dollar values are converted using lagged exchange rates (generally by no more than six months). The GDP estimates of the Inter-American Development Bank, usually lower than those derived from official exchange rates, are used for Latin American countries. For former communist countries, PPP rather than market exchange rates are sometimes used for dollar conversions of both GDP and defence expenditures, and this is marked.

The arguments for using PPP are strongest for Russia and China. Both the UN and IMF have issued caveats concerning the reliability of official economic statistics on transitional economies, particularly those of Russia and some Eastern European and Central Asian countries. Non-reporting, lags in the publication of current statistics and frequent revisions of recent data (not always accompanied by timely revision of previously published figures in the same series) pose transparency and consistency problems. Another problem arises with certain transitional economies whose productive capabilities are similar to those of developed economies, but where cost and price structures are often much lower than world levels. PPP dollar values are used in preference to market exchange rates in cases where using such exchange rates may result in excessively low dollar-conversion values for GDP and defence expenditure.

Demographic data

Population aggregates are based on the most recent official census data or, in their absence, demographic statistics taken from *World Population Projections* published annually by the World Bank. Data on ethnic and religious minorities are also provided under country entries where a related security issue exists.

MILITARY CAPABILITY

In February 1999, well before the crisis in Kosovo led to the NATO air campaign and the deployment of more forces to the Balkans, US President Bill Clinton, in the administration's defence budget for 2000, called for an increase in defence spending of some $112 billion for the period 2000–05. While this is a modest rise in relation to the overall size of the budget, it reverses years of decline. A significant proportion of the extra money is for equipment modernisation, readiness and unforeseen contingencies, but there is also an important recognition that more resources need to be devoted to recruiting and retaining military personnel in both the active and reserve armed forces. The budget for 2000 contains the largest military pay increase since 1982. The deployment of US forces as part of the NATO-led peacekeeping operation in Kosovo (KFOR) means that the military is faced with yet another long-term deployment overseas. The plan to 'put people first', as Defense Secretary William Cohen described it in his 1999 budget statement, accounted for $36.5bn of the requested $112bn increase.

The biggest programmes in dollar terms are still in aviation. With procurement of more modern weapons set to reach nearly $62bn in 2001, there is little doubt that the US will retain, and increase, its lead in the quality of deployed weapons and military technology. Programmes covered by the planned expenditure include:

Aviation

- Air capability modernisation involves the largest single acquisition programme, the Joint Strike Fighter (JSF). The programme's object is a family of aircraft, with variants configured to meet different requirements. The new aircraft will replace the F-16 in the Air Force, the F/A-18C in the Navy, and the F/A-18C/D and AV-8B for the Marines. Plans for the JSF to continue in its development phase until 2001, with delivery to start in 2005, are unchanged.
- The F-22 is due to replace the F-15C/D in the air superiority role, but it is also intended to have an air-to-ground capability. If the project goes forward, F-22 production is planned to build up to 36 aircraft per year by 2004. However, Congress has expressed concern over costs, which are reportedly running at up to $165 million per aircraft, and has deleted funds for production from the 2000 budget request. There have been calls to end the programme and divert the savings to the JSF and to modernising the existing fleet.
- The enlargement of the B-2 bomber force continues, and the 509th Bomber Wing is due to have 20 operational aircraft by July 2000, at a cost of about $1.3bn per aircraft.
- The mid-1999 inventory of four E-8Cs, the Joint Surveillance Target Attack Radar System (JSTARS), will increase to 14 by 2003, which will significantly enhance the battle management capabilities of the armed forces as a whole.
- The Navy's F/A-18E/F will provide much greater survivability and payload over earlier F/A-18 models. The new model is expected to be in service by 2001 and is intended to fill the capability gap until the JSF comes into service.
- Strategic airlift will be enhanced by completing the purchase of 120 C-17s by 2003, with further acquisitions planned for 2004 and 2005. The C-5 transport and the KC-135 will benefit from major avionics upgrades and other enhancements.

Land Forces

- Modernisation of land forces includes upgrades of primary weapons systems such as the *Abrams* tank, the *Bradley* armoured fighting vehicle and *Apache Longbow* helicopter. Major development programmes include the *Comanche* helicopter and *Crusader* artillery system. The Marine Corps will benefit from the introduction of V-22 *Osprey* tilt-rotor aircraft, the Advanced Amphibious Assault Vehicle, and upgrades of utility and attack helicopters.

Navy

- Planned modernisation of naval forces continues to include procurement of the DDG-21 destroyer (equipped with a new land-attack missile), the LPD-17 amphibious transport dock ship, the T-ADC (X) logistics-support ship, and the new nuclear-powered attack submarine (NSSN) (*Virginia* class), which is to be brought into service in 2004. The production rate after 2005 is not yet decided; it could be two or three per year to bring total SSN strength to 50. The ninth and last *Nimitz* class aircraft carrier (CVN-77) is to be delivered in 2003. The programmes for the next generation aircraft carrier (CVX) and destroyer, equipped with a new land-attack cruise missile, continue. The CVX is not scheduled to enter service until 2015. As planned, seven of the 19 *Bob Hope* and *Watson* class heavy-lift ships for rapid transport of army divisions will be in service by the end of 1999.

Reserve Forces

The upgrading of reserve forces and their integration with the active component continues, and is becoming even more important in view of increasing domestic and overseas commitments. Over $1bn was added to the 2000 defence budget specifically for activities such as reserve support for combatant commands and programmes to encourage the backing of civilian employers, which is vital if there is to be increased use of National Guard and reserve personnel. The 2000 budget plans strongly support the larger part that Reserve components are to play in reinforcing the armed forces' capability to fulfil their role of bolstering the civilian authorities' response to domestic incidents involving weapons of mass destruction (WMD).

Missile Defence

Increasing concern about ballistic-missile threats to the continental US from, for example, North Korea, has increased the emphasis on national missile defence (NMD), and the 2000 budget increases NMD funding by $3.9bn to $10.5bn over the six years 1999–2005. The total includes funding for NMD deployment, but a decision on deployment is not expected until June 2000 when it is likely to be based primarily on the maturity of the technology demonstrated during development and testing. The aim of the envisaged NMD system is the defence of all 50 US states against a limited strategic ballistic-missile attack mounted by a state with modest capabilities. The hope is that such a system would also provide some capability against a limited accidental or unauthorised launch of strategic ballistic missiles from a state with a full range of capabilities.

Meanwhile, systems under the continuing Theater Missile Defence (TMD) programmes are aimed at countering threats against US forces deployed overseas. Lower-tier programmes to defend against shorter-range missiles include the *Patriot* Advanced Capability (PAC) 3 and Navy Area systems, while the main upper-tier programmes are the Theater High Altitude Area Defense (THAAD) and the Navy Theater Wide systems. An airborne laser system is being developed to protect against shorter-range missiles during their boost phase.

Strategic Weapons

As Russia has not yet ratified the Strategic Arms Reduction Treaty (START) II, the US is making a modest budget provision of $51m against the possibility that START I levels of strategic forces will be maintained for longer than expected. If Russia ratifies START II, and the implementation process begins, as amended by the 1997 Helsinki Summit letters, accountable warheads will be reduced to 3,000–3,500 by the end of 2007 with no more than 1,750 warheads carried on submarine-launched ballistic missiles (SLBMs), and with the strategic nuclear-delivery vehicles to be dismantled under START II being deactivated by 31 December 2003. This timetable technically still stands, but its implementation will be put in doubt if Russian ratification is delayed much beyond the end of 1999. The Helsinki Summit letters also envisaged a START III process that would reduce warheads to overall limits of 2,000–2,500. The plan was to begin these negotiations once Russia ratified START II.

The numbers of delivery vehicles for strategic nuclear weapons according to the declarations made under the START I Memoranda of Understanding and the 1 January 1999 Lisbon Protocols are as shown in Table 1 below.

Table 1 **Aggregate numbers of strategic offensive delivery vehicles**						
As declared on 1 January 1999		**US**	**Russia**	**Belarus**	**Kazakstan**	**Ukraine**	**Totals**
	ICBM	701	756	0	0	44[1]	1,501
	SLBM	464	592	0	0	0	1,056
	bbr	315	74	0	0	43	432

Note [1]There are no warheads with these missiles.

Cooperative Threat Reduction Programme

At a bilateral meeting on 15–16 June 1999, the US and Russia signed a protocol to continue the Cooperative Threat Reduction (CTR) programme until June 2006. Projects under way at that date included:

- Accelerating the elimination of Russian missiles, bombers, submarines and land-based missile launchers to meet the START I requirements;
- Improving the safety, security, control and accounting of nuclear warheads in transport and at all of Russia's nuclear-weapon storage sites;
- Ending Russia's production of weapon-grade plutonium;
- Building a facility for storing nuclear material from up to 12,500 dismantled nuclear warheads;
- Assisting Russia to implement the 1993 Chemical Weapons Convention by dismantling former chemical weapon production facilities and helping to destroy chemical weapons.

The CTR programme, also known as the 'Nunn–Lugar' programme after its original sponsoring US senators, also operates in other former Soviet Union countries.

DEFENCE SPENDING

Financial Year 1999

The administration's budget request for Financial Year (FY) 1999 asked for $270.6bn for national defence. Congress added supplemental defence appropriations as it had in the three previous years, and the addition of $5.6bn resulted in an increased budget authorisation of $276.2bn. Major changes included additional funds for readiness, for contingency operations in Bosnia, and for intelligence and Year 2000 information technology programmes, all under the Operations and Maintenance (O&M) budget, and for research and development (R&D) on ballistic-missile defence.

Financial Year 2000

The Clinton administration's FY2000 budget request for national defence, details of which were released on 1 February 1999, contains the first sustained, long-term increase in defence funding since the Cold War, with proposals to make an additional $112bn available to the DoD in FY2000–2005. The FY2000 request is for $280.8bn, up $10.2bn from the FY1999 request and up $4.9bn from last year's projection for FY2000. The $112bn increase, made up of an $84bn rise from FY1999 six-year spending plans, and $28bn in savings from lower inflation, lower fuel prices and other adjustments, is modest in real terms since most of the new money simply reverses the large cuts in previous years' plans, and defence spending will continue to decline until 2001. From 2001–05, the defence budget will increase by only 4.5% in real terms overall, or less than 1% each year. This compares with a decline in US defence spending of 37% in real terms between 1985 and 2000.

Table 2 National Defense Budget Authority, FY1998–2005

(US$m)	1998	1999	2000	2001	2002	2003	2004	2005
		Estimate	Projection	Projection	Projection	Projection	Projection	Projection
Military Personnel	69,822	70,932	73,724	76,307	78,417	80,914	83,748	86,700
O&M	97,214	98,058	103,535	103,854	104,964	107,760	111,178	114,400
Procurement	44,772	48,951	53,021	61,783	62,297	66,552	69,211	75,100
RDT&E	37,090	36,635	34,374	34,290	34,680	34,518	35,015	34,200
Military Construction	5,463	5,079	2,297	7,079	4,246	4,342	4,452	4,800
Family Housing	3,829	3,580	3,141	3,827	3,614	3,744	3,851	3,900
Other incl Net Receipts	346	-672	-2,867	-771	51	869	104	-200
Total DoD	258,536	262,563	267,225	286,369	288,269	298,699	307,559	318,900
Department of Energy (defence-related)	11,704	12,520	12,352	12,912	12,900	12,874	12,835	12,825
Other (defence-related)	1,014	1,147	1,223	1,230	1,242	1,251	1,263	1,275
Total National Defence	271,254	276,230	280,800	300,511	302,411	312,824	321,657	333,000
Real growth per annum (%)	-1.4	-0.4	-0.5	4.5	-1.8	1.0	0.2	1.0

About $37bn of the $112bn additional funding is allocated to personnel budgets for measures to support recruitment and retention. The six-year budget plan includes a 4.4% pay increase (the largest military pay-rise since 1982) and improved retirement benefits for long-service personnel. To improve readiness, there is increased funding under O&M budgets for training (including more flying hours), maintenance and spare parts. Procurement budgets are set to exceed the target levels of the 1997 Quadrennial Defense Review (QDR), which planned for spending on equipment to rise to $60bn by 2001. The FY2000–05 projection sets procurement at $53bn in FY2000, rising to $61.8bn in FY2001, and to $75.1bn in FY2005.

Ballistic Missile Defence
The FY2000 budget request for R&D in ballistic missile defence (BMD) is $4.2bn, while substantial new resources are requested for the NMD programme. Total NMD funding for FY1999–2005 is $10.5bn, an increase of $6.6bn over previously planned levels, including $600m supplemental funding in FY1999 and $1.287bn in FY2000. The FY2000 request for TMD is $3bn.

Funding for Contingency Operations
The FY2000 budget request includes $1.8bn for Bosnia-related and $1.1bn for Iraq-related operations. Neither the FY1999 nor the FY2000 budget requests included funding for contingencies arising from the Kosovo crisis. A supplementary FY1999 budget request was presented to Congress in April 1999 asking for an additional $6bn for Kosovo-related operations. This was mostly for the DoD, including $287m for Kosovo deployment and $3bn for continuing air operations over six months and other support costs for US forces around Kosovo. For munitions, $698m was requested for such items as upgrades and replenishment of air- and sea-launched *Tomahawk* cruise missiles and winding up production of the Joint Direct Attack Munition (JDAM), and $850m as a readiness and contingency

reserve fund. The request also included an additional $274m for air operations over Iraq since December 1998, including *Operation Desert Fox*, and additional funds for DoD costs related to disaster relief following Hurricane *Mitch* in Central America and Hurricane *Georges* in the Caribbean. In the event, Congress increased the FY1999 supplementary allocation to $15bn, including $12bn for the Kosovo air campaign and related costs.

Foreign Military Assistance

The FY2000 request for International Security Assistance (funded under the US Agency for International Development, now part of the State Department) is $6.2bn, compared to $6bn in FY1999. Israel and Egypt continue to take most of the military equipment grant allocation. Israel will receive $1.92bn in FY2000, an increase of $120m, while Egypt will get $1.3bn as in previous years. The economic assistance allocation to both countries is cut: Israel's to $930m from $1.08bn and Egypt's to $715m from $775m. Jordan's allocation of military aid rises from $45m to $75m in FY2000. Under the Wye Peace Accord programme, the administration is requesting that the three parties, Israel, Jordan and the Palestinian National Authority (PNA), receive a total of $1.9bn in FY1999–2001. Israel is set to receive $1.2bn, the PNA $400m and Jordan $200m, provided that Israel carries out its troop withdrawal commitments under the Accord.

Cooperative Threat Reduction Assistance

The FY2000–2005 plan calls for $4.2bn to assist threat-reduction programmes in the countries of the Former Soviet Union. This includes $2.9bn for the DoD's share of the CTR programme, of which $476m is for FY2000. The Department of Energy (DoE)'s Former Soviet Union-related WMD programmes receive $276m in FY2000, including $145m (1999 $100m) for International Materials Protection Control and Accounting (MPC&A). There is also a significant increase in State Department funding (from $41m to $251m) for programmes aiming to prevent the proliferation of WMD-related expertise and technology.

Table 3 FY1998–2000 Budget Authority for Threat Reduction Assistance in the Former Soviet Union

(US$m)	FY1998	FY1999 Estimate	FY2000 Request
Department of Defense (DoD)	382	440	476
Department of Energy (DoE)	212	237	276
State Department	20	41	251
Total	614	718	1,003

Table 4 US government programmes for nuclear non-proliferation assistance to the Former Soviet Union

Programme	Year commenced	US Agency funding	Funding received to 1998 (US$m)
Initiatives for Proliferation Prevention	1994	DoE	114
Cooperative Threat Reduction [1]	1992	DoD	1,346
Defense Enterprise Fund	1994	DoD	67
Materials Control, Protection and Accounting	1994	DoE	428
International Science and Technology Center	1994	State Department	215
Nuclear Cities Initiative [2]	1998	DoE	0

Notes   [1] Figures for CTR exclude chain-of-custody activities, arctic nuclear waste, and funds to other agencies for defence conversion.
[2] The DoE plans to spend about $600m on the Nuclear Cities Initiative over the next five years.

Table 5 US National Defense Budget Function and other selected budgets, 1992–2004

(US$bn)	National Defense Budget Function[1]		Department of Defense		Atomic Energy Defense Activities	International Security Assistance	Veterans Administration	Total Federal Government Expenditure[2]	Total Federal Budget Deficit[3]
FY	(BA)	(outlay)	(BA)	(outlay)	(outlay)	(outlay)	(outlay)	(outlay)	(outlay)
1992	295.1	302.3	282.1	274.7	10.6	7.5	34.1	1,042.7	386.4
1993	281.1	292.4	267.2	271.4	11.0	7.6	35.7	1,060.9	355.4
1994	263.3	282.3	251.4	265.8	11.9	6.6	37.6	1,073.5	298.5
1995	266.3	273.6	255.7	258.4	11.8	5.3	37.9	1,102.0	263.2
1996	266.0	266.0	254.4	253.2	11.6	4.6	37.0	1,139.2	222.1
1997	270.3	271.7	258.0	258.3	11.3	4.6	39.3	1,158.2	147.9
1998	271.3	270.2	258.5	256.1	11.3	5.1	41.8	1,205.5	92.0
1999	276.2	277.6	262.6	263.6	12.0	5.7	43.5	1,257.1	110.5
2000[R]	280.8	274.8	267.2	260.8	12.1	5.6	44.0	1,268.2	67.5
2001[P]	300.5	282.7	286.4	268.6	12.3	5.8	45.3	1,278.7	52.7
2002[P]	302.4	292.8	288.3	278.3	12.5	5.8	46.0	1,288.6	17.3
2003[P]	312.8	304.7	298.7	290.2	12.5	5.9	46.8	1,336.3	23.9
2004[P]	321.7	314.4	308.6	300.0	12.5	6.0	47.9	1,378.5	4.0

FY = Fiscal Year (1 October–30 September), [R] = Request, [P] = Projection

Notes [1] The National Defense Budget Function subsumes funding for the DoD, the DoE Atomic Energy Defense Activities and some smaller support agencies (including Federal Emergency Management and Selective Service System). It does not include funding for International Security Assistance (under International Affairs), the Veterans Administration, the US Coast Guard (Department of Transport), nor for the National Aeronautics and Space Administration (NASA). Funding for civil projects administered by the DoD is excluded from the figures cited here.
[2] The figures for Federal Government Expenditure and Federal Budget Deficit differ from previous figures cited in *The Military Balance* because US Government Trust Funds are no longer included. If Trust Funds were included, net US Government expenditure would show a surplus rather than deficit from 1998 [+$69.0bn] through to 2004 [+$207.6bn].
[3] Early in each calendar year, the US government presents its defence budget to Congress for the next fiscal year which begins on 1 October. It also presents its Future Years' Defense Program (FYDP), which covers the next fiscal year plus the following five. Until approved by Congress, the Budget is called the Budget Request; after approval, it becomes the Budget Authority.
[4] Definitions of US budget terms: *Authorisation* establishes or maintains a government programme or agency by defining its scope. Authorising legislation is normally a prerequisite for appropriations and may set specific limits on the amount that may be appropriated. An authorisation, however, does not make money available. *Budget Authority* is the legal authority for an agency to enter into obligations for the provision of goods or services. It may be available for one or more years. *Appropriation* is one form of Budget Authority provided by Congress for funding an agency, department or programme for a given length of time and for specific purposes. Funds will not necessarily all be spent in the year in which they are initially provided. *Obligation* is an order placed, contract awarded, service agreement undertaken or other commitment made by federal agencies during a given period which will require outlays during the same or some future period. *Outlays* are money spent by a federal agency from funds provided by Congress. Outlays in a given fiscal year are a result of obligations that in turn follow the provision of Budget Authority.

Table 6 Major US research and development (R&D) programmes, FY1998–2000

Type	Model	1998 value	1999 value	2000 value	Comment
(values in US$m)					
DoD					
BMD	TMD	3,047	2,834	2,962	
	of which				
	THAAD	387	434	612	
	Navy Area	292	243	268	
	Navy Theater	438	344	350	
	Joint TMD	684	200	196	

Type	Model	1998 value	1999 value	2000 value	Comment
	Space-based laser	118	152	139	
	Airborne laser	154	257	309	
	Family of systems		96	142	
	Technical ops		185	191	
	MEADS	50	10	49	With Ge,'It. $150m committed over 3 years in FY2000
	Patriot PAC-3	243	241	109	
BMD	NMD	936	1,093	1,287	
sat	*Discoverer* 2			60	Radar sat programme in project definition late 1998
sat					SIGINT sat $1bn development programme since 1994
Joint					
FGA	JSF	913	923	477	
hel	V-22 *Osprey*	488	346	183	
UAV	UAV	517	665	610	
ASM	JASSM	167	131	168	
AAM	AIM-9X *Sidewinder*	106	117	142	For development. Production starts in FY2000
Air Force					
FGA	F-22	2,011	1,571	1,222	Requirement 339. $19bn dev, $48bn prod
FGA	JSF	444	455	235	
laser	YAL-1A ABL	154	257	309	
BMD	SBIRS-High	338	539	329	Space-based infra-red sensor – high Earth orbit
BMD	SBIRS-Low	214	192	229	Space-based infra-red sensor – low Earth orbit
Army					
lt tk	TRACER				With UK in devpt. Programme worth up to $4.8bn
SP arty	*Crusader*	301	314	344	Requirement for 824 between 2005–14. Prod in 2003
hel	RAH-66 *Comanche*	263	365	427	Req for 1,292 for $34bn, incl $5.4bn R&D, from 2006
hel	CH-47 *Chinook*				Upgrade costing $2.1bn for delivery 2003–12
C3I	FBCB2				$20bn planned spend on digitisation 2000–05
Navy & Marines					
CVN	CVNX-1		190		Construction to start FY2001 for delivery 2006
CVN	CVNX-2				
SSN	NSSN	465	358	357	Plans for 20 units. Construction to start 1999
DD	DD-21		84		$25bn programme for 32 warships. Funding in FY2004
FGA	JSF	448	469	242	
arty	Xm777 155mm				Dev since 1997. Requirement for 450 FY2003–6
IT	IT-21				$3bn programme to 2003

Table 7 Major US equipment orders, FY1998–2000

Type	Model	FY1998 units	FY1998 value	FY1999 units	FY1999 value	FY2000 units	FY2000 value	Comment
(values in US$m)								
DoD								
BMD	*Patriot* PAC-3	48	317	60	246	60	301	54 systems for $7.6bn
BMD	TMD		14.2		23			
BMD	Navy Area		14.9		43		55	
Joint								
tpt	C-130J	9	545	7	494		43	28 on order late 1998
trg	JPATS	22	125	22	150	21	167	711 planned for USAF and USN
hel	V-22 *Osprey*	7	1,186	7	1,060	10	1,169	Requirement for 458
PGM	JDAM	2,202	101	2,527	107	6,195	174	
ASM	JSOW	180	167	414	131	808	168	
AAM	AMRAAM	293	202	280	187	310	207	

Type	Model	FY1998 units	FY1998 value	FY1999 units	FY1999 value	FY2000 units	FY2000 value	Comment
AAM	AIM-9X *Sidewinder*		106		117		142	Production starts in FY2000
UAV	*Predator*	20	136	15	114	3	38	
Air Force								
bbr	B-2		650		425		375	21 units on order
FGA	F-16	3	210	1	207	10	441	*Falcon* multi-mission fighter
FGA	F-22		73	2	795	6	1,852	Requirement for 339 units
tpt	C-17	9	2,367	13	3,192	15	3,562	120 on order up to 2003
C3	E-8C JSTARS	1	433	2	663	1	483	Requirement for 13
sat	NAVSTAR GPS	3	259		188		270	Global Positioning System
sat	MILSTAR		610		547		361	
sat	DSP		103		101		119	
launcher	*Titan*		516		661		477	Defence-support programme
Army								
MBT	M1A2	120	622	120	702	120	658	Upgrade of 368 M1A1, 68 new M1A2
AIFV	M2A3	72	302	73	441	72	349	1,100 to A3 model, deliveries from Nov 1998
MRL	MLRS	21	176	24	152	47	193	
MRL	ATACMS	109	17,305	96	182	110	200	
arty	SADARM	300	76	100	63	227	74	
ATGW	*Javelin*	894	146	3,316	349	2,682	411	AAWS-M
veh	FHTV	286	112	489	196	450	190	Family of hy tac veh
wpn	FMTV	1,179	205	1,439	335	2,179	428	Family of med tac wpn
veh	HMMWV	1,768	121	671	64	867	99	
SAM	*Avenger*			20	35	20	34	
attack hel	AH-64D	16	506	20	631	24	774	*Apache Longbow*. Req for 530
ATGM	*Longbow*	1,100	231	2,000	345	2,200	294	
hel	UH-60 *Blackhawk*	28	283	29	274	8	103	hel
sat	DSCS		102		126		89	
digitisation							2,900	$20bn planned spend 2000–5
Navy & Marines								
SLBM	*Trident 2*	5	306	5	374	12	537	
SLCM	*Tomahawk*	65	129	114	202	148	198	
SSN	SSN-21 *Seawolf*		222		58		66	
SSN	NSSN	1	2,510	1	1,996		749	Req for 30 costing $64bn
CVN	CVN-68	1	1,708					
CVN	CVN-77				213		1	10th & last *Nimitz*-class CVN for $5bn
DDG	DDG-51	4	3,622	3	2,899	3	2,928	Req for 57 at $54bn to 2003–4
LPD	LPD-17		231	1	638	2	1,523	*San Antonio* Class. 12 planned
AK	ADCC (X)					1	453	
FGA	F/A-18E/F	20	2,424	30	3,178	36	3,066	Req fell to 548–785 under QDR
FGA	AV-8B	12	334	12	389	12	346	Upgrade. 72 re-manufactured AV-8Bs
EW	EA-6B *Prowler*		117		160		248	
RECCE	EC-2C *Hawkeye*	4	376	3	461	3	412	Total of 21 on order for $1.3bn
TRG	T-45TS	15	296	15	316	15	358	
hel	MV-22 *Osprey*	7	677	7	662	10	867	First delivery May 1999
hel	CH-60	1	59	5	176	13	326	
hel	SH-60R		82		226	7	349	
SAM	*Standard*	100	178	100	224	90	213	
ATGW	*Javelin*	380	58	741	83	954	93	
IT	IT-21							$3bn programme 1997–2001

United States   US

	1997	1998	1999	2000
GDP	$8.1tr	$8.5tr		
per capita	$29,600	$31,100		
Growth	3.9%	3.9%		
Inflation	2.4%	1.5%		
Publ debt	59.1%	57.4%		
Def bdgt				
BA	$270.3bn	$271.3bn		
Outlay	$271.7bn	$270.2bn		
Request				
BA			$276.2bn	$280.8bn
Outlay			$277.6bn	$274.8bn
Population				273,133,000
Age	*13–17*	*18–22*		*23–32*
Men	9,515,000	9,273,000		19,586,000
Women	9,066,000	8,844,000		18,777,000

Total Armed Forces

ACTIVE 1,371,500

(incl 199,900 women, excl Coast Guard)

RESERVES 1,303,300

(incl Stand-by Reserve)

READY RESERVE 1,274,600

Selected Reserve and Individual Ready Reserve to
augment active units and provide reserve
formations and units
NATIONAL GUARD 468,700
Army (ARNG) 362,400 **Air Force** (ANG) 106,300
RESERVE 784,600
Army 421,500 **Navy** 196,700 **Marines** 96,200 **Air
Force** 70,200

STAND-BY RESERVE 28,700

Trained individuals for mob **Army** 740 **Navy** 11,700
Marines 260 **Air Force** 16,000

US Strategic Command (US STRATCOM)

HQ: Offutt AFB, NE (manpower incl in Navy and Air
Force totals)

NAVY up to 432 SLBM in 18 SSBN

(Plus 16 *Poseidon* C-3 launchers in one op ex SSBN
redesignated SSN (32 msl), START accountable)

SSBN 18 *Ohio*

10 (SSBN-734) with up to 24 UGM-133A *Trident* D-5
(240 msl)
8 (SSBN-726) with up to 24 UGM-93A *Trident* C-4
(192 msl)

AIR FORCE

ICBM (Air Force Space Command (AFSPC)) 550

11 missile sqn
500 *Minuteman* II and III (LGM-30G)
50 *Peacekeeper* (MX; LGM-118A) in mod
AC (Air Combat Command (ACC)): 178 active hy
bbr (315 START-accountable)
14 bbr sqn (7 B-1, 5 B-52)
7 sqn (2 ANG) with 91 B-1B
5 sqn (1 AFR) with 70 B-52H (with AGM-86 ALCM)
2 sqn with 17 B-2A
FLIGHT TEST CENTRE 3
1 B-52, 2 B-1 (not START-accountable)

Strategic Recce/Intelligence Collection (Satellites)

IMAGERY Improved *Crystal* (advanced **KH-11**)
visible and infra-red imagery (perhaps 3 op,
resolution 6in)
Lacrosse (formerly *Indigo*) radar-imaging satellite
(resolution 1–2m)
ELECTRONIC OCEAN RECCE SATELLITE (EORSAT)
to detect ships by infra-red and radar
**NAVIGATIONAL SATELLITE TIMING AND RANG-
ING** (NAVSTAR) 24 satellites, components of Global
Positioning System (GPS); block 2R system with
accuracy to 1m replacing expired satellites
ELINT/SIGINT 2 *Orion* (formerly *Magnum*), 2
Trumpet (successor to *Jumpseat*), 3 name unknown,
launched August 1994, May 1995, April 1996
NUCLEAR DETONATION DETECTION SYSTEM
detects and evaluates nuclear detonations; sensors
to be deployed in NAVSTAR satellites

Strategic Defences

US Space Command (HQ: Peterson AFB, CO)
North American Aerospace Defense Command
(NORAD), a combined US–Canadian org (HQ:
Peterson AFB, CO)
US Strategic Command (HQ: Offutt AFB, NE)

EARLY WARNING

DEFENSE SUPPORT PROGRAM (DSP) infra-red
surveillance and warning system. Detects missile
launches, nuclear detonations, aircraft in after
burner, spacecraft and terrestrial infra-red events.
Approved constellation: 3 op satellites and 1 op
on-orbit spare
**BALLISTIC-MISSILE EARLY-WARNING
SYSTEM (BMEWS)** 3 stations: Clear (AK), Thule
(Greenland), Fylingdales Moor (UK). Primary
mission to track ICBM and SLBM; also used to
track satellites
SPACETRACK USAF radars at Incirlik (Turkey),
Eglin (FL), Cavalier AFS (ND), Clear, Thule,
Fylingdales Moor, Beale AFB (CA), Cape Cod
(MA); optical tracking systems in Socorro (NM),
Maui (HI), Diego Garcia (Indian Ocean)

USN SPACE SURVEILLANCE SYSTEM
(NAVSPASUR) 3 transmitting, 6 receiving-site field
    stations in south-east US
PERIMETER ACQUISITION RADAR ATTACK
CHARACTERISATION SYSTEM (PARCS) 1
    north-facing phased-array system at Cavalier AFS
    (ND); 2,800km range
PAVE PAWS phased-array radars in Massachusetts,
    GA; 5,500km range
MISCELLANEOUS DETECTION AND TRACK-
ING RADARS US Army Kwajalein Atoll (Pacific)
    USAF Ascension Island (Atlantic), Antigua
    (Caribbean), Kaena Point (HI), MIT Lincoln
    Laboratory (MA)
GROUND-BASED ELECTRO-OPTICAL DEEP
SPACE SURVEILLANCE SYSTEM (GEODSS)
    Socorro, Maui, Diego Garcia

AIR DEFENCE

RADARS
OVER-THE-HORIZON-BACKSCATTER RADAR
(OTH-B) 1 in Maine (mothballed), 1 in Mountain
    Home AFB (mothballed); range 500nm (mini-
    mum) to 3,000nm
NORTH WARNING SYSTEM to replace DEW line
    15 automated long-range (200nm) radar stations
    40 short-range (110–150km) stations
DEW LINE system deactivated
AC ANG 90
    4 sqn: 3 with 45 F-15A/B, 1 with 15 F-16C/D
    ac also on call from Navy, USMC and Air Force
AAM *Sidewinder, Sparrow,* AMRAAM

Army 469,300

(71,000 women)
3 Army HQ, 4 Corps HQ (1 AB)
2 armd div (3 bde HQ, 5 tk, 4 mech inf, 3 SP arty bn; 1
    MLRS bn, 1 AD bn; 1 avn bde)
2 mech div (3 bde HQ, 5 tk, 4 mech inf, 3 SP arty bn; 1
    MLRS bn, 1 ADA bn; 1 avn bde)
1 mech div (3 bde HQ, 4 tk, 5 mech inf, 3 SP arty bn; 1
    MLRS bn, 1 ADA bn; 1 avn bde)
1 mech div (3 bde HQ, 4 tk, 3 mech inf, 2 air aslt inf, 3
    SP arty bn; 1 ADA bn; 1 avn bde)
2 lt inf div (3 bde HQ, 9 inf, 3 arty, 1 AD bn; 1 avn bde)
1 air aslt div (3 bde HQ, 9 air aslt, 3 arty bn; 2 avn bde
    (7 hel bn: 3 ATK, 2 aslt, 1 comd, 1 med tpt))
1 AB div (3 bde HQ, 9 AB, 1 lt tk, 3 arty, 1 AD, 1 air cav,
    3 avn bde)
5 avn bde (1 army, 3 corps, 1 trg)
3 armd cav regt (1 hy, 1 lt, 1 trg)
6 arty bde (3 with 1 SP arty, 2 MLRS bn; 1 with 3 arty, 1
    MLRS bn; 1 with 3 MLRS bn; 1 with 1 MLRS bn)
3 indep inf bn, 1 AB Task Force
9 *Patriot* SAM bn (5 with 6 bty, 2 with 4 bty, 2 with 3 bty)
2 *Avenger* SAM bn

READY RESERVE
ARMY NATIONAL GUARD (ARNG) 362,400 (35,700
    women): capable after mob of manning 8 div (3
    armd, 4 mech, 1 lt inf) • 1 mech div HQ • 1 inf div
    HQ • 18 indep bde, incl 15 enhanced (3 armd, 4
    mech, 7 inf, 1 armd cav), 1 armd, 1 lt inf, 1 inf scout
    (3 bn) • 16 fd arty bde HQ • Indep bn: 3 inf, 36 arty,
    18 avn, 9 AD (1 *Patriot,* 8 *Avenger*), 37 engr
ARMY RESERVE (AR) 421,500 (49,700 women): 7 trg
    div, 5 exercise div, 13 AR/Regional Spt Cmd
    (Of these, 208,000 Standing Reservists receive
    regular trg and have mob assignment; the remain-
    der receive limited trg, but as former active-duty
    soldiers could be recalled in an emergency)

EQUIPMENT
MBT some 7,684: 40 M-60A3, 7,644 M-1 *Abrams* incl
    M-1A1, M-1A2
RECCE 113 Tpz-1 *Fuchs*
AIFV 6,715 M-2/-3 *Bradley*
APC 17,800 M-113A2/A3 incl variants
TOTAL ARTY 5,699
    TOWED 1,593: **105mm:** 458 M-102, 420 M-119;
        155mm: 715 M-198
    SP 2,555: **155mm:** 2,526 M-109A1/A2/A6;
        203mm: 29 M-110A1/A2
    MRL 227mm: 857 MLRS (all ATACMS-capable)
    MOR 879: **120mm:** 879 M-120/121; plus **81mm:**
        1,067 M-251
ATGW 8,452 TOW (1,237 HMMWV, 500 M-901,
    6,715 M-2/M-3 *Bradley*), 24,400 *Dragon,* 500 *Javelin*
RL 84mm: AT-4
SAM FIM-92A *Stinger,* 767 *Avenger* (veh-mounted
    Stinger), 80 *Linebacker* (4 *Stinger* plus 25mm gun),
    485 *Patriot*
SURV Ground 122 AN/TPQ-36 (arty), 70 AN/
    TPQ-37 (arty), 59 AN/TRQ-32 (COMINT), 29
    AN/TSQ-138 (COMINT), 39 AN/TSQ-138A, 68
    AN/TLQ-17A (EW) **Airborne** 4 *Guardrail* (RC-
    12D/H/K, 3 RU-21H ac), 6 EO-5ARL (DHC-7), 35
    OV/RV-1D
AMPH 51 ships:
    6 *Frank Besson* LST: capacity 32 tk
    34 LCU-2000
    11 LCU-1600
    Plus craft: some 82 LCM-8
UAV 7 *Hunter* (5 in store)
AC some 249: 1 **BN-2T**, 30 **C-12C/R**, 74 **C-12D/-J**, 3
    C-20, 3 **C-21**, 51 **C-23A/B**, 11 **C-26**, 2 **C-31**, 2 **C-182**,
    2 **O-2**, 1 **PA-31**, 37 **RC-12D/H/K/N**, 12 **RC-12P/Q**,
    2 **T-34**, 12 **UC-35**, 4 **UV-18A**, 2 **UV-20A**
HEL some 4,923 (1,437 armed): 457 **AH-1S**, 746 **AH-
    64A/D**, 40 **AH-6/MH-6**, 809 **UH-1H/V**, 1,372 **UH-
    60A/L**, 4 **UH-60Q**, 60 **MH-60L/K**, 66 **EH-60A
    (ECM)**, 466 **CH/MH-47D/E**, 386 **OH-58A/C**, 380
    OH-58D (incl 194 armed), 135 **TH-67** *Creek*, 2
    RAH-66

Navy (USN) 369,800

(52,800 women)
5 Fleets: **2nd** Atlantic, **3rd** Pacific, **5th** Indian Ocean,
Persian Gulf, Red Sea, **6th** Mediterranean, **7th** W.
Pacific; plus Military Sealift Command, Naval Reserve
Force (NRF)

SUBMARINES 76

STRATEGIC SUBMARINES 18 (see p. 20)
TACTICAL SUBMARINES 57 (incl about 8 in refit)
  SSGN 33
  2 *Seawolf* (SSN-21) with up to 45 *Tomahawk* SLCM
    plus 660mm TT; about 50 tube-launched msl and
    Mk 48 HWT
  23 imp *Los Angeles* (SSN-751) with 12 *Tomahawk*
    SLCM (VLS), 533mm TT (Mk 48 HWT, *Harpoon*,
    Tomahawk)
  8 mod *Los Angeles* (SSN-719) with 12 *Tomahawk*
    SLCM (VLS), 533mm TT (Mk 48 HWT, *Harpoon*,
    Tomahawk)
  SSN 24
  20 *Los Angeles* (SSN-688) with Mk 48 HWT, *Harpoon*,
    Tomahawk SLCM
  4 *Sturgeon* (SSN-637) with Mk 48 HWT, *Tomahawk*
OTHER ROLES 1 ex-SSBN (SSBN 642) (special ops,
  included in the START-accountable launcher figures)

PRINCIPAL SURFACE COMBATANTS 130

AIRCRAFT CARRIERS 12
  CVN 9
  8 *Nimitz* (CVN-68) (one in refit)
  1 *Enterprise* (CVN-65) (in refit until Jan 2000)
  CV 3
  2 *Kitty Hawk* (CV-63)
  1 *J. F. Kennedy* (CV-67) (in reserve)
  AIR WING 11 (10 active, 1 reserve); average Air
  Wing comprises 9 sqn
    3 with 12 F/A-18C, 1 with 14 F-14, 1 with 8 S-3B
    and 2 ES-3, 1 with 6 SH-60, 1 with 4 EA-6B,
    1 with 4 E-2C, 1 spt with C-2

CRUISERS 27
CG 27 *Ticonderoga* (CG-47 *Aegis*)
  5 *Baseline* 1 (CG-47–51) with 2 x 2 SM-2 MR SAM/
    ASROC, 2 x 4 *Harpoon* SSM, 2 127mm guns, 2 x 3
    ASTT, 2 SH-2F or SH-60B hel
  22 *Baseline* 2/3 (CG-52) with 2 VLS Mk 41 (61 tubes
    each) for combination of SM-2 ER SAM, and
    Tomahawk; other weapons as *Baseline* 1

DESTROYERS 54
DDG 54
  28 *Arleigh Burke* (DDG-51 *Aegis*) with 2 VLS Mk 41
    (32 tubes fwd, 64 tubes aft) for combination of
    Tomahawk, SM-2 ER SAM and ASROC; plus 2 x 4
    Harpoon SSM, 1 127mm gun, 2 x 3 ASTT, 1 SH-60B
    hel
  26 *Spruance* (DD-963) with 2 VLS Mark 41 for
    combination of *Tomahawk* and ASROC, *Harpoon*
    SSM, *Sea Sparrow* SAM, 2 127mm gun, 2 x 3 ASTT,

2 SH-60B hel

FRIGATES 37
FFG 37 *Oliver Hazard Perry* (FFG-7) (10 in reserve) all
  with 2 x 3 ASTT; 24 with 2 SH-60B hel; 27 with 2 SH-
  2F hel; all 1 SM-1 MR SAM/*Harpoon* SSM

PATROL AND COASTAL COMBATANTS 21

(mainly responsibility of Coast Guard)
PATROL, COASTAL 13 *Cyclone* PFC with SEAL team
PATROL, INSHORE 8<

MINE WARFARE 27

MINELAYERS none dedicated, but mines can be laid
  from attack submarines, aircraft and surface ships.
MCM 27
  1 *Inchon* MCCS in reserve
  2 *Osprey* (MHC-51) MHC, 10 *Osprey* in reserve
  10 *Avenger* (MCM-1) MCO, 4 *Avenger* in reserve

AMPHIBIOUS 42

LCC 2 *Blue Ridge*, capacity 700 tps
LHD 6 *Wasp*, capacity 1,894 tps, 60 tk; with 5 AV-8B ac,
  42 CH-46E, 6 SH-60B hel; plus 3 LCAC, 2 RAM
LHA 5 *Tarawa*, capacity 1,900 tps, 100 tk, 4 LCU or 1
  LCAC, 6 AV-8B ac, 12 CH-46E, 9 CH-53E hel, 2 RAM
LPD 11 *Austin*, capacity 900 tps, 4 tk; with 6 CH-46E hel
LSD 16
  8 *Whidbey Island* with 4 LCAC, capacity 500 tps, 40 tk
  4 *Harpers Ferry* with 2 LCAC, capacity 500 tps, 40 tk
  4 *Anchorage* with 3 LCAC, capacity 330 tps, 38 tk
LST 2 *Newport*, capacity 347 tps, 10 tk, both in reserve
CRAFT 202
  82 LCAC, capacity 1 MBT; about 37 LCU-1610,
    capacity 1 MBT; 8 LCVP; 75 LCM; plus numerous
    LCU

NAVAL RESERVE SURFACE FORCES 20

  1 CV (*J. F. Kennedy*) fully op with assigned air wg, 10
  FFG, 4 MCM, 10 MHC, 2 LST, 1 MCCS (*Inchon*)
  generally crewed by 70% active and 30% reserve,
  plus 28 MIUW units

NAVAL INACTIVE FLEET about 26

  2 CV, 1 FFG, 2 BB, 7 LST, 4 LKA, 5 AO, 3 AF, 1 AK, 1
  AG plus 35 misc service craft

MILITARY SEALIFT COMMAND (MSC)

MSC operates about 110 ships around the world
carrying the designation "USNS" (United States Naval
Ships). They are not commissioned ships and are
manned by civilians. Some also have small military
departments assigned to carry out specialised military
functions such as communications and supply
operations. MSC ships carry the prefix "T" before their
normal hull numbers.

Naval Auxiliary Force 34
7 AE • 6 AF • 2 AH • 12 AO • 7 AT/F

Special Mission Ships 26
3 AG • 1 AR/C • 3 AGOS (counter-drug ops) • 11

AGOS • 8 AGHS

Prepositioning Program/Maritime Prepositioning Program 32

1 ro-ro AK • 3 heavy ro-ro AK • 1 flo-flo AK • 4 AK • 13 MPS AK • 4 LASH • 2 AOT • 2 AVB • 1 AG • 1 AO

Sealift Force 24

8 AKR • 11 ro-ro AKR • 5 AOT

Additional Military Sealift

Ready Reserve Force 80

27 breakbulk, 31 ro-ro, 4 LASH, 3 'Seebee', 4 tkr, 2 tps, 9 AG (crane at 4–10 days' readiness, maintained by Department of Transport)

National Defence Reserve Fleet (NDRF) 48

38 dry cargo, 8 tkr, 2 tps

Augment Forces

14 cargo handling bn (12 in reserve)

COMMERCIAL SEALIFT about 327

US-flag (152) and effective US-controlled (EUSC, 175) ships potentially available to augment military sealift

NAVAL AVIATION 76,548

(6,167 women)
incl 12 carriers, 11 air wg (10 active, 1 reserve) **Flying hours** F-14: 216; F-18: 252
Average air wg comprises 9 sqn

3 with 12 F/A-18C, 1 with 10 F-14, 1 with 8 S-3B, 1 with 6 SH-60, 1 with 4 EA-6B, 1 with 4 E-2C, 1 spt with C-2

AIRCRAFT

FTR 12 sqn
5 with F-14A, 4 with F-14B, 3 with F-14D
FGA/ATTACK 24 sqn with F/A-18C/D
ELINT 4 sqn
2 with EP-3, 2 with ES-3A
ECM 14 sqn with EA-6B
MR 6 land-based sqn with P-3CIII
ASW 10 sqn with S-3B
AEW 10 sqn with E-2C
COMD 2 sqn with E-6A (TACAMO)
OTHER 4 sqn
2 with C-2A, 2 with C-130T
TRG 11 sqn
2 'Aggressor' with F/A-18
9 trg with T-2C, T-34C, T-44, T-45A

HELICOPTERS

ASW 20 sqn
10 with SH-60B (LAMPS Mk III)
10 with SH-60F/HH-60H
MCM 2 sqn with MH-53E
MISC 6 sqn
5 with CH-46, 1 with MH-53E

TRG 2 sqn with TH-57B/C

NAVAL AVIATION RESERVE 23,480

(3,840 women)
FTR ATTACK 2 sqn with F-18
FTR 1 sqn with F-18
AEW 2 sqn with E-2C
ECM 1 sqn with EA-6B
MPA 9 sqn: 1 with P-3C, 1 with EP-3J
FLEET LOG SPT 1 wg
8 sqn with C-9B/DC-9, 4 sqn with C-130T
TRG 2 aggressor sqn (1 with F/A-18, 1 with F-5E/F)
HEL 1 wg
ASW 3 sqn: 2with SH-2G, 1 with SH-3H
MSC 3 sqn: 2 with HH-60H, 1 with UH-3H

AIRCRAFT

(Naval Inventory includes Marine Corps ac and hel)
1,510 cbt ac; 506 armed hel

235* **F-14** (112 **-A** (ftr, incl 14 NR) plus 30 in store, 77 **-B** (ftr), 46 **-D** (ftr)) • 515* **F/A-18** (114 **-A** (FGA, incl 34 NR, 84 MC (48 MCR)), 28 **-B** (FGA, incl 2 NR (4 TACAMO MC)), 332 **-C** (FGA, incl 79 MC), 34 **-D** (FGA, incl 90 MC), 5 **-E**, 2 **-F**) • 22* **F-5E/F** (trg, incl 13 MCR) • 57* **TA-4J** (trg) plus 3 in store • 95 **EA-6B** (ECM, incl 4 NR, 18 MC) • 124 **E-6B**, 167* **AV-8B** (FGA) plus 5 in store • 2* **TAV-8B** (trg) plus 2 in store • 74 **E-2** (72 **-C** (AEW, incl 11 NR) plus 3 in store, 2 **TE-2C** (trg) • 273 **P-3** (3 **-B**, plus 29 in store, 231* **-C** (MR, incl 70, NR) plus 13 in store, 14 **EP-3** (ELINT), 13 **NP-3D** (trials), 10 **U/VP-3A** (utl/VIP), 2 **TP-3A** (trg) plus 9 in store) • 132 **S-3** plus 21 in store (116 **-B** (ASW) plus 1 in store, 16 **ES-3A** (ECM)) • 105 **C-130** (20 **-T** (tpt NR), 80 **-KC-130F/R/T** (incl 78 MC (28 MCR)), 1 **-TC-130G/Q** (tpt/trg), 4 **LC-130** (Antarctic)) • 2 **CT-39G** (1 MC incl 1 MCR) • 38 **C-2A** (tpt), 17 **C-9B** (tpt, 15 NR, 2 MC), 12 **DC-9** (incl 10 NR) (tpt), 7 **C-20**, 2 **-D** (VIP/NR), 5 **-G** (tpt/4 NR, 1 MCR) • 59 **UC-12** (utl) 42 **-B** (incl 12 MC, 5 MCR), 6 **-F** (incl 4 MC), 10 **-M** (1 **NU-1B** (utl)) • 2 **U-6A** (utl) • 107 **T-2C** (trg) plus 13 in store • 1 **T-39D** (trg) • 55 **T-44** (trg) • 71 **T-45** (trg) plus 7 in store • 313 **T-34C** (incl 2 MC) • 11 **T-38A/B** (trg) • 20 **TC-12B** • 2 **TC-18F** (trg)

HELICOPTERS

106 **UH-1N** (utl, incl 103 MC (20 MCR)) • 26 **HH-1H** (utl, incl 7 MC) plus 10 in store • 151 **CH-53E** (tpt, incl 16 MCR) plus 150 MC • 47 **CH-53D** (tpt MC) • 43 **MH-53E** (tpt, incl 12 NR, 5 MC) • 242 **SH-60** (166 **-B**, 76 **-F**) • 38 **HH-60H** (cbt spt, incl 16 NR) plus 1 in store • 14 **SH-2G** (ASW, 14 NR) plus 3 in store • 8 **VH-60** (ASW/SAR MC) • 7 **SH-3H** (ASW/SAR incl 6 NR) plus 15 in store • 52 **UH-3H** (ASW/SAR incl 10 NR) plus 3 in store • 27 **CH-46D** (tpt, trg) • 233 **CH-46E** (tpt, incl 232 MC (25 MCR)) • 53 **UH/HH-46D** (utl incl 9 MC) • 118 **TH-57** (45 **-B** (trg), 73 **-C** (trg) (plus B-2, C-12 in store)) • 14 **VH-3A/D** (VIP, 11 MC) • 204 **AH-1W** (atk, incl 197 MC (37 MCR)) plus 11 in store • 42 **CH-53D** (tpt, incl 42 MC) plus 25 in store

TILT ROTOR 1 (MC)
MISSILES
  AAM AIM-120 AMRAAM, AIM-7 *Sparrow*, AIM-54A/C *Phoenix*, AIM-9 *Sidewinder*
  ASM AGM-45 *Shrike*, AGM-88A HARM; AGM-84 *Harpoon*, AGM-119 *Penguin* Mk-3, AGM-114 *Hellfire*

Marine Corps (USMC) 171,000

(9,800 women)

GROUND
3 div
  1 with 3 inf regt (10bn), 1 tk, 2 lt armd recce (LAV-25), 1 aslt amph, 1 cbt engr bn, 1 arty regt (4 bn), 1 recce coy
  1 with 3 inf regt (9 bn), 1 tk, 1 lt armd recce (LAV-25), 1 aslt amph, 1 cbt engr bn, 1 arty regt (4 bn), 1 recce bn
  1 with 2 inf regt (6 bn), 1 cbt aslt bn (1 AAV, 1 LAR coy), 1 arty regt (2 bn), 1 cbt engr, 1 recce coy
3 Force Service Spt Gp
1 bn Marine Corps Security Force (Atlantic and Pacific)
Marine Security Guard bn (1 HQ, 7 region coy)

RESERVES (MCR)
1 div (3 inf (9 bn), 1 arty regt (5 bn); 2 tk, 1 lt armd recce (LAV-25), 1 aslt amph, 1 recce, 1 cbt engr bn)
1 Force Service Spt Gp
EQUIPMENT
  MBT 403 M-1A1 *Abrams*
  LAV 401 LAV-25 (**25mm gun**) plus 334 variants incl 50 Mor, 95 ATGW (see below)
  AAV 1,321 AAV-7A1 (all roles)
  TOWED ARTY 105mm: 331 M-101A1; **155mm**: 599 M-198
  MOR 81mm: 613 (incl 50 LAV-M)
  ATGW 1,145 TOW, 1,121 *Dragon*, 95 LAV-TOW
  RL 83mm: 1,454 SMAW; **84mm**: 1,300 AT-4
  SURV 22 AN/TPQ-36 (arty)
AVIATION 36,400
(1,280 women)
Flying hours 264
3 active air wg and 1 MCR air wg
Flying hours cbt aircrew: 264
AIR WING no standard org, but a notional wg comprises
  AC 130 fixed-wing: 48 **F/A-18A/C/D**, 60 **AV-8B**, 10 **EA-6B**, 12 **KC-130**
  HEL 167: 12 **CH-53D**, 32 **CH-53E**, 36 **AH-1W**, 27 **UH-1N**, 60 **CH-46E**
  1 MC C² system, wg support gp
AIRCRAFT
  FTR/ATTACK 18 sqn with 216 F/A-18A/C/D (4 MCR sqn)
  FGA 7 sqn with 112 AV-8B

ECM 4 sqn with 22 EA-6B
TKR 6 sqn with 79 KC-130F/R/T (4 MCR sqn)
TRG 4 sqn
  1 with 14 AV-8B, 8 TAV-8B
  1 with 41 F/A-18A/B/C/D, 3 T-34C
  1 with 12 F-5E, 1 F-5F
  1 with 8 KC-130F
HELICOPTERS
  ARMED 6 lt attack/utl with 108 AH-1W and 54 UH-1N
  TPT 15 **med** sqn with 180 CH-46E, 4 sqn with 32 CH-53D; 6 **hy** sqn with 96 CH-53E
  TRG 4 sqn
    1 with 20 AH-1W, 10 UH-1N, 4 HH-1N
    1 with 20 CH-46
    1 with 6 CH-53D
    1 with 15 CH-53E, 5 MH-53E
  SAM 3+ bn
    2+ bn (5 bty), 1 MCR bn with *Stinger* and *Avenger*
  UAV 2 sqn with *Pioneer*
RESERVES 9,000
(500 women); 1 air wg
AIRCRAFT
  FTR/ATTACK 4 sqn with 48 F-18A
    1 *Aggressor* sqn with 13 F5-E/F
  TKR 2 tkr/tpt sqn with 28 KC-130T
HELICOPTERS
  ARMED 2 attack/utl sqn with 36 AH-1W, 18 UH-1N
  TPT 4 sqn
    2 **med** with 24 CH-46E, 2 **hy** with 16 CH-53E
  SAM 1 bn (2 bty) with *Stinger* and *Avenger*
EQUIPMENT (incl MCR): 442 cbt ac; 175 armed hel
Totals included in the Navy inventory
AIRCRAFT
259 **F-18A/-B/-C/-D** (FGA incl 48 MCR) • 154 **AV-8B**, 14* **TAV-8B** (trg) • 21 **EA-6B** (ECM) • 13* **F-5E/F** (trg, MCR) • 79 **KC-130F/R/T** (tkr, incl 28 MCR) • 2 **C-9B** (tpt) • 1 **C-20G** (MCR) (tpt) • 3 **CT-39G** (1 MCR) • 18 **UC-12B/F** (utl, incl 3 MCR) • 3 **T-34C** (trg)
HELICOPTERS
175 **AH-1W** (GA, incl 37 MCR) • 103 **UH-1N** (utl, incl 20 MCR) • 7 **HH-1H** (utl) • 231 **CH-46E** (tpt incl 25 MCR) • 9 **UH/HH-46D** (utl) • 149 **CH-53-E** (tpt, incl 16 MCR) • 5 **MH-53E**, 47 **CH-53D** (tpt) • 8 **VH-60** (VIP tpt) • 11 **VH-3A/D** (VIP tpt)
TILT ROTOR 12 MV-22B
MISSILES
  SAM 1,929 *Stinger*, 235 *Avenger*
  AAM *Sparrow* AMRAAM, *Sidewinder*
  ASM *Maverick*, *Hellfire*, TOW

Coast Guard (active duty) 35,100 military, 6,000 civilian

(includes 3,400 women)

By law a branch of the Armed Forces; in peacetime operates under, and is funded by, the Department of Transport

Bdgt Authority

1995	$3.7bn	*1998*	$3.9bn
1996	$3.7bn	*1999*	$3.9bn
1997	$3.8bn	*2000*	request $4.1bn

PATROL VESSELS 174

OFFSHORE 78

12 *Hamilton* high-endurance with HH-60J LAMPS HU-65A *Dolphin* hel, all with 76mm gun
13 *Bear* med-endurance with 76mm gun, HH-65A hel
16 *Reliance* med-endurance with 25mm gun, hel deck
2 *Vindicator* (USN *Stalwart*) med-endurance cutter
3 other med-endurance cutters (inactive status)
32 buoy tenders

INSHORE 85

49 *Farallon*, 30 *Point Hope*, 6 *Baracuda*

SPT AND OTHER 11

2 icebreakers, 8 icebreaking tugs, 1 trg

AVIATION (3,700 personnel)

AC 20 HU-25 (plus 21 support or in store), 26 HC-130H (plus 4 support), 2 RU-38A, 35 HH-60J (plus 7 support), 80 HH-65A (plus 13 support), 1 VC-4A, 1 C-20B

RESERVES 14,400

Air Force 361,400

(66,300 women) **Flying hours** ftr 212, bbr 215
Air Combat Comd (ACC) 4 air force, 23 ac wg **Air Mobility Comd** (AMC) 2 air force, 13 ac wg
The US Air Force is altering its posture from being US-based to rapidly deployable. Ten Air Expeditionary Wings (AEW) have been nominated, each with about 15,000 personnel and up to 200 aircraft. Two AEWs, with their mix of aircraft assets, will be on deployment readiness at all times.

TACTICAL 52 ftr sqn

incl active duty sqn ACC, USAFE and PACAF (sqn may be 12 to 24 ac)
14 with F-15, 6 with F-15E, 23 with F-16C/D (incl 3 AD), 7 with A-10/OA-10, 2 with F-117

SUPPORT

RECCE 3 sqn with U-2R and RC-135
AEW 1 Airborne Warning and Control wg, 6 sqn (incl 1 trg) with E-3
EW 2 sqn with EC-130
FAC 7 tac air control sqn, mixed A-10A/OA-10A
TRG 36 sqn
  1 *Aggressor* with F-16
  35 trg with **ac** F-15, F-16, A-10/OA-10, T-37, T-38, AT-38, T-1A, -3A, C-5, -130, -141 **hel** HH-60, U/TH-1

TPT 28 sqn
  17 strategic: 5 with C-5 (1 trg), 9 with C-141 (2 trg), 3 with C-17
  11 tac airlift with C-130
  Units with C-135, VC-137, C-9, C-12, C-20, C-21
TKR 23 sqn
  19 with KC-135 (1 trg), 4 with KC-10A
SAR 8 sqn (incl STRATCOM msl spt), HH-60, HC-130N/P
MEDICAL 3 medical evacuation sqn with C-9A
WEATHER RECCE WC-135
TRIALS weapons trg units with **ac** A-10, F-4, F-15, F-16, F-111, T-38, C-141 **hel** UH-1
UAV *Global Hawk* and *Darkstar*, 2 sqn with *Predators*

RESERVES

AIR NATIONAL GUARD (ANG) 106,300

(17,100 women)
  BBR 2 sqn with B-1B
  FTR 6 AD sqn with F-15, F-16
  FGA 43 sqn
    6 with A-10/OA-10
    31 with F-16 (incl 3 AD)
    6 with F-15A/B (incl 3 AD)
  TPT 27 sqn
    24 tac (1 trg) with C-130E/H
    3 strategic: 1 with C-5, 2 with C-141B
  TKR 23 sqn with KC-135E/R (11 with KC-135E, 12 with KC-135R)
  SPECIAL OPS 1 sqn (AFSOC) with EC-130E
  SAR 3 sqn with **ac** HC-130 **hel** HH-60
  TRG 7 sqn

AIR FORCE RESERVE (AFR) 70,200

(14,700 women), 35 wg
  BBR 1 sqn with B-52H
  FGA 7 sqn
    4 with F-16C/D, 3 with A-10/OA-10 (incl 1 trg)
  TPT 19 sqn
    7 strategic: 2 with C-5A, 5 with C-141B
    11 tac with 8 C-130H, 3 C-130E
    1 weather recce with WC-130E/H
  TKR 7 sqn with KC-135E/R (5 KC-135R, 2 KC-135E)
  SAR 3 sqn (ACC) with **ac** HC-130N/P **hel** HH-60
  ASSOCIATE 20 sqn (personnel only)
    4 for C-5, 8 for C-141, 1 aero-medical for C-9, 2 C-17A, 4 for KC-10, 1 for KC-135

AIRCRAFT

LONG-RANGE STRIKE/ATTACK 208 cbt ac: 94 B-52H (70 in service, 23 in store, 1 test) • 93 B-1B (91 in service, 2 test) • 21 B-2A (17 in service, 4 test)
RECCE 32 U-2R/S • 4 TU-2 R/S • 21 RC-135S/U/V/W • SR-71 (6 in store) • (232 RF-4C in store)
COMD 33 E-3B/C • 4 E-4B • 3 EC-135 (plus 26 in store)
TAC 2,598 cbt ac (incl ANG, AFR plus 1,004 in store); no armed hel: F-4 (300 -D, -E, -G models in store) • 714 F-15 (496 -A/B/C/D (ftr incl 99 ANG, 13 test,

205 -**E** (FGA) (plus 95 F-15A/B/C/D/E in store)) •
1,443 **F-16** (99 -**A** (incl 96 ANG), 51 -**B** (incl 35
ANG), 1,106 -**C** (incl 407 ANG, 58 AFR), 187 -**D**
(incl 39 ANG, 17 AFR) (plus 384 F-16A/B in store))
• 45 **F-117** (46 (FGA), 6* (trg), plus 1 test) • 4 **F-22A**
• 234 **A-10A** (FGA, incl 84 ANG, 46 AFR), plus 178
in store • 130* **OA-10A** (FAC incl 18 ANG, 7 AFR) •
3 **EC-18B/D** (Advanced Range Instrumentation)(3
in store) • 8 **E-8C** (JSTARS) • 1 **TE-8A** • 2 **E-9A** • 2
WC-135H/J (AFR) • 3 **WC-135W** • 3 **OC-135**
('Open Skies' Treaty) • 21* **AC-130H/U** (special ops,
USAF) • 31 **HC-130N/P** • 31 **EC-130E/H/J** (special
ops incl 8 SOF) • 10 **LC-130H/R** (ANG) • 66 **MC-130E/H/P** (special ops) • 16 **WC-130H/J/W**
(weather recce, 10 AFR)(plus 6 in store) • 1 **EC-137D**, 3 **WC-135H/J/W**

TPT 126 **C-5** (74 -**A** (strategic tpt, incl 14 ANG, 32
AFR), 50 -**B**, 2 -**C**) • 48 **C-17A** • 2 **C-38** (ANG) •
158 **C-141B** (incl 18 ANG, 45 AFR)(plus 72 in store)
• 519 **C-130B/E/H/J** (tac tpt, incl 214 ANG, 104
AFR), plus 47 in store • 6 **C-135B/C/E** • 4 **C-137B/C** (VIP tpt) • 23 **C-9A/C** • 38 **C-12C/-D/-J** (liaison)
• 12 **C-20** (2 -**A**, 5 -**B**, 3 -**C**, 2 -**H**) • 77 **C-21A** • 3 **C-22B** (ANG) • 3 **C-23A** • 2 **VC-25A** • 11 **C-26A/B**
(ANG) • 10 **C-27A** (tpt) in store • 1 **C-18B** in store
• 4 **C-32A** • 2 **C-37A** • 2 **C-38A**

TKR 547 **KC-135** (222 ANG, 75 AFR) • 59 **KC-10A**
tkr/tpt

TRG 180 **T-1A** • 112 **T-3A** • 414 **T-37B** • 413 **T-38** • 1
T-39B (25 in store) • 3 **T-41** • 10 **T-43A** • 2 **TC-135S/W** • 2 **UV-18B** • 77 **AT-38B** • 2 **TC-18E** • 1 **CT-43A**

HELICOPTERS

40 **MH-53-J** *Pave Low* (special ops) • 9 **MH-60G** (incl
6 SOC) • 8 **HH-1H** • 90 **HH-60G** (incl 24 AFR, 17
ANG) • 63 **UH-1N**, 6 **TH-53A**

UAV

High Level – **RQ-4A** *Global Hawk* and **RQ-3A** *Darkstar*
Tactical – 10 **RQ-1A** *Predator*

MISSILES

AAM 9,200+ AIM-9P/L/M *Sidewinder*, 4,300+ AIM-7E/F/M *Sparrow*, 4,500+ AIM 120 A/B AMRAAM
ASM 27,000+ AGM-65A/B/D/G *Maverick*, 8,000+
AGM-88A/B HARM, 70+ AGM-84B *Harpoon*,
1,100 AGM-86B ALCM, 200+ AGM-86C ALCM,
400+ AGM-129A, 100+ AGM-130A, 110+ AGM-142A/B/C/D

CIVIL RESERVE AIR FLEET (CRAF) 683

commercial ac (numbers fluctuate)
  LONG-RANGE 501
    passenger 271 (A-310, B-747, B -757, B-767, DC-10,
    L-1011, MD-11)
    cargo 230 (B-747, DC-8, DC-10, L-1011, MD-11)
  SHORT-RANGE 95
    passenger 81 (A-300, B-727, B-737, MD-80/83)
    cargo 14 (L-100, B-727, DC-9)
  DOMESTIC AND AERO-MEDICAL 34 (B-767)

Special Operations Forces (SOF)

Units only listed
ARMY (15,300)
5 SF gp (each 3 bn) • 1 Ranger inf regt (3 bn) • 1
special ops avn regt (3 bn) • 1 Psychological Ops gp (5
bn) • 1 Civil Affairs bn (5 coy) • 1 sigs, 1 spt bn
RESERVES (2,800 ARNG, 7,800 AR)
  2 ARNG SF gp (3 bn) • 12 AR Civil Affairs HQ (4
  comd, 8 bde) • 2 AR Psychological Ops gp • 36 AR
  Civil Affairs 'bn' (coy)
NAVY (4,000)
1 Naval Special Warfare Comd • 1 Naval Special
Warfare Centre • 3 Naval Special Warfare gp • 6
Naval Special Warfare units • 6 SEAL teams • 2 SEAL
delivery veh teams • 2 Special Boat sqn • 6 DDS
RESERVES (1,400)
  1 Naval Special Warfare Comd det • 6 Naval Special
  Warfare gp det • 3 Naval Special Warfare unit det • 5
  SEAL team det • 2 Special Boat unit • 2 Special Boat
  sqn • 1 SEAL delivery veh det • 1 CINCSOC det
AIR FORCE (9,320): (AFRES 1,260) (ANG 750)
1 air force HQ, 1 wg, 14 sqn
7 with AC-130H, 12 AC-130U, 5 MC-130E, 21 MC-130H, 19 MC-130P, 34 MH53J
7 with MH-60G, 5 C-130E. AETC (Air Education
  and Training Command) 1 wg, 2 sqn: 3 MC-130H,
  4 MC-130P, 5 MH-53J, 4 TH-53A
RESERVES
1 wg, 2 sqn:
8 MC-130E, 4 MC-130P, 2 C-130E
ANG
1 wg, 2 sqn:
5 EC-130E

Deployment

Commanders' NATO appointments also shown
(e.g., COMEUCOM is also SACEUR)

EUROPEAN COMMAND (EUCOM)
some 97,510 incl 20,500 in HQ and centrally controlled
formations/units. Plus 14,000 Mediterranean 6th Fleet:
HQ Stuttgart-Vaihingen (Commander is SACEUR)
ARMY (65,700) HQ US Army Europe (USAREUR),
Heidelberg
NAVY HQ US Navy Europe (USNAVEUR), London
  (Commander is also CINCAFSOUTH)
AIR FORCE (31,250) HQ US Air Force Europe
  (USAFE), Ramstein (Commander is COMAIRCENT)
USMC 950

GERMANY
ARMY (51,870)
  V Corps with 1 armd(-), 1 mech inf div(-), 1 arty, 1 AD
    (1 *Patriot* (6 bty), 1 *Avenger* bn), 1 engr, 1 avn bde
  Army Prepositioned Stocks (APS) for 4 armd/mech

bde, approx 57% stored in Ge
EQPT (incl APS in Ge, Be, Lux and Nl)
some 805 MBT, 738 AIFV, 857 APC, 441 arty/MRL/mor, 138 ATK hel
AIR FORCE (15,270), 72 cbt ac
1 air force HQ: USAFE
1 ftr wg: 3 sqn (2 with 54 F-16C/D, 1 with 12 A-10 and 6 OA-10)
1 airlift wg: incl 16 C-130E and 9 C-9A, 9C-21, 2C-20, 1CT-43
NAVY 300
USMC 200

BELGIUM
ARMY 970; approx 22% of POMCUS
NAVY 100
AIR FORCE 500

GREECE
NAVY 240; base facilities at Soudha Bay, Makri (Crete)
AIR FORCE 160; air base gp. Facilities at Iraklion (Crete)
ARMY 10
USMC 10

ITALY
ARMY 2,400; HQ: Vicenza. 1 inf bn gp, 1 arty bty
EQPT for Theater Reserve Unit/Army Readiness Package South (TRU/ARPS), incl 122 MBT, 133 AIFV, 81 APC, 56 arty/MLRS/mor
NAVY 4,400; HQ: Gaeta; bases at Naples, La Maddalena, 1 MR sqn with 9 P-3C at Sigonella
AIR FORCE 3,400; 1 AF HQ (16th Air Force), 1 ftr wg, 2 sqn with 36 F-16C/D
Deliberate Force Component 86 F-16C, 4 AC-130, 8 EC-130, 26 F-15, 18 F-15C, 21 EA-6B, 10 KC-135, 12 F-117, 7 UH-60, 22 A-10, 4 U-2, 3 P-3, 9 MH-53, 3 MC-130, 4 MH-60
USMC 200

LUXEMBOURG
ARMY approx 21% of APS

MEDITERRANEAN
NAVY some 14,000 (incl 2,100 Marines). 6th Fleet (HQ Gaeta, Italy): typically 4 SSN, 1 CVBG (1 CV, 5 surface combatants, 1 fast spt ship), 2 AO, 1 AE, 1 AF, 1 AT/F. MPS-1 (4 ships with equipment for 1 MEF (fwd)). Marine personnel: some 2,000. MEU (SOC) embarked aboard Amphibious Ready Group ships

NETHERLANDS
ARMY 380; approx 7% of APS
AIR FORCE 290
NAVY 10
USMC 10

NORWAY
prepositioning incl 24 M-109, 8 M-198 arty, no aviation assets

AIR FORCE 50
NAVY 10

PORTUGAL
(for Azores, see Atlantic Command)
NAVY 50
AIR FORCE 930
ARMY 20
USMC 20

SPAIN
NAVY 1,760; base at Rota
AIR FORCE 240
USMC 120

TURKEY
ARMY 290
NAVY 20, spt facilities at Izmir and Ankara
AIR FORCE 1,900; facilities at Incirlik. 1 wg (ac on det only), numbers vary (incl F-15, F-16, EA-6B, KC-135, E-3B/C, C-12, HC-130, HH-60)
Installations for SIGINT, space tracking and seismic monitoring
USMC 220

UNITED KINGDOM
ARMY 380
NAVY 1,220; HQ: London, admin and spt facilities, 1 SEAL det
AIR FORCE 9,400
1 air force HQ (3rd Air Force): 1 ftr wg, 53 cbt ac, 2 sqn with 26 F-15E, 1 sqn with 27 F-15C/D
1 special ops gp
1 air refuelling wg with 15 KC-135
1 recce sqn
1 naval air flt
USMC 170

PACIFIC COMMAND (USPACOM)
HQ: Hawaii

ALASKA
ARMY 6,600; 1 lt inf bde
AIR FORCE 9,400; 1 air force HQ (11th Air Force): 1 ftr wg with 2 sqn (1 with 18 F-16, 1 with 6 A-10, 6 OA-10), 1 wg with 2 sqn with 36 F-15C/D, 1 sqn with 18 F-15E, 1 sqn with 10 C-130H, 2 E-3B, 3 C-12, 1 air tkr wg with 8 KC-135R

HAWAII
ARMY 15,500; HQ: US Army Pacific (USARPAC): 1 lt inf div (2 lt inf bde)
AIR FORCE 4,500; HQ: Pacific Air Forces (PACAF): 1 wg with 2 C-135B/C, 1 wg (ANG) with 15 F-15A/B, 4 C-130H and 8 KC-135R
NAVY 7,500; HQ: US Pacific Fleet
Homeport for some 22 SSN, 3 CG, 4 DDG, 2 FFG, 4 spt and misc ships
USMC 7,000; HQ: Marine Forces Pacific

SINGAPORE
NAVY 90; log facilities

AIR FORCE 40 det spt sqn
USMC 20

JAPAN

ARMY 1,800; 1 corps HQ, base and spt units
AIR FORCE 13,900; 1 air force HQ (5th Air Force):
90 cbt ac
1 ftr wg, 2 sqn with 36 F-16 • 1 wg, 3 sqn with 54
F-15C/D • 1 sqn with 15 KC-135 • 1 SAR sqn with
8 HH-60 • 1 sqn with 2 E-3 AWACS • 1 Airlift Wg
with 16 C-130 E/H, 4 C-21, 3 C-9 • 1 special ops
gp with 4 MC-130P and 4 MC-130E
NAVY 5,200; bases: **Yokosuka** (HQ 7th Fleet)
homeport for 1 CV, 6 surface combatants **Sasebo**
homeport for 4 amph ships, 1 MCM sqn
USMC 19,200; 1 MEF

SOUTH KOREA

ARMY 27,500; 1 Army HQ (UN command), 1 inf
div with 2 bde (2 mech inf, 2 air aslt, 2 tk bn), 2 SP
arty, 2 MLRS, 1 AD bn, 1 avn, 1 engr bde, 1 air cav
bde (2 ATK hel bn), 1 *Patriot* SAM bn (Army tps)
EQPT incl 116 MBT, 126 AIFV, 111 APC, 45 arty/
MRL/mor
AIR FORCE 8,600; 1 air force HQ (7th Air Force): 2
ftr wg, 90 cbt ac; 3 sqn with 72 F-16, 1 sqn with 6
A-10, 12 OA-10, 1 special ops sqn, 5 MH-53J
NAVY 300
USMC 130

GUAM

ARMY 40
AIR FORCE 2,000; 1 air force HQ (13th Air Force)
NAVY 1,850; MPS-3 (4 ships with eqpt for 1 MEB)
Naval air station, comms and spt facilities

AUSTRALIA

AIR FORCE 260
NAVY some 40; comms facility at NW Cape, SEWS/
SIGINT station at Pine Gap, and SEWS station at
Nurrungar

DIEGO GARCIA

NAVY 650; MPS-2 (5 ships with eqpt for 1 MEB)
Naval air station, spt facilities
AIR FORCE 20

THAILAND

ARMY 40
NAVY 10
AIR FORCE 30
USMC 40

US WEST COAST

MARINES 1 MEF

AT SEA

PACIFIC FLEET 132,300 USN, 12,850 reserve,
30,450 civilians (HQ: Pearl Harbor) **Main base**
Pearl Harbor **Other bases** Bangor, Everett,
Bremerton (WA), San Diego (CA)
Submarines 8 SSBN, 30 SSN
Surface Combatants 3 CVN, 2 CV, 13 CG/CGN, 13

DDG, 11 DD, 16 FFG
Amph 1 comd, 3 LHA, 3 LPH, 6 LPD, 8 LSD, 1 LST,
plus 1 AG, 59 MSC ships
Surface Combatants divided between two fleets
3rd Fleet (HQ: San Diego) covers Eastern and
Central Pacific, Aleutian Islands, Bering Sea;
typically 3 CVBG, 4 URG, amph gp
7th Fleet (HQ: Yokosuka) covers Western Pacific,
Japan, Philippines, ANZUS responsibilities, Indian
Ocean; typically 2 CVBG, 1 URG, amph ready gp
(1 MEU embarked), 2 MCM
Aircraft 363 tactical, 203 helicopter, 77 P-3, 162 other

CENTRAL COMMAND (USCENTCOM)

commands all deployed forces in its region; HQ:
MacDill AFB, FL
ARMY 2,070
AT SEA
5th Fleet HQ Manama. Average US Naval Forces
deployed in Indian Ocean, Persian Gulf, Red Sea:
1 CVBG, 1 URG (forces provided from Atlantic
and Pacific), 2 MCM

BAHRAIN

NAVY 680
USMC 220
ARMY 10
AIR FORCE 20

KUWAIT

ARMY 3,000; prepositioned eqpt for 1 armd bde (2
tk, 1 mech bn, 1 arty bn)
NAVY 10
AIR FORCE 2,100 (force structure varies)
USMC 80

OMAN

AIR FORCE 630
NAVY 60

QATAR

ARMY 30; prepositioned eqpt for 1 armd bde
(forming)

SAUDI ARABIA

ARMY 650; 1 *Patriot* SAM, 1 sigs unit incl those on
short-term (6 months) duty
AIR FORCE 4,800. Units on rotational detachment,
ac numbers vary (incl F-15, F-16, F-117, C-130, KC-
135, U-2, E-3)
NAVY 20
USMC 250

UAE

AIR FORCE 390

SOUTHERN COMMAND (USSOUTHCOM)

HQ: Miami, FL
ARMY 2,100; HQ: US Army South, Fort Clayton: 1
inf, 1 avn bn
USMC 100
AIR FORCE 1,600; 1 wg (1 C-21, 9 C-27, 1 CT-43)

HONDURAS
ARMY 160
USMC 70
AIR FORCE 170

ATLANTIC COMMAND (USACOM)
HQ: Norfolk, VA (CINC has op control of all CONUS-based army and air forces)

US EAST COAST
USMC 19,200; 1 MEF

BERMUDA
NAVY 800

CUBA
NAVY 590 (Guantánamo)
USMC 490 (Guantánamo)

HAITI
USMC 230

ICELAND
NAVY 960; 1 MR sqn with 6 P-3, 1 UP-3
USMC 80
AIR FORCE 600; 6 F-15C/D, 1 KC-135, 1 HC-130, 4 HH-60G

PORTUGAL (AZORES)
NAVY 10; limited facilities at Lajes
AIR FORCE periodic SAR detachments to spt space shuttle ops

UNITED KINGDOM
NAVY 1,220; comms and int facilities, Edzell, Thurso

AT SEA
ATLANTIC FLEET (HQ: Norfolk, VA) **Other main bases** Groton (CT), King's Bay (GA), Mayport (FL)
Submarines 10 SSBN, 16 SSGN, 35 SSN
Surface Combatants 6 CV/CVN, 23 CG/CGN, 21 DDG, 23 FFG. Amph: 1 LCC, 2 LHA, 4 LPH, 6 LPD, 5 LSD, 6 LST, 1 LKA
Surface Forces divided into 2 fleets:
2nd Fleet (HQ: Norfolk) covers Atlantic; typically 4–5 CVBG, amph gp, 4 URG
6th Fleet (HQ: Gaeta, Italy) under op comd of EUCOM, typically 1 CG, 3 DDG, 2 FFG, 3 SSN, amph gp

Continental United States (CONUS)

major units/formations only listed
930,800 personnel

ARMY (USACOM)
340,300 provides general reserve of cbt-ready ground forces for other comd
Active 1 Army HQ, 3 Corps HQ (1 AB), 1 armd, 2 mech, 1 lt inf, 1 AB, 1 air aslt div; 6 arty bde; 2 armd cav regt, 6 AD bn (1 *Avenger*, 5 *Patriot*)
Reserve (ARNG): 3 armd, 4 mech, 1 lt inf div;18 indep bde

NAVY 186,200
AIR FORCE 276,200
USMC 128,100

US STRATEGIC COMMAND (USSTRATCOM)
HQ: Offutt AFB, NE
See entry on p. 20

AIR COMBAT COMMAND (ACC)
HQ: Langley AFB, VA. Provides strategic AD units and cbt-ready Air Force units for rapid deployment

SPACE COMMAND (AFSPACECOM)
HQ: Peterson AFB, CO. Provides ballistic-missile warning, space control, satellite operations around the world, and maintains ICBM force

US SPECIAL OPERATIONS COMMAND (USSOCOM)
HQ: MacDill AFB, FL. Comd all active, reserve and National Guard special ops forces of all services based in CONUS. See p. 26

US TRANSPORTATION COMMAND (USTRANSCOM)
HQ: Scott AFB, IL. Provides all common-user airlift, sealift and land transport to deploy and maintain US forces on a global basis

AIR MOBILITY COMMAND (AMC)
HQ: Scott AFB, IL. Provides strategic, tac and special op airlift, aero-medical evacuation, SAR and weather recce

Forces Abroad

UN AND PEACEKEEPING
BOSNIA (SFOR II): 8,360; 1 inf bde plus spt tps
CROATIA (SFOR): 150. **SFOR AIR ELEMENT** (OP JOINT GUARD) 3,200. Forces are deployed to **Bosnia, Croatia, Hungary, Italy, France, Germany** and the **United Kingdom**. Aircraft include F/A-16, A-10, AC-130, MC-130, C-130, E-3, U-2, EC-130, RC-135, EA-6B, MH-53J and *Predator* UAV. **EGYPT** (MFO): 918; 1 inf, 1 spt bn. **GEORGIA** (UNOMIG): 1 Obs. **HUNGARY** (SFOR): 640. 230 Air Force *Predator* UAV. **IRAQ/KUWAIT** (UNIKOM): 8 Obs. **MIDDLE EAST** (UNTSO): 1 Obs. **WESTERN SAHARA** (MINURSO): 15 Obs. **SAUDI ARABIA** (*Southern Watch*) **Air Force** units on rotation, numbers vary (incl F-15, F-16, F-117, C-130, KC-135, E-3). **TURKEY** (*Northern Watch*) **Air Force** 1,400; 1 tac, 1 Air Base gp (ac on det only), numbers vary but include F-16, F-15, EA-6B, KC-135, E3B/C, C-12, HC-130

Paramilitary

CIVIL AIR PATROL (CAP) 53,000
(1,900 cadets); HQ, 8 geographical regions, 52 wg, 1,700 units, 535 CAP ac, plus 4,700 private ac

MILITARY DEVELOPMENTS

Regional Trends

The dominating military event in Europe during 1999, the NATO-led military campaign in Yugoslavia, has had a substantial impact on the development of the military and political aspects of security policy both within the region and beyond. In Western Europe it has inspired European Union countries to accelerate their plans for developing a more substantial European military capability – although much has to be done before this aspiration can be realised in even a modest way. The disparity between US military capability to conduct the missions now required of NATO forces and that of the European NATO members was thrown into stark relief by the US dominance in the air campaign. Relations between the NATO countries and Russia were severely challenged by the Kosovo crisis, but they were improving modestly by the time the NATO-led Kosovo Force (KFOR), was deployed. There was a deeper impact on Russia domestically, which led to a more assertive military establishment despite the crippling economic circumstances which damaged military reform. *Operation Allied Force* has had reverberations beyond Europe, particularly influencing perceptions of NATO's ability to conduct operations outside its members' territories. Some of these perceptions over-estimate both NATO's readiness and its capability to embark on major military operations further afield. Tensions and conflicts persist in parts of Europe other than the Balkans, for example the disputes between Armenia and Azerbaijan over Nagorno Karabakh, within Georgia and between Greece and Turkey over Cyprus.

Kosovo

In terms of its military outcome, it is hard to judge *Operation Allied Force* other than as a success. After the air campaign from 24 March to 10 June 1999, the NATO ground force, KFOR was introduced on 12 June and Yugoslav forces were withdrawn from Kosovo by 20 June. By the end of July, 720,000 of the around one million refugees from the province had returned home. However, a great deal of investment of military capability in a deployed peacekeeping force, as well as economic and social support will be needed over a long period before the military result can be translated into a lasting peace. The experience in Bosnia-Herzegovina, where the 60,000-strong force deployed in 1995 had been scaled down to a little over 20,000 by mid-1999, suggests that the demands of Kosovo might decline over a period of some five years. Nevertheless, maintaining a force of some 20,000 over a decade or more will impose a strain on the NATO countries' regular forces.

NATO air forces carried out nearly 10,000 bombing missions during the 79-day air campaign, and deployed just over 1,000 aircraft at the height of the action, only two of which were lost to enemy fire. The US provided over 70% of the aircraft for the campaign with the remainder coming from 13 countries (Belgium, Canada, Denmark, France, Germany, Italy, Netherlands, Norway, Portugal, Spain, Turkey, the UK and the US). The US preponderance is even more marked in terms of the estimated amount of weapons delivered, of which the US accounted for over 80%. The main reason for this was that the US has a far superior capability to deliver weapons, in all weather conditions, from the altitude of 5,000 metres laid down by NATO to minimise aircraft and aircrew losses. Where cruise missiles were concerned, the US delivered well over 90% of those launched from either air or sea. The UK, with its submarine-launched missile capability, was the only other NATO country able to contribute cruise missiles during the campaign. A total of 240 sea-launched *Tomahawk* Land-Attack Missiles (TLAM) were fired during the campaign of which the US launched 220 and the UK 20. The US fired 60 air-launched cruise missiles (ALCM).

Although nine NATO navies contributed warships, the US was also dominant at sea, providing most of the carrier-based air effort and vessels to deliver TLAMs. The nature of the air- and missile-support for the operation meant that surface ships were able to lie well back from the coast where they were vulnerable only to submarine attack. Here the Netherlands and Italy were able to play an important role with their anti-submarine warfare (ASW) diesel submarines (SSKs) to protect against a possible attempt by the Yugoslavs to deploy their two operational diesel submarines. SSKs are the best defence in these circumstances, particularly in countering a threat moving out from relatively shallow coastal waters. The UK and the US no longer have SSKs, and France is about to retire the two in its fleet, thus smaller NATO navies were able to make an important contribution.

The deployment of KFOR in June 1999 demonstrated a different kind of disparity, this time between the UK and the other European members of NATO. One of the major problems experienced by the force was getting sufficient numbers of troops to all parts of Kosovo quickly enough to establish security for returning refugees and, in particular, to deter reprisals by the ethnic Albanian population against the Serbs. On the initial deployment on 12 June, the KFOR commander had some 20,000 troops available to him, but the build-up to the planned total of some 52,000 was slow. The UK, having the only all-professional force amongst the larger European countries and thus having the capability to deploy fully trained personnel quickly, initially provided the largest contingent of all the NATO countries and twice as many troops as any other European member. By 7 August, there were over 38,000 KFOR troops deployed in Kosovo and about 7,000 in the Former Yugoslav Republic of Macedonia, with the UK providing just over 10,000. Maintaining the force over a long period will be a challenge for all participants, given their other commitments such as the NATO Stabilisation Force (SFOR) in neighbouring Bosnia-Herzegovina. These commitments, along with other deployments, will severely inhibit the NATO Europeans' capability for new operations elsewhere.

NATO

The military campaign against Yugoslavia had been underway for nearly a month when the NATO allies gathered for their fiftieth anniversary summit meeting in Washington on 23–24 April 1999, where, as scheduled, they endorsed a new strategic concept for the Alliance. While it does not embody radical change, the new concept confirms the development of NATO towards the task of fulfilling peacekeeping missions and operations beyond the borders of its members. The summit also approved a revised command structure and support for combined joint task forces (CJTFs), whether led through the normal command structure or composed of purely European forces, through the Western European Union (WEU) or other European arrangements.

A new development at the Washington summit meeting was NATO's Defence Capabilities Initiative (DCI), whose aim is to improve defence capabilities 'to ensure effectiveness of future multinational operations across the full spectrum of Alliance missions in the present and foreseeable security environment'. The Initiative is intended to focus particularly on improving interoperability among NATO forces as well as members of the Partnership for Peace (PFP) programme. The new strategic concept brought no change in the Alliance's nuclear strategy. This means that, theoretically, any NATO country may accept the basing of nuclear weapons on their territory, but the so-called three 'noes' still apply – the Alliance has 'no intention, no plan, and no reason' to deploy nuclear weapons on the territories of the new members from the former Eastern block. The number of sub-strategic nuclear weapons in Western Europe has fallen substantially since 1991. All nuclear artillery and ground-launched short-range nuclear missiles have been withdrawn from all NATO forces. The sub-strategic capability now consists of only a few hundred free-fall bombs and the UK's 200 or so warheads in their *Trident* ballistic-missile submarines (SSBNs), which are now assigned a sub-strategic as well as strategic role. France's nuclear capability is not assigned to NATO. The NATO capability compares with Russia's sub-strategic nuclear arsenal which is estimated to contain between 20,000 and 30,000 warheads.

The door to NATO's further enlargement was left open by the April 1999 summit declaration: 'No European democratic country whose admission would fulfil the objectives of the (Washington) Treaty will be excluded from consideration'. An enhanced partnership programme has been approved to assist aspiring countries to prepare for membership, whose main vehicle is an enhanced and more operational PFP. In particular, an Operational Capabilities Concept is being developed to improve the ability of PFP countries to contribute to NATO-led operations. The Planning and Review Process (PARP), under which the ability of PFP countries to interoperate with NATO forces can be assessed, is being strengthened. The PARP sets out 45 interoperability objectives for the assessment process, mainly in the combat-support and logistic areas. More controversially, NATO ministers, at the NATO ministerial meeting in autumn 1999, are likely to agree a set of priority goals for operational capabilities to be achieved as part of the qualification for membership.

NATO–Russia

When the NATO campaign in Kosovo began, Russia withdrew from activities under the NATO–Russia Founding Act and withdrew its mission to NATO, and meetings of the Joint Permanent Council (JPC) ceased. However, the need to coordinate peacekeeping activities may help repair relations over time. Once the bombing in Kosovo had ended, and the dust had settled after a small Russian force had raced to Slatina airfield near Pristina, the *modus operandi* for integrating Russian forces into KFOR was worked out quickly. Under an agreement with the US, the Russians can deploy up to 2,850 troops in up to five battalions in agreed areas in the French, German and US sectors of KFOR. They can also deploy up to 750 troops for the airfield and logistics base operations at Slatina. The JPC restarted its meetings in June, although only to discuss the practicalities of peacekeeping operations in the Balkans.

NATO–Ukraine

Cooperation between NATO and Ukraine under the 'Charter on a Distinctive Partnership' is gathering momentum and more substance. Ukraine has put in hand a State Programme of Cooperation with NATO, which extends to 2001, and broadens the areas of collaboration. In April 1999, Ukraine formally designated its Yavoriv training area as a PFP training centre and multilateral exercises have already taken place there. The joint Polish–Ukrainian peacekeeping battalion formed in 1999 has real substance and will be a model for Ukrainian participation in other multinational peacekeeping units. Consultations with NATO on defence-industrial restructuring, armed-forces restructuring and retirement and retraining of military personnel are particularly valuable to Ukraine. Given the difficult economic situation, the armed forces are in urgent need of modernisation and upgrading. For example, none of the submarines in the Ukrainian fleet is operational and only a small proportion of the surface combatants can be sustained at sea to form a naval task force on their own. Complementary to the cooperation with NATO, Ukraine is making a major effort to profit from bilateral military programmes, particularly with Poland, the UK and US.

European Security and Defence Identity

There has been a drive to add impetus to the development of the European Security and Defence Identity (ESDI) which predates NATO's 1999 Kosovo campaign. The reinvigoration effort was initiated by the UK in October 1998 when it indicated, at an informal EU summit in Austria, that it would no longer object to military cooperation within the EU provided that it was militarily sound and did not harm the transatlantic security relationship. This important shift in UK policy was followed up at the December 1998 Anglo-French summit in St Malo where a joint declaration set out the need for the EU to have an 'autonomous military capability', but one which still drew on NATO as well as other European assets. The momentum was maintained at the June 1999 EU summit in Cologne, with determination now reinforced by the experience of *Operation Allied Force*, which was then reaching its closing stages. It was agreed at the Cologne summit that:

- the Western European Union (WEU)'s military functions (essentially those of a small military contingency planning staff) should be transferred to the EU and its mission ended; no decision was taken on whether the WEU should be merged with the EU or dissolved;
- the EU General Affairs Council (GAC) should be expanded to include defence ministers by the end of 2000, and its work on security policy should be backed by a Political and Security Committee and a Military Committee;
- a High Representative should be appointed to oversee the implementation of the EU's Common and Foreign and Security Policy; then NATO Secretary-General, Javier Solana, was selected.

These limited steps contrast starkly with the ambitious objective stated at Cologne of 'a capacity for autonomous action backed by credible military forces'. Perhaps necessarily at this stage, the focus has been on institutional arrangements rather than military capabilities. However, the latter did move to centre stage at the Anglo-Italian summit in July 1999, at which a proposal was made 'to set criteria for improved and strengthened European defence capabilities and effective performance'. The proposal included:

- developing goals for enhanced military capabilities linked to 'national capability objectives' for achieving the goals;
- instituting a system of peer review, to take place at an EU GAC meeting at least once every six months, to measure progress against an agreed set of criteria;
- taking account of work in NATO on a Defence Capabilities Initiative;
- Creating a 'road map' for achieving more effective defence procurement, including the harmonisation of military requirements and collaborative arms procurement.

EU countries can be expected to try to develop force-modernisation convergence criteria for strengthened European defence. However, even if the EU adopts the ideas of the Anglo-Italian summit and peer pressure is applied, independent European capabilities for major combined-arms operations remain a distant prospect. However, the process should achieve a limited improvement (mainly in the fields of coordination, training and readiness) in Europe's abilities to conduct peacekeeping and military support of humanitarian operations that require only lightly armed forces. Where these are concerned, the key factors are the numbers of armed forces personnel available to be deployed and the capability to move them to the theatre of operations. However, developing an autonomous combined-arms capability to conduct offensive operations, or at least to be prepared to do so, as in the case of the 60,000 strong NATO deployment immediately following the Dayton Agreement on Bosnia-Herzegovina, is a far bigger undertaking. While the decline in defence spending since 1991 appears to have levelled out, the NATO Europeans collectively spend about half as much on defence as the US. They will have to raise defence outlays significantly above current plans to acquire the more advanced weapons, command-and-control systems, surveillance and target-acquisition equipment and logistic and transport support needed for an independent capability. Another key ingredient in enhanced capability is the professionalisation of armed forces. The UK has longstanding all-professional forces, and some progress has been made elsewhere, for example in Belgium and the Netherlands, which now have fully professional armed forces and France whose professional armed forces will be slightly larger than those of the UK by 2003. Among the other larger European countries, Italy and Spain have begun the professionalisation process, but for historical and domestic political reasons, Germany seems unable to take this step at present.

However, Germany has enhanced the number of professionals available for military missions abroad and they acquitted themselves well in the Balkans. A German general (Klaus Reinhardt) is set to take over from the British commander of KFOR in autumn 1999.

Tensions and Conflict

Apart from the Balkans, the main areas of conflict, or potential for conflict in Europe, were unchanged in 1998–99. Tense situations remain in the Caucasus region, in the province of Abkhazia in Georgia and between Armenia and Azerbaijan over Nagorno Karabakh. Talks between the Georgian government and representatives of the Abkhazian separatists, held under UN sponsorship in Istanbul in June 1999, resulted in agreement to exchange prisoners and set up working groups to deal with the return of refugees. A final declaration issued in Istanbul said that both sides agreed to develop a series of joint projects, such as building dams and power plants, and work towards establishing a 'security line' along the internal border of the disputed province. While there are positive signs of progress, the potential for conflict remains, particularly over the return of refugees. The conflict over Nagorno Karabakh has been running since 1988 when the Armenian ethnic majority in the enclave tried to break away from Azerbaijan. More than 20,000 people died and one million more were displaced in the ensuing fighting before a cease-fire was agreed in 1994. Talks between the presidents of Azerbaijan and Armenia were held in Geneva in June 1999, but no progress towards a settlement was achieved. Sporadic fighting still occurs, there is continuous potential for wider conflict, and Armenia and Azerbaijan continue to strengthen their military capabilities. The even longer-running dispute between the Greek and Turkish communities in Cyprus also remains unresolved. Tensions arose between Turkey and Cyprus in late 1998 and early 1999 over the Cypriot purchase of Russian S-300 surface-to-air missiles (SAMs). The problem was resolved, at least temporarily, in February 1999, when Greece agreed to allow the missiles to be stationed on Crete, although they remain the property of the Cypriot government. Despite efforts by the EU, the UN and individual governments, particularly the US and the UK, no progress has been made in resolving the underlying dispute.

Terrorism

Domestic terrorism continues to decline in Western Europe, although resolution of the conflicts remains a painfully slow process. This is particularly true in the UK where terrorist incidents in Northern Ireland have declined sharply overall, but the peace process is very hesitant. In Spain, the armed wing of the Basque separatist organisation *Euskadi ta Askatasuna* (ETA) declared a cease-fire in September 1998 and the Spanish government had released 22 members of the group's political wing by July 1999. Although there has been sporadic violence since the cease-fire began, the government has offered to improve prison conditions for ETA members convicted of terrorist offences if the group declares a permanent end to armed action. Talks on ending the 30-year old conflict continue.

DEFENCE SPENDING

NATO Europe and Canada

Defence expenditure by NATO European countries has fallen by 22% in real terms since 1992, but the rate of decline slowed in 1998, when spending, measured in constant 1997 US dollars, fell by only 1% to $171 billion from $173bn in 1997. However, in 1999, while spending levels are similar in nominal terms to 1998 levels, the depreciation of the euro since its introduction in January 1999 means that the dollar value of most European defence budgets is some 7% down in real terms on 1998. Sustaining defence budgets, even at these reduced levels, is a political challenge for the majority of NATO European governments. This is particularly so for those countries within the euro zone which have not yet managed to meet the Maastricht Treaty criteria for government debt (Germany, France, Italy, Austria, Netherlands, and Spain, according to June 1999 figures published by the OECD). At the same time, many governments have to balance costly priorities such as professionalisation and equipment modernisation within static or shrinking defence budgets. There is no sign that any European country shares the US intention to increase defence spending (particularly on procurement) over the next five years, as set out in its plan for the year 2000.

The enlargement of NATO to include Poland, Hungary and the Czech Republic does not herald a significant increase in Alliance spending overall because of the economic problems of the three new members. Although all three set higher targets for defence spending, they are likely to give greater priority to wider economic and social objectives in order to meet the criteria for EU membership. They, along with Estonia, Cyprus and Slovenia, are negotiating a target date of 2002 for EU membership; the most likely formal entry date is 2005. Concern about the cost of NATO enlargement, within both the new and the longstanding member states, has largely subsided. It is now recognised that the incremental costs will be carried mainly by the new member states, and that neither unilateral (US) nor multilateral (NATO common-funded) contributions will be substantial. According to Polish Ministry of National Defence estimates (February 1998), Poland's direct costs of joining NATO will amount to some $3bn in the period 1998–10, or about 5% of the annual defence budget. The indirect costs (of achieving interoperability with NATO Armed Forces and of equipment modernisation) are expected to be some $8.3bn over 15 years.

Contingency and peacekeeping operations are an increasing drain on Europe's stretched defence budgets. NATO's common-funded budget (for which all member states are assessed on economic criteria) has no formal mechanism for spreading the cost of contingencies. Consequently, the US carried around 80% of the incremental cost of the Kosovo air campaign and supporting force deployments, with the UK and France contributing most of the balance. Governments were at pains to play down the direct costs of the campaign, which *The Military Balance* estimates to be some $11bn, including the wear-and-tear costs of much higher than normal rates of equipment use.

Research, Development and Procurement Spending

The continuing decline in European procurement is raising concerns that the NATO European defence capability is becoming increasingly inferior to that of the US. The lessons from *Operation Allied Force* underlined the transatlantic asymmetry in certain weapon categories, and have added a new set of procurement challenges for the European allies. Their overall defence spending in 1999 is about half that of the US, and their spending on military research and development is just one quarter of US levels. The Europeans appear to have no collective plans to address the growing capability gap. At the same time, the fall in the purchasing power of European defence budgets as a result of the weakening euro makes US technology more expensive at the moment it is most needed. Weak European currencies also increase the competitiveness of European defence exports, giving the major European governments the incentive to make defence exports a policy priority rather than face unpopular decisions on defence budget increases. In the case of the larger European NATO member states, it seems unlikely that current procurement commitments can be sustained under existing budget plans.

Equipment programmes

European equipment programmes continue to be characterised by over-commitment and under-funding. Frequently the result is technical under-performance, delayed schedules, and substantial cost overruns. An analysis in *The Military Balance 1998/99* (Transatlantic Defence Industries and NATO Armaments Cooperation, pp. 273–283) concluded that similar shortcomings were becoming a feature of US procurement programmes. The analysis suggested that the most promising solution lay in NATO-wide programmes, administered by a central NATO procurement organisation and sourced from a competitive transatlantic defence industry. No progress has been made since 1998 on either the policy-making or the institutional fronts. In Europe, development of the Joint Armaments Co-operation Organisation (JACO), also known as *Organisme Conjoint en Matière d'Armement* (OCCAR), has been slowed by continuing disputes over workshare allocations (*juste retour*). New JACO programmes have been hard hit. The UK withdrew from the three-nation *Horizon* frigate programme in April 1999, effectively terminating it, while the three-nation armoured vehicle programme (MRAV/GTK/VBCI) has been in limbo since France's effective withdrawal in October 1998. Long-running programmes, now managed by JACO, such as the *Tiger* helicopter, are the subjects of tortuous renegotiations and delays. Meanwhile NATO's Conference of National Armaments Directors (CNAD) remains an ineffective forum for NATO armaments cooperation, since there is no consensus among NATO governments as to how the organisation should be further empowered. After a study lasting over a year, CNAD circulated an internal report on Alliance collective procurement in September 1998, but there has since been no public sign of action to implement radical change, despite advance publicity suggesting a major shift in approach.

As stated in the last edition of *The Military Balance*, there are formidable barriers to NATO procurement reform despite the evidence that the purchasing power of all NATO defence-equipment budgets is falling sharply in the face of supplier-price escalation. Governments of countries with large arms production capabilities have become more open over the past year to the possibility of foreign ownership of national defence industries and the development of a competitive, transatlantic defence industry, but most of those governments still operate protectionist, preferential procurement policies and practices. Even when they buy foreign equipment, they insist on expensive offsets and *juste retour* arrangements. The clear evidence of the inadequacy of such policies makes it difficult for governments to defend them. The US has focused its criticism on the technology gap between the US and Europe. However, while the gap exists in certain weapon categories, the US does not have technological superiority in all conventional weapon sectors. Such a generalisation blocks exploration of areas where Europe and the US might best cooperate in developing and producing conventional weapons. Once suitable programmes are identified, there is every possibility that a combined purchase would recreate the economies in technology development and scale that once justified exclusive national and Europe-only collaborative projects. But such economies on a purely European basis no longer bring rewards because of escalating research and development costs and shrinking production volumes. Cooperative procurement of certain conventional weapon systems on a NATO-wide scale would also ease the way for the US to provide Europe with those weapons and technologies where the US has a clear superiority. Such a division of effort would reduce the element of duplication in NATO procurement without compromising competition, hence driving costs down. For their part, the Europeans have helped to generate US distrust of cooperative programmes through poor management of European collaborative projects and of those few NATO programmes in which the US and the Europeans have worked together. The management of such a new division of effort in NATO procurement would undoubtedly require the abandonment of long-held prejudices on both sides of the Atlantic. At present, it appears that both policy makers and procurement staffs seem prepared to accept the eroding purchasing power of their defence procurement budgets, so long as whatever remains is spent at home. The costs of failing to overcome the formidable political obstacles and sectional interests opposed to achieving an efficient level of armaments cooperation

Table 8 Defence R&D and procurement spending in NATO and non-NATO Western Europe, 1995–1999

(Constant 1997 US$million)

	Defence Budget					Research and development (R&D)					Equipment procurement				
	1995	1996	1997	1998	1999	1995	1996	1997	1998	1999	1995	1996	1997	1998	1999
NATO															
Be	3,534	3,186	2,806	2,723	2,588	2	2	2	1	2	293	217	192	203	183
Da	3,250	3,099	2,726	2,652	2,395	5	5	5	5	5	406	384	339	351	322
Fr	42,240	37,861	32,711	30,703	28,353	5,525	4,932	3,821	3,254	3,148	7,952	7,588	6,465	5,620	5,242
Ge	34,625	32,745	26,641	26,002	23,790	1,981	1,850	1,487	1,410	1,262	3,969	3,705	2,956	3,455	3,715
Gr	3,473	3,598	3,648	3,867	3,675	8	9	18	23	21	1,022	1,146	1,146	1,287	1,273
It	16,619	20,680	18,237	17,495	15,609	579	756	751	533	298	1,642	2,026	2,100	2,394	1,905
Lu	128	124	109	105	98	0	0	0	0	0	3	7	6	5	5
Nl	8,775	8,249	6,992	6,869	6,797	79	121	102	99	64	1,338	1,578	1,324	1,581	1,380
No	3,901	3,820	3,597	3,099	3,070	48	36	22	21	21	826	839	906	773	691
Por	1,869	1,755	1,698	1,554	1,564	4	4	4	4	4	140	263	352	365	400
Sp	7,243	7,014	5,942	5,888	5,464	299	282	242	198	170	998	1,243	1,012	781	744
Tu	6,006	5,175	8,110	8,191	8,556	12	14	40	45	42	2,392	2,309	2,568	2,933	3,028
UK	35,725	34,196	35,736	36,111	33,254	3,408	3,422	3,491	3,785	3,909	7,334	8,189	8,466	9,354	8,263
Sub-total	167,389	161,502	148,955	145,260	135,213	11,951	11,433	9,984	9,378	8,946	28,314	29,496	27,834	29,102	27,152
Cz	966	1,009	988	1,081	1,110	25	28	24	19	15	119	142	135	149	176
Hu	806	597	666	647	661	1	5	2	12	12	87	83	130	179	179
Pl	3,580	3,150	3,073	3,258	3,094	33	61	55	93	76	305	559	475	505	468
Sub-total	5,352	4,755	4,727	4,986	4,866	59	93	80	124	103	511	784	739	833	822
Total	172,740	166,257	153,682	150,246	140,079	12,010	11,527	10,065	9,502	9,050	28,825	30,280	28,573	29,935	27,974
Ca	8,663	7,908	7,162	6,200	6,498	85	93	75	113	110	1,791	2,165	1,878	1,441	1,258
US (DoD)	274,624	271,739	257,975	253,423	252,379	36,597	35,722	36,404	36,469	35,324	46,251	43,332	42,930	43,887	47,052
US and Ca	283,287	279,646	265,137	259,623	258,878	36,682	35,815	36,479	36,582	35,434	48,042	45,497	44,808	45,328	48,310
Total	456,028	445,903	418,819	409,869	398,957	48,692	47,342	46,544	45,932	44,337	76,867	75,777	73,381	75,263	76,284
Non-NATO															
A	2,195	2,001	1,710	1,764	1,591	10	10	10	10	10	451	371	310	400	288
SF	2,227	1,976	1,834	1,829	1,493	11	9	9	9	13	792	742	670	866	591
Irl	723	757	771	780	580	0	0	0	0	0	27	25	27	33	20
Swe	6,290	6,253	5,021	5,241	4,350	163	160	158	160	95	2,485	1,943	1,671	1,895	2,205
CH	5,121	4,534	3,727	3,556	3,040	101	97	77	69	62	2,168	1,839	1,647	1,518	1,315
Total	16,555	15,521	13,063	13,169	11,053	286	276	254	248	180	5,924	4,920	4,325	4,712	4,419

Note Hungary figures include arms-for-debt transactions.

are likely to be high, not only in economic, but also in military terms. Effective transatlantic cooperation in armaments procurement is essential to ensure that NATO armed forces are properly equipped for the missions that will face them over the coming years.

The European Fighter Aircraft (EFA) programme is the most expensive current European collaborative programme, and is a good example of the strengths and weaknesses of European cooperation. The order for the first batch of 148 aircraft was placed in January 1998. While *Eurofighter* has avoided outright cancellation (the possible fate of the US F-22), it is unlikely that the requirement for 620 aircraft can withstand the current and future budgetary constraints and the review of equipment requirements following the military campaign in the Balkans. Meanwhile first deliveries of 294 to the French Air Force of the domestically-produced *Rafale* fighter, ground attack aircraft (FGA) take place in 1999. Sweden's purchase of 204 of the JAS-9 *Gripen* aircraft remains firm for the moment, despite the fact that its purchase is consuming much of the Swedish procurement budget. The production schedule has been extended to 2007 and intensive effort is going into marketing the aircraft for export. The manufacturers of all three types (*Eurofighter*, *Rafale* and *Gripen*) are drawing encouragement from the uncertainty over the US F-22 FGA, which if cancelled will improve the export prospects for these types – a telling reflection of the over capacity that exists in this most prestigious of weapons sectors. The uncertainty over the F-22 has also improved the prospects for the US Joint Strike Fighter (JSF) programme, of which the UK is a full partner and Norway, Denmark, and the Netherlands have joined as single associate partners. Singapore and Turkey have contracted for customer status without industrial participation, rather than associate partner or observer status. Canada and Italy have observer status and Israel is considering joining. The JSF could prove to be a new model for NATO equipment cooperation after decades of expensive wrangling, protectionism and delay.

Non-NATO Europe

Defence spending by the European countries outside Europe increased by some $500m (2%) in real terms in 1998 to over $27bn. There are wide regional variations in spending trends. Countries with relatively large defence expenditures, mainly non-NATO EU countries, continue to cut their spending. In non-NATO EU countries and Switzerland, 1999 defence budgets show little change on 1998 when measured in nominal national currencies, but inflation-adjustment shows a fall in real terms. Budgets expressed in dollar terms also show a fall, given the continuing weakness of European currencies against the US dollar. However spending is higher in some areas, such as the Transcaucasus, the Baltic states, and in Cyprus where the defence budget rose to C£300m ($530m) in 1999 from C£265m ($515m) in 1998. In the Transcaucasus, real military spending in Azerbaijan and Armenia continues at higher levels than official defence budgets suggest. Azerbaijan's official defence budget in 1999 is m472bn ($120m) compared to m463bn ($119m) in 1998, while Armenia's 1999 budget rises to d40bn ($75m) against d33bn ($66m) in 1998. *The Military Balance* estimates actual outlays at approaching double these figures. In the Balkans, Slovenia reported defence expenditure of t53bn ($305m) in 1998, very similar to official spending levels in 1997. Croatia's 1999 budget is k6.1bn ($815m), compared to a budget of k7.5bn and outturn of k6.2bn ($1bn) in 1998. In the Federal Republic of Yugoslavia (Serbia and Montenegro), the official 1999 defence budget was d11.4bn ($990m) rising to d14.4bn ($1,250m) after 1999 supplementary allocations to fund military and armed police operations in Kosovo and contingencies associated with *Operation Allied Force*.

Ukraine's real military spending is difficult to analyse, given the extensive military-related spending excluded from the defence budget. The 1999 defence budget under the federal budget is h1.7bn, unchanged from the initial level in 1998 (which was later cut to h1.5bn). The dollar value, however, has fallen to $429m from the initial 1998 level of $700m. The outturn in 1998 was h1.2bn, excluding military pensions of some h500m. The internal security budget including the National

Guard, Border Guard, Interior Troops and Civil Defence, as well civil policing, is also h1.7bn ($700m) in 1999 compared to h1.6bn in 1998. Excluded from the 1999 defence budget are military-related activities such as international operations (h520m), research and development – some of which is military or dual-use (h511m), defence conversion (h90m), military pensions, and unspecified military spending by regional authorities (notably in the Crimea). Ukrainian arms sales in 1998 were worth over $500m, slightly up on 1997.

Table 9 Arms orders and deliveries, NATO Europe and Canada, 1997–1999

Supplier	Classification	Designation	Units	Order Date	Delivery Date	Comment
Belgium						
Sgp	tpt	A-310	2	1996	1998	Second aircraft delivered May 1998
US	FGA	F-16	48	1993	1998	Mid-Life Update. 88 AMRAAM on order
US	FGA	F-16	18	1999	2000	Upgrade; option on 18 exercised
Fr	arty	105mm	14	1996	1996	Deliveries continue in 1997
A	APC	*Pandur*	54	1997	1998	
Il	UAV	*Hunter*	18	1998	2000	
Canada						
UK	SSK	*Upholder*	4	1998	2000	Deliveries to 2001
dom	MCMV	*Kingston*	12	1992	1996	Deliveries continue to 1999
US	hel	B-412EP	100	1992	1994	Deliveries to 1998 at 3 per month
CH	AD Guns	GDF-005	20	1996	1997	Upgrade
dom	LAV	LAV-25	240	1996	1998	105 in 1997, 47 1998; deliveries continue
dom	LAV	LAV-25	120	1998	2001	Follow-on order after initial batch of 240
UK	ACV	API-88/400	2	1996	1998	Delivery May 1998
US	APC	M-113	400	1997	1998	Life extension update; deliveries continue
Ge	MBT	*Leopard* 1	114	1997	1999	*Leopard* C1A5 Upgrade
col	hel	EH-101	15	1998	2001	Ca designation AW520; deliveries to 2002
Czech Republic						
dom	MBT	T-72	250	1995	2000	Upgrade prog. Rescheduled in 1999
dom	trg	L-39	27	1997	1999	Originally for Nga; delivery to Cz airforce delayed
dom	FGA	L-159	72	1997	1999	
col	UAV	*Sojka*3	8	1998	2000	Upgraded *Sojka* III. Developed with Hu
RF	cbt hel	Mi-24	7	1999	1999	Arms for debt
Denmark						
US	FGA	F-16	63	1993	1998	Mid-Life Update; deliveries continue 1999
dom	AFV	*Hydrema*	12	1996	1997	Mine-clearing AFV. Deliveries to 1998
dom	PCI	MHV-800	6	1997	1997	12 ordered 1991–92. 3rd batch delivery 1997
Ge	MBT	*Leopard* 2A4	51	1998	2000	Ex-Ge Army
UK	hel	*Lynx*	8	1998	2000	Upgrade to *Super Lynx* standard
CH	APC	*Piranha* III	2	1998	1999	Option for 20 more; UN peacekeeping use
Ge	APC	M-113	100	1999	2000	Upgrade. Deliveries until 2001
France						
dom	SSBN	*Le Triomphant*	3	1986	1996	Deliveries to 2001; 4th order 2000 for 2007
dom	SLBM	M-45		1994	1996	Longer range varient of M-4
dom	SLBM	M-51		1996	2008	To replace M-45; development continues
col	UAV	*Eagle*				Development with UK
col	Sat	*Helios* 1A	2	1994	1995	With Ge, It, Sp. *Helios*1B for launch in 1999
col	Sat	*Helios* 2	1	1994	2002	Development with Ge
col	Sat	*Horus*		1994	2005	Fr has withdrawn funding
col	sat	*Skynet* 5	4	1998	2005	Comms; development in 1998; with Ge, UK
col	ASSM	ANNG		1985	2005	In development with Ge

Supplier	Classification	Designation	Units	Order Date	Delivery Date	Comment
dom	FGA	*Rafale*	60	1984	1999	Deliveries of first ten 1999–2001
dom	FGA	*Rafale*	234	1984	1999	Deliveries of first 3 began 1999. ISD 2005
dom	FGA	*Mirage* 2000-D	86	1991	1994	45 delivered by Jan 1997. Deliveries to 2000
dom	FGA	*Mirage* 2000-5F	37	1993	1998	Mirage 2000-C upgrade, deliveries to 2002
col	ALCM	SCALP	600	1994	2000	2 orders for delivery over 11 years
col	AAM	*Mica*	225	1998	1999	
col	tpt	FLA	52	1989	2005	Development. Prog status uncertain
Sp	tpt	CN 235	7	1996	1998	Offset for Spanish AS-532 purchase
dom	recce	*Falcon*-50	4	1997	1998	Deliveries to 2000
dom	SSN	SSN	6	1998	2010	Design studies approved Oct 1998
dom	CVN	R 91	1	1986	1999	Sea trials mid 1998. To commission 1999
US	AEW	E2-D	3	1994	1999	1st delivered in Jan 1999
col	FF	*Horizon*	2	1994	2003	Fr withdrew 1999
dom	FF	*Lafayette*	6	1990	1996	Deliveries to 2003
col	torpedo	MU-90	150	1991	2000	With It and Ge. Deliveries 2000–2
col	SAM	FSAF		1990	2006	Future surface-to-air-family; with It, UK
Be	MHC	*Tripartite*	3	1996	1997	Be Navy surplus
dom	LSD	TCD 90	2	1994	1998	2 on order
dom	LSD	*Foudre*	2	1986	1990	2nd of class delivered 1998
dom	PCI	*Stellis*	4	1994	1997	
col	hel	AS-532	4	1995	1999	Combat SAR, requirement for 6
col	hel	AS-532	4	1992	1996	Battlefield radar system *Horizon*; to 1998
col	hel	AS-555	44	1988	1990	Deliveries through 1990s
col	hel	AS 565	8	1996	1997	7 delivered in 1997; 1 delivered in 1998
col	hel	NH-90	160	1987	2003	With Ge, It, Nl; prod orders delayed.
col	hel	EC-120		1990		In development with PRC, Sgp
col	hel	*Tiger*	215	1984	2003	With Ge; 1st batch of 80 ordered in 1999
col	ATGW	*Trigat*		1988	2004	With UK, Ge
col	hel	BK-117	32	1997	1999	
dom	MBT	*Leclerc*	406	1985	1992	153 delivered by end 1998; to 2002
dom	AIFV	AMX-10	300	1999	2001	Upgrade
dom	APC	VBL	120	1996	1998	20 delivered in 1998
col	APC	VBCI	50	1998	2004	Dev; with Ge (GTK) and UK (MRAV)
dom	SAM	*Mistral*	1,130	1996	1997	To 2002
dom	MSL	*Eryx*	6,400	1997	1997	To 2002
dom	MSL	LAW	30,800	1997	1997	For delivery 1997–2002
col	ASM	*Vesta*		1997	2005	In development
col	radar	*Cobra*	10	1986	2002	Counter-battery radar; dev with UK, Ge

Germany

col	Sat	*Helios* 1A	2	1994	1995	With Fr, It, Sp, *Helios* 1B for launch in 1999
col	Sat	*Helios* 2	1	1994	2001	Development with Fr, It
col	Sat	*Horus*	1	1994	2005	Development with Fr
col	sat	Skynet 5	4	1997	2005	With UK, Fr
col	FGA	EF-2000	180	1985	2001	With UK, It, Sp; 44 ordered late 1998
col	ASM	*Taurus*		1998	2001	Dev with Swe (KEPD-350)
col	AAM	IRIS-T		1997	2003	Development with It, Swe, Gr, Ca, No
col	tpt	FLA	75	1989	2008	Development. Status uncertain
dom	hel	BO-105	17	1996	1996	Deliveries completed in 1997
col	hel	EC-135	15	1997	1998	For *Tiger* hel trg. Deliveries start mid-1998
col	tpt hel	AS-532	3	1994	1997	
col	hel	AS-365	13	1997	1998	Delivery from 1998–2001
col	hel	NH-90	272	1987	2003	With Fr, It, Nl; production orders delayed
dom	FFG	Type F 124	3	1996	2002	Deliveries 2002–6. Possible 1 more unit
dom	FFG	Type F 125	8	1999	2010	Feasibility study stage

Supplier	Classification	Designation	Units	Order Date	Delivery Date	Comment
UK	hel	*Lynx*	7	1996	1999	
UK	hel	*Lynx*	17	1998	2000	Upgrade to *Super Lynx* standard
col	torpedo	MU-90	600	1998	2000	
dom	SSK	Type 212	4	1994	2003	Deliveries to 2006
dom	MHC	Type 332	12	1988	1992	Deliveries to 1998
dom	AOE	Type 702	2	1996	2002	
dom		Type 751	1	1999	2002	Defence research and test ship
dom	Corvette	Type 130	5	1999	2004	
col	APC	GTK	200	1998	2004	With Fr (VBCI), UK (MRAV); dev delayed
dom	APC	TPz KRK	50	1998	1999	
col	recce	*Fennek*	164	1994	2000	Joint dev project with Nl. Prod in 2000
dom	SPA	PzH 2000	186	1986	1998	Req 594 units; 4 delivered 1998
dom	AAA	*Gepard*	147	1996	1999	Upgrade. 1st of 147 delivered Jan 1999
dom	SAM	*Wiesel* 2	50	1998	1999	
US	SAM	*Patriot*		1998		Upgrade to PAC-3 configuration
col	hel	*Tiger*	212	1984	1905	With Fr. 1st order for 80 placed 1998
col	ATGW	*Trigat*		1988	2004	
Greece						
Fr	SAM	*Crotale* NG	11	1999	2001	9 for air force; 2 for navy
US	FGA	F-4	38	1996	1999	Upgrade in Ge; deliveries to 2000
US	FGA	F-16	80	1985	1988	Deliveries of 2nd batch of 40 1997–99
US	AAM	AIM-120B	90	1997	1999	In addition to previous 150 AMRAAM
US	FGA	F-16	58	1999	2001	
Fr	FGA	*Mirage* 2000-5	25	1999	2001	Delivery to 2003
Br	AEW	RJ-145	4	1998	2000	Interim lease from Swe of Saab 350 *Argus*
US	DDG	*Kidd*	4	1998	1999	Deliveries to 2000.
Ge	FFG	*Meko*	4	1988	1992	Deliveries to 1998; last 2 built in Gr
Swe	PCI	CB 90	3	1996	1998	
US	SAM	*Patriot* PAC-3	5	1998	2001	5 batteries, option for 1 more
RF	SAM	SA-15	32	1998	1999	aka Tor-M1; for deployment in Cy
Fr	hel	AS-532	4	1999	1999	
dom	AIFV	*Kentaurus*		1994	2000	In development and trials in late 1998
US	hel	CH-47D	7	1995	1998	In addition to 9 in inventory
US	SP arty	M-109A5	12	1997	1999	135 delivered previously; option for further 12
Nl	FFG	*Kortenaer*	1	1997	1997	Total of 6 delivered since 1981
Ge	MBT	*Leopard* 1A5	170	1997	1998	In addition to previous delivery of 75
US	SAM	*Stinger*	188	1998	2000	
Ge	SSK	Type 214	4	1998	2003	1 built in Ge; 3 in Gr
It	AK	AK	1	1999	2002	
US	trg	T-6A	45	1998	2000	Completion of deliveries 2003
US	MRL	MLRS	18	1999	2002	
US	MRL	ATACM	81	1996	1998	
Hungary						
Fr	SAM	*Mistral*	45	1996	1998	27 launchers, 110 msl delivered in 1998
Bel	MBT	T-72	100	1994	1996	Ex-Bel, 31 delivered in 1996
RF	APC	BTR-80	555	1993	1996	190 delivered 1996, 130 1997
Italy						
col	sat	*Helios* 1A	1	1994	1995	With Fr, Ge, Sp. *Helios* 1B for launch 1999
US	FGA	AV-8B	18	1990	1994	Deliveries to 1997
col	FGA	*Tornado* F-3	24	1993	1996	Deliveries 1996–97
col	FGA	EF-2000	121	1985	2002	With UK, Ge, Sp; 29 ordered
col	SAM	FSAF		1990	2006	Future surface-to-air-family, with Fr, UK
It	tpt	P-180	12	1997	1998	

Supplier	Classification	Designation	Units	Order Date	Delivery Date	Comment
col	tpt	FLA	44	1989	2008	With Fr, Ge, Sp, Be, Por, Tu, UK
US	tpt	C-130J	18	1997	1999	Options for 14 more
Fr	tpt	*Falcon* 900EX	2	1997	1999	
dom	trg	MB-339CD	15	1990	1996	Deliveries to 1998
col	hel	NH 90	214	1987	2003	With Fr, Ge, Nl; production order delayed
dom	hel	AB-412	80	1988	1990	Licence; deliveries of ±10 a year 1990–97
dom	CV	Project NUM	1	1996	2004	Partly funded 1996 budget
col	FF	*Horizon*	4	1994	2003	It withdrew 1999
dom	PCC	*Aliscarfi*	4	1999	2001	1st batch of 4; 2nd expected after 2003
dom	LPD	*San Giorgio*	2	1999	2001	Upgrade to carry 4 hel
dom	AGI	A-5353	2	1998	2000	2nd for delivery 2001
dom	AO	*Etna*	1	1994	1998	
dom	PCO	*Esploratore*	4	1993	1997	Deliveries to 2000
Ge	SSK	Type 212	2	1997	2005	Licence-built in It; options for 2 more
col	hel	EH101	16	1993	1999	With UK. Navy require 38
dom	hel	A-129	66	1978	1990	Deliveries through 1998
dom	MBT	C1 *Ariete*	200	1982	1995	Deliveries to 2001
dom	AIFV	VCC-80	200	1982	1999	First ordered 1998. Aka *Dardo*
Ge	SP arty	PzH 2000	70	1999	2001	
dom	APC	*Puma*	600	1988	1999	Deliveries to 2004

NATO

UK	trg	*Hawk*	18	1997	1999	Option for 8 more
US	AWACS	E3-A	18	1997	1999	NATO fleet upgrade
US	trg	T-6A	24	1997	1999	Deliveries to 2000
US	C&C	ACCS	1	1999	2005	Air Command and Control System

Netherlands

SF	APC	XA-188	90	1996	1998	24 delivered in 1998
US	hel	CH-47C	7	1995	1999	
Ge	MBT	*Leopard* 2A5	330	1994	1996	Upgrade programme
col	hel	NH-90	20	1987	2003	With Fr, Ge, It
Fr	hel	AS-532	17	1993	1996	Deliveries to 1997
dom	LPD	*Rotterdam*	1	1993	1998	Hangar space for 4 hel
US	FGA	F-16	136	1993	1997	Update programme continues to 2001
US	hel	AH-64A	12	1995	1997	Lease until arrival of AH-64D
US	hel	AH-64D	30	1995	1998	4 delivered in 1998
dom	FFG	LCF	4	1995	2001	2 ordered in 1995; 2 more ordered 1997

Norway

Ge	AFV	*Leopard* 1	73	1998	1999	Deliveries to 2000; for mineclearing
Swe	LCA	90-H	16	1995	1997	Deliveries to 1998
dom	MCMV	M-350	5	1989	1996	Deliveries to 1997
Swe	AIFV	CV-90	104	1990	1996	Option for 70 more. Deliveries 1996–99
US	FGA	F-16	58	1993	1997	Mid-Life Update programme to 2001
US	AAM	AMRAAM	500	1993	1995	84 delivered 1998; deliveries to 2000
US	APC	M-113	205	1995	1997	Surplus from US, Ge, Nl
US	MRL	MLRS	12	1995	1997	Deliveries to 1998
Fr	ATGW	*Eryx*	424	1996	1997	
dom	FAC	*Skjold*	8	1996	1999	Deliveries to 2004
US	MPA	PC-3	4	1997	1999	Upgrade
US	FGA	F-16	25	1998	2001	
UK	arty	105mm	21	1997	1998	

Poland

dom	hel	W-3	11	1994	1998	1 for Navy. First 4 delivered July 1998
Il	ATGW	NT-D		1997		For W-3 *Huzar* attack hel. Canc in 1999
Ge	FGA	MiG-29	22	1999	2002	Upgrade

Supplier	Classification	Designation	Units	Order Date	Delivery Date	Comment
RF	recce	Su-22M4	15	1994	1997	Upgrade
dom	AIFV	BWP 2000		1989		Development
dom	trg	I-22	17	1995	1997	
Pl	SAR	PLZ M-28	3	1998	1999	
UK	SPA	AS-90	80	1999	2001	Licence
Spain						
It	SAM	*Spada* 2000	2	1996	1998	First of two batteries delivered
col	tpt	FLA	36	1989	2008	With Fr, Ge, It, Be, Por, Tu, UK
col	MHC	*Segura*	4	1989	1999	Deliveries to 2000
dom	LPD	*Galicia*	2	1991	1998	Second for delivery 2000
US	FGA	AV-8B	8	1992	1997	
dom	FFG	F-100	4	1992	2002	Deliveries to 2006
US	FGA	F/A-18A	30	1994	1995	EX-USN, deliveries continue to 1998
US	AAM	AIM-120B	100	1998	1999	
col	FGA	EF-2000	87	1994	2001	With Ge, It, UK; 20 ordered late 1998
col	sat	*Helios* 1A	1	1994	1995	With Fr, Ge, It. *Helios* 1B for launch in 1999
Fr	hel	AS-532	18	1995	1996	1st delivery in 1996. Deliveries to 2003
US	tpt	C-130	12	1995	1999	Upgrade programme
A	AIFV	*Pizarro*	144	1996	1998	Licence. Requirement for 463
Ge	MBT	*Leopard* 2	235	1998	2002	Built in Sp. Includes 16 ARVs
dom	arty	SBT-1		1997	2000	Development
dom	MPA	P-3	7	1997	2002	Upgrade
Turkey						
US	APC	M-113	1698	1988	1992	Final deliveries in 1999
Ge	PCM	P-330	3	1993	1998	1st built Ge; 2nd and 3rd Tu; to 1999
US	FFG	*Perry*	11	1996	1998	Delivery of five 1998–99
Il	FGA	F-4	54	1996	1999	Upgrade; deliveries to 2002
Il	AGM	*Popeye* 1	50	1997	1999	For use with upgraded F-4 ac
Il	FGA	F-5	48	1998	2001	IAI awarded contract to upgrade 48 Tu F-5
US	FGA	F-16	240	1984	1987	All but 8 assembled in Tu; to 1999
US	FGA	F-16	32	1999	2002	License; following orders of 240 in 2 batches
US	AAM	AIM-120B	138	1997	2000	
Ge	FFH	*Meko*-200	8	1985	1987	7 by 1999; final delivery 2000, 4 built in Tu
Ge	SSK	*Preveze*	8	1987	1994	Delivery of first 5 to 2003
US	TKR AC	KC-135R	9	1994	1995	Deliveries in 1995 and 1998
US	tpt hel	CH-47	4	1996	1999	
UK	SAM	*Rapier*	78	1996	1998	Upgrade programme
UK	SAM	*Rapier* MK 2	840	1999	2000	Licence; 80 a year for 10 years
US	MRL	ATACM	72	1996	1998	36 msl delivered in 1998
Fr	hel	AS-532	20	1996	1999	Deliveries to 2001
US	asw hel	SH-60B	8	1997	2000	
dom	APC	RN-94	5	1997		Development
Sp	tpt	CN-235	43	1990	1992	41 delivered by 1998
Sp	MPA	CN-235	9	1997	2000	
Fr	MHC	*Circe*	5	1997	1998	Ex-Fr Navy. 3 in 1998, 2 in 1999
It	SAR hel	AB-412	5	1998	2000	
US	hel	CH-53E	8	1998	2003	
US	SAM	*Stinger*	208	1999	2001	
US	hel	S-70	50	1999	1999	Deliveries to 2001
Ge	MHC		6	1999	1999	1 delivered; 5 under license in Tu
dom	PCC		10	1999	2000	For coastguard
UK						
dom	SSBN	*Vanguard*	4	1982	1993	Deliveries to 1999
US	SLBM	*Trident* D-5	48	1982	1994	Deliveries to 1999; original order 96

Supplier	Classification	Designation	Units	Order Date	Delivery Date	Comment
col	sat	*Skynet* 5	4	1993	2005	With Fr and Ge
col	AEW	ASTOR	5	1997	2003	
col	bbr	FOAS		1997	2020	Future Offensive Air System, feasibility study with Fr
dom	FGA	*Tornado* GR4 ID	142	1994	1998	Upgrade; deliveries to 2003
dom	FGA	*Tornado* F-3	100	1996	1998	Upgrade
US	AAM	AIM-120		1994	1998	
dom	AAM	ASRAAM	1300	1981	1998	
col	FGA	EF-2000	232	1984	2002	1st batch of 55 ordered end 1998
dom	ASM	*Brimstone*		1996	2001	1st 12 to be delivered 2001
col	ASM	*Storm Shadow*	900	1996	2001	
col	FGA	JSF	150	1996	2012	Development with US
dom	MPA	*Nimrod* 2000	21	1996	2003	Upgrade
col	tpt	FLA	45	1993	2005	Dev with Fr, Ge, Sp, Be, Por, Tu, It
US	tpt	C-130J	25	1994	1999	Option for 20 more
Ge	trg	*Grob*-115D	85	1998	2000	
col	hel	EH 101	22	1987	2000	With It; for RAF; aka *Merlin* HM Mk.3
US	hel	CH-47	14	1995	1997	Deliveries to 2000. Total *Chinnook* buy 58
Fr	trg hel	AS-550	12	1996	1997	
dom	CV	CV	2	1998	2012	Under 1998 Strategic Defence Review
dom	FGA	*Sea Harrier*	35	1985	1994	Upgrade programme; deliveries to 1999
dom	FGA	*Sea Harrier*	18	1990	1995	Deliveries to 1999
dom	SSN	*Swiftsure*	5	1988	2003	Upgrade of existing submarines
dom	SSN	*Trafalger*	7	1988	2003	Upgrade of existing submarines
dom	SSN	*Astute*	3	1991	2005	
US	SLCM	TLAM	30	1999	2002	
US	SLCM	*Tomahawk*	65	1995	1998	
dom	FFG	Type 23	13	1984	1997	aka *Duke* Class
dom	FFG	*Duke*	3	1996	1999	Deliveries to 2000; last three of Type 23
col	FFG	*Horizon*	12	1996	2003	Development with Fr, It; cancelled 1999
col	SAM	PAAMS		1994	2003	Dev with Fr, It. Part of FSAF programme
dom	DD	Type 45		1999		Project definition. Instead of *Horizon*
col	hel	EH 101	44	1979	1999	With It; for RN; aka *Merlin* HM Mk.1
dom	hel	*Lynx*	50	1992	1995	Upgrade. Completion in 1998–99
dom	PCI	*Archer*	2	1997	1998	
US	PFC		5	1996	1997	Ex-US 42 and 65 foot patrol boats
dom	MHC	*Sandown*	12	1985	1989	8 delivered by 1999; deliveries to 2001
dom	LPD	*Albion*	2	1991	2002	Deliveries to 2003
dom	LPH	*Ocean*	1	1993	1998	
dom	AGOS	*Scott*	1	1995	1997	
dom	AO	*Fast Fleet Tanker*	2	1997	2000	
dom	AK	*Sea Chieftain*	1	1997	1998	18 month lease. Heavy sealift
Swe	APC	BvS 10	125	1999	2001	
dom	MBT	*Challenger* 2	386	1993	1998	78 delivered 1998
dom	APC	*Stormer*	18	1996	1998	
col	lt tk	TRACER	200	1998	2007	With US; in feasibility phase
col	APC	MRAV	200	1998	2002	Multi-Role Armoured Vehicle; with Fr, Ge
US	hel	AH-64D	67	1996	2000	Deliveries to 2003
dom	UAV	*Phoenix*	50	1985	1998	Upgrade programme planned
col	radar	*Cobra*		1986	1999	Counter-battery radar in dev with Fr, Ge
col	UAV	*Sender*		1999		Development with US
col	ATGW	*Trigat*		1988	2004	With Fr, Ge

Table 10 **Arms orders and deliveries, non-NATO Europe, 1997–1999**					

Supplier	Classification	Designation	Units	Order Date	Delivery Date	Comment
Armenia						
PRC	AAA	*Typhoon*	8	1998	1999	
Azerbaijan						
Kaz	FGA	MiG-25	8	1996	1998	
Austria						
col	lt tk	ULAN	112	1999	2002	Delivery to 2004
US	SPA	M109A2	46	1996	1998	27 delivered in 1998
dom	APC	*Pandur*	269	1997	1999	
Ge	ATGW	*Jaguar*	90	1997	1998	
Nl	MBT	*Leopard* 2A4	114	1997	1998	79 delivered in 1998
Swe	FGA	J-35	5	1999	1999	
Bosnia-Herzegovina						
US	hel	UH-1	15	1996	1998	Part of US-funded Equip and Train prog
UAE	arty	105mm	36	1996	1998	
Et	arty	122mm	12	1996	1998	
Et	arty	130mm	12	1996	1998	
US	arty	155mm	116	1996	1997	Part of US-funded Equip and Train prog
Et	AD Guns	23mm	18	1996	1998	
UAE	MBT	AMX-30	36	1996	1997	
R	arty	122mm	18	1996	1998	
R	arty	130mm	8	1996	1998	
Bulgaria						
US	hel	B-206	6	1998	1999	2 delivered
RF	AIFV	BMP-1/2	100	1994	1996	Deliveries continued in 1997
RF	MBT	T-72	100	1994	1996	Deliveries continued in 1997
Croatia						
dom	MBT	M-84		1992	1996	In production
dom	MBT	*Degman*		1995	2001	
dom	FAC	*Kralj Petar Kre*	2	1989	1992	Second delivered in 1999
dom	MHC	*Rhino*	1	1995	1999	
dom	PCI		1	1996	1998	Deliveries to 2002
US	hel	B-206	10	1996	1997	
CH	trg	PC-9	20	1997	1997	Upgrade
US	FGA	F-16	18	1999	2001	Ex-US inventory
Cyprus						
Il	PCI		1	1996	1997	Reportedly torpedo boat
RF	MBT	T-80	40	1996	1998	2nd batch; following earlier delivery of 41T-80U
It	SAM	*Aspide*	44	1996	1998	32 delivered by 1998; 12 more ordered
RF	SAM	S-300	48	1997	1999	msl. Delivered to Gr, based in Crete
Gr	MBT	AMX-30	37	1997	1997	Last ten delivered in 1998
Estonia						
Ge	MCI	Type 394	2	1996	1997	Free transfer
SF	arty	105mm	18	1996	1997	105mm. Deliveries 1997-98
SF	ML		2	1998	1999	Free transfer
Finland						
dom	AIFV	TA 2000	150	1998		Development
dom	APC	XA-185	450	1982	1983	XA180/185 series. Deliveries to 1999
dom	APC	XA-200	48	1999	1999	Deliveries to 2001
dom	PFM	*Rauma*	5	1987	1990	Developed from *Helsinki* class; 1990–97
CH	UAV	*Ranger*	9	1999	1999	Under licence from Il
US	FGA	F/A-18C/D	64	1992	1995	Deliveries to 2000, 57 for assembly in SF.

Supplier	Classification	Designation	Units	Order Date	Delivery Date	Comment
						14 delivered 1998
US	AAM	AIM-120		1993	1997	
RF	SAM	BuK-M1		1996	1997	aka SA-11, arms for debt deal
SF	arty	K-98	24	1996	1998	
dom	ACV	RA-140	10	1997	1998	Mine-clearing vehicle
dom	PFM	*Hamina*	2	1997	1998	
Georgia						
Ukr	PCI	*Zhuk*	1	1996	1997	Free transfer
Tu	PCI	SG-48	1	1997	1998	Free transfer
Ge	MSC	*Lindau*	2	1997	1998	Free transfer; deliveries to 1999
Ukr	PFM	*Konotop*	1	1999	1999	
UK	PFC		2	1998	1999	Free transfer
US	hel	UH-1	10	1999	1999	
Ireland						
UK	recce	*Defender*4000	1	1994	1997	
UK	OPV	*Guardian*	1	1997	1999	65% funded by European Commission
UK	arty	105mm	12	1996	1998	
Latvia						
SF	OPV	OPV	1	1996	1997	3rd vessel donated to Border Guard by SF
Lithuania						
Cz	trg	L-39	2	1997	1998	To join 4 L-39C trg ac purchased in 1992
Former Yugoslav Republic of Macedonia						
Ge	APC	BTR-70	60	1998	1998	Free transfer
Kaz	APC	BTR-80	12	1997	1998	
Bg	arty	152mm	10	1998	1998	Free transfer
Bg	arty	76mm	72	1998	1998	aka ZIS-3. Free transfer
US	ACV	HMMWV	41	1998	1998	Free transfer
Bg	MBT	T-55	150	1998	1999	36 type T-55AM2
Bg	arty	122mm	142	1998	1999	Free transfer
US	arty	105mm	18	1998	1999	Free transfer
Tu	FGA	F-5A/B	20	1998	1999	Free transfer
Malta						
Nl	hel	SA-316	2	1996	1997	Free transfer
UK	MPA	BN2B	2	1997	1998	
Romania						
dom	FGA	MiG-21	110	1994	1997	Upgrade programme, with Il
US	tpt	C-130	5	1995	1998	
R	trg	IAR-99	40	1998	2001	26 for delivery in 2001
dom	hel	IAR-330L	26	1995	1998	Upgrade
Il	UAV	*Shadow*	6	1995	1998	
US	cbt hel	AH-1RO	96	1997		Licence. Derivative of AH-1W. Delayed
Ge	AAA	35mm	43	1997	1999	
Slovakia						
Cz	APC	OT-64	100	1997	1998	Also 2 BVP-2 from Ukr for delivery to Indo
RF	trg	*Yak*-130	12	1997	1999	RF debt repayment. Delayed or cancelled
dom	MBT	M-2 *Moderna*		1995	2000	T-72 upgrade programme
RF	SAM	S-300		1997		Part of debt repayment. Cancelled in 1999
col	hel	EC-135	12	1997	1999	
col	hel	AS-532	5	1997	1999	
col	hel	AS-550	2	1997	1999	
dom	arty	*Zuzana* 2000	8	1997	1998	155mm. Deliveries 1998
Slovenia						
A	APC	*Pandur*	70	1998	1999	

Supplier	Classification	Designation	Units	Order Date	Delivery Date	Comment
Il	mor	120mm	56	1996	1998	Mortar
Il	arty	M845	18	1996	1998	155mm 45 cal. towed arty
Il	trg	PC-9	9	1997	1998	Upgrade
CH	trg	PC-9	2	1997	1998	
dom	MBT	M-55	30	1998	1999	T-55 upgrade involving 105mm L-7 gun
dom	MBT	T-84	40	1999	2002	Upgrade
Sweden						
dom	FGA	JAS-39	204	1981	1995	Deliveries to 2007. 18 delivered in 1998
US	AAM	AMRAAM	110	1994	1998	Option for a further 700
col	AAM	IRIS-T		1997	2003	Development with Ge
col	ASM	KEPD 350		1997	2003	Dev with Ge to 2002. Also KEPD 150
dom	AEW	*Saab* 340	6	1993	1997	Deliveries 1997–98.
Fr	hel	AS532	12	1998	2001	Deliveries 2002
dom	SSK	A-19 *Gotland*	3	1986	1996	Deliveries to 1997
dom	corvette	*Visby*	4	1995	2001	Deliveries to 2003
dom	PCI	*Tapper*	12	1992	1993	Deliveries to 1999. Coastal arty
dom	MCM	YSB	4	1994	1996	Deliveries to 1998
dom	LCA	90	199	1988	1989	To 2001. 100 delivered by 1997
dom	LCA	*Transportbat*	14	1997	1999	
dom	ACV	M 10	6	1997	1998	
dom	PCI	KBV 201	2	1999	2002	
dom	AIFV	CV-90	600	1984	1993	200 delivered by 1998; to 2004
Ge	MBT	*Leopard* 2	120	1994	1998	New-build *Leopard* 2A5; to 2002
Ge	MBT	*Leopard* 2	160	1994	1997	Ex-Ge Army. Upgrade
Ge	ARV	*Buffel*	10	1999	2002	
Ge	APC	MT-LB	584	1994	1995	Deliveries to 1998. Last 34 delivered 1998
CH	APC	*Pirahna*	8	1996	1998	Command variant. Deliveries continue.
dom	SPA	*Karelin*	50	1998		155mm. Development
Fr	UAV	*Ugglan*	3	1997		
Switzerland						
US	FGA	F/A-18C/D	34	1993	1997	Most assembled in CH, deliveries 1997–99
US	AAM	AIM-120	100	1993	1998	
Fr	hel	AS-532	12	1997	2000	Deliveries to 2002
US	AD System	*Florako*	1	1999	2007	Upgrade
Il	UAV	*Ranger*	4	1995	1998	Licensed, 28 UAVs. Deliveries to 1999
dom	AD	*Skyguard*	100	1997	1999	Upgrade
US	SPA	M-109	456	1997	1998	Upgrade, deliveries to 2000
dom	AIFV	*Eagle* 1	154	1995	1995	Deliveries to 1997
dom	APC	*Eagle* 2	205	1997	1999	Deliveries 2003
Ukraine						
col	tpt	AN-70		1991		In development with RF
dom	CGH	*Ukraina*	1	1990	2000	

Belgium   Be

	1997	1998	1999	2000
GDP	fr8.7tr	fr9.1tr		
	($244bn)	($250bn)		
per capita	$23,000	$24,200		
Growth	3.2%	2.9%		
Inflation	1.6%	1.0%		
Publ debt	115.9%	115.9%		
Def exp	fr135bn	fr137bn		
	($3.8bn)	($3.8bn)		
Def bdgt		fr102.5bn	fr100.8bn	fr102.3bn
		($2.8bn)	($2.5bn)	($2.6bn)
$1=franc	35.8	36.3	39.6	
Population				10,115,000
Age	*13–17*	*18–22*		*23–32*
Men	308,000	317,000		710,000
Women	294,000	305,000		688,000

Total Armed Forces

ACTIVE 41,750

(incl 1,250 Medical Service, 2,570 women)

RESERVES 152,050 (to be 62,000)

Army 105,200 **Navy** 6,250 **Air Force** 20,700 **Medical Service** 19,900

Army 26,400

(incl 1,500 women)
1 joint service territorial comd (incl 2 engr, 2 sigs bn)
1 op comd HQ
1 mech inf div with 3 mech inf bde (each 1 tk, 2 mech inf, 1 SP arty bn) (2 bde at 70%, 1 bde at 50% cbt str), 1 AD arty bn, 2 recce coy (Eurocorps); 1 recce bn (MNDC)
1 cbt spt div (11 mil schools forming, 1 arty, 1 engr bn – augment mech inf div, plus 1 inf, 1 tk bn for bde at 50% cbt str)
1 para-cdo bde (3 para-cdo, 1 ATK/recce bn, 1 arty, 1 AD bty, 1 engr coy)
1 lt avn gp (2 ATK, 1 obs bn)

RESERVES
Territorial Defence 11 lt inf bn (9 province, 1 gd, 1 reserve)

EQUIPMENT
  MBT 155: 132 *Leopard* 1A5, 23 *Leopard* 1A1
  RECCE 141 *Scimitar* (29 in store)
  AIFV 220 YPR-765 (plus 52 'look-alikes')
  APC 187 M-113 (plus 112 'look-alikes'), 115 *Spartan* (plus 79 'look-alikes'), 4 YPR-765, some *Pandur* (being delivered)
  TOTAL ARTY 243
    TOWED 19: **105mm**: 5 M-101, 14 LG Mk II
    SP 132: **105mm**: 19 M-108 (trg); **155mm**: 112 M-109A2, plus 1A3 (trials)
    MOR **107mm**: 90 M-30; **120mm**: 2 (for sale), plus **81mm**: 100
  ATGW 476: 420 *Milan* (incl 218 YPR-765 (24 in store), 56 M-113 (4 in store))
  AD GUNS **35mm**: 51 *Gepard* SP (all for sale)
  SAM 118 *Mistral*
  AC 10 BN-2A *Islander*
  HELICOPTERS 78
    ASLT 28 A-109BA
    OBS 18 A-109A
    SPT 32 SA-318 (5 in store)
  UAV 28 *Epervier*

Navy 2,600

(incl 270 women)
BASES Ostend, Zeebrugge. Be and Nl Navies under joint op comd based at Den Helder (Nl)
FRIGATES 3
FFG 3 *Wielingen* with 2 dual role (Fr L-5 HWT), 1 x 6 ASW mor, 4 MM-38 *Exocet* SSM, 1 100mm gun and 8 *Sea Sparrow* SAM
MINE COUNTERMEASURES 11
    4 *Van Haverbeke* (US *Aggressive* MSO) (incl 1 used for trials)
    7 *Aster* (tripartite) MHC
SUPPORT AND MISCELLANEOUS 5
    2 log spt/comd with hel deck, 1 AGOR, 1 sail trg **hel** 3 SA-316B, 1 PC/R
    ADDITIONAL IN STORE 1 FF for sale

Air Force 11,500

(incl 800 women)
Flying hours 165
FGA 2 sqn with F-16A/B
FGA/RECCE 1 sqn with F-16A/B
FTR 3 sqn with F-16A/B
TPT 2 sqn
    1 with 11 C-130H
    1 with 2 Airbus A310-200, 3 HS-748, 5 *Merlin* IIIA, 2 *Falcon* 20, 1 *Falcon* 900
TRG 4 sqn
    2 with *Alpha Jet*
    1 with SF-260
    1 with CM-170
SAR 1 sqn with *Sea King* Mk 48
EQUIPMENT
  90 cbt ac (plus 59 in store), no armed hel
  AC 90 **F-16** (81 **-A**, 19 **-B** (plus 32 in store)) • 11 C-130 (tpt) • 2 Airbus A310-200 (tpt) • 3 HS-748 (tpt) • 2 *Falcon* 20 (VIP) • 1 *Falcon* 900B • 5 SW 111 *Merlin* (VIP, photo, cal) • 11 CM-170 (trg, liaison) • 33 SF-260 (trg) • 31 *Alpha Jet* (trg)
  HEL 5 (SAR) *Sea King*

IN STORE 27 *Mirage* 5 (12 -BA, 12 -BR, 3 -BD)
MISSILES
AAM AIM-9 *Sidewinder*, AIM-120 AMRAAM
ASM AGM-65G *Maverick*
SAM 24 *Mistral*

Forces Abroad

GERMANY 2,100; 1 mech inf bde (1 inf, 1 arty bn, 1 recce coy)
STANAVFORLANT/STANAVFORMED
1 FF (part time basis)
1 MHC
MCMFORMED
1 MCMV (part time basis)
UN AND PEACEKEEPING
ALBANIA (AFOR II): some **BOSNIA/CROATIA** (SFOR II): up to 550. SFOR **Air Component** 3 F-16. (UNMOP): 1 obs **INDIA/PAKISTAN** (UNMOGIP): 2 obs **MIDDLE EAST** (UNTSO): 6 obs **YUGOSLAVIA** (Joint Guardian): to be some 1,100

Foreign Forces

NATO HQ NATO Brussels; HQ SHAPE Mons
WEU Military Planning Cell
US 1,570: **Army** 970 **Navy** 100 **Air Force** 500

Canada
Ca

	1997	1998	1999	2000
GDP	C$874bn	C$896bn		
	($631bn)	($604bn)		
per capita	$22,700	$23,700		
Growth	5.2%	3.2%		
Inflation	1.6%	1.0%		
Publ debt	92.7%	89.8%		
Def exp	C$10.8bn	C$10.0bn		
	($7.8bn)	($6.8bn)		
Def bdgt		C$9.4bn	C$9.7bn	C$9.9bn
		($6.3bn)	($6.7bn)	($6.8bn)
US$1=C$	1.38	1.48	1.47	
Population				29,236,000
Age	*13–17*	*18–22*	*23–32*	
Men	991,000	976,000	2,088,000	
Women	947,000	942,000	2,042,000	

Canadian Armed Forces are unified and org in functional comds. Land Force Comd has op control of TAG. Maritime Comd has op control of maritime air. This entry is set out in traditional single-service manner.

Total Armed Forces

ACTIVE 60,600

(incl 6,100 women). Some 15,700 are not identified by service

RESERVES 43,300

Primary 28,600 **Army** (Militia) (incl comms) 22,200 **Navy** 4,000 **Air Force** 2,100 **Primary Reserve List** 300 *Supplementary* **Ready Reserve** 14,700

Army (Land Forces) 20,900

(incl 1,600 women)
1 Task Force HQ • 3 mech inf bde gp, each with 1 armd regt, 3 inf bn (1 lt), 1 arty, 1 engr regt, 1 AD bty • 1 indep AD regt • 1 indep engr spt regt

RESERVES

Militia 20,100 (excl comms); 18 armd, 19 arty, 51 inf, 12 engr, 20 log bn level units, 14 med coy
Canadian Rangers 3,250; 127 patrols
EQUIPMENT
MBT 114 *Leopard* C-1
RECCE 5 *Lynx* (in store), 195 *Cougar*, 203 *Coyote*
APC 1,743: 1,214 M-113 A2 (82 in store), 61 M-577, 269 *Grizzly*, 199 *Bison*, some *Kodiak* (being delivered)
TOWED ARTY 213: **105mm**: 185 C1/C3 (M-101), 28 LG1 Mk II
SP ARTY 155mm: 76 M-109A4
MOR 81mm: 167
ATGW 150 TOW (incl 72 TUA M-113 SP), 425 *Eryx*
RL 66mm: M-72
RCL 84mm: 1,040 *Carl Gustav*; **106mm**: 111
AD GUNS 35mm: 34 GDF-005 with *Skyguard*; **40mm**: 57 L40/60 (in store)
SAM 22 ADATS, 96 *Javelin*, *Starburst*

Navy (Maritime Command) 9,000

(incl 2,800 women)
SUBMARINES 1
SSK 1 *Ojibwa* (UK *Oberon*) with Mk 48 HWT (equipped for, but not with, *Harpoon* USGW)
PRINCIPAL SURFACE COMBATANTS 16
DESTROYERS 4
DDG 4 modified *Iroquois* with 1 Mk-41 VLS for 29 SM-2 MR, 2 CH-124 *Sea King* ASW hel (Mk 46 LWT), 6 ASTT, plus 1 76mm gun
FRIGATES 12
FFG 12 *Halifax* with 1 CH-124A *Sea King* ASW hel (Mk 46 Mod 5 LWT), 2 x 2 ASTT, 8 *Harpoon* SSM and 16 *Sea Sparrow* SAM
PATROL AND COASTAL COMBATANTS 14
12 *Kingston* MCDV, 2 *Fundy* PCC (trg)

MINE COUNTERMEASURES 2

2 *Anticosti* MSO (converted offshore spt vessels)

SUPPORT AND MISCELLANEOUS 7

2 *Protecteur* AO with 3 *Sea King*, 1 AOT, 2 AGOR, 1 diving spt, 1 *Riverton* spt

DEPLOYMENT AND BASES

NATIONAL Ottawa (Chief of Maritime Staff)

ATLANTIC Halifax (National and Marlant HQ; Commander Marlant is also OMCANLANT): 1 SS, 2 DDG, 7 FFG, 1 AOR, 1 AGOR, 6 MCDV, 1 MSO; 2 MR plus 1 MR (trg) sqn with CP-140 and 3 CP-140A, 1 ASW and 1 ASW (trg) hel sqn with 26 CH-125 hel

PACIFIC Esquimalt (HQ): 2 DDG, 5 FFG, 1 AOR, 5 MCDV, 1 MSO; 1 MR sqn with 4 CP-140 and 1 ASW hel sqn with 6 CH-124 hel

RESERVES

4,000 in 24 div: patrol craft, coastal def, MCM, Naval Control of Shipping, augmentation of regular units

Air Force (Air Command) 15,000

(incl 1,700 women)

Flying hours 210

1 Air Div with 13 wg responsible for operational readiness, combat air-support, air tpt, SAR, MR and trg

EARLY WARNING Canadian NORAD Regional HQ at North Bay: 47 North Warning radar sites: 11 long-range, 36 short-range; Regional Op Control Centre (ROCC) (2 Sector Op Control Centres (SOCC)): 4 Coastal Radars and 2 Transportable Radars. Canadian Component – NATO Airborne Early Warning (NAEW)

EQUIPMENT

140 (incl 18 MR) cbt **ac**, 30 armed **hel**

AC 5 sqns of 122 **CF-18** (83 **-A**, 39 **-B**) • 4 sqns with 18 **CP-140** (MR) and 3 **CP-140A** (environmental patrol) • 4 sqns with 32 **CC-130E/H** (tpt) and 5 **KCC-130** (tkr) • 1 sqn with 5 **CC-150** (Airbus A-310) and 5 Boeing CC-137 • 1 sqn with 7 **CC-109** (tpt) and 16 11 **CC-144** (EW trg, coastal patrol, VIP/tpt) • 4 sqns with 7 **CC-138** (SAR/tpt), 10 **CC-115** (SAR/tpt), 45 **CT-133** (EW trg/tpt plus 9 in store)

HEL 15 **CH-113** (SAR/tpt) • 3 sqns of 30 **CH-124** (ASW, afloat) • 100 **CH-146** (tpt, SAR) of which 30 armed • 8 **CH-118** (EW)

TRG 2 Flying Schools 130 **CT-114** *Turor*, 6 **CT-142 hel** 9 **CH-139** *Jet Ranger*

AAM AIM-7M *Sparrow*, AIM-9L *Sidewinder*

Forces Abroad

UN AND PEACEKEEPING

BOSNIA (SFOR II): 1,380: 1 inf bn, 1 armd recce, 1 engr sqn; **SFOR Air Component** 6 CF-18 **CAR**

(MINURCA): 29 **CROATIA** (UNMOP): 1 obs **CY-PRUS** (UNFICYP): 2 **EGYPT** (MFO): 28 **KOSOVO**: 1,002 **MIDDLE EAST** (UNTSO): 11 obs **SYRIA/ISRAEL** (UNDOF): 188: log unit

Paramilitary 9,350

Canadian Coast Guard has merged with **Department of Fisheries and Oceans**. Both are civilian-manned.

CANADIAN COAST GUARD (CCG) 4,700

some 137 vessels incl 19 navaids/tender, 23 survey/research, 17 icebreaker, 39 cutter, 22 lifeboat, 10 utility, 4 ACV, 3 trg; plus **hel** 1 S-61, 6 Bell-206L, 5 Bell-212, 16 BO-105

DEPARTMENT OF FISHERIES AND OCEANS (DFO) 4,650

some 90 vessels incl 35 AGOR/AGHS, 38 patrol, 17 icebreakers

Czech Republic   Cz

	1997	1998	1999	2000
GDP	Kc1.6tr	Kc1.8tr		
	($52bn)	($55bn)		
per capita	$13,100	$13,000		
Growth	1.0%	-2.7%		
Inflation	8.5%	10.7%		
Debt	$21.4bn	$23.6bn		
Def exp	Kc31.3bn	Kc37.3bn		
	($987m)	($1,155m)		
Def bdgt		Kc35.3bn	Kc41.4bn	Kc44.9bn
		($1,125m)	($1,163m)	($1,270m)
FMA (US)	$0.7m	$1.4m	$1.4m	$1.6m
$1=koruna	31.7	32.2	35.7	
Population				10,480,000
(Slovak 3%, Polish 0.6%, German 0.5%)				
Age	*13–17*	*18–22*		*23–32*
Men	360,000	416,000		780,000
Women	344,000	399,000		752,000

Total Armed Forces

ACTIVE 58,200

(incl 25,000 conscripts; about 17,500 MoD, centrally controlled formations and HQ units)

Terms of service 12 months

Army 25,300

(incl 15,500 conscripts)

1 rapid-reaction bde (2 mech, 1 AB, 1 recce, 1 arty bn)

2 mech bde (each with 4 mech, 1 recce, 1 arty, 1 ATK, 1 AD bn)

1 combined msl regt

7 trg and mob base (incl arty, AD, engr)

RESERVES

14–15 territorial def bde

EQUIPMENT

MBT 938 (202 in store): 202 T-54, 195 T-55, 541 T-72M (250 to be upgraded)
RECCE some 182 BRDM, OT-65
AIFV 804: 615 BMP-1, 174 BMP-2, 15 BRM-1K
APC 403 OT-90, 12 OT-64 plus 568 'look-alikes'
TOTAL ARTY 754
    TOWED 122mm: 148 D-30
    SP 370: **122mm**: 91 2S1; **152mm**: 273 *Dana* (M-77)
    MRL 122mm: 149 RM-70
    MOR 93: **120mm**: 85 M-1982, 8 MSP-85
SSM FROG-7, SS-21
ATGW 721 AT-3 *Sagger* (incl 621 on BMP-1, 100 on BRDM-2), 21 AT-5 *Spandrel*
AD GUNS 30mm: M-53/-59
SAM SA-7, ε140 SA-9/-13
SURV GS-13 (veh), *Small Fred/Small Yawn* (veh, arty)

Air Force 15,400

(incl AD and 8,500 conscripts); 94 cbt ac, 34 attack hel
Organised into two main structures - Tactical Air Force and Air Defence
Flying hours 50
FGA/RECCE 2 sqn with 32 Su-22, MK/UM3K
FTR 1 sqn with 38 MiG-21
TPT 2 sqn with 14 L-410, 8 An-24/26/30, 2 Tu-154 **hel** 2 Mi-2, 4 Mi-8, 1 Mi-9, 10 Mi-17
HEL 2 sqn (aslt/tpt/attack) with 24 Mi-2, 3 Mi-8/20, 24 Mi-17, 34* Mi-24, 11 PZL W-3
TEST AC The Test Centre has been disbanded but the following ac have not yet been redistributed: 7* Mig-21, 2 L-29, 2 L-39, 4 Mi-17, 1 Mi-2
TRG 1 regt with **ac** 18 L-29, 14 L-39C, 17* L-39ZO, 3 L-39MS, 8 Z-142C **hel** 8 Mi-2
AAM AA-2 *Atoll*, AA-7 *Apex*, AA-8 *Aphid*
SAM SA-2, SA-3, SA-6

Forces Abroad

UN AND PEACEKEEPING

BOSNIA (SFOR II): up to 560; 1 mech inf bn
CROATIA (UNMOP): 1 obs; (SFOR): 7 **GEORGIA** (UNOMIG): 4 obs **TAJIKISTAN** (UNMOT): 2 obs

Paramilitary 5,600

BORDER GUARDS 4,000

(1,000 conscripts)

INTERNAL SECURITY FORCES 1,600

(1,500 conscripts)

Denmark   Da

	1997	1998	1999	2000
GDP	kr1,118bn	kr1,167bn		
	($169bn)	($174bn)		
per capita	$23,200	$24,200		
Growth	3.1%	3.0%		
Inflation	2.3%	1.8%		
Publ debt	59.5%	59.5%		
Def exp	kr18.5bn	kr19.1bn		
	($2.8bn)	($2.9bn)		
Def bdgt		kr18.1bn	kr18.6bn	kr18.5bn
		($2.7bn)	($2.6bn)	($2.5bn)
$1=kroner	6.60	6.70	7.00	
Population				5,256,000
Age	*13–17*		*18–22*	*23–32*
Men	145,000		159,000	385,000
Women	140,000		154,000	372,000

Total Armed Forces

ACTIVE 24,300

(excluding civilians but incl 461 central staff; about 7,880 conscripts; 1,020 women)
Terms of service 4–12 months (up to 24 months in certain ranks)

RESERVES 81,200

Army 58,000 **Navy** 8,400 **Air Force** 14,800
Home Guard (*Hjemmevaernet*) (volunteers to age 50)
61,500 **Army** 49,700 **Navy** 4,300 **Air Force** 7,500

Army 15,300

(incl 6,800 conscripts, 470 women)
1 op comd, 1 land comd (east) • 1 mech inf div (3 mech inf bde (1 reserve) each 2 mech, inf, 1 tk, 1 arty bn), 1 recce, 1 mech inf, 1 AD, 1 engr bn (reserve), div arty (reserve)) • 1 rapid-reaction bde with 2 mech inf, 1 tk, 1 SP arty bn (20% active cbt str) • 1 mech inf bde with 2 mech inf, 1 tk, 1 arty bn • 1 recce, 1 indep AD, 1 indep engr bn • Army avn (1 attack hel coy, 1 recce hel det) • 1 SF unit

RESERVES

7 mil region (regt cbt gp or 1–2 inf bn), 4 regt cbt gp HQ, 1 mech inf, 4 mot inf, 2 inf • 1 arty comd, 1 arty, 1 AD, 2 engr bn

EQUIPMENT

MBT 337: 220 *Leopard* 1A5 (58 in store), 10 *Leopard* 2, 54 *Centurion*, 53 M-41DK-1
RECCE 36 Mowag *Eagle*
AIFV 50 M-113A2 (with **25mm** gun)
APC 263 M-113 (plus 223 'look-alikes' incl SP mor)
TOTAL ARTY 503
    TOWED 105mm: 134 M-101; **155mm**: 24 M-59, 97

M-114/39; **203mm**: 8 M-115
SP **155mm**: 76 M-109
MRL **227mm**: 4 MLRS
MOR **120mm**: 160 Brandt; **81mm**: 338 (incl 53 SP)
ATGW 140 TOW (incl 56 SP)
RL **84mm**: AT-4
RCL 1,151: **84mm**: 1,131 *Carl Gustav*; **106mm**: 20 M-40
SAM *Stinger*
SURV *Green Archer*
ATTACK HEL 12 AS-550C2
SPT HEL 13 Hughes 500M/OH-6

Navy 4,300

(incl 570 conscripts, 230 women)
BASES Korsør, Frederikshavn
SUBMARINES 5
SSK 5
3 *Tumleren* (mod No *Kobben*) with Swe FFV Type 61 HWT
2 *Narhvalen*, with FFV Type 61 HWT
FRIGATES 3
FFG 3 *Niels Juel* with 8 *Harpoon* SSM and 8 *Sea Sparrow* SAM, 1 76mm gun
PATROL AND COASTAL COMBATANTS 38
MISSILE CRAFT 7 *Willemoes* PFM with 2 x 4 *Harpoon* SSM, 2 or 4 533mm TT, 1 76mm gun (plus 3 in reserve)
PATROL CRAFT 31
  OFFSHORE 5
  1 *Beskytteren* PCO, 4 *Thetis* PCO all with 1 *Lynx* hel
  COASTAL 17
  14 *Flyvefisken* (Stanflex 300) PFC, 3 *Agdlek* PCC
  INSHORE 9
  9 *Barsøe* PCC
MINE WARFARE 10
(All units of *Flyvefisken* class can also lay up to 60 mines)
MINELAYERS 6
  4 *Falster* (400 mines), 2 *Lindormen* (50 mines)
MINE COUNTERMEASURES 4
  1 *Sund* (US MSC-128)
  3 *Flyvefisken* (SF300) MHC
SUPPORT AND MISCELLANEOUS 15
  2 AOT (small), 4 icebreakers (civilian-manned), 1 tpt, 6 environmental protection, 1 Royal Yacht, 1AE
HEL 8 *Lynx* (up to 4 embarked)

COASTAL DEFENCE

1 coastal fortress; **150mm** guns, coastal radar
2 mobile coastal missile batteries: 2 x 8 *Harpoon*
RESERVES (Home Guard)
40 inshore patrol craft

Air Force 4,700

(incl 510 conscripts, 320 women)

Flying hours 180
TACTICAL AIR COMD
FGA/FTR 4 sqn with 69 F-16A/B (60 operational, 9 attritional reserve)
TPT 1 sqn with 4 C-130H, *Challenger*-604, *Gulfstream* G-III
SAR 1 sqn with 8 S-61A hel
TRG 1 flying school with SAAB T-17
AIR DEFENCE GROUP
2 SAM bn: 8 bty with 36 I HAWK, 32 **40mm**/L70
CONTROL/REPORTING GROUP
5 radar stations, one in the Faroe Islands
EQUIPMENT
  69 cbt ac, no armed hel
  AC 69 **F-16A/B** (FGA/ftr) • 3 **C-130H** (tpt) • 2 *Challenger*-604 (tpt) • 28 **SAAB T-17** • *Gulfstream* G-III
  HEL 8 **S-61** (SAR)
MISSILES
  ASM AGM-12 *Bullpup*
  AAM AIM-9 *Sidewinder*
  SAM 36 I HAWK

Forces Abroad

UN AND PEACEKEEPING

ALBANIA (AFOR II): some BOSNIA (SFOR II): up to 630; 1 inf bn gp incl 1 tk sqn (10 *Leopard* MBT); aircrew with NATO E-3A operations; Air Force personnel in tac air-control parties (TACP) CROATIA (UNMOP): 1 obs GEORGIA (UNOMIG): 5 obs INDIA/PAKISTAN (UNMOGIP): 7 obs IRAQ/KUWAIT (UNIKOM): 7 obs MIDDLE EAST (UNTSO): 9 obs TAJIKISTAN (UNMOT): 3 obs YUGOSLAVIA (Joint Guardian): to be 850

Foreign Forces

NATO HQ Allied Forces Baltic Approaches (BALTAP)

France				Fr
	1997	**1998**	**1999**	**2000**
GDP	fr8.1tr	fr8.5tr		
	($1.4tr)	($1.4tr)		
per capita	$22,000	$23,100		
Growth	2.3%	3.2%		
Inflation	1.2%	0.9%		
Publ debt	65.3%	66.5%		
Def exp	fr242bn	fr240bn		
	($41.5bn)	($40.6bn)		
Def bdgt		fr184.8bn	fr190.0bn	
		($31.3bn)	($29.5bn)	
$1=franc	5.84	5.90	6.44	

Population			59,165,000
Age	*13–17*	*18–22*	*23–32*
Men	1,967,000	1,971,000	4,320,000
Women	1,878,000	1,885,000	4,153,000

Total Armed Forces

ACTIVE 317,300

(incl 22,790 women, 103,500 conscripts; 5,200 **Central Staff**, 8,600 (2,300 conscripts) *Service de santé*, 400 *Service des essences* not listed)
Terms of service 10 months (can be voluntarily extended to 12–24 months)

RESERVES 419,000

Army 242,500 Navy 97,000 **Air Force** 79,500
Potential 1,096,500 **Army** 782,000 **Navy** 97,000 **Air Force** 179,500

Strategic Nuclear Forces (8,700)

(**Navy** 4,700 **Air Force** 3,100 *Gendarmerie* 600)
NAVY 64 SLBM in 4 SSBN
   SSBN 4
   2 *L'Inflexible* with 16 M-4/TN-70 or -71; plus SM-39 *Exocet* USGW and 4 533mm HWT
   2 *Le Triomphant* with 16 M-45/TN-75 SLBM; plus SM-39 *Exocet* and 4 533mm HWT
   36 *Super Etendard* strike **ac** (ASMP); plus 16 in store
AIR FORCE
   3 sqn with 60 *Mirage* 2000 N(ASMP)
   TKR 1 sqn with 11 C-135FR, 3 KC-135
   RECCE 1 sqn with 5 *Mirage* IV P

Army 178,300

(incl 13,490 women, 84,340 conscripts) regt normally bn size
1 Int and EW bde
1 corps with 1 armd, 1 mtn inf div
Summary of div cbt units
   3 armd regt • 4 arty regt • 3 mech inf regt • 2 recce sqn • 3 mot inf regt • 2 ATK sqn • 3 mtn inf regt
Corps units: 1 armd recce, 1 mot inf, 1 arty bde (1 MLRS, 2 *Roland* SAM (each of 4 bty), 1 HAWK SAM regt • 1 air mobile bde with 2 cbt hel regt (**hel** 26 SA-330, 48 SA-342 HOT ATK, 20 SA-341 gunships) • 1 engr bde (4 regt)
1 armd div (in Eurocorps): 2 armd, 1 mech inf, 2 arty regt
1 Fr/Ge bde (2,500): Fr units incl 1 lt armd, 1 mot inf regt; 1 recce sqn
Rapid Action Force (FAR) (41,500)
   1 para div: 6 para inf, 1 armd cavalry, 1 arty, 1 engr regt • 1 lt armd marine div: 2 APC inf, 2 lt armd, 1 arty, 1 engr regt • 1 lt armd div: 2 armd cavalry, 2 APC inf, 1 arty, 1 engr regt • 1 air-mobile div: 1 inf, 3

cbt hel, 1 spt hel regt (245 **hel** 63 SA-330, 90 SA-342/HOT, 20 AS-532, 72 SA-341 (30 gun, 42 recce/liaison))
Corps units: 1 arty bde (1 MLRS, 1 *Roland* SAM, 1 HAWK SAM regt) • 1 engr regt
Territorial def forces incl spt of UN missions: 7 regt

FOREIGN LEGION (8,200)

1 armd, 1 para, 6 inf, 1 engr regt (incl in units listed above)

MARINES (31,000)

(incl 12,000 conscripts, mainly overseas enlisted)
1 div (see FAR), 4 regt in France (see div cbt units above), 11 regt overseas

SPECIAL OPERATIONS FORCES

(see also above) 1 Marine para regt, 1 para regt, 2 hel units (EW, special ops)

RESERVES

Indiv reinforcements for 1 corps (incl Eurocorps) and FAR (75,000)
Territorial def forces: 10 regt, 75 coy (all arms), 12 coy (engr, tpt, log)

EQUIPMENT

   MBT 1,207: 985 AMX-30B2 (incl 662 in store), 222 *Leclerc*
   RECCE 337 AMX-10RC, 192 ERC-90F4 *Sagaie*, 155 AML-60/-90, 899 VBL M-11
   AIFV 713 AMX-10P/PC
   APC 3,820 VAB (incl variants)
   TOTAL ARTY 1,055
     TOWED 155mm: 113 BF-50, 105 TR-F-1
     SP 155mm: 272 AU-F-1
     MRL 227mm: 58 MLRS
     MOR 507: **120mm**: 361 RT-F1, 146 M-51
   ATGW 660 *Eryx*, 1,405 *Milan*, HOT (incl 125 VAB SP)
   RL 19,540: **89mm**: 9,850; **112mm**: 9,690 APILAS
   AD GUNS 20mm: 774 53T2
   SAM 605: 69 HAWK, 156 *Roland* I/II, 380 *Mistral*
   SURV RASIT-B/-E (veh, arty), RATAC (veh, arty)
   AC 2 Cessna *Caravan* II , 5 PC-6
   HELICOPTERS 518
     ATTACK 342: 157 SA-341F, 155 SA-342M, 30 SA-342AATCP
     RECCE 4 AS-532 *Horizon*
     SPT 172: 24 AS-532, 18 AS-555, 130 SA-330
   UAV 6 CL-289 (AN/USD-502), 2 *Crecerelle*, 4 *Hunter*

Navy 62,600

(incl 2,900 Marines, 3,500 Naval Air, 3,000 women, 8,160 conscripts)
COMMANDS SSBN (ALFOST) HQ Paris **Atlantic** (CECLANT) HQ Brest **North Sea/Channel** (COMAR CHERBOURG) HQ Cherbourg **Mediterranean** (CECMED) HQ Toulon **Indian Ocean** (ALINDIEN) HQ afloat **Pacific Ocean** (ALPACI) HQ Papeete
ORGANIC COMMANDS ALFAN (Surface Ships)

ALGASA (Surface Ships ASW) **ALMINES** (mine warfare) **ALAVIA** (naval aviation) **COFUSCO** (Marines) **ALFOST** (Submarines)

BASES France Cherbourg, Brest (HQ), Lorient, Toulon (HQ) **Overseas** Papeete (HQ) (Tahiti), La Réunion, Noumea (New Caledonia), Fort de France (Martinique), Cayenne (French Guiana)

SUBMARINES 12

STRATEGIC SUBMARINES 4 SSBN (see **Strategic Nuclear Forces**)

TACTICAL SUBMARINES 8
  SSN 6 *Rubis* ASW/ASUW with F-17 HWT, L-5 LWT and SM-39 *Exocet* USGW
  SSK 2 *Agosta* with F-17 HWT and L-5 LWT, SM-39 *Exocet* USGW

PRINCIPAL SURFACE COMBATANTS 41

CARRIERS 1 *Clémenceau* CVS (32,700t), capacity 40 ac (typically 2 flt with 16 *Super Etendard*, 1 with 6 *Alizé*; 1 det with 2 *Etendard* IVP, 8 *Crusader* F8/P, 2 *Super Frelon*, 2 *Dauphin* hel)

CRUISERS 1 *Jeanne d'Arc* CCH (trg/ASW) with 6 MM-38 *Exocet* SSM, 4 100mm guns, capacity 8 SA-319B hel

DESTROYERS 4

DDG 4
  2 *Cassard* with 1 x 1 *Standard* SM-1 MR; plus 8 MM-40 *Exocet* SSM, 1 100mm gun, 2 ASTT, 1 *Panther* hel
  2 *Suffren* with 1 x 2 *Masurca* SAM; plus 1 *Malafon* SUGW, 4 ASTT, 4 MM-38 *Exocet* SSM, 2 100mm guns

FRIGATES 35

FFG 35
  6 *Floréal* with 2 MM-38 *Exocet* SSM, 1 AS-365 hel and 1 100mm gun
  7 *Georges Leygues* with 2 *Lynx* hel (Mk 46 LWT), 2 ASTT; plus 5 with 8 MM-40, 2 with 4 MM-38 *Exocet* SSM, all with 1 100mm gun and CN SAM
  3 *Tourville* with 2 *Lynx* hel, 1 *Malafon* SUGW, 2 ASTT; plus 4 MM-38 *Exocet* SSM, 2 100mm guns, CN SAM
  16 *D'Estienne d'Orves* with 4 ASTT, 6 ASW mor; plus 10 with 2 MM-38, 6 with 4 MM-40 *Exocet* SSM, all with 1 100mm gun
  3 *La Fayette* with 8 MM-40 *Exocet* SSM, CN-2 SAM, 1 100mm gun, 1 *Panther* hel

PATROL AND COASTAL COMBATANTS 40

PATROL, OFFSHORE 1 *Albatross* PCO (Public Service Force)

PATROL, COASTAL 23
  10 *L'Audacieuse*, 8 *Léopard* PCC (instruction), 3 *Flamant* PCC, 1 *Sterne* PCC, 1 *Grebe* PCC (Public Service Force)

PATROL, INSHORE 16
  2 *Athos* PCI, 2 *Patra* PCI, 1 *La Combattante* PCI, 6 *Stellis* PCI, 5 PCI< (manned by *Gendarmarie Maritime*)

MINE WARFARE 22

COMMAND AND SUPPORT 2 Loire MCCS

MINELAYERS 0, but submarines and *Thetis* (trials ship) have capability

MINE COUNTERMEASURES 20
  13 *Eridan* MHC, 4 *Vulcain* MCM diver spt, 3 *Antares* (route survey/trg)

AMPHIBIOUS 9
  2 *Foudre* LPD, capacity 450 tps, 30 tk, 4 *Cougar* hel, 2 CDIC LCT or 10 LCM
  2 *Ouragan* LPD: capacity 350 tps, 25 tk, 2 *Super Frelon* hel or 4 *Puma* hel
  5 *Champlain* LSM: capacity 140 tps, tk
  Plus craft: 5 LCT, 21 LCM

SUPPORT AND MISCELLANEOUS 36

UNDER WAY SUPPORT 5 *Durance* AO with 1 SA-319 hel

MAINTENANCE AND LOGISTIC 18
  1 AOT, 1 *Jules Verne* AR with 2 SA-319 hel, 2 *Rhin* depot/spt, with hel; 8 tpt, 6 AT/F (3 civil charter)

SPECIAL PURPOSES 7
  5 trial ships, 2 *Glycine* trg

SURVEY/RESEARCH 6
  5 AGHS, 1 AGOR

DEPLOYMENT

CECLAND (HQ, Brest): 4 SSBN, 2 SS, 1 CCH, 5 DDH, 9 FFG, 3 MCMV, 1 MCCS, 10 MHC, 1 diver spt, 3 AGS, 1 AGOR

COMAR CHERBOURG (HQ, Cherbourg): 1 clearance diving ship

CECMED (HQ, Toulon): 6 SSN, 1 CV, 5 DDH, 4 DDG, 4 FFH, 7 FFA, 3 LSD, 3 AOR, 1 LSM, 4 LCT, 2 diver spt, 3 MHC, 1 AR

NAVAL AIR (3,500)

Flying hours *Etendard* and *Crusader*: 180–220 (night qualified pilots)

NUCLEAR STRIKE 2 flt with *Super Etendard* (ASMP nuc ASM)

FTR 1 sqn with F-8E (FN) *Crusader*

RECCE 1 sqn with *Etendard* IV P

AEW 2 flt with *Alizé*

MR 4 flt with N-262 *Frégate*

MP 2 sqn with *Atlantique*

ASW 2 sqn with *Lynx*

AEW 1 E-2C

TRG 3 units with N-262 *Frégate*, *Rallye* 880, CAP 10, 1 unit with SA-316B

COMMANDOS 1 aslt sqn with SA-321

MISC 1 SAR unit with SA-321, SA-365, 1 unit with SA-365F, SA-319, 2 liaison units with EMB-121

EQUIPMENT
  61 cbt ac (plus 35 in store); 25 armed hel (plus 9 in store)
  AC 29* *Super Etendard* plus 23 in store (52 to be mod for ASMP) • 9* *Crusader* plus 2 in store • 5* *Etendard* IV P • 7 *Alizé* (AEW) plus 2 in store • 18* *Atlantique* 2 (MP) plus 8 in store • 13 *Nord* 262 (MR/trg) • 8 *Xingu* (misc) • 7 *Rallye* 880 • 8

CAP-10 (trg) • 5 *Falcon* 10MER (trg)
HEL 25 *Lynx* (ASW) plus 8 in store • 10 **SA-321**
(SAR, trg) plus 4 in store • 13 **AS-565SA** (SAR,
trg) plus 2 in store

MISSILES

ASM *Exocet* AM-39
AAM R-550 *Magic* 2

MARINES (2,900)

COMMANDO UNITS (400) 4 aslt gp
1 attack swimmer unit
FUSILIERS-MARIN (2,500) 14 naval-base protection gp
PUBLIC SERVICE FORCE naval personnel perform-
ing general coast guard, fishery, SAR, anti-pollution
and traffic surv duties: 1 *Albatross*, 1 *Sterne*, 1 *Grebe*, 1
Flamant PCC; **ac** 4 N-262 **hel** 4 SA-365 (ships incl in
naval patrol and coastal totals). Comd exercised
through *Maritime Préfectures* (Premar): *Manche*
(Cherbourg), *Atlantique* (Brest), *Méditerranée* (Toulon)

Air Force 76,400

(incl 6,300 women, 11,000 conscripts, 5,600 civilians,
incl strategic nuc forces)
Flying hours 180

AIR SIGNALS AND GROUND ENVIRONMENT COMMAND

CONTROL automatic *STRIDA* II, 6 radar stations, 1
sqn with 4 E3F
SAM 10 sqn (1 trg) with *Crotale*, *Aspic*, SATCP and AA
gun bty (**20mm**)

AIR COMBAT COMMAND

FTR 5 sqn with *Mirage* 2000C/B
FGA 7 sqn
3 with *Mirage* 2000D • 2 with *Jaguar* A • 2 with
Mirage F1-CT
RECCE 2 sqn with *Mirage* F-1CR
TRG 3 OCU sqn
1 with *Jaguar* A/E • 1 with F1-C/B • 1 with *Mirage*
2000/BC
EW 1 sqn with C-160 ELINT/ESM

AIR MOBILITY COMMAND (CFAP)

TPT 11 sqn
1 hy with DC-8F, A310-300
5 tac with C-160/-160NG, C-130H
5 lt tpt/trg/SAR/misc with C-160, DHC-6, CN235,
Falcon 20, *Falcon* 50, *Falcon* 900, TBM-700, N-262,
AS-555
EW 1 sqn with DC-8 ELINT
HEL 6 sqn with AS-332, SA-330, AS-555, AS-355, SA-319
TRG 1 OCU with C-160, N-262, 1 OCU with SA-319,
AS-555, SA-330

AIR TRAINING COMMAND

TRG *Alpha Jet*, EMB-121, TB-30, EMB-312, CAP-10/-
20/-231, CR-100, N262

EQUIPMENT

531 cbt ac, no armed hel
AC 345 *Mirage* (10 **F-1B** (OCU), 10 **F-1C** (OCU plus
6 in Djibouti), 40 **F-1CR** (recce), 40 **F-1CT** (FGA), 5
MIVP (recce), 120 **-M-2000B/C** (95 -C (ftr), 25 -B
(OCU)), 60 **-M-2000N** (strike, FGA), 60 **-M-2000D**)
• 67 *Jaguar* (FGA) (plus 54 in store) • 119* *Alpha
Jet* (trg, plus 29 in store) • 4 **E-3F** (AEW) • 2 **A
310-300** (tpt) • 3 **DC-8F** (tpt) • 14 **C-130** (5 -**H**
(tpt), 9 -**H**-30 (tpt)) • 11 **C-135FR** (tkr) • 60 **C-160**
(40 -**AG**, 20 -**NG** (tpt of which 14 tkr)) • 3 **KC-135**
• 10 **CN-235M** (tpt) • 19 **N-262** • 17 *Falcon* (7 -
20), 4 -**50** (VIP), 2 -**900** (VIP)) • 13 **TBM-700** (tpt) •
6 **DHC-6** (tpt) • 49 **EMB-121** (trg) • 97 **TB-30** (trg
plus 50 in store) • 4 **CAP-10/20/231** (trg) • 48
EMB-312 (trg) • 2 **CR-100** (trg)
HEL 3 **SA-319** (*Alouette* III) • 29 **SA-330** (26 tpt,
SAR, 3 OCU) (*Puma*) • 7 **AS-332** (tpt/VIP) (*Super
Puma*) • 3 **AS-532** (tpt) (*Cougar*) • 6 **AS-355**
(*Ecureuil*) • 43 **AS-555** (34 tpt, 9 OCU) (*Fennec*)

MISSILES

ASM ASMP, AS-30/-30L
AAM *Super* 530F/D, R-550 *Magic* 1/II, AIM-9
Sidewinder, *Mica*

Forces Abroad

GERMANY 3,300: incl elm Eurocorps
ANTILLES (HQ Fort de France) 2,200: 3 marine inf
regt (incl 2 SMA), 1 marine inf bn, 1 air tpt unit **ac** 2
C-160 **hel** 2 SA-330, 2 SA-319, 1 FFG (1 AS-365 hel),
2 PCI, 1 LSM, 1 spt *Gendarmerie* 860
FRENCH GUIANA (HQ Cayenne) 2,200: 2 marine inf
(incl 1 SMA), 1 Foreign Legion regt, 2 PCI 1 *Atlantic*
ac, 1 air tpt unit **hel** 4 SA-330, 3 AS-555 *Gendarmerie*
600
INDIAN OCEAN (Mayotte, La Réunion) 2,850: 2
Marine inf (incl 1 SMA) regt, 1 spt bn, 1 Foreign
Legion coy, 1 air tpt unit **ac** 2 C-160 **hel** 2 AS 555, 1
LSM, 1 spt *Gendarmerie* 850 **Navy** Indian Ocean
Squadron, Comd ALINDIEN (HQ afloat): 1 FFG (2
AS-365 hel), 2 PCI, 1 AOR (comd), reinforcement 2
FFG, 1 *Atlantic* ac
NEW CALEDONIA (HQ Nouméa) 2,300: 1 Marine inf
regt; some 12 AML recce, 5 **120mm** mor; 1 air tpt
unit, det **ac** 2 CN-235 **hel** 2 AS-555, 5 SA-330 **Navy** 2
FFG (2 AS-365 hel), 2 PCI, 1 LSM, 1 AGS, 1 spt **ac** 2
Guardian MR *Gendarmerie* 1,050
POLYNESIA (HQ Papeete) 2,000 (incl *Centre
d'Expérimentation du Pacifique*): 1 Marine inf regt, 1
Foreign Legion bn, 1 air tpt unit; 2 CN-235, 3 AS-332
Gendarmerie 600 **Navy** 1 FFG, 3 patrol combatants,
1 amph, 1 AGHS, 5 spt **ac** 3 *Guardian* MR
CHAD 900: 2 inf coy, 1 AML sqn (-) **ac** 2 C-160, 1 C-
130, 3 *Mirage* FICT, 2 *Mirage* FICR
CÔTE D'IVOIRE 570: 1 marine inf bn (18 AML-60/-
90) **hel** 1 AS-555

DJIBOUTI 2,600: 1 marine inf(-), 1 Foreign Legion regt(-); 26 ERC-90 recce, 6 **155mm** arty, 16 AA arty; 3 amph craft, 1 sqn with **ac** 6 *Mirage* F-1C (plus 4 in store), 1 C-160 **hel** 1 SA-319, 2 SA-330
GABON 700: 1 marine inf bn (4 AML-60) **ac** 1 C-160 **hel** 1 AS-555
SENEGAL 1,200: 1 marine inf bn (14 AML-60/-90) **ac** 1 *Atlantic* MR, 1 C-160 tpt **hel** 1 SA-319

UN AND PEACEKEEPING

ALBANIA (AFOR II): some **BOSNIA** (SFOR II): 3,000: 2 mech inf bde, 1 N-262. (UNMIBH): 1 **CROATIA:** SFOR Air Component 11 *Jaguar*, 10 Mirage 2000C/D, 1 E-3F, 1 KC-135, 1 N-262 **EGYPT** (MFO): 17; 1 DHC-6 **GEORGIA** (UNOMIG): 5 obs **IRAQ/KUWAIT** (UNIKOM): 11 obs **ITALY** (SFOR Air Component): 10 *Mirage* 2000C/D, 1 C-135, 1 E-3F, 11 *Jaguar*, 1 N-262, 3 SA-330 (*Puma*) **LEBANON** (UNIFIL): 246: elm 1 log bn **MIDDLE EAST** (UNTSO): 3 obs **SAUDI ARABIA** (*Southern Watch*): 170; 5 *Mirage* 2000C, 3 F-1CR, 1 C-135 **WESTERN SAHARA** (MINURSO): 25 obs (*Gendarmerie*) **YUGOSLAVIA** (Joint Guardian): 4,100 (to be 6,000)

Paramilitary 94,300

GENDARMERIE 94,300

(incl 3,600 women, 13,700 conscripts, 1,600 civilians) **Territorial** 61,000 **Mobile** 17,000 **Schools** 5,600 **Overseas** 3,200 **Maritime, Air** (personnel drawn from other dept.) **Republican Guard, Air tpt, Arsenals** 5,000 **Administration** 2,500 **Reserves** 50,000
   EQPT 28 VBC-90 armd cars; 155 VBRG-170 APC; 826 **60mm, 81mm** mor; 5 PCIs (listed under Navy), plus 35 other patrol craft and 4 AT **hel** 12 SA-319, 30 AS-350

Foreign Forces

SINGAPORE AIR FORCE 200: 18 TA-4SU *Skyhawks* (Cazaux AFB)

Germany   Ge

	1997	1998	1999	2000
GDP	DM3.6tr	DM3.8tr		
	($2.1tr)	($2.1tr)		
per capita	$21,900	$23,000		
Growth	2.2%	2.8%		
Inflation	1.8%	1.0%		
Publ debt	63.6%	63.1%		
Def exp	DM57.6bn	DM58.1bn		
	($33.2bn)	($33.0bn)		
Def bdgt		DM46.7bn	DM47.5bn	DM49.9bn
		($26.5bn)	($24.7bn)	($26.0bn)
$1=DM	1.73	1.76	1.92	

Population			82,057,000
Age	*13–17*	*18–22*	*23–32*
Men	2,338,000	2,263,000	5,662,000
Women	2,213,000	2,162,000	5,463,000

Total Armed Forces

ACTIVE some 332,800
(incl 142,000 conscripts, 1,440 women)
Terms of service 10 months; 12–23 months voluntary

RESERVES 344,700
(men to age 45, officers/NCO to 60) **Army** 276,000 **Navy** 8,700 **Air Force** 60,000

Army 228,300

(incl 112,000 conscripts)
ARMY FORCES COMMAND
1 air-mobile force comd (div HQ) with 2 AB (1 Crisis Reaction Force (CRF)) • 1 cdo SF bde • 1 army avn bde with 5 regt • 1 SIGINT/ELINT bde • 1 spt bde
ARMY SUPPORT COMMAND
3 log, 1 medical bde
CORPS COMMANDS
I Ge/Nl Corps 2 MDC/armd div
II Corps 2 MDC/armd div; 1 MDC/mtn div
IV Corps 1 MDC/armd inf div; 1 armd inf div; 1 MDC
Corps Units 2 spt bde and Ge elm of Ge/Nl Corps, 1 air mech bde (CRF), 1 ATGW hel regt
Military District Commands (MDC)/Divisions
6 MDC/div; 1 div; 1 MDC comd and control 9 armd bde, 7 armd inf and the Ge elm of the Ge/Fr bde, 2 armd (not active), 2 armd inf (not active), 1 inf, 1 mtn bde. Bde differ in their basic org, peacetime str, eqpt and mob capability; 4 (2 armd, 1 inf and Ge/Fr bde) are allocated to the CRF, the remainder to the Main Defence Forces (MDF). The MDC also comd and control 27 Military Region Commands (MRC). One armd div earmarked for Eurocorps, another for Allied Rapid Reaction Corps (ARRC). 7 recce bn, 7 arty regt, 7 engr bde and 7 AD regt available for cbt spt
EQUIPMENT
   MBT 3,136: 1,315 *Leopard* 1A1/A3/A4/A5 (incl 327 to be destroyed), 1,821 *Leopard* 2 (225 to be upgraded to A5)
   RECCE 523: 409 SPz-2 *Luchs*, 114 TPz-1 *Fuchs* (NBC)
   AIFV 2,118 *Marder* A2/A3, 343 *Wiesel* (210 TOW, 133 20mm gun)
   APC 814 TPz-1 *Fuchs* (incl variants), 2,492 M-113 (incl variants, 320 arty obs)
   TOTAL ARTY 2,068
      TOWED 353: **105mm**: 18 Geb H, 143 M-101; **155mm**: 192 FH-70
      SP 155mm: 571 M-109A3G, 4 PzH 2000

MRL 232: **110mm**: 78 LARS; **227mm**: 154 MLRS
MOR 908: **120mm**: 393 Brandt, 515 Tampella
ATGW 1,960: 1,648 *Milan*, 225 RJPz-(HOT) *Jaguar* 1,
87 RJPz-(TOW) *Jaguar* 2
AD GUNS 1,529: **20mm**: 1,150 Rh 202 towed;
35mm: 379 *Gepard* SP (147 being upgraded)
SAM 143 *Roland* SP, *Stinger*
SURV 19 *Green Archer* (mor), 110 RASIT (veh, arty),
73 RATAC (veh, arty)
HELICOPTERS 624
ATTACK 204 PAH-1 (BO-105 with HOT)
SPT 396: 151 UH-1D, 108 CH-53G, 95 BO-105M,
42 *Alouette* II
UAV CL-289 (AN/USD-502)
MARINE (River Engineers) 13 LCM

Navy 28,100

(incl 4,200 Naval Air, 6,800 conscripts, 490 women)
FLEET COMMAND Type comds Frigate, Patrol Boat,
MCMV, Submarine, Support Flotillas, Naval Air **Spt
comds** Naval Comms, Electronics
BASES Glücksburg (Maritime HQ), Wilhelmshaven,
Kiel, Olpenitz, Eckernförde, Warnemünde
SUBMARINES 14
SSK 12 Type 206/206A SSC with *Seeaal* DM2 A3 HWT
SSC 2 Type 205
PRINCIPAL SURFACE COMBATANTS 14
DESTROYERS 2
DDG 2 *Lütjens* (mod US *Adams*) with 1 x 1 SM-1 MR
SAM/*Harpoon* SSM launcher, 2 127mm guns; plus 8
ASROC (Mk 46 LWT), 6 ASTT
FRIGATES 12
FFG 12
8 *Bremen* with 2 *Lynx* hel (ASW/OTHT), 2 x 2 ASTT;
plus 8 *Harpoon* SSM
4 *Brandenburg* with 4 MM-38 *Exocet* SSM, 1 VLS Mk-
41 SAM, 2 RAM, 21 Mk-49 SAM, 1 76mm gun, 4
324mm TT, 2 *Lynx* hel
PATROL AND COASTAL COMBATANTS 28
MISSILE CRAFT 28
10 *Albatross* (Type 143) PFM with 4 *Exocet* SSM, and
2 533mm TT
10 *Gepard* (T-143A) PFM with 4 *Exocet* SSM
8 *Tiger* (Type 148) PFM with 4 *Exocet* SSM
MINE COUNTERMEASURES 34
10 *Hameln* (T-343) comb ML/MCC
4 HL 351 *Troika* MSC control and guidance, each
with 3 unmanned sweep craft
3 converted *Lindau* (T-331) MHC
12 *Frankenthal* (T-332) MHC
4 *Frauenlob* MSI
1 MCM/T-742A diver spt ship
AMPHIBIOUS craft only
5 LCU/LCM

SUPPORT AND MISCELLANEOUS 42
UNDER WAY SUPPORT 2 *Spessart* AO
MAINTENANCE AND LOGISTIC 26
6 *Elbe* spt, 4 small (2,000t) AOT, 4 *Lüneburg* log spt, 2
AE, 8 AT, 2 icebreakers (civil)
SPECIAL PURPOSE 10
3 AGI, 2 trials, 3 multi-purpose (T-748), 2 trg
RESEARCH AND SURVEY 4
1 AGOR, 3 AGHS (civil-manned for Ministry of
Transport)

NAVAL AIR (4,200)
Flying hours *Tornado*: 160
3 wg, 8 sqn, plus 2 sqn GBAD *Roland*
1 wg with *Tornado*, 2 sqn FGA/recce, 1 sqn trg, 1 sqn
·GBAD *Roland*
1 wg with MPA/SIGINT/SAR/pollution control/
tpt, 2 sqn with *Atlantic* (MPA/SIGINT), Do-228
(pollution control/tpt), 1 sqn with *Lynx* (ASW/
ASUW)
1 SAR/ASUW/tpt wg with 1 sqn *Sea King* Mk 41 hel
EQUIPMENT
52 cbt ac, 39 armed hel
AC 52 *Tornado* • 17 *Atlantic* (13 MR, 4 ELINT) • 2
Do-228 (pollution control) • 2 **Do-228** (tpt)
HEL 17 *Sea Lynx* **Mk 88** (ASW/ASUW) • 22 *Sea
King* **Mk 41** (SAR/tpt/ASUW)
MISSILES
ASM *Kormoran*, *Sea Skua*, HARM
AAM AIM-9 *Sidewinder*, *Roland*

Air Force 76,400

(23,200 conscripts, 950 women)
Flying hours 150
AIR FORCE COMMAND
2 TAC cmds, 4 air div
FGA 4 wg with 8 sqn *Tornado*
FTR 4 wg (with F-4F (7 sqn); MiG-29 1 sqn)
RECCE 1 wg with 2 sqn *Tornado*
ECR 1 wg with 2 sqn *Tornado*
SAM 6 mixed wg (each 1 gp *Patriot* (6 sqn) plus 1 gp
HAWK (4 sqn plus 2 reserve sqn)); 14 sqn *Roland*
RADAR 2 tac Air Control regts, 8 sites; 11 remote
radar posts
TRANSPORT COMMAND (GAFTC)
TPT 3 wg, 4 sqn with *Transall* C-160, incl 1 (OCU) with
C-160, 4 sqn (incl 1 OCU) with Bell UH-1D, 1 special
air mission wg with Boeing 707-320C, Tu-154,
Airbus A-310, VFW-614, CL-601, L-410S (VIP), 3 AS-
532U2 (VIP)
TRAINING
FGA OCU with 13 *Tornado*
FTR OCU with 23 F-4F
NATO joint jet pilot trg (Sheppard AFB, TX) with 35 T-
37B, 40 T-38A; primary trg sqn with Beech *Bonanza*
(Goodyear AFB, AZ), GAF Air Defence School (Fort

Bliss TX)

EQUIPMENT

451 cbt ac (36 trg (overseas)) (plus 106 in store); no attack hel

AC 154 **F-4** (147 -**F** (FGA, ftr), 7 -**E** (OCU, in US being wfs) • 274 *Tornado* (185 FGA, 35* ECR, 40 Recce, 14* OCU • 23 **MiG-29** (19 (ftr), 4* -**UB** (trg)) • 106 *Alpha Jet* (in store) • 84 *Transall* **C-160** (tpt, trg) • 2 **Boeing 707** (VIP) • 5 **A-310** (VIP, tpt) • 1 **Tu-154** • 7 **CL-601** (VIP) • 4 **L-410-S** (VIP) • 35 **T-37B** • 40 **T-38A**

HEL 99 **UH-1D** (95 SAR, tpt, liaison; 4 VIP) • 3 **AS-532U2** (VIP)

MISSILES

ASM AGM-65 *Maverick*, AGM-88A HARM

AAM AIM-9 *Sidewinder*, AA-8 *Aphid*, AA-10 *Alamo*, AA-11 *Archer*

SAM HAWK, *Roland*, *Patriot*

Forces Abroad

NAVY 1 DDG/FFG with STANAVFORLANT, 1 DDG/FFG with STANAVFORMED, 1 MCMV with STANAVFORCHAN, 3 MPA in ELMAS/Sardinia **US Army** trg area with 40 *Leopard* 2 MBT, 32 *Marder* AIFV, 12 M-109A3G **155mm** SP arty. **Air Force** 812 flying trg at Goodyear, Sheppard, Holloman AFBs, NAS Pensacola, Fort Rucker AFBs with 35 T-37, 40 T-38, 24 F-4F; 14 *Tornado*, missile trg at Fort Bliss

UN AND PEACEKEEPING

ALBANIA (AFOR II): some **BOSNIA** (SFOR II): 2,738; 56 SPz-2 *Luchs* recce, 98 TPz-1 *Fuchs* APC, 7 CH-53 hel, 1 CL-289 UAV **SFOR Air Component** 14 *Tornado* 2 C-160 **GEORGIA** (UNOMIG): 1 obs **IRAQ/KUWAIT** (UNIKOM): 15 **YUGOSLAVIA** (Joint Guardian): 4,400 (to be 8,000)

Foreign Forces

NATO HQ Allied Land Forces Central Europe (LANDCENT), HQ Allied Rapid Reaction Corps (ARRC), HQ Allied Air Forces Central Europe (AIRCENT), HQ Allied Land Forces Jutland and Schleswig-Holstein (LANDJUT), HQ Multi-National Division (Central) (MND(C)), HQ Allied Command Europe Mobile Force (AMFL), Airborne Early Warning Force: 17 E-3A *Sentry*, 2 Boeing-707 (trg)
BELGIUM 2,100: 1 mech inf bde(-)
FRANCE 3,300: incl elm Eurocorps
NETHERLANDS 3,000: 1 lt bde
UK 20,800: **Army** 18,300: 1 corps HQ (multinational), 1 armd div **Air Force** 2,500: 1 air base, 3 sqn with ac 39 *Tornado* GR1, 1 RAF regt sqn with *Rapier* SAM
US 68,820: **Army** 53,600: 1 army HQ, 1 corps HQ; 1 armd (-), 1 mech inf div (-) **Navy** 290 **USMC** 200 **Air Force** 14,700: HQ USAFE, (HQ 17th Air Force), 1 tac ftr wg with 4 sqn FGA/ftr, 1 cbt spt wg, 1 air-control wg, 1

tac airlift wg; 1 air base wg, 54 F-16C/D, 12 A-10, 6 OA-10, 16 C-130E, 9 C-9A, 9 C-21, 2 C-20, 1 CT-43

Greece   Gr

	1997	1998	1999	2000
GDP	dr32.7tr	dr35.7tr		
	($120bn)	($121bn)		
per capita	$12,500	$13,100		
Growth	3.2%	3.5%		
Inflation	5.6%	4.7%		
Publ debt	106.3%	106.3%		
Def exp	dr1.5tr	dr1.7tr		
	($5.5bn)	($5.8bn)		
Def bdgt		dr1,170bn	dr1,220bn	
		($4.0bn)	($3.8bn)	
FMA (US)	$123m	$15m	$0.025m	$0.035m
$1=drachma	273	296	319	
Population[a]			10,645,000 (Muslim 1%)	
Age	*13–17*	*18–22*	*23–32*	
Men	344,000	383,000	825,000	
Women	323,000	363,000	788,000	

[a] Excl ε350–400,000 Albanians working in Greece in 1999

Total Armed Forces

ACTIVE 165,670

(incl 105,820 conscripts, 5,520 women)
Terms of service **Army** up to 19 months **Navy** up to 21 months **Air Force** up to 21 months

RESERVES some 291,000

(to age 50) **Army** some 235,000 (Field Army 200,000, Territorial Army/National Guard 35,000) **Navy** about 24,000 **Air Force** about 32,000

Army 116,000

(incl 88,500 conscripts, 2,700 women)

FIELD ARMY

3 Mil Regions • 1 Army, 5 corps HQ • 5 div HQ (1 armd, 3 mech, 1 inf) • 4 inf div (3 inf, 1 arty regt, 1 armd bn) • 5 indep armd bde (each 2 armd, 1 mech inf, 1 SP arty bn) • 7 mech bde (2 mech, 1 armd, 1 SP arty bn) • 5 inf bde • 1 army avn bde with 5 avn bn (incl 1 ATK) • 1 amph bn • 4 recce bn • 5 fd arty bn • 1 indep avn coy • 10 AD arty bn • 2 SAM bn with I HAWK Units are manned at 3 different levels
  Cat A 85% fully ready **Cat B** 60% ready in 24 hours
  Cat C 20% ready in 48 hours

TERRITORIAL DEFENCE

Higher Mil Comd of Interior and Islands HQ
4 Mil Comd HQ (incl Athens) • 1 inf div • 4 AD arty

bn • 2 inf regt • 1 army avn bn • 1 para regt • 8 fd
arty bn

RESERVES 34,000

National Guard internal security role

EQUIPMENT

    MBT 1,735: 714 M-48 (15 A3, 699 A5), 669 M-60 (357
A1, 312 A3), 352 *Leopard* (105 -1CR, 170 -1V, 77 -
1A5)

    RECCE 130 M-8, 13 VBL

    AIFV 500 BMP-1

    APC 308 *Leonidas* Mk1/Mk2, 1,669 M-113A1/A2

    TOTAL ARTY 1,886

    TOWED 730: **105mm**: 18 M-56, 445 M-101;
    155mm: 267 M-114

    SP 398: **105mm**: 72 M-52A1; **155mm**: 133 M-109A1/
A2, **175mm**: 12 M-107; **203mm**: 181 M-110A2

    MRL 122mm: 116 RM-70; **227mm**: 18 MLRS (incl
ATACMS)

    MOR 107mm: 624 M-30 (incl 191 SP); plus **81mm**:
2,800

    ATGW 290 *Milan*, 336 TOW (incl 212 M-901), 262
AT-4 *Spigot*

    RL 64mm: 21,625 RPG-18; **66mm**: 12,000 M-72

    RCL 84mm: 2000 *Carl Gustav*; **90mm**: 1,314 EM-67;
106mm: 1,291 M-40A1

    AD GUNS 23mm: 506 ZU-23-2

    SAM 838 *Stinger*, 42 I HAWK, 12 SA-8B, S-300 in
Crete, originally intended for Cyprus

    SURV AN/TPQ-36 (arty, mor)

    AC 43 U-17A

    HELICOPTERS

        ATTACK 20 AH-64A

        SPT 9 CH-47D (1 in store), 76 UH-1H, 30 AB-
205A, 14 AB-206

Navy 19,500

(incl 9,800 conscripts, 1,300 women)

BASES Salamis, Patras, Soudha Bay

SUBMARINES 8

SSK 8

    4 *Glavkos* (Ge T-209/1100) with 533mm TT, and
Harpoon USGW (1 in refit)

    4 *Poseidon* (Ge T-209/1200) with 533mm TT and
Harpoon USGW

PRINCIPAL SURFACE COMBATANTS 17

DESTROYERS 4

DDG 4 *Kimon* (US *Adams*) (US lease) with 1 SM-1; plus
1 x 8 ASROC, 2 x 3 ASTT, 2 127mm guns, 6 *Harpoon*
SSM

FRIGATES 13

FFG 13

    4 *Hydra* (Ge MEKO 200) with 6 ASTT; 8 *Harpoon* SSM
and 1 127mm gun (1 SH-60 hel, 1 DC)

    2 *Elli* (Nl *Kortenaer* Batch 2) with 2 AB-212 hel, 4
ASTT; 8 *Harpoon* SSM

    4 *Aegean* (Nl *Kortenaer* Batch 1) with 2 AB-212 hel, 2
x 2 ASTT, 8 *Harpoon* SSM

    3 *Makedonia* (ex-US *Knox*) (US lease) with 8 ASROC,
4 ASTT; plus *Harpoon* SSM (from ASROC
launcher), 1 127mm gun

PATROL AND COASTAL COMBATANTS 42

CORVETTES 5 *Niki* (ex-Ge *Thetis*) (ASW) with 4 ASW
RL, 4 533mm TT

MISSILE CRAFT 19

    13 *Laskos* (Fr *La Combattante* II, III, IIIB) PFM, 8 with
4 MM-38 *Exocet*, 5 with 6 *Penguin* SSM, all with 2
533mm TT

    4 *Votis* (Fr *La Combattante* IIA) PFM 2 with 4 MM-38
Exocet, 2 with *Harpoon*

    2 *Stamou* with 4 SS-12 SSM

TORPEDO CRAFT 8

    4 *Hesperos* (Ge *Jaguar*) PFT with 4 533mm TT

    4 *Andromeda* (No *Nasty*) PFT with 4 533mm TT

PATROL CRAFT 10

    COASTAL 4

    2 *Armatolos* (Dk *Osprey*) PCC, 2 *Pirpolitis* PCC

    INSHORE 6

    2 *Tolmi*, 4 PCI

MINE WARFARE 16

MINELAYERS 2 *Aktion* (US LSM-1) (100–130 mines)

MINE COUNTERMEASURES 14

    8 *Alkyon* (US MSC-294) MSC

    6 *Atalanti* (US *Adjutant*) MSC, plus 4 MSR

AMPHIBIOUS 10

    2 *Chios* LST with hel deck: capacity 300 tps, 4 LCVP
plus veh

    1 *Nafkratoussa* (US *Cabildo*) LSD: capacity 200 tps, 18
tk, 1 hel

    2 *Inouse* (US *County*) LST: capacity 400 tps, 18 tk

    3 *Ikaria* (US LST-510): capacity 200 tps, 16 tk

    2 *Roussen* (US LSM-1) LSM, capacity 50 tps, 4 tk

    Plus about 57 craft: 2 LCT, 6 LCU, 11 LCM, some 31
LCVP, 7 LCA

SUPPORT AND MISCELLANEOUS 14

    2 AOT, 4 AOT (small), 1 *Axios* (ex-Ge *Lüneburg*) log
spt, 1 AE, 5 AGHS, 1 trg

NAVAL AIR (250)

6 cbt ac, 15 armed hel

AC 6 P-3B (MR)

HEL 2 sqn with 8 AB-212 (ASW), 2 AB-212 (EW), 2 SA-
319 (ASW), 5 S-70B (ASW)

Air Force 30,170

(incl 7,521 conscripts, 1,520 women)

TACTICAL AIR FORCE

8 cbt wg, 1 tpt wg

FGA 10 sqn

    2 with A-7H, 2 with A-7E, 2 with F-16CG/DG, 1
with F-4E, 3 with F-5A/B, NF-5A/B, RF-5A

FTR 8 sqn

2 with *Mirage* F-1CG, 2 with *Mirage* 2000 EG/BG, 2
  with F-4E, 2 with F-16 CG/DG
RECCE 1 sqn with RF-4E
TPT 3 sqn with C-130H/B, YS-11, C-47, Do-28,
  Gulfstream
LIAISON 4 T-33A
HEL 1 sqn with AB-205A, AB-212, Bell 47G
AD 1 bn with *Nike Hercules* SAM (36 launchers), 12 bty
  with *Skyguard/Sparrow* SAM, twin **35mm** guns

AIR TRAINING COMMAND

TRG 4 sqn
  1 with T-41A, 1 with T-37B/C, 2 with T-2E

EQUIPMENT

458 cbt ac, no armed hel
AC 90 **A-7 H** (FGA), 4 **TA-7H** (FGA) • 87 **F-5A/B**, 10
  NF-5A, 1 **NF-5B** • 95 **F-4E/RF-4E** • 75 **F-16CG**
  (FGA)/DG (trg) • 27 *Mirage* **F-1 CG** (ftr) • 34
  Mirage **2000** (**EG** (FGA)/**BG*** (trg)) • 4 **C-47** (tpt)
  • 10 **C-130H** (tpt) • 5 **C-130B** (tpt) • 10 **CL-215**
  (tpt, fire-fighting) • 13 **Do-28** (lt tpt) • 1
  Gulfstream **I** (VIP tpt) • 35* **T-2E** (trg) • 30 **T-33A**
  (liaison) • 34 **T-37B/C** (trg) • 20 **T-41D** (trg) • 1
  YS-11-200 (tpt)
HEL 13 **AB-205A** (SAR) • 1 **AB-206** • 4 **AB-212** (VIP,
  tpt) • 7 **Bell 47G** (liaison)

MISSILES

ASM AGM-65 *Maverick*, AGM-88 HARM
AAM AIM-7 *Sparrow*, AIM-9 *Sidewinder* L/P, R-550
  Magic 2, AIM 120 AMRAAM, *Super* 530D
SAM 1 bn with 36 *Nike Hercules*, 12 bty with
  Skyguard, 40 *Sparrow*, **35mm** guns

Forces Abroad

CYPRUS 1,250: incl 1 mech bde and officers/NCO
seconded to Greek-Cypriot forces
UN AND PEACEKEEPING
ADRIATIC (*Sharp Guard* if re-implemented): 2 MSC
ALBANIA (AFOR II): some **BOSNIA** (SFOR II): 250
SFOR Air Component 1 C-130 **GEORGIA**
(UNOMIG): 4 obs **IRAQ/KUWAIT** (UNIKOM): 6 obs
WESTERN SAHARA (MINURSO): 1 obs **YUGOSLA-
VIA** (Joint Guardian): 550 (to be 1,000)

Paramilitary 4,000

COAST GUARD AND CUSTOMS 4,000

some 100 patrol craft, **ac** 2 Cessna *Cutlass*, 2 TB-20
Trinidad

Foreign Forces

US 420: **Navy** 240; facilities at Soudha Bay **Air Force**
160; air base gp; facilities at Iraklion **Army** 10

Hungary   Hu

	1997	1998	1999	2000
GDP	f8.6tr	f10.3tr		
	($46bn)	($48bn)		
per capita	$7,000	$7,600		
Growth	4.0%	5.0%		
Inflation	18.3%	14.4%		
Debt	$24.3bn	$25.2bn		
Def exp	f124bn	f142bn		
	($666m)	($660m)		
Def bdgt		f142bn	f168bn	f202bn
		($660m)	($688m)	($722m)
FMA (US)	$1.0m	$1.5m	$1.5m	$1.6m
$1 =forint	187	214	244	
Population				10,028,000

(Romany 4%, German 3%, Serb 2%, Romanian 1%,
Slovak 1%)

Age	*13–17*	*18–22*	*23–32*
Men	336,000	390,000	703,000
Women	317,000	366,000	659,000

Total Armed Forces

ACTIVE 43,440

(incl 22,900 conscripts; 8,150 HQ staff and centrally
controlled formations/units)
Terms of service 9 months

RESERVES 90,300

Army 74,900 **Air Force** 15,400 (to age 50)

Land Forces 23,500

(incl 17,800 conscripts)
Land Forces HQ • 1 Mil District HQ
2 mech div
  1 with 3 mech inf, 1 engr bde, 1 arty, 1 ATK, 1 recce bn
  1 with 2 trg centres
Corps tps
  1 army maritime wing, 1 counter mine bn
MoD tps (Budapest): 1 MP regt

RESERVES

4 mech inf bde
EQUIPMENT
  MBT 807: 569 T-55 (209 in store), 238 T-72
  RECCE 104 FUG D-442
  AIFV 490 BMP-1, 12 BRM-1K, 70 BTR-80A
  APC 786: 420 BTR-80, 336 PSZH D-944 (83 in store),
    30 MT-LB (plus some 369 'look-alike' types)
  TOTAL ARTY 839
    TOWED 532: **122mm**: 230 M-1938 (M-30) (24 in
    store); **152mm**: 302 D-20 (218 in store)
    SP 122mm: 151 2S1 (18 in store)
    MRL 122mm: 56 BM-21

MOR 120mm: 100 M-120 (2 in store)
ATGW 369: 115 AT-3 *Sagger*, 30 AT-4 *Spigot* (incl
BRDM-2 SP), 224 AT-5 *Spandrel*
ATK GUNS 85mm: 162 D-44 (all in store); **100mm**:
106 MT-12
AD GUNS 57mm: 186 S-60 (43 in store)
SAM 243 SA-7, 60 SA-14, 45 *Mistral*
SURV PSZNR-5B, SZNAR-10

Army Maritime Wing (290)

BASE Budapest

RIVER CRAFT 50

6 *Nestin* MSI (riverine), some 44 An-2 mine warfare/
patrol boats

Air Force 11,500

(incl 5,100 conscripts)
AIR DEFENCE COMMAND
136 cbt ac, 86 attack hel
Flying hours 50
FTR 2 regt with 86 MiG-21bis/MF/UM, 27 MiG-29, 11
MiG-23, 12 Su-22
ATTACK HEL 86 Mi-24
SPT HEL 33 Mi-2, 50 Mi-8/-17
TPT 4 An-26, 4 Z-43
TRG 19 L-39, 12 Yak-52
AAM AA-2 *Atoll*, AA-8 *Aphid*, AA-10 *Alamo*, AA-11
Archer
ASM AT-2 *Swatter*, AT-6 *Spiral*
SAM 2 regt with 66 SA-2/-3/-5, 12 SA-4, 20 SA-6

Forces Abroad

UN AND PEACEKEEPING
BOSNIA (SFOR II): 4 obs **CROATIA** (SFOR II): 310; 1
engr bn **CYPRUS** (UNFICYP): 109 **EGYPT** (MFO): 41
mil pol **GEORGIA** (UNOMIG): 5 obs **INDIA/
PAKISTAN** (UNMOGIP): 1 obs **IRAQ/KUWAIT**
(UNIKOM): 5 obs

Paramilitary 14,000

BORDER GUARDS (Ministry of Interior) 12,000 (to
reduce)
11 districts/regts plus 1 Budapest district (incl 7 rapid-
reaction coy; 33 PSZH, 68 BTR-80 APC)
INTERNAL SECURITY FORCES (Police) 2,000
33 PSZH, 40 BTR-80APC

Iceland — Icl

	1997	1998	1999	2000
GDP	K530bn	K586bn		
	($7.5bn)	($8.3bn)		
per capita	$22,400	$23,900		
Growth	5.2%	5.0%		
Inflation	1.8%	1.7%		
Publ debt	52.7%	48.3%		
Sy exp[a]	K1.1bn	K1.3bn		
	($15m)	($18m)		
Sy bdgt[a]			K1.4bn	
			($19m)	
$1=kronur	70.9	71.0	75.5	

[a] Iceland has no Armed Forces. Sy bdgt is mainly for Coast
Guard

Population			280,000	
Age	*13–17*	*18–22*	*23–32*	
Men	11,000	11,000	22,000	
Women	10,000	10,000	20,000	

Total Armed Forces

ACTIVE Nil

Paramilitary 120

COAST GUARD 120
BASE Reykjavik
PATROL CRAFT 4
2 *Aegir* PCO with hel, 1 *Odinn* PCO with hel deck, 1
PCI<
AVN ac 1 F-27, **hel** 1 SA-365N, 1 SA-332, 1 AS-350B

Foreign Forces

NATO Island Commander Iceland (ISCOMICE,
responsible to CINCEASTLANT)
US 1,640: **Navy** 960; MR: 1 sqn with 4 P-3C **Marines**
80 **Air Force** 600; 4 F-15C/D, 1 HC-130, 1 KC-135, 4
HH-60G
NETHERLANDS 16: **Navy** 1 P-3C

Italy — It

	1997	1998	1999	2000
GDP	L1,951tr	L2,017tr		
	($1.1tr)	($1.2tr)		
per capita	$20,700	$21,500		
Growth	1.5%	1.4%		
Inflation	2.0%	2.0%		
Publ debt	122.4%	119.9%		
Def exp	L38.7tr	L40.1tr		
	($22.7bn)	($23.1bn)		

contd	1997	1998	1999	2000
Def bdgt		L31.0tr	L30.9tr	
		($17.8bn)	($16.2bn)	
$1=lira	1,703	1,736	1,900	
Population				57,917,000
Age	*13–17*	*18–22*	*23–32*	
Men	1,572,000	1,821,000	4,515,000	
Women	1,494,000	1,738,000	4,367,000	

Total Armed Forces

ACTIVE 265,500

(incl 126,100 conscripts)
Terms of service all services 10 months

RESERVES 72,000 (immediate mobilisation)
Army 29,000 (500,000 obligation to age 45) **Navy**
28,000 (to age 39 for men, variable for officers to 73)
Air Force 15,000 (to age 25 or 45 (specialists))

Army 165,600

(incl 95,800 conscripts)
1 Op Comd HQ, 3 mil region HQ
1 Projection Force with 1 mech, 1 airmobile, 1 AB bde,
   1 amph, 1 engr, 1 avn regt
1 mtn force with 3 mtn bde, 1 engr, 1 avn regt, 1 alpine
   AB bn
2 defence force
   1 with 1 armd, 1 mech, 1 armd cav bde, 1 engr regt
   1 with 3 mech, 1 armd bde, 1 engr, 1 avn regt
1 spt comd with
   1 AD div: 3 HAWK SAM, 2 AAA regt
   1 arty bde: 1 hy arty, 3 arty, 1 NBC regt
   1 avn div: 2 avn regt, 2 avn bn

EQUIPMENT
MBT 1,322: 868 *Leopard* (incl 115 -1A5), 380 *Centauro*
   B-1, 74 *Ariete*
APC 1,221 (incl variants) M-113, 1,729 VCC1/-2, 157
   Fiat 6614, some *Puma*
AAV 15 LVTP-7
TOTAL ARTY 1,334
   TOWED 368: **105mm**: 150 Model 56 pack; **155mm**:
   164 FH-70, 54 M-114 (in store)
   SP 286: **155mm**: 260 M-109G/-L; **203mm**: 26 M-
   110A2 (in store)
   MRL 227mm: 22 MLRS
   MOR 120mm: 658; **81mm**: 1,200 (386 in store)
ATGW 426 TOW 2B (incl 243 SP), 1,000 *Milan*
RL 1,120 *Panzerfaust* 3
RCL 80mm: 690 *Folgore*
AD GUNS 25mm: 275 SIDAM SP
SAM 60 HAWK, 113 *Stinger*, 23 *Skyguard/Aspide*
AC 6 SM-1019, 3 Do-228, 1 P-180
HELICOPTERS
   ATTACK 45 A-129

ASLT 27 A-109, 62 AB-206
SPT 86 AB-205A, 68 AB-206 (obs), 14 AB-212, 23 AB-
   412, 36 CH-47C
UAV 5 *Mirach* 20

Navy 38,000

(incl 2,500 Naval Air, 1,000 Marines and 11,000
conscripts)
COMMANDS 1 Fleet Commander CINCNAV (also
NATO COMEDCENT) **Area Commands** 5 Upper
Tyrrhenian, Adriatic, Ionian and Strait of Otranto,
Sicily, Sardinia
BASES La Spezia (HQ), Taranto (HQ), Ancona (HQ),
Brindisi, Augusta, Messina (HQ), La Maddalena (HQ),
Cagliari, Naples (HQ), Venice
SUBMARINES 8
SSK 8
   4 *Pelosi* (imp *Sauro*) with Type 184 HWT
   4 *Sauro* with Type 184 HWT (includes 2 non-op,
      undergoing mod)
PRINCIPAL SURFACE COMBATANTS 30
CARRIERS 1 *G. Garibaldi* CVV. Total ac capacity 16
   AV-8B *Harrier* V/STOL or 18 SH-3 *Sea King* hel.
   Usually a mix
CRUISERS 1 *Vittorio Veneto* CGH with 1 x 2 SM-1 ER
   SAM, 6 AB-212 ASW hel (Mk 46 LWT); 4 *Teseo* SSM,
   2 x 3 ASTT
DESTROYERS 4
DDG 4
   2 *Luigi Durand de la Penne* (ex-*Animoso*) with 1 SM-1
      MR SAM, 8 *Teseo* SSM, 2 AB-312 hel, 1 127mm
      gun, 6 ASTT
   2 *Audace*, with 1 SM-1 MR SAM, 4 *Teseo* SSM, 2 AB-
      212 hel, 1 127mm gun, 6 ASTT
FRIGATES 24
FFG 16
   8 *Maestrale* with 2 AB-212 hel, 2 533mm DP TT; 4
      Teseo SSM, 1 127mm gun
   4 *Lupo* with 1 AB-212 hel, 2 x 3 ASTT; 8 *Teseo* SSM, 1
      127mm gun
   4 *Artigliere* (ex-*Lupo* for Iraq) with 8 *Teseo* SSM, 8
      Aspide SAM, 1 127mm gun, 1 AB-212 hel
FF 8 *Minerva* with 6 ASTT
PATROL AND COASTAL COMBATANTS 16
MISSILE CRAFT 4 *Sparviero* PHM with 2 *Teseo* SSM
PATROL, OFFSHORE 6
   4 *Cassiopea* with 1 AB-212 hel
   2 *Storione* (US *Aggressive*) ex-MSO
PATROL, COASTAL 6
   3 *Bambu* (ex-MSC) PCC
   3 *Esplatore* PCO
MINE COUNTERMEASURES 13
   1 MHC (ex *Alpino*)
   4 *Lerici* MHC
   8 *Gaeta* MSC

NATO

NATO and Non-NATO Europe

AMPHIBIOUS 3

2 *San Giorgio* LPD: capacity 350 tps, 30 trucks, 2 SH-3D or CH-47 hel, 7 craft

1 *San Giusto* LPD: capacity as above

Plus some 33 craft: about 3 LCU, 10 LCM and 20 LCVP

SUPPORT AND MISCELLANEOUS 82

2 *Stromboli* AO, 8 AT, 44 coastal AT, 8 water tkr, 4 trials, 5 trg, 3 AGOR, 2 ARS, 1 *Etna* AOR, 2 diving tender, 3 AR

SPECIAL FORCES (Special Forces Command – COMSUBIN)

3 gp; 1 underwater ops; 1 school; 1 research

MARINES (San Marco gp) (1,000)

1 bn gp, 1 trg gp, 1 log gp

EQUIPMENT

30 VCC-1 APC, 10 LVTP-7 AAV, 16 **81mm** mor, 8 **106mm** RCL, 6 *Milan* ATGW

NAVAL AIR (2,500)

18 cbt ac, 80 armed hel

FGA 1 sqn with 16 AV-8B plus and 2*TAV-8B plus

ASW 5 hel sqn with 21 SH-3D, 45 AB-212

HEL 8* SH-3D (amph aslt), 6* AB-212 (amph aslt)

AAM AIM-9L *Sidewinder*

ASM *Marte* Mk 2, AS-12

Air Force 61,900

(incl 19,300 conscripts)

FGA 8 sqn

4 with *Tornado* 1 IDS • 4 with AMX (50% of 1 *Tornado* and 1 AMX sqn devoted to recce)

FTR 6 sqn

4 with F-104 ASA • 2 with *Tornado* F-3

RECCE 2 sqn with AMX

MR 2 sqn with *Atlantic* (OPCON to Navy)

EW 1 ECM/recce sqn with G-222VS, PD-808, P-180, P-166DL-3

TPT/TAC 3 sqn

2 with G-222 • 1 with C-130H

TKR/CAL 1 sqn with B707-320, G-222 RM

TPT/VIP 2 sqn with ac *Gulfstream* III, *Falcon* 50, DC-9 hel SH-3D

TRG 1 OCU with TF-104G; 5 sqn with ac *Tornado*, AMX-T, MB-339A, SF-260M, MB-339 (Aerobatic Team) hel 1 sqn with NH-500

SAR 4 sqn with HH-3F

5 det with AB-212

AD 3 SAM sqn with *Nike Hercules*, 14 SAM sqn with *Spada*

EQUIPMENT

321 cbt ac, no armed hel

AC 115 *Tornado* (91 IDS, 24 F-3) • 101 **F-104** (80 ASA, 21 TF-104G) • 80 **AMX** (60 (FGA), 20 -T

(trg)) (plus 21 FGA and 2 T in store), 75 MB-339 (62 trg, 13 Acrobatic Team) (plus 16 in store), 11* **MB-339CD** • 14* *Atlantic* (MR) (plus 4 in store) • 4 **Boeing-707-320** (tkr/tpt) • 10 **C-130H** (tpt) • 32 **G-222** (28 tpt, 4 cal) • 2 **DC9-32** (VIP) • 2 *Gulfstream* III (VIP) • 4 *Falcon* 50 (VIP) • 7 **P-166** (2 -M, 5 -DL3 (liaison and trg)) • 18 **P-180** (liaison) • 1 **PD-808** (ECM, cal, tpt) • 26 **SF-260M** (trg) • 30 **SIAI-208** (liaison)

HEL 21 **HH-3F** (SAR) • 2 **SH-3D** (liaison/VIP) • 27 **AB-212** (SAR) • 51 **NH-500D** (trg)

MISSILES

ASM AGM-88 HARM, *Kormoran*

AAM AIM-9L *Sidewinder*, *Aspide*

SAM *Nike Hercules*, *Aspide*

Forces Abroad

GERMANY 92: **Air Force, NAEW Force**

MALTA 16: **Air Force** with 2 AB-212

US 33: **Air Force** flying trg

UN AND PEACEKEEPING

ALBANIA (AFOR II): 2,531 **BOSNIA** (SFOR II): 2,313: 1 mech inf bde gp **EGYPT** (MFO): 77 **FORMER YUGOSLAVIA** (ECMM): 32. (IPTF): 22 **GUATE-MALA** (MINUGUA): 7 **HEBRON** (TIPHZ): 27 **INDIA/PAKISTAN** (UNMOGIP): 7 obs **IRAQ/ KUWAIT** (UNIKOM): 4 obs **ISRAEL** (UNTSO): 8 **KOSOVO** (Joint Guarantor): 1,106. (KVM): 12. (EE): 12 **LEBANON** (UNIFIL): 44; hel unit **MALTA** (MIATM): 47 **MIDDLE EAST** (UNTSO): 8 obs **MOROCCO** (DIATM): 1 **WESTERN SAHARA** (MINURSO): 5 obs

Paramilitary 255,700

CARABINIERI 113,200 (Ministry of Defence)

Territorial 5 bde, 18 regt, 94 gp **Trg** 1 bde **Mobile def** 1 div, 2 bde, 1 cav regt, 1 special ops gp, 13 mobile bn, 1 AB bn, avn and naval units

EQPT 40 Fiat 6616 armd cars; 40 VCC2, 91 M-113 APC **hel** 24 A-109, 4 AB-205, 39 AB-206, 24 AB-412

PUBLIC SECURITY GUARD 79,000 (Ministry of Interior)

11 mobile units; 40 Fiat 6614 APC ac 5 P-68 **hel** 12 A-109, 20 AB-206, 9 AB-212

FINANCE GUARDS 63,500 (Treasury Department)

14 Zones, 20 Legions, 128 gp ac 5 P-166-DL3 **hel** 15 A-109, 65 Breda-Nardi NH-500M/MC/MD; 3 PCI; plus about 300 boats

HARBOUR CONTROL (*Capitanerie di Porto*)

(subordinated to Navy in emergencies): some 12 PCI, 130+ boats and 4 AB-412 (SAR)

Foreign Forces

NATO HQ Allied Forces Southern Europe
(AFSOUTH), HQ 5 Allied Tactical Air Force (5 ATAF)
US 10,400: **Army** 2,400; 1 inf bn gp **Navy** 4,400 **Air
Force** 3,400 **USMC** 200
DELIBERATE FORGE COMPONENTS Be 11 F-16A,
Ca 12 CF-18, **Da** 8 F-16, **Fr** 20 *Mirage* 2000C/D, 1 C-160,
1E-3F, 8 *Jaguar*, **Ge** 10 *Tornado* PA, **NATO** 5 E-3A, **Nl** 22
F-16, 1 P-3, **No** 6 F-16, **NZ** 1 C-130, **Po** 3 F-16, **Sp** 6 EF-
18, 1 KC-130, **Tu** 10 F-16C, **UK** 12 *Harrier* GR-7, 1
Nimrod, 3 L1011K, 3 E-3D *Sentry* **US** 86 F-16C, 4 AC-
130, 8 EC-130, 26 F-15, 18 F-15C, 21 EA-6B, 10 KC-135,
12 F-117, 7 UH-60, 22 A-10, 4 U-2, 3 P-3, 9 MH-53, 3
MC-130, 4 MH-60
SUPPORT COMPONENTS (for NATO ops in Kosovo)
Sp 1 CASA 212, **US** 4 C-12, 1 LJ-35, 1 BE-20, 4 C-130, 3
KC-135, 4 H-53, 2 H-3, 1 C-5, 3 P-3, 1 C-9, 2 C-2

Luxembourg Lu

	1997	1998	1999	2000
GDP	fr556bn	fr584bn		
	($16bn)	($16bn)		
per capita	$25,300	$27,300		
Growth	4.7%	5.7%		
Inflation	1.4%	1.0%		
Publ debt	6.5%	6.5%		
Def exp	fr4.8bn	fr5.1bn		
	($134m)	($142m)		
Def bdgt		fr3.9bn	fr4.0bn	
		($107m)	($102m)	
$1 = franc	35.8	36.3	39.6	
Population	4 17,000 (ε124,000 foreign citizens)			
Age	*13–17*	*18–22*	*23–32*	
Men	12,000	12,000	28,000	
Women	12,000	12,200	29,000	

Total Armed Forces

ACTIVE 768

Army 768

1 lt inf bn, 2 recce coy, 1 to Eurocorps/BE div, 1 to
AMF(L)
EQUIPMENT
   MOR 81mm: 6
   ATGW 6 TOW
   RL LAW

Air Force

(none, but for legal purposes NATO's E-3A AEW ac
have Lu registration)

1 sqn with 17 E-3A *Sentry* (NATO standard), 2 Boeing
707 (trg)

Forces Abroad

UN AND PEACEKEEPING
BOSNIA (SFOR II): 23 **Deliberate Force Air
Component** 5 E-3A

Paramilitary 612

GENDARMERIE 612

Netherlands Nl

	1997	1998	1999	2000
GDP	gld703bn	gld738bn		
	($360bn)	($372bn)		
per capita	$21,700	$22,800		
Growth	3.6%	3.8%		
Inflation	2.2%	1.9%		
Publ debt	67.4%	67.4%		
Def exp	gld13.3bn	gld13.4bn		
	($6.8bn)	($6.8bn)		
Def bdgt		gld14.1bn	gld15.1bn	
		($7.1bn)	($7.0bn)	
$1 = guilder	1.95	1.98	2.16	
Population			15,724,000	
Age	*13–17*	*18–22*	*23–32*	
Men	447,000	463,000	1,169,000	
Women	428,000	442,000	1,108 ,000	

Total Armed Forces

ACTIVE 56,380
(incl 3,600 Royal Military Constabulary, 800 Inter-
Service Organisation; 1,920 women)

RESERVES 75,000
(men to age 35, NCOs to 40, officers to 45) **Army**
60,000 **Navy** some 5,000 **Air Force** 10,000 (immediate
recall)

Army 27,000

1 Corps HQ (Ge/Nl), 1 mech div HQ • 3 mech inf bde
(2 cadre) • 1 lt bde • 1 air-mobile bde (3 inf bn) • 1 fd
arty, 1 AD gp • 1 engr gp
Summary of cbt arm units
   7 tk bn • 7 armd inf bn • 3 air-mobile bn • 3 recce bn
   • 7 arty bn • 1 AD bn • 2 MLRS bty

RESERVES
(cadre bde and corps tps completed by call-up of
reservists)

National Command (incl Territorial Comd): 3 inf, 1 SF, 2 engr bn spt units, could be mob for territorial defence
Home Guard 3 sectors; lt inf weapons
EQUIPMENT
   MBT 359: *Leopard* 1A4 (in store; for sale), *Leopard* 2 (180 to be A5)
   AIFV 383 YPR-765, 65 M-113C/-R all with **25mm**
   APC 269 YPR-765 (plus 491 look-a-likes)
   TOTAL ARTY 376
      TOWED 155mm: 80 M-114/39, 15 FH-70 (trg)
      SP 155mm: 126 M-109A3
      MRL 227mm: 22 MLRS
      MOR 81mm: 40; **120mm**: 133
   ATGW 753 (incl 135 in store): 427 *Dragon*, 326 (incl 90 YPR-765) TOW
   RL 84mm: *Carl Gustav,* AT-4
   RCL 106mm: 185 M-40 (in store)
   AD GUNS 35mm: 77 *Gepard* SP (60 to be up-graded); **40mm**: 60 L/70 towed
   SAM 312 *Stinger*
   SURV AN/TPQ-36 (arty, mor)
   MARINE 1 tk tpt, 3 coastal, 3 river patrol boats

Navy 13,800

(incl 950 Naval Air, 2,800 Marines, 1,200 women)
BASES Netherlands Den Helder (HQ). Nl and Be Navies under joint op comd based Den Helder
Overseas Willemstad (Curaçao)
SUBMARINES 4
SSK 4 *Walrus* with Mk 48 HWT; plus provision for *Harpoon* USGW
PRINCIPAL SURFACE COMBATANTS 16
DESTROYERS 4
DDG (Nl desig = FFG) 4
   2 *Tromp* with 1 SM-1 MR SAM; 8 *Harpoon* SSM, 2 120mm guns, 1 *Lynx* hel (ASW/OTHT), 6 ASTT (Mk 46 LWT)
   2 *Van Heemskerck* with 1 SM-1 MR SAM; 8 *Harpoon* SSM, 4 ASTT
FRIGATES 12
FFG 12
   8 *Karel Doorman* with 8 *Harpoon* SSM, 4 ASTT; 1 *Lynx* (ASW/OTHT) hel
   4 *Kortenaer* with 2 *Lynx* (ASW/OTHT) hel, 4 ASTT; 8 *Harpoon* SSM
MINE WARFARE 17
MINELAYERS none, but *Mercuur*, listed under spt and misc, has capability
MINE COUNTERMEASURES 17
   15 *Alkmaar* (tripartite) MHC
   2 *Dokkum* MSC
AMPHIBIOUS 1
   1 *Rotterdam* LPD: capacity 4 LCU or 6 LCA, 600 troops

SUPPORT AND MISCELLANEOUS 13
   1 *Amsterdam* AOR (4 *Lynx* or 3 NH-90 or 2 EH-101 hel), 1 *Mercuur* torpedo tender, 2 trg, 4 *Cerberus* div spt, 1 *Zuideruis* AOR (2 *Lynx* hel), 1 *Pelikaan* spt, 1 AGOR, 2 AGHS

NAVAL AIR (950)
MR 1 sqn with F-27M (see Air Force)
MR/ASW 2 sqn with P-3C
ASW/SAR 2 sqn with *Lynx* hel
EQPT 13 cbt ac, 22 armed hel
AC 13 P-3C (MR)
HEL 22 *Lynx* (ASW, SAR)

MARINES (2,800)
3 Marine bn (1 cadre); 1 spt bn

RESERVES
1 Marine bn
EQUIPMENT
   TOWED ARTY 105mm: 8 lt
   MOR 81mm: 18; **120mm**: 14
   ATGW *Dragon*
   RL AT-4
   SAM *Stinger*

Air Force 11,980

(incl 720 women)
Flying hours 180
FTR/FGA 6 sqn with F-16A/B
FTR/RECCE 1 sqn with F-16A(R)
MR 2 F-27M (assigned to Navy)
TPT 1 sqn with F-50, F-60, C-130H-30, KDC-10 (tkr/tpt), *Gulfstream*
TRG 1 sqn with PC-7
HEL
   1 sqn with AH-64A/D
   1 sqn with AH-64D
   1 sqn with BO-105
   1 sqn with AS-532U2, SA-316
   1 sqn with CH-47D
   SAR 1 sqn with AB-412 SP
AD 8 bty with HAWK SAM (4 in Ge), 4 bty with *Patriot* SAM (in Ge)
EQUIPMENT
   170 cbt ac (plus 11 in store), 42 armed hel
   AC 170 **F-16A/B** (plus 11 in store): 92 F-16A, 21 F-16A(R) and 25 F-16B to be converted under European mid-life update programme • 2 **F-27M** (MR) • 2 **F-50** • 4 **F-60** • 2 **C-130H-30** • 2 **KDC-10** (tkr/tpt) • 1 *Gulfstream* IV • 10 **PC-7** (trg)
   HEL 3 **AB-412** SP (SAR) • 9 **SA-316** • 27 **BO-105** • 12* **AH-64A** (leased from US Army pending delivery of AH-64D) • 30* **AH-64D** • 13 **CH-47D** • 17 **AS-532U2**
MISSILES
   AAM AIM-9/L/N *Sidewinder*, AGM-88 HARM

SAM 48 HAWK, 5 *Patriot*, 100 *Stinger*
AD GUNS 25 VL 4/41 *Flycatcher* radar, 75 L/70
40mm systems

Forces Abroad

GERMANY 3,000: 1 lt bde (1 armd inf, 1 tk bn), plus
spt elms
ICELAND 16: **Navy** 1 P-3C
NETHERLANDS ANTILLES Netherlands, Aruba
and the Netherlands Antilles operate a Coast Guard
Force to combat org crime and drug smuggling. Comd
by Netherlands Commander Caribbean. HQ Curaçao,
bases Aruba and St Maarten **Navy** 20 (to expand); 1
frigate, 1 amph cbt det, 2 P-3C **Air Force** 25; 2 F-27MPA

UN AND PEACEKEEPING

ALBANIA (AFOR II): some **BOSNIA** (SFOR II): 1,220:
1 mech inf bn gp. (UNMIBH): 1 **CYPRUS** (UNFICYP):
102 **ITALY**: 155 (SFOR Air Component) 9 F-16, 1 C-
130, 1 F-60, 1 KDC-10 **MIDDLE EAST** (UNTSO): 10
obs **YUGOSLAVIA** (Joint Guardian): 400 (to be 2,000)

Paramilitary 3,600

ROYAL MILITARY CONSTABULARY (*Koninklijke Marechaussee*) 3,600

(500 conscripts); 3 'div' comprising 10 districts with 72
'bde'

Foreign Forces

NATO HQ Allied Forces Central Europe
US 690: **Army** 380 **Air Force** 290 **Navy** 10 **USMC** 10

Norway   No

	1997	1998	1999	2000
GDP	kr1,085bn	kr1,101bn		
	($153bn)	($146bn)		
per capita	$24,100	$25,000		
Growth	3.4%	2.0%		
Inflation	2.6%	2.2%		
Publ debt	33.4%	33.4%		
Def exp	kr23.0bn	kr24.1bn		
	($3.3bn)	($3.2bn)		
Def bdgt		kr25.3bn	kr25.4bn	
		($3.4bn)	($3.2bn)	
$1 =kroner	7.07	7.55	7.96	
Population				4,425,000
Age	*13–17*	*18–22*	*23–32*	
Men	138,000	142,000	334,000	
Women	130,000	133,000	314,000	

Total Armed Forces

ACTIVE 31,000

(incl 16,500 conscripts; 400 Joint Services org, 500
Home Guard permanent staff)
Terms of service **Army**, **Navy**, **Air Force**, 12 months, plus
4–5 refresher trg periods

RESERVES

234,000 mobilisable in 24–72 hours; obligation to 44
(conscripts remain with fd army units to age 35,
officers to age 55, regulars to age 60)
Army 101,000 **Navy** 22,000 **Air Force** 25,000 **Home
Guard** some 83,000 on mob

Army 15,200

(incl 10,000 conscripts, 665 recalled reservists)
2 Comd, 4 district comd, 14 territorial regt
North Norway 1 inf/ranger bn, border gd, cadre and
trg units for 1 div (1 armd, 2 inf bde) and 1 indep mech
inf bde
South Norway 2 inf bn (incl Royal Guard), indep units
plus cadre units for 1 mech inf and 1 armd bde

RESERVES

17 inf, 3 ranger plus some indep coy and spt units. 1
arty bn; 10 inf coy, engr coy, sigs units

LAND HOME GUARD 77,000

18 districts each divided into 2–6 sub-districts and
some 465 sub-units (pl)

EQUIPMENT

MBT 170 *Leopard* (111 -1A5NO, 59 -1A1NO)
AIFV 53 NM-135 (M-113/**20mm**), ε50 CV 9030N
APC 194 M-113 (incl variants), 31 XA-186 *Sisu*
TOTAL ARTY 222
TOWED 84: **105mm**: 36 M-101; **155mm**: 48 M-114
SP 155mm: 126 M-109A3GN
MRL 227mm: 12 MLRS
MOR 81mm: 454 (40 SP incl 28 M-106A1, 12 M-125A2)
ATGW 320 TOW-1/-2 incl 126 NM-142 (M-901), 424
  Eryx
RCL 84mm: 2,517 *Carl Gustav*
AD GUNS 20mm: 252 Rh-202 (192 in store)
SAM 300 RBS-70 (120 in store)
SURV *Cymberline* (mor)

Navy 8,200

(incl 160 Coastal Defence, 270 Coast Guard and 3,300
conscripts)
OPERATIONAL COMMANDS: 2 JOINT OPERA-
TIONAL COMMANDS, COMNAVSONOR and
COMNAVNON with regional naval commanders and
7 regional Naval districts
BASES Horten, Haakonsvern (Bergen), Olavsvern
(Tromsø)

SUBMARINES 12
SSK 6 *Ulla* with 8 533mm TT
SSC 6 *Kobben* with 8 533mm TT
FRIGATES 4
FFG 4 *Oslo* with 6 ASTT, 6 *Terne* ASW RL, 4 *Penguin* 1
SSM, *Sea Sparrow* SAM
PATROL AND COASTAL COMBATANTS 22
MISSILE CRAFT 22
14 *Hauk* PFM with 6 *Penguin* 1 SSM, 2 (Swe TP-613)
HWT
8 *Storm* PFM with 6 *Penguin* 1 SSM, 1 76mm gun
MINE WARFARE 14
MINELAYERS 3
2 *Vidar*, coastal (300–400 mines), 1 *Tyr* (amph craft
also fitted for minelaying)
MINE COUNTERMEASURES 11
4 *Oskøy* MHC, 5 *Alta* MSC, 2 diver spt
AMPHIBIOUS craft only
5 LCT, 8 S90N LCA
SUPPORT AND MISCELLANEOUS 7
1 *Horten* sub/patrol craft depot ship, 1 *Mariata*
AGOR (civ manned), 1 *Valkyrien Torpedo* recovery,
1 *Sverdrup* II, 1 Royal Yacht, 2 *Hessa* trg
ADDITIONAL IN STORE 1 *Sauda* MSC

NAVAL HOME GUARD 5,000
on mob assigned to 10 sub-districts incl 33 areas.
Some 400 fishing craft

COASTAL DEFENCE
FORTRESS 17 **75mm**: 6; **120mm**: 3; **127mm**: 6;
150mm: 2 guns; 6 cable mine and 4 torpedo bty

COAST GUARD (270)
PATROL AND COASTAL COMBATANTS 18
PATROL, OFFSHORE 11
3 *Nordkapp* with 1.*Lynx* hel (SAR/recce), fitted for 6
Penguin Mk 2 SSM, 1 *Nornen*, 7 chartered (partly
civ manned)
PATROL INSHSORE 7 PCI plus 7 cutters
AVN ac 2 P-3N *Orion* **hel** 6 *Lynx* Mk 86 (Air Force-
manned)

Air Force 6,700

(incl 3,200 conscripts, 185 women)
Flying hours 180
OPERATIONAL COMMANDS 2 joint with
COMSONOR and COMNON
FGA 4 sqn with F-16A/B
FTR 1 trg sqn with F-5A/B
MR 1 sqn with 6 P-3D/N *Orion* (2 assigned to Coast
Guard)
TPT 3 sqn
1 with C-130, 1 with DHC-6, 1 with *Falcon* 20C
(CAL, ECM)
TRG MFI-15

SAR 1 sqn with *Sea King* Mk 43B
TAC HEL 2 sqn with Bell-412SP
SAM 6 bty NASAMS, 6 bty RB-70
AAA 10 bty L70 (with Fire-Control System 2000) org
into 5 gps
EQUIPMENT
79 cbt ac (incl 4 MR), no armed hel
AC 15 F-5A/B (ftr/trg) • 58 F-16A/B • 6* P-3 (4 -D
(MR), 2 -N (Coast Guard)) • 6 C-130H (tpt) • 3
Falcon 20C (EW/tpt Cal) • 3 DHC-6 (tpt) • 15
MFI-15 (trg)
HEL 18 Bell 412 SP (tpt) • 12 *Sea King* Mk 43B
(SAR) • 6 *Lynx* Mk 86 (Coast Guard)
MISSILES
ASM CRV-7, *Penguin* Mk-3, AGM-88 HARM
AAM AIM-9L/N *Sidewinder*, AIM 120 AMRAAM

AA HOME GUARD
(on mob under comd of Air Force): 2,500; 2 bn (9 bty)
AA **20mm** NM45

Forces Abroad

UN AND PEACEKEEPING
BOSNIA (SFOR II): up to 700: 1 inf bn **CROATIA**
(UNMOP): 1 obs **EGYPT** (MFO): 5 Staff Officers
MIDDLE EAST (UNTSO): 12 obs **YUGOSLAVIA**
(Joint Guardian): some 100 (to be 800)

Foreign Forces

US 60. Prepositioned eqpt for **Marines**: 1 MEB **Army**: 1
arty bn **Air Force**: ground handling eqpt
Ge prepositioned eqpt for 1 arty bn
NATO HQ Allied Forces North Europe (HQ North)

Poland Pl

	1997	1998	1999	2000
GDP	z445bn	z551bn		
	($136bn)	($159bn)		
per capita	$7,000	$7,500		
Growth	6.7%	4.8%		
Inflation	15.9%	11.7%		
Debt	$39bn	$43bn		
Def exp	z10.1bn	z11.9bn		
	($3.1bn)	($3.4bn)		
Def bdgt		z11.7bn	z12.6bn	z14.4bn
		($3.4bn)	($3.2bn)	($3.6bn)
FMA (US)	$1.0m	$1.6m	$1.6m	$1.6m
$1 = zloty	3.28	3.48	3.91	
Population				38,854,000
(German 1.3%, Ukrainian 0.6%, Belarussian 0.5%)				
Age	*13–17*	*18–22*	*23–32*	
Men	1,653,000	1,628,000	2,736,000	
Women	1,570,000	1,551,000	2,619,000	

Total Armed Forces

ACTIVE 240,650

(incl 141,600 conscripts; 25,750 centrally controlled staffs, units/formations)
Terms of service 12 months

RESERVES 406,000

Army 343,000 **Navy** 14,000 (to age 50) **Air Force** 49,000 (to age 60)

Army 142,500

(incl 101,670 conscripts)
4 Mil Districts/Army HQ
Pomerania 2 mech div (incl 1 coast def), 1 arty, 1 engr, 1 territorial def bde, 1 SSM, 1 cbt hel, 2 AA arty, 1 SA-6 regt
Silesia 3 mech, 1 armd cav div, 1 mtn, 2 arty, 2 engr, 1 AD arty bde, 2 SSM regt
Warsaw 3 mech div, 1 arty, 1 engr, 1 territorial def bde, 1 cbt hel regt
Krakow 1 air cavalry div HQ, 1 armd, 1 mech, 1 air aslt, 1 mtn, 1 territorial def bde, 1 mech, 2 engr, 1 recce regt
Div tps: 10 SA-6/-8 regt
General Staff tps: 1 special ops, 1 gd regt
EQUIPMENT
  MBT 1,675: T-55, T-72, PT-91
  RECCE 510 BRDM-2
  AIFV 1,405: 1,367 BMP-1, 38 BRM-1
  APC 35 OT-64 plus some 693 'look-alike' types
  TOTAL ARTY 1,580
    TOWED 440: **122mm**: 280 M-1938 (M-30); **152mm**: 160 M-1938 (ML-20)
    SP 652: **122mm**: 533 2S1; **152mm**: 111 *Dana* (M-77); **203mm**: 8 2S7
    MRL 258: **122mm**: 228 BM-21, 30 RM-70
    MOR 230: **120mm**: 214 M-120, 16 2B11/2S12
  SSM launchers: 35 FROG, SS-C-2B
  ATGW 403: 263 AT-3 *Sagger*, 115 AT-4 *Spigot*, 18 AT-5 *Spandrel*, 7 AT-6 *Spiral*
  ATK GUNS 85mm: 711 D-44
  AD GUNS 1,116: **23mm**: ZU-23-2, ZSU-23-4 SP; **57mm**: S-60
  SAM 1,290: SA-6/-7/-8/-9/-13
  HELICOPTERS
    ATTACK 22 PZL-W3, 38 Mi-24, 34 Mi-2URP
    SPT 18 Mi-2URN
    TPT 36 Mi-8/Mi-17, 31 Mi-2
  SURV GS-13 (arty), 1 L219/200 PARK-1 (arty), *Long Trough* ((SNAR-1) arty), *Pork Trough* ((SNAR-2/-6) veh, arty), *Small Fred/Small Yawn* (veh, arty), *Big Fred* ((SNAR-10) veh, arty)

Navy 17,100

(incl 2,460 Naval Aviation, 9,500 conscripts)

BASES Gdynia, Hel, Swinoujscie; Kolobrzeg, Gdansk (Coast Guard), Darlowa, Siemirowice-Cewice (Naval Air Brigade)
SUBMARINES 3
SSK 3
  1 *Orzel* SS (RF *Kilo*) with 533mm TT
  2 *Wilk* (RF *Foxtrot*) with 533mm TT
PRINCIPAL SURFACE COMBATANTS 2
DESTROYERS 1
DDG 1 *Warszawa* DDG (Sov mod *Kashin*) with 2 x 2 SA-N-1 *Goa* SAM, 4 SS-N-2C *Styx* SSM, 5 533mm TT, 2 ASW RL
FRIGATES 1
FF 1 *Kaszub* with 2 ASW RL, 4 533mm TT, 76mm gun
PATROL AND COASTAL COMBATANTS 40
CORVETTES 4 *Gornik* (Sov *Tarantul* I) with 2 x 2 SS-N-2C *Styx* SSM, 76mm gun
MISSILE CRAFT 7 Sov *Osa* I PFM with 4 SS-N-2A SSM
PATROL CRAFT 29
  COASTAL 3 *Sassnitz* with 1 x SA-N-5 SAM, 1 x 76mm gun
  INSHORE 26
  8 *Obluze* PCI, 11 *Pilica* PCI, 7 *Puck* (OSA 1) PCI
MINE WARFARE 24
MINELAYERS none, but SS, *Krogulec* MSC and *Lublin* LSM have minelaying capability
MINE COUNTERMEASURES 24
  5 *Krogulec* MSC (non-op), 13 *Goplo* (*Notec*) MSI, 4 *Mamry* (*Notec*) MHI, 2 *Leniwka* MSI
AMPHIBIOUS 5
  5 *Lublin* LSM, capacity 135 tps, 9 tk
  Plus craft: 3 *Deba* LCU (none employed in amph role), 2 LCU
SUPPORT AND MISCELLANEOUS 18
  1 *Polochny C* comd ship, 1 *Polochny B* AK, 2 AGI, 3 AGS, 2 ARS, 5 AT, 4 AOT

NAVAL AVIATION (2,460)
28 cbt ac, 11 armed hel
Flying hours (MiG-21) 60
7 sqn
  2 with 28 MiG-21 BIS/UM
  1 with 5 PZL-3RM (SAR), 2 PZL-W3T (tpt), 3 An-28 (tpt), 25 Mi-2 (tpt)
  1 ASW with 11 Mi-14PL
  1 SAR with 3 Mi-14 PS, 3 Mi-2RM
  1 SAR with 3 PZL An-28RM, 6 PZL An-2
  1 Recce with 17 PZL TS-11 *Iskra*

Air Force 55,300

(incl AD tps, 30,430 conscripts); 297 cbt ac, 32 attack hel
Flying hours 60
FTR 2 AD Corps
  7 regt with 133 MiG-21/U, 27 MiG-23, 22 MiG-29/U
FGA 4 regt with 99 Su-22

RECCE 16* MiG-21R/U
TPT 2 regt with 32 An-2, 10 An-26, 5 An-28, 13 Yak-40, 2 Tu-154
HEL 32* PZL-W3W, 35 Mi-2, 5 Mi-8
TRG 183 TS-11 *Iskra*, 11 PZL I-22 *Iryda*, 25 PZL-130 *Orlik*
IN STORE 13 MiG-17, 1 MiG-21
AAM AA-2 *Atoll*, AA-8 *Aphid*
ASM AS-7 *Kerry*
SAM 5 bde; 1 indep regt with about 200 SA-2/-3/-4/-5

Forces Abroad

UN AND PEACEKEEPING
ALBANIA (AFOR II): some **BOSNIA** (SFOR II): 450: 1 AB bn **CROATIA** (UNMOP): 1 obs **GEORGIA** (UNOMIG): 4 obs **IRAQ/KUWAIT** (UNIKOM): 5 obs **LEBANON** (UNIFIL): 636: 1 inf bn, mil hospital **ROK** (Neutral Nations Supervisory Commission – NNSC): staff **SYRIA** (UNDOF): 353: 1 inf bn **TAJIKISTAN** (UNMOT): 3 obs **WESTERN SAHARA** (MINURSO): 3 obs **YUGOSLAVIA** (Joint Guardian): 750: 1 AB bn

Paramilitary 23,400

BORDER GUARDS (Ministry of Interior and Administration) 13,500

12 district units, 2 trg centres
MARITIME BORDER GUARD
about 28 patrol craft: 2 PCC, 9 PCI and 17 PC1<
PREVENTION UNITS OF POLICE (OPP-Ministry of Interior) 7,000
(1,000 conscripts)

Portugal   Por

	1997	1998	1999	2000
GDP	esc17.9tr	esc18.9tr		
	($102bn)	($105bn)		
per capita	$13,900	$14,800		
Growth	3.7%	3.9%		
Inflation	2.1%	2.8%		
Publ debt	61.5%	57.7%		
Def exp	esc419bn	esc429bn		
	($2.4bn)	($2.4bn)		
Def bdgt		esc286bn	esc320bn	
		($1.6bn)	($1.6bn)	
FMA (US)	$0.8m	$0.8m	$0.7m	$0.7m
$1 = escudo	175	180	197	
Population				9,874,000
Age	*13–17*	*18–22*	*23–32*	
Men	337,000	379,000	812,000	
Women	318,000	363,000	793,000	

Total Armed Forces

ACTIVE 49,700
(6,470 conscripts, 2,300 women)
Terms of service **Army** 4–8 months **Navy** and **Air Force** 4–12 months

RESERVES 210,930
(all services) (obligation to age 35) **Army** 210,000 **Navy** 930

Army 25,650

(incl 5,500 conscripts)
5 Territorial Comd (1 mil governance, 2 mil zone, 2 mil region) • 1 mech inf bde (2 mech, 1 tk, 1 fd arty bn) • 3 inf bde (on mob), 1 AB bde • 1 lt intervention bde • 3 mech, 1 tk, 1 composite regt (3 inf bn, 2 AA bty) • 3 armd cav regt • 8 inf regt • 2 fd, 1 AD, regt • 2 engr regt • 1 MP regt • 1 special ops centre

EQUIPMENT
MBT 187: 86 M-48A5, 101 M-60 (8 -A2, 86 -A3)
RECCE 15 V-150 *Chaimite*, 18 ULTRAV M-11
APC 249 M-113, 44 M-557, 81 V-200 *Chaimite*
TOTAL ARTY 318
  TOWED 134: **105mm**: 51 M-101, 24 M-56, 21 L119; **155mm**: 38 M-114A1
  SP 155mm: 6 M-109A2
  MOR 178: **107mm**: 62 M-30 (incl 14 SP); **120mm**: 118 *Tampella*; **81mm**: incl 22 SP
  COASTAL 20: **150mm**: 8; **152mm**: 6; **234mm**: 6 (inactive)
  RCL 84mm: 162 *Carl Gustav*; **89mm**: 53; **90mm**: 46; **106mm**: 128 M-40
  ATGW 45 TOW (incl 18 M-113, 4 M-901), 66 *Milan* (incl 6 ULTRAV-11)
  AD GUNS 85, incl **20mm**: Rh202; **40mm**: L/60
  SAM 15 *Stinger*, 37 *Chaparral*

DEPLOYMENT
AZORES AND MADEIRA 2,250; 3 composite regt (3 inf bn, 2 AA bty)

Navy 16,600

(incl 1,540 Marines, 970 conscripts, 120 recalled reserves)
COMMANDS Naval Area Comd, 4 Subordinate Comds Azores, Madeira, North Continental, South Continental
BASES Lisbon (Alfeite), 4 spt bases Lega da Palmeira (North), Portindo (South), Funchal (Madeira), Ponta Delgada (Azores)
SUBMARINES 3
SSK 3 *Albacora* (Fr *Daphné*) with 12 550mm TT
FRIGATES 6
FFG 3 *Vasco Da Gama* (MEKO 200) with 6 ASTT (US

Mk 46), plus 8 *Harpoon* SSM, 8 *Sea Sparrow* SAM, 1 100mm gun (with 2 *Super Lynx* hel in some)
FF 3 *Commandante João Belo* (Fr *Cdt Rivière*) with 6 ASTT, 2 x 100mm gun
PATROL AND COASTAL COMBATANTS 30
PATROL, OFFSHORE 10
  6 *João Coutinho* PCO, hel deck
  4 *Baptista de Andrade* PCI, hel deck
PATROL, COASTAL 9 *Cacine* PCC
PATROL, INSHORE 10
  5 *Argos*
  5 *Albatros*
RIVERINE 1 *Rio Minho*
AMPHIBIOUS craft only
  1 LCU
SUPPORT AND MISCELLANEOUS 13
  1 *Berrio* (UK *Green Rover*) AO, 8 AGHS, 2 trg, 1 ocean trg, 1 div spt
AIR 5 *Lynx*-Mk 95

MARINES (1,500)
3 bn (2 lt inf, 1 police), spt units
EQUIPMENT
  MOR 120mm: 36

Air Force 7,445

Flying hours F-16: 180; A-7P: 160
1 op air com (COFA)
FGA 2 sqn
  1 with F-16A/B, 1 with *Alpha Jet*
SURVEY 1 sqn with C-212
MR 1 sqn with P-3P
TPT 4 sqn
  1 with C-130H, 1 with C-212, 1 with *Falcon 20* and *Falcon 50*, 1 with SA-330 hel
SAR 2 sqn
  1 with SA-330 hel, 1 with SA-330 hel and C-212
LIAISON 1 sqn with Reims-Cessna FTB-337G
TRG 2 sqn
  1 with *Socata TB-30 Epsilon*, 1 with *Alpha Jet*
EQUIPMENT
  60 cbt ac (plus 16 in store), no attack hel
  AC 35 *Alpha Jet* (FGA trg) (plus 15 in store) • 20 F-16A/B (17 -A, 3 -B) • 5* P-3P (MR) (plus 1 in store) • 6 C-130H (tpt plus SAR) • 24 C-212 (20 -A (12 tpt/SAR, 1 Nav trg, 2 ECM trg, 5 fisheries protection), 4 -B (survey)) • 12 **Cessna 337** (liaison) • 1 *Falcon 20* (tpt, cal) • 3 *Falcon 50* (tpt) • 16 *Epsilon* (trg)
  HEL 10 **SA-330** (SAR/tpt) • 18 **SA-316** (trg, utl)
  MISSILES
  ASM AGM-65B/G *Maverick*, AGM-84A *Harpoon*
  AAM AIM-9 *Sidewinder*

Forces Abroad
SAO TOME & PRINCIPE
5 Air Force, 1 C212
UN AND PEACEKEEPING
BOSNIA (SFOR II): 335: 1 inf bn(-) **CROATIA** (UNMOP): 1 obs **WESTERN SAHARA** (MINURSO): 4 obs **YUGOSLAVIA** (Joint Guardian): to be some 300

Paramilitary 40,900
NATIONAL REPUBLICAN GUARD 20,900
Commando Mk III APC **hel** 7 SA-315
PUBLIC SECURITY POLICE 20,000

Foreign Forces
NATO HQ IBERLANT area at Lisbon (Oeiras)
US 1,020: **Navy** 50 **Air Force** 930 **Army** 20 **USMC** 20

Spain | | | | Sp

	1997	1998	1999	2000
GDP	pts77.9tr ($532bn)	pts82.7tr ($553bn)		
per capita	$16,000	$16,900		
Growth	3.5%	3.8%		
Inflation	1.9%	1.8%		
Publ debt	74.4%	73.3%		
Def exp	pts1.1tr ($7.7bn)	pts1.1tr ($7.4bn)		
Def bdgt		pts897bn ($5.9bn)	pts928bn ($6.0bn)	
$1=peseta	146	149	163	
Population				39,218,000
Age	*13–17*	*18–22*		*23–32*
Men	1,263,000	1,508,000		3,331,000
Women	1,187,000	1,425,000		3,181,000

Total Armed Forces

ACTIVE 186,500
(incl 102,700 conscripts (to be reduced), some 3,800 women)
Terms of service 9 months

RESERVES 447,900
Army 436,000 **Navy** 3,900 **Air Force** 8,000

Army 120,000

(incl 81,000 conscripts, 2,290 women)
8 Regional Op Comd incl 2 overseas: 1 mech div (1 armd, 2 mech bde) • 2 armd cav bde (1 cadre) • 1 mtn

bde • 3 lt inf bde (cadre) • 1 air-portable bde • 1 AB bde • Spanish Legion: 1 bde (3 lt inf, 1 arty, 1 engr bn, 1 ATK coy), 2 regt (each with 1 mech, 1 mot bn, 1 ATK coy) • 3 island garrison: Ceuta and Melilla, Balearic, Canary • 1 arty bde; 1 AD regt • 1 engr bde • 1 Army Avn bde (1 attack, 1 tpt hel bn, 4 utl units) • 1 AD comd: 5 AD regt incl 1 HAWK SAM, 1 composite *Aspide*/**35mm**, 1 *Roland* bn • 1 Coastal Arty Comd (2 coast arty regt) • 3 special ops bn • Rapid Action Force (FAR) formed from 1 Spanish Legion, 1 AB and 1 air-portable bde (see above)

EQUIPMENT

MBT 660: 210 AMX-30 ER1/EM2, 131 M-48A5E, 211 M-60A3TTS, 108 *Leopard* 2 A4 (Ge tempy transfer)

RECCE 340 BMR-VEC (100 **90mm**, 208 **25mm**, 32 **20mm** gun)

AIFV 5 *Pizarro*

APC 1,997: 1,311 M-113 (incl variants), 686 BMR-600, 6 BLR

TOTAL ARTY 1,129 (excluding coastal)

TOWED 498: **105mm**: 262 M-26, 170 M-56 pack, 46 L 118; **155mm**: 20 M-114

SP 208: **105mm**: 48 M-108; **155mm**: 96 M-109A1; **203mm**: 64 M-110A2

COASTAL ARTY 53: **6in**: 44; **305mm**: 6; **381mm**: 3

MRL 140mm: 14 *Teruel*

MOR 120mm: 409 (incl 169 SP); plus **81mm**: 1,314 (incl 187 SP)

ATGW 442 *Milan*, 28 HOT, 200 TOW

RCL 106mm: 638

AD GUNS 20mm: 329 GAI-BO1; **35mm**: 92 GDF-002 twin; **40mm**: 183 L/70

SAM 24 I HAWK, 18 *Roland*, 13 *Skyguard*/*Aspide*, 108 *Mistral*

HELICOPTERS 178 (28 attack)

3 AS-532UL, 53 HU-10B, 70 HA/HR-15 (31 with **20mm** guns, 28 with HOT, 9 trg), 6 HU-18, 11 HR-12B, 18 HT-21, 17 HT-17 (incl 12-D models)

SURV 2 AN/TPQ-36 (arty, mor)

DEPLOYMENT

CEUTA AND MELILLA 8,100; 2 armd cav, 2 Spanish Legion, 2 mot inf, 2 engr, 2 arty regt; 2 lt AD bn, 1 coast arty bn

BALEARIC ISLANDS 2,200; 1 mot inf regt: 3 mot inf bn; 1 mixed arty regt: 1 fd arty, 1 AD; 1 engr bn

CANARY ISLANDS 4,300; 3 mot inf regt each 2 mot inf bn; 1 mot inf bn, 2 mixed arty regt each: 1 fd arty, 1 AD bn; 2 engr bn

Navy 36,950

(incl 860 Naval Air, 6,900 Marines, 10,700 conscripts and 830 women) plus 7,900 civilians

FLEET COMMANDS 5

NAVAL ZONES Cantabrian, Strait (of Gibraltar), Mediterranean, Canary (Islands)

BASES El Ferrol (La Coruña) (Cantabrian HQ), San Fernando (Cadiz) (Strait HQ), Rota (Cadiz) (Fleet HQ), Cartagena (Murcia) (Mediterranean HQ), Las Palmas (Canary Islands HQ), Palma de Mallorca and Mahón (Menorca)

SUBMARINES 8

SSK 8

4 *Galerna* (Fr *Agosta*) with 20 L-5 HWT

4 *Delfin* (Fr *Daphné*) with 12 L-5 HWT

PRINCIPAL SURFACE COMBATANTS 18

CARRIERS 1 (CVV) *Príncipe de Asturias* (16,200t); air gp: typically 6 to 10 AV-8S/EAV-8B FGA, 4 to 6 SH-3D ASW hel, 2 SH-3D AEW hel, 2 utl hel

FRIGATES 17

FFG 17

6 *Santa Maria* (US *Perry*) with 1 x 1 SM-1 MR SAM/*Harpoon* SSM launcher, 2 SH-60B hel, 6 ASTT; 1 76mm gun, 1–2 S-70L hel

5 *Baleares* with 1 x 1 SM-1 MR SAM, 8 ASROC, 4 324mm and 2 484mm ASTT; 8 *Harpoon* SSM, 1 127mm gun

6 *Descubierta* with 6 ASTT, 1 x 2 ASW RL; 8 *Harpoon* SSM

PATROL AND COASTAL COMBATANTS 32

PATROL, OFFSHORE 6

4 *Serviola*, 1 *Chilreu*, 1 *Alboran*

PATROL, COASTAL 10 *Anaga* PCC

PATROL, INSHORE 16

6 *Barceló* PFI, 10 PCI<

MINE COUNTERMEASURES 13

3 *Guadalete* (US *Aggressive*) MSO

8 *Júcar* (US *Adjutant*) MSC

2 *Segura* MSC

AMPHIBIOUS 4

1 *Castilla* (US *Paul Revere*) amph tpt, capacity: 1,600 tps; plus some 15 amph craft

2 *Hernán Cortés* (US *Newport*) LST, capacity: 400 tps, 500t vehicles, 3 LCVPs, 1 LCPL

1 *Galicia* LPD, capacity 620 tps, 6 LCVP

Plus 13 craft: 3 LCT, 2 LCU, 8 LCM

SUPPORT AND MISCELLANEOUS 34

1 AOR, 2 AO, 5 AT/F, 3 diver spt, 2 tpt/spt, 3 water carriers, 6 AGHS, 1 AGOR, 1 ARS, 1 AK, 5 trg craft, 4 sail trg

NAVAL AIR (860)

(incl 290 conscripts)

Flying hours 160

FGA 1 sqn with 9 AV-8B/9 AV-8B plus

LIAISON 1 sqn with 3 *Citation* II

HELICOPTERS 5 sqn

ASW 2 sqn

1 with SH-3D/G *Sea King* (mod to SH-3H standard)

1 with SH-60B (LAMPS-III fit)

COMD/TPT 1 sqn with 10 AB-212 and 4 AB-204

TRG 1 sqn with 10 Hughes 500

AEW 1 flt with SH-3D (*Searchwater* radar)
EQUIPMENT
  18 cbt ac, 25 armed hel
  Flying hours 160
  AC 9 **EAV-8B**, 9 **EAV-8B** plus (trg) • 3 *Citation* II
    (liaison)
  HEL 10 **AB-212** (ASW/SAR) • 12 **SH-3D** (9 -H
    ASW, 3 -D AEW) •10 **Hughes 500** (trg) • 6 **SH-
    60B** (ASW)

MARINES (6,900)
(incl 2,800 conscripts)
1 marine bde (3,000); 2 inf, 1 spt bn; 3 arty bty
5 marine garrison gp
EQUIPMENT
  MBT 16 M-60A3
  AFV 17 *Scorpion* lt tk, 16 LVTP-7 AAV, 35 BLR APC
  TOWED ARTY 105mm: 12 M-56 pack
  SP ARTY 155mm: 6 M-109A
  ATGW 12 TOW, 18 *Dragon*
  RL 90mm: C-90C
  RCL 106mm: 54
  SAM 12 *Mistral*

Air Force 29,100

(incl 11,000 conscripts, 685 women)
Flying hours EF-18: 180; F-5: 220; *Mirage* F-1: 180
CENTRAL AIR COMMAND (MACEN) 4 wg
FTR 2 sqn with EF-18 (F-18 *Hornet*)
RECCE 1 sqn with RF-4C
TPT 7 sqn
  2 with C-212, 2 with CN-235, 1 with *Falcon* (20, 50,
    900), 1 with Boeing 707 (tkr/tpt), 1 with AS-332
    (tpt)
SPT 5 sqn
  1 with CL-215, 1 with C-212 (EW) and *Falcon* 20, 1
    with C-212, AS-332 (SAR), 1 with C-212 and
    Cessna *Citation*, 1 with Boeing 707
TRG 4 sqn
  1 with C-212, 1 with Beech (*Baron*), 1 with C-101, 1
    with Beech (*Bonanza*)
EASTERN AIR COMMAND (MALEV) 2 wg
FTR 4 sqn
  2 with EF-18 (F-18 *Hornet*), 1 with EF-18 (/trg/FTR),
    1 with *Mirage* F1
TPT 2 sqn
  1 with C-130H, 1 tkr/tpt with KC-130H
SPT 1 sqn with **ac** C-212 (SAR) **hel** AS-330
STRAIT AIR COMMAND (MAEST) 4 wg
FTR 3 sqn
  2 with *Mirage* F-1 CE/BE
  1 with EF/A-18
FGA 2 sqn with F-5B
MR 1 sqn with P-3A/B
TRG 6 sqn

2 hel with *Hughes* 300C, S-76C, 1 with C-212, 1 with
  E-26 (*Tamiz*), 1 with C-101, 1 with C-212
CANARY ISLANDS AIR COMMAND (MACAN) l wg
FGA 1 sqn with *Mirage* F-1EE
TPT 1 sqn with C-212
SAR 1 sqn with **ac** F-27 **hel** AS-332 (SAR)
LOGISTIC SUPPORT COMMAND (MALOG)
1 trials sqn with C-101, C-212 and F-5A, EF/A-18
EQUIPMENT
  208 cbt ac, no armed hel
  AC 87 **EF/A-18** A/B (ftr, OCU) • 35 **F-5B** (FGA) • 65
    Mirage **F-1CF/-BE/-EE** • 14* **RF-4C** (recce) 7* **P-3**
    (2 -A (MR), 5 -B (MR)) • 4 **Boeing 707** (tkr/tpt) •
    12 **C-130:** 7 -H (tpt), 5 **KC-130H** (tkr) • 78 **C-212**
    (34 tpt, 9 SAR, 6 recce, 26 trg, 2 EW, 1 trials) • 2
    Cessna 560 *Citation* (recce) • 78 **C-101** (trg) • 15
    CL-215 (spt) • 5 *Falcon* **20** (3 VIP tpt, 2 EW) • 1
    Falcon **50** (VIP tpt) • 2 *Falcon* **900** (VIP tpt) • 21
    Do-27 (U-9, liaison/trg) • 3 **F-27** (SAR) • 37 **E-26**
    (trg) • 20 **CN-235** (18 tpt, 2 VIP tpt) • 5 **E-20**
    (*Baron*) trg • 25 **E-24** (*Bonanza*) trg
  HEL 5 **SA-330** (SAR) • 16 **AS-332** (10 SAR, 6 tpt) •
    13 **Hughes 300C** (trg) • 8 **S-76C** (trg)
MISSILES
  AAM AIM-7 *Sparrow*, AIM-9 *Sidewinder*, AIM-120
    AMRAAM, R-530
  ASM *Maverick, Harpoon,* AGM-88A HARM
  SAM *Mistral, Skyguard/Aspide*

Forces Abroad

UN AND PEACEKEEPING
ALBANIA (AFOR II): some **BOSNIA** (SFOR II): 1,600:
1 inf bn gp, 12 obs, 2 TACP. SFOR **Air Component** 8
F/A-18, 2 KC-130 (tkr), 1 CASA-212 (spt ac) **YUGO-
SLAVIA** (Joint Guardian): some (to be 1,200)

Paramilitary 75,760

GUARDIA CIVIL 75,000
(incl 2,200 conscripts); 9 regions, 19 inf *tercios* (regt)
  with 56 rural bn, 6 traffic security gp, 6 rural special
  ops gp, 1 special sy bn; 22 BLR APC, 18 Bo-105, 5
  BK-117 hel
GUARDIA CIVIL DEL MAR 760
32 PCI

Foreign Forces

US 2,120: **Navy** 1,760 **Air Force** 240 **USMC** 120

Turkey   Tu

	1997	1998	1999	2000
GDP	L28,721tr	L49,079tr		
	($184bn)	($188bn)		
per capita	$6,000	$6,300		
Growth	6.3%	3.8%		
Inflation	85.7%	69.7%		
Debt	$85bn	$96bn		
Def exp	L1,232tr	L2,179tr		
	($8.1bn)	($8.4bn)		
Def bdgt		L2,021tr	L3,818tr	
		($7.8bn)	($8.9bn)	
FMA (US)	$177m	$22m	$1.5m	$1.5m
$1 = lira	151,865	260,724	428,920	

Population	65,161,000 (Kurds ε20–23%)		
Age	*13–17*	*18–22*	*23–32*
Men	3,267,000	3,257,000	5,953,000
Women	3,164,000	3,082,000	5,644,000

Total Armed Forces

ACTIVE ε639,000

(incl ε528,000 conscripts) *Terms of service* 18 months

RESERVES 378,700

(all to age 41) **Army** 258,700 **Navy** 55,000 **Air Force** 65,000

Army ε525,000

(incl ε462,000 conscripts)
4 army HQ: 9 corps HQ • 1 mech div (1 mech, 1 armd bde) • 1 mech div HQ • 1 inf div • 14 armd bde (each 2 armd, 2 mech inf, 2 arty bn) • 17 mech bde (each 2 armd, 2 mech inf, 1 arty bn) • 9 inf bde (each 4 inf, 1 arty bn) • 4 cdo bde (each 4 cdo bn) • 1 inf regt • 1 Presidential Guard regt • 5 border def regt • 26 border def bn

RESERVES

4 coastal def regt • 23 coastal def bn

EQUIPMENT

Figures in ( ) were reported to CFE on 1 Jan 1999
  MBT 4,205 (2,554): 2,876 M-48 A5T1/T2, 932 M-60 (658 -A3, 274-A1), 397 *Leopard* (170-1A1, 227-1A3)
  RECCE some *Akrep*
  TOTAL AIFV/APC (2,515)
  AIFV 450 AIFV
  APC 830 AAPC, 2,813 M-113/-A1/-A2
  TOTAL ARTY 4,453 (2,811)
    TOWED 1,552 incl: **105mm**: M-101A1; **150mm**: 62 Skoda (in store); **155mm**: 517 M-114A1\A2, 171 M-59 (in store); **203mm**: 162 M-115
    SP 820: **105mm**: 362 M-52A1, 26 M-108T; **155mm**: 4 M-44A1, 164 M-44T1; **175mm**: 36 M-107;

203mm: 9 M-55, 219 M-110A2
  MRL 60: **107mm**: 48; **227mm**: 12 MLRS (incl ATACMS)
  MOR 2,021: **107mm**: 1,264 M-30 (some SP); **120mm**: 757 (some 179 SP); plus **81mm**: 3,792 incl SP
  ATGW 943: 186 *Cobra*, 365 TOW SP, 392 *Milan*
  RL M-72
  RCL 57mm: 923 M-18; **75mm**: 617; **106mm**: 2,329 M-40A1
  AD GUNS 1,664: **20mm**: 439 GAI-DO1; **35mm**: 120 GDF-001/-003; **40mm**: 803 L60/70, 40 T-1, 262 M-42A1
  SAM 108 *Stinger*, 789 *Redeye* (being withdrawn)
  SURV AN/TPQ-36 (arty, mor)
  AC 168: 3 Cessna 421, 34 *Citabria*, 4 B-200, 4 T-42A, 98 U-17B, 25 T-41D
  ATTACK HEL 37 (26) AH-1W/P
  SPT HEL 253: 8 S-70A, 19 AS-532UL, 12 AB-204B, 64 AB-205A, 23 AB-206, 2 AB-212, 28 H-300C, 3 OH-58B, 94 UH-1H
  UAV CL-89 (AN/USD-501), *Gnat* 750, *Falcon* 600

Navy 51,000

(incl 3,100 Marines, 34,500 conscripts)
BASES Ankara (Navy HQ and COMEDNOREAST), Gölcük (HQ Fleet), Istanbul (HQ Northern area and Bosphorus), Izmir (HQ Southern area and Aegean), Eregli (HQ Black Sea), Iskenderun, Aksaz Bay, Mersin (HQ Mediterranean)

SUBMARINES 15

SSK 15
  6 *Atilay* (Ge Type 209/1200) with SST-4 HWT
  3 *Canakkale/Burakreis*† (plus 2 non-op) (US *Guppy*) with Mk 37 HWT
  2 *Hizirreis* (US *Tang*) with Mk 37 HWT
  4 *Preveze* (Ge Type 209/1400)

PRINCIPAL SURFACE COMBATANTS 21

FRIGATES 21
  FFG 19
  5 *Gaziantep* (US *Perry*) with 4 *Harpoon* SSM, 36 *SM-IMR*, 6 ASTT, 1 OTO Melara 76mm gun
  4 *Yavuz* (Ge MEKO 200) with 1 AB-212 hel (ASW/OTHT), 6 ASTT; 8 *Harpoon* SSM, 1 127mm gun
  8 *Muavenet* (US *Knox*-class) with 8 ASROC, 4 ASTT; plus *Harpoon* (from ASROC launcher), 1 127mm gun
  2 *Barbaros* (MOD Ge MEKO 200) with 8 *Harpoon* SSM, 8 *Sea Sparrow* SSM, 1 127mm gun, 6 324mm TT, 1 AB-212 hel
  FF 2 *Berk* with 6 ASTT, 2 Mk 11 *Hedgehog*

PATROL AND COASTAL COMBATANTS 50

MISSILE CRAFT 19
  1 *Kilic* with 8 x *Harpoon* SSM, 1 x 76mm gun
  8 *Dogan* (Ge Lürssen-57) PFM with 8 *Harpoon* SSM
  8 *Kartal* (Ge *Jaguar*) PFM with 4 *Penguin* 2 SSM, 2

533mm TT
2 *Yildiz* with 8 *Harpoon* SSM, 1 76mm gun
PATROL CRAFT 31
  COASTAL 10
  1 *Girne* PFC, 6 *Sultanhisar* PCC, 3 *Trabzon* PCC (1
    used as AGI)
  INSHORE 21
  1 *Bora* (US *Asheville*) PFI, 12 AB-25 PCI, 4 AB-21, 4
    PGM-71
MINE WARFARE 29
MINELAYERS 3
  1 *Nusret* (400 mines), 1 *Mersin* (US LSM) coastal (400
    mines), 1 *Mehmetcik* (plus 3 ML tenders)
  (*Bayraktar, Sarucabey* and *Çakabey* LST have
  minelaying capability)
MINE COUNTERMEASURES 26
  5 *Circe* MHC
  11 *Selcuk* (US *Adjutant*) MSC
  6 *Karamürsel* (Ge *Vegesack*) MSC
  4 *Foça* (US *Cape*) MSI (plus 8 MCM tenders)
AMPHIBIOUS 8
  1 *Osman Gazi* LST: capacity 980 tps, 17 tk, 4 LCVP
  2 *Ertugal* LST (US *Terrebonne Parish*): capacity 400 tps,
    18 tk
  2 *Bayraktar* LST (US LST-512): capacity 200 tps, 16 tk
  2 *Sarucabey* LST: capacity 600 tps, 11 tk
  1 *Çakabey* LSM: capacity 400 tps, 9 tk
  Plus about 59 craft: 35 LCT, 2 LCU, 22 LCM
SUPPORT AND MISCELLANEOUS 27
  1 *Akar* AO, 5 spt tkr, 2 Ge *Rhein* plus 3 other depot
    ships, 3 ARS, 2 AGHS, 3 tpt, 5 AT, 2 AR, 1 div spt

NAVAL AVIATION
13 armed hel
ASW 3 AB-204AS, 13* AB-212 ASW
TRG 7 TB-20

MARINES (3,100)
1 regt, HQ, 3 bn, 1 arty bn (18 guns), spt units

Air Force 63,000

(incl 31,500 conscripts) 2 tac air forces, 1 tpt comd, 1 air
trg comd, 1 air log comd
Flying hours 180
FGA 11 sqn
  1 OCU with F-5A/B, 4 (1 OCU) with F-4E, 6 (1
    OCU) with F-16C/D
FTR 7 sqn
  2 with F-5A/B, 2 with F-4E, 3 with F-16C/D
RECCE 2 sqn with RF-4E
TPT 5 sqn
  1 with C-130B/E, 1 with C-160D, 2 with CN-235, 1
    VIP tpt unit with *Gulfstream, Citation* and CN 235
TKR 2 KC-135R
LIAISON 10 base flts with ac T-33 hel UH-1H
TRG 3 sqn

1 with T-41, 1 with SF-260D, 1 with T-38 trg schools
  with **ac** CN-235 **hel** UH-1H
SAM 4 sqn with 92 *Nike Hercules*, 2 sqn with 86 *Rapier*
EQUIPMENT
440 cbt ac, no attack hel
  AC 175 **F-16C/D** (149 -C, 26 -D) • 87 **F-5A/B** (FGA
    • 178 **F-4E** (92 FGA, 47 ftr, 39 RF-4E (recce)) • 13
    C-130 (tpt) • 7 **KC-135R** • 19 **C-160D** (tpt) • 2
    Citation **VII** (VIP) • 44 **CN-235** (tpt) • 38 **SF-**
    260D (trg) • 34 **T-33** (trg) • 60 **T-37** trg • 70 **T-38**
    (trg) • 28 **T-41** (trg)
  HEL 20 **UH-1H** (tpt, liaison, base flt, trg schools)
MISSILES
  AAM AIM-7E *Sparrow*, AIM 9 S *Sidewinder*, AIM-120
    AMRAAM
  ASM AGM-65 *Maverick*, AGM-88 HARM, *Popeye* 1

Forces Abroad

CYPRUS 30–33,000: 1 corps; 282 M-48A5 MBT; 200 M-
113, 50 AAPC APC; 126 **105mm**, 36 **155mm**, 8 **203mm**
towed; 26 **155mm** SP; 30 **120mm**, 102 **107mm**, 175
81mm mor; **20mm, 35mm**; 84 **40mm** AA guns; **ac** 3 **hel**
4 **Navy** 1 PCI
UN AND PEACEKEEPING
ALBANIA (AFOR II): some **BOSNIA** (SFOR II): 1,300;
1 inf bn gp **GEORGIA** (UNOMIG): 5 obs **IRAQ/**
KUWAIT (UNIKOM): 6 obs **ITALY** (SFOR Air
Component): 18 F-16 C **YUGOSLAVIA** (Joint
Guardian): ε500

Paramilitary 202,200

GENDARMERIE/NATIONAL GUARD 200,000
(Ministry of Interior, Ministry of Defence in war)
50,000 reserve; some *Akrep* recce, 535 BTR-60/-80, 25
  Condor APC **ac** 2 Dornier 28D, 0-1E **hel** 19 Mi-17, 8
  AB-240B, 6 AB-205A, 8 AB-206A, 1 AB-212, 14 S-70A
COAST GUARD 2,200
(incl 1,400 conscripts); 48 PCI, 16 PCI<, plus boats, 2
  tpt

Opposition

KURDISTAN WORKERS PARTY (PKK) ε5,000
plus 50,000 spt militia

Foreign Forces

NATO HQ Allied Land Forces South Eastern Europe
(LANDSOUTHEAST), HQ 6 Allied Tactical Air Force
(6 ATAF)
OPERATION NORTHERN WATCH
UK Air Force 160; 4 *Jaguar* GR-3A/-B, 2 VC-10 (tkr)
US 2,420: **Army** 290 **Navy** 20 **Air Force** 1,900; 1 wg (ac

on det only), numbers vary (incl F-16, F-15C, KC-135, E-3B/C, C-12, HC-130, HH-60) **USMC** 220
US Installations for seismic monitoring
ISRAEL Periodic det of F-16 at Akinci

United Kingdom   UK

	1997	1998	1999	2000
GDP	£786bn	£812bn		
	($1.3tr)	($1.3tr)		
per capita	$20,700	$21,600		
Growth	3.5%	2.1%		
Inflation	3.2%	3.4%		
Publ debt	59.1%	56.6%		
Def exp	£21.8bn	£22.5bn		
	($35.7bn)	($37.4bn)		
Def bdgt		£22.5bn	£22.3bn	
		($37.4bn)	($34.6bn)	
$1 = pound	0.61	0.60	0.64	
Population				58,763,000

(**Northern Ireland** 1,600,000: Protestant 56%, Roman Catholic 41%)

Age	13–17	18–22	23–32
Men	1,883,000	1,817,000	4,194,000
Women	1,796,000	1,732,000	4,025,000

Total Armed Forces

ACTIVE 212,400

(incl 15,860 women, and 4,150 locally enlisted personnel)

RESERVES

Army 191,000 (Regular 140,000) **Territorial Army** (TA) 51,000 (to be 41,200) **Navy/Marines** 26,300 (Regular 22,600, Volunteer Reserves 3,700) **Air Force** 47,000 (Regular 45,000, Volunteer Reserves 2,000)

Strategic Forces (1,900)

SLBM 48 msl in 3 SSBN
  SSBN 3
  3 *Vanguard* SSBN each capable of carrying 16 *Trident* (D5); will not deploy with more than 48 warheads per boat, but each msl could carry up to 8 MIRV (some *Trident* D5 missiles loaded with single warheads for sub-strategic role)
EARLY WARNING
Ballistic-Missile Early-Warning System (BMEWS) station at Fylingdales

Army 113,500

(incl 7,400 women, 4,150 enlisted outside the UK, of whom 3,800 are Gurkhas)

regt normally bn size
1 Land Comd HQ • 3 Mil Districts incl 1 UK Spt Comd (Germany) (UKSC(G)), 3 (regenerative) div HQ (former mil districts) • 1 armd div with 3 armd bde, 3 arty, 4 engr, 1 avn, 1 AD regt • 1 mech div with 2 mech (*Warrior/Saxon*), 1 AB bde, 3 arty, 3 engr, 1 avn, 1 AD regt • ARRC Corps tps: 3 armd recce, 2 MLRS, 2 AD, 1 engr regt (EOD) • 1 air-mobile bde • 1 Air Spt bde • 14 inf bde HQ (3 control ops in N. Ireland, remainder mixed regular and TA for trg/administrative purposes only)
Summary of combat arm units
  8 armd regt • 3 armd recce regt • 4 mech inf bn (*Saxon*) • 8 armd inf bn (*Warrior*) • 25 lt inf bn (incl 2 air mobile, 2 Gurkha) • 3 AB bn (2 only in para role) • 1 SF (SAS) regt • 11 arty regt (2 MLRS, 5 SP, 3 fd (1 cdo, 1 AB, 1 air-mobile), 1 trg) • 4 AD regt (2 *Rapier*, 2 *Javelin*) • 10 engr regt • 5 avn regt (2 ATK, 2 air mobile, 1 general)

HOME SERVICE FORCES

N. Ireland 4,500: 6 inf bn (2,700 full-time)
Gibraltar 350: 1 regt (150 full-time)
Falkland Island Defence Force 60

RESERVES

Territorial Army 1 armd recce, 4 lt recce, 1 NBC def, 1 armd delivery regt, 31 inf bn, 2 AB (not in role), 2 SF (SAS), 4 arty (1 MLRS, 2 fd, 1 obs), 3 AD, 9 engr, 1 avn regt

EQUIPMENT

Figures in ( ) were reported to CFE on 1 Jan 1999
  MBT 542: 91 *Challenger* 2, 396 *Challenger*, 55 *Chieftain*
  LT TK 17 *Scorpion* (in store - for disposal)
  RECCE 315 *Scimitar*, 136 *Sabre*, 11 *Fuchs*
  TOTAL AIFV/APC (2,396)
  AIFV 528 *Warrior* (plus 208 'look-alikes'), 11 AFV 432 *Rarden*
  APC 809 AFV 432 (plus 887 'look-alikes'), 526 FV 103 *Spartan*, 592 *Saxon* (incl 'look-alikes'), 2 *Saracen* (plus 2 in store)
  TOTAL ARTY 425
    TOWED 182: **105mm**: 143 L-118, 7 L-119; **140mm**: 1 5.5in; **155mm**: 31 FH-70
    SP 155mm: 179 AS-90
    MRL 227mm: 64 MLRS
  MOR 81mm: 543 (incl 110 SP)
  ATGW 793 *Milan*, 48 *Swingfire* (FV 102 *Striker* SP), TOW
  RL 94mm: LAW-80
  RCL 84mm: 302 *Carl Gustav* (in store)
  SAM 135 *Starstreak* (SP), some 298 *Javelin* and *Starburst*, 79 *Rapier* (some 24 SP)
  SURV 33 *Cymbeline* (mor)
  AC 7 BN-2
  ATTACK HEL 269 (249): 154 SA-341, 115 *Lynx* AH-1/-7/-9
  TRG HEL 12 AS 350 *Ecureuil*

UAV *Phoenix*
LANDING CRAFT 2 LCL, 6 RCL, 4 LCVP, 4
workboats

Navy (RN) 43,700

(incl 6,740 Fleet Air Arm, 6,740 Royal Marines Command, 3,300 women)
ROYAL FLEET AUXILIARY (RFA)
(2,400 civilians) mans major spt vessels
MARINE SERVICES
(280 MoD civilians and 780 commercial contractors)
203 craft, provides harbour/coastal services
BASES UK Northwood (HQ Fleet,
CINCEASTLANT), Devonport (HQ), Faslane,
Portsmouth **Overseas** Gibraltar
SUBMARINES 15
STRATEGIC SUBMARINES 3 SSBN
TACTICAL SUBMARINES 12
  SSN 12
  5 *Swiftsure* with *Spearfish* or *Tigerfish* HWT and *Sub-
    Harpoon* SSM, one (*Splendid*) with 12 *Tomahawk
    Block* III TLAM (C) (1 in refit)
  7 *Trafalgar* with *Spearfish* and *Tigerfish* HWT and *Sub-
    Harpoon* SSM (2 in refit)
PRINCIPAL SURFACE COMBATANTS 34
CARRIERS 3: 2 mod *Invincible* CVS each with **ac** 8 FA-
  2 *Sea Harrier* V/STOL **hel** 12 *Sea King*, up to 9 ASW,
  3 AEW; plus 1 *Invincible* in extended refit
  Full 'expeditionary air group' comprises 8 *Sea
  Harrier* FA-2, 8 RAF *Harrier* GR-7, 2 *Sea King* ASW, 4
  Sea King AEW
DESTROYERS
  DDG 11 Type 42 with 2 *Sea Dart* SAM; plus 1 *Lynx*
    hel, 6 ASTT, 1 114mm gun (2 in refit)
FRIGATES 20
  FFG 20
  4 *Cornwall* (Type 22 Batch 3) with 1 *Sea King* or 2
    Lynx hel (*Sting Ray* LWT), 6 ASTT; 8 *Harpoon* SSM,
    1 114mm gun, *Seawolf* SAM (1 in refit)
  3 *Broadsword* (Type 22 Batch 2) with 2 *Lynx* hel (2
    with 1 *Sea King*), 6 ASTT, 4 MM 38 *Exocet* SSM,
    Seawolf SAM
  13 *Norfolk* (Type 23) with 1 *Lynx* hel, 4 ASTT, plus 8
    Harpoon SSM, 1 114mm gun, *Seawolf* VL SAM (1 in
    refit)
PATROL AND COASTAL COMBATANTS 24
PATROL, OFFSHORE 8
  2 *Castle*, 5 *Island*, 1 *River* PCO
PATROL, INSHORE 16
  16 *Archer* (incl 4 trg)
MINE WARFARE 19
MINELAYER no dedicated minelayer, but all
  submarines have limited minelaying capability
MINE COUNTERMEASURES 21
  13 *Hunt* MCC (4 mod *Hunt* MCC/PCC), 8 *Sandown*

MHO (5 batch 1, 3 batch 2)
AMPHIBIOUS 8
  2 *Fearless* LPD (incl 1 in extended readiness) with 4
    LCU, 4 LCVP; capacity 350 tps, 15 tk, 3 hel
  1 *Ocean* LPH with 4 LVCP, capacity 800 tps, 18 hel
  5 *Sir Bedivere* LSL; capacity 340 tps, 16 tk, 1 hel (RFA
    manned)
  Plus 23 craft: 9 LCU, 14 LCVP
  (see Army for additional amph lift capability)
SUPPORT AND MISCELLANEOUS 21
UNDER WAY SUPPORT 9
  2 *Fort Victoria* AOR, 2 *Olwen*, 3 *Rover* AO, 2 *Fort
    Grange* AF
MAINTENANCE AND LOGISTIC 4 AOT
SPECIAL PURPOSE 2
  1 *Endurance*, 1 AVB
SURVEY 6
  1 *Scott*, 2 *Bulldog*, 1 *Roebuck*, 1 *Herald*, 1 *Gleaner*

FLEET AIR ARM (6,740)
(incl 330 women)
Flying hours *Harrier*: 275
A typical CVS air group consists of 8 FA-2 *Harrier*, 7
Sea King (ASW), 3 *Sea King* (AEW) (can carry 8 RAF
GR-7 *Harrier* instead of 4 *Sea King*)
FTR/ATK 2 ac sqn with *Sea Harrier* F/A2 plus 1 trg
  sqn with *Harrier* T-4/-8
ASW 5 hel sqn with *Sea King* Mk-5/6
ASW/ATK 2 sqn with *Lynx* HAS-3 HMA8 (in indep flt)
AEW 1 hel sqn with *Sea King* AEW-2
COMMANDO SPT 3 hel sqn with *Sea King* HC-4
SAR 1 hel sqn with *Sea King* MK-5
TRG 1 sqn with *Jetstream*
FLEET SPT 13 *Mystère-Falcon* (civil registration), 1
  Cessna *Conquest* (civil registration), 1 Beech *Baron*
  (civil registration) 5 GROB 115 (op under contract)
TPT *Jetstream*
EQUIPMENT
  33 cbt ac (plus 21 in store), 109 armed hel (plus 29 in
    store)
  AC 28 *Sea Harrier* FA-2 (plus 19 in store) • 5* T-4/T-8
    (trg) plus 2 in store • 15 *Hawk* (spt) • 10 *Jetstream* •
    7 T-2 (trg) • 3 T-3 (spt)
  HEL 92 *Sea King* (49 HAS-5/6, 33 HC-4, 10 AEW-2)
    • 36 *Lynx* HAS-3 • 23 *Lynx* HAS-8, 12 EH-101
    Merlin
MISSILES
  ASM *Sea Skua*, *Sea Eagle*
  AAM AIM-9 *Sidewinder*, AIM-120C AMRAAM

ROYAL MARINES COMMAND (6,740, incl RN and
Army)
1 cdo bde: 3 cdo; 1 cdo arty regt (Army); 1 cdo log regt;
1 HQ and sig sqn, 1 cdo AD bty (Army), 2 cdo engr (1
Army, 1 TA), 1 LCA sqn. Serving with RN/Other
comd: 1 sy gp, Special Boat Service, 1 cdo lt hel sqn, 2
LCA sqn, 3 dets/naval parties

EQUIPMENT

MOR 81mm
ATGW *Milan*
SAM *Javelin*
HEL 9 SA-341 (*Gazelle*); plus 3 in store, 6 *Lynx* AH-7
AMPH 24 RRC, 4 LACV

Air Force (RAF) 55,200

(incl 5,164 women)

Flying hours Tornado GRI/4 210, F3 183; *Harrier*: 186; *Jaguar*: 203

FGA/BBR 6 sqn with *Tornado* GRI/4

FGA 5 sqn
3 with *Harrier* GR-7, 2 with *Jaguar* GR-3/3A

FTR 5 sqn with *Tornado* F-3 plus 1 flt in the Falklands

RECCE 4 sqn
2 with *Tornado* GR-1A/4A, 1 with *Canberra* PR-9, 1 with *Jaguar* GR-3/3A

MR 3 sqn with *Nimrod* MR-2

AEW 2 sqn with E-3D *Sentry*

ELINT 1 ELINT with *Nimrod* R-1

TPT/TKR 3 sqn
1 with VC-10 C1, VC-10 K-2/-3/-4, and 1 with *Tristar* K-1/KC-1/-2A, plus 1 VC-10 flt in the Falklands

TPT 4 sqn with *Hercules* C-1/-3, 1 comms sqn with **ac** HS-125, BAe 146 **hel** AS-355 (*Twin Squirrel*)

TARGET FACILITY/CAL 1 sqn with *Hawk* T-1/T-1A

OCU 6: *Tornado* GR-1/4, *Tornado* F-3, *Jaguar* GR-3/3A/T2A, *Harrier* GR-7/-T10, *Hercules* C-1/-3, *Nimrod* MR-2

TRG *Hawk* T-1/-1A/-1W, *Jetstream* T-1, *Bulldog* T-1, G.115E *Tutor*, HS-125 *Dominie* T-1, *Tucano* T-1

TAC HEL 8 sqn
1 with CH-47 (*Chinook*) and SA-341 (*Gazelle* HT3), 1 with *Wessex* HC-2, 2 with SA-330 (*Puma*), 1 with CH-47 and *Sea King* HAR3, 2 with CH-47, 1 with *Wessex* HC-2 and SA-330 (*Puma*)

SAR 2 hel sqn with *Sea King* HAR-3/3A

TRG *Sea King* (including postgraduate training on 203(R) sqn), Tri-Service Defence Helicopter School with AS-350 (*Single Squirrel*) and Bell 412

EQUIPMENT

462 cbt ac, incl 24 MR (plus 132 in store), no armed hel

AC 246 *Tornado* (101 **GR-1/4**, 26 **GR-1A/4A**, 26 **GR-1B/4B**, 93 **F-3** (plus 68 *Tornado* in store)• 53 *Jaguar* (43 **GR-3/3A**, 10 **T-2A/B** (plus 26 in store)) • 64 *Harrier* (53 **GR-7**, 11 **T-10** (plus 22 **GR-7** in store)) • 125 *Hawk* **T-1/1-A-W** (incl 75* (T1-A)) (plus 16 in store) • 7 *Canberra* (2 **T-4**, 5 **PR-9**) • 27 *Nimrod* (3 **R-1** (ECM), 24* **MR-2** (MR) • 7 *Sentry* (**E-3D**) (AEW) • 9 *Tristar* (2 **K-1** (tkr/pax), 4 **KC-1** (tkr/pax/cgo), 2 **C-2** (pax), 1 **C-2A** (pax) • 24 **VC-10** (12 **C-1K** (tkr/cgo), 3 **K-2** (tkr), 4 **K-3** (tkr), 5 **K-4**)(tkr)(plus 2 **K-2** (tkr) in store) • 55 *Hercules* C-1/

C-3 • 6 **BAe-125 CC-3** (comms), 6 **CC-2/-3** (liaison) • 2 *Islander* **CC-MK2** • 3 **BAe-146** (VIP tpt) • 82 *Tucano* (trg) (plus 46 in store) • 11 *Jetstream* (trg) • 110 *Bulldog* (trg)(plus 5 in store) • 10 *Dominie* (trg) • 2 *Tutor* (trg)

HEL 15 *Wessex* • 38 **CH-47** (*Chinook*) • 39 **SA-330** (**Puma**) • 25 *Sea King* • 38 **AS-350B** (*Single Squirrel*) • 3 **AS-355** (*Twin Squirrel*) • 9 Bell-412EP

MISSILES

ASM AGM-84D-1 *Harpoon, Sea Eagle*
AAM ASRAAM, AIM-9L *Sidewinder, Sky Flash*
ARM ALARM

ROYAL AIR FORCE REGIMENT

5 fd sqn, 4 gd based air defence sqns with 24 *Rapier* field standard C fire units; 1 gd based air defence conversion unit

RESERVES (Royal Auxiliary Air Force/RAF Volunteer Reserve): 3 field sqns, 1 gd based AD sqn, 3 Maritime HQ Units, 1 sqn Air Movements, 2 medical sqns, 2 Intelligence sqns, 1 Photographic Interpretation and Imaging Analysis sqn, 1 Public Relations sqn, 2 Training and Standardisation sqns, 5 role support sqns covering Helicopter Support, Air Tpt/Tkr, Offensive Support, Air Defence and Strike Attack

Deployment

ARMY

LAND COMMAND
Assigned to ACE Rapid Reaction Corps **Germany** 1 armd div plus Corps cbt spt tps **UK** 1 mech inf div, 1 air mobile bde (assigned to MND(C)); additional TA units incl 8 inf bn, 2 SAS, 3 AD regt **Allied Command Europe Mobile Force** (*Land*) (AMF(L)): UK contribution 1 inf BG (incl 1 inf bn, 1 arty bty, 1 sigs sqn)

HQ NORTHERN IRELAND
(some 9,300 (incl 200 RN, 1,200 RAF), plus 4,600 Home Service); 3 inf bde HQ, up to 12 major units in inf role (5 in province, 1 committed reserve, up to 6 roulement inf bn), 1 engr, 1 avn regt, 6 Home Service inf bn.
The roles of the remainder of Army regular and TA units incl Home Defence and the defence of Dependent Territories, the Cyprus Sovereign Base Areas and Brunei.

NAVY

FLEET (CinC is also CINCEASTLANT and COMNAVNORTHWEST): almost all regular RN forces are declared to NATO, split between SACLANT and SACEUR
MARINES 1 cdo bde (declared to SACLANT)

AIR FORCE

STRIKE COMMAND responsible for all RAF front-line forces. Day-to-day control delegated to 3 Groups

No. 1 (Offensive Support and Suppport Helicopters) **No. 11/18** (Air Defence/Maritime) **No. 38** (Air Transport/AAR)
PERSONNEL AND TRAINING COMMAND responsible for personnel management and ground/ flying trg; incl Training Group Defence Agency, Personnel Management Agency and Armed Forces Personnel Administration Agency
LOGISTIC COMMAND responsible for log spt for RAF units world-wide; Joint Service spt for RN and Army units for rationalised eqpt

Forces Abroad

ANTARCTICA 1 ice patrol ship (in summer only)
ASCENSION ISLAND RAF 27
BELIZE Army 180
BRUNEI Army some 1,050: 1 Gurkha inf bn, 1 hel flt (3 hel)
CANADA Army 200 trg and liaison unit **RAF** 155; routine training deployment of **ac** *Tornado, Harrier, Jaguar*
CYPRUS 3,200: **Army** 2,000; 2 inf bn, 1 engr spt sqn, 1 hel flt **RAF** 1,200; 1 hel sqn (5 *Wessex* HC-2), plus **ac** on det
FALKLAND ISLANDS Army 1 inf coy gp, 1 engr sqn (fd, plant) **RN** 1 DDG/FFG, 1 OPV, 1 spt, 1 AR **RAF**, 4 *Tornado* F-3, 1 *Hercules* C-1, 1 VC-10 K-2 (tkr), 2 *Sea King* HAR-3, 2 CH-47 hel, 1 sqn RAF regt (*Rapier* SAM)
GERMANY about 20,800: **Army** 18,300; 1 corps HQ (multinational), 1 armd div **RAF** 2,500; 3 sqn with 39 *Tornado*, 1 RAF regt sqn with *Rapier* SAM
GIBRALTAR 330: **Army** 60; Gibraltar regt (350) **RN/ Marines** 270; 2 PCI; Marine det, 2 twin *Exocet* launchers (coastal defence), base unit **RAF** some 118; periodic ac det
INDIAN OCEAN (*Armilla Patrol*): 2 DDG/FFG, 1 spt **Diego Garcia** 1 Marine/naval party
NEPAL Army 90 (Gurkha trg org)
WEST INDIES 1 DDG/FFG, 1 spt
UN AND PEACEKEEPING
ALBANIA (AFOR II): 130 (elm multinational HQ)
BAHRAIN (*Southern Watch*): RAF 50 2 VC-10 (tkr)
BOSNIA (SFOR II): 4,500 (incl log and spt tps in Croatia); 1 Augmented Brigade HQ (multinational) with 2 recce sqn, 1 armd inf bn, 1 tk sqn, 2 arty bty, 1 engr regt, 1 hel det **hel** 2 *Sea King* MK4 (RN), 8 *Lynx* AH-7 (Army), 3 *Gazelle* (Army) 3 CH-47 *Chinook* (RAF); 1 RFA (Split, Croatia) **CYPRUS** (UNFICYP): 306: 1 bn in inf role, 1 hel flt, engr spt (incl spt for UNIFIL) **FYROM** (OSCE): 2 *Puma* (RAF) **GEORGIA** (UNOMIG): 7 obs **IRAQ/KUWAIT** (*Southern Watch*) RAF 400; 12 *Tornado* GRI. (UNIKOM): 11 obs **ITALY** (SFOR Air Component): 350; 8 *Harrier* GR-7, 2 K-1 *Tristar* (tkr), 2 E-3D *Sentry* **MACEDONIA** 2 *Puma* (RAF) **SAUDI ARABIA** (*Southern Watch*): RAF 200; 6

Tornado F3 **SIERRA LEONE** (UNOMSIL): 5 obs
TURKEY (*Northern Watch*): RAF: 160; 4 *Jaguar* GR-3/ 3A, 2 VC-10 tkr **YUGOSLAVIA** (Joint Guardian): ε9,600: 1 corps HQ (multinational), 1 armd bde with 1 armd, 1 armd inf, 3 inf (incl 1 AB, 1 Gurkha) bn, 1 arty, 2 engr regt
MILITARY ADVISERS 455 in 30 countries

Foreign Forces

US 11,170: **Army** 380 **Navy** 1,220 **Air Force** 9,400; 1 Air Force HQ (3rd Air Force) 1 ftr wg, 53 cbt ac, 2 sqn with 26 F-15E, 1 sqn with 27 F-15C/D, 1 air refuelling wg with 15 KC-135, 1 Special Ops Gp, 5 MC-130P, 5 MC-130H, 1 C-130E, 8 MH-53J, 1 Recce sqn, 2 RC-135Js (ac not permanently assigned), 1 naval air flt, 2 C-12
USMC 170
NATO HQ Allied Forces North-west Europe (AFNORTHWEST), HQ Allied Naval Forces North-west Europe (NAVNORTHWEST), HQ Allied Air Forces North-west Europe (AIR NORTH WEST), HQ Eastern Atlantic Area (EASTLANT), HQ Maritime Forces Northern Sub-Area (NORLANT), HQ Maritime Forces Central Sub-Area (CENTLANT), HQ Maritime Forces Eastern Atlantic (AIREASTLANT), HQ Submarines Eastern Atlantic (SUBEASTLANT)

Non-NATO Europe

Albania   Alb

	1997	1998	1999	2000
GDP	leke386bn	leke452bn		
	($1.4bn)	($1.5bn)		
per capita	$3,400	$3,700		
Growth	-7.0%	8.0%		
Inflation	33.2%	20.1%		
Debt	$826m	$900m		
Def exp	εleke14.0bn	εleke15.0bn		
	($94m)	($100m)		
Def bdgt			leke5.8bn	
			($43m)	
FMA[a] (US)	$0.7m	$0.6m	$0.6m	$0.6m
FMA (Tu)			$5m	
$1 = leke	149	151	134	

[a] *Operation Alba 1997* ε$175m

Population			3,741,000

(Muslim 70%, Albanian Orthodox 20%, Roman Catholic 10%; Greek ε3–8%)

Age	13–17	18–22	23–32
Men	186,000	174,000	325,000
Women	170,000	160,000	301,000

Total Armed Forces

The Albanian armed forces are in the process of being re-constituted under Plan 2000. The army is to consist of 7 divs, plus a cdo bde of 3 bn. Restructuring is planned for completion by the beginning of year 2000, but is unlikely to be met. Personnel str and eqpt details are those reported prior to the unrest and should be treated with caution.

EQUIPMENT

MBT 138 T-34 (in store), 721 T-59
LT TK 35 Type-62
RECCE 15 BRDM-1
APC 103 PRC Type-531
TOWED ARTY 122mm: 425 M-1931/37, M-30, 208 PRC Type-60; **130mm:** 100 PRC Type-59-1; **152mm:** 90 PRC Type-66
MRL 107mm: 270 PRC Type-63
MOR 82mm: 259; **120mm:** 550 M-120; **160mm:** 100 M-43
RCL 82mm: T-21
ATK GUNS 45mm: M-1942; **57mm:** M-1943; **85mm:** 61 D-44 PRC Type-56; **100mm:** 50 Type-86
AD GUNS 23mm: 12 ZU-23-2/ZPU-1; **37mm:** 100 M-1939; **57mm:** 82 S-60; **85mm:** 30 KS-12; **100mm:** 56 KS-19

Navy ε2,500

BASES Durrës, Sarandë, Shëngjin, Vlorë
PATROL AND COASTAL COMBATANTS† 21
TORPEDO CRAFT 11 PRC *Huchuan* PHT with 2 533mm TT
PATROL CRAFT 10
  1 Sov *Kronstadt* PCO, 1 PRC *Shanghai* II, 3 Sov Po-2 PFI, 5 (US) PB Mk3 (for Coast Guard use)
MINE COUNTERMEASURES† 6
  3 Sov T-43 MSO (in reserve), 3 Sov T-301 MSI
SUPPORT 3
  1 AO†, 1 AGOR, 1 AT†

Air Force 4,500

98 cbt act, no armed hel
Flying hours 10–15
FGA 1 air regt with 10 J-2 (MiG-15), 14 J-6 (MiG-17), 23 J-6 (MiG-19)
FTR 2 air regt
  1 with 20 J-6 (MiG-19), 10 J-7 (MiG-21)
  1 with 21 J-6 (MiG-19)
TPT 1 sqn with 10 C-5 (An-2), 3 Il-14M, 6 Li-2 (C-47)
HEL 1 regt with 20 Z-5 (Mi-4)
TRG 8 CJ-5, 15 MiG-15UTI, 6 Yak-11
SAM† some 4 SA-2 sites, 22 launchers

Forces Abroad

UN AND PEACEKEEPING

BOSNIA (SFOR II): 100 **GEORGIA** (UNOMIG): 1 obs

Paramilitary

INTERNAL SECURITY FORCE 'SPECIAL POLICE':

1 bn (Tirana) plus pl sized units in major towns
BORDER POLICE (Ministry of Public Order): ε500

Foreign Forces

NATO (AFOR2): ε5,500 (to be 2,500): Be, Ca, Da, Fr, Ge, Gr, It, Nl, Pl, Sp, Tu, UK, US. **Non-NATO:** A, Lat, L, R, Slvk, Slvn, UAE

Armenia
Arm

	1997	1998	1999	2000
GDP	d762bn	d952bn		
	($1.5bn)	($1.8bn)		
per capita	$2,600	$2,900		
Growth	3.3%	6.9%		
Inflation	13.9%	21.9%		
Debt	$798m	$822m		
Def exp	εd68bn	εd75bn		
	($138m)	($149m)		
Def bdgt		d33bn	d40bn	
		($66m)	($75m)	
$1=dram	491	505	536	
Population				3,967,000

(Armenian Orthodox 94%, Russian 2%, Kurd 1%)

Age	*13–17*	*18–22*	*23–32*
Men	184,000	172,000	290,000
Women	179,000	169,000	281,000

Total Armed Forces some 53,400

incl 1,400 MoD and comd staff
Terms of service conscription, 18 months

RESERVES

some mob reported, possibly 300,000 with mil service within 15 years

Army some 52,000

(incl 3,700 Air and AD Component; conscripts)
4 Army Corps HQ
  1 with 1 mot rifle bde, 1 MRR
  1 with 3 MRR
  1 with 1 mot rifle bde, 3 MRR, 1 tk bn
  1 with 3 MRR, 1 tk bn, 2 arty regt (1 SP), 1 ATK regt
1 mot rifle trg bde

1 SAM bde, 2 SAM regt
1 mixed avn regt, 1 avn sqn
1 SF, 1 engr regt
EQUIPMENT (CFE-declared totals as at 1 Jan 1999)
  MBT 102 T-72
  AIFV 158 BMP-1/-2, 10 BMD-1
  APC 14 BTR-60, 32 BTR-70, 4 BTR-80
  TOTAL ARTY 225
  TOWED 121: **122mm**: 59 D-30; **152mm**: 2 D-1, 34
    D-20, 26 2A36
  SP 38: **122mm**: 10 2S1; **152mm**: 28 2S3
  MRL 122mm: 47 BM-21
  MOR 120mm: 19 M-120
  SSM 8 *Scud* (reported)
  ATK GUNS 105: **85mm**: D-44; **100mm**: T-12
  ATGW 18 AT-3 *Sagger*, 27 AT-6 *Spiral*
  SAM 25 SA-2/-3, 27 SA-4, 20 SA-8, SA-13
  SURV GS-13 (veh), *Long Trough* ((SNAR-1) arty),
    Pork Trough ((SNAR-2/-6) arty), *Small Fred/Small*
    Yawn (arty), *Big Fred* ((SNAR-10) veh/arty)
  AIR COMPONENT (3,700 incl AD):
    FGA 6 cbt ac, 13 armd hel
      5* Su-25, 1* MiG-25 1 hel sqn with 9 Mi-2, 7
      Mi-24 (attack), 7 Mi-8, 6* Mi-24K/P/R/MT
    AIR TRG CENTRE 9 Mi-2 hel, 24 ac (An-2, Yak-
      52, Yak-55, Yak-18T)

Paramilitary 1,000

MINISTRY OF INTERIOR ε1,000
4 bn: 34 BMP-1, 33 BTR-60/-70/-152

Foreign Forces

RUSSIA 3,100: **Army** 2 mil base (bde+) with 74 MBT,
17 APC, 148 ACV, 84 arty/MRL/mor **Air Defence** 1
sqn MiG-29

Austria   A

	1997	1998	1999	2000
GDP	OS2.5tr	OS2.6tr		
	($220bn)	($212bn)		
per capita	$21,600	$22,500		
Growth	2.1%	3.3%		
Inflation	1.4%	0.9%		
Publ Debt	63.1%	63.1%		
Def exp	OS21.8bn	OS22.3bn		
	($1.8bn)	($1.8bn)		
Def bdgt			OS22.3bn	OS22.5bn
			($1.8bn)	($1.8bn)
$1 = OS (Austrian schilling)				
	12.2	12.4	13.5	

Population			8,107,000
Age	*13–17*	*18–22*	*23–32*
Men	242,000	245,000	608,000
Women	231,000	235,000	586,000

Total Armed Forces

(Air Service forms part of the Army)

ACTIVE some 40,500

(incl 28,400 active and short term; 16,600 conscripts;
excl ε5,000 civilians; some 66,000 reservists a year
undergo refresher trg, a proportion at a time)
Terms of service 7 months recruit trg, 30 days reservist
refresher trg during 10 years (or 8 months trg, no
refresher); 60–90 days additional for officers, NCO and
specialists

RESERVES

100,700 ready (72 hrs) reserves; 990,000 with reserve
trg, but no commitment. Officers, NCO and specialists
to age 65, remainder to age 50

Army some 40,500 (to be 26,100)

(incl 16,600 conscripts)
2 corps
  1 with 2 inf bde (each 3 inf bn), 1 mech inf bde (2
    mech inf, 1 tk, 1 recce, 1 SP arty bn), 1 SP arty regt,
    1 recce, 2 engr, 1 ATK bn
  1 with 1 inf bde (3 inf bn), 1 mech inf bde (1 mech
    inf, 2 tk, 1 SP arty bn), 1 SP arty regt, 1 recce, 1
    engr bn
  1 Provincial mil comd with 1 inf regt (plus 5 inf bn
    on mob)
  8 Provincial mil comd (15 inf bn on mob)
EQUIPMENT
  MBT 169 M-60A3 (being withdrawn), 114 *Leopard*
    2A4
  APC 465 Saurer 4K4E/F, 269 *Pandur*
  TOWED ARTY 105mm: 108 IFH (M-2A1)
  SP ARTY 155mm: 178 M-109/-A2/-A5Ö
  FORTRESS ARTY 155mm: 24 SFK M-2 (deactivated)
  MRL 128mm: 18 M-51 (in store)
  MOR 81mm: 498; **120mm**: 242 M-43
  ATGW 226 RBS-56 *Bill*, 87 RJPz-(HOT) *Jaguar* 1
  RCL 2,196 incl **74mm**: *Miniman*; **84mm**: *Carl Gustav*;
    106mm: 445 M-40A1 (in store)
  ANTI-TANK GUNS
    SP 105mm: 284 *Kuerassier* JPz SK (50 in store)
    TOWED 85mm: 205 M-52/-55 (in store)
    STATIC 105mm: some 227 L7A1 (*Centurion* tk)
  AD GUNS 20mm: 426

MARINE WING
  (under School of Military Engineering)
  2 river patrol craft<; 10 unarmed boats

Air Force (4,250)

(3,400 conscripts); 53 cbt ac, no armed hel
Flying hours 130
1 air div HQ, 3 air regt, 3 AD regt, 1 air surv regt
FTR/FGA 1 wg with 24 SAAB J-35Oe
HELICOPTERS
  LIAISON 11 OH-58B, 11 AB-206A
  TPT 22 AB-212; 8 AB-204 (9 in store)
  SAR 24 SA-319 *Alouette* III
TPT 2 *Skyvan* 3M
LIAISON 14 O-1 (L-19A/E), 12 PC-6B
TRG 16 PC-7, 29* SAAB 105Oe
AD 76 *Mistral*; 132 **20mm** AA guns: 74 Twin **35mm** AA
  towed guns with *Skyguard* radars; air surv *Goldhaube*
  with *Selenia* MRS-403 3D radars

Forces Abroad

UN AND PEACEKEEPING
ALBANIA (AFOR): some **BOSNIA** (SFOR II): 200
CYPRUS (UNFICYP): 241: 1 inf bn **GEORGIA**
(UNOMIG): 4 obs **MIDDLE EAST** (UNTSO): 6 obs
SYRIA (UNDOF): 428: 1 inf bn **TAJIKISTAN**
(UNMOT): 2 obs **WESTERN SAHARA** (MINURSO):
6 obs

Azerbaijan   Az

	1997	1998	1999	2000
GDP	m15.4tr	m16.3tr		
	($3.9bn)	($4.2bn)		
per capita	$1,600	$1,800		
Growth	5.8%	9.5%		
Inflation	4.0%	-0.8%		
Debt	$567m	$684m		
Def exp	εm580bn	εm750bn		
	($146m)	($193m)		
Def bdgt		m463bn	m472bn	
		($119m)	($120m)	
FMA (Tu)			$3m	
$1 = manat	3,985	3,890	3,950	
Population				7,284,000

(Daghestani 3%, Russian 2%, Armenian 2–3% (mostly
in Nagorno-Karabakh))

Age	*13–17*	*18–22*	*23–32*
Men	400,000	357,000	613,000
Women	378,000	336,000	631,000

Total Armed Forces

ACTIVE 69,900

(incl 4,000 MOD and centrally controlled units/
formations)

Terms of service 17 months, but can be extended for
ground forces

RESERVES
some mob 575,700 with mil service within 15 years

Army 55,600

3 Army Corps HQ • 1 MRD • 18 MR bde • 2 arty bde,
1 ATK regt
EQUIPMENT (CFE declared totals as at 1 Jan 1998)
  MBT 259: 136 T-72, 123 T-55
  AIFV 254: 94 BMP-1, 90 BMP-2, 3 BMP-3, 44 BMD-
    1/-2, 23 BRM-1
  APC 74: 25 BTR-60, 28 BTR-70, 11 BTR-80, 10 BTR-D
  TOTAL ARTY 303
    TOWED 153: **122mm**: 97 D-30; **152mm**: 32 D-20,
      24 2A36
    SP 122mm: 14 2S1
    COMBINED GUN/MOR 120mm: 28 2S9
    MRL 122mm: 56 BM-21
    MOR 120mm: 52 PM-38
  SAM 60+ SA-4/-8/-13
  SURV GS-13 (veh); *Long Trough* ((SNAR-1) arty),
    Pork Trough ((SNAR-2/-6) arty), *Small Fred/Small
    Yawn* (veh, arty), *Big Fred* ((SNAR-10) veh, arty)

Navy 2,200

BASE Baku
PRINCIPAL SURFACE COMBATANTS 1
FRIGATES FF 1 *Petya* II with 4 76mm gun, 5 406mm
  TT (non-op)
PATROL AND COASTAL COMBATANTS 9
MISSILE CRAFT 2 *Osa* II PFM with 4 SS-N-2B *Styx* SSM
PATROL, INSHORE 7
  5 *Stenka* PFI, 1 *Zhuk* PCI, 1 *Svetlyak* PCI
MINE COUNTERMEASURES 5
  3 *Sonya* MSC, 2 *Yevgenya* MSI
AMPHIBIOUS 4
  4 *Polnochny* LSM capacity 180 tps
SUPPORT AND MISCELLANEOUS 3
  1 *Vadim Popov* (research), 2 *Balerian Uryvayev*
  (research)

Air Force and Air Defence 8,100

49 cbt ac, 15 attack hel
FGA regt with 4* Su-17, 4* Su-24, 2* Su-25, 5* MiG-21,
  28 L-29, 12 L-39
FTR sqn with 29* MiG-25, 3* MiG-25UB
RECCE sqn with 2* MiG-25
TPT 4 ac (1 An-12, 3 Yak-40)
HEL 1 regt with 7 Mi-2, 13 Mi-8, 15* Mi-24
IN STORE 33 **ac** MiG-25, MiG-21, Su-24
SAM 100 SA-2/-3/-5

Paramilitary ε15,000+

MILITIA (Ministry of Internal Affairs) 10,000+
   EQPT incl 3 T-55 MBT; 17 ACV incl BMP-1, BMD,
   BTR-60/-70/-80; 2 122mm D-30 arty; 2 120mm
   mor
BORDER GUARD (Ministry of Internal Affairs) ε5,000
   EQPT incl 100 BMP-2 AIFV, 19 BTR-60/-70/-80 APC

Opposition

ARMENIAN ARMED GROUPS

ε20–25,000 in Nagorno-Karabakh
(incl ε8,000 personnel from Armenia)
   EQPT (reported) 316 incl T-72, T-55 MBT; 324 ACV
   incl BTR-70/-80, BMP-1/-2; 322 arty incl D-44, 102
   D-30, 53 D-20, 99 2A36, 44 BM-21, KS-19

Belarus   Bel

	1997	1998	1999	2000
GDP	r351tr	r662tr		
	($13bn)	($14bn)		
per capita	$6,300	$7,000		
Growth	10.0%	8.3%		
Inflation	64%	73%		
Debt	$991m	$2,250m		
Def exp	εr11.7tr	εr26.7tr		
	($451m)	($462m)		
Def bdgt		r6.1tr	r22,565tr	
		($106m)	($46m)	
FMAᵃ (US)	$0.3m	$0.1m		
$1 =rubel	30,740	57,850	489,132	

ᵃ Excl US Cooperative Threat Reduction programme:
1992–96 $119m budget, of which $44m spent by Sept 1996.
Programme continues through 1999

Population			10,470,000
(Russian 13%, Polish 4%, Ukrainian 3%)			
Age	*13–17*	*18–22*	*23–32*
Men	404,000	389,000	706,000
Women	390,000	380,000	705,000

Total Armed Forces

ACTIVE 80,900
(incl 15,100 in centrally controlled units and MoD staff,
2,100 women; 40,000 conscripts)
Terms of service 18 months

RESERVES some 289,500
with mil service within last 5 years

Army 43,350

MoD tps: 2 MRD (1 trg), 1 arty div (5 'bde')
2 SSM, 1 ATK, 1 *Spetsnaz*
3 Corps
   1 with 3 indep mech, 1 SAM bde, 1 arty, 1 MRL, 1
   ATK regt
   1 with 1 SAM bde, 1 arty, 1 MRL regt
   1 with 1 SAM bde, 1 arty, 1 ATK, 1 MRL regt
EQUIPMENT
   MBT 1,778 (295 in store): 62 T-55, 1,621 T-72, 95 T-80
   AIFV 1,583 (94 in store): 75 BMP-1, 1,228 BMP-2,
   161 BRM, 119 BMD-1
   APC 930 (254 in store): 188 BTR-60, 449 BTR-70, 193
   BTR-80, 30 BTR-D, 70 MT-LB
   TOTAL ARTY 1,515 (158 in store) incl
   TOWED 440: **122mm**: 190 D-30; **152mm**: 6 M-1943
   (D-1), 58 D-20, 136 2A65, 50 2A36
   SP 586: **122mm**: 239 2S1; **152mm**: 166 2S3, 120 2S5;
   152mm: 13 2S19; **203mm**: 48 2S7
   COMBINED GUN/MOR 120mm: 54 2S9
   MRL 358: **122mm**: 232 BM-21, 1 9P138; **130mm**: 1
   BM-13; **220mm**: 84 9P140; **300mm**: 40 9A52
   MOR 120mm: 77 2S12
   ATGW 480: AT-4 *Spigot*, AT-5 *Spandrel* (some SP),
   AT-6 *Spiral* (some SP), AT-7 *Saxhorn*
   SSM 60 *Scud*, 36 FROG/SS-21
   SAM 350 SA-8/-11/-12/-13
   SURV GS-13 (arty), *Long Trough* ((SNAR-1) arty),
   Pork Trough ((SNAR-2/-6) arty), *Small Fred/Small
   Yawn* (veh, arty), *Big Fred* ((SNAR-10) veh, arty)

Air Force 22,450

(incl 10,200 Air Defence); 152 cbt ac, 44 attack hel
Flying hours 28
FGA 20 Su-24, 42 Su-25
FTR 61 MiG-29, 23 Su-27
RECCE 6* Su-24
HELICOPTERS
   ATTACK 44 Mi-24 (30 in store)
   EW 3 Mi-8
   CBT SPT unknown number of Mi-8, Mi-24
TPT ac 16 Il-76, 3 An-12, 7 An-24, 1 An-26, 1 Tu-134, Il-
20 **hel** 10 Mi-26 (4 in store), 5 Mi-6

AIR DEFENCE (10,000)
SAM 175 SA-3/-5/-10

Paramilitary 8,000

BORDER GUARDS (Ministry of Interior) 12,000
MINISTRY OF INTERIOR TROOPS 11,000
MILITIA (Ministry of Interior) 87,000

Bosnia-Herzegovina   BiH

	1997	1998	1999	2000
GDP	ε$4.1bn	ε$4.9bn		
per capita	ε$5,300	ε$6,400		
Growth	30%	20%		
Inflation	14%	6%		
Debt	$2.8bn	$3.4bn		
Def exp[a]	$327m	$397m		
Def bdgt[a]		$227m	$318m	
FMA[b][c] (US)	$0.5m	$0.6m	$0.6m	$0.6m
$1=convertible mark				
	150	151	185	

[a] Excl Bosnian Serb def exp
[b] Eqpt and trg valued at ε$450m from US, Sau, Kwt, UAE, Et and Tu in 1996–99
[c] UNMIBH **1997** $190m **1998** $190m; SFOR **1997** ε$4bn **1998** $4bn

Population			ε4,000,000
(Bosnian Muslim 44%, Serb 33%, Croat 17%)			

Age	*13–17*	*18–22*	*23–32*
Men	193,000	183,000	342,000
Women	183,000	173,000	322,000

Total Armed Forces

ACTIVE see individual entries below

The data outlined below represent the situation prior to the signing of a comprehensive peace agreement on 14 December 1995. BiH and HVO forces are to merge and form the armed forces of a Muslim–Croat Federation with a probable structure of 4 Corps, 15 bde (incl 1 rapid-reaction) and an arty div. It is reported that this force will be equipped with 273 MBT (200), 227 ACV (200), 1,000 arty (1,000), 14 attack hel. Figures in ( ) denote eqpt delivered in country, but under US control

Army (BiH) some 40,000

1 'Army' HQ • 3 'Corps' HQ • 10 div HQ • 1 armd, 10 mot inf, 4 arty bde

RESERVES 150,000: 59 inf, 1 arty bde

EQUIPMENT
  MBT 150: T-34, T-55, AMX-30, M-60A3
  RECCE 44 AML-90
  APC 150 incl M-113A2
  TOTAL ARTY (incl hy mor) 2,000
    ARTY incl **105mm**: 36 L-118; **122mm**: 12 D-30; **130mm**: M-59; **155mm**: 126 M-114; **203mm**
    MRL incl **262mm**: M-87 *Orkan*
    MOR 82mm; 120mm
  ATGW 100 AT-3 *Sagger*, *Red Arrow* (TF-8) reported
  AD GUNS 20mm; 23mm: 19 ZU-23; **30mm**
  SAM SA-7/-14
  HEL 10 Mi-8/-17, 15 UH-1H
  AC 3 UTVA-75

Other Forces

CROAT (Croatian Defence Council (HVO)) 16,000
4 MD • 4 gd, 2 arty bde, 1 inf bn, 1 MP bn

  RESERVES 30,000: 12 Home Guard inf regt, 6 Home Guard inf bn

  EQUIPMENT
  MBT 75, incl T-34, T-55, M-84/T-72M, M-47
  AFV 80 M-60, M-80
  TOTAL ARTY some 400 incl
    TOWED incl **76mm**: M-48; **105mm**: M-56; **122mm**: D-30; **130mm**: M-46
    MRL 122mm: BM-21; **128mm**: M-63, M-77
    MOR 82mm
  ATGW AT-3 *Sagger*, AT-4 *Fagot*, AT-6 (reported)
  RL ε100 *Armbrust*, M-79, RPG-7/-22
  RCL 84mm: 30 *Carl Gustav*
  AD GUNS 20mm: M-55, Bov-3; **30mm**: M-53; **57mm**: S-60
  SAM SA-7/-9/-14/-16
  HEL Mi-8, Mi-24, MD-500

SERB (Army of the Serbian Republic of Bosnia and Herzegovina–VRS) 30,000+
4 'Corps' HQ • 38 inf/armd/mot inf bde • 1 SF 'bde' • 12 arty/ATK/AD regt
RESERVES 80,000

  EQUIPMENT
  MBT 300 incl T-34, T-55, M-84, T-72
  APC 360
  TOTAL ARTY some 1,000 incl
    TOWED 122mm: D-30, M-1938 (M-30); **130mm**: M-46; **152mm**: D-20
    SP 122mm: 2S1
    MRL 128mm: M-63; **262mm**: M-87 *Orkan*
    MOR 120mm
  SSM FROG-7
  AD GUNS 975: incl **20mm**, **23mm** incl ZSU 23-4; **30mm**: M53/59SP; **57mm**: ZSU-57-2; **90mm**
  SAM SA-2, some SA-6/-7B/-9/-13
  AC 6 *Orao*, 13 *Jastreb*, 1 *Super Galeb*
  HEL 20 SA-341, 10 Mi-8

Foreign Forces

NATO (SFOR II): about 31,000: Be, Ca, Da, Fr, Ge, Gr, It, Lu, Nl, No, Por, Sp, Tu, UK, US **Non-NATO** Alb, A, Cz, Ea, Et, HKJ, Hu, Lat, L, Mor, Pl, R, RSA, RF, Ukr

Bulgaria   Bg

	1997	1998	1999	2000
GDP	L17tr	L22tr		
	($10.2bn)	($10.7bn)		
per capita	$4,000	$4,200		
Growth	-7.4%	3.5%		
Inflation	1,082%	22.3%		
Debt	$10.0bn	$10.3bn		
Def exp	L570bn	L700bn		
	($339m)	($398m)		
Def bdgt		L488bn	L588bn	L702bn
		($277m)	($307m)	($351m)
FMA (US)	$0.9m	$1.0m	$1.0m	$1.0m
$1=leva	1,682	1,760	1,913	
Population				8,400,000

(Turkish 9%, Macedonian 3%, Romany 3%)

Age	13–17	18–22	23–32
Men	289,000	308,000	590,000
Women	274,000	292,000	565,000

Total Armed Forces

ACTIVE ε80,760

(perhaps 49,800 conscripts; incl about 12,500 centrally controlled, 1,300 MoD staff, but excl some 10,000 construction tps)
Terms of service 12 months

RESERVES 303,000

Army 250,500 **Navy** (to age 55, officers 60 or 65) 7,500
Air Force (to age 60) 45,000

Army 43,400

(incl ε33,300 conscripts)
3 Mil Districts/Corps HQ
  1 with 1 MRD, 1 tk, 2 mech bde • 1 with 1 MRD, 1 Regional Training Centre (RTC), 1 tk bde • 1 with 2 MRD, 2 tk, 1 mech bde
Army tps: 4 *Scud*, 1 SS-23, 1 SAM bde, 2 arty, 1 MRL, 3 ATK, 3 AD arty, 1 SAM regt
1 AB bde

EQUIPMENT

MBT 1,475: 1,042 T-55, 433 T-72
ASLT GUN 68 SU-100
RECCE 58 BRDM-1/-2
AIFV 100 BMP-1, 114 BMP-23, BMP-30
APC 1,772: 759 BTR-60, 1,013 MT-LB (plus 1,270 'look-alikes')
TOTAL ARTY 1,744 (CFE total as at 1 Jan 99)
  TOWED 100mm: M-1944 (BS-3); **122mm:** 195 M-30, M-1931/37 (A-19); **130mm:** 72 M-46; **152mm:** M-1937 (ML-20), 206 D-20
  SP 122mm: 686 2S1

MRL 122mm: 222 BM-21
MOR 120mm: M-38, 2B11, B-24, 359 *Tundzha* SP
SSM launchers: 28 FROG-7, 36 *Scud*, 8 SS-23
ATGW 200 AT-3 *Sagger*
ATK GUNS 85mm: 150 D-44; **100mm:** 200 T-12
AD GUNS 400: **23mm:** ZU-23, ZSU-23-4 SP; **57mm:** S-60; **85mm:** KS-12; **100mm:** KS-19
SAM 20 SA-3, 27 SA-4, 20 SA-6
SURV GS-13 (veh), *Long Trough* ((SNAR-1) arty), *Pork Trough* ((SNAR-2/-6) arty), *Small Fred/Small Yawn* (veh, arty), *Big Fred* ((SNAR-10) veh, arty)

Navy ε5,260

(incl ε2,000 conscripts)
BASES Coastal Varna (HQ), Atya **Danube** Vidin (HQ), Balchik, Sozopol. Zones of operational control at Varna and Burgas

SUBMARINES 1

SSK 1 *Pobeda* (Sov *Romeo*)-class with 533mm TT†

FRIGATES 1

FF 1 *Smeli* (Sov *Koni*) with 1 x 2 SA-N-4 *Gecko* SAM, 2 x 12 ASW RL; plus 2 x 2 76mm guns

PATROL AND COASTAL COMBATANTS 23

CORVETTES 7
  4 *Poti* with 2 ASW RL, 4 ASTT
  1 *Tarantul* II with 2 x 2 SS-N-2C *Styx* SSM, 2 x 4 SA-N-5 *Grail* SAM; 1 76mm gun
  2 *Pauk* I with 1 SA-N-5 *Grail* SAM, 2 x 5 ASW RL; 4 406mm TT
MISSILE CRAFT 6 *Osa* I/II PFM with 4 SS-N-2A/B *Styx* SSM
PATROL, INSHORE 10
  10 *Zhuk* PFI

MINE WARFARE 20

MINE COUNTERMEASURES 20
  4 *Sonya* MSC, 16 MSI (4 *Vanya*, 4 *Yevgenya*, 6 *Olya*, 2 PO-2)

AMPHIBIOUS 2 Sov *Polnocny A* LSM, capacity 150 tps, 6 tk

  Plus 6 LCU

SUPPORT AND MISCELLANEOUS 16

  3 AGS, 3 AO, 1 diving tender, 1 degaussing, 1 AT, 7 AG

NAVAL AVIATION

9 armed hel
HEL 1 ASW sqn with 6 Mi-14, 3 Ka-25
COASTAL ARTY 2 regt, 20 bty
GUNS 100mm: ε150; **130mm:** 4 SM-4-1
SSM SS-C-1B *Sepal*, SSC-3 *Styx*

NAVAL GUARD

3 coy

Air Force 18,300

(14,500 conscripts); 227 cbt ac, 43 attack hel, 1 Tactical Aviation corps, 1 AD corps
Flying hours 30–40
FGA 3 regt
  1 with 39 Su-25
  2 with 41 MiG-21, 1 regt with 32 MiG-23
FTR 4 regt with some 40 MiG-23, 23 MiG-21, 21 MiG-29
RECCE 1 regt with 21 Su-22, 10 MiG-21
TPT 1 regt with 2 Tu-134, 3 An-24, 4 An-26, 5 L-410, 3 Yak-40 (VIP)
SURVEY 1 An-30
HEL 2 regt with 32 Mi-2, 9 Mi-8, 31 Mi-17, 43 Mi-24 (attack), 2 Bell-206 (another 4 to be delivered this year)
TRG 3 trg regt with 6 Yak-18, 73 L-29, 35 L-39, MiG-21UM, MiG-23UB, MiG-29UB
MISSILES
  ASM AS-7 *Kerry*
  AAM AA-2 *Atoll*, AA-7 *Apex*, AA-8 *Aphid*
  SAM SA-2/-3/-5/-10 (20 sites, some 110 launchers)

Forces Abroad

UN AND PEACEKEEPING
BOSNIA (SFOR II): 1 pl **TAJIKISTAN** (UNMOT): 3 obs

Paramilitary 34,000

BORDER GUARDS (Ministry of Interior) 12,000
12 regt; some 50 craft incl about 12 Sov PO2 PCI<
SECURITY POLICE 4,000
RAILWAY AND CONSTRUCTION TROOPS 18,000

Croatia   Cr

	1997	1998	1999	2000
GDP	k123bn	k126bn		
	($20.1bn)	($16.8bn)		
per capita	$6,300	$6,500		
Growth	6.5%	3.0%		
Inflation	3.6%	5.4%		
Debt	$6.3bn	$8.5bn		
Def exp	k7.6bn	k8.9bn		
	($1.2bn)	($1.4bn)		
Def bdgt		k7.5bn	k6.1bn	
		($1.2bn)	($815m)	
FMA[a] (US)	$0.4m	$0.4m	$0.4m	$0.6m
$1 =kuna	6.10	6.36	7.47	

[a] UNTAES **1997** $266m; UNMOP (UNMIBH) **1997** $190m
1998 $190m

Population	ε4,794,000 (Serb 3%, Slovene 1%)		
Age	*13–17*	*18–22*	*23–32*
Men	165,000	168,000	331,000
Women	156,000	159,000	318,000

Total Armed Forces

ACTIVE 61,000
(incl conscripts)
Terms of service 10 months

RESERVES 220,000
Army 150,000 **Home Defence** 70,000

Army 53,000

(incl ε20,000 conscripts)
6 Mil Districts • 8 Guard bde (each 3 mech, 1 tk, 1 arty bn) • 3 inf 'bde' (each 3 inf bn, 1 tk, 1 arty unit) • 1 mixed arty/MRL bde • 1 ATK bde • 4 AD bde • 1 engr bde

RESERVES
26 inf 'bde' (incl 1 trg), 39 Home Def regt
EQUIPMENT
  MBT 300: T-34, T-55, M-84/T-72M
  LT TK 1 PT-76
  RECCE 7 BRDM-2
  AIFV 109 M-80
  APC 18 BTR-50, 20 M-60PB plus 7 'look-alikes'
  TOTAL ARTY some 1,500
    TOWED 427: **76mm:** ZIS-3; **85mm; 105mm:** 100 M-56, 50 M-2A1; **122mm:** 50 M-1938, 40 D-30; **130mm:** 83 M-46; **152mm:** 20 D-20, 21 M-84; **155mm:** 37 M-1; **203mm:** 22 incl some **SP 122mm:** 8 2S1
    MRL 122mm: 40 BM-21; **128mm:** 200 M-63/-91; **262mm:** 2 M-87 *Orkan*
    MOR 388 incl: **82mm; 120mm:** 325 M-75, 6 UBM-52; **240mm:** reported
  ATGW AT-3 *Sagger* (9 on BRDM-2), AT-4 *Spigot*, AT-7 *Saxhorn*, Milan reported
  RL 73mm: RPG-7/-22. **90mm:** M-79
  ATK GUNS 100mm: 133 T-12
  AD GUNS 600+: **14.5mm:** ZPU-2/-4; **20mm:** BOV-1 SP, M-55; **30mm:** M-53/59, BOV-3SP

Navy 3,000

BASES Split, Pula, Sibenik, Ploce, Dubrovnik **Minor facilities** Lastovo, Vis
SUBMARINES 1
SSI 1 *Velebit* (Mod *Una*) for SF ops (4 SDV or 4 mines)
PATROL AND COASTAL COMBATANTS 13
CORVETTES 1 *Kralj Petar* with 4 or 8 Saab RBS-15 SSM
MISSILE CRAFT 2
  1 *Rade Koncar* PFM with 4 RBS-15 SSM
  1 *Dubrovnik* (Mod Sov *Osa* 1) no missiles, can lay mines
PATROL, INSHORE 10
  4 *Mirna*, 1 RLM-301, 5 riverine

MINE WARFARE 2

MINELAYERS 2 *Cetina* (*Silba*-class, LCT hull), 94 mines

AMPHIBIOUS craft only

2 *Silba* LCT, 1 DTM LCT/ML, 1 DSM-501 LCT/ML, 7 LCU

SUPPORT AND MISCELLANEOUS 5

1 *Spasilac* ARS, 1 Sov *Moma* AGHS, 1 AE, 2 AT

MARINES

2 indep inf coy

COASTAL DEFENCE

some 10 coast arty bty, 2 RBS-15 SSM bty (reported)

Air Force 5,000

(incl 1,320 conscripts)

44+ cbt ac, 15 armed hel

Flying hours 80

FGA/FTR 2 sqn with 20 MiG-21 bis/4 MiG-21 UM, some *Kraguj* and *Jastreb*

TPT 4 An-2, 2 An-26, 2 An-32, 5 UTVA, 2 Do-28, 2 MD-500

HEL 16 Mi-8/17, 15* Mi-24, 2 MD-500, 1 UH-1, 9 Bell-206B

TRG 20* PC-9, 1 *Galeb*

AAM AA-2 *Atoll*, AA-8 *Aphid*

SAM SA-6, SA-7, SA-9, SA-10 (non-op), SA-13, SA-14/-16

Paramilitary 40,000

POLICE 40,000 armed

COAST GUARD boats only

Foreign Forces

UN (UNMOP): 27 obs from 23 countries; (SFOR II): not known

Cyprus   Cy

	1997	1998	1999	2000
GDP	C£4.4bn	C£4.7bn		
	($8.7bn)	($9.1bn)		
per capita	$11,700	$12,300		
Growth	2.5%	5.0%		
Inflation	3.6%	2.2%		
Debt	$6.7bn	$7.2bn		
Def exp	C£259m	C£256m		
	($505m)	($499m)		
Def bdgt		C£265m	C£300m	
		($515m)	($530m)	
$1 = pound	0.51	0.51	0.57	

UNFICYP **1997** $46m **1998** $45m

Population		870,000 (Turkish 23%)	
Age	*13–17*	*18–22*	*23–32*
Men	32,000	29,000	54,000
Women	30,000	27,000	51,000

Total Armed Forces

ACTIVE 10,000

(incl 8,700 conscripts; 445 women)

Terms of service conscription, 26 months, then reserve to age 50 (officers 65)

RESERVES

88,000 **first-line** (age 20–34), 43,000 **second-line** (age 35–50)

National Guard 10,000

(incl 8,700 conscripts) (all units classified non-active under Vienna Document)

1 Corps HQ, 1 air comd, 1 naval comd • 2 lt inf div HQ • 2 lt inf bde HQ • 1 armd bde (3 bn) • 1 arty comd (regt) • 1 ATK bn (div unit) • 1 SF comd (regt of 3 bn)

EQUIPMENT

MBT 104 AMX-30 (incl 52 -B2), 41 T-80U

RECCE 124 EE-9 *Cascavel*, 15 EE-3 *Jararaca*

AIFV 27 VAB-VCI, 43 BMP-3

APC 268 *Leonidas*, 118 VAB (incl variants), 16 AMX-VCI

TOWED ARTY 75mm: 4 M-116A1 pack; **88mm:** 36 25-pdr (in store); **100mm:** 20 M-1944; **105mm:** 72 M-56; **155mm:** 12 TR F1

SP ARTY 155mm: 12 F3

MRL 128mm: 18 FRY M-63

MOR 376+: **81mm:** 170 E-44, 70+ M1/M29 (in store); **107mm:** 20 M-30/M-2; **120mm:** 116 RT61

ATGW 45 *Milan* (15 on EE-3 *Jararaca*), 22 HOT (18 on VAB)

RL 66mm: M-72 LAW; **73mm:** 850 RPG-7; **112mm:** 1,000 *Apilas*

RCL 90mm: 40 EM-67; **106mm:** 144 M-40A1

AD GUNS 20mm: 36 M-55; **35mm:** 24 GDF-003 with *Skyguard*; **40mm:** 20 M-1 (in store)

SAM 60 *Mistral* (some SP), 12 *Aspide*, SA-10 (S-300 deployed on Greek island of Crete)

MARITIME WING

1 *Salamis* PFI (plus 11 boats)

1 coastal def SSM bty with 3 MM-40 *Exocet*

AIR WING

AC 1 BN-2 *Islander*, 2 PC-9

HEL 3 Bell 206C, 4 SA-342 *Gazelle* (with HOT), 2 Mi-2 (in store)

Paramilitary some 750

ARMED POLICE about 500

1 mech rapid-reaction unit (350), 2 VAB/VTT APC, 1 BN-2A *Maritime Defender* ac, 2 Bell 412 hel

MARITIME POLICE 250

2 *Evagoras* PFI, 1 *Shaltag* PFI, 5 SAB-12 PCC

Foreign Forces

GREECE 1,250: 1 mech inf bde incl 950 (ELDYK) (Army); 2 mech inf, 1 armd, 1 arty bn, plus ε200 officers/NCO seconded to Greek-Cypriot National Guard, 61 M-48A5 MOLF MBT, 80 *Leonidas* APC (from National Guard), 12 M-114 155mm towed arty, 6 M-110A2 203mm SP arty

UK (in Sovereign Base Areas) 3,200: **Army** 2,000; 2 inf bn, 1 eng spt sqn, 1 hel flt **Air Force** 1,200; 1 hel sqn, plus ac on det

UN (UNFICYP) some 1,228: 3 inf bn (Arg, A, UK), tps from Ca, SF, Hu, Irl, Nl, Slvn, plus 35 civ pol from 2 countries

'Turkish Republic of Northern Cyprus'

Data presented here represent the *de facto* situation on the island. This in no way implies international recognition as a sovereign state

	1997	1998	1999	2000
GNP	ε$909m	ε$950m		
per capita	ε$4,800	ε$5,100		
Def exp	ε$600m	ε$700m		
(Tu)				
Def bdgt			TL17.3tr	
			($41m)	
Population				ε210,000

Total Armed Forces

ACTIVE some 4,500

Terms of service conscription, 24 months, then reserve to age 50

RESERVES 26,000

11,000 **first-line** 10,000 **second-line** 5,000 **third-line**

Army some 4,500

7 inf bn

Paramilitary

ARMED POLICE ε150

1 Police SF unit

COAST GUARD

(operated by TRNC Security Forces)

1 *Raif Denktash* PCC • 2 ex-US Mk5 PCC • 2 SG45/SG46 PCC

Foreign Forces

TURKEY

ARMY 30–33,000 (mainly conscripts)

1 Corps HQ, 2 Inf div, 1 armd bde

EQUIPMENT

MBT 300+ M-48A5 T1/T2, 8 M-48A2 (trg)

APC 208 AAPC, 255 M-113

TOWED ARTY 105mm: 126 M-101A1; **155mm:** 36 M-114A2; **203mm:** 8 M-115

SP ARTY 105mm: 26 M-52A1; **155mm:** 36 M-44T

MOR 81mm: 175; **107mm:** 102 M-30; **120mm:** 30 HY-12

ATGW 48 *Milan*, 36 TOW

RL 66mm: M-72 LAW

RCL 90mm: M-67; **106mm:** 176 M-40A1

AD GUNS 20mm: Rh 202; **35mm:** GDF-003; **40mm:** M-1

SAM 50+ *Stinger*

SURV AN/TPQ-36

AC 3 U-17. Periodic det of F-16C/D, F-4E

HEL 4 UH-1H. Periodic det of S-70A, AS-532UL, AH-1P

NAVY

1 *Caner Goyneli* PCI

Estonia   Ea

	1997	1998	1999	2000
GDP	kn65.0bn	kn83.7bn		
	($4.7bn)	($5.5bn)		
per capita	$8,000	$8,600		
Growth	9.9%	4.0%		
Inflation	11.2%	10.7%		
Debt	$1,067m	$3,300m		
Def exp[a]	kn900m	kn980m		
	($65m)	($70m)		
Def bdgt		kn843m	kn1,134m	kn1,292m
		($60m)	($74m)	($84m)
FMA (US)	$0.6m	$0.7m	$0.7m	$0.8m
$1 = kroon	13.9	14.1	15.4	

[a] Incl exp on paramilitary forces

Population				1,445,000
(Russian 9%, Ukrainian 3%, Belarussian 2%)				
Age	*13–17*	*18–22*		*23–32*
Men	59,000	56,000		104,000
Women	56,000	54,000		101,000

Total Armed Forces

ACTIVE some 4,800

(incl 2,870 conscripts)
Terms of service 12 months

RESERVES some 14,000
Militia

Army 4,320

(incl 2,600 conscripts)
4 Defence Regions, 14 Defence Districts, 5 inf, 1 arty •
1 guard, 1 recce bn • 1 peace ops centre

RESERVES

Militia 7,500, 15 *Kaitseliit* (Defence League) units
EQUIPMENT
RECCE 7 BRDM-2
APC 32 BTR-60/-70/-80
TOWED ARTY 105mm: 19 M 61-37
MOR 81mm: 44; **120mm**: 14
ATGW 10 *Mapats*, 3 RB-56 *Bill*
RL 82mm: 200 B-300
RCL 84mm: 109 *Carl Gustav*; **90mm**: 100 PV-1110;
   106mm: 30 M-40A1
AD GUNS 23mm: 100 ZU-23-2

Navy 340

(incl 220 conscripts)
Lat, Ea and L have set up a joint Naval unit BALTRON
BASES Tallinn (HQ BALTRON), Miinisadam (Navy
and BALTRON)
PATROL CRAFT 3
  PATROL, INSHORE 3
  2 *Grif* (RF *Zhuk*) PCI, 1 *Ahti* (*Da Maagen*) PCI
MINE WARFARE 4
MINELAYERS 2
  2 *Rymaettylae*
MINE COUNTERMEASURES 2
  2 *Kalev* (Ge *Frauenlob*) MSI
SUPPORT AND MISCELLANEOUS 2
  1 *Mardus* AK, 1 *Laine* (Ru *Mayak*) AK

Air Force 140

(incl 50 conscripts)
Flying hours 70
  ac 2 An-2 (another expected this year), 1 PZL-140
  Wilga **hel** 3 Mi-2

Forces Abroad

UN AND PEACEKEEPING
BOSNIA (SFOR II): 46 **MIDDLE EAST** (UNTSO): 1 obs

Paramilitary 2,800

BORDER GUARD (Ministry of Internal Affairs) 2,800
(360 conscripts); 1 regt, 3 rescue coy; maritime elm of
Border Guard also fulfils task of Coast Guard
  BASES Tallinn
  PATROL CRAFT 20
  PATROL, OFFSHORE 3
  1 *Kou* (*Silma*), 1 *Linda* (*Kemio*), 1 *Valvas* (US *Bittersweet*)
  PATROL, COASTAL 6
  3 PVL-100 (*Koskelo*), 1 *Pikker*, 1 *Torm* (*Arg*), 1 *Maru*
  (*Viima*)
  PATROL, INSHORE 11
  3 PVK-001 (Type 257 KBV), 1 PVK-025 (Type 275
  KBV), 5 PVK-006 (RV), 1 PVK-010 (RV 90), 1 PVK-
  017, plus 2 LCU
  SPT AND MISC 1 *Linda* (SF *Kemio*) PCI (trg)
  AVN 2 L-410 UVP-1 *Turbolet*, 5 Mi-8

Finland SF

	1997	1998	1999	2000
GDP	m622bn	m660bn		
	($120bn)	($124bn)		
per capita	$19,600	$20,900		
Growth	5.5%	4.7%		
Inflation	1.2%	1.4%		
Publ debt	49.8%	49.8%		
Def exp	m10.2bn	m10.1bn		
	($2.0bn)	($1.9bn)		
Def bdgt[a]		m10.0bn	m9.0bn	
		($1.8bn)	($1.5bn)	
$1=markka	5.19	5.34	5.84	

[a] Excl supplementary multi-year budget for procurement
of m6.1bn ($1.1bn) approved in April 1998

Population			5,167,000
Age	*13–17*	*18–22*	*23–32*
Men	168,000	169,000	342,000
Women	158,000	160,000	327,000

Total Armed Forces

ACTIVE 31,700
(incl 23,100 conscripts, some 500 women)
Terms of service 6–12 months (12 months for officers, NCO
and soldiers with special duties)

RESERVES some 540,000 (to be 430,000)
Total str on mob some 540,000 (all services), with 300,000
in general forces (bde etc) and 200,000 in local forces.
Some 30,000 reservists a year do refresher trg: total
obligation 40 days (75 for NCO, 100 for officers) between
conscript service and age 50 (NCO and officers to age 60)

Army 24,000

(incl 19,000 conscripts)
(all bdes reserve, some with peacetime trg role)
3 Mil Comd
  1 with 6 mil provinces, 2 armd (1 trg), 3 *Jaeger* (trg), 9 inf
  1 with 2 mil provinces, 3 *Jaeger* (trg) bde
  1 with 4 mil provinces, 4 *Jaeger* (trg), 5 inf bde
Other units
  4 AD regt, 4 engr bn

RESERVES

some 200 local bn and coy

EQUIPMENT

MBT 70 T-55M, 160 T-72
AIFV 163 BMP-1PS, 110 BMP-2 (incl 'look-alikes')
APC 120 BTR-60, 450 XA-180/185 *Sisu*, 220 MT-LBV (incl 'look-alikes')
TOWED ARTY 105mm: 54 H 61-37; **122mm**: 486 H 63 (D-30); **130mm**: 36 K 54, **152mm**: 324 incl: H 55 (D-20), H 88-40, H 88-37 (ML-20), H 38 (M-10); **155mm**: 108 M-74 (K-83), 24 K 98
SP ARTY 122mm: 72 PsH 74 (2S1); **152mm**: 18 *Telak* 91 (2S5)
MRL 122mm: 24 Rak H 76 (BM-21), 36 Rak H 89 (RM-70)
MOR 81mm: 800; **120mm**: 789: KRH 40, KRH 92
ATGW 100: incl 24 M-82 (AT-4 *Spigot*), 12 M-83 (BGM-71D TOW 2), M-82M (AT-5 *Spandrel*)
RL 112mm: APILAS
RCL 66mm: 66 KES-75, 66 KES-88; **95mm**: 100 SM-58-61
AD GUNS 23mm: 400 ZU-23; **30mm**; **35mm**: GDF-005, *Marksman* GDF-005 SP; **57mm**: 12 S-60 towed, 12 ZSU-57-2 SP
SAM SAM-78 (SA-7), SAM-79 (SA-3), SAM-86M (SA-18), SAM-86 (SA-16), 20 SAM-90 (*Crotale* NG), 18 SAM-96 (SA-11)
SURV *Cymbeline* (mor)
HEL 3 Hughes 500D/E, 7 Mi-8

Navy 5,000

(incl 2,600 conscripts)
BASES Upinniemi (Helsinki), Turku
4 functional sqn (2 missile, 2 mine warfare). Approx 50% of units kept fully manned; others in short-notice storage, rotated regularly

PATROL AND COASTAL COMBATANTS 15

CORVETTES 2 *Turunmaa* with 1 120mm gun, 2 x 5 ASW RL
MISSILE CRAFT 9
  4 *Helsinki* PFM with 4 x 2 MTO-85 (Swe RBS-15SF) SSM
  4 *Rauma* PFM with 2 x 2 and 2 x 1 MTO-85 (Swe RBS-15SF) SSM, 1 x 6 *Mistral* SAM
  1 *Hamina* PFM with 6 RBS 15 SF SSM, 1 x 6 *Mistal* SAM

PATROL CRAFT, INSHORE 4
  2 *Rihtniemi* with 2 ASW RL
  2 *Ruissalo* with 2 ASW RL
MINE WARFARE 23
MINELAYERS 10
  2 *Hämeenmaa*, 150–200 mines, plus 1 x 6 Matra Mistral SAM
  1 *Pohjanmaa*, 100–150 mines; 2 x 5 ASW RL
  3 *Pansio* aux minelayer, 50 mines
  4 *Tuima* (ex-PFM), 20 mines
MINE COUNTERMEASURES 13
  6 *Kuha* MSI, 7 *Kiiski* MSI
AMPHIBIOUS craft only
  3 *Kampela* LCU tpt, 3 *Kala* LCU
SUPPORT AND MISCELLANEOUS 37
  1 *Kustaanmiekka* command ship, 5 *Valas* tpt, 6 *Hauki* tpt, 4 *Hila* tpt, 2 *Lohi* tpt, 1 *Aranda* AGOR (Ministry of Trade control), 9 *Prisma* AGS, 9 icebreakers (Board of Navigation control)
COASTAL DEFENCE
1 coastal bde (trg) with **100mm**: D-10T (tank turrets); **130mm**: 195 K-54 (static) arty
COASTAL SSM 5 RBS-15

Air Force 2,700

(incl 1,500 conscripts); 85 cbt ac, no armed hel, 3 AD areas: 3 ftr wg
Flying hours 150
FTR 3 wg
  2 with 21 F/A-18C, 7 F/A-18D, 20 *Hawk* 5/51A
  1 re-equipping with F/A-18 but still using SAAB 35 *Drakens* (reducing from 25) until 2001
OCU 5* SAAB SK-35C, 7* F/A-18D
RECCE some *Hawk* Mk 51 (incl in ftr sqn). One F-27 ESM/Elint
SURVEY 3 *Learjet* 35A (survey, ECM trg, target-towing)
TPT 1 ac sqn with 2 F-27, 3 Learjet-35A
TRG 22 *Hawk* Mk 51, 28 L-70 *Vinka*
LIAISON 13 Piper (7 *Cherokee Arrow*, 6 *Chieftain*), 9 L-90 *Redigo*
AAM AA-2 *Atoll*, AA-8 *Aphid*, AIM-9 *Sidewinder*, RB-27, RB-28 (*Falcon*), AIM-20 AMRAAM

Forces Abroad

UN AND PEACEKEEPING

CROATIA (UNMOP): 1 obs **CYPRUS** (UNFICYP): 9 **INDIA/PAKISTAN** (UNMOGIP): 5 obs **IRAQ/KUWAIT** (UNIKOM): 7 obs **LEBANON** (UNIFIL): 494: 1 inf bn **MIDDLE EAST** (UNTSO): 11 obs

Paramilitary 3,400

FRONTIER GUARD (Ministry of Interior) **3,400**
(on mob 23,000); 4 frontier, 3 Coast Guard districts, 1 air

comd; 5 offshore, 2 coastal, 4 inshore patrol craft (plus boats and ACVs); air patrol sqn with **hel** 3 AS-332, 4 AB-206L, 4 AB-412 **ac** 2 Do-228 (Maritime Surv)

Georgia Ga

	1997	1998	1999	2000
GDP	lari.5.7bn	lari 6.8bn		
	($4.3bn)	($4.4bn)		
per capita	$4,300	$4,600		
Growth	11.0%	4.0%		
Inflation	7.3%	3.6%		
Debt	$1.6bn	$1.8bn		
Def exp	lari 143m	lari 170m		
	($109m)	($110m)		
Def bdgt[a]		lari 82m	lari 55m	
		($53m)	($24m)	
FMA[b] (US)	$0.3m	$0.4m	$0.4m	$0.4m
FMA (Tu)			$3.8m	
$1 = lari	1.31	1.55	2.25	

[a] Abkhazia def bdgt 1997 $5m
[b] UNOMIG **1997** $18m **1998** $19m

Population				5,448,000

(Armenian 8%, Azeri 6%, Russian 6%, Ossetian 3%, Abkhaz 2%)

Age	13–17	18–22	23–32
Men	214,000	207,000	380,000
Women	206,000	199,000	360,000

Total Armed Forces

ACTIVE 26,300
(incl 10,550 MoD and centrally controlled units)
Terms of service conscription, 2 years

RESERVES up to 250,000
with mil service in last 15 years

Army 12,600

up to 24,000 planned
6 mech inf bde (incl 1 national gd, plus trg centre) • 1 arty bde (3 bn) • 1 marine inf bn, 1 peacekeeping bn
EQUIPMENT
   MBT 79: 48 T-55, 31 T-72
   AIFV/APC 111: 67 BMP-1, 11 BMP-2, 11 BRM-1K, 19 BTR-70, 3 BTR-80
   TOWED ARTY 85mm: D-44; **100mm**: KS-19 (ground role); **122mm**: 57 D-30; **152mm**: 3 2A36, 11 2A65
   SP ARTY 152mm: 1 2S5, 1 2S19
   MRL 122mm: 18 BM-21
   MOR 120mm: 16 M-120
   SAM some SA-13

Navy 750

BASES Tbilisi (HQ), Poti
PATROL AND COASTAL COMBATANTS 13
PATROL CRAFT 13
   2 *Zhuk* PCI, 5 ex trawlers, 4 cutters, 1 *Stenka* PCI, 1*Konotop* (Ukr *Matka*) PHM
MINE COUNTERMEASURES 4 *Yevgenya* MHC
AMPHIBIOUS craft only
   2 LCT, 4 LCM

Air Force 2,400

ac some 5 Su-25, 5 Su-17; **hel** 1 Mi-2, 6 Mi-6, 4 Mi-8, 3 Mi-24
TRG 10 L-29

AIR DEFENCE
SAM 75 SA-2/-3/-4/-5/-7

Opposition

ABKHAZIA ε5,000
50+ T-72, T-55 MBT, 80+ AIFV/APC, 80+ arty
SOUTH OSSETIA ε2,000
5–10 MBT, 30 AIFV/APC, 25 arty incl BM-21

Paramilitary ε6,500

BORDER GUARD ε6,500
   COAST GUARD
   3 *Zhuk* PCI

Foreign Forces

RUSSIA 5,000: **Army** 3 mil bases (each = bde+) 140 T-72 MBT, 500 ACV, 173 arty incl **122mm** D-30, 2S1; **152mm** 2S3; **122mm** BM-21 MRL; **120mm** mor plus 118 ACV and some arty deployed in Abkhazia **Air Force** 1 composite regt, some 35 tpt **ac** and **hel** incl An-12, An-26 and Mi-8
PEACEKEEPING: ε1,500; 2 MR, 1 inf bn (Russia)
UN (UNOMIG): 100 obs from 22 countries

Ireland Irl

	1997	1998	1999	2000
GDP	I£47bn	I£55bn		
	($75bn)	($78bn)		
per capita	$18,700	$20,700		
Growth	9.8%	10.4%		
Inflation	1.5%	2.4%		
Publ debt	56.6%	56.6%		
Def exp	I£491m	I£558m		
	($767m)	($796m)		

contd	1997	1998	1999	2000
Def bdgt		I£558m	I£586m	
		($796m)	($758m)	
$1=pound	0.64	0.71	0.77	
Population				3,698,000
Age	*13–17*	*18–22*	*23–32*	
Men	157,000	168,000	326,000	
Women	148,000	159,000	308,000	

Total Armed Forces

ACTIVE 11,500

(incl 200 women)

RESERVES 14,800

(obligation to age 60, officers 57–65) **Army** first-line 500, second-line 14,000 **Navy** 300

Army 9,300

3 inf bde each 3 inf bn, 1 arty regt, 1 cav recce sqn, 1 engr coy
Army tps: 1 lt tk sqn, 1 AD regt, 1 Ranger coy
Total units: 9 inf bn • 1 UNIFIL bn *ad hoc* with elm from other bn, 1 lt tk sqn, 3 recce sqn, 3 fd arty regt (each of 2 bty) • 1 indep bty, 1 AD regt (1 regular, 3 reserve bty), 4 fd engr coy, 1 Ranger coy

RESERVES

4 Army Gp (garrisons), 18 inf bn, 6 fd arty regt, 3 cav sqn, 3 engr sqn, 3 AD bty

EQUIPMENT

LT TK 14 *Scorpion*
RECCE 15 AML-90, 32 AML-60
APC 47 Panhard VTT/M3, 10 *Timoney* Mk 6, 2 A-180 *Sisu*
TOWED ARTY 88mm: 42 25-pdr; **105mm**: 18 L-118
MOR 81mm: 400; **120mm**: 67
ATGW 21 *Milan*
RL 84mm: AT-4
RCL 84mm: 444 *Carl Gustav*; **90mm**: 96 PV-1110
AD GUNS 40mm: 24 L/60, 2 L/70
SAM 7 RBS-70

Naval Service 1,100

BASE Cork, Dublin
PATROL AND COASTAL COMBATANTS 7
PATROL OFFSHORE 7
1 *Eithne* with 1 *Dauphin* hel, 3 *Emer*, 1 *Deirdre*, 2 *Orla* (UK *Peacock*)

Air Corps 1,060

7 cbt ac, 15 armed hel; 3 wg (1 trg)
CCT 1 sqn

1 with 7 SF-260WE,
MR 2 CN-235MP
TPT 1 *Super King Air* 200, 1 *Gulfstream* IV
LIAISON 1 sqn with 6 Cessna Reims FR-172H, 1 FR-172K
HEL 4 sqn
1 Army spt with 8 SA-316B (*Alouette* III)
1 Navy spt with 2 SA-365FI (*Dauphin*)
1 SAR with 3 SA-365FI (*Dauphin*)
1 trg with 2 SA-342L (*Gazelle*)

Forces Abroad

UN AND PEACEKEEPING

BOSNIA (SFOR II): 50 **CROATIA** (UNMOP): 1 obs
CYPRUS (UNFICYP): 19 **IRAQ/KUWAIT** (UNIKOM): 5 obs **LEBANON** (UNIFIL): 608: 1 bn; 4 AML-90 armd cars, 10 *Sisu* APC, 4 **120mm** mor **MIDDLE EAST** (UNTSO): 10 obs **WESTERN SAHARA** (MINURSO): 7 obs

Latvia Lat

	1997	1998	1999	2000
GDP	L3.3bn	L3.8bn		
	($5.6bn)	($6.4bn)		
per capita	$5,600	$6,000		
Growth	6.6%	3.6%		
Inflation	8.5%	4.5%		
Debt	$2,775m	$3,154m		
Def exp[a]	εL90.9m	εL95m		
	($156m)	($160m)		
Def bdgt		L23.2m	L35.4m	L47.2m
		($39m)	($58m)	($78m)
FMA (US)	$0.5m	$0.8m	$0.7m	$0.8m
FMA (Swe)		$1.5m		
$1=lats	0.58	0.59	0.61	

[a] Incl exp on paramilitary forces.

Population			2,450,000

(Russian 34%, Belarussian 5%, Ukrainian 3%, Polish 2%)

Age	*13–17*	*18–22*	*23–32*
Men	97,000	93,000	167,000
Women	94,000	89,000	163,000

Total Armed Forces

ACTIVE 5,730

(incl 2,120 conscripts; 1,300 National Guard and 830 in centrally controlled units)
Terms of service 12 months

RESERVES 14,500
National Guard

Army 2,550

(incl 1,760 conscripts)
1 mobile rifle bde with 1 inf bn • 1 recce bn • 1 HQ bn
• 1 arty unit • 1 peacekeeping coy • 1 SF team

RESERVES
National Guard 5 bde each of 5–7 bn
EQUIPMENT
  RECCE 2 BRDM-2
  APC 13 *Pskbil* m/42
  TOWED ARTY 100mm: 26 K-53
  MOR 82mm: 5; 120mm: 26
  AD GUNS 14.5mm: 12 ZPU-4

Navy 840

(incl 360 conscripts, 250 Coastal Defence)
Lat, Ea and L have set up a joint Naval unit BALTRON with
bases at Liepaja, Riga, Ventspils, Tallin (Ea), Klaipeda (L)
BASES Liepaja, Riga, Ventspils
PATROL CRAFT 12
  1 *Osa* PFM (unarmed), 1 *Storm* PCC (unarmed), 2
  Ribnadzor PC, 5 KBV 236 PC, 3 PCH
MINE COUNTERMEASURES 3
  2 *Kondor* II MCO, 1 *Lindou*

SUPPORT AND MISCELLANEOUS 3
  1 *Nyrat* AT, 1 *Goliat* AT, 1 diving vessel

COASTAL DEFENCE (250)
1 coastal def bn
10 patrol craft: 2 *Ribnadzor* PCC, 5 KBV 236 PC, 3 PCH

Air Force 210

AC 2 An-2, 1 L-410
HEL 3 Mi-2

Forces Abroad

UN AND PEACEKEEPING
ALBANIA (AFOR): some **BOSNIA** (SFOR II): 40

Paramilitary 3,720

BORDER GUARD (Ministry of Internal Affairs) 3,500
1 bde (7 bn)

Lithuania   L

	1997	1998	1999	2000
GDP	L38bn	L43bn		
	($9.6bn)	($10.7bn)		
per capita	$5,300	$5,700		
Growth	5.7%	5.1%		
Inflation	8.9%	5.0%		
Debt	$1,787m	$3,514m		
Def exp	L540m	L545m		
	($135m)	($136m)		
Def bdgt		L615m	L724m	L945m
		($154m)	($181m)	($236m)
FMA (US)	$0.5m	$0.7m	$0.7m	$0.8m
$1=litas	4.0	4.0	4.0	
Population				3,700,000
(Russian 9%, Polish 8%, Belarussian 2%)				
Age	*13–17*	*18–22*		*23–32*
Men	142,000	136,000		260,000
Women	137,000	132,000		254,000

Total Armed Forces

ACTIVE 12,130
(incl 3,560 conscripts; 2,000 Voluntary National
Defence Force) *Terms of service* 12 months

RESERVES 355,650
27,700 **first line** (ready 72 hrs, incl 11,100 Voluntary
National Defence Service), 327,950 **second line** (age up
to 59)

Army 7,840

(incl 2,890 conscripts)
1 motor rifle bde (6 bn) • 1 Jaeger, 1 Guard, 1 engr bn •
1 peacekeeping coy
EQUIPMENT
  RECCE 11 BRDM-2
  APC 14 BTR-60, 13 *Pskbil* m/42
  MOR 120mm: 36 M-43
  RL 82mm: 170 RPG-2
  RCL 84mm: 119 *Carl Gustav*

RESERVES
Voluntary National Defence Service: 10 Territorial
Defence regt, 38 territorial def bn, 134 territorial def
coy, 2 air sqn

Navy 1,320

(incl 670 conscripts)
Lat, Ea and L have set up a joint Naval unit BALTRON
BASES Klaipeda, HQ BALTRON Tallinn (Ea)
FRIGATES 2
FF 2 Sov *Grisha III*, with 2 x 12 ASW RL, 4 533mm TT

PATROL AND COASTAL COMBATANTS 4

1 *Storm* PCI, 1 SK-21 PCI, 1 SK-23 PCI, 1 SK-24 PCI

SUPPORT AND MISCELLANEOUS 1

1 *Valerian Uryvayev* AGOR

Air Force 970

no cbt ac

Flying hours 60

Air Force HQ, 3 Air Bases, 1 Air Control Centre, 3 Air Surveillance coy

AC 4 L-39, 2 L-410, 3 AN-26, 1 AN-24

HEL 3 Mi-8, 5 Mi-2

Forces Abroad

UN AND PEACEKEEPING

ALBANIA (AFOR): some **BOSNIA** (SFOR II): 41

Paramilitary 3,900

BORDER POLICE 3,500

COAST GUARD 400

Macedonia, Former Yugoslav Republic of			**FYROM**

	1997	1998	1999	2000
GDP	ε$1.3bn	ε$1.4bn		
per capita	$3,600	$3,800		
Growth	1.5%	5.0%		
Inflation	1.1%	0.6%		
Debt	$1.1bn	$1.3bn		
Def exp	d6.6bn	εd7.9bn		
	($132m)	($139m)		
Def bdgt		d3.7bn	d3.9bn	
		($68m)	($68m)	
FMA[ab] (US)	$0.5m	$3.4m	$0.5m	$0.5m
$1 = dinar	50.0	54.5	57.0	

[a] UNPREDEP **1997** $45m **1998** $21m
[b] UNPREDEP figures exclude US costs paid as voluntary contributions

Population		2,303,000

(Albanian 22%, Turkish 4%, Romany 3%, Serb 2%)

Age	*13–17*	*18–22*	*23–32*
Men	96,000	93,000	176,000
Women	87,000	84,000	161,000

Total Armed Forces

ACTIVE ε16,000

(incl 8,000 conscripts; about 1,000 HQ staff) *Terms of service* 9 months

RESERVES 102,000 planned

Army ε15,000

3 Corps HQ (cadre), 3 bde
1 border gd bde

EQUIPMENT

MBT 4 T-34

RECCE 10 BRDM-2, 41 HMMWV

APC 60 BTR-70, 12 BTR-80

TOWED ARTY 400 incl **76mm**: M-48, M-1942;
  105mm: 18 M-56, 18 M-2A1; **152mm**: 10-18 D-20

MRL 128mm: 70 M-71 (single barrel), 12 M-77

MOR 150 **60mm** and **120mm**

ATGW AT-3 *Sagger*

RCL 57mm; **82mm**

MARINE WING (400)

9 river patrol craft

Air Force (under 700)

ac 4 *Zlin*-242 (trg), 10 UTVA-75 **hel** 4 Mi-17

AD GUNS 50: **20mm**; **40mm**

SAM 30 SA-7

Paramilitary 7,500

POLICE 7,500

(some 4,500 armed)

Foreign Forces

UN (KFOR) about 8,000 providing logistic spt for tps deployed in the Yugoslav province of Kosovo

---

Malta				**M**

	1997	1998	1999	2000
GDP	ML1.3bn	ML1.3bn		
	($3.3bn)	($3.4bn)		
per capita	$8,300	$8,900		
Growth	4.8%	4.1%		
Inflation	3.1%	2.4%		
Debt	$978m	$990m		
Def exp	ML11.8m	ML11.5m		
	($31m)	($30m)		
Def bdgt		ML11.5m	ML12.0m	
		($30m)	($29m)	
FMA (US)	$0.1m	$0.1m	$0.1m	$0.1m
$1 = lira	0.39	0.39	0.41	
Population				377,000
Age	*13–17*	*18–22*	*23–32*	
Men	14,000	14,000	26,000	
Women	14,000	14,000	25,000	

Total Armed Forces

ACTIVE 1,900

Armed Forces of Malta 1,900

Comd HQ, spt tps
No. 1 Regt (inf bn): 3 rifle, 1 spt coy
No. 2 Regt (composite regt)
 1 air wg (76) with **ac** 4 O-1 *Bird Dog*, 2 BN-2B *Islander*
 hel 2 SA-316A, 3 SA-316B, 2 NH-369M Hughes, 1
 AB-206A, 4 AB-47G2
 1 maritime sqn (210) with 3 ex-GDR *Kondor* 1 PCC,
 4 PCI, 3 harbour craft, 1 LCVP
 1 AD bty; **14.5mm**: 50 ZPU-4; **40mm**: 40 Bofors
No. 3 Regt (Depot Regt): 1 engr sqn, 1 workshop, 1
 ordnance, 1 airport coy

Foreign Forces

ITALY 47 **Air Force** 2 AB-212 **hel**

Moldova   Mol

	1997	1998	1999	2000
GDP	L9.5bn	L9.9bn		
	($1.2bn)	($1.2bn)		
per capita	$3,600	$3,500		
Growth	1.3%	-5.0%		
Inflation	11.0%	7.7%		
Debt	$969m	$1,212m		
Def exp[a]	L245m	L280m		
	($53m)	($52m)		
Def bdgt		L96m	L74m	
		($20m)	($7m)	
FMA (US)	$0.3m	$0.5m	$0.5m	$0.6m
$1=leu	4.62	5.37	11.11	

[a] Incl exp on paramilitary forces

Population			4,414,000

(Moldovan/Romanian 65%, Ukrainian 14%, Russian
13%, Gaguaz 4%, Bulgarian 2%, Jewish <1.5%)

Age	13–17	18–22	23–32
Men	202,000	184,000	298,000
Women	187,000	180,000	299,000

Total Armed Forces

ACTIVE 10,650
(incl ε5,200 conscripts) *Terms of service* up to 18 months

RESERVES some 66,000

Army 9,600

(incl ε5,200 conscripts)

3 MR bde • 1 arty bde • 1 gd, 1 SF, 1 indep engr bn
EQUIPMENT
 AIFV 54 BMD-1
 APC 11 BTR-80, 11 BTR-D, 2 BTR-60PB, 131 TAB-71,
 plus 135 'look-alikes'
 TOTAL ARTY 153
 TOWED ARTY 122mm: 17 M-30; **152mm**: 32 D-20,
 21 2A36
 COMBINED GUN/MOR 120mm: 9 2S9
 MRL 220mm: 14 9P140 *Uragan*
 MOR 82mm: 54; **120mm**: 60 M-120
 ATGW 70 AT-4 *Spigot*, 19 AT-5 *Spandral*, 27 AT-6
 Spiral
 RCL 73mm: SPG-9
 ATK GUNS 100mm: 36 MT-12
 AD GUNS 23mm: 30 ZU-23; **57mm**: 12 S-60
 SURV GS-13 (arty), 1 L219/200 PARK-1 (arty), *Long
 Trough* ((SNAR-1) arty), *Pork Trough* ((SNAR-2/-6)
 veh, arty), *Small Fred/Small Yawn* (veh, arty), *Big
 Fred* ((SNAR-10) veh, arty)

Air Force 1,050

(incl Defence Aviation)
TPT 1 mixed sqn **ac** 3 An-72, 1 Tu-134, (6 MiG-29 in
store) **hel** 8 Mi-8
SAM 1 bde with 25 SA-3/-5

Paramilitary 3,400

INTERNAL TROOPS (Ministry of Interior) 2,500
OPON (Ministry of Interior) 900 (riot police)

Opposition

DNIESTR 5,000 (up to 10,000 reported)
incl Republican Guard (Dniestr bn), Delta bn, ε1,000
Cossacks

Foreign Forces

RUSSIA 2,600: 1 op gp
PEACEKEEPING: 2 inf bn (-) **Russia** (500) 3 inf bn

Romania   R

	1997	1998	1999	2000
GDP	lei 250tr	lei 339tr		
	($35bn)	($38bn)		
per capita	$4,600	$4,500		
Growth	-6.6%	-5.5%		
Inflation	155%	59%		
Debt	$10.4bn	$9.1bn		
Def exp	lei 5.7tr	lei 7.9tr		
	($793m)	($887m)		

contd	1997	1998	1999	2000
Def bdgt		lei 8.0tr	lei 9.6tr	
		($900m)	($607m)	
FMA (US)	$1.1m	$1.0m	$1.3m	$1.2m
$1 =lei	7,168	8,876	15,835	
Population		22,732,000 (Hungarian 9%)		
Age	*13–17*	*18–22*	*23–32*	
Men	874,000	924,000	1,835,000	
Women	843,000	890,000	1,773,000	

Total Armed Forces

ACTIVE 207,000

(incl 108,600 conscripts, and 36,700 in centrally controlled units)
Terms of service All services 12 months

RESERVES 470,000

Army 400,000 **Navy** 30,000 **Air Force** 40,000

Army 106,000

(incl 71,000 conscripts)
3 Army HQ, 7 Corps HQ each with 2–3 mech 1 tk, 1 mtn, 1 arty, 1 ATK bde
Army tps: 1 arty, 1 ATK, 1 SAM bde, 1 engr regt
Defence Staff tps: 2 AB (Air Force), 1 gd bde
Land Force tps: 1 SAM, 2 engr regt
Determining the manning state of units is difficult. The following is based on the latest available information: one-third at 100%, one-third at 50–70%, one-third at 10–20%
EQUIPMENT
  MBT 1,253: 821 T-55, 30 T-72, 314 TR-85, 88 TR-580
  ASLT GUN 84 SU-100
  RECCE 121 BRDM-2, 49 ABC-M
  AIFV 177 MLI-84
  APC 1,619: 167 TAB-77, 384 TABC-79, 920 TAB-71, 88 MLVM, 60 TAB ZIMBRU, plus 1,015 'look-alikes'
  TOTAL ARTY 1,276
    TOWED 748: **122mm**: 204 M-1938 (M-30) (A-19); **130mm**: 70 Gun 82; **150mm**: 12 Skoda (Model 1934); **152mm**: 114 Gun-how 85, 294 Model 81, 54 M-1937 (ML-20)
    SP 48: **122mm**: 6 2S1, 42 Model 89
    MRL 122mm: 148 APR-40
    MOR 120mm: 332 M-1982
  SSM launchers: 9 FROG
  ATGW 174 AT-3 *Sagger* (incl BRDM-2), 54 AT-5 *Spandrel*
  ATK GUNS 57mm: M-1943; **85mm**: D-44; **100mm**: 877 Gun 77, 75 Gun 75
  AD GUNS 1,093: **30mm**; **37mm**; **57mm**; **85mm**; **100mm**
  SAM 62 SA-6/-7/-8
  SURV GS-13 (arty), 1 L219/200 PARK-1 (arty), *Long*

Trough ((SNAR-1) arty), *Pork Trough* ((SNAR-2/-6) veh, arty), *Small Fred/Small Yawn* (veh, arty), *Big Fred* ((SNAR-10) veh, arty)
  UAV 6 *Shadow-600*

Navy 20,800

(incl 12,600 conscripts; incl 10,200 Naval Inf and Coastal Defence)
Navy HQ with 1 Naval fleet, 1 Danube flotilla, 1 Naval inf corps
Naval fleet with 1 missile, torpedo, minelayer, minesweeper bde
Danube flotilla with 1 riverine naval and 1 river bde
BASES Coastal Mangalia, Constanta **Danube** Braila, Giurgiu, Tulcea, Galati
SUBMARINES 1
SSK 1 Sov Kilo with 533mm TT
PRINCIPAL SURFACE COMBATANTS 7
DESTROYERS 1
  DDG 1 *Muntena* with 4 x 2 SS-N-2C *Styx* SSM, plus SA-N-5 *Grail* SAM, 2 IAR-316 hel, 2 x 3 533mm TT, RBU 6000
FRIGATES 6
  FF 6
  4 *Tetal* 1 with 2 ASW RL, 4 ASTT
  2 *Tetal* II with 2 ASW RL, 4 ASTT, plus 1 SA-316 hel
PATROL AND COASTAL COMBATANTS 68
CORVETTES 3 *Zborul* (Sov *Tarantul* I) with 2 x 2 SS-N-2C *Styx* SSM, 1 76mm gun
MISSILE CRAFT 3 Sov *Osa* I PFM with 4 SS-N-2A *Styx* SSM
TORPEDO CRAFT 31
  12 *Epitrop* PFT with 4 533mm TT
  19 PRC *Huchuan* PHT with 2 533mm TT
PATROL CRAFT 31
  OFFSHORE 4 *Democratia* (GDR M-40) PCO
  RIVERINE 27
  some 6 *Brutar* with 1 100mm gun, 1 122mm RL, 3 *Kogalniceanu* with 2 x 100mm gun, 18 *VB 76* PCI
MINE WARFARE 37
MINELAYERS 2 *Cosar*, capacity 100 mines
MINE COUNTERMEASURES 35
  4 *Musca* MSC, 6 T-301 MSI, 25 VD141 MSI
SUPPORT AND MISCELLANEOUS 11
  2 *Constanta* log spt with 1 *Alouette* hel, 3 AOT, 2 AGOR, 1 trg, 2 AT, 1 tkr
HELICOPTERS 7
  3 1AR-316, 4 Mi-14 PL

NAVAL INFANTRY (10,200)
1 Corps HQ
2 mech, 1 mot inf, 1 arty bde, 1 ATK, 1 marine bn
EQUIPMENT
  MBT 120 TR-580
  APC 208: 172 TAB-71, 36 TABC-79 plus 101 'look-alikes'

TOTAL ARTY 138
   TOWED 90: **122mm**: 54 M-1938 (M-30); **152mm**:
   36 Model 81
   MRL **122mm**: 12 APR-40
   MOR **120mm**: 36 Model 1982
   ATK GUNS **100mm**: 57 Gun 77

COASTAL DEFENCE

4 coastal arty bty with 32 **130mm**

Air Force 43,500

(incl 5,500 AB; 25,000 conscripts); 367 cbt ac, 16 attack
hel
Flying hours 40
Air Force comd: 2 Air and Air Defence Corps, each
   with 2 Air Flotilla, 6-7 air bases, 4-6 air defence
   artillery bde or rgt, 2 para bde
FGA 2 regt with 73 IAR-93
FTR 6 regt with 215 MiG-21, 40 MiG-23, 18 MiG-29
RECCE 1 sqn with 12* Il-28 (recce/ECM), 9* MiG-21
TPT ac 6 An-24, 11 An-26, 2 Boeing 707, 4 C-130B **hel** 5
   IAR-330, 9 Mi-8, 4 SA-365
SURVEY 3 An-30
HELICOPTERS
   ATTACK 16 IAR 316A
   CBT SPT 74 IAR-330, 88 IAR-316, 15 Mi-8, 2 Mi-17
TRG ac 45 L-29, 32 L-39, 14 IAR-99, 36 IAR-823, 23
   Yak-52
AAM AA-2 *Atoll*, AA-3 *Anab*, AA-7 *Apex*, AA-11 *Archer*
ASM AS-7 *Kerry*
AD 2 div bde
   20 SAM sites with 120 SA-2, SA-3 *Strella*

Forces Abroad

UN AND PEACEKEEPING
ALBANIA (AFOR): some **BOSNIA** (SFOR II): 200: 1
engr bn **IRAQ/KUWAIT** (UNIKOM): 5 obs

Paramilitary 75,900

BORDER GUARDS (Ministry of Interior) 22,900
(incl conscripts) 6 bde, 7 naval gp
   33 TAB-71 APC, 18 SU-100 aslt gun, 12 M-1931/37
   (A19) **122mm** how, 18 M-38 **120mm** mor, 7 PRC
   Shanghai II PFI
GENDARMERIE (Ministry of Interior) 53,000

Slovakia   Slvk

	1997	1998	1999	2000
GDP	Ks654bn	Ks717bn		
	($19.5bn)	($20.4bn)		
per capita	$7,100	$7,600		
Growth	6.5%	4.4%		

contd	1997	1998	1999	2000
Inflation	6.1%	6.7%		
Debt	$10.7bn	$12.0bn		
Def exp	Ks13.9bn	Ks14.6bn		
	($414m)	($415m)		
Def bdgt		Ks14.6bn	Ks13.8bn	
		($416m)	($311m)	
FMA (US)	$0.6m	$0.6m	$0.6m	$0.7m
$=koruna	33.6	35.2	44.4	
Population				5,280,000

(Hungarian 11%, Romany ε5%, Czech 1%)

Age	13–17	18–22	23–32
Men	225,000	234,000	415,000
Women	217,000	227,000	405,000

Total Armed Forces

ACTIVE 44,880
(incl 13,600 conscripts; 2,180 centrally controlled staffs,
6,900 log and spt)
Terms of service 12 months

RESERVES ε20,000 on mob
National Guard Force

Army 23,800

(incl 13,600 conscripts)
2 Corps HQ
3 tk bde (each 3 tk, 1 mech, 1 recce, 1 arty bn)
3 mech inf bde (each 3 mech inf, 1 tk, 1 recce, 1 arty bn)

RESERVES
National Guard Force 6 bde plus 32 indep coy
EQUIPMENT
   MBT 478 (103 in store): 272 T-72M, 206 T-55
   RECCE 129 BRDM, 90 OT-65, 72 BPVZ
   AIFV 383 BMP-1, 93 BMP-2
   APC 207 OT-90
   TOTAL ARTY 383 (68 in store)
      TOWED 122mm: 76 D-30
      SP 191: **122mm**: 49 2S1; **152mm**: 134 *Dana* (M-77);
      155mm: 8 *Zuzana* 2000
      MRL 122mm: 87 RM-70
      MOR 120mm: 29 M-1982
   SSM 9 FROG-7, SS-21, SS-23, *Scud*
   ATGW 538 (incl BMP-1/-2 and BRDM mounted):
      AT-3 *Sagger*, AT-5 *Spandrel*
   AD GUNS ε200: **30mm**: M-53/-59, *Strop* SP; **57mm**:
      S-60
   SAM SA-7, ε48 SA-9/-13
   SURV GS-13 (veh), *Long Trough* (SNAR-1), *Pork
      Trough* ((SNAR-2/-6) arty), *Small Fred/Small Yawn*
      (veh, arty), *Big Fred* ((SNAR-10) veh, arty)

Air Force 12,000

102 cbt ac, 19 attack hel
Flying hours 45
FGA 20 Su-22, 12 Su-25
FTR 38 MiG-21, 24 MiG-29
RECCE 8* MiG-21 RF
TPT 1 An-12, 2 An-24, 2 An-26, 4 L410M
TRG 14 L-29, 20 L-39
ATTACK HEL 19 Mi-24
ASLT TPT 13 Mi-2, 7 Mi-8, 17 Mi-17
AAM AA-2 *Atoll*, AA-7 *Apex*, AA-8 *Aphid*, AA-10
 Alamo, AA-11 *Archer*
AD SA-2, SA-3, SA-6, SA-10B

Forces Abroad

UN AND PEACEKEEPING

ALBANIA (AFOR): some **MIDDLE EAST** (UNTSO):
2 obs **SYRIA** (UNDOF): 35

Paramilitary 2,600

INTERNAL SECURITY FORCES 1,400

CIVIL DEFENCE TROOPS 1,200

Slovenia				**Slvn**
	1997	**1998**	**1999**	**2000**
GDP	t2.9tr	t3.6tr		
	($18.2bn)	($21.8bn)		
per capita	$10,200	$10,800		
Growth	3.8%	3.9%		
Inflation	9.1%	6.5%		
Debt	$4.3bn	$4.9bn		
Def exp	t53bn	t61bn		
	($329m)	($367m)		
Def bdgt		t41.4bn	t67bn	
		($241m)	($347m)	
FMA (US)	$0.4m	$0.6m	$0.7m	$0.7m
$1=tolar	160	166	192	
Population				2,017,000
(Croat 3%, Serb 2%, Muslim 1%)				
Age	*13–17*	*18–22*		*23–32*
Men	70,000	75,000		148,000
Women	66,000	71,000		145,000

Total Armed Forces

ACTIVE 9,550

(incl 4,200 conscripts) *Terms of service* 7 months

RESERVES 61,000

Army (incl 300 maritime)

Army 9,550

(incl 4,200 conscripts)
7 Mil Regions, 27 Mil Districts • 7 inf bde (each 1
active, 3 reserve inf bn) • 1 SF 'bde' • 1 SAM 'bde' (bn)
• 2 indep mech bn • 1 avn 'bde' • 1 arty bn

RESERVES

2 indep mech, 1 arty, 1 coast def, 1 ATK bn

EQUIPMENT

 MBT 44 M-84, 46 T-55, 6 T-34
 RECCE 16 BRDM-2
 AIFV 52 M-80
 APC 29 *Valuk* (*Pandur* – being delivered)
 TOWED ARTY 105mm: 18 M-2; **155mm:** 18 Il
 SP ARTY 122mm: 8 2S1
 MRL 128mm: 56 M-71 (single tube), 4 M-63
 MOR 120mm: 120 M-52
 ATGW AT-3 *Sagger* (incl 12 BOV-1SP)

MARITIME ELEMENT (100)

(effectively police) (plus 300 reserve)
BASE Koper
1 PCI

AIR ELEMENT (120)

8 armed hel
AC 3 PC-9, 3 *Zlin*-242, 1 LET L-410, 3 UTVA-75
HEL 1 AB-109, 3 B-206, 8* B-412
SAM 9 SA-9
AD GUNS 20mm: 9 SP; **30mm:** 9 SP; **57mm:** 21 SP

Forces Abroad

UN AND PEACEKEEPING

CYPRUS (UNFICYP): 15

Paramilitary 4,500

POLICE 4,500

armed (plus 5,000 reserve) **hel** 2 AB-206 *Jet Ranger*, 1
 AB-109A, 1 AB-212, 1 AB-412

Sweden				**Swe**
	1997	**1998**	**1999**	**2000**
GDP	Skr1.7tr	Skr1.8tr		
	($218bn)	($227bn)		
per capita	$20,700	$21,700		
Growth	1.8%	2.9%		
Inflation	1.0%	0.0%		
Publ Debt	77.2%	75.5%		
Def exp	Skr41.8bn	Skr44.9bn		
	($5.5bn)	($5.6bn)		
Def bdgt		Skr38.1bn	Skr38.7bn	Skr39.6bn
		($4.8bn)	($4.5bn)	($4.6bn)
$1=kronor	7.63	7.95	8.56	

Population			8,915,000
Age	*13–17*	*18–22*	*23–32*
Men	265,000	265,000	607,000
Women	250,000	251,000	578,000

Total Armed Forces

ACTIVE 53,100

(incl 35,600 conscripts and active reservists)
Terms of service **Army, Navy** 7–15 months **Air Force** 8–12 months

RESERVES[a] 570,000

(obligation to age 47) **Army** (incl Local Defence and Home Guard) 450,000 **Navy** 50,000 **Air Force** 70,000

[a] About 48,000 reservists carry out refresher trg each year; length of trg depends on rank (officers up to 31 days, NCO and specialists, 24 days, others 17 days). Commitment is five exercises during reserve service period, plus mob call-outs

Army 35,100

(incl 24,200 conscripts and active reservists)
3 joint (tri-service) comd each with: Army div and def districts, Naval Comd (2 in Central Joint Comd)
Air Comd, logistics regt
No active units (as defined by Vienna Document)
3 div with total of 6 mech, 4 inf, 3 arctic bde, 3 arty regt HQ, 12 arty bn
15 def districts

EQUIPMENT
- **MBT** 60 *Centurion*, 239 Strv-103B (in store), 160 Strv-121 (*Leopard* 2), 78 Strv-122 (*Leopard* 2 (S))
- **LT TK** 211 Ikv-91
- **AIFV** 647 Pbv-302, 202 Strf-9040, 361 Pbv-501 (BMP-1)
- **APC** 550 Pbv 401A (MT-LB), 96 *Pskbil* M/42 (plus 323 ACV 'look-a-likes')
- **TOWED ARTY** 105mm: 127 m/40; 155mm: 206 FH-77A, 168 Type F
- **SP ARTY** 155mm: 24 BK-1C
- **MOR** 81mm: 160; 120mm: 525
- **ATGW** 55 TOW (Pvrbv 551 SP), RB-55, RB-56 *Bill*
- **RL** 84mm: AT-4
- **RCL** 84mm: *Carl Gustav*; 90mm: PV-1110
- **AD GUNS** 40mm: 600
- **SAM** RBS-70 (incl Lvrbv SP), RB-77 (I HAWK), RBS-90
- **SURV** *Green Archer* (mor)
- **AC** 1 C-212
- **HEL** see under Air Force 'Armed Forces Helicopter Wing'

Navy 9,200

(incl 1,100 Coastal Defence, 320 Naval Air, 4,200 conscripts and 2,500 reserve officers)
BASES Muskö, Karlskrona, Härnösand, Göteborg (spt only)

SUBMARINES 9
SSK 9
- 3 *Gotland* with 4 533mm TT, TP-613 and TP-431/451 (AIP powered)
- 4 *Västergötland* with 6 533mm TT, TP-613 and TP-431/451
- 2 *Näcken* with 6 533mm TT, TP-613 and TP-421

PATROL AND COASTAL COMBATANTS 24
MISSILE CRAFT 24 PFM
- 4 *Göteborg* with 4 x 2 RBS-15 SSM; 4 400mm TT, 4 ASW mor
- 2 *Stockholm* with 4 x 2 RBS-15 SSM; 2 Type 613 533mm, 4 400mm TT, 4 ASW mor
- 4 *Hugin* with 6 RBS-12 *Penguin* SSM
- 8 *Kaparen* with 6 RBS-12 *Penguin* SSM
- 6 *Norrköping* with 4 x 2 RBS-15 SSM, 2-6 Type 613 533mm TT

MINE WARFARE 25
MINELAYERS 2
- 1 *Carlskrona* (200 mines) trg, 1 *Visborg* (200 mines)
  (Mines can be laid by all submarine classes)
MINE COUNTERMEASURES 23
- 4 *Styrsö* MCMV, 1 *Utö* MCMV spt, 1 *Skredsvic* MCM/diver support, 7 *Landsort* MCMV, 2 *Gassten* MSO, 1 *Vicksten* MSO, 3 *Gilloga* MSC, *4 *Hisingen* diver support

SUPPORT AND MISCELLANEOUS 28
- 1 AGI, 1 ASR/ARS, 2 AGHS, 7 icebreakers, 16 AT, 1 SES PCI (trials)

COASTAL DEFENCE (1,100)
2 mobile coastal arty bde: 5 naval bde, 6 amph, 3 mobile arty (**120mm**), 12 specialist protection (incl inf, static arty (**75mm, 105mm, 120mm**), SSM and mor units)

EQUIPMENT
- **APC** 5 *Piranha*
- **GUNS** 40mm, incl L/70 AA; 75mm, 105mm, 120mm 24 CD-80 *Karin* (mobile); 120mm *Ersta* (static)
- **MOR** 81mm, 120mm: 70
- **SSM** 90 RBS-17 *Hellfire*, 6 RBS-15KA
- **SAM** RBS-70
- **MINELAYERS** 5 inshore
- **PATROL CRAFT** 12 PCI
- **AMPH** 16 LCM, 52 LCU, 123 LCA

Air Force 8,800

(incl 3,000 conscripts and 1,700 active reservists); 253 cbt ac, no armed hel

Flying hours 110–140

3 Air Comd

FGA/RECCE 2 sqn with 36 SAAB AJS-37/AJSH-37/
AJSF-37, 1 (OCU) with 14 SAAB SK-37

MULTI-ROLE (FTR/FGA/RECCE) 2 sqn with 70
SAAB JAS-39 (third sqn forming 1999)

FTR 8 sqn with 133 SAAB JA-37

SIGINT 2 S-102B *Korpen* (*Gulfstream* IV)

AEW 4 S-100B *Argus* (SAAB-340B)

TPT 1 sqn with 8 C-130, 3 *King Air* 200, 1 *Metro* III, 13
SK-60D/E, 1 Tp-100A (SAAB 340B) (VIP), 1 Tp-
102A (*Gulfstream* IV) (VIP)

TRG 122 Sk-60, 38 SK-61 (*Bulldog*)

AAM RB-71 (*Skyflash*), RB-74 AIM 9L (*Sidewinder*),
AIM 120 (AMRAAM)

ASM RB-15F, RB-75 (*Maverick*), BK-39

AD semi-automatic control and surv system, *Stric*,
coordinates all AD components. *Stric* will replace
from 1997 and will be fully operational by 2000

ARMED FORCES HELICOPTER WING
(1,000 personnel from all three services)

HEL 15 Hkp-3c tpt/SAR, 14 Hkp-4 ASW/tpt/SAR, 25
Hkp-5b (*Hughes* 300c) trg, 19 Hkp-6a (Bell-206) utl,
10 Hkp-6b, 20 Hkp-9a, 12 Hkp-10 (*Super Puma*)
SAR, 5 Hkp-11 SAR, 1 C-212 ASW, MP

Forces Abroad

UN AND PEACEKEEPING

BOSNIA (SFOR II): 510 **CROATIA** (UNMOP): 1 obs.
(SFOR): 1 **GEORGIA** (UNOMIG): 5 obs **INDIA/
PAKISTAN** (UNMOGIP): 8 obs **IRAQ/KUWAIT**
(UNIKOM): 5 obs **MIDDLE EAST** (UNTSO): 11 obs
ROK (NNSC): 5 staff

Paramilitary 600

COAST GUARD 600

1 *Gotland* PCO and 1 KBV-171 PCC (fishery protection), some 65 PCI

AIR ARM 2 C-212 MR

CIVIL DEFENCE shelters for 6,300,000

All between ages 16–25 liable for civil defence duty

VOLUNTARY AUXILIARY ORGANISATIONS some
35,000

Switzerland CH

	1997	1998	1999	2000
GDP	fr372bn	fr383bn		
	($256bn)	($265bn)		
per capita	$27,500	$28,600		
Growth	1.8%	2.1%		
Inflation	0.5%	-0.6%		
Publ Debt	48.0%	48.0%		

contd	1997	1998	1999	2000
Def exp	fr5.6bn	fr5.3bn		
	($3.8bn)	($3.6bn)		
Def bdgt		fr5.3bn	fr5.0bn	fr4.8bn
		($3.6bn)	($3.2bn)	($3.1bn)
$1=franc	1.45	1.45	1.58	
Population				7,080,000
Age	*13–17*	*18–22*		*23–32*
Men	207,000	210,000		554,000
Women	195,000	204,000		560,000

Total Armed Forces

ACTIVE about 3,470

plus recruits (2 intakes in 1999 (total ε24,200) each for 15
weeks only)

Terms of service 15 weeks compulsory recruit trg at age
19–20, followed by 10 refresher trg courses of 3 weeks
over a 22-year period between ages 20–42. Some
196,400 attended trg in 1998

RESERVES 384,900

Army 352,860 (to be mobilised)

Armed Forces Comd (All units non-active/Reserve
status)

Comd tps: 2 armd bde, 2 inf, 1 arty, 1 airport, 2 engr regt

3 fd Army Corps, each 2 fd div (3 inf, 1 arty regt), 1
armd bde, 1 arty, 1 engr, 1 cyclist, 1 fortress regt, 1
territorial div (5/6 regt)

1 mtn Army corps with 3 mtn div (2 mtn inf, 1 arty
regt), 3 fortress bde (each 1 mtn inf regt), 2 mtn inf, 2
fortress, 1 engr regt, 1 territorial div (6 regt), 2
territorial bde (1 regt)

EQUIPMENT

MBT 769 (incl 27 in store): 186 Pz-68, 186 Pz-68/88,
370 Pz-87 (*Leopard* 2)

RECCE 154 *Eagle*

AIFV 513 (incl 6 in store): 192 M-63/73, 315 M-63/
89 (all M-113 with **20mm**)

APC 836 M-63/73 (M-113) incl variants, 186 *Piranha*

TOTAL ARTY 796 (incl 22 in store)

　TOWED 105mm: 216 Model-46/91

　SP 155mm: 558 PzHb 66/74/-74/-79/-88
　(M-109U)

MOR 81mm: 1,469 M-33, M-72; **120mm:** 534: 402 M-
87, 132 M-64 (M-113)

ATGW 3,012 *Dragon*, 303 TOW-2 SP (MOWAG)
Piranha

RL 13,484 incl: **60mm:** *Panzerfaust*; **83mm:** M-80

SAM some *Stinger*

HEL 60 *Alouette* III

MARINE

10 *Aquarius* patrol boats

Air Force 32,024 (to be mobilised)

(incl AD units, mil airfield guard units); 171 cbt ac, no armed hel
1 Air Force bde, 1 AAA bde, 1 Air-Base bde and 1 Comd-and-Control bde
Flying hours: 150–200; reserves 50–70
FTR 9 sqn
  6 with 89 *Tiger* II/F-5E, 12 *Tiger* II/F-5F
  1 with 29 *Mirage* IIIS, 4 -III DS
  2 with 14 F/A-18 C and 7 F/A-18D
RECCE 3 sqn with 16* *Mirage* IIIRS 2
TPT 1 sqn with 16 PC-6, 1 *Learjet* 35A, 2 Do-27, 1 *Falcon*-50
HEL 3 sqn with 15 AS-332 M-1 (*Super Puma*), 12 SA-316 (*Alouette* III)
TRG 19 *Hawk* Mk 66, 38 PC-7, 11 PC-9 (tgt towing)
UAV *Ranger*/ADS 95 (4 to be deployed in 1999)
AAM AIM-9 *Sidewinder*, AIM-26 *Falcon*, AIM-120 AMRAAM

AIR DEFENCE

1 SAM regt with 3 bn each with 2 or 3 bty; 59 B/L-84 (*Rapier*)
7 AD Regt (each with 2 or 3 bn; each bn of 3 bty; 35mm AD guns, Skyguard fire control radar)

Forces Abroad

UN AND PEACEKEEPING

CROATIA (UNMOP): 1 obs **GEORGIA** (UNOMIG): 4 obs **KOREA** (NNSC): 5 Staff **MIDDLE EAST** (UNTSO): 7 obs

Paramilitary

CIVIL DEFENCE 295,000 (not part of Armed Forces)

Ukraine   Ukr

	1997	1998	1999	2000
GDP	h92bn	h118bn		
	($50bn)	($48bn)		
per capita	$4,400	$4,500		
Growth	-3.2%	-2.0%		
Inflation	15.9%	10.6%		
Debt	$10.4bn	$11.5bn		
Def exp[a]	h2.5bn	h3.4bn		
	($1.3bn)	($1.4bn)		
Def bdgt		h1.7bn	h1.7bn	
		($700m)	($429m)	
FMA[b] (US)	$1.0m	$1.3m	$2.2m	$1.3m
$1=hryvnia	1.86	2.45	3.97	

[a] Incl exp on paramilitary forces
[b] Excl US Cooperative Threat Reduction programme: **1992–**

96 $395m, of which $171m spent by Sept 1996. Programme continues through 2000

Population			49,980,000
(Russian 22%, Polish ε4%, Jewish 1%)			
Age	*13–17*	*18–22*	*23–32*
Men	1,894,000	1,860,000	3,557,000
Women	1,828,000	1,816,000	3,534,000

Total Armed Forces

ACTIVE ε311,400
(excl Strategic Nuclear Forces and Black Sea Fleet; incl 43,500 in central staffs and units not covered below)
Terms of service **Army**, **Air Force** 18 months **Navy** 2 years

RESERVES some 1,000,000
mil service within 5 years

Strategic Nuclear Forces

(to be eliminated under START)
ICBM 44 SS-24 *Scalpel* (RS-22); silo-based (without warheads)
BBR 43
  20 Tu-95H16
  5 Tu-95H6 (with AS-15 ALCM)
  18 Tu-160 (with AS-15 ALCM) (START accountable – 8 to be returned to Russia in late 1999)

Ground Forces 154,900

3 Op Comd (North, South, West)
MoD tps: 1 air mobile bde, 1 SSM div (3 *Scud* bde), 1 arty (trg), 2 engr bde
WESTERN OP COMD
Comd tps 1 arty div (2 arty, 1 MRL bde), 1 air mobile, 1 *Spetsnaz* bde, 2 avn gp
2 Corps 1 with 2 mech div, 2 mech, 1 SSM, 1 arty bde, 1 MRL, 1 ATK regt
  1 with 2 mech div, 1 mech, 1 SSM, 1 arty bde, 1 MRL, 1 ATK regt
SOUTHERN OP COMD
Comd tps 1 mech, 1 air mobile, 1 arty div (1 arty, 1 MRL, 1 ATK bde), 1 air mobile, 1 SSM bde, 1 avn gp
2 Corps 1 with 1 tank, 2 mech div, 2 arty bde, 1 MRL regt
  1 with 2 mech, 1 arty, 1 *Spetsnaz* bde, 1 MRL, 1 ATK regt
NORTHERN OP COMD
Comd tps 1 mech, 1 trg div (include 1 active tank regt), 1 tank, 1 SSM bde
1 Corps with 1 tank, 1 mech, 1 trg div, 1 arty, 1 SSM bde, 1 MRL, 1 ATK regt, 2 avn gp
EQUIPMENT
  MBT 4,014 (933 in store): 154 T-55, 1 T-62, 2,281 T-64, 1,305 T-72, 273 T-80

RECCE some 1,500

AIFV 3,079 (321 in store): 1,010 BMP-1, 458 BRM-1K, 1,468 BMP-2, 5 BMP-3, 61 BMD-1, 78 BMD-2

APC 1,823 (238 in store): 203 BTR-60, 1,105 BTR-70, 473 BTR-80, 42 BTR-D; plus 2,000 MT-LB, 4,700 'look-alikes'

TOTAL ARTY 3,739 (544 in store)

  TOWED 1,139: **122mm**: 435 D-30, 3 M-30; **152mm**: 219 D-20, 8 ML-20, 185 2A65, 289 2A36

  SP 1,307: **122mm**: 642 2S1; **152mm**: 501 2S3, 24 2S5, 40 2S19, **203mm**: 100 2S7

  COMBINED GUN/MOR 120mm: 62 2S9, 2 2B16

  MRL 625: **122mm**: 364 BM-21, 24 9P138; **132mm**: 4 BM-13; **220mm**: 139 9P140; **300mm**: 94 9A52

  MOR 604: **120mm**: 346 2S12, 257 PM-38; **160mm**: 1 M-160

SSM 132 Scud, 140 FROG/SS-21

ATGW AT-4 Spigot, AT-5 Spandrel, AT-6 Spiral

SAM SA-4/-6/-8/-11/-12A/-15

ATTACK HEL 236 Mi-24

SPT HEL 4 Mi-2, 31 Mi-6, 162 Mi-8, 17 Mi-26

SURV SNAR-10 (Big Fred), Small Fred (arty)

Navy† ε13,000

(incl nearly 2,500 Naval Aviation, ε3,000 Naval Infantry, 2,000 conscripts)

On 31 May 1997, Russian President Yeltsin and Ukrainian President Kuchma signed an inter-governmental agreement on the status and terms of the Black Sea Fleet's deployment on the territory of Ukraine and parameters for the Fleet's division. The Russian Fleet will lease bases in Sevastopol for the next 20 years. It is based at Sevastopol and Karantinnaya Bays and jointly with Ukrainian warships at Streletskaya Bay. The overall serviceability of the Fleet is very low

BASES Sevastopol, Donuzlav, Odessa, Kerch, Ochakov, Chernomorskoye (Balaklava, Nikolaev construction and repair yards)

SUBMARINES 1

SSK 1 Foxtrot (Type 641) (non-op)

PRINCIPAL SURFACE COMBATANTS 8

CRUISERS 1

CG 1 Ukraina

FRIGATES 7

FFG 3

  2 Krivak 1 with 4 SS-N-14 Silex SSM/ASW, 2 SA-N-4 Gecko SAM, 4 76mm gun, 8 533mm TT

  1 Krivak 2 with 4 SS-N-14 Silex SSM, 2 100mm gun, 8 533mm TT

FF 4

  1 Krivak 3 with 2 SA-N-4 Gecko SAM, 1 100mm gun, 8 533mm TT, 1 KA-27 hel

  3 Grisha II/V with 2 SA-N-4 Gecko SAM, 1 76mm gun, 4 533mm TT

PATROL AND COASTAL COMBATANTS 8

  2 Pauk 1 PFT with 4 SA-N-5 Grail SAM, 1 76mm

gun, 4 406mm TT

  5 Matka PHM with 2 SS-N-2C Styx SSM, 1 76mm gun

  1 Zhuk PCI

MINE COUNTERMEASURES 5

  1 Yevgenya MHC, 2 Sonya MSC, 2 Natya MSC

AMPHIBIOUS 7

  4 Pomornik ACV with 2 SA-N-5 capacity 30 tps and crew

  1 Ropucha LST with 4 SA-N-5 SAM, 2 x 2 57mm gun, 92 mines; capacity 190 tps or 24 veh

  1 Alligator LST with 2/3 SA-N-5 SAM capacity 300 tps and 20 tk

  1 Polnocny LSM capacity 180 tps and 6 tk

SUPPORT AND MISCELLANEOUS 9

  1 Mod Kamkatka research, 2 Vytegrales AK, 1 Lama msl spt, 1 Mod Moma AGI, 1 Primore AGI, 1 Kashtan buoytender, 1 Passat AGOS, 1 Elbrus ASR

NAVAL AVIATION (2,500)

ASW 11 Be-12, 2 Ka-27E

TPT 8 An-26, 1 An-24, 5 An-12, 5 Mi-6, 1 Il-18, 1 Tu-134

MISC HEL 28 Ka-25, 42 Mi-14 plus 14 Su-17 (non-op)

NAVAL INFANTRY (1,250)

2 inf bn

Air Force 100,000

some 521 cbt ac (plus 542 in store MiG-21, MiG-23, MiG-25, MiG-27, MiG-29, Su-24, Su-25, Su-27, Mi-6/8, Tu-22M, Il-76, L-39, Yak-28), no attack hel

3 air corps

BBR 1 div HQ, 2 regt with 25 Tu-22M (others in store)

FGA/BBR 2 div HQ, 5 regt (1 trg) with 140 Su-24

FGA 2 regt with 63 Su-25

FTR 2 div, 6 regt with 30 MiG-23, 178 MiG-29, 44 Su-27

RECCE 2 regt (1 trg) with 14* Tu-22, 5* Su-17, 22* Su-24

TPT 78 Il-76, 45 An-12/An-24/An-26/An-30/Tu-134, Il-78 (tkr/tpt)

TRG 7 regt with 174 L-39

SPT HEL 3 Mi-6, 65 Mi-8

SAM 825: SA-2/-3/-5/-10/-12A

Forces Abroad

UN AND PEACEKEEPING

BOSNIA (SFOR II): 400 **CROATIA** (UNMOP): 1 obs
TAJIKISTAN (UNMOT): 2 obs

Paramilitary

MVS (Ministry of Internal Affairs) 42,000, 4 regions, internal security tps, 85 ACV, 6 ac, 8 hel

NATIONAL GUARD 26,600

4 div, 1 armd regt, 1 hel bde, 60 MBT, 500 ACV, 12

attack hel
BORDER GUARD 34,000
HQ and 3 regions, 200 ACV
MARITIME BORDER GUARD
The Maritime Border Guard is an independent
subdivision of the State Commission for Border
Guards, is not part of the Navy and is org with:
  4 cutter, 2 river bde • 1 gunship, 1 MCM sqn • 1 aux
  ship gp • 1 trg div • 3 air sqn
  PATROL AND COASTAL COMBATANTS 36
    3 *Pauk* 1 with 4 SA-N-5 SAM, 1 76mm gun, 4
      406mm TT
    3 *Muravey* PHT with 1 76mm gun, 2 406mm TT
    10 *Stenka* PFC with 4 30mm gun, 4 406mm TT
    20 *Zhuk* PCI
  AIRCRAFT
    An-24, An-26, An-72, An-8, Ka-27
COAST GUARD 14,000
3 patrol boats, 1 water jet boat, 1 ACV, 1 landing ship,
  1 OPV, 1 craft
CIVIL DEFENCE TROOPS (Ministry of Emergency
  Situations): some 9,500; 4 indep bde, 4 indep regt

Foreign Forces

Naval Inf (Russia) ε1,500

Yugoslavia, Federal Republic of (Serbia–Montenegro)   FRY

	1997	1998	1999	2000
GDP	d92bn	d106bn		
	($16bn)	($17bn)		
per capita	$5,000	$5,300		
Growth	7.4%	4.0%		
Inflation	9.0%	15.0%		
Debt	$14bn	$15bn		
Def exp	εd8.5bn	εd17bn		
	($1.5bn)	($1.6bn)		
Def bdgt		d6.6bn	d14.4bn	
		($599m)	($1.3bn)	
$1 =new dinar	5.71	10.9	11.5	

Population				ε10,600,000

Serbia ε9,900,000 (Serb 66%, Albanian 17% (90% in
Kosovo), Hungarian 4%, mainly in Vojvodina)
Montenegro ε700,000 (Montenegrin 62%, Serb 9%,
Albanian 7%)
(ε2,032,000 Serbs were living in the other Yugoslav
republics before the civil war)

Age	13–17	18–22	23–32
Men	417,000	425,000	836,000
Women	394,000	402,000	795,000

The data outlined below represents the situation
prior to the implementation of *Operation Allied Force*
on 24 March 1999. Details should therefore be
treated with caution

Total Armed Forces

ACTIVE some 108,700
(43,000 conscripts) *Terms of service* 12–15 months

RESERVES some 400,000

Army (JA) some 85,000

(37,000 conscripts)
3 Army, 7 Corps (incl 1 capital def) • 3 div HQ • 6 tk
bde • 1 gd bde (-), 1 SF bde • 4 mech bde • 1 AB bde •
8 mot inf bde (incl 1 protection) • 5 mixed arty bde • 7
AD bde • 1 SAM bde

RESERVES
  27 mot inf, 42 inf, 6 mixed arty bde
EQUIPMENT
  MBT 785 T-55, 239 M-84 (T-74; mod T-72), 181 T-34,
    65 T-72
  LT TK 40 PT-76
  RECCE 80 BRDM-2
  AIFV 568 M-80
  APC 169 M-60P, 68 BOV VP M-86
  TOWED 105mm: 265 M-56, 15 M-18, 54 M2A1;
    122mm: 90 M-38, 310 D-30; **130mm:** 276 M-46;
    152mm: 25 D-20, 52 M-84; **155mm:** 139 M-1, 6 M-
    65
  SP 122mm: 80 2S1
  MRL 107mm; 122mm: BM-21; **128mm:** 103 M-63, 64
    M-77, **262mm:** M-87 *Orkan*
  MOR 82mm: 1,100; **120mm:** 6 M-38/-39, 123 M-52,
    320 M-74, 854 M-75
  SSM 4 FROG
  ATGW 80 AT-3 *Sagger* incl SP (BOV-1, BRDM-1/2),
    AT-4 *Fagot*
  RCL 57mm: 1,550; **82mm:** 1,500 M-60PB SP; **105mm:**
    650 M-65
  ATK GUNS 1,250 incl: **90mm:** M-36B2 (incl SP), M-
    3; **100mm:** 138 T-12, MT-12
  AD GUNS 2,000: **20mm:** M-55/-75, BOV-3 SP triple;
    30mm: M-53, M-53/-59, BOV-30 SP; **57mm:** ZSU-
    57-2 SP
  SAM 60 SA-6, SA-7/-9/-13/-14/-16

Navy 7,000

(incl 3,000 conscripts and 900 Marines)
BASES Kumbor, Tivat, Bar, Novi Sad (River Comd)
(Most former Yugoslav bases are now in Croatian
hands)

SUBMARINES 5

SSK 2
1 *Sava* with 533mm TT (plus 1 non-op)
1 *Heroj* with 533mm TT
SSI 3 *Una* SSI for SF ops (non-op)

FRIGATES 4

FFG 4
2 *Kotor* with 4 SS-N-2C *Styx* SSM, 1 x 2 SA-N-4 *Gecko* SAM, 2 x 12 ASW RL, 2 x 3 ASTT
2 *Split* (Sov *Koni*) with 4 SS-N-2C *Styx* SSM, 1 x 2 SA-N-4 *Gecko* SAM, 2 x 12 ASW RL

PATROL AND COASTAL COMBATANTS 30

MISSILE CRAFT 8
5 *Rade Koncar* PFM with 2 SS-N-2B *Styx* SSM (some †)
3 *Mitar Acev* (Sov *Osa* I) PFM with 4 SS-N-2A *Styx* SSM
PATROL CRAFT 22†
PATROL, INSHORE 4 *Mirna*
PATROL, RIVERINE about 18 < (some in reserve)
MINE COUNTERMEASURES 10
2 *Vukov Klanac* MHC, 1 UK *Ham* MSI, 7 *Nestin* MSI

AMPHIBIOUS 1
1 *Silba* LCT/ML: capacity 6 tk or 300 tps, 1 x 4 SA-N-5 SAM, can lay 94 mines
plus craft:
8 Type 22 LCU
6 Type 21 LCU
4 Type 11 LCVP

SUPPORT AND MISCELLANEOUS 9
1 PO-91 *Lubin* tpt, 1 water carrier, 4 AT, 2 AK, 1 degaussing

MARINES (900)
2 mot inf 'bde' (2 regt each of 2 bn) • 1 lt inf bde (reserve) • 1 coast arty bde • 1 MP bn

Air Force 16,700

(3,000 conscripts); 238 cbt ac, 52 armed hel
2 Corps (1 AD)
FGA 4 sqn with 30 *Orao* 2, 50 *Galeb*, 9 *Super Galeb* G-4
FTR 5 sqn with 47 MiG-21F/PF/M/bis, 17 MiG-21U, 15 MiG-29
RECCE 2 sqn with some 20* *Orao*, 18* MiG-21R
ARMED HEL 44 Gazelle
ASW 1 hel sqn with 3* Mi-14, 3* Ka-25, 2* Ka-28
TPT 15 An-26, 4 CL-215 (SAR, fire-fighting), 2 *Falcon* 50 (VIP), 6 Yak-40
LIAISON ac 32 UTVA-66 **hel** 14 *Partizan*
TRG ac 16* *Super Galeb*, 16* *Orao*, 25 UTVA, 15 UTVA-75 **hel** 16 *Gazelle*
AAM AA-2 *Atoll*, AA-8 *Aphid*, AA-10 *Alamo*, AA-11 *Archer*
ASM AGM-65 *Maverick*, AS-7 *Kerry*
AD 8 SAM bn, 8 sites with 24 SA-2, 16 SA-3
15 regt AD arty

Paramilitary

MINISTRY OF INTERIOR TROOPS str n.k.
internal security; eqpt incl 150 AFV, 170 mor, 16 hel

UN and Peacekeeping

KFOR (Kosovo Peace Implementation Force): some 34,000 (to be 55,000). Tps from A, Be, Ca, Da, Fr, Ge, Gr, Hu, It, Nl, No, Pl, Por, R, RF, SF, Sp, UK, Ukr, US. Small contingents are to be provided by Arg, Bg, Ea, HKJ, Lat, L, Slvk, Slvn, Swe, UAE

MILITARY DEVELOPMENTS

Overall Trends

Russian military developments in late 1998 and in 1999 were influenced most by the profound financial crisis of August 1998, the NATO action in the Balkans and the conflict in the North Caucasus region. Economic difficulties put a brake on military reform, but the armed forces gained the necessary resources for additional exercises and improving readiness as part of Russia's domestic reaction to NATO's campaign in Yugoslavia. The overall state of operational readiness of all except the nuclear forces remains low due to lack of resources for training, maintenance and new equipment. At the same time there are more demands on the military (including the Interior Troops) in the North Caucasus region as conflict has increased around the borders of Chechnya, particularly in Daghestan. Despite the problems, a much better capability to deploy large combined-arms forces than might be expected was demonstrated in major exercises during 1999.

Military Reform

The first phase of military reform, involving personnel reductions and the reorganisation of the military districts and the armed-forces command structure, was completed by the end of 1998, according to the Russian Ministry of Defence (MOD). The next phase through to 2001 is focused on operational readiness and modernisation of equipment. In April 1999, Defence Minister Marshall Igor Sergeyev announced that the force reductions had reached 1.2 million personnel and there would be no further cuts, although some units may be enlarged within the reduced overall force level. Among those that may be strengthened are airborne forces, which have formed the backbone of Russian peacekeeping contingents abroad and for whom there is an increased demand. In 1998 the MOD discharged 109,000 officers as well as cutting many posts and streamlining and reducing infrastructure and training establishments. The reductions, however, were not accompanied by the implementation of the plans (set out in a 1996 presidential decree) for the creation of fully professional armed forces. On the contrary, in December 1998 President Boris Yeltsin signed a decree stating that the armed forces were no longer obliged to use only contract (professional) NCOs and soldiers in armed-conflict situations, but they could also call on conscripts. The decree stipulated that the plan for professional armed forces would be implemented 'once the necessary conditions (mainly economic) emerge', which makes implementation a distant prospect. The armed forces will have difficulty in maintaining personnel even at the new lower level. There are already a large number of unfilled posts and conscription is not bringing in the full numbers liable for call-up.

Restructuring the military districts was to be completed by the end of 1999. The first step was the merger of the Siberian and Trans-Baikal military districts authorised by the Chief of the General Staff, General Anatolyi Kvashnin, on 21 November 1998. The merger of the Volga and Ural Districts is the final step. From 2000 on, the military districts will be made up of Moscow, Leningrad, North Caucasus, Volga-Ural, Siberian and Far Eastern. In addition, Kaliningrad is designated a 'special region' where all land sea and air forces are under the joint Baltic Command as an operational strategic group. A similar combined-arms group has been created on the Kamchatka peninsula where the commander of the Kamchatka Flotilla runs the joint headquarters. Once the Interior Troops and other paramilitary forces complete their reorganisation in line with the Ministry of Defence (MOD) districts, joint command arrangements will be put in place to control all types of armed forces within each military district.

The transition to a four-service structure for the armed forces (Army, Navy, Air Force and Strategic Forces) has been completed. The last step was a merger between the Air and Air Defence Forces which was finalised by the end of 1998. The Army was substantially reduced from a level of 420,000 to around 348,000. The field element of the land forces is organised into 24 operational divisions of various kinds, with the remaining 13 being either training or cadre formations. By mid-1999 three divisions and four brigades in the Leningrad, Moscow, North Caucasus and Siberian Military districts, were designated 'permanent readiness units', which are defined as units manned to at least 80% of full personnel strength and with 100% of their weapons and equipment and are required to be fully trained and operationally ready. Formations not in this category may be fully equipped but with perhaps only 10–15% of their personnel. The plan is that such formations should be capable of operational readiness in 30 days. The next stage of military reform will be focused on increasing the number of 'permanent readiness' units and on the modernisation and upgrading of weapons and equipment. According to the 'State Programme on Military Construction to 2005', the armed forces plan to create up to ten 'permanent readiness' units, made up initially of one naval infantry, seven army and two air force divisions. Priority is being given to units in Moscow, Leningrad and North Caucasus Military Districts and to the Kaliningrad Special Region and the Black Sea Fleet. The fleet requires special attention mainly because the poor state of its support ships means that it cannot be sustained at sea for a reasonable length of time. Also, of the 12 submarines based in the Crimea, only one appears to be operational.

Exercise Activity

The first stage of the Russian military reform process was tested in a series of exercises in 1999. The first large-scale exercise, *Air bridge-99*, was conducted from 14–18 March. More than 100 aircraft and 12,000 personnel from Moscow and Leningrad Military Districts took part along with elements from Air Defence units, the Military Transport Aviation Command and the Air Force's 6th Army. Elements from the Baltic Operational Strategic Group also participated. The largest armed forces exercise in the last 14 years, *West-99*, took place at the end of June 1999. Four military districts (Leningrad, Moscow, North Caucasus and Volga–Ural) and three navies (Northern, Baltic and Black Sea) took part in joint manoeuvres. The Interior Troops of three military districts also participated as well as the armed elements of the Federal Security Service, the Federal Border Guard Service, the Emergency Ministry and the Federal Agency for Government Communications and Information. According to the Russian MOD, the main aim of *Airbridge-99* and *West-99* – which were first planned in 1998 – was to practice the newly established commands in the armed forces and coordination with commands of other armed organisations and agencies of the Russian Federation. In *West-99*, for the first time since the end of the Cold War, a single command controlled forces from different government departments and military districts over a large geographical area. Also for the first time, the exercises included a unified Russia–Belarussian group of forces. This group is likely to conduct more joint planning and exercises in future. Russia and Belarus are also planning to establish a unified air-defence system supported by the Baranovichi early-warning station in Belarus which is expected to become operational by the end of 1999. The recently reformed Strategic Aviation Force took part and flew missions out over the North Atlantic. According to Defence Minister Sergeyev, the Russian armed forces were rehearsing 'one provision of Russian military doctrine – the use of nuclear forces when all measures of conventional defence against the aggression have failed'. According to the exercise scenario, the opening engagement came from an 'unidentified' military bloc in the West, which delivered cruise missiles into Kaliningrad and Belarus territory. The Far East Military District and the Pacific Fleet conducted separate exercises on 19–30 April and the Caspian Flotilla on 14–29 April.

According to bilateral agreements, joint planning and exercises will also be carried out in Armenia between local forces and Russian armed forces stationed in the country. This Russian contingent was reinforced with the S-300B air-defence system and eight MiG-29 (bringing the total to 13) combat aircraft in 1999. Russia also announced plans to strengthen the integrated Commonwealth of Independent States (CIS) air-defence system, which was established by a 1996 treaty and includes the air-defence forces of Armenia, Belarus, Kazakstan, Kyrgyzstan, Russia and Tajikistan. A joint exercise involving all these countries was conducted in April 1999.

The scale of the exercise activity in 1999, particularly the combined arms exercises involving different command organisations, indicates that, with forward planning, the military chain of command can be counted upon to deploy significant numbers of troops, aircraft and ships. It is, however, difficult to assess the combat efficiency or state of operational readiness of those involved from the information available. Factors such as morale and the quality of training standards are vital in influencing how units will perform in difficult operational conditions

Nuclear Forces

While the economic crisis was the critical factor hindering the progress of military reform in the conventional armed forces, where nuclear forces were concerned, the obstacle was of a different character. There has been growing disagreement within the military establishment about the strategy for nuclear-forces reform. For example, shortly after the approval of the 'State Programme for Military Construction until 2005' in August 1999, disagreements emerged between Minister of Defence Sergeyev and the Chief of the General Staff Kvashnin. In October 1998, Sergeyev persuaded President Yeltsin to sign a special decree which initiated a transition from a four- to a three-service structure for the armed forces and the creation of a separate Unified Command for Strategic Nuclear Forces (UC SNF). The plan is that the UC SNF, reporting directly to the Minister of Defence, would assume command of all nuclear forces, based on the Strategic Rocket Forces, and would include all the Naval and Air Force components. As a result, the General Staff would be left in charge of three services – Navy, Air Force and the substantially reduced Army. The General Staff, along with other high level MOD officials, are categorically opposed to the creation of a UC SNF, and, in a very public debate, expressed concern at the danger of concentrating all operational command of strategic and tactical nuclear forces into the hands of one man. After almost a year of controversy, all work on setting up the UC SNF was stopped when the NATO air campaign in Kosovo began. *Operation Allied Force* caused the Russian government to raise the priority allocated to maintaining an effective nuclear force. In this situation, the process of establishing a UC SNF would have resulted – at least in the short term – in a reduction in readiness. It is unclear whether the decision to drop the UC SNF idea is permanent or whether the plan will be implemented at a later stage of the reform.

The central role of the nuclear forces in Russian defence doctrine was emphasised at a special Security Council meeting on development of Russian nuclear weapons, which took place on 28 April 1999, soon after the beginning of the NATO campaign against Yugoslavia. After the meeting, the then Secretary of the Security Council, Vladimir Putin (appointed Prime Minister in August 1999) announced that President Yeltsin had signed two decrees on a programme for the further development of strategic and tactical nuclear weapons. He said that the Security Council had also agreed that Russia would conduct a series of sub-critical nuclear tests in 1999 at Novaya Zemlya (Russia had already conducted five such tests between 14 September and 13 December 1998). The stated aim was to test the operational capability and safety of nuclear warheads. Russian officials claim that these tests did not violate the terms of the Comprehensive Nuclear Test Ban Treaty (CTBT). Special emphasis was placed on the need to strengthen Russian nuclear forces by extending the life of existing systems and by speeding up the deployment of a new generation of missiles and warheads such as the SS-27 (*Topol*-M). By the end of 1998 Russia had deployed ten *Topol*-M systems which became operational in the Tatischevo division. Two successful flight tests were conducted in 1999, and Russia plans to deploy another ten systems during the year.

It was also decided not to decommission *Delta* III submarines from the Pacific Fleet but to modernise them and extend their life until 2005. The new *Dolgoruky*-class ballistic-missile submarine (SSBN) will not be entering service in 2002 as planned. It is now scheduled for 2006. The operational life of the SS-18s will be extended for at least two years. They are due to be decommissioned by 31 December 2003 in accordance with the Strategic Arms Reduction Treaty (START) II, assuming it is ratified by Russia.

START

On 2 July 1999, the Federation Council approved the federal law on 'The Funding of the State Defence Order for Strategic Nuclear Forces' which establishes a minimum funding level under each article of the Defence Order for strategic nuclear forces for each year until 2005, and overall until 2010. The new legislation followed the approval by the Security Council in 1998 of the federal programme for the development of strategic nuclear forces. The adoption of these two documents could play a positive role in Russia's ratification of the Strategic Arms Reduction Treaty (START) II since these legal steps were specified as key requirements for consideration of the treaty by the Russian *Duma*. The debate and vote on START II in the *Duma* was cancelled in April 1999 because of the NATO campaign in Yugoslavia. Following the cease-fire, the then Russian Prime Minister Sergei Stepashin pledged to continue pressing the *Duma* to achieve ratification by the end of 1999. Although Stepashin was replaced as Prime Minister in August 1999, the government went ahead with talks with the US on details of the START III Treaty on 18–19 August. The US side made it clear that full negotiations on START III could not begin before START II had been ratified, but agreed to begin consultations about its provisions, as well as on the 1972 Anti-Ballistic Missile (ABM) Treaty, in the light of the enhanced US national missile defence programme. From a purely military perspective Russia needs START II and III to be implemented as it will have difficulty in maintaining its strategic forces at higher levels due to obsolescence of some systems and the cost of necessary modernisation. Another important development in US–Russia relations, which proceeded unaffected by the Kosovo crisis, was the agreement on the extension of the Co-operative Threat Reduction (CTR) Program (also known as the Nunn-Lugar program) in June 1999. The CTR programme is designed to assist Russia (and other former Soviet states) in the safe and secure destruction of nuclear weapons when they are withdrawn from service. The programme also provides support for Russia in the dismantling of its chemical weapons under the terms of the 1993 Chemical Weapons Convention.

External Influences

Among the most important external factors influencing Russian strategic thinking and the military reform process in 1999 were the new NATO strategic concept and NATO's military action against Yugoslavia. Before these events, the Russian MOD had declared that it was revising its military doctrine on the assumption that Russia did not have external threats to its security and that the likelihood of large-scale conflict was very low. The main provisions of a new Russian military doctrine were drawn up in 1993 and from these a draft national security concept was developed in 1997. However, the drafts were never formally agreed. In the light of events in 1999, as perceived in Moscow, work has started on elaborating a new doctrine that is due to be complete by the end of 1999.

Another effect of NATO action in Yugoslavia on Russian military policy was the decision to withdraw from activities under the 1997 NATO–Russia Founding Act after the air-strikes started. In

July 1999, meetings of the Joint Permanent Council under the Act resumed, but discussion was restricted to cooperation in peacekeeping operations, in particular within the NATO-led Kosovo Force (KFOR). Russia also declared that it has suspended its participation in the NATO Partnership for Peace (PFP) activities, although it played only a small part in this programme from the start. At the same time Russia strengthened its military links with its traditional partners in Asia and the Middle East, including China, India, Iran, Iraq and Syria. As in the past, economic factors play an important role in these relations. China and India are Russia's two biggest customers for major weapon systems, while Russian industrial exports to Iran (nuclear power equipment) and energy supplies (oil and natural gas contracts in both Iran and Iraq) are also important.

Another Russian response to NATO's Kosovo campaign was reflected in its attempts to strengthen its military cooperation with its closest allies in the Commonwealth of Independent States (CIS). The actions included the joint-command arrangements with Belarus armed forces, the reinforcement of Russian forces in Armenia and the formal establishment of a Russian military base in Tajikistan. The 1999 agreement with Tajikistan regularises the presence of the 201st Motor Rifle Division (6,500 strong) and Border Troops that have been in the country since 1993. Russia also tried to extend the 1992 CIS Collective Security Treaty, which expired in May 1999, but was only partially successful as four states (Georgia, Azerbaijan, Uzbekistan and Moldova) refused to extend their membership. All except for Uzbekistan still have Russian troops on their soil, and even Uzbekistan still houses the early warning station at Gaballa. However, reductions have taken place in other CIS countries during 1999. Russian Border Troops will be withdrawn from Kyrgyzstan by the end of August and from Georgia (Abkhazia) by September 1999. In Georgia's case, some 8,000 Russian regular armed forces remain in place.

Domestic Conflict

The most serious domestic challenge for the Russian armed forces remains in the North Caucasus region. By August 1999 the conflict with armed groups based in Chechnya had become more intense, with a number of villages in neighbouring Daghestan being seized by the insurgents. The groups are Islamic militants and, while not supported directly by the Chechen leadership, they claim to be seeking to establish an independent Islamic republic in Daghestan. The conflict may escalate. However, the diverse ethnic composition of Daghestan's population makes the situation even more complex than that in the 1994–96 Chechen conflict. It will be as difficult for the Islamic militants to garner coherent support for their cause in Daghestan as it will be for the Russian armed and interior forces to count on local sympathies for their operations. This portends a chaotic situation and an unpredictable outcome. The Russian armed forces' lack of trained professional troops – many of the best of which are used on peacekeeping operations abroad – will limit their ability to conduct an effective ground campaign. In an effort to avoid casualties in combat at close-quarters, extensive use was (at least in August 1999) being made of air-strikes and artillery.

DEFENCE SPENDING

External events in 1999 have entrenched domestic opposition both to armed forces' reform, and to the restructuring of the defence industry. At the same time, lack of resources as a result of continuing weak performance by the Russian economy ties the hands of government in these as in other areas. The military claims that essential reform of the armed forces cannot take place without substantial increases in the defence budget. The result is a stalemate which continues to slow down change in both the armed forces and in industry. Because of the tensions over NATO action in the Balkans and domestic political uncertainty, details of the 1999 defence budget were classified for the first time since the formation of the Russian Federation in 1991.

The 1999 Federal Budget (excluding Social Expenditures and Special Funds), released on 25 February 1999, estimated revenues at R474bn and expenditures at R575bn, making for a deficit of R101bn or 2.5% of gross domestic product (GDP). GDP was forecast to be 4,000bn redenominated roubles in 1999 with annual consumer price inflation running at 30% and an average exchange rate of R21.5 to the US dollar. The original defence budget topline was R94bn, comprising 16.3% of the

Table 11 Estimated Russian defence budget by function, 1999

(Redenominated roubles m)	Budget
Personnel	33,900
Operations and Maintenance	29,600
Procurement	23,800
R&D	14,000
Infrastructure	3,500
Nuclear	1,900
MOD	500
Other	1,800
Defence Budget	**109,000**

federal budget. Of this, R92bn is intended for 'organisational development and maintenance of the RF Armed Forces', and R2bn goes to the Ministry of Atomic Energy's military programme, mobilisation, and reservist training. Since the budget's release, an additional R15bn have been added to fund arms procurement.

As usual, the defence lobby in the *Duma* protested that the budget was inadequate. The effect of the NATO air-strikes on Yugoslavia was to coalesce parliamentary support for a stronger defence posture, but the government has responded with mixed signals. In May 1999, then Prime Minister Stepashin prepared the *Duma* for an increase in the 2000 defence budget to 3.5% of GDP. However, the draft budget for 2000, as of June 1999, calls for 2.2% of GDP to be spent on defence or R111bn under June 1999 economic assumptions.

Table 12 Official Russian defence budgets and outlays, 1993–1999

(Redenominated roubles m)   * = revised

	1993	1993*	1994	1995	1995*	1996	1997	1997*	1998	1999	1999*
Defence budget	3,116	8,327	40,626	48,577	59,379	80,185	104,300	83,000	81,765	93,702	109,000
Federal budget (%)	16.6	n.a.	20.9	19.6	21.3	18.4	19.7	19.7	16.4	16.3	19.0
Defence outlay	n.a.	7,210	28,028	n.a.	47,800	63,900		n.a.	79,700	56,700	n.a.	n.a.

Official defence outlays for 1998 were R57bn (16.4% of government spending, excluding Social Expenditures and Special Funds) compared to a budget of R82bn (16.4%). As in previous years, fiscal revenues failed to match government expectations and the Finance Ministry sequestered defence funds on a *pro rata* basis. The actual allocations to defence in 1998 were 71% of the budget for the year.

Estimates of Russian Military Spending

The secrecy surrounding the 1999 defence budget added a further dimension of uncertainty to estimates of Russia's real military expenditure. Press reports suggest that the 1999 budget lies in the range of 2.7–3.5% of GDP (R107–140bn), depending on whether military pensions and funding for military reform are classified as a cost to defence or the state. In 1998 the MOD succeeded in having military pensions moved from the defence budget to the social budget. Irrespective of budget heading, however, the government continues to classify military pensions as a cost to defence, and it seems likely that the costs of military reform are classified in the same way. Significant funding for military-related activities is excluded from the defence budget, and appears in the federal budget under another heading. When military-related spending taking place outside the domain of the

MOD is taken into account, the total military spend rose from 2.3% to 3.8% of GDP under the original 1999 budget. Industrial subsidies and Science and Technology allocations under the Ministry of the Economy budget, together with funding from regional and local governments and revenue from arms exports, further inflate the real military spend to over 5% of GDP.

Table 13 Russia: defence budget and military-related expenditure, 1999

Budget heading		Budget (rouble m)
Defence budget excluding military pensions and reform		**93,702**
of which	Defence	91,620
	Military programme of Ministry of Atomic Energy	1,933
	Mobilisation	150
	Military pensions	1,3380
	Military reform	2,475
Paramilitary Forces		**17,156**
of which	Internal troops	4,043
	Border Guards	5,402
	Ministry of Emergencies and Civil Defence	322
	Federal Railway Police	954
	Federal Service of Special Construction	360
	Pensions for Paramilitary Forces	6,075
Other military-related budgets		**24,525**
of which	International treaty obligations	6,136
	Mobilisation of the economy	450
	Salaries of military personnel outside military organisations	871
	Subsidies to closed military cities and regions	2,360
	Defence industry conversion and restructuring	1,259
	Nuclear, biological and chemical clean-up and rehabilitation programmes	546
Undistributed funds		**12,903**
Total		**151,238**

Table 14 Independent estimates of Russian military expenditure

	IMF % GDP	SIPRI 1997 $bn	SIPRI % GDP	IISS 1997 $bn	IISS % GDP	ACDA 1997 $bn	ACDA % GDP	NATO % GDP
1992	4.7	50	5.5	146	10.8	178	20	>10
1993	4.4	44	5.3	114	8.9	137	17	>10
1994	4.6	42	5.8	101	8.3	99	14	>10
1995	2.9	25	3.7	86	7.4	79	11	>7
1996	3.6	24	3.7	73	6.5	n.a.	n.a.	7
1997	3.3	25	3.8	64	5.8	n.a.	n.a.	<7
1998	2.5	n.a.	3.2	55	5.2	n.a.	n.a.	4.4

The lack of transparency of Russian military accounting, coupled with the non-convertibility of the rouble, continues to make estimates of Russia's real military spending imprecise and vulnerable to misinterpretation. At the market exchange rate, Russia's defence budget for 1999 amounts to $4bn – roughly equivalent to Singapore's annual defence spending. This figure totally belies the real value of the resources allocated to the military, which is masked by the pervasive practices of nonpayment and barter. The impact of these practices is that up to 75% of all defence-related financial transactions effectively fall outside the defence budget. The situation is further complicated by poor accounting practices that result in funds not going to the intended destination due to either inefficiency or corruption. Estimates in the public domain vary considerably according to the definition of military spending and the purchasing power attributed to the rouble. While few would dispute that Russia's military effort has contracted enormously since the Cold War, the evidence suggests that real military spending still accounted for at least 5% of GDP or some $55bn in 1998.

Weapon Programmes

Series production of ballistic missiles is now confined to the new SS-27 (*Topol*-M2) inter-continental ballistic missile (ICBM). The SS-NX-28 submarine-launched ballistic missile (SLBM) was cancelled in August 1998 after three test failures. At the same time, work was suspended on the missile's intended platform, the *Dolgoruky* SSBN, until new design criteria for the SLBM and SSBN could be established. Refurbishment of the road-mobile SS-25 ICBMs has continued with the aim of prolonging their service life. Development of the SS-X-26, the successor to the *Scud* SRBM, should be complete in 1999. In 1998, the Air Force took delivery of 12 variants of the Su-30 fighter, ground-attack aircraft (FGA) together with the first 20 MiG-29SMT upgrades, with another 24 expected to be delivered in 1999 out of a total of 180 upgrades on order. In 1999 the Air Force also ordered the Il-112V transport aircraft to replace its AN-26 fleet. The Army was expecting to receive 30 T-90 main battle tanks (MBTs) in 1999, as well as the first consignment of new armoured vehicles based on the existing BTR-80.

Arms Exports

Given the fall in government contracts and the need for hard currency, exports are an increasingly vital source of revenue for defence companies. Russian arms exports increased in 1998 to an estimated $2.9bn from $2.5bn in 1997. *Rosvooruzheniye* accounts for 80% of the total, with sales in 1998 of some $2.3bn. The other leading exporters are *Promeksport* and *Rossyskii Teknologii*. Exports are expected to grow in 1999 despite fierce competition in the global arms market.

A confluence of events in 1998–99 has served to stimulate Russian arms sales. The rouble's devaluation following Russia's August 1998 financial crisis lowered the price of its equipment in global markets. This factor was particularly important where less affluent importers were concerned, notably those at war in the Horn of Africa, Central Africa and Angola. While China, India and Iran remain Russia's largest customers, it returned to being the largest equipment supplier to Syria in 1998 and Libya in 1999.

Table 15 **Russia: estimated production of major weapon systems, 1990–1998**									
Equipment	1990 (USSR)	1991 (USSR)	1992	1993	1994	1995	1996	1997	1998
MBT	1,600	850	500	200	40	30	5	5	15
AIFV and APC	3,400	3,000	700	300	380	400	250	350	250
SP arty	500	300	200	100	85	15	20	10	10
Bbr	40	30	20	10	2	2	1	0	0
FGA	430	250	150	100	50	20	25	35	40
Transport Aircraft	120	60	5	5	5	4	3	0	0
Hel	450	350	175	150	100	95	75	70	40
SS	12	6	6	4	4	3	2	2	2
Major Surface Ships	2	3	1	1	0	1	1	0	0
ICBM/SLBM	115	100	55	35	25	10	10	10	15
SRBM	0	0	80	105	55	45	35	30	0

Russia   RF

	1997	1998	1999	2000
GDP[a]	r2,563bn	r2,685bn		
	($1.1tr)	($1.1tr)		
per capita	$6,800	$6,600		
Growth	0.8%	-4.6%		
Inflation	14.6%	27.8%		
Debt	$126bn	$153bn		
Def exp[a]	$64bn	$55bn		
Def bdgt[a]		r82bn	r109bn	r111bn
		($35bn)	($31bn)	($30bn)
FMA[b] (US)	$0.7m	$0.9m	$0.9m	$0.9m
FMA (Ge)	**1991–97** $5.0bn			
$1=rouble*	5.78	9.71	24.7	

* (redenominated)

[a] PPP est

[b] Under the US Cooperative Threat Reduction programme, $2.8bn has been authorised by the US to support START implementation and demilitarisation in Russia, Ukraine, Belarus and Kazakstan. Russia's share is 60–65%.

Population				146,300,000

(Tatar 4%, Ukrainian 3%, Chuvash 1%, Bashkir 1%, Belarussian 1%, Moldovan 1%, other 8%)

Age	13–17	18–22	23–32
Men	5,868,000	5,551,000	10,170,000
Women	5,647,000	5,398,000	9,933,000

Total Armed Forces

ACTIVE 1,004,100

(incl perhaps 330,000 conscripts, 145,000 women; about 200,000 MoD staff, centrally controlled units for EW, trg, rear services, not incl elsewhere)
Terms of service 18–24 months. Women with medical and other special skills may volunteer

RESERVES some 20,000,000

some 2,400,000 with service within last 5 years; Reserve obligation to age 50

Strategic Deterrent Forces ε149,000

(incl 49,000 assigned from Air Force and Navy)

NAVY (ε13,000)
332 msl in 21 operational SSBN†
SSBN 21 (all based in Russian ports)
  3 *Typhoon* with 20 SS-N-20 *Sturgeon* (60 msl)
  7 *Delta* IV with 16 SS-N-23 *Skiff* (112 msl)
  7 *Delta* III with 16 SS-N-18 *Stingray* (112 msl)
  4 *Delta* I with 12 SS-N-8 *Sawfly* (48 msl)
(The following non-op SSBNs remain START-account-able, with a total of 260 msl)
  3 *Typhoon* with 60 SS-N-20
  6 *Delta* III with 96 SS-N-18
  2 *Delta* II with 32 SS-N-8

  6 *Delta* I with 72 SS-N-8
In the 1 January START I declaration, Russia stated a total of 592 'deployed' SLBMs. The above figures represent holdings as of 1 August 1999.

STRATEGIC MISSILE DEFENCE TROOPS (ε100,000 incl 50,000 conscripts)

5 rocket armies, org in div, regt, bn and bty, launcher gp normally with 10 silos (6 for SS-18) and one control centre; 12 SS-24 rail each 3 launchers
ICBM 771
  180 SS-18 *Satan* (RS-20) at 4 fields; mostly mod 4/5, 10 MIRV;
  160 SS-19 *Stiletto* (RS-18) at 4 fields; mostly mod 3, 6 MIRV;
  46 SS-24 *Scalpel* (RS-22) 10 MIRV; 10 silo, 36 rail;
  370 SS-25 *Sickle* (RS-12M); 360 mobile, single-warhead; 10 variant for silo launcher; 10 bases with some 40 units
  15 SS-27 (*Topol*-M2) (20 additional missiles planned to become operational in 2000)
ABM 100: 36 SH-11 (mod *Galosh*), 64 SH-08 *Gazelle*
WARNING SYSTEMS
ICBM/SLBM launch-detection capability, others include photo recce and ELINT
RADARS
OVER-THE-HORIZON-BACKSCATTER (OTH-B)
2 in the Ukraine, at Nikolaev and Mukachevo, covering US and polar areas. (While these facilities are functioning, they are not tied in with the Russian air defence system because of outstanding legal difficulties with Ukraine.)
1 near Yeniseysk, covering China
LONG-RANGE EARLY-WARNING ABM-ASSOCIATED
7 long-range phased-array systems **Operational** Moscow, Olenegorsk (Kola), Gaballa (Azerbaijan), Pechora (Urals), Balkhash (Kazakstan), Mishelevka (Irkutsk). Azerbaijan and Kazakstan sites not functioning because of outstanding legal difficulties. **Under construction** Baranovichi (Belarus) – planned to become operational in 2000
11 *Hen House*-series; range 6,000km, 6 locations covering approaches from the west and south-west, north-east and south-east and (partially) south. Engagement, guidance, battle management: 1 *Pill Box* phased-array at Pushkino (Moscow)

Army ε348,000

(incl ε185,000 conscripts)
6 Mil Districts (MD)
5 Army HQ, 6 Corps HQ
6 TD (3 tk, 1 motor rifle, 1 arty, 1 SAM regt; 1 armd recce bn; spt units)
20 MRD (incl trg) (3 motor rifle, 1 arty, 1 SAM regt; 1 indep tk, 1 ATK, 1 armd recce bn; spt units)
4 ABD (each 2/3 para, 1 arty regt) (plus 1 trg div)

4 MG/arty div

3 arty div; no standard org: perhaps 4 bde (12 bn):
152mm SP, 152mm towed and MRL: plus ATK bde
Some 32 arty bde/regt; no standard org, perhaps 4
bn: 2 each of 24 152mm towed guns, 2 each of 24
152mm SP guns, some only MRL
4 hy arty bde (each with 4 bn of 12 203mm 2S7 SP
guns)

12 indep bde (11 MR, 1 tk)

2 AB bde (1 trg)

7 SF (*Spetsnaz*) bde (5 op incl 1 trg, 3 cadre)

13 SSM bde

9 ATK, 21 SAM bde/regt

21 hel regt (9 attack, 7 aslt tpt, 5 trg)

Other Front and Army tps
engr, pontoon-bridge, pipe-line, signals, EW, CW
def, tpt, supply bde/regt/bn

EQUIPMENT

Figures in () were reported to CFE on 1 Jan 1999 and
include those held by Naval Infantry and Coastal
Defence units

MBT about 15,500 (5,510), incl: T-55 (22), T-62 (92),
T-64A/-B (203), T-72L/-M (2,031) and T-80/-U/
UD/UM (3,159), T-90 (2), plus some 11,000 in
store east of Urals (incl Kazakstan, Uzbekistan)

LT TK 200 PT-76 (2)

RECCE some 2,000 BRDM-2

TOTAL AIFV/APC ε26,300 (10,062)

AIFV (6,725): BMP-1 (1,671), BMP-2 (3,255), BMP-3
(27), some 1,600 BMD-1/-2/-3 (AB) (1,176), BRM
(564), BTR-80A (32)

APC (3,337): BTR-60P/-70/-80 (2,071), BTR-D (485);
MT-LB (781), plus 'look-alikes'

TOTAL ARTY ε15,700 (6,299), plus some 13,000,
mainly obsolete types, in store east of the Urals
TOWED (2,075) incl: **122mm**: M-30 (16); D-30
(887); **130mm**: M-46 (1); **152mm**: ML-20 (1); D-20
(229), *Giatsint-B* 2A36 (524), MSTA-B 2A65 (417);
203mm: B-4M
SP (2,636) incl: **122mm**: *Gvozdika* 2S1 (625);
152mm: *Acatsia* 2S3 (1,060), *Giatsint-S* 2S5 (494),
MSTA-S 2S19 (420); **203mm**: *Pion* 2S7 (37)
COMBINED GUN/MOR (434): **120mm**: *Nona-S*
2S9 SP (414), *Nona-K* 2B16 (2), 2 S23 (18)
MRL (900) incl: **122mm**: BM-21 (362), BM-13 (6),
9P138 (13); **220mm**: 800 (414) 9P140 *Uragan*;
300mm: 105 (105) *Smerch* 9A52
MOR (254) incl: **120mm**: 2S12 (168), PM-38 (68);
160mm: M-160; **240mm**: *Tulpan* 2S4 SP (18)

SSM (nuclear-capable) ε200 SS-21 *Scarab* (*Tochka*),
ε116 *Scud-B*/-C mod (R-17) (FROG (*Luna*) units
mostly disbanded)

ATGW AT-2 *Swatter*, AT-3 *Sagger*, AT-4 *Spigot*, AT-5
Spandrel, AT-6 *Spiral*, AT-7 *Saxhorn*, AT-9, AT-10

RL 64mm: RPG-18; **73mm**: RPG-7/-16/-22/-26;
105mm: RPG-27/-29

RCL 73mm: SPG-9; **82mm**: B-10

ATK GUNS 57mm: ASU-57 SP; **76mm**; **85mm**: D-

44/SD-44, ASU-85 SP; **100mm**: 526 T-12/-12A/M-
55 towed

AD GUNS 23mm: ZU-23, ZSU-23-4 SP; **37mm;**
57mm: S-60, ZSU-57-2 SP; **85mm**: M-1939;
100mm: KS-19; **130mm**: KS-30

SAM
500 SA-4 A/B *Ganef* (twin) (Army/Front weapon)
400 SA-6 *Gainful* (triple) (div weapon)
400 SA-8 *Gecko* (2 triple) (div weapon)
200 SA-9 *Gaskin* (2 twin) (regt weapon)
250 SA-11 *Gadfly* (quad) (replacing SA-4/-6)
100 SA-12A/B (*Gladiator/Giant*)
350 SA-13 *Gopher* (2 twin) (replacing SA-9)
100 SA-15 (replacing SA-6/SA-8)
SA-19 (2S6 SP) (8 SAM, plus twin **30mm** gun)
SA-7, SA-14 being replaced by SA-16, SA-18 (man-
portable)

HELICOPTERS some 2,300
ATTACK 1,000 Mi-24 (757), Ka-50 *Hokum* (4)
TPT some 1,300 incl 35 Mi-6, 651 Mi-8/-17 (some
armed), Mi-26 (hy)

Navy 171,500

(incl ε16,000 conscripts, ε13,000 Strategic Forces,
ε35,000 Naval Aviation, 9,500 Coastal Defence Forces/
Naval Infantry)

SUBMARINES 70+

STRATEGIC 21 (see p. 112)

TACTICAL 44
SSGN 9 *Oscar* II with 24 SS-N-19 *Shipwreck* USGW
(VLS); plus T-65 HWT
SSN 19
8 *Akula* with T-65 HWT, SS-N-21 *Sampson* SLCM
3 *Sierra* with T-65 HWT, SS-N-21 *Sampson* SLCM
1 *Yankee* 'Notch' with 20+ SS-N-21 *Sampson* SLCM
7 *Victor* III with T-65 HWT, SS-N-15 *Starfish*
SSK 16
12 *Kilo*, 3 *Tango*, 1 *Foxtrot* (all with T-53 HWT)

OTHER ROLES 5
3 *Uniform* SSN, 1 *Yankee* SSN, 1 *X-Ray* SSK trials

RESERVE probably some *Foxtrot*, *Tango* and *Kilo*

PRINCIPAL SURFACE COMBATANTS 35

CARRIERS 1 *Kuznetsov* CVV (67,500t) capacity 20
fixed wing ac (Su-33) and 15–17 ASW hel with 12
SS-N-19 *Shipwreck* SSM, 4 x 6 SA-N-9 *Gauntlet* SAM,
8 CADS-1, 2 RBU-12 (not fully op)

CRUISERS 7
CGN 2 *Kirov* with 12 x 8 SA-N-6 *Grumble* SAM, 20
SS-N-19 *Shipwreck* SSM, 3 Ka-25/-27 hel, SA-N-4
Gecko SAM, SS-N-15 *Starfish* SUGW, 2 x 130mm
gun, 10 x 533mm ASTT
CG 5
3 *Slava* with 8 x 8 SA-N-6 *Grumble* SAM, 8 x 2 SS-N-
12 *Sandbox* SSM, 1 Ka-25/-27 hel (AEW/ASW); 8
533mm TT, 1 x 2 130mm guns
1 *Kara* with 2 x 4 SS-N-14 *Silex* SUGW, 10 533mm TT,
1 Ka-25 hel, 2 x 2 SA-N-3 *Goblet* SAM, (1 (*Azov*)

with 3 x 8 SA-N-6, only 1 SA-N-3 and other differences), 2 SA-N-4 *Gecko* SAM

1 *Kynda* with 8 SS-N-3B SSM, 2 SA-N-1 *Goa* SAM, 6 533mm TT

DESTROYERS 17

DDG 17

7 *Sovremennyy* with 2 x 4 SS-N-22 *Sunburn* SSM, 2 x 1 SA-N-7 *Gadfly* SAM, 2 x 2 130mm guns, 1 Ka-25 (B) hel (OTHT), 4 533mm TT

1 mod *Kashin* with 4 SS-N-2C *Styx* SSM, 2 x 2 SA-N-1 *Goa* SAM, 5 533mm TT (non-op)

1 *Kashin* with 2 x 12 ASW RL, 5 533mm TT, 2 x 2 SA-N-1 *Goa* SAM

7 *Udaloy* (ASW) with 2 x 4 SS-N-14 *Silex* SUGW, 2 x 12 ASW RL, 8 533mm TT, 2 Ka-27 hel, 2 100mm guns

1 *Udaloy* II with 8 x 4 SS-N-22 *Sunburn* SSM, 8 SA-N-9 *Gauntlet* SAM, 2 Cads-N-1, 8 SA-N-11 *Grisson* SAM, 10 533mm TT, 2 Ka-27 hel, 2 100mm guns

FRIGATES 10

FFG 10

2 *Krivak* II with 1 x 4 SS-N-14 *Silex* SUGW, 8 533mm TT, 2 x 12 ASW RL, 2 100mm guns

7 *Krivak* I (weapons as *Krivak* II, but with 2 twin 76mm guns)

1 *Neustrashimyy* with 2 x 12 ASW RL, SA-N-9 *Gauntlet* SAM, 6 533mm ASTT

PATROL AND COASTAL COMBATANTS 112

CORVETTES 27

27 *Grisha* I, -III, -IV, -V, with 2 x 12 ASW RL, 4 533mm TT

LIGHT FRIGATES 12

12 *Parchim* II (ASW) with 2 x 12 ASW RL, 4 406mm ASTT

MISSILE CRAFT 56

28 *Tarantul*, 1 -I, 5 -II, both with 2 x 2 SS-N-2C *Styx* SSM; 22 -III with 2 x 2 SS-N-22 *Sunburn* SSM

22 *Nanuchka* 4 -I, 17 -III and 1 -IV, with 2 x 3 SS-N-9 *Siren* SSM

2 *Dergach* ACV with 8 x SS-N-22 *Sunburn* SSM, 1 SAN-4 *Gecko* SAM, 1 76mm gun

3 *Matka* PHM with 2 x 1 SS-N-2C *Styx* SSM

1 *Sarancha* PGG with hel

TORPEDO CRAFT 8 *Turya* PHT with 4 533mm TT

PATROL CRAFT 9

COASTAL 9

6 *Pauk* PFC (ASW) with 2 ASW RL, 4 ASTT

1 *Babochka* PHT (ASW) with 8 ASTT

2 *Mukha* PHT (ASW) with 8 ASTT

MINE WARFARE about 72

MINE COUNTERMEASURES about 72

OFFSHORE 15

2 *Gorya* MCO

13 *Natya* I and -II MSO

COASTAL 27

27 *Sonya* MSC

INSHORE 30

30 MSI<

AMPHIBIOUS about 25

LPD 1 *Ivan Rogov* with 4–5 Ka-27 hel, capacity 520 tps, 20 tk

LST 23

19 *Ropucha*, capacity 225 tps, 9 tk

4 *Alligator*, capacity 300 tps, 20 tk

LSM 1 *Polnocny*, capacity 180 tps, 6 tk

Plus about 21 craft: about 6 *Ondatra* LCM; about 15 LCAC and SES (incl 4 *Pomornik*, 3 *Aist*, 3 *Tsaplya*, 1 *Lebed*, 1 *Utenok*, 2 *Orlan* WIG and 1 *Utka* WIG (wing-in-ground-experimental))

Plus about 80 smaller craft

SUPPORT AND MISCELLANEOUS about 436

UNDER WAY SUPPORT 28

1 *Berezina*, 5 *Chilikin*, 22 other AO

MAINTENANCE AND LOGISTIC about 271

some 15 AS, 38 AR, 20 AOT, 8 msl spt/resupply, 90 AT, 9 special liquid carriers, 8 water carriers, 17 AK, 46 AT/ARS, 13 ARS, 7 AR/C

SPECIAL PURPOSES about 53

some 17 AGI (some armed), 1 msl range instrumentation, 7 trg, about 24 icebreakers (civil-manned), 4 AH

SURVEY/RESEARCH about 84

some 19 naval, 61 civil AGOR, 4 specialist support vessels

MERCHANT FLEET (aux/augmentation)

1,448 ocean-going vehicles over 1,000 tonnes; 266 AOT, 113 dry bulk; 24 AK, 11 ro-ro, 9 pax; 1,025 other (breakbulk, partial AK, refrigerated AK, specialised AK and LASH)

NAVAL AVIATION (ε35,000)

some 329 cbt ac; 387 armed hel

Flying hours 40

HQ Naval Air Force

FLEET AIR FORCES 4

each org in air div, each with 2–3 regt of HQ elm and 2 sqn of 9–10 ac each; recce, ASW, tpt/utl org in indep regt or sqn

BBR some 71

5 regt with some 71 Tu-22M (AS-4 ASM)

FGA 75 Su-24, 9 Su-25, 30 Su-27

ASW ac 9 Tu-142, 35 Il-38, 54 Be-12 **hel** 70 Mi-14, 53 Ka-25, 119 Ka-27

MR/EW ac incl 14 Tu-95, 8 Tu-22, 24 Su-24, 7 An-12, 2 Il-20 **hel** 20 Ka-25

MCM 25 Mi-14 hel

CBT ASLT 25 Ka-29 hel

TPT ac 120 An-12, An-24, An-26 **hel** 70 Mi-6/-8

ASM AS-4 *Kitchen*, AS-7 *Kerry*, AS-10 *Karen*, AS-11 *Kilter*, AS-12 *Kegler*, AS-13 *Kingbolt*, AS-14 *Kedge*

COASTAL DEFENCE (9,500)

(incl Naval Infantry, Coastal Defence Troops)

NAVAL INFANTRY (Marines)

1 inf div (2,500: 3 inf, 1 tk, 1 arty bn) (Pacific Fleet)

1 indep bde (4 inf, 1 tk, 1 arty, 1 MRL, 1 ATK bn), 3
indep regt, 1 indep bn
3 fleet SF bde (1 op, 2 cadre): 2–3 underwater, 1 para
bn, spt elm
EQUIPMENT
MBT 130: T-55, T-72, T-80
RECCE 60 BRDM-2/*Sagger* ATGW
APC some 1,500: BTR-60/-70/-80, 250 MT-LB
TOTAL ARTY 321
SP 122mm: 96 2S1; **152mm:** 18 2S3
MRL 122mm: 96 9P138
COMBINED GUN/MOR 120mm: 100 2S9
SP, 11 2S23 SP
ATGW 72 AT-3/-5
AD GUNS 23mm: 60 ZSU-23-4 SP
SAM 250 SA-7, 20 SA-8, 50 SA-9/-13
COASTAL DEFENCE TROOPS (5,000)
(all units reserve status)
1 coastal defence div
1 coastal defence bde
1 arty regt
2 SAM regt
EQUIPMENT
MBT 350 T-64
AIFV 450 BMP
APC 280 BTR-60/-70/-80, 400 MT-LB
TOTAL ARTY 364 (152)
TOWED 280: **122mm:** 140 D-30; **152mm:** 40
D-20, 50 2A65, 50 2A36
SP 152mm: 48 2S5
MRL 122mm: 36 BM-21

NAVAL DEPLOYMENT

NORTHERN FLEET (Arctic and Atlantic)
(HQ Severomorsk)
BASES Kola peninsula, Severodovinsk
SUBMARINES 39
strategic 15 SSBN **tactical** 24 (4 SSGN, 14 SSN, 3
SSK, 3 SSN other roles)
PRINCIPAL SURFACE COMBATANTS 12
1 CV, 3 cruisers, 6 DDG, 2 FFG
OTHER SURFACE SHIPS about 30 patrol and coastal
combatants, 25 MCM, 8 amph, some 130 spt and misc
NAVAL AVIATION
104 cbt ac; 85 armed hel
BBR 37 Tu-22M
FTR/FGA 30 Su-24/-25, 24 Su-27
ASW ac 11 Il-38, 5 Be-12 **hel** (afloat), 55 Ka-27
MR/EW ac 2 An-12
MCM 8* Mi-14 hel
CBT ASLT HEL 12 Ka-29
COMMS 5 Tu-142

BALTIC FLEET (HQ Kaliningrad)
BASES Kronstadt, Baltiysk
SUBMARINES 2
2 SS

PRINCIPAL SURFACE COMBATANTS 6
2 DDG, 4 FFG
OTHER SURFACE SHIPS about 30 patrol and coastal
combatants, 19 MCM, 5 amph, some 130 spt and misc
NAVAL AVIATION
50 cbt ac, 37 armed hel
FGA 2 regt: 20 Su-24, 28 Su-27
ASW hel 22* Ka-27
MR/EW ac 2 An-12, 5 Su-24
MCM 6 Mi-14 BT hel
CBT ASLT HEL 4 Ka-29

BLACK SEA FLEET (HQ Sevastopol)
The Russian Fleet is leasing bases in Sevastopol for the
next 20 years; it is based at Sevastopol and Karantinnaya
Bays, and jointly with Ukrainian warships at Stralet-
skaya Bay. The Fleet's overall serviceability is low.
BASES Sevastopol, Temryuk, Novorossiysk
SUBMARINES 12 (only one op)
11 SSK, 1 SSK other roles
PRINCIPAL SURFACE COMBATANTS 7
3 cruisers, 2 DDG, 2 FFG
OTHER SURFACE SHIPS about 19 patrol and coastal
combatants, 20 MCM, 5 amph, some 90 spt and misc
NAVAL AVIATION
14 cbt ac; 63 armed hel
ASW ac 10* Be-12 **hel** 35 Mi-14, 25* Ka-25, 5* Ka-27
MR/EW ac 4 An-12 **hel** 3 Ka-25
MCM 5 Mi-14 BT hel

CASPIAN SEA FLOTILLA
BASE Astrakhan (Russia)
The Caspian Sea Flotilla has been divided among
Azerbaijan (about 25%), and Russia, Kazakstan and
Turkmenistan, which are operating a joint flotilla under
Russian command currently based at Astrakhan.
SURFACE COMBATANTS about 37
10 patrol and coastal combatants, 6 MCM, some 6
amph, about 15 spt

PACIFIC FLEET (HQ Vladivostok)
BASES Vladivostok, Petropavlovsk Kamchatskiy,
Magadan, Sovetskaya Gavan
SUBMARINES 17+
strategic 6 SSBN **tactical** 11 (5 SSGN, 5 SSN, 1 SSN
other roles)
PRINCIPAL SURFACE COMBATANTS 10
1 cruiser, 7 DDG, 2 FFG
OTHER SURFACE SHIPS about 41 patrol and coastal
combatants, 33 MCM, 4 amph, some 57 spt and misc
NAVAL AVIATION (Pacific Fleet Air Force)
(HQ Vladivostok) 71 cbt ac, 71 cbt hel
BBR 1 regt with 9 Tu-22M
ASW ac 27 Tu-142, 20 Il-38 **hel** 30 Ka-27; ashore 25
Mi-14
MR/EW ac some 8 An-12
MCM hel 6 Mi-14 BT
CBT ASLT HEL 10 Ka-29
COMMS 7 Tu-142

Air Force (Integrated Air Force and Air Defence Forces) (VVS) ε184,600

On 1 March 1998, the Air Defence Troops (PVO) amalgamated with the Air Force (VVS) under one Air Force Command. The Air Force now comprises some 1,800 combat aircraft: 2 Air Armies (Long Range Aviation (LRA) and Military Transport Aviation (VTA)), and 6 Tactical/Air Defence formations. The Tactical/Air Defence role includes air defence, interdiction, recce and tactical air support. LRA (6 div) and VTA (9 regt) are subordinated to central air force command. The VVS/PVO armies and independent corps are subordinated to commanders of military districts.

Flying hours Average annual flying time for LRA and Tactical/Air Defence is about 20 hours, and approximately 60 hours for VTA.

LONG-RANGE AVIATION COMMAND (37th Air Army)

2 div and 1 combat conversion unit
BBR (START-accountable) 74 hy bbr; 68 Tu-95, 6 Tu-160 (8 further Tu-160 to come from Ukraine in late 1999). (Test ac: 7 Tu-95, 5 Tu-160)
158 Tu-22M/MR (92 in store)
TKR 20 Il-78
TRG 10 Tu-22M-2/3, 30 Tu-134

TACTICAL AVIATION

6 formations – 3 armies of VVS and PVO (Rostov-on-Don, St Petersburg and Khabarovsk), and 3 independent corps of VVS and PVO (Novosibirsk, Yekaterinburg and Chita)
Flying hours 20
BBR/FGA some 575: 350 Su-24, 225 Su-25
FTR some 880: incl 260 MiG-29, 340 Su-27, 280 MiG-31
RECCE some 135: incl 15 MiG-25, 120 Su-24
AEW AND CONTROL 20 A-50
ECM 60 Mi-8
TRG 1 centre for op conversion: some 90 ac incl 20 MiG-29, 35 Su-24, 15 Su-25
  1 centre for instructor trg: 65 ac incl 10 MiG-25, 20 MiG-29, 15 Su-24, 10 Su-25, 10 Su-27
AAM AA-8 *Aphid*, AA-10 *Alamo*, AA-11 *Archer*
ASM AS-7 *Kerry*, AS-10 *Karen*, AS-11 *Kilter*, AS-12 *Kegler*, AS-13 *Kingbolt*, AS-14 *Kedge*, AS-17 *Krypton*, AS-18 *Kazoo*
SAM 37 SAM regt, some 2,150 launchers in some 225 sites
  50 SA-2 *Guideline* (being replaced by SA-10)
  200 SA-5 *Gammon* (being replaced by SA-10)
  some 1,900 SA-10
DECOMMISSIONED AIRCRAFT IN STORE 300 ac inc MiG-23, MiG-25

MILITARY TRANSPORT AVIATION COMMAND
(VTA) (61st Air Army)

2 div, each 4 regt, each 30 ac; 1 indep regt
  EQUIPMENT
  some 280 ac, incl Il-76M/MD, An-12, An-22, An-124
CIVILIAN FLEET 1,500 medium- and long-range passenger ac, incl some 350 An-12 and Il-76

AIR FORCE AVIATION TRAINING SCHOOLS

TRG 5 military aviation institutes subordinate to Air Force HQ: some 1,000 ac incl L-39, L-29, Tu-134, Mig-23, MiG-29, Su-22, Su-25, Su-27
DECOMMISSIONED AIRCRAFT IN STORE some 1,000 ac incl MiG-23, MiG-27, Su-17, Su-22
COMBAT AIRCRAFT (CFE totals as at 1 Jan 1999 for all air forces less maritime)
  ac 3,966: 193 Su-17 • 70 Su-22 • 737 Su-24 • 376 Su-25 • 337 Su-27 • 563 MiG-23 • 234 MiG-25 • 179 MiG-27 • 708 MiG-29 • 383 MiG-31 • 186 Tu-22M
  hel 805: 720 Mi-24 • 38 Mi-24(K) • 43 Mi-24(R) • 4 Ka-50

Deployment

The manning state of Russian units is difficult to determine. The following assessment of units within the Atlantic to the Urals (ATTU) region is based on the latest available information. Above 75% – none reported; above 50% – possibly 2 TD, 6 MRD, 4 ABD, 1 arty and 1 AB bde. The remainder are assessed as 20–50%. Units outside the ATTU are likely to be at a lower level. All bde are maintained at or above 50%. TLE in each MD includes active and trg units and in store

KALININGRAD OPERATIONAL STRATEGIC GROUP

These forces are now commanded by The Ground and Coastal Defence Forces of the Baltic Fleet.
GROUND 10,400: 2 MRD, 1 tk, 1 SSM, 1 SAM bde/regt, 1 attack hel regt, 829 MBT, 860 ACV, 330 arty/MRL/mor, 18 *Scud/Scarab*, 24 attack hel

NAVAL INFANTRY (1,800)

1 regt (25 MBT, 34 arty/MRL) (Kaliningrad)

COASTAL DEFENCE

2 arty regt (133 arty)
1 SSM regt: some 8 SS-C-1b *Sepal*
AD 1 regt: 28 Su-27 (Baltic Fleet)
SAM 50

RUSSIAN MILITARY DISTRICTS

LENINGRAD MD (HQ St Petersburg)

GROUND 38,000: 1 ABD; plus 2 indep MR bde, 2 arty bde/regt, 1 SSM, 1 *Spetsnaz*, 4 SAM bde, 1 ATK, 1 MRL, 1 aslt tpt hel regt, 323 MBT, 490 ACV, 940 arty/MRL/mor, 18 *Scud/Scarab*
NAVAL INFANTRY (1,700)
1 regt (77 MBT, 100 ACV, 41 arty)
COASTAL DEFENCE
1 Coastal Defence (360 MT-LB, 134 arty), 1 SAM regt
AIR 6th Air Army has 334 combat ac. It is divided into two PVO corps, 1 bbr div (66 Su-24), 1 recce regt (26

MiG-25, 20 Su-24), 1 ftr div (35 Su-27, 60 MiG-29), 1
hel ECM sqn (20 Mi-8)
AD 7 regt: 100 MiG-31, 90 Su-27
SAM 525

MOSCOW MD (HQ Moscow)

GROUND 95,900: 1 Army HQ, 1 Corps HQ, 2 TD, 1
MRD, 2 ABD, plus 1 arty div HQ, 5 arty bde/regt, 3
SSM, 1 indep MR, 1 *Spetsnaz*, 4 SAM bde, 3 attack hel,
1 aslt tpt hel regt, 2,000 MBT, 2,400 ACV, 1,700 arty/
MRL/mor, 48 *Scud/Scarab*, 180 attack hel
AIR 2 PVO divs, one mixed div incl air aslt regt, one
mil depot storing 43 MiG-25. 494 cbt ac: MiG-25/-
29/-31, Su-24/-25/-27: 2 hel ECM sqn with 51 Mi-8
SAM 850

VOLGA–URAL MD (HQ Yekaterinburg)

GROUND 1 TD, 2 MRD, 2 AB, 2 *Spetsnaz*, 3 arty/regt,
1 ATK bde/regt, 2 SSM bde, 1 SAM bde, 1 aslt tpt
hel, 1 hel trg regt, 2,120 MBT, 2,700 ACV, 1,400 arty/
MRL/mor, 36 *Scarab*, 24 attack hel
AIR Although Volga–Ural provides air defence cover
for Siberian and Far East MDs, two PVO regts have
been disbanded. Volga–Ural hosts air force aviation
and trg schools, trg regts of tac aviation, storage
bases
AD MiG-23, MiG-25, MiG-31, Su-27
SAM 600

NORTH CAUCASUS MD (HQ Rostov-on-Don)

GROUND 79,500: 1 Army HQ, 1 Corps HQ, 2 MRD, 1
ABD, 3 MR bde, 1 *Spetsnaz*, 1 arty bde, 1 SSM, 4
SAM bde, 1 ATK, 2 attack hel, 1 aslt tpt hel regt, 600
MBT, 1,900 ACV, 730 arty/MRL/mor, 18 *Scud/
Scarab*, 10 attack hel
NAVAL INFANTRY (ε1,500)
1 regt (36 MBT, 130 APC, 24 arty (2S1, 2S9))
AIR 4th Air Army: 1 bbr div (112 Su-24), 1 recce regt
(50 Su-24), 1 air aslt div (116 Su-25, 35 Su-22), 1 ftr
corps of 4 regt (105 MiG-29, 58 Su-27), 1 hel ECM
sqn with 45 Mi-8, trg regt of tac aviation and Air
Force aviation schools
SAM 125

SIBERIAN MD (HQ Chita)

GROUND 2 Corps HQ, 3 TD (1 trg), 2 MRD, 1 arty div,
2 MG/arty div, 3 MR bde, 10 arty bde/regt, 2 SSM, 1
AB, 2 SAM, 2 *Spetsnaz* bde, 4 ATK, 1 attack hel, 4,468
MBT, 6,000 ACV, 4,300 arty/MRL/mor, 36 *Scud/
Scarab*, 18 SS-21, 35 attack hel
AIR Covering Siberian Zone and Far Eastern MD:
FGA 315 Su-24/25
FTR 100 Su-27/MiG-29
RECCE 100 Su-24
AD See Volga–Urals MD

FAR EASTERN MD (HQ Khabarovsk)

GROUND 2 Army, 2 Corps HQ, 10 MRD (2 trg), plus
2 MG/arty div, 1 arty div, 9 arty bde/regt, 1 MR, 1
AB, 3 SSM, 5 SAM, 1 *Spetsnaz*, 1 ATK bde, 2 attack
hel, 2 aslt tpt hel regt, 3,900 MBT, 6,400 ACV, 3,000

arty/MRL/mor, 54 *Scud/Scarab*, 120 attack hel
NAVAL INFANTRY (2,500)
1 div HQ, 3 inf, 1 tk and 1 arty bn
COASTAL DEFENCE
1 div
AIR See Siberian MD
AD See Volga–Ural MD

Forces Abroad ε30,000

Declared str of forces deployed in Armenia and Georgia as
at 1 Jan 1999 was 10,700. These forces are now subordinate
to the North Caucasus MD. Total probably excludes locally
enlisted personnel.

ARMENIA

GROUND (3,100); 2 mil base, 74 MBT, 17 APC, 148
ACV, 84 arty/MRL/mors
AD 1 sqn: 14 MiG-29, 1 S-300 bty

GEORGIA

GROUND (5,000); 3 mil bases (each = bde+), 140 T-
72 MBT, 500 ACV, 173 arty incl **122mm** D-30, 2S1
SP; **152mm** 2S3; **122mm** BM-21 MRL; **120mm**
mor, 5 attack hel. Plus 118 ACV and some arty
deployed in Abkhazia
AD 60 SA-6
AIR 1 composite regt with some 35 **ac** An-12, An-26
hel Mi-8

MOLDOVA (Dniestr)

GROUND 2,600; 1 op gp, 117 MBT, 133 ACV, 128
arty/MRL/mor. These forces are now subordinate to the Moscow MD

TAJIKISTAN

GROUND (ε8,200); 1 MRD, 190 MBT, 303 ACV, 180
arty/MRL/mor; plus 14,500 Frontier Forces
(Russian officers, Tajik conscripts)

UKRAINE

NAVAL INFANTRY (ε1,500); 1 regt (36 MBT, 100
APC, 24 arty (2S1, S29))
AFRICA 100
CUBA some 800 SIGINT and ε10 mil advisers
SYRIA 150
VIETNAM 700; naval facility and SIGINT station.
Used by RF aircraft and surface ships on reduced basis

Peacekeeping

BOSNIA (SFOR II): 1,400; 2 AB bn
GEORGIA/ABKHAZIA ε1,500; 1 AB regt, 2 MR bn
GEORGIA/SOUTH OSSETIA 1,700; 1 MR bn
MOLDOVA/TRANSDNIESTR 500; 1 MR bn
YUGOSLAVIA (KFOR): 3,600

UNITED NATIONS

BOSNIA (UNMIBH): 1 plus 36 civ pol **CROATIA**
(UNPSG): 31 plus 1 civ pol; (UNMOP): 1 obs **GEOR-
GIA**: (UNOMIG) 3 obs **IRAQ/KUWAIT** (UNIKOM):
11 obs **MIDDLE EAST** (UNTSO): 4 obs **WESTERN
SAHARA** (MINURSO): 25 obs

Paramilitary ε478,000 active

FEDERAL BORDER GUARD SERVICE ε196,000
directly subordinate to the President; 10 regional directorates, 7 frontier gps

EQUIPMENT
1,000 ACV (incl BMP, BTR), 90 arty (incl 2S1, 2S9, 2S12)

ac some 70 Il-76, Tu-134, An-72, An-24, An-26, Yak-40, 16 SM-92 **hel** some 200+ Mi-8, Mi-24, Mi-26, Ku-27

PATROL AND COASTAL COMBATANTS about 237
PATROL, OFFSHORE 23
7 *Krivak*-III with 1 Ka-27 hel, 1 100mm gun, 12 *Grisha*-II, 4 *Grisha*-III
PATROL, COASTAL 35
20 *Pauk*, 15 *Svetlyak*
PATROL, INSHORE 95
65 *Stenka*, 10 *Muravey*, 20 *Zhuk*
RIVERINE MONITORS about 84
10 *Yaz*, 7 *Piyavka*, 7 *Vosh*, 60 *Shmel*
SUPPORT AND MISCELLANEOUS about 26
8 *Ivan Susanin* armed icebreakers, 18 *Sorum* armed AT/F

INTERIOR TROOPS 140,000
6 districts, some 20 'div' incl 5 indep special purpose div (ODON – 2 to 5 op regt), 29 indep bde incl 10 indep special designation bde (OBRON – 3 mech, 1 mor bn); 65 regt/bn incl special motorised units, avn

EQUIPMENT
incl 1,700 ACV (incl BMP-1/-2, BTR-80), 20 D-30

FORCES FOR THE PROTECTION OF THE RUSSIAN FEDERATION 25,000
org incl elm of Ground Forces (1 mech inf bde, 1 AB regt, 1 Presidential Guard regt)

FEDERAL SECURITY SERVICE ε4,000 armed incl Alfa, Beta and Zenit cdo units

FEDERAL COMMUNICATIONS AND INFORMATION AGENCY ε54,000

RAILWAY TROOPS ε59,000 in 4 rly corps, 28 rly bde

MILITARY DEVELOPMENTS

Regional Trends

The Middle East and North Africa region continues to be the world's leading arms market, both in absolute terms and as a proportion (7%) of gross domestic product (GDP). While there have been some positive political developments, they have yet to lead to a reduction in demand for advancing military capabilities, and the underlying security uncertainties persist. This situation could change in 2000. The accession to power in May 1999 of the new Israeli government led by Ehud Barak – with its 15-month plan to restart the Middle East peace process and, in particular, to open a dialogue with Syria – has already been influential in, for example, reducing the intensity of the conflict in south Lebanon. The smooth transitions of power to King Abdullah in Jordan in February 1999 and to King Mohammed VI in Morocco in July are both encouraging signs for stability. Further justification for optimism derives from the more flexible approach taken by Algerian President Abdelaziz Bouteflika in dealing with Islamic political and armed opposition. In the Gulf, however, insecurities arise from the failure to resolve the issue of Iraq's weapons of mass destruction (WMD) programmes and the hesitant nature of domestic political reform in Iran.

Middle East

The principal military impact of the new Israeli government's policy has been the sharp reduction of military action in south Lebanon. However, exchanges between *Hizbollah* and the 1,500 Israeli troops and 2,500-strong Israeli-backed South Lebanon Army (SLA) in the 'security zone' along the Israeli border still occur from time to time. Barak has strongly indicated that Israel is prepared to withdraw from south Lebanon subject to progress in negotiations with Syria and Lebanon over the security of Israel's northern border. There have been signs of *rapprochement* between Israel and Syria that could lead to serious negotiations over the Golan Heights and other issues. However, these signs have not prevented either Syria or Israel from upgrading their military capabilities. Syrian President Hafez al-Assad visited Moscow in July 1999 where he signed a deal under which Russia is to supply $2 billion-worth of weapons and equipment – including Su-27 and MiG-29SMT combat aircraft and T-80 tanks – to upgrade outdated Syrian weapon systems. A significant addition to Israel's capabilities was the July 1999 delivery of the first of three German *Dolphin*-class submarines, which have a missile-launch capability, and the 1999 order of 50 F-16 aircraft.

The Gulf

The ending of inspections in Iraq following the withdrawal of the UN Special Commission (UNSCOM) in December has resulted in the containment of Iraq's WMD capabilities being left to the US and UK air forces. Attempts to agree on a new inspection system, linked to a commitment to lift sanctions, failed to make progress by August 1999. It would be difficult for Iraq to deploy significant systems capable of delivering WMD, or to restart or rebuild a major production facility, without such activities being detected and attacked. The four nights of bombing during *Operation Desert Fox* in December 1998, following the withdrawal of the UN inspectors, would have set back attempts to rebuild important WMD capabilities. Nevertheless, significant research and development, as well as planning for a breakout production capability, could be taking place. The US and UK continue to enforce the no-fly zones over Iraq. These are designed to inhibit major conventional-force actions against the *Shi'a* population south of the 33rd Parallel and the Kurdish areas north of the 36th Parallel, as well as threats to Iraq's neighbours, especially Kuwait. The Gulf Cooperation Council (GCC) states are becoming less cohesive, due in some cases to domestic pressures for political reform and succession issues. Particularly notable are Qatar's increasingly independent foreign policy and challenges in the Kuwaiti parliament to the high levels of defence spending. These developments will introduce uncertainties into defence alliances and into major arms transactions with outside powers.

Iran

In 1998 and 1999, Iran's relations and dialogue with the US and other Western powers improved greatly as, despite setbacks, President Mohammad Khatami made modest progress with domestic political reform. In March 1999, Khatami made the first visit to Western Europe by an Iranian leader since the 1979 revolution. This was followed by the first visit of a Western warship to Iran for 20 years when an Italian frigate visited Bandar Abbas in April 1999. Optimism about the reform process in Iran must, however, be tempered by the events of July 1999, when violence erupting from student demonstrations resulted in repressive actions by the security forces and additional restrictions on press freedom. While there have not been significant changes in Iranian military capabilities, the armed forces once again demonstrated their ability to mobilise and deploy large numbers of troops. In September and October 1998, in response to the August kidnapping and killing by *Taleban* forces of Iranian diplomats in the Afghan city of Mazar-e Sharif, the Iranian Revolutionary Guard Corps (IRGC) and then the regular armed forces deployed to the Zabol region near the Afghan border. Some reports indicate that up to 200,000 troops were involved. Although this estimate is probably too high, it is clear that a combined armed force of well over 100,000 was deployed. No doubt the presence of the regular armed forces was intended to be a necessary damper on the zeal of the IRGC and prevented unwanted border incursions. Nonetheless, the major deployment was a salutary lesson to the *Taleban* and others in the region that Iran can muster large conventional force capabilities at short notice when it feels that vital interests are threatened. Since July 1998, when Iran demonstrated its missile capabilities by testing the 1,000–1,500 kilometre *Shihab* 3 medium-range ballistic missile (MRBM), concerns have been aroused in the region and beyond both about the need for missile defence and about possible Iranian WMD programmes. In February 1999, the government declared that its current missile programmes were complete, and that the longer-range *Shihab* 4 ballistic missile in development, reportedly derived from Russian SS-4 technology, was intended for satellite launches only.

North Africa

The continuing civil war in Algeria has accounted for the deaths of about 80,000 people since 1992. The principal active armed opposition group, the *Groupe Islamique Armée* (GIA), continues its campaign, mainly against civilians rather than the security forces. The other main armed opposition group, the *Armée Islamique du Salut* (AIS), which had announced a cease-fire in June 1998, stated in July 1999 that it had ended the armed struggle. This move was in the context of President Bouteflika's plan for a 'law on civil concord', under which an amnesty is to be granted to members of groups such as the GIA and the AIS and their relatives. The amnesty does not apply to those directly involved in terrorism acts. In July 1999, the government released some 2,300 people who had been jailed for minor offences related to the activities of the armed groups. Bouteflika's plan, already approved by the country's legislative assemblies, was due to be put to a national referendum in September 1999. Partly as a result of these moves, Algeria's difficult relations with its two strategic partners, France and Morocco, have improved considerably.

The accession of King Mohammed VI in July 1999 passed off smoothly and promises the development of a more democratic style of government in Morocco. It is not yet clear that this will lead to a solution to the Western Sahara issue. Mohammed has already indicated that he will not stand in the way of the long-deferred referendum on the region's future status, due to take place in December 1999. At the same time, conscious of the strongly entrenched positions among those in and close to the government, he has made clear that the region was 'an integral part' of Moroccan territory. However, renewed armed conflict is now an even more remote possibility.

Libya finally responded to UN demands to hand over for trial suspects in the 1988 bombing of the Pan American flight over the UK. It has also admitted responsibility for the 1989 UTA aircraft bombing over Niger and has agreed to pay compensation. As a result, the UN Security Council lifted its sanctions in April 1999. The immediate consequence has been improved diplomatic and trading relations with Western, mainly European, powers. It remains to be seen if this will help allay concerns over proliferation of missiles and WMD programmes in the longer term.

DEFENCE SPENDING

In 1998, regional military expenditure increased by about 7% in real terms to $61bn, measured in 1997 US dollars, from $57bn in 1997. The weak oil price extending between April 1998 and March 1999 affected the economies and government revenues of the region's oil-producing countries. Regional GDP declined by 1% in 1998, according to provisional estimates. The continued growth in military spending despite economic decline is unsurprising given the continuing regional tensions.

However, 1999 defence budgets indicate a fall in regional spending of some 5% over 1998, with most regional budgets drafted before the March 1999 recovery in crude-oil prices (from under $11 to $17–18 per barrel). This upturn increased the revenues of many regional governments above previous expectations. As a result, 1999 defence budgets may be supplemented during the year. Commitments to equipment modernisation in the region have been generally sustained, although the pace of new orders slowed in 1998 and 1999. Syria and Libya have made known their substantial procurement requirements, particularly after the UN lifted its sanctions on Libya.

Israel

The underlying uncertainties of the Middle East peace process have kept Israel's defence budget at 10–12% of GDP in recent years. The 1999 budget, excluding US Foreign Military Assistance (FMA), is NS27.8bn, up from an initial NS25.1bn in 1998, later revised to NS27.5bn. However, currency depreciation meant the budget declined in real terms from $7.2bn to $6.8bn. Significant military-related expenditure is excluded from Israel's defence budget. For example, in fiscal year (FY) 2000, US Foreign Military Financing (FMF) will rise from $1.8bn to $1.92bn for procurement, but there will be a further cut in military-related economic assistance (steady at around $1.2bn for many years) from $1.1bn to $930 million. Under the October 1998 Wye Memorandum, Israel also stands to receive an additional $1.2bn in FMA from the US in FY1999–01 if the agreement is implemented. The $1.83bn of US FMF is divided as follows: $470m is to be converted to shequals and spent inside Israel, $5m is to be spent in Europe (on procurement and upkeep of defence attachés) and the remainder is to be spent in the US. Because US funding was released early, the Israeli Ministry of Defence gains an extra $100m from interest. One of the largest of Israel's indirect security expenditures is on military pensions, which amounted to some NS2.3bn in 1997 (at 1999 prices) and will increase considerably over the next decade. The 1999 budget proposal contains an increase of NS63m for disabled veterans. Another expenditure under a new law provides education grants for former conscripts – some NS667m for 1999.

Initial deployment of the joint US–Israel *Arrow* anti-ballistic missile (ABM) is planned for late 1999 or early 2000. In 1998, the Israeli Air Force took delivery of the first four of 25 F-15I aircraft, equipped with the US advanced medium-range air-to-air missile (AMRAAM), and the new Israeli *Python*-4 air-to-air missile (AAM), under a contract valued at $2.2bn over ten years. The Air Force has ordered 50 more F-16s from the US in 1999. The Navy took delivery in March 1999 of the first of three *Dolphin*-class submarines supplied by Germany under a bilateral FMA programme. Each submarine is estimated to cost $300m and it is reported that Germany is contributing $750m towards the total cost.

The value of Israeli arms exports fell to $1.3bn in 1998 from $1.5bn in 1997, but Israel remains one of the top five exporters in the international arms trade. A growing proportion of its trade takes the form of firm-to-firm transactions with West European and US defence companies.

Iran

Iran's defence budget for 1999 is R100 trillion ($5.7bn), marginally less than 1998's R101tr ($5.8bn). Official figures show that Tehran's defence spending has almost tripled since 1993. Iran assembled 100 T-72 main battle tanks (MBTs) and 100 BMP-2 armoured personnel carriers (APCs) from kits supplied by Russia in 1998.

Syria and Lebanon

Syria's 1998 official defence budget of S£39.5bn ($878m), which accounts for over a quarter of government expenditure, was similar to actual spending in 1997. The budget covers personnel and operations and maintenance (O&M), but details of procurement spending were not released. The prolonged dispute with Russia, its major equipment supplier, over Syria's Soviet-era debt (estimated by Russia at $11bn) has meant that Syria's procurement activity has been constrained since the end of the Cold War. Reports in 1999 suggest that the dispute has been resolved and that Damascus intends to purchase a range of Russian equipment including S-300 surface-to-air missile (SAM) systems. The 1999 defence budget, including procurement, is estimated at S£67bn ($1.5bn). Lebanon's defence budget has declined from L£901bn ($594m) in 1998 to L£846bn ($560m) in 1999.

Jordan

Jordan's 1999 defence budget rose to D347m ($488m) from D318m ($447m) in 1998. FMF funding from the US for FY1998–2000 amounts to $170m, with a further $200m due under the Wye Memorandum if the agreement is implemented. Under a March 1999 agreement, the Army is to receive 150 *Challenger* 1 MBTs from the UK, with deliveries commencing before the end of 1999.

Gulf Cooperation Council States

Defence-spending in the GCC states is particularly sensitive to oil prices, since oil accounts for the larger part of government revenues. The onset of weak oil prices in April 1998 came too late to change 1998 defence budgets, but caused reductions in several budgets for 1999. The recovery of the oil market in March 1999 came too late to influence these cuts. GDP in the GCC states (which account for half of the region's defence spending) declined by $24bn (9%) in 1998. The economies of Saudi Arabia (-10.8%), Kuwait (-14%), the United Arab Emirates (UAE) (-6%), Oman (-7%) and Bahrain (-3%) were all badly affected. Only Qatar thrived, with its continued spectacular growth (12%) in 1998, fuelled by the strength of liquefied natural gas exports. Despite economic weakness elsewhere, GCC defence-spending obligations in 1998 grew by an estimated 8%, carried forward by the momentum of equipment-programme commitments. Government spending cuts mostly affected non-defence budgets, particularly capital spending for civil programmes. There were also small reductions in salaries for government employees, including the armed forces. Defence budgets for 1999 suggest a real decline of 5% over 1998 levels. The high spending levels of Saudi Arabia and Kuwait will dip in 1999 and 2000 as their post-Gulf War modernisation programmes reach completion. In contrast, spending levels in the UAE and, on a smaller scale, Qatar and Bahrain will increase in 1999–2000 during the delivery phases of committed equipment programmes.

Saudi Arabia's defence spending in 1998 was R78bn ($21bn), compared to R68bn ($18bn) in 1997. Arms imports cost an estimated $10bn in 1998, compared to $11bn in 1997, mainly as a result of continuing combat aircraft deliveries. Saudi government revenues fell by over 30% in 1998 as a result of weak oil prices, forcing the government to borrow from the private sector. Nevertheless, defence spending commitments were maintained. The 1999 defence budget (formulated before the March 1999 oil-price recovery) is an estimated R69bn ($18bn), in a government budget that plans for a 13% drop in expenditure over 1998. Delivery of 72 F-15S fighters ordered from the US in 1992 are past the half-way stage and will continue until 2000. The accumulation of the Kingdom's estimated $7bn debt to the US has required the government to increase payments to the US for the *Peace Sun* F-15 support and C2 *Peace Shield* programmes. Meanwhile, deliveries of 48 *Tornado* bombers ordered in 1993 from the UK under the bilateral *Al-Yamamah* II programme were completed in October 1998.

Kuwait's defence budget in 1998, excluding some military expenses, procurement and other capital spending, was D472m ($1.6bn) with a further D88m ($289m) for the National Guard. Kuwait pays two-thirds of the annual cost of the United Nations Iraq-Kuwait Observer Mission (UNIKOM) (total cost $52m in 1998). In 1997, the government reported total defence outlays of D778m ($2.6bn), D314m ($1bn) for Public Order and Safety, and D301m ($1bn) in unspecified outlays. Official defence and security outlays in 1998 were D903m ($3bn). *The Military Balance* estimates defence outlays at $3.6bn in 1997, falling to $3.4bn in 1998. Kuwait's rearmament programme following the 1991 war with Iraq is nearly complete. Delivery from France of eight *Um Almaradin* (formerly known as *Combattante)* fast patrol craft, armed with British *Sea Skua* missiles, got under way in 1998 and continued in 1999. Delivery of 16 AH-64D attack helicopters is in progress, and is due to be completed in 2000. Deliveries of 27 PLZ45 155mm guns from China were due to be completed by the end of 1999. The order for 48 M-109 155mm guns from the US was confirmed in late 1998. The 1999 budget takes into account a 3% decline in overall government expenditure, with defence spending in 1999 likely to be lower than the 1998 level as new equipment deliveries decline.

Defence spending in the UAE (estimated at $3bn in 1998) will rise substantially as progress payments for new aircraft on order commence, despite the 5% reduction in the government's overall budget for 1999. The UAE order from France in December 1997 for 30 new *Mirage* 2000-9 (plus 33 upgrades to 2000-9 standard for its existing *Mirage* fighters) was confirmed in November 1998. At the same time an order was placed for the Anglo-French *Black Shahine* air-launched cruise missile (ALCM) (based on the French APACHE and UK *Storm Shadow* ALCM). According to some US officials, the transaction might have breached the Missile Technology Control Regime (MTCR) guidelines. Meanwhile, the contract for 80 F-16 Block 60 fighters from the US, ordered in May 1998, has been delayed and is now not expected to be signed until autumn 1999. The other major order is for 18 *Hawk* 200 single-seat multi-role combat aircraft from the UK, first mooted in April 1998, but the contract has yet to be confirmed. If all these contracts are honoured, the combined value of the UAE's fighter acquisitions since late 1997 would exceed $11bn.

Oman's defence spending has consistently exceeded budget under the 1996–2000 five-year plan. Outlays in 1997 were R760m ($2bn), compared to a budget of R698m ($1.8bn). Official outlays in 1998 were reported as R676m ($1.8bn). The 1999 government budget has been cut by 7%, and the defence budget has dropped to R613m ($1.6bn). The 10-year basing agreement with the US (originating in 1979 and renewed in 1989) expired in June 1999. Oman placed an order with a joint UK–Italian consortium to modernise its air-defence radar network in June 1999. Defence spending in Bahrain and Qatar has risen in line with recent equipment modernisation. Bahrain ordered 8 F-16C/Ds from the US in January 1998 for delivery beginning in 2001. Qatar took delivery of the last two of four *Barzan* fast attack craft from the UK in April 1998, and delivery of 12 *Mirage* 2000-5 fighters from France was due to be completed in 1999.

The Gulf States did not commit themselves directly to contributing towards the costs of the *Desert Fox* and *Desert Thunder* operations undertaken against Iraq by the US and UK in December

1998, or of their aftermath. Saudi Arabia pays a third (about $300m a year) of the standing cost of the joint US–UK *Northern* and *Southern Watch* operations. The increased momentum of US–UK operations over Iraq during the first half of 1999 cost them an estimated $300m in addition to the standing costs of *Northern* and *Southern Watch*.

Egypt

Official figures for the 1997–98 Egyptian defence budget show outlays of E£7.8bn ($2.3bn), excluding US FMA for equipment purchases ($1.3bn) and economic aid ($815m). US FMF funding for Egypt in FY1998–2000 has remained at $1.3bn per year, while economic aid from the US has been cut in 1999 to $775m and $715m in 2000. The 1998–99 defence budget was set at E£6.9bn ($2.1bn). The government's overall budget for 1999–2000 increased by 8% over 1998. Defence spending levels in 1999 are likely to be similar to 1998.

Deliveries under the follow-on order for 21 F-16C/Ds from the US (assembled in Turkey) began in June 1999 and are set to continue until 2000. The last of ten SH-2G naval helicopters was delivered in April 1999. The order for an additional 80 M1 *Abrams* MBTs (assembled in Egypt), after delivery of 555 units (mostly assembled in Egypt) ended in late 1998, has not been confirmed. Instead, the Egyptian Tank Plant is to produce under licence 50 M88A2 *Hercules* armoured recovery vehicles (ARVs), with final deliveries to the Army planned for 2002.

Algeria and Morocco

Algeria's 1999 defence budget increased in nominal terms to D121bn from D112bn the previous year, but declined in dollar terms from $1.9bn to $1.8bn in line with the weakening dinar. The Algerian civil war has almost doubled the country's defence budget since 1992, and actual outlays are likely to be higher than budgeted. Delivery of Kh-35 ASSMs from Russia is scheduled for 1999. The armed forces also took delivery of 27 T-72 tanks, 32 BMP-2 APCs and 14 Mi-24 attack helicopters from Ukraine in 1998. In Morocco, defence spending increased sharply in 1998 to D16bn ($1.7bn), up from D13bn ($1.4bn) in 1997.

Table 16 Arms orders and deliveries, Middle East and North Africa, 1997–1999

Supplier	Classification	Designation	Units	Order Date	Delivery Date	Comment
Algeria						
Slvk	APC	BVP-2	48	1994	1995	Deliveries complete 1996
Tu	LACV	*Scorpion*	700	1995	1996	Deliveries continuing
Bel	FGA	Su-24	2	1996	1997	
RSA	UAV	*Seeker*		1997	1997	
Ukr	MBT	T-72	27	1997	1998	
Ukr	AIFV	BMP-2	32	1997	1998	
Ukr	cbt hel	Mi-24	14	1997	1998	
Bel	FGA	MiG-29	36	1998	1999	Reportedly in exchange for 120 MiG-21s
RF	ASSM	Kh-35	96	1998	1999	For FACs. 2 batches of 48 ordered
RF	FGA	Su-24	3	1999	2000	
Bahrain						
US	MRL	ATACMS		1999	2001	
US	hel	AH-1	16	1994	1995	6 in1995, 10 1997. With ATGW
US	SP arty	M-110	49	1995	1997	Ex-US Army
US	FF	FFG-7	1	1995	1997	
US	SAM	*Hawk*	8	1996	1997	Deliveries to 1998. 8 btys
US	APC	M-113	301	1989	1992	Final delivery 1997
US	FGA	F-16C/D	10	1998	2000	AMRAAM-equipped; option for 2 more

Supplier	Classification	Designation	Units	Order Date	Delivery Date	Comment
Egypt						
US	APC	M-113	2,000	1980	1982	Delivered throughout 1997
US	MBT	M1A1	555	1988	1993	Order for 555 complete by end-1998
US	ARV	M88A2	50	1998	2002	1st of 2 contracts. 2nd for parts
US	hel	AH-64	36	1990	1994	24 delivered by 1995; 12 more 1997–99
US	FGA	F-16C/D	46	1991	1994	Deliveries completed 1996, assembled Tu
US	FGA	F-16C/D	21	1996	1999	2 delivered per month until 2000
US	FGA	F-16	24	1999	2001	12 x 1 seater; 12 x 2 seater
US	FFG	*Knox*	6	1993	1994	Leased. 4 more acquired 1998
US	FF	*Perry*	3	1994	1996	Deliveries to 1998
US	hel	SH-2G	10	1994	1997	Deliveries to 1999
US	arty	SP 122 SPG	24	1996	1998	2nd order
RF	hel	Mi-17	20	1997	1997	
US	hel	CH-47D	4	1997	1999	Also updates for 6 CH-47Cs to D
US	SAM	*Avenger*	50	1998	2001	
dom	APC	*Al-Akhbar*		1998	2001	Development complete
US	SAM	*Patriot*	384	1998	2001	384 missiles; 48 launchers
RF	SAM	*Pechora*	50	1999	2003	Upgrade to *Pechora*-2
US	LST	*Newport*	1	1999	2000	
PRC	trg	K-8		1999	2001	
US	AEW	E-2C	5	1999	2002	Upgrade
Iran						
RF	MBT	T-72	100	1989	1998	Kits for local assembly
RF	AIFV	BMP-2	200	1989	1998	Kits for local assembly
RF	SS	*Kilo*	3	1989	1996	Last delivered 1997
dom	SSM	*Shihab*-2		1994	1998	Dom produced *Scud*
dom	SSM	*Shihab*-3		1994	1999	Reportedly based on DPRK *No-dong* 1
dom	MRBM	*Shihab*-4		1994		Development. Reportedly based on RF SS-4
dom	ICBM	*Shihab*-5		1994		Dev. Possibly based on *Taepo-dong*
PRC	FGA	F-7	10	1996	1998	
Fr	trg	TB-200	6	1995	1997	
Fr	trg	TB-21	6	1995	1997	
PRC	tpt	Y-7	14	1996	1998	Deliveries 1998–2006
Iraq						
Ir	FGA	Mig-29	29	1999	1999	Held since 1990; returned by Ir 1999
Israel						
US	tpt hel	S-70A	15	1995	1998	1st 2 deliveries complete
US	tpt	C-135	1	1995	1997	
dom	PFM	*Saar* 4.5	6	1990	1994	Upgrade. 4th delivered 1998 Deliveries of last 2 pending
dom	sat	*Ofek*-3	1	1990	1995	Already launched
dom	sat	*Ofek*-4	1	1990	1999	Launch failed
col	BMD	*Nautilus*		1992	2000	Joint development with US
col	BMD	*Arrow*	2	1986	1999	Deployment to begin 1999; with US
dom	ATGW	LAHAT		1991	1999	Development completed end-1999
Ge	SSK	*Dolphin*	3	1991	1998	1st delivered 1998. Funded by Ge
US	MRL	MLRS	42	1994	1995	Deliveries: 16 in 1997, completed 1998
Fr	hel	AS-565	8	1994	1997	5 delivered 1997
US	FGA	F-15I	25	1994	1998	Deliveries: 4 in 1998, continue to 2000
US	AAM	AIM-120B	64	1998	1999	
dom	sat	*Amos*-1	1	1995		Development slowed by lack of funds
dom	MBT	*Merkava* 3		1983	1989	In production
dom	MBT	*Merkava* 4		1991	2001	In development

Supplier	Classification	Designation	Units	Order Date	Delivery Date	Comment
dom	UAV	*Silver Arrow*		1997		Prototype unveiled April 1998
US	LST	*Newport*	1	1997	1999	
US	cbt hel	AH-64	42	1998	2001	Upgrade to *Longbow* standard.
US	FGA	F-16I	50	1999	2003	With *Popeye* 2 and *Python* 4 AAM
Jordan						
US	SP arty	M-110	18	1996	1998	
US	MBT	M-60A3	50	1996		38 delivered 1997
US	tpt	C-130H	1	1995	1997	
US	tac hel	UH-1H	18	1995	1996	
Pi	FGA	F-5	2	1996	1997	
US	FGA	F-16A/B	16	1995	1997	Deliveries complete April 1998
US	hel	UH-60L	4	1995	1998	
UK	MBT	*Challenger* 1		1999	1999	
UK	recce	*Scorpion*		1999	2001	Upgrade
US	APC	M-113		1999		
Tu	tpt	CN-235	2	1999	2001	One year lease
US	MBT	M1A2	218	1992	1994	Deliveries 1994–97.
US	SAM	*Patriot*	5	1992	1995	5 batteries and 210 missiles
UK	AIFV	*Warrior*	254	1993	1995	Deliveries 1995–97
RF	AIFV	BMP-3	126	1994	1995	Deliveries 1995–97
Fr	PFM	*Um Almaradin*	8	1995	1998	4 delivered. Deliveries continue to 2000
UK	ASSM	*Sea Skua*	60	1997	1998	
Fr	recce	VBL	20	1995	1997	
UK	SAM	*Starburst*	48	1995	1997	
A	APC	*Pandur*	70	1996	1997	Option for 130 more
PRC	SP arty	PLZ 45 155mm	27	1997	1999	Option for 27 more
Aus	APC	S-600	22	1997	1998	
RSA	mor	81mm		1997	1997	
US	cbt hel	AH-64	16	1997	2000	*Longbow* radar not fitted
US	SP arty	M-109A6	48	1998		Includes spt veh. Order frozen late 1998
Lebanon						
US	APC	M113	88	1995	1997	
Mauritania						
Fr	PCI	VSA 14	1	1994	1996	
PRC	tpt	Y-7	1	1995	1997	
Morocco						
Fr	OPV	OPV 64	5	1993	1995	Deliveries completed 1997
US	arty	M-110	60	1995	1997	
Fr	AK	*Dakhla*	1	1995	1997	1,500 tonne AK
Fr	arty	*Canon* 155 F3	18	1997	1997	
Fr	arty	AMX13	10	1997	1997	
Fr	FF	*Floreal*	2	1998	2001	
Oman						
UK	corvette	VT-83	2	1992	1996	Deliveries 1996–97
UK	APC	*Piranha*	80	1993	1994	Final deliveries 1997. Options on 46 more
Fr	APC	VBL	51	1995	1997	Deliveries to 1998
UK	ftr	*Jaguar*	15	1997	1999	Upgrade to bring up to RAF standard
UK	MBT	*Challenger* 2	20	1997	1999	Following purchase of 24 1993–96
Qatar						
UK	APC	*Piranha* II	40	1995	1997	2 delivered 1997, 26 1998
UK	FAC	*Barzan*	4	1992	1995	Deliveries completed 1997
Fr	FGA	*Mirage* 2000-5	12	1994	1997	3 delivered 1997, 8 1998

Supplier	Classification	Designation	Units	Order Date	Delivery Date	Comment
UK	PFC	M-160	7	1995	1996	3 delivered 1996
UK	trg	*Hawk* 100	15	1996	1999	
Fr	MBT	AMX-30	10	1997	1998	Military aid from Fr

Saudi Arabia

US	APC	M113	56	1995	1997	
UK	MHC	*Sandown*	3	1988	1991	Deliveries 1991, 1993, 1997
US	SAM	*Patriot* PAC2	20	1990	1993	Part of *Peace Shield* contract
Ca	LAV	LAV-25	1,117	1990	1992	800 delivered by 1998
UK	FGA	*Tornado* IDS	48	1993	1996	Deliveries completed 1998
UK	trg	*Hawk*	20	1993	1996	Deliveries to 1997. Part of *Al-Yamamah* II
Fr	FFG	F-3000	3	1994	2001	1st to commission 2001, 2nd 2003, 3rd 2005
US	construction	*Jizan*	1	1996	1999	Military city and port
Fr	hel	AS-532	12	1996	1998	4 delivered 1998
Fr	APC	VBL	2	1997	1997	
US	AWACS	E-3	5	1997	2000	Upgrade
It	SAR hel	AB-412TP	40	1998	2000	

Syria

RF	ATGW	AT-14	1,000	1997	1998	Missiles
Ukr	MBT	T-55MV	200	1995	1997	
PRC	SSM	M-9		1995	1997	Operational status not known
RF	SAM	S-300		1997		Unconfirmed

Tunisia

US	hel	HH-3	4	1996	1998	

United Arab Emirates

Fr	MBT	*Leclerc*	390	1993	1994	Also 46 ARVs. Deliveries to 2000
Nl	SP arty	M-109	87	1995	1997	Ex-Nl Army. US made. Upgraded 1999
Fr	hel	AS-565	6	1995	1998	For *Kortenaer* frigates
Nl	FF	*Kortenaer*	2	1996	1997	Ex-Nl, 2nd delivery 1998
Fr	hel	AS-332	5	1996	1998	Upgrade of anti-ship and ASW eqpt
Ge	trg	G-115 TA	12	1996	1997	UAE has option for further 12
RF	tpt	Il-76	4	1997	1998	On lease
US	FAC	TNC-45	6	1997	1999	Deliveries to 2000
Tu	APC	M-113	136	1997	1999	
Indo	tpt	CN-235	7	1997		
US	cbt hel	AH-64A	10	1997	1999	
Fr	hel	*Gazelle*	5	1997	1999	Option for further 5
Fr	FGA	*Mirage* 2000	30	1997	2000	*Mirage* 2000-9
Fr	FGA	*Mirage* 2000	33	1997	2000	Upgrade to 2000-9 standard
UK	ALCM	*Al-Hakim*	416	1992	1998	All delivered 1998
Fr	ALCM	*Black Shahine*		1998	2000	For new and upgraded *Mirage* 2000-9
UK	trg	*Hawk*-200	18	1998	2001	Following delivery of 26 1992–6
Indo	MPA	CN-235	4	1998		
UK	PFC	*Protector*	2	1998	1999	
US	FGA	F-16	80	1999	2002	

Yemen

Fr	APC	AML	5	1996	1998	
Fr	FAC	*Vigilante*	6	1996	1997	Commissioning delayed
Cz	trg	L-39C	12	1999	1999	Deliveries began late 1999
RF	FGA	Su-27	14	1999	2001	

Algeria   Ag

	1997	1998	1999	2000
GDP	D2.7tr	D2.9tr		
	($46bn)	($49bn)		
per capita	$6,400	$6,600		
Growth	1.3%	2.4%		
Inflation	3.8%	2.9%		
Debt	$31bn	$32bn		
Def exp	D122bn	D140bn		
	($2.1bn)	($2.4bn)		
Def bdgt		D112bn	D121bn	
		($1.9bn)	($1.8bn)	
FMA (US)	$0.1m	$0.1m	$0.1m	$0.2m
$1 = dinar	57.7	58.7	68.0	
Population				29,600,000
Age	*13–17*	*18–22*	*23–32*	
Men	1,923,000	1,740,000	2,780,000	
Women	1,790,000	1,626,000	2,610,000	

Total Armed Forces

ACTIVE ε122,000

(incl ε75,000 conscripts)
Terms of service **Army** 18 months (6 months basic, 12 months civil projects)

RESERVES

Army some 150,000, to age 50

Army 105,000

(incl ε75,000 conscripts)
6 Mil Regions; re-org into div structure on hold
2 armd div (each 3 tk, 1 mech regt) • 2 mech div (each 3 mech, 1 tk regt) • 1 AB div • 1 indep armd bde • 4–5 indep mot/mech inf bde • 6 arty, 1 ATK, 5 AD bn
EQUIPMENT
   MBT 951: 324 T-54/-55, 332 T-62, 295 T-72
   RECCE 75 BRDM-2
   AIFV 700 BMP-1, 225 BMP-2
   APC 530 BTR-50/-60, 150 OT-64, some BTR-80 (reported)
   TOWED ARTY 122mm: 28 D-74, 100 M-1931/37, 60 M-30 (M-1938), 198 D-30; **130mm**: 10 M-46; **152mm**: 20 ML-20 (M-1937)
   SP ARTY 185: **122mm**: 150 2S1; **152mm**: 35 2S3
   MRL 122mm: 48 BM-21; **140mm**: 48 BM-14-16; **240mm**: 30 BM-24
   MOR 82mm: 150 M-37; **120mm**: 120 M-1943; **160mm**: 60 M-1943
   ATGW AT-2 *Swatter*, AT-3 *Sagger*
   RCL 82mm: 120 B-10; **107mm**: 58 B-11
   ATK GUNS 57mm: 156 ZIS-2; **85mm**: 80 D-44; **100mm**: 12 T-12, 50 SU-100 SP
   AD GUNS 14.5mm: 80 ZPU-2/-4; **20mm**: 100;

23mm: 100 ZU-23 towed, 210 ZSU-23-4 SP; **37mm**: 150 M-1939; **57mm**: 75 S-60; **85mm**: 20 KS-12; **100mm**: 150 KS-19; **130mm**: 10 KS-30
   SAM SA-7/-8/-9

Navy ε7,000

(incl ε500 Coast Guard)
BASES Mers el Kebir, Algiers, Annaba, Jijel
SUBMARINES 2
SSK 2 Sov *Kilo* with 533mm TT
FRIGATES 3
FF 3 *Mourad Rais* (Sov *Koni*) with 4 x 76mm gun, 2 x 12 ASW RL
PATROL AND COASTAL COMBATANTS 19
CORVETTES 5
   3 *Rais Hamidou* (Sov *Nanuchka* II) with 4 SS-N-2C *Styx* SSM, 2 C-58
   2 *Djebel Chioise*
MISSILE CRAFT 11 *Osa* with 4 SS-N-2 *Styx* SSM (2 non-op)
PATROL CRAFT 5
   INSHORE 3 *El Yadekh* PCI
MINE COUNTERMEASURES 11
   11 Sov T-43 MSC
AMPHIBIOUS 3
   2 *Kalaat beni Hammad* LST: capacity 240 tps, 10 tk, hel deck
   1 *Polnocny* LSM: capacity 180 tps, 6 tk
SUPPORT AND MISCELLANEOUS 3
   1 *El Idrissi* AGHS, 1 div spt, 1 *Poluchat* torpedo recovery vessel

COAST GUARD (ε500)
   Some 7 PRC *Chui-E* PCC, about 6 *El Yadekh* PCI, 16 PCI<, 1 spt, plus boats

Air Force 10,000

181 cbt ac, 65 armed hel
Flying hours ε160
FGA 3 sqn
   1 with 10 Su-24, 2 with 40 MiG-23BN
FTR 5 sqn
   1 with 10 MiG-25, 1 with 30 MiG-23B/E, 3 with 70 MiG-21MF/bis (36 MiG-29 likely to replace some MiG-21s)
RECCE 1 sqn with 4* MiG-25R, 1 sqn with 6* MiG-21
MR 2 sqn with 15 *Super King Air* B-200T
TPT 2 sqn with 10 C-130H, 6 C-130H-30, 5 Il-76
VIP 2 *Falcon* 900, 3 *Gulfstream* III, 2 F-27
HELICOPTERS
   ATTACK 35 Mi-24, 1 with 30 Mi-8/-17
   TPT 2 Mi-4, 5 Mi-6, 46 Mi-8/17, 10 AS 355
   TRG 3* MiG-21U, 5* MiG-23U, 3* MiG-25U, 6 T-34C, 30 L-39, plus 30 ZLIN-142

UAV *Seeker*
AAM AA-2, AA-6
AD GUNS 3 bde+: 725 **85mm, 100mm, 130mm**
SAM 3 regt with 100 SA-3, SA-6, SA-8

Paramilitary ε181,200

GENDARMERIE 60,000 (Ministry of Defence)
6 regions; 44 Panhard AML-60/M-3, BRDM-2 recce,
200 *Fahd* APC **hel** Mi-2
NATIONAL SECURITY FORCES 20,000 (Directorate
of National Security)
small arms
REPUBLICAN GUARD 1,200
AML-60, M-3 recce
LEGITIMATE DEFENCE GROUPS ε100,000
self-defence militia, communal guards

Opposition

GROUPE ISLAMIQUE ARMÉE (GIA) small groups each
ε50–100; total less than 3,000
ARMED FRONT FOR ISLAMIC *JIHAD* (FIDA) small
groups
ISLAMIC LEAGUE FOR THE CALL AND *JIHAD*
(LIDD) small groups

Bahrain   Brn

	1997	1998	1999	2000
GDP	D2.3bn	D2.3bn		
	($6.1bn)	($6.0bn)		
per capita	$8,900	$8,600		
Growth	3.0%	-2.8%		
Inflation	1.0%	-0.2%		
Debt	$2.8bn	$2.0bn		
Def exp	D137m	D151m		
	($364m)	($402m)		
Def bdgt[a]		D112m	D115m	
		($298m)	($306m)	
FMA (US)	$0.1m	$0.3m	$0.2m	$0.2m
$1 = dinar	0.38	0.38	0.38	
[a] Excl procurement				
Population				626,000

(Nationals 63%, Asian 13%, other Arab 10%, Iranian
8%, European 1%)

Age	*13–17*	*18–22*	*23–32*
Men	32,000	25,000	40,000
Women	31,000	24,000	40,000

Total Armed Forces

ACTIVE 11,000

Army 8,500

1 armd bde (-) (2 tk, 1 recce bn) • 1 inf bde (2 mech, 1
mot inf bn) • 1 arty 'bde' (1 hy, 2 med, 1 lt, 1 MRL bty)
• 1 SF, 1 *Amiri* gd bn • 1 AD bn (2 SAM, 1 AD gun bty)
EQUIPMENT
MBT 106 M-60A3
RECCE 22 AML-90, 8 *Saladin*, 8 *Ferret*, 8 Shorland
AIFV 25 YPR-765 (with **25mm**)
APC some 10 AT-105 *Saxon*, 110 Panhard M-3, 220
M-113A2
TOWED ARTY 105mm: 8 lt; **155mm**: 28 M-198
SP ARTY 203mm: 62 M-110
MRL 227mm: 9 MLRS
MOR 81mm: 9; **120mm**: 9
ATGW 15 TOW
RCL 106mm: 30 M-40A1; **120mm**: 6 MOBAT
AD GUNS 35mm: 12 Oerlikon; **40mm**: 12 L/70
SAM 40+ RBS-70, 15 *Stinger*, 7 *Crotale*, 8 I HAWK

Navy 1,000

BASE Mina Sulman
PRINCIPAL SURFACE COMBATANTS 1
FRIGATES
FFG 1 *Sabah* (US OH *Perry*) with 4 *Harpoon* SSM, 1
Standard SAM, 1 76mm gun (hel deck)
PATROL AND COASTAL COMBATANTS 12
CORVETTES 2 *Al Manama* (Ge Lürssen 62m) with 2 x
2 MM-40 *Exocet* SSM, 1 x 76mm gun, hel deck
MISSILE CRAFT 4 *Ahmad el Fateh* (Ge Lürssen 45m)
with 2 x 2 MM-40 *Exocet*
PATROL CRAFT 4
INSHORE 4
2 *Al Riffa* (Ge Lürssen 38m) PFI
2 *Swift* FPB-20
SUPPORT AND MISCELLANEOUS 5
4 *Ajeera* LCU-type spt
1 *Tiger* ACV, **hel** 2 B-105

Air Force 1,500

24 cbt ac, 26 armed hel
FGA 1 sqn with 8 F-5E, 4 F-5F
FTR 1 sqn with 8 F-16C, 4 F-16D
TPT 2 *Gulfstream* (1 -II, 1 -III; VIP), 1 Boeing 727
HEL 1 sqn with 12 AB-212 (10 armed), 14 AH-1E
(ATK), 5 Bo-105, 1 UH-60L (VIP), 1 S-70A (VIP)
MISSILES
ASM AS-12, AGM-65 *Maverick*
AAM AIM-9P *Sidewinder*, AIM-7F *Sparrow*

Paramilitary ε10,150

POLICE 9,000 (Ministry of Interior)
2 Hughes 500, 2 Bell 412, 1 BO-105 hel

NATIONAL GUARD ε900

3 bn; 1 PCI, some 20 PCI<, 2 spt/landing craft, 1 hovercraft

COAST GUARD ε250 (Ministry of Interior)

1 PCI, some 20 PCI<, 2 spt/landing craft, 1 hovercraft

Foreign Forces

US Air Force periodic detachments of ftr and support ac **Navy** (HQ CENTCOM and 5th Fleet) 900
UK RAF 40 (*Southern Watch*), 2 VC-10 tkr

Egypt   Et

	1997	1998	1999	2000
GDP	E£256bn	E£280bn		
	($65bn)	($69bn)		
per capita	$4,400	$4,600		
Growth	5.6%	5.6%		
Inflation	4.6%	3.5%		
Debt	$30bn	$32bn		
Def exp	εE£9.3bn	εE£9.6bn		
	($2.7bn)	($2.8bn)		
Def bdgt		E£6.9bn	E£7.6bn	
		($2.0bn)	($2.2bn)	
FMAᵃ (US)	$2.1bn	$2.1bn	$2.1bn	$2.0bn
$1=pound	3.39	3.39	3.39	
ᵃ UNTSO **1997** $27m **1998** $27m				
Population				61,703,000
Age	*13–17*		*18–22*	*23–32*
Men	3,560,000		3,122,000	4,984,000
Women	3,364,000		2,943,000	4,683,000

Total Armed Forces

ACTIVE 450,000

(incl some 320,000 conscripts)
Terms of service 3 years (selective)

RESERVES 254,000

Army 150,000 **Navy** 14,000 **Air Force** 20,000 **AD** 70,000

Army 320,000

(perhaps 250,000+ conscripts)
4 Mil Districts, 2 Army HQ • 4 armd div (each with 2 armd, 1 mech, 1 arty bde) • 8 mech inf div (each with 2 mech, 1 armd, 1 arty bde) • 1 Republican Guard armd bde • 4 indep armd bde • 1 air-mobile bde • 2 indep inf bde • 1 para bde • 4 indep mech bde • 6 cdo gp • 15 indep arty bde • 2 SSM bde (1 with FROG-7, 1 with Scud-B)

EQUIPMENTᵃ

 MBT 840 T-54/-55, 260 *Ramses* II (mod T-54/55), 500 T-62, 1,700 M-60 (400 M-60A1, 1,300 M-60A3), 555 M1A1 *Abrams*
 RECCE 300 BRDM-2, 112 *Commando Scout*
 AIFV 220 BMP-1 (in store), 260 BMR-600P, 310 YPR-765 (with **25mm**)
 APC 650 *Walid*, 165 *Fahd*/-30, 1,075 BTR-50/OT-62 (most in store), 2,320 M-113A2 (incl variants), 70 YPR-765
 TOWED ARTY 122mm: 36 M-31/37, 359 M-1938, 156 D-30M; **130mm**: 420 M-46
 SP ARTY 122mm: 76 SP 122, **155mm**: 175 M-109A2
 MRL 122mm: 96 BM-11, 60 BM-21/*as-Saqr*-10/-18/-36
 MOR 82mm: 540 (some 50 SP); **120mm**: 1,800 M-38; **160mm**: 60 M-160
 SSM 12 FROG-7, *Saqr*-80 (trials), 9 *Scud*-B
 ATGW 1,400 AT-3 *Sagger* (incl BRDM-2); 220 *Milan*; 200 *Swingfire*; 530 TOW (incl I-TOW, TOW-2A (with 52 on M-901, 210 on YPR-765 SP))
 RCL 107mm: B-11
 AD GUNS 14.5mm: 200 ZPU-4; **23mm**: 280 ZU-23-2, 118 ZSU-23-4 SP, 36 *Sinai*; **37mm**: 200 M-1939; **57mm**: 200 S-60, 40 ZSU-57-2 SP
 SAM 2,100 SA-7/'*Ayn as-Saqr*, 20 SA-9, 26 M-54 SP *Chaparral*
 SURV AN/TPQ-37 (arty/mor), RASIT (veh, arty), *Cymbeline* (mor)
 UAV R4E-50 *Skyeye*

ᵃ Most Sov eqpt now in store, incl MBT and some cbt ac

Navy ε20,000

(incl ε2,000 Coast Guards and ε10,000 conscripts)
BASES Mediterranean Alexandria (HQ), Port Said, Mersa Matruh, Safaqa, Port Tewfig **Red Sea** Hurghada (HQ)

SUBMARINES 4

SSK 4 PRC *Romeo* with sub-*Harpoon* and 533mm TT

PRINCIPAL SURFACE COMBATANTS 11

DESTROYERS 1 *El Fateh* (UK 'Z') (trg) with 4 114mm guns, 5 533mm TT

FRIGATES 10

 FFG 9

 3 *Mubarak* (ex-US *OH Perry*) with 4 *Harpoon* SSM, 36 *Standard* SAM, 1 76mm gun, 2 hel

 2 *El Suez* (Sp *Descubierta*) with 2 x 3 ASTT, 1 x 2 ASW RL; plus 2 x 4 *Harpoon* SSM

 2 *Al Zaffir* (PRC *Jianghu* I) with 2 ASW RL; plus 2 CSS-N-2 (*HY* 2) SSM

 2 *Damyat* (US *Knox*) with 8 *Harpoon* SSM, 127mm gun, 4 324mm TT

 FF 1 *Tariq* (UK *Black Swan*) with 6 102mm gun

PATROL AND COASTAL COMBATANTS 39

MISSILE CRAFT 24

 5 *Ramadan* with 4 *Otomat* SSM

 5 Sov *Osa* I with 4 SS-N-2A *Styx* SSM (2 non-op)

4 *6th October* with 2 *Otomat* SSM
4 Sov *Komar* with 2 SSN-2A *Styx* (2 non-op)
6 PRC *Hegu* (*Komar*-type) with 2 SSN-2A *Styx* SSM (2 non-op)

PATROL CRAFT 15
4 PRC *Hainan* PFC with 6 324mm TT, 4 ASW RL (plus 4 in reserve)
6 Sov *Shershen* PFI; 2 with 4 533mm TT and BM-21 (8-tube) 122mm MRL; 4 with SA-N-5 and 1 BM-24 (12-tube) 240mm MRL
5 PRC *Shanghai* II PFI

MINE COUNTERMEASURES 14
5 *Aswan* (Sov *Yurka*) MSC (1 non-op)
6 *Assiout* (Sov T-43 class) MSC (op status doubtful)
3 *Swiftship* MHI
plus 2 route survey boats

AMPHIBIOUS 3
3 Sov *Polnocny* LSM, capacity 100 tps, 5 tk
plus craft: 9 *Vydra* LCU, capacity 200 tps

SUPPORT AND MISCELLANEOUS 20
7 AOT (small), 5 trg, 6 AT, 1 diving spt, 1 *Tariq* (ex-UK FF) trg

NAVAL AVIATION
24 armed Air Force hel 5 *Sea King* Mk 47 (ASW, anti-ship), 9 SA-342 (anti-ship), 10 SH-2G

COASTAL DEFENCE (Army tps, Navy control)
GUNS 130mm: SM-4-1
SSM *Otomat*

Air Force 30,000

(incl 10,000 conscripts); 583 cbt ac, 129 armed hel
FGA 7 sqn
2 with 41 *Alpha Jet*, 2 with 44 PRC J-6, 2 with 28 F-4E, 1 with 20 *Mirage* 5E2
FTR 21 sqn
2 with 25 F-16A, 6 with 74 MiG-21, 6 with 114 F-16C, 3 with 53 *Mirage* 5D/E, 3 with 53 PRC J-7, 1 with 18 *Mirage* 2000C
RECCE 2 sqn with 6* *Mirage* 5SDR, 14* MiG-21
EW ac 2 C-130H (ELINT), 4 Beech 1900 (ELINT) **hel** 4 *Commando* 2E (ECM)
AEW 5 E-2C
MR 2 Beech 1900C surv ac
TPT 19 C-130H, 5 DHC-5D, 1 *Super King Air*, 3 *Gulfstream* III, 1 *Gulfstream* IV, 3 *Falcon* 20
HELICOPTERS
ASW 9* SA-342L, 5* *Sea King* 47, 10* SH-2G (with Navy)
   ATTACK 4 sqn with 69 SA-342K (44 with HOT, 25 with 20mm gun), 36 AH-64A
   TAC TPT hy 15 CH-47C, 14 CH-47D **med** 66 Mi-8, 25 *Commando* (3 VIP), 2 S-70 (VIP) **lt** 12 Mi-4, 17 UH-12E (trg), 2 UH-60A, 2 UH-60L (VIP), 3 AS-61
TRG incl 4 DHC-5, 54 EMB-312, 10* F-16B, 29* F-16D,

36 *Gumhuria*, 16* JJ-6, 40 L-29, 48 L-39, 30* L-59E, MiG-21U, 5* *Mirage* 5SDD, 3* *Mirage* 2000B
UAV 29 Teledyne-Ryan 324 *Scarab*
MISSILES
ASM AGM-65 *Maverick*, Exocet AM-39, AS-12, AS-30, AS-30L HOT
ARM *Armat*
AAM AA-2 *Atoll*, AIM-7E/F/M *Sparrow*, AIM-9F/L/P *Sidewinder*, MATRA R-530, MATRA R-550 *Magic*

Air Defence Command 80,000

(incl 50,000 conscripts)
4 div: regional bde, 100 AD arty bn, 40 SA-2, 53 SA-3, 14 SA-6 bn, 12 bty I HAWK, 12 bty *Chaparral*, 14 bty *Crotale*
EQUIPMENT
AD GUNS some 2,000: **20mm, 23mm, 37mm, 57mm, 85mm, 100mm**
SAM some 282 SA-2, 212 SA-3, 56 SA-6, 78 I HAWK, 36 *Crotale*
AD SYSTEMS some 18 *Amoun* (*Skyguard*/RIM-7F *Sparrow*, some 36 twin **35mm** guns, some 36 quad SAM); *Sinai*-23 short-range AD (Dassault 6SD-20S radar, **23mm** guns, '*Ayn as-Saqr* SAM)

Forces Abroad

Advisers in Oman, Saudi Arabia, Zaire
UN AND PEACEKEEPING
CAR (MINURCA): 328

Paramilitary 230,000 active

CENTRAL SECURITY FORCES 150,000 (Ministry of Interior)
110 *Hotspur Hussar*, *Walid* APC
NATIONAL GUARD 60,000
8 bde (each of 3 bn; cadre status); lt wpns only
BORDER GUARD FORCES 20,000
19 Border Guard Regt; lt wpns only
COAST GUARD ε2,000 (incl in Naval entry)
   PATROL, INSHORE 40
   20 *Timsah* PCI, 9 *Swiftships*, 5 *Nisr*†, 6 *Crestitalia* PFI<, plus some 60 boats

Foreign Forces

PEACEKEEPING
MFO Sinai: some 1,896 from **Aus, Ca, Co, Fji, Fr, Hu, It, No, NZ, Ury, US**

Middle East and North Africa

Iran   Ir

	1997	1998	1999	2000
GDP[a]	r279tr	r330tr		
	($85bn)	($89bn)		
per capita	$5,200	$5,300		
Growth	3.2%	2.5%		
Inflation	17.2%	22.0%		
Debt	$18.8bn	$20.6bn		
Def exp[a]	r8.2tr	r10.1tr		
	($4.7bn)	($5.8bn)		
Def bdgt		r10.1tr	r10.0tr	
		($5.8bn)	($5.7bn)	
$1 =rial[b]	1,753	1,753	1,753	

[a] Excl defence industry funding
[b] Market rate **1999** $1=r9,400

Population				72,664,000

(Persian 51%, Azeri 24%, Gilaki/Mazandarani 8%, Kurdish 7%, Arab 3%, Lur 2%, Baloch 2%, Turkman 2%)

Age	*13–17*	*18–22*	*23–32*
Men	4,438,000	3,694,000	5,582,000
Women	4,259,000	3,555,000	5,276,000

Total Armed Forces

ACTIVE 545,600

(perhaps 250,000 plus conscripts)
Terms of service 21 months

RESERVES

Army 350,000, ex-service volunteers

Army ε350,000

(perhaps 220,000 conscripts)
4 Corps HQ • 4 armd div (each 3 armd, 1 mech bde, 4–5 arty bn) • 6 inf div (each 4 inf bde, 4–5 arty bn) • 1 AB bde • 1 cdo div, 1 SF div • some indep armd, inf, cdo bde • 5 arty gps • Army avn

EQUIPMENT† (overall totals incl those held by Revolutionary Guard Corps Ground Forces)
  MBT some 1,345 incl: 400 T-54/-55 and PRC Type-59, some 75 T-62, 480 T-72, 140 *Chieftain* Mk 3/5, 150 M-47/-48, 100 M-60A1
  LT TK 80 *Scorpion*
  RECCE 35 EE-9 *Cascavel*
  AIFV 300 BMP-1, 140 BMP-2
  APC 300 BTR-50/-60, 250 M-113
  TOWED 2,170: **105mm**: 130 M-101A1; **122mm**: 600 D-30, 100 PRC Type-54; **130mm**: 1,100 M-46/Type-59; **152mm**: 30 D-20; **155mm**: 20 WAC-21, 70 M-114; 100 GHN-45; **203mm**: 20 M-115
  SP 290: **122mm**: 60 2S1; **155mm**: 160 M-109; **170mm**: 10 M-1978; **175mm**: 30 M-107; **203mm**: 30 M-110
  MRL 764+: **107mm**: 600 PRC Type-63; **122mm**: 50

Hadid/Arash/Noor, 100 BM-21, 5 BM-11; **240mm**: 9 M-1985; **320mm**: *Oghab*; **333mm**: *Shahin* 1/-2; **355mm**: *Nazeat*
  MOR 6,500 incl: **60mm**; **81mm**; **82mm**; **107mm**: 4.2in M-30; **120mm**
  SSM ε10 *Scud*-B/-C (210 msl), ε25 CSS-8 (200 msl), *Fajr*, *Shehab* 3
  ATGW TOW, AT-3 *Sagger* (some SP)
  RL 73mm: RPG-7
  RCL 75mm: M-20; **82mm**: B-10; **106mm**: M-40; **107mm**: B-11
  AD GUNS 1,700: **14.5mm**: ZPU-2/-4; **23mm**: ZU-23 towed, ZSU-23-4 SP; **35mm**; **37mm**: M-1939, PRC Type-55; **57mm**: ZSU-57-2 SP
  SAM SA-7
  AC incl 50 Cessna (150, 180, 185, 310), 19 F-27, 8 *Falcon* 20
  HEL 100 AH-1J **attack**; 40 CH-47C **hy tpt**; 130 Bell 214A, 35 AB-214C; 40 AB-205A; 90 AB-206; 12 AB-212; 30 Bell 204; 5 Hughes 300C; 9 RH-53D; 10 SH-53D, 10 SA-319; 45 UH-1H

Revolutionary Guard Corps (*Pasdaran Inqilab*) some 125,000

GROUND FORCES some 100,000

grouped into perhaps 16–20 div incl 2 armd, 5 mech, 10 inf, 1 SF and 15–20 indep bde, incl inf, armd, para, SF, 5 arty gp (incl SSM), engr, AD and border defence units, serve indep or with Army; eqpt incl 470 tk, 620 APC/ACV, 360 arty, 40 RL and 140 AD guns, all incl in army inventory; controls *Basij* (see *Paramilitary*) when mob

NAVAL FORCES some 20,000

BASES Al Farsiyah, Halul (oil platform), Sirri, Abu Musa, Larak
some 40 Swe Boghammar Marin boats armed with ATGW, RCL, machine guns; 5 *Hudong* with C-802 SSM; controls coast-defence elm incl arty and CSSC-3 (*HY* 2) *Seersucker* SSM bty. Under joint command with Navy

MARINES some 5,000 1 bde

Navy 20,600

(incl Naval Air and 2,600 Marines)
BASES Bandar Abbas (HQ), Bushehr, Kharg, Bandar-e-Anzelli, Bandar-e-Khomeini, Chah Bahar
SUBMARINES 5
SSK 3 Sov *Kilo* SS with 6 533mm TT (possibly wake homing)
SSI 2
PRINCIPAL SURFACE COMBATANTS 3
FRIGATES
FFG 3 *Alvand* (UK Vosper Mk 5) with 1 x 4 *Sea Killer* II, with 4 x C-802 SSM, 1 x 3 AS mor, 1 x 114mm gun

PATROL AND COASTAL COMBATANTS 64

CORVETTES 2 *Bayandor* (US PF-103) with 2 x 76mm gun

MISSILE CRAFT 20

10 *Kaman* (Fr *Combattante* II) PFM 5 of which have 2 or 4 C-802 SSM

10 *Houdong* PFM with 4 C-802 SSM

PATROL, INSHORE 42

3 *Zafar*, 3 *Parvin* PCI, 1 ex-Irq *Bogomol* PFI, some 35 other PFI<, plus some 9 hovercraft< (not all op), 60+ small craft

MINE WARFARE 7

MINE LAYERS

2 *Hejaz* LST

MINE COUNTERMEASURES 5

1 *Shahrokh* MSC (in Caspian Sea as trg ship)

2 *Riazi* (US *Cape*) MSI

2 292 MSC

AMPHIBIOUS 9

4 *Hengam* LST, capacity 225 tps, 9 tk, 1 hel

3 *Iran Hormuz* 24 (ROK) LSM, capacity 140 tps, 9 tk

2 *Foque* LSL

Plus craft: 3 LCT, 6 ACV

SUPPORT AND MISCELLANEOUS 25

1 *Kharg* AOE with 2 hel, 2 *Bandar Abbas* AOR with 1 hel, 1 AR, 4 water tkr, 7 *Delvar* and 9 *Hendijan* spt vessels, 1 AT, 1 *Hamzeh* msc trg

NAVAL AIR (2,000)

8 cbt ac, 9 armed hel

MR 3 P-3F, 5 Do-228

ASW 1 hel sqn with ε3 SH-3D, 6 AB-212 ASW

MCM 1 hel sqn with 2 RH-53D

TPT 1 sqn with 4 *Commander*, 4 F-27, 1 *Falcon* 20 ac AB-205, AB-206 **hel**

MARINES (2,600) 2 bde

Air Force ε50,000

(incl 25,000 Air Defence); some 304 cbt ac (serviceability probably about 60% for US ac types and about 80% for Chinese/Russian ac); no armed hel

FGA 9 sqn

4 with some 50 F-4D/E, 4 with some 60 F-5E/F, 1 with 30 Su-24 (including former Irq ac)

FTR 7 sqn

4 with 60 F-14, 1 with 24 F-7, 2 with 30 MiG-29 (incl former Irq ac)

MR 5* C-130H-MP

RECCE 1 sqn (det) with some 15* RF-4E

TKR/TPT 1 sqn with 3 Boeing 707, 1 Boeing 747

TPT 5 sqn with 6 Boeing 747F, 1 Boeing 727, 18 C-130E/H, 3 *Commander* 690, 15 F-27, 4 *Falcon* 20 1 *Jetstar*, 10 PC-6B, 2 Y-7

HEL 2 AB-206A, 39 Bell 214C, 5 CH-47

TRG incl 26 Beech F-33A/C, 15 EMB-312, 40 PC-7, 7 T-

33, 5* MiG-29B, 5* FT-7, 20* F-5B, 8 TB-21, 4 TB-200

MISSILES

ASM AGM-65A *Maverick*, AS-10, AS-11, AS-14, C-801

AAM AIM-7 *Sparrow*, AIM-9 *Sidewinder*, AIM-54 *Phoenix*, probably AA-8, AA-10, AA-11 for MiG-29, PL-7

SAM 16 bn with 100 I HAWK, 5 sqn with 30 *Rapier*, 15 *Tigercat*, 45 HQ-2J (PRC version of SA-2), 10 SA-5, FM-80 (PRC version of *Crotale*), SA-7, *Stinger*

Forces Abroad

LEBANON: ε150 Revolutionary Guard

SUDAN: mil advisers

Paramilitary 40,000 active

BASIJ ('Popular Mobilisation Army') (R) ε200,000 peacetime volunteers, mostly youths; str up to 1,000,000 during periods of offensive ops. Small arms only; not currently embodied for mil ops

LAW-ENFORCEMENT FORCES (Ministry of Interior) ε40,000

incl border-guard elm ac Cessna 185/310 lt hel ε24 AB-205/-206; about 90 patrol inshore, 40 harbour craft

Opposition

NATIONAL LIBERATION ARMY (NLA) some 15,000

Iraq-based; org in bde, armed with captured eqpt. Perhaps 160+ T-54/-55 tanks, BMP-1 AIFV, D-30 **122mm** arty, BM-21 **122mm** MRL, Mi-8 hel

KURDISH DEMOCRATIC PARTY OF IRAN (KDP-Iran) ε1,200–1,800

KURDISH COMMUNIST PARTY OF IRAN (KOMALA-Iran) based in Iraq ε200

Iraq   Irq

	1997	1998	1999	2000
GDP	ε$17bn	ε$19bn		
Growth	ε10%	ε12%		
Inflation	ε45%	ε45%		
Debt	ε$23bn	ε$23bn		
Def exp	ε$1.3bn	ε$1.3bn	ε$1.4bn	
$1=dinar[a]	0.31	0.31	0.31	

[a] Market rate **1999** $1=d1,600

Population				23,846,000

(Arab 75–80% (of which Shi'a Muslim 55%, Sunni Muslim 45%), Kurdish 20–25%)

Age	13–17	18–22	23–32
Men	1,457,000	1,237,000	1,828,000
Women	1,393,000	1,187,000	1,768,000

Total Armed Forces

ACTIVE ε429,000

Terms of service 18–24 months

RESERVES ε650,000

Army ε375,000

(incl ε100,000 recalled Reserves)
7 corps HQ • 3 armd div, 3 mech div*a* • 12 inf div*a* • 6
Republican Guard Force div (2 armd, 3 mech, 1 inf) • 4
Special Republican Guard bde • 7 cdo bde • 2 SF bde
EQUIPMENT*b*
  MBT perhaps 2,200, incl 1,500 T-55/-62 and PRC
    Type-59, 700 T-72
  RECCE BRDM-2, AML-60/-90, EE-9 *Cascavel*, EE-3
    Jararaca
  AIFV perhaps 900 BMP-1/-2
  APC perhaps 2,000, incl BTR-50/-60/-152, OT-62/-
    64, MTLB, YW-701, M-113A1/A2, Panhard M-3,
    EE-11 *Urutu*
  TOWED ARTY perhaps 1,800, incl **105mm**: incl M-56
    pack; **122mm**: D-74, D-30, M-1938; **130mm**: incl M-
    46, Type 59-1; **155mm**: some G-5, GHN-45, M-114
  SP ARTY 150, incl **122mm**: 2S1; **152mm**: 2S3;
    155mm: M-109A1/A2, AUF-1 (GCT)
  MRL perhaps 150, incl **107mm**; **122mm**: BM-21;
    127mm: ASTROS II; **132mm**: BM-13/-16; **262mm**:
    Ababeel
  MOR 81mm; **120mm**; **160mm**: M-1943; **240mm**
  SSM up to 6 *Scud* launchers (ε27 msl) reported
  ATGW AT-3 *Sagger* (incl BRDM-2), AT-4 *Spigot*
    reported, SS-11, *Milan*, HOT (incl 100 VC-TH)
  RCL 73mm: SPG-9; **82mm**: B-10; **107mm**
  ATK GUNS 85mm; **100mm** towed
  HELICOPTERS ε500 (120 armed)
    ATTACK ε120 Bo-105 with AS-11/HOT, Mi-24,
    SA-316 with AS-12, SA-321 (some with *Exocet*),
    SA-342
    TPT ε350 **hy** Mi-6 **med** AS-61, Bell 214 ST, Mi-4,
    Mi-8/-17, SA-330 **lt** AB-212, BK-117 (SAR),
    Hughes 300C, Hughes 500D, Hughes 530F
  SURV RASIT (veh, arty), *Cymbeline* (mor)

a All divisions less Republican Guard at a reported 50% cbt
effectiveness
b 50% of all eqpt lacks spares

Navy ε2,000

BASES Basra (limited facilities), Az Zubayr, Umm
Qasr (currently closed for navy, commercials only)
FRIGATES 2
FFG 2 *Mussa Ben Nussair* (It *Assad*) with 2 *Otomat* SSM,
  1 *Aspide* SAM, 1 76mm gun, 1 AB 212 hel (1 cur-
  rently in Italy, 1 non-op)

PATROL AND COASTAL COMBATANTS 6
MISSILE CRAFT 1 Sov *Osa* I with 4 SS-N-2A *Styx* SSM
PATROL, INSHORE 5
  1 Sov *Bogomol* PFI, 3 PFI, 1 PCI (all non-op)
  plus 80 boats
MINE COUNTERMEASURES 4
  2 Sov *Yevgenya*, 2 *Nestin* MSI
SUPPORT AND MISCELLANEOUS 3
  1 *Damen* AGS, 1 *Aka* (Yug *Spasilac*-class) AR, 1 yacht
    with hel deck
  (Plus 1 *Agnadeen* (It *Stromboli*) AOR laid-up in
    Alexandria, 3 *Al Zahraa* ro-ro AK with hel deck,
    capacity 16 tk, 250 tps, inactive in foreign ports)

Air Force ε35,000

Serviceability of fixed-wg ac about 55%, serviceability
of hel poor
Flying hours senior pilots 90–120, junior pilots as low
as 20
BBR ε6, incl H-6D, Tu-22
FGA ε130, incl MiG-23BN, *Mirage* F1EQ5, Su-7, Su-20,
  Su-25
FTR ε180 incl F-7, MiG-21, MiG-23, MiG-25, *Mirage* F-
  1EQ, MiG-29
RECCE incl MiG-25
TKR incl 2 Il-76
TPT incl An-2, An-12, An-24, An-26, Il-76
TRG incl AS-202, EMB-312, some 50 L-39, *Mirage* F-
  1BQ, 25 PC-7, 30 PC-9
MISSILES
  ASM AM-39, AS-4, AS-5, AS-11, AS-9, AS-12, AS-
    30L, C-601
  AAM AA-2/-6/-7/-8/-10, R-530, R-550

Air Defence Command ε17,000

  AD GUNS ε6,000: **23mm**: ZSU-23-4 SP; **37mm**: M-
    1939 and twin; **57mm**: incl ZSU-57-2 SP; **85mm**;
    100mm; **130mm**
  SAM 575 launchers SA-2/-3/-6/-7/-8/-9/-13/-14/-
    16, *Roland*, *Aspide*

Paramilitary 45–50,000

SECURITY TROOPS ε15,000
BORDER GUARDS ε20,000
lt wpns and mor only
SADDAM'S *FEDAYEEN* ε10–15,000

Opposition

KURDISH DEMOCRATIC PARTY (KDP) ε15,000
(plus 25,000 tribesmen); small arms, some Iranian lt
arty, MRL, mor, SAM-7

PATRIOTIC UNION OF KURDISTAN (PUK) ε10,000 (plus 22,000 tribesmen); 450 mor (**60mm, 82mm, 120mm**); **106mm** RCL; some 200 **14.5mm** AA guns; SA-7 SAM

SOCIALIST PARTY OF KURDISTAN ε500

SUPREME COUNCIL FOR ISLAMIC RESISTANCE IN IRAQ (SCIRI)

ε4,000; ε1 'bde'; Iran-based; Iraqi dissidents, ex-prisoners of war

Foreign Forces

UN (UNIKOM): some 909 tps and 149 mil obs from 28 countries

Israel				II

	1997	1998	1999	2000
GDP	NS340bn	NS370bn		
	($95bn)	($97bn)		
per capita	$18,000	$18,200		
Growth	2.4%	2.0%		
Inflation	9.0%	7.0%		
Debt	$56bn	$55bn		
Def exp	εNS39bn	εNS41bn		
	($11.3bn)	($11.3bn)		
Def bdgt		NS25.1bn	NS27.6bn	
		($6.6bn)	($6.7bn)	
FMAᵃ (US)	$3bn	$3bn	$3bn	$3bn
$1=new sheqalim				
	3.45	3.80	4.12	

ᵃ UNDOF **1997** $38m **1998** $35m

Population*b*				6,007,000

(Jewish 82%, Arab 14%, Christian 3%, Druze 2%, Circassian ε3,000)

Age	*13–17*	*18–22*	*23–32*
Men	278,000	269,000	516,000
Women	263,000	258,000	508,000

b Incl ε180,000 Jewish settlers in Gaza and the West Bank, ε217,000 in East Jerusalem and ε15,000 in Golan

Total Armed Forces

ACTIVE 173,500

(107,500 conscripts)
Terms of service **officers** 48 months **men** 36 months **women** 21 months (Jews and Druze only; Christians, Circassians and Muslims may volunteer). Annual trg as cbt reservists to age 41 (some specialists to age 54) for men, 24 (or marriage) for women

RESERVES 425,000

Army 400,000 **Navy** 5,000 **Air Force** 20,000. Reserve service can be followed by voluntary service in Civil Guard or Civil Defence

Strategic Forces

Israel is widely believed to have a nuclear capability with up to 100 warheads. Delivery means could include ac, *Jericho* 1 SSM (range up to 500km), *Jericho* 2 (range ε1,500-2,000km)

Army 130,000

(85,000 conscripts, male and female); some 530,000 on mob
3 territorial, 1 home front comd • 3 corps HQ • 3 armd div (2 armd, 1 arty bde, plus 1 armd, 1 mech inf bde on mob) • 2 div HQ (op control of anti-*intifada* units) • 3 regional inf div HQ (border def) • 4 mech inf bde (incl 1 para trained) • 3 arty bn with MLRS

RESERVES
8 armd div (2 or 3 armd, 1 affiliated mech inf, 1 arty bde) • 1 air-mobile/mech inf div (3 bde manned by para trained reservists) • 10 regional inf bde (each with own border sector)

EQUIPMENT
  MBT 3,800: 800 *Centurion*, 300 M-48A5, 300 M-60/A1, 600 M-60A3, 400 *Magach* 7, 200 Ti-67 (T-54/-55), 100 T-62, 1,100 *Merkava* I/II/III
  RECCE about 400, incl RAMTA RBY, BRDM-2, ε8 *Fuchs*
  APC 5,500 M-113A1/A2, ε200 *Nagmashot* (*Centurion*), ε200 *Achzarit, Puma*, BTR-50P, 4,000 M-2/-3 half-track (most in store)
  TOWED ARTY 420: **105mm**: 70 M-101; **122mm**: 100 D-30; **130mm**: 100 M-46; **155mm**: 50 Soltam M-68/-71, 50 M-839P/-845P, 50 M-114A1
  SP ARTY 1,010: **105mm**: 34 M-7; **155mm**: 150 L-33, 120 M-50, 530 M-109A1/A2; **175mm**: 140 M-107 (being phased out); **203mm**: 36 M-110
  MRL 200+: **122mm**: 50 BM-21; **160mm**: LAR-160; **227mm**: 48 MLRS; **240mm**: 30 BM-24; **290mm**: 20+ MAR-290.
  MOR 60mm: ε5,000; **81mm**: 1,600; **120mm**: 900; **160mm**: 240 (some SP)
  SSM 20 *Lance* (in store), some *Jericho* 1/2
  ATGW 300 TOW (incl *Ramta* (M-113) SP), 900 *Dragon*, AT-3 *Sagger*, 25 *Mapats*
  RL 82mm: B-300
  RCL 106mm: 250 M-40A1
  AD GUNS 20mm: 850: incl TCM-20, M-167 *Vulcan*, 35 M-163 *Vulcan*/M-48 *Chaparral* gun/msl, *Machbet Vulcan*/*Stinger* gun/msl SP system; **23mm**: 100 ZU-23 and 60 ZSU-23-4 SP; **37mm**: M-39; **40mm**: L-70
  SAM 250 *Stinger*, 1,000 *Redeye*, 48 *Chaparral*
  SURV EL/M-2140 (veh), AN/TPQ-37 (arty), AN/PPS-15 (arty)

Navy ε6,500

(incl 2,500 conscripts), 11,500 on mob
BASES Haifa, Ashdod, Eilat
SUBMARINES 4
SSK 1 *Dolphin* (Ge prob Type 212 variant)
SSC 3 *Gal* (UK Vickers) with Mk 37 HWT, *Harpoon* USGW (plus 1 in maintenance)
PATROL AND COASTAL COMBATANTS 53
CORVETTES 3 *Eilat* (*Sa'ar* 5) with 8 *Harpoon* SSM, 8 *Gabriel* II SSM, 2 *Barak* VLS SAM (2 32 mls), 6 324mm ASTT plus 1 SA-366G hel
MISSILE CRAFT 14
  2 *Aliya* with 4 *Harpoon* SSM, 4 *Gabriel* SSM, 1 SA-366G *Dauphin* hel (OTHT)
  6 *Hetz* (*Sa'ar* 4.5) with 4 *Harpoon* SSM, 6 *Gabriel* SSM and *Barak* SSM VLS (plus 1 trials)
  4 *Reshef* (*Sa'ar* 4) with 2–4 *Harpoon* SSM, 4–6 *Gabriel* SSM
  2 *Mivtach* with 2–4 *Harpoon* SSM, 3–5 *Gabriel* SSM
PATROL, INSHORE 36
  13 *Super Dvora* PFI<, some with 2 324mm TT, 3 *Nashal* PCI, 17 *Dabur* PFI with 2 324mm TT, 3 Type-1012 *Bobcat* catamaran PCC
AMPHIBIOUS craft only
  1 *Ashdod* LCT, 1 US type LCM

NAVAL COMMAND 300 mainly underwater trained

Air Force 37,000

(20,000 conscripts, mainly in AD), 57,000 on mob; 459 cbt ac (plus perhaps 250 stored including significant number of *Kfir* C7), 133 armed hel
Flying hours regulars: 188; reserves: 75
FGA/FTR 12 sqn
  2 with 50 F-4E-2000, 20 F-4E
  2 with 73 F-15 (38 -A, 8 -B, 16 -C, 11 -D)
  1 with 25 F-15I
  7 with 237 F-16 (92 -A, 17 -B, 79 -C, 49 -D)
FGA 1 sqn with 25 A-4N
RECCE 10* RF-4E
AEW 6 Boeing 707 with *Phalcon* system
EW 3 Boeing 707 (ELINT/ECM), 6 RC-12D, 3 IAI-200, 15 Do-28, 10 *King Air* 2000
MR 3 IAI-1124 *Seascan*
TKR 3 KC-130H
TPT 1 wg incl 5 Boeing 707 (3 tpt/tkr), 12 C-47, 22 C-130H
LIAISON 2 *Islander,* 20 Cessna U-206, 10 *Queen Air* 80
TRG 77 CM-170 *Tzukit,* 28 *Super Cub,* 9* TA-4H, 10* TA-4J, 4 *Queen Air* 80
HELICOPTERS
  ATTACK 21 AU-1G, 36 AH-1F, 30 Hughes 500MD, 42 AH-64A
  ASW 4* AS-565A, 2 x SA-366G
  TPT 38 CH-53D, 10 UH-60; 15 S-70A *Blackhawk,* 54 Bell 212, 43 Bell 206

UAV *Scout, Pioneer, Searcher, Firebee, Samson, Delilah, Hunter Silver Arrow*
MISSILES
  ASM AGM-45 *Shrike,* AGM-62A *Walleye,* AGM-65 *Maverick,* AGM-78D *Standard,* AGM-114 *Hellfire,* TOW, *Popeye* I + II
  AAM AIM-7 *Sparrow,* AIM-9 *Sidewinder,* AIM-120B AMRAAM, R-530, *Shafrir, Python* III, *Python* IV
  SAM 17 bty with MIM-23 I HAWK, 3 bty *Patriot,* 8 bty *Chapparal, Stinger*

Forces Abroad

TURKEY: occasional det of Air Force F-16 ac to Akinci air base

Paramilitary ε6,050

BORDER POLICE 6,000
  some *Walid* 1, 600 BTR-152 APC
COAST GUARD ε50
  1 US PBR, 3 other patrol craft

Foreign Forces

UN (UNTSO): 141 mil obs from 21 countries

Jordan HKJ

	1997	1998	1999	2000
GDP	D5.0bn	D6.0bn		
	($7.1bn)	($7.1bn)		
per capita	$4,400	$4,500		
Growth	5.0%	2.2%		
Inflation	3.1%	4.5%		
Debt	$8.2bn	$7.7bn		
Def exp	D352m	D390m		
	($496m)	($548m)		
Def bdgt		D318m	D347m	
		($447m)	($488m)	
FMA[a] (US)	$32m	$52m	$47m	$77m
$1=dinar	0.71	0.71	0.71	
[a] Excl US military debt waiver **1997** $15m **1998** $12m			

Population	5,020,000 (Palestinian ε50–60%)		
Age	*13–17*	*18–22*	*23–32*
Men	269,000	242,000	439,000
Women	261,000	235,000	423,000

Total Armed Forces

ACTIVE ε104,000

RESERVES 35,000 (all services)
Army 30,000 (obligation to age 40)

Army 90,000

2 armd div (each 2 tk, 1 mech inf, 1 arty, 1 AD bde)
2 mech inf div (each 2 mech inf, 1 tk, 1 arty, 1 AD bde)
1 indep Royal Guard bde
1 SF bde (2 SF, 2 AB, 1 arty bn)
1 fd arty bde (4 bn)
Southern Mil Area (3 inf, 1 recce bn)

EQUIPMENT

MBT some 1,204: 300 M-47/-48A5 (in store), 354 M-60A1/A3, 270 *Khalid/Chieftain*, 280 *Tariq* (*Centurion*)
LT TKS 19 *Scorpion*
AIFV some 35 BMP-2
APC 1,400 M-113
TOWED ARTY 115: **105mm**: 50 M-102; **155mm**: 30 M-114 towed, 10 M-59/M-1; **203mm**: 25 M-115 towed (in store)
SP ARTY 406: **105mm**: 30 M-52; **155mm**: 20 M-44, 220 M-109A1/A2; **203mm**: 136 M-110
MOR 81mm: 450 (incl 130 SP); **107mm**: 50 M-30; **120mm**: 300 Brandt
ATGW 330 TOW (incl 70 SP), 310 *Dragon*
RL 94mm: 2,500 LAW-80; **112mm**: 2,300 APILAS
RCL 106mm: 330 M-40A1
AD GUNS 368: **20mm**: 100 M-163 *Vulcan* SP; **23mm**: 52 ZSU-23-4 SP; **40mm**: 216 M-42 SP
SAM SA-7B2, 50 SA-8, 50 SA-13, 300 SA-14, 240 SA-16, 250 *Redeye*
SURV AN-TPQ-36/-37 (arty, mor)

Navy ε480

BASE Aqaba
PATROL AND COASTAL COMBATANTS 3
PATROL CRAFT, INSHORE 3
3 *Al Hussein* (Vosper 30m) PFI
Plus 3 *Al Hashim* (Rotork) PCI< and 4 other armed boats

Air Force 13,500

(incl 3,400 AD); 93 cbt ac, 16 armed hel
Flying hours 180
FGA 3 sqn with 50 F-5E/F
FTR 3 sqn
2 with 25 *Mirage* F-1 CJ/EJ/BJ
1 with 16 F-16A/B (12 -A, 4 -B)
TPT 1 sqn with 8 C-130 (3 -B, 5 -H), 4 C-212A
VIP 1 sqn with **ac** 2 *Gulfstream* III, IL-1011 **hel** 3 S-70, Bo-105
HELICOPTERS 3 sqn
ATTACK 2 with 16 AH-1S (with TOW ASM)
TPT 1 with 9 AS-332M, 3 Bo-105, 8 Hughes 500D, 18 UH-1H, 8 UH-60 *Blackhawk*
TRG 4 sqn with 16 *Bulldog*, 15 C-101, 12 PA-28-161, 6 PA-34-200, 2* *Mirage* F-1B
AD 2 bde: 14 bty with 80 I HAWK

MISSILES

ASM TOW, AGM-65D *Maverick*
AAM AIM-9 *Sidewinder*, MATRA R-530, MATRA R-550 *Magic*

Forces Abroad

UN AND PEACEKEEPING

CROATIA (UNMOP): 1 obs **GEORGIA** (UNOMIG): 6 obs **TAJIKISTAN** (UNMOT): 5 obs

Paramilitary ε10,000 active

PUBLIC SECURITY DIRECTORATE (Ministry of Interior) ε10,000
(incl Police Public Sy bde); some *Scorpion* lt tk, 25 EE-11 *Urutu*, 30 *Saracen* APC
CIVIL MILITIA 'PEOPLE'S ARMY' (R) ε20,000
(to be 5,000) **men** 16–65 **women** 16–45

Kuwait   Kwt

	1997	1998	1999	2000
GDP	D9.2bn ($30bn)	D8.1bn ($27bn)		
per capita	$15,700	$13,500		
Growth	-1.0%	-14.0%		
Inflation	0.8%	0.1%		
Debt	$8.3bn	$9.0bn		
Def exp[a]	D1.1bn ($3.6bn)	D1.1bn ($3.4bn)		
Def bdgt		D863m ($2.8bn)	D903m ($3.0bn)	
$1=dinar	0.30	0.31	0.31	

[a] UNIKOM **1997** $50m **1998** $52m

Population				2,200,000

(Nationals 35%, other Arab 35%, South Asian 9%, Iranian 4%, other 17%)

Age	*13–17*	*18–22*		*23–32*
Men	117,000	98,000		146,000
Women	87,000	74,000		109,000

Total Armed Forces

ACTIVE 15,300

(some conscripts)
Terms of service voluntary, conscripts 2 years

RESERVES 23,700

obligation to age 40; 1 month annual trg

Land Force 11,000

(incl 1,600 foreign personnel)

2 armd bde • 1 force arty bde • 1 mech inf bde • 1 force engr bde • 1 recce (mech) bde

ARMY

1 reserve bde • 1 Amiri gd bde • 1 cdo bn

EQUIPMENT

MBT 150 M-84 (ε50% in store), 218 M-1A2 (being delivered), 17 *Chieftain* (in store)

AIFV 46 BMP-2, 55 BMP-3, 254 *Desert Warrior*

APC 60 M-113, 40 M-577, 40 *Fahd* (in store)

SP ARTY 155mm: 23 M-109A2, 18 GCT (in store), 18 F-3

MRL 300mm: 27 *Smerch* 9A52

MOR 81mm: 44; **107mm**: 6 M-30

ATGW 118 TOW/TOW II (incl 8 M-901 ITV; 66 HMMWV)

Navy ε1,800

(incl 400 Coast Guard)

BASE Ras al Qalaya

PATROL AND COASTAL COMBATANTS 11

MISSILE CRAFT 6

4 *Um Almaradim* PFM (Fr P-37 BRL) with 4 *Sea Skua* SSM, 1 x 6 Sadral SAM, 1 x 40mm gun (2 more to commission in late 1999/early 2000)

1 *Istiqlal* (Ge Lürssen FPB-57) PFM with 2 x 2 MM-40 *Exocet* SSM

1 *Al Sanbouk* (Ge Lürssen TNC-45) with 2 x 2 MM-40 *Exocet*

PATROL INSHORE 5

1 *Al Shaheed* PCI

4 *Inttisar* OPV

plus about 30 boats

SUPPORT AND MISCELLANEOUS 6

2 LCM, 4 spt

Air Force ε2,500

76 cbt ac, 20 armed hel

Flying hours 210

FTR/FGA 40 F/A-18 (-C 32, -D 8)

FTR 8 *Mirage* F1-CK/BK

CCT 1 sqn with 12 *Hawk* 64, 16 Shorts *Tucano*

TPT ac 3 L-100-30, 1 DC-9 **hel** 4 AS-332 (tpt/SAR/attack), 8 SA-330

TRG/ATK hel 16 SA-342 (with HOT)

AIR DEFENCE

4 *Hawk* Phase III bty with 24 launchers

6 bty *Amoun* (each bty, 1 *Skyguard* radar, 2 *Aspide* launchers, 2 twin **35mm** Oerlikon), 48 *Starburst*

Paramilitary 5,000 active

NATIONAL GUARD 5,000

3 gd, 1 armd car, 1 SF, 1 mil police bn; 20 VBL recce, 70 *Pandur* APC

COAST GUARD

4 *Inttisar* (Aust 31.5m) PFI, 3 LCU

Plus some 30 armed boats

Foreign Forces

UN (UNIKOM) some 909 tps and 149 obs from 28 countries

UK Air Force (Southern Watch) 12 Tornado-GR1/1A

US 5,190 **Army** 3,000; prepositioned eqpt for 1 armd bde (2 tk, 1 mech, 1 arty bn) **Air Force** 2,100 (Southern Watch) Force structure varies with aircraft detachments **Navy** 10 **USMC** 80

Lebanon   RL

	1997	1998	1999	2000
GDP	LP23tr	LP25tr		
	($15bn)	($16bn)		
per capita	$4,800	$4,900		
Growth	4.0%	3.0 %		
Inflation	7.8%	2.0%		
Debt	$4.2bn	$6.2bn		
Def exp	LP1,041bn	LP871bn		
	($676m)	($575m)		
Def bdgt		LP901bn	LP846bn	
		($594m)	($560m)	
FMA[a] (US)	$0.5m	$0.6m	$0.6m	$0.6m
$1=pound	1,540	1,515	1,512	

[a] UNIFIL **1997** $121m **1998** $143m

Population				4,277,000

(Christian 30%, Druze 6%, Armenian 4%, excl ε300,000 Syrian nationals and ε500,000 Palestinian refugees)

Age	13–17	18–22	23–32
Men	210,000	196,000	385,000
Women	214,000	201,000	398,000

Total Armed Forces

ACTIVE 67,900 (incl 27,400 conscripts)

Terms of Service 1 year

Army 65,000 (incl conscripts)

11 inf bde (-) • 1 Presidential Guard bde • 1 cdo/Ranger, 5 SF regt • 2 arty regt • 1 air aslt regt • 1 mne cdo regt • 1 mtn inf coy

EQUIPMENT

MBT some 92 M-48A1/A5, 212 T-54/-55

RECCE 67 AML

APC 1,164 M-113A1/A2, 80 VAB-VCI, 37 Panhard M3/VTT

TOWED ARTY 105mm: 13 M-101A1; **122mm**: 62 incl M-1938, D-30; **130mm**: 11 M-46; **155mm**: 12

Model 50, 18 M-114A1, 35 M-198
MRL 122mm: 23 BM-21
MOR 81mm: 93; **82mm**: 111; **120mm**: 108
ATGW ENTAC, *Milan*, 20 BGM-71A TOW
RL 85mm: RPG-7; **89mm**: M-65
RCL 106mm: M-40A1
AD GUNS 20mm; 23mm: ZU-23; **40mm**: 10 M-42A1

Navy 1,200

BASES Juniye, Beirut
PATROL AND COASTAL COMBATANTS 7
PATROL CRAFT, INSHORE 7
5 UK *Attacker* PCI<, 2 UK *Tracker* PCI, plus 27 armed boats
AMPHIBIOUS 2
2 *Sour* (Fr *Edic*) LST (96 tps)

Air Force 1,700

EQUIPMENT
HELICOPTERS
TPT 16 UH-1H
TRG 3† *Bulldog*

Paramilitary ε13,000 active

INTERNAL SECURITY FORCE ε13,000 (Ministry of Interior)
(incl Regional and Beirut *Gendarmerie* coy plus Judicial Police); 30 *Chaimite* APC
CUSTOMS
2 *Tracker* PCI<, 5 *Aztec* PCI<

Opposition

MILITIAS
Most militias, except *Hizbollah* and the South Lebanon Army, have been substantially disbanded and hy wpn handed over to the National Army.
HIZBOLLAH ('Party of God'; Shi'a, fundamentalist, pro-Iranian): ε3–500 (-) active; about 3,000 in spt
EQUIPMENT arty, MRL, RL, RCL, ATGW (AT-3 *Sagger*, AT-4 *Spigot*), AA guns, SAM
SOUTH LEBANESE ARMY (SLA) 2,500 active (was mainly Christian but increasingly Shi'a, some Druze; trained, equipped and supported by Israel; occupies the 'Security Zone' between Israeli border and area controlled by UNIFIL and also the reduced Jezzine Pocket up to KFAR HOUNE)
EQUIPMENT
MBT 30 T-54/-55
APC M-113, BTR-50
TOWED ARTY **122mm**: D-30; **130mm**: M-46; **155mm**: M-1950
MOR some **160mm**

Foreign Forces

UN (UNIFIL): some 4,496; 6 inf bn 1 each from **Fji**, **Gha**, **Ind**, **Irl**, **N**, **SF**, plus spt units from **Fr**, **It**, **Pl**
IRAN ε150 Revolutionary Guard
SYRIA 22,000 **Beirut** elm 1 mech inf bde, 5 SF regt **Metn** elm 1 mech inf bde **Bekaa** 1 mech inf div HQ, elm 2 mech inf, elm 1 armd bde **Tripoli** 1 SF regt **Batrum** 1 SF Regt **Kpar Fallus** elm 3 SF regt

Libya   LAR

	1997	1998	1999	2000
GDP	ε$26bn	ε$26bn		
per capita	$5,700	$5,600		
Growth	ε2.6%	ε-1.8%		
Inflation	ε25%	ε24%		
Debt	ε$4.1bn	ε$3.8bn		
Def exp	εD480m	εD560m		
	($1.3bn)	($1.5bn)		
Def bdgt		εD495m	εD580m	
		($1.3bn)	($1.3bn)	
$1 = dinar[a]	0.38	0.38	0.45	
[a] Market rate 1999 $1=D3–4				
Population				6,203,000
Age	13–17	18–22	23–32	
Men	362,000	301,000	458,000	
Women	348,000	290,000	438,000	

Total Armed Forces

ACTIVE ε65,000
(incl ε40,000 conscripts)
Terms of service selective conscription, 1–2 years

RESERVES some 40,000
People's Militia

Army ε35,000

(ε25,000 conscripts)
7 Mil Districts • 5 elite bde (regime sy force) • 10 tk bn • 22 arty bn • 21 inf bn • 8 AD arty bn • 8 mech inf bn • 15 para/cdo bn • 5 SSM bde
EQUIPMENT
MBT 560 T-55, 280 T-62, 145 T-72 (plus some 1,040 T-54/-55, 70 T-62, 115 T-72 in store†)
RECCE 250 BRDM-2, 380 EE-9 *Cascavel*
AIFV 1,000 BMP-1
APC 750 BTR-50/-60, 100 OT-62/-64, 40 M-113, 100 EE-11 *Urutu*, some BMD
TOWED ARTY some 720: **105mm**: some 60 M-101; **122mm**: 270 D-30, 60 D-74; **130mm**: 330 M-46; **152mm**: M-1937
SP ARTY: 450: **122mm**: 130 2S1; **152mm**: 60 2S3, 80

DANA; **155mm:** 160 *Palmaria*, 20 M-109
MRL 107mm: Type 63; **122mm:** 350 BM-21/RM-70,
    300 BM-11
MOR 82mm; 120mm: M-43; **160mm:** M-160
SSM launchers: 40 FROG-7, 80 *Scud*-B
ATGW 3,000: *Milan*, AT-3 *Sagger* (incl BRDM SP),
    AT-4 *Spigot*
RCL 106mm: 220 M-40A1
AD GUNS 600: **23mm:** ZU-23, ZSU-23-4 SP; **30mm:**
    M-53/59 SP
SAM SA-7/-9/-13, 24 quad *Crotale*
SURV RASIT (veh, arty)

Navy 8,000

(incl Coast Guard)
BASES Major: Tripoli, Benghazi, Tobruk, Khums
Minor: Derna, Zuwurah, Misonhah
SUBMARINES
SSK 4 *Al Badr* † (Sov *Foxtrot*) with 533mm and 406mm
    TT (2 non-op)
FRIGATES 2
FFG 2 *Al Hani* (Sov *Koni*) with 4 ASTT, 2 ASW RL; plus
    4 SS-N-2C SSM (1 non-op)
PATROL AND COASTAL COMBATANTS 32
CORVETTES 3
    3 *Ean al Gazala* (Sov *Nanuchka* II) with 2 x 2 SS-N-2C
      Styx SSM
MISSILE CRAFT 21
    9 *Sharaba* (Fr *Combattante* II) with 4 *Otomat* SSM, 1 x
      76mm gun (5 non-op)
    12 *Al Katum* (Sov *Osa* II) with 4 SS-N-2C SSM (6 non-
      op)
PATROL, INSHORE 8
    4 *Garian*, 3 *Benina*, 1 Sov *Poluchat*
MINE COUNTERMEASURES 8
    8 *Ras al Gelais* (Sov *Natya* MSO)
    (*El Temsah* and about 5 other ro-ro tpt have mine-
    laying capability)
AMPHIBIOUS 5
    2 *Ibn Ouf* LST, capacity 240 tps, 11 tk, 1 SA-316B hel
    3 Sov *Polnocny* LSM, capacity 180 tps, 6 tk (1 non-op)
    Plus craft: 3 LCT
SUPPORT AND MISCELLANEOUS 10
    1 *Zeltin* log spt/dock, 1 *Tobruk* trg, 1 ARS, 1 diving
    spt, 1 *El Temsah* and about 5 other ro-ro tpt
COASTAL DEFENCE
1 SSC-3 *Styx* bty
NAVAL AVIATION
32 armed hel
HEL 2 sqn
    1 with 25 Mi-14 PL (ASW), 1 with 7 SA-321 (Air
    Force assets)

Air Force 22,000

(incl Air Defence Command; ε15,000 conscripts) 420
cbt ac, 52 armed hel (many ac in store, number n.k.)
Flying hours 85
BBR 1 sqn with 6 Tu-22
FGA 13 sqn
    12 with 40 MiG-23BN, 15 MiG-23U, 30 *Mirage* 5D/
      DE, 14 *Mirage* 5DD, 14 *Mirage* F-1AD, 6 Su-24, 45
      Su-20/-22
    1 with 30 J-1 *Jastreb*
FTR 9 sqn with 50 MiG-21, 75 MiG-23, 60 MiG-25, 3 -
    25U, 15 *Mirage* F-1ED, 6 -BD
RECCE 2 sqn with 4 *Mirage* 5DR, 7 MiG-25R
TPT 9 sqn with 15 An-26, 12 Lockheed (7 C-130H, 2 L-
    100-20, 3 L-100-30), 16 G-222, 20 Il-76, 15 L-410
ATTACK HEL 40 Mi-25, 12 Mi-35
TPT HEL hy 18 CH-47C **med** 34 Mi-8/17 **lt** 30 Mi-2, 11
    SA-316, 5 AB-206
TRG ac 80 *Galeb* G-2 **hel** 20 Mi-2 **other ac** incl 1 Tu-22,
    150 L-39ZO, 20 SF-260WL
MISSILES
    ASM AT-2 *Swatter* ATGW (hel-borne), AS-7, AS-9,
      AS-11
    AAM AA-2 *Atoll*, AA-6 *Acrid*, AA-7 *Apex*, AA-8
      Aphid, R-530, R-550 *Magic*

AIR DEFENCE COMMAND

Senezh AD comd and control system
4 bde with SA-5A: each 2 bn of 6 launchers, some 4 AD
    arty gun bn; radar coy
5 Regions: 5–6 bde each 18 SA-2; 2–3 bde each 12 twin
    SA-3; ε3 bde each 20–24 SA-6/-8

Paramilitary

CUSTOMS/COAST GUARD (Naval control)
a few patrol craft incl in naval totals, plus armed boats

Mauritania				RIM
	1997	**1998**	**1999**	**2000**
GDP	OM165bn	OM180bn		
	($1.1bn)	($1.2bn)		
per capita	$1,800	$1,800		
Growth	5.1%	3.9%		
Inflation	4.6%	7.1%		
Debt	$2.5bn	$2.5bn		
Def exp	OM3.7bn	OM4.7bn		
	($24m)	($26m)		
Def bdgt			εOM5.4bn	
			($26m)	
FMA (Fr)	$1.1m	$1.0m	$1.2m	
$1=OM (Mauritanian ougiya)				
	152	184	207	

Population			2,538,000
Age	*13–17*	*18–22*	*23–32*
Men	140,000	117,000	184,000
Women	137,000	112,000	179,000

Total Armed Forces

ACTIVE ε15,650

Terms of service conscription 24 months authorised

Army 15,000

6 Mil Regions • 7 mot inf bn • 3 arty bn • 8 inf bn • 4 AD arty bty • 1 para/cdo bn • 1 Presidential sy bn • 2 Camel Corps bn • 1 engr coy • 1 armd recce sqn

EQUIPMENT
MBT 35 T-54/-55
RECCE 60 AML (20 -60, 40 -90), 40 *Saladin*, 5 *Saracen*
TOWED ARTY 105mm: 35 M-101A1/HM-2; **122mm**: 20 D-30, 20 D-74
MOR 81mm: 70; **120mm**: 30
ATGW *Milan*
RCL 75mm: M-20; **106mm**: M-40A1
AD GUNS 23mm: 20 ZU-23-2; **37mm**: 15 M-1939; **57mm**: S-60; **100mm**: 12 KS-19
SAM SA-7

Navy ε500

BASES Nouadhibou, Nouakchott
PATROL CRAFT 7
OFFSHORE 3
1 *Aboubekr Ben Amer* (Fr OPV 54) OPV
1 *N'Madi* (UK *Jura*) PCO (fishery protection)
1 *El Nasr* (Fr *Patra*) PCO
INSHORE 4
4 *Mandovi* PCI

Air Force 150

7 cbt ac, no armed hel
CCT 5 BN-2 *Defender*, 2 FTB-337 *Milirole*
MR 2 *Cheyenne* II
TPT 2 Cessna F-337, 1 DHC-5D, 1 *Gulfstream* II

Paramilitary ε5,000 active

GENDARMERIE (Ministry of Interior) ε3,000
6 regional coy
NATIONAL GUARD (Ministry of Interior) 2,000
plus 1,000 auxiliaries
CUSTOMS
1 *Dah Ould Bah* (Fr *Amgram* 14)

Morocco   Mor

	1997	1998	1999	2000
GDP	D319bn	D347bn		
	($34bn)	($36bn)		
per capita	$3,600	$3,800		
Growth	-2.4%	6.7%		
Inflation	0.9%	2.7%		
Debt	$22bn	$23bn		
Def exp	D13.2bn	D16bn		
	($1.4bn)	($1.7bn)		
Def bdgt			D17.3bn	
			($1.7bn)	
FMA[a] (US)	$0.8m	$0.9m	$2.9m	$3.2m
$1 =dirham	9.53	9.60	9.94	

[a] MINURSO **1997** $29m **1998** $23m

Population			29,829,000
Age	*13–17*	*18–22*	*23–32*
Men	1,720,000	1,555,000	2,589,000
Women	1,663,000	1,502,000	2,512,000

Total Armed Forces

ACTIVE 196,300

(incl ε100,000 conscripts)
Terms of service conscription 18 months authorised; most enlisted personnel are volunteers

RESERVES

Army 150,000; obligation to age 50

Army 175,000

(ε100,000 conscripts)
2 Comd (Northern Zone, Southern Zone) • 3 mech inf bde • 1 lt sy bde • 2 para bde • 8 mech inf regt •
Indep units
  12 arty bn • 3 mot (camel corps) bn • 1 AD gp • 2 cav bn • 10 armd bn • 1 mtn bn • 37 inf bn • 7 engr bn • 4 cdo units • 2 AB bn

ROYAL GUARD 1,500
1 bn, 1 cav sqn
EQUIPMENT
MBT 224 M-48A5, 300 M-60 (60 -A1, 240 -A3)
LT TK 100 SK-105 *Kuerassier*
RECCE 16 EBR-75, 80 AMX-10RC, 190 AML-90, 38 AML-60-7, 20 M-113
AIFV 60 *Ratel* (30 -20, 30 -90), 45 VAB-VCI, 10 AMX-10P
APC 420 M-113, 320 VAB-VTT, some 45 OT-62/-64 may be op
TOWED ARTY 105mm: 35 lt (L-118), 20 M-101, 36 M-1950; **130mm**: 18 M-46; **155mm**: 20 M-114, 35 FH-70, 26 M-198
SP ARTY 105mm: 5 Mk 61; **155mm**: 126 F-3, 44 M-

109, 20 M-44; **203mm**: 60 M-110
MRL 122mm: 39 BM-21
MOR 81mm: 1,100; **120mm**: 600 (incl 20 VAB SP)
ATGW 440 *Dragon*, 80 *Milan*, 150 TOW (incl 42 SP),
50 AT-3 *Sagger*
RL 89mm: 150 3.5in M-20
RCL 106mm: 350 M-40A1
ATK GUNS 90mm: 28 M-56; **100mm**: 8 SU-100 SP
AD GUNS 14.5mm: 200 ZPU-2, 20 ZPU-4; **20mm**:
40 M-167, 60 M-163 *Vulcan* SP; **23mm**: 90 ZU-23-2;
100mm: 15 KS-19 towed
SAM 37 M-54 SP *Chaparral*, 70 SA-7
SURV RASIT (veh, arty)
UAV R4E-50 *Skyeye*

Navy 7,800

(incl 1,500 Marines)
BASES Casablanca, Agadir, Al Hoceima, Dakhla,
Tangier
FRIGATES 1 *Lt Col. Errhamani* (Sp *Descubierta*) with 2 x
3 ASTT (Mk 46 LWT), 1 x 2 375mm AS mor (fitted for 4
MM-38 *Exocet* SSM)
PATROL AND COASTAL COMBATANTS 27
MISSILE CRAFT 4 *Cdt El Khattabi* (Sp *Lazaga* 58m)
PFM with 4 MM-38 *Exocet* SSM
PATROL CRAFT 23
COASTAL 17
2 *Okba* (Fr PR-72) PFC
6 *LV Rabhi* (Sp 58m B-200D) PCC
4 *El Hahiq* (Dk *Osprey* 55) PCC (incl 2 with customs)
5 *Rais Bargach* (navy marine for fisheries dept)
INSHORE 6 *El Wacil* (Fr P-32) PFI< (incl 4 with
customs)
AMPHIBIOUS 4
3 *Ben Aicha* (Fr *Champlain* BATRAL) LSM, capacity
140 tps, 7 tk
1 *Sidi Mohammed Ben Abdallah* (US Newport) LST,
capacity 400 troops
Plus craft: 1 *Edic*-type LCT
SUPPORT AND MISCELLANEOUS 4
2 log spt, 1 tpt, 1 AGOR (US lease)

MARINES (1,500)
1 naval inf bn

Air Force 13,500

89 cbt ac, 24 armed hel
Flying hours F-5 and *Mirage*: over 100
FGA 10 F-5A, 3 F-5B, 16 F-5E, 4 F-5F, 14 *Mirage* F-1EH
FTR 1 sqn with 15 *Mirage* F-1CH
RECCE 2 C-130H (with side-looking radar), 4* OV-10
EW 2 C-130 (ELINT), 1 *Falcon* 20 (ELINT)
TKR 1 Boeing 707, 2 KC-130H (tpt/tkr)
TPT 11 C-130H, 7 CN-235, 3 Do-28, 3 *Falcon* 20, 1
Falcon 50 (VIP), 2 *Gulfstream* II (VIP), 5 *King Air* 100,

3 *King Air* 200
HELICOPTERS
ATTACK 24 SA-342 (12 with HOT, 12 with cannon)
TPT hy 7 CH-47 **med** 27 SA-330, 27 AB-205A **lt** 20
AB-206, 3 AB-212, 4 SA-319
TRG 10 AS-202, 2 CAP-10, 4 CAP-230, 12 T-34C, 23*
Alpha Jet
LIAISON 2 *King Air* 200, 2 UH-60 *Blackhawk*
AAM AIM-9B/D/J *Sidewinder*, R-530, R-550 *Magic*
ASM AGM-65B *Maverick* (for F-5E), HOT

Forces Abroad

UN AND PEACEKEEPING
BOSNIA (SFOR II): ε800; 1 mot inf bn

Paramilitary 42,000 active

GENDARMERIE ROYALE 12,000

1 bde, 4 mobile gp, 1 para sqn, air sqn, coast guard unit
EQPT 18 boats **ac** 2 *Rallye* **hel** 3 SA-315, 3 SA-316, 2
SA-318, 6 *Gazelle*, 6 SA-330, 2 SA-360
FORCE AUXILIAIRE 30,000
incl 5,000 Mobile Intervention Corps
CUSTOMS/COAST GUARD
4 *Erraid* PCI, 32 boats, 3 SAR craft

Opposition

POLISARIO ε3–6,000
Mil wing of Sahrawi People's Liberation Army, org in
bn
EQPT 100 T-55, T-62 tk; 50+ BMP-1, 20–30 EE-9
Cascavel MICV; 25 D-30/M-30 **122mm** how; 15
BM-21 **122mm** MRL; 20 **120mm** mor; AT-3 *Sagger*
ATGW; 50 ZSU-23-2, ZSU-23-4 **23mm** SP AA
guns; SA-6/-7/-8/-9 SAM (Captured Moroccan
eqpt incl AML-90, *Eland* armd recce, *Ratel* 20,
Panhard APC, Steyr SK-105 *Kuerassier* lt tks)

Foreign Forces

UN (MINURSO) some 27 tps, 204 mil obs in Western
Sahara from 24 countries

Oman   O

	1997	1998	1999	2000
GDP	R6.2bn	R5.5bn		
	($16.2bn)	($14.2bn)		
per capita	$9,100	$8,300		
Growth	3.6%	-7.0%		
Inflation	-0.2%	-5.7%		
Debt	$3.4bn	$3.9bn		

contd	1997	1998	1999	2000
Def exp	R760m	R740m		
	($2.0bn)	($1.8bn)		
Def bdgt[a]		R655m	R613m	
		($1.7bn)	($1.6bn)	
FMA[b] (US)	$0.2m	$0.2m	$0.2m	$0.3m
$1 = rial	0.38	0.38	0.38	

[a] Five-year plan 1996–2000 allocates R3.3bn ($8.6bn) for defence
[b] Excl ε$100m over 1990–99 from US Access Agreement renewed in 1990

Population		2,213,000 (expatriates 27%)	
Age	*13–17*	*18–22*	*23–32*
Men	126,000	101,000	149,000
Women	122,000	99,000	138,000

Total Armed Forces

ACTIVE 43,500
(incl Royal Household tps, and some 3,700 foreign personnel)

Army 25,000

(regt are bn size)
1 armd, 2 inf bde HQ • 2 armd regt (3 tk sqn) • 1 armd recce regt (3 sqn) • 4 arty (2 fd, 1 med (2 bty), 1 AD (2 bty)) regt • 8 inf regt (incl 2 Baluch) • 1 inf recce regt (3 recce coy), 2 indep recce coy • 1 fd engr regt (3 sqn) • 1 AB regt • Musandam Security Force (indep rifle coy)

EQUIPMENT
MBT 6 M-60A1, 93 M-60A3, 24 *Qayid al-Ardh* (*Chieftain* Mk 7/-15) (in store), 18 *Challenger* 2
LT TK 37 *Scorpion*
RECCE 41 VBL
APC 6 *Spartan*, 13 *Sultan*, 4 *Stormer*, 80 *Piranha*
TOWED ARTY 91: **105mm**: 42 ROF lt; **122mm**: 25 D-30; **130mm**: 12 M-46, 12 Type 59-1
SP ARTY **155mm**: 18 G-6
MOR **81mm**: 69; **107mm**: 20 4.2in M-30
ATGW 18 TOW, 50 *Milan* (incl 2 VCAC)
AD GUNS **23mm**: 4 ZU-23-2; **35mm**: 10 GDF; **40mm**: 12 Bofors L/60
SAM *Blowpipe*, 28 *Javelin*, 34 SA-7

Navy 4,200

BASES Seeb (HQ), Wudam (main base), Raysut, Ghanam Island, Alwi
PATROL AND COASTAL COMBATANTS 13
MISSILE CRAFT 4 *Dhofar*, 1 with 2 x 3 MM-40 *Exocet* SSM, 3 with 2 x 4 MM-40 *Exocet* SSM
PATROL CRAFT 7
3 *Al Bushra* (Fr P-400) with 1 76m gun, 4 406mm TT
4 *Seeb* (Vosper 25m) PCI<

CORVETTES 2 *Qahir Al Amwaj* with 8 MM-40 *Exocet* SSM, 8 *Crotale* SAM, 1 76mm gun, 6 x 324mm TT, hel deck
AMPHIBIOUS 1
1 *Nasr el Bahr* LST†, capacity 240 tps, 7 tk, hel deck
Plus craft: 3 LCM, 1 LCU
SUPPORT AND MISCELLANEOUS 5
1 *Al Sultana*, 1 *Al Mabrukah* trg with hel deck (also used in offshore patrol role), 1 supply, 1 AGHS, 1 Royal Yacht plus craft

Air Force 4,100

40 cbt ac, no armed hel
FGA 2 sqn with 8 *Jaguar* S(O) Mk 1, 4 T-2
FGA/RECCE 12 *Hawk* 203
CCT 1 sqn with 12* BAC-167 Mk 82, 4* *Hawk* 103
TPT 3 sqn
 1 with 3 BAC-111
 2 with 15 *Skyvan* 3M (7 radar-equipped, for MR), 3 C-130H
HEL 2 med tpt sqn with 20 AB-205, 3 AB-206, 3 AB-212, 5 AB-214
TRG 4 AS-202-18, 7 MFI-17B *Mushshak*
AD 2 sqn with 28 *Rapier* SAM, *Martello* radar
AAM AIM-9P *Sidewinder*

Royal Household 6,500

(incl HQ staff) 2 SF regt (1,000)
Royal Guard bde (5,000) 9 VBC-90 lt tk, 14 VAB-VCI APC, 9 VAB-VDAA, *Javelin* SAM
Royal Yacht Squadron (based Muscat) (150) 1 Royal Yacht, 3,800t with hel deck, 1 *Fulk Al Salamah* tps and veh tpt with up to 2 AS-332C *Puma* hel, 1 *Zinat Al Bihaar Dhow*
Royal Flight (250) ac 2 Boeing-747 SP, 1 DC-8-73CF, 2 *Gulfstream* IV hel 3 AS-330, 2 AS-332C, 1 AS-332L

Paramilitary 4,400 active

TRIBAL HOME GUARD (*Firqat*) 4,000
org in teams of ε100
POLICE COAST GUARD 400
3 CG 29 PCI, plus 14 craft
POLICE AIR WING
ac 1 Do-228, 2 CN 235M, 1 BN-2T Islander hel 3 Bell 205A, 6 Bell 214ST

Foreign Forces

US 690 **Air Force**: 630 **Navy** 60

Palestinian Autonomous Areas of Gaza and Jericho GzJ

	1997	1998	1999	2000
GDP	ε$3.4bn	ε$3.5bn		
per capita	$1,600	$1,600		
Growth	ε1.0%	ε2.0%		
Inflation	ε9.0%	ε7.0%		
Debt	ε$290m	ε$500m		
Sy bdgt	ε$250m	ε$300m	ε$500m	
FMA (US)	$75m	$85m	$100m	$100m
Population				ε2,900,000

West Bank and Gaza excluding East Jerusalem ε2,900,000 (Israeli ε180,000 excl East Jerusalem) **Gaza** ε1,200,000 (Israeli ε6,100) **West Bank excl East Jerusalem** ε1,700,000 (Israeli ε174,000) **East Jerusalem** Israeli ε217,000, Palestinian ε86–200,000

Age	*13–17*	*18–22*	*23–32*
Men	163,000	140,000	233,000
Women	158,000	134,000	222,000

Total Armed Forces

ACTIVE Nil

Paramilitary ε35,000

PUBLIC SECURITY 6,000 Gaza, 8,000 West Bank

CIVIL POLICE 4,000 Gaza, 6,000 West Bank

PREVENTIVE SECURITY 1,200 Gaza, 1,800 West Bank

GENERAL INTELLIGENCE 3,000

MILITARY INTELLIGENCE 500

PRESIDENTIAL SECURITY 3,000

Others include **Coastal Police, Civil Defence, Air Force, Customs and Excise Police Force, University Security Service**
    EQPT incl small arms, 45 APC **ac** 1 Lockheed *Jet Star* **hel** 2 Mi-8, 2 Mi-17

PALESTINIAN GROUPS

All significant Palestinian factions are listed irrespective of where they are based. Est number of active 'fighters' are given; these could perhaps be doubled to give an all-told figure. In 1991, the Lebanon Armed Forces (LAF), backed by Syria, entered refugee camps in southern Lebanon to disarm many Palestinian groups of their heavier weapons, such as tk, arty and APCs. The LAF conducted further disarming operations against *Fatah* Revolutionary Council (FRC) refugee camps in spring 1994.

PLO (Palestine Liberation Organisation) **Leader** Yasser Arafat
    FATAH Political wing of the PLO
    PNLA (Palestine National Liberation Army) ε8,000
        Effectively mil wing of the PLO **Based** Ag, Et, RL, LAR, HKJ, Irq, Sdn, Ye. Units closely monitored

by host nations' armed forces.

PLF (Palestine Liberation Front) ε300–400 **Leader** Al Abas; **Based** Irq **Tal al Yaqub faction** ε100–150 **Based** Syr

DFLP (Democratic Front for the Liberation of Palestine) ε500–600 **Leader** Hawatmah; **Based** Syr, RL, elsewhere **Abd Rabbu faction** ε150–20 **Based** HKJ

PFLP (Popular Front for the Liberation of Palestine) ε800 **Leader** Habash; **Based** Syr, RL, Occupied Territories

PSF (Popular Struggle Front) ε600–700 **Leader** Samir Ghansha; **Based** Syr

ARAB LIBERATION FRONT ε500 **Based** RL, Irq

GROUPS OPPOSED TO THE PLO

FATAH **DISSIDENTS** (Abu Musa gp) ε1,000 **Based** Syr, RL

FRC (*Fatah* Revolutionary Council, Abu Nidal Group) ε300 **Based** RL, Syr, Irq, elsewhere

PFLP (GC) (Popular Front for the Liberation of Palestine (General Command)) ε600 **Leader** Jibril

PFLP (SC) (Popular Front for the Liberation of Palestine – Special Command) ε50–100 **Based** RL, Irq, Syr

SAIQA ε1,000 **Leader** al-Khadi; **Based** Syr

HAMAS ε300 **Based** Occupied Territories

PIJ (Palestine Islamic *Jihad*) ε350 all factions **Based** Occupied Territories

PALESTINE LIBERATION FRONT Abd al-Fatah Ghanim faction **Based** Syr

PLA (Palestine Liberation Army) ε4,500 **Based** Syr

Qatar Q

	1997	1998	1999	2000
GDP	R36bn	R41bn		
	($9.8bn)	($11.2bn)		
per capita	$17,600	$19,700		
Growth	15.5%	11.5%		
Inflation	2.6%	2.6%		
Debt	$8bn	$8.6bn		
Def exp	εR4.9bn	εR4.9bn		
	($1.3bn)	($1.3bn)		
Def bdgt		εR4.5bn	εR4.7bn	
		($1.2bn)	($1.3bn)	
$1 = rial	3.64	3.64	3.64	
Population				681,000

(nationals 25%, expatriates 75%, of which Indian 18%, Iranian 10%, Pakistani 18%)

Age	*13–17*	*18–22*	*23–32*
Men	25,000	20,000	35,000
Women	27,000	20,000	32,000

Total Armed Forces

ACTIVE ε11,800

Army 8,500

1 Royal Guard regt • 1 SF 'bn' (coy) • 1 tk bn • 1 fd
arty regt • 4 mech inf bn • 1 mor bn

EQUIPMENT
> **MBT** 44 AMX-30
> **RECCE** 16 VBL, 12 AMX-10RC, 8 V-150
> **AIFV** 40 AMX-10P
> **LAV** 36 *Piranha* II
> **APC** 160 VAB, 12 AMX-VCI
> **TOWED ARTY 155mm**: 12 G5
> **SP ARTY 155mm**: 28 F-3
> **MRL** 4 ASTROS II
> **MOR 81mm**: 24 L16 (some SP); **120mm**: 15 Brandt
> **ATGW** 100 *Milan*, HOT (incl 24 VAB SP)
> **RCL 84mm**: *Carl Gustav*

Navy ε1,800

(incl Marine Police)
BASE Doha

PATROL AND COASTAL COMBATANTS 7
MISSILE CRAFT 3 *Damsah* (Fr *Combattante* III) with 2
x 4 MM-40 *Exocet* SSM
PATROL, INSHORE 4 *Barzan* (UK *Vita*) PCI with 8
Exocet SSM, 6 *Mistral* SAM, 1 76mm gun
Plus some 40 small craft operated by Marine Police

COASTAL DEFENCE
> 4 x 3 *quad* MM-40 *Exocet* bty

Air Force 1,500

18 cbt ac, 18 armed hel
FGA/FTR 2 sqn
> 1 with 6 *Alpha* jets
> 1 with 9 *Mirage* - 2000-5 EDA, 3 *Mirage* - 2000-5 DDA
TPT 1 sqn with 2 Boeing 707, 1 Boeing 727, 2 *Falcon*
900, 1 *Airbus* A340
ATTACK HEL 10 SA-342L (with HOT), 8 *Commando*
Mk 3 (*Exocet*)
TPT 4 *Commando* (3 Mk 2A tpt, 1 Mk 2C VIP)
LIAISON 2 SA-341G
MISSILES
> **ASM** Exocet AM-39, *HOT*, *Apache*
> **AAM** MATRA R550 *Magic*, MATRA *Mica*
> **SAM** 9 *Roland* 2, *Mistral*, *Stinger*, SA-7 *Grail*

Foreign Forces

US: **Army** 30; prepositioned eqpt for 1 armd bde
(forming)

Saudi Arabia Sau

	1997	1998	1999	2000
GDP	R547bn	R498bn		
	($146bn)	($133bn)		
per capita	$9,600	$8,500		
Growth	1.9%	-10.8%		
Inflation	1.0%	-0.2%		
Debt	$21bn	$22bn		
Def exp	R68bn	R78bn		
	($18.2bn)	($20.9bn)		
Def bdgt		R69bn	R69bn	
		($18.4bn)	($18.4bn)	
$1=rial	3.75	3.75	3.75	
Population				18,000,000

(nationals 73%, of which Bedouin up to 10%, Shi'a
6%, expatriates 27%, of which Asians 20%, Arabs
6%, Africans 1% and Europeans <1%)

Age	*13–17*	*18–22*	*23–32*
Men	1,304,000	1,088,000	1,615,000
Women	1,167,000	968,000	1,376,000

Total Armed Forces

ACTIVE ε105,500
(plus 57,000 active National Guard)

Army 70,000

3 armd bde (each 3 tk, 1 mech, 1 fd arty, 1 recce, 1 AD,
1 ATK bn) • 5 mech bde (each 3 mech, 1 tk, 1 fd arty, 1
AD, 1 spt bn) • 1 AB bde (2 AB bn, 3 SF coy) • 1 Royal
Guard regt (3 bn) • 8 arty bn • 1 army avn comd

EQUIPMENT
> **MBT** 315 M-1A2 *Abrams* (ε200 in store), 290 AMX-
> 30 (50% in store), 450 M60A3
> **RECCE** 235 AML-60/-90
> **AIFV** 570+ AMX-10P, 400 M-2 *Bradley*
> **APC** 1,750 M-113 (incl variants), 150 Panhard M-3
> **TOWED ARTY 105mm**: 100 M-101/-102; **155mm**:
> 50 FH-70 (in store), 90 M-198, M-114; **203mm**: 8
> M-115 (in store)
> **SP ARTY 155mm**: 110 M-109A1B/A2, 90 GCT
> **MRL** 60 ASTROS II
> **MOR** 400, incl: **107mm**: 4.2in M-30; **120mm**: 110
> Brandt
> **SSM** some 10 PRC CSS-2 (40 msl)
> **ATGW** TOW-2 (incl 200 VCC-1 SP), M-47 *Dragon*,
> HOT (incl 90 AMX-10P SP)
> **RCL 84mm**: 300 *Carl Gustav*; **90mm**: M-67; **106mm**:
> M-40A1
> **HEL** 12 AH-64, 12 S-70A-1, 10 UH-60 (tpt, 4
> medevac), 6 SA-365N (medevac), 15 Bell 406CS
> **SAM** *Crotale*, *Stinger*, 500 *Redeye* **SURV** AN/TPQ-
> 36/-37 (arty, mor)

Navy ε13,500

(incl 3,000 Marines)

BASES Riyadh (HQ Naval Forces) **Western Fleet**
Jiddah (HQ), Yanbu **Eastern Fleet** Al-Jubayl (HQ), Ad-
Dammam, Ras al Mishab, Ras al Ghar, Jubail

FRIGATES 8

FFG 8

4 *Madina* (Fr F-2000) with 4 533mm, 1 SA 365F hel, 8
  Otomat 2 SSM, 8 *Crotale* SAM, 1 100mm gun (1 in
  refit)
4 *Badr* (US Tacoma) with 2 x 4 *Harpoon* SSM, 2 x 3
  ASTT (Mk 46 LWT), 1 76mm gun

PATROL AND COASTAL COMBATANTS 26

MISSILE CRAFT 9 *Al Siddiq* (US 58m) PFM with 2 x 2
  Harpoon, 1 76mm gun
PATROL CRAFT 17 US Halter Marine PCI< (some
  with Coast Guard) plus 40 craft

MINE COUNTERMEASURES 7

3 *Al Jawf* (UK *Sandown* MHO)
4 *Addriyah* (US MSC-322) MCC

AMPHIBIOUS (craft only)

4 LCU, 4 LCM

SUPPORT AND MISCELLANEOUS 7

2 *Boraida* (mod Fr *Durance*) AO with 1 or 2 hel, 3 AT/
  F, 1 ARS, 1 Royal Yacht with hel deck

NAVAL AVIATION

31 armed hel
  19 AS-565 (4 SAR, 15 with AS-15TT ASM), 12 AS-
  332B/F (6 tpt, 6 with AM-39 *Exocet*)

MARINES (3,000)

1 inf regt (2 bn) with 140 BMR-600P

Air Force 18,000

432 cbt ac
FGA 7 sqn
  3 with 56 F-5E, 14 F-5F
  4 with 90 *Tornado* IDS
FTR 24 *Tornado* ADV, 70 F-15C, 25 F-15D, 72 F-15S
  (being delivered)
RECCE 1 sqn with 10* RF-5E (plus 10 *Tornado* in FGA
  sqn)
AEW 1 sqn with 5 E-3A
TKR 8 KE-3A (tkr/tpt), 7 KC-130H
OCU 2 sqn with 14* F-5B, 7* F-5F
TPT 3 sqn with 41 C-130 (7 -E, 34 -H), 8 L-100-30HS
  (hospital ac)
HEL 2 sqn with 22 AB-205, 25 AB-206B, 27 AB-212, 12
  AS-332 B/F, 12 AS-532A2
TRG 30* *Hawk* Mk 65, 20* *Hawk* Mk 65A, 50 PC-9, 1
  Jetstream 31, 4 Cessna 172
ROYAL FLT ac 1 Boeing-747SP, 1 Boeing-737-200, 4
  BAe 125-800, 2 C-140, 4 CN-235, 2 *Gulfstream* III, 2
  Learjet 35, 6 VC-130H, 1 Cessna 310 **hel** 3 AS-61, AB-
  212, 1 -S70

MISSILES

ASM AGM-65 *Maverick*, AS-15, AS-30, *Sea Eagle*,
  Shrike AGM-45, ALARM
AAM AIM-9J/L/P *Sidewinder*, AIM-7F *Sparrow*,
  Skyflash

Air Defence Forces 4,000

33 SAM bty
  16 with 128 I HAWK
  17 with 68 *Shahine* fire units and AMX-30SA 30mm
    SP AA guns
73 *Shahine/Crotale* fire units as static defence

EQUIPMENT

AD GUNS 20mm: 92 M-163 *Vulcan*; **30mm**: 50 AMX-
  30SA; **35mm**: 128; **40mm**: 150 L/70 (in store)
SAM 141 *Shahine*, 128 MIM-23B I HAWK, 40 *Crotale*

National Guard 77,000

(57,000 active, 20,000 tribal levies)
3 mech inf bde, each 4 all arms bn
5 inf bde
1 ceremonial cav sqn

EQUIPMENT

LAV 450 LAV-25
APC 290 V-150 *Commando* (plus 810 in store), 440
  Piranha
TOWED ARTY 105mm: 40 M-102; **155mm**: 30 M-198
MOR 81mm
RCL 106mm: M-40A1
ATGW TOW

Paramilitary 15,500+ active

FRONTIER FORCE 10,500

COAST GUARD 4,500

EQPT 4 *Al Jouf* PFI, about 30 PCI<, 16 hovercraft, 1
  trg, 1 Royal Yacht (5,000t) with 1 Bell 206B hel,
  about 350 armed boats

GENERAL CIVIL DEFENCE ADMINISTRATION UNITS

10 KV-107 **hel**

SPECIAL SECURITY FORCE 500

UR-416 APC

Foreign Forces

PENINSULAR SHIELD FORCE ε7,000

1 inf bde (elm from all GCC states)
FRANCE (Southern Watch) 170; 5 *Mirage* 2000C, 3 F-
1CR, 3 C 135FR
UK ε200; (Southern Watch) ε200; 6 *Tornado* GR-1A
US 5,720 **Army** 650 incl 1 *Patriot* SAM, 1 sigs unit and
those on short-term duty (6 months) **Air Force**
(Southern Watch) 4,800; units on rotational det,

numbers vary (incl: F-15, F-16, F-117, C-130, KC-135, U-2, E-3) **Navy** 20 **USMC** 250

Syria   Syr

	1997	1998	1999	2000
GDP	S£729bn	S£755bn		
	($35bn)	($37bn)		
per capita	$6,600	$6,800		
Growth	5.0%	4.3%		
Inflation	2.5%	1.0%		
Debt	$21bn	$21bn		
Def exp	S£51bn	S£63bn		
	($2.2bn)	($2.7bn)		
Def bdgt		S£63bn	S£67bn	
		($2.7bn)	($2.9bn)	
$1 = pound[a]	11.2	11.2	11.2	

[a] Market rate 1999 $1=S£45

Population				16,404,000
Age	*13–17*	*18–22*	*23–32*	
Men	1,007,000	823,000	1,208,000	
Women	970,000	798,000	1,173,000	

Total Armed Forces

ACTIVE ε316,000

Terms of service conscription, 30 months

RESERVES (to age 45) 396,000
Army 300,000 **Navy** 4,000 **Air Force** 92,000

Army ε215,000

(incl conscripts)
3 corps HQ • 7 armd div (each 3 armd, 1 mech bde, 1 arty regt) • 3 mech div (-) (each 2 armd, 2 mech bde, 1 arty regt) • 1 Republican Guard div (3 armd, 1 mech bde, 1 arty regt) • 1 SF div (3 SF regt) • 4 indep inf bde • 1 Border Guard bde • 2 indep arty bde • 2 indep ATK bde • 9 indep SF regt • 1 indep tk regt • 3 SSM bde (each of 3 bn): 1 with FROG, 1 with *Scud*-B/-C, 1 with SS-21 • 1 coastal def SSM bde with SS-C-1B *Sepal* and SS-C-3 *Styx*

RESERVES

30 inf, arty regt

EQUIPMENT

MBT 4,650: 2,150 T-55/MV, 1,000 T-62M/K, 1,500 T-72/-72M (incl some 1,200 in static positions and in store)
RECCE 850 BRDM-2, 85 BRDM-2 Rkh
AIFV 2,250 BMP-1, 100 BMP-2, some BMP-3
APC 1,500 BTR-40/-50/-60/-152
TOWED ARTY some 1,480, incl: **122mm**: 100 M-1931/-37 (in store), 150 M-1938, 450 D-30; **130mm**: 700 M-46; **152mm**: 20 D-20, 50 M-1937; **180mm**: 10

S23
SP ARTY 122mm: 400 2S1; **152mm**: 50 2S3
MRL 107mm: 200 Type-63; **122mm**: 280 BM-21
MOR 82mm: 200; **120mm**: 600 M-1943; **160mm**: 100 M-160; **240mm**: ε8 M-240
SSM launchers: 18 FROG-7, some 18 SS-21, 26 *Scud*-B/-C; 4 SS-C-1B *Sepal*, 6 SS-C-3 *Styx* coastal
ATGW 3,000 AT-3 *Sagger* (incl 2,500 SP), 150 AT-4 *Spigot*, 40 AT-5 *Spandrel*, AT-10, AT-14 Komet (reported) and 200 *Milan*
AD GUNS 2,060: **23mm**: 650 ZU-23-2 towed, 400 ZSU-23-4 SP; **37mm**: 300 M-1939; **57mm**: 675 S-60, 10 ZSU-57-2 SP; **100mm**: 25 KS-19
SAM 4,000 SA-7, 20 SA-9, 35 SA-13

Navy ε6,000

BASES Latakia, Tartus, Minet el-Baida
SUBMARINES 3
SSK 3 Sov *Romeo* with 533mm TT (all non-op)
FRIGATES 2
FF 2 Sov *Petya* II with 4 ASW RL, 5 533mm TT
PATROL AND COASTAL COMBATANTS 20
MISSILE CRAFT 10
10 Sov *Osa* I and II PFM with 4 SS-N-2 *Styx* SSM
PATROL CRAFT 10
8 Sov *Zhuk* PFI<
about 2 *Hamelin* PFI< (ex-PLF)
MINE COUNTERMEASURES 5
1 Sov T-43 MSC, 1 *Sonya* MSC, 3 *Yevgenya* MSI
AMPHIBIOUS 3
3 *Polnocny* LSM, capacity 100 tps, 5 tk
SUPPORT AND MISCELLANEOUS 4
1 spt, 1 trg, 1 div spt, 1 AGOR

NAVAL AVIATION

24 armed hel
ASW 20 Mi-14, 4 Ka-28 (Air Force manpower)

Air Force 40,000

589 cbt ac; 72 armed hel (some may be in store)
Flying hours 30
FGA 9 sqn
5 with 90 Su-22, 2 with 44 MiG-23 BN, 2 with 20 Su-24
FTR 17 sqn
8 with 170 MiG-21, 5 with 90 MiG-23, 2 with 30 MiG-25, 2 with 20 MiG-29
RECCE 6 MiG-25R, 8 MiG-21H/J
TPT 4 An-24, civil-registered **ac** incl 5 An-26, 2 *Falcon* 20, 4 Il-76, 7 Yak-40, 1 *Falcon* 900, 6 Tu-134 **hel** 10 Mi-2, 100 Mi-8/-17
ATTACK HEL 49 Mi-25, 23 SA-342L
TRG incl 80* L-39, 20 MBB-223, 20* MiG-21U, 6* MiG-23UM, 5* MiG-25U, 6 *Mashshak*

MISSILES
ASM AT-2 *Swatter*, AS-7 *Kerry*, AS-12, HOT
AAM AA-2 *Atoll*, AA-6 *Acrid*, AA-7 *Apex*, AA-8
Aphid, AA-10 *Alamo*

Air Defence Command ε55,000

25 AD bde (some 130 SAM bty)
Some 480 SA-2/-3, 200 SA-6 and 4,000 AD arty
2 SAM regt (each 2 bn of 2 bty) with some 48 SA-5, 60
SA-8

Forces Abroad

LEBANON 22,000; 1 mech div HQ, elm 1 armd, 4
mech inf bde, elm 10 SF, 2 arty regt

Paramilitary ε108,000

GENDARMERIE 8,000 (Ministry of Interior)
WORKERS' MILITIA (PEOPLE'S ARMY) (*Ba'ath* Party)
ε100,000

Foreign Forces

UN (UNDOF) 1,029; contingents from **A** 428 **Ca** 183 **J**
30 **Pl** 353 **Slvk** 35
RUSSIA ε150 advisers, mainly AD

Tunisia				**Tn**
	1997	1998	1999	2000
GDP	D21bn	D23bn		
	($19bn)	($20bn)		
per capita	$6,000	$6,400		
Growth	5.4%	5.0%		
Inflation	3.7%	3.7%		
Debt	$10bn	$11bn		
Def exp	D369m	D405m		
	($334m)	($355m)		
Def bdgt		D398m	D421m	
		($340m)	($351m)	
FMA (US)	$0.8m	$0.9m	$2.9m	$3.2m
$1=dinar	1.11	1.17	1.20	
Population				9,811,000
Age	*13–17*	*18–22*	*23–32*	
Men	519,000	487,000	842,000	
Women	497,000	468,000	817,000	

Total Armed Forces

ACTIVE ε35,000
(incl ε23,400 conscripts)
Terms of service 12 months selective

Army 27,000

(incl 22,000 conscripts)
3 mech bde (each with 1 armd, 2 mech inf, 1 arty, 1 AD
regt) • 1 Sahara bde • 1 SF bde • 1 engr regt
EQUIPMENT
MBT 54 M-60A3, 30 M-60A1
LT TK 55 SK-105 *Kuerassier*
RECCE 24 *Saladin*, 35 AML-90
APC 140 M-113A1/-A2, 18 EE-11 *Urutu*, 110 Fiat F-
6614
TOWED ARTY 105mm: 48 M-101A1/A2; **155mm**:
12 M-114A1, 57 M-198
MOR 81mm: 95; **107mm**: 66 4.2in
ATGW 65 TOW (incl some SP), 500 *Milan*
RL 89mm: 300 LRAC-89, 300 3.5in M-20
RCL 57mm: 140 M-18; **106mm**: 70 M-40A1
AD GUNS 20mm: 100 M-55; **37mm**: 15 Type-55/-65
SAM 48 RBS-70, 25 M-48 *Chaparral*
SURV RASIT (veh, arty)

Navy ε4,500

(incl ε700 conscripts)
BASES Bizerte, Sfax, Kelibia
PATROL AND COASTAL COMBATANTS 21
MISSILE CRAFT 6
3 *La Galite* (Fr *Combattante* III) PFM with 8 MM-40
Exocet SSM
3 *Bizerte* (Fr P-48) with 8 SS-12 SSM
PATROL, INSHORE 15
3 *Utique* (mod PRC *Shanghai* II) PCI, 2 *Tazarka* (UK
Vosper 31m) PCI, some 10 PCI<
SUPPORT AND MISCELLANEOUS 2
1 *Salambo* (US *Conrad*) survey/trg, 1 AGS

Air Force 3,500

(incl 700 conscripts); 44 cbt ac, 7 armed hel
FGA 15 F-5E/F
CCT 3 MB-326K, 2 MB-326L
TPT 5 C-130B, 2 C-130H, 1 *Falcon* 20, 3 LET-410
LIAISON 2 S-208M
TRG 18 SF-260 (6 -C, 12* -W), 5 MB-326B, 12* L-59
ARMED HEL 5 SA-341 (attack) 2 HH-3 (ASW)
TPT HEL 1 wg with 15 AB-205, 6 AS-350B, 1 AS-365, 6
SA-313, 3 SA-316, 2 UH-1H, 2 UH-1N
AAM AIM-9J *Sidewinder*

Paramilitary 12,000

NATIONAL GUARD 12,000 (Ministry of Interior)
incl Coastal Patrol with 5 (ex-GDR) *Kondor* I-class
PCC, 5 (ex-GDR) *Bremse*-class PCI<, 4 *Gabes* PCI<, plus
some 10 other PCI< **ac** 5 P-6B **hel** 8 SA-318/SA-319

United Arab Emirates — UAE

	1997	1998	1999	2000
GDP	D176bn ($48bn)	D170bn ($46bn)		
per capita	$16,600	$15,400		
Growth	2.6%	-5.6%		
Inflation	4.0%	3.1%		
Debt	$12.2bn	$13.0bn		
Def exp	εD8.9bn ($2.1bn)	εD11.0bn ($3.0bn)		
Def bdgt[a]		εD13.7bn ($3.7bn)	εD14.0bn ($3.8bn)	
$1=dirham	3.67	3.67	3.67	

[a] Including extra-budgetary funding for procurement

Population				2,650,000

(nationals 24%, expatriates 76%, of which Indian 30%, Pakistani 20%, other Arab 12%, other Asian 10%, UK 2%, other European 1%)

Age	*13–17*	*18–22*	*23–32*
Men	86,000	82,000	142,000
Women	84,000	77,000	104,000

Total Armed Forces

The Union Defence Force and the armed forces of the UAE (Abu Dhabi, Dubai, Ras Al Khaimah and Sharjah) were formally merged in 1976 and centred on Abu Dhabi. Dubai still maintains its independence, and other emirates to a smaller degree.

ACTIVE ε64,500 (perhaps 30% expatriates)

Army 59,000

(incl **Dubai** 15,000) **MoD** Dubai **GHQ** Abu Dhabi
INTEGRATED 1 Royal Guard 'bde' • 1 armd bde • 2 mech inf bde • 2 inf bde • 1 arty bde (3 regt)
NOT INTEGRATED 2 inf bde (Dubai)
EQUIPMENT
  MBT 45 AMX-30, 36 OF-40 Mk 2 (*Lion*), 156 *Leclerc*
  LT TK 76 *Scorpion*
  RECCE 49 AML-90, 20 *Saladin* (in store)
  AIFV 18 AMX-10P, 415 BMP-3
  APC 80 VCR (incl variants), 370 Panhard M-3, 120 EE-11 *Urutu*, some AAPC
  TOWED ARTY 105mm: 26 ROF lt; 130mm: 20 PRC Type-59-1
  SP ARTY 155mm: 18 Mk F-3, 72 G-6, 87 M-109A3
  MRL 70mm: 18 LAU-97; 122mm: 48 FIROS-25 (ε24 op)
  MOR 81mm: 114 L16; 120mm: 21 Brandt
  SSM 6 *Scud*-B (Dubai only)
  ATGW 230 *Milan*, *Vigilant*, 25 TOW, HOT (20 SP)
  RCL 84mm: Carl Gustav; 106mm: 12 M-40
  AD GUNS 20mm: 42 M-3VDA SP; 30mm: 20 GCF-BM2
  SAM 20+ *Blowpipe*, *Mistral*

Navy ε1,500

BASE Abu Dhabi
NAVAL FACILITIES Dalma, Mina Zayed, Ajman **Dubai** Mina Rashid, Mina Jabal, Al Fujairah **Ras al Khaimah** Mina Sakr **Sharjah** Mina Khalid, Khor Fakkan
FRIGATES
FFG 2 *Abu Dhabi* (NL *Kortenaer*) with 8 *Harpoon* SSM, 8 *Sea Sparrow* SAM, 1 x 76mm gun, 4 x 324mm TT, 2 x AS565 hel
PATROL AND COASTAL COMBATANTS 19
  CORVETTES 2 *Muray Jip* (Ge Lürssen 62m) with 2 x 2 MM-40 *Exocet* SSM, plus 1 SA-316 hel
  MISSILE CRAFT 8
    6 *Ban Yas* (Ge Lürssen TNC-45) with 2 x 2 MM-40 *Exocet* SSM
    2 *Mubarraz* (Ge Lürssen 45m) with 2 x 2 MM-40 *Exocet* SSM, plus 1 x 6 *Sadral* SAM
  PATROL, INSHORE 9
    6 *Ardhana* (UK Vosper 33m) PFI
    3 *Kawkab* PCI< plus boats
AMPHIBIOUS (craft only)
    3 *Al Feyi* LCT, 2 other LCT
SUPPORT AND MISCELLANEOUS 2
    1 div spt, 1 AT

Air Force 4,000

(incl Police Air Wing) 99 cbt ac, 49 armed hel
Flying hours 110
FGA 3 sqn
  1 with 9 *Mirage* 2000E
  1 with 17 *Hawk* 102
  1 with 17 *Hawk* Mk 63/63A/63C (FGA/trg)
FTR 1 sqn with 22 *Mirage* 2000 EAD
CCT 1 sqn with 8 MB-326 (2 -KD, 6 -LD), 5 MB-339A
OCU *5 *Hawk* Mk 61, *2 MB-339A, *6 *Mirage* 2000 DAD
RECCE 8* *Mirage* 2000 RAD
TPT incl 1 BN-2, 4 C-130H, 2 L-100-30, 4 C-212, 7 CN-235M-100, 4 Il-76 (on lease)
HELICOPTERS
  ATTACK 5 AS-332F (anti-ship, 3 with *Exocet* AM-39), 10 SA-342K (with HOT), 7 SA-316/-319 (with AS-11/-12), 20 AH-64A, 7 AS-565 *Panther*
  TPT 2 AS-332 (VIP), 1 AS-350, 26 Bell (8 -205, 9 -206, 5 -206L, 4 -214), 10 SA-330, 2 *King Air* 350 (VIP)
  SAR 3 Bo-105, 3 *Agusta* -109 K2
TRG 30 PC-7, 5 SF-260 (4 -TP, 1 -W), 12 Grob G-115TA
MISSILES
  ASM HOT, AS-11/-12, AS-15 *Exocet* AM-39, *Hellfire*, Hydra-70, PGM1, PGM2
  AAM R-550 *Magic*, AIM 9L
AIR DEFENCE
1 AD bde (3 bn)
5 bty I HAWK
12 *Rapier*, 9 *Crotale*, 13 RBS-70, 100 *Mistral* SAM

Paramilitary

COAST GUARD (Ministry of Interior)
some 40 PCI<, plus boats

Foreign Forces

US Air Force 390

Yemen, Republic of				Ye

	1997	1998	1999	2000
GDP	R741bn	R816bn		
	($5.7bn)	($6.0bn)		
per capita	$1,400	$1,400		
Growth	5.2%	2.7%		
Inflation	6.3%	11.1%		
Debt	$3.9bn	$4.0bn		
Def exp	R53bn	R54bn		
	($411m)	($396m)		
Def bdgt			R55bn	
			($374m)	
FMA (US)	$0.05m	$0.1m	$0.1m	$0.1m
$1=rial	129	136	152	
Population	18,000,000 (**North** 79% **South** 21%)			
Age	*13–17*	*18–22*		*23–32*
Men	939,000	772,000		1,259,000
Women	913,000	739,000		1,146,000

Total Armed Forces

ACTIVE 66,300

(incl conscripts)
Terms of service conscription, 3 years

RESERVES perhaps 40,000
Army

Army 61,000

(incl conscripts)
9 armd bde • 1 SF bde • 18 inf bde • 5 arty bde • 7 mech
bde • 3 SSM bde • 2 AB/cdo bde • 1 central guard force
• 3 AD arty bn • 2 AD bn (1 with SA-2 SAM)

EQUIPMENT
  MBT 1,320: 290 T-34, 720 T-54/-55, 250 T-62, 60 M-
    60A1
  RECCE 60 AML-245, 130 AML-90, 160 BRDM-2
  AIFV 300 BMP-1/-2
  APC 60 M-113, 580 BTR-40/-60/-152
  TOWED ARTY some 452: **100mm**: 50 M-1944, 45
    M-1955; **105mm**: 35 M-101A1; **122mm**: 30 M-
    1931/37, 50 M-1938, 130 D-30; **130mm**: 90 M-46;
    152mm: 10 D-20; **155mm**: 12 M-114
  ASLT GUNS 100mm: 30 SU-100

  COASTAL ARTY 130mm: 36 SM-4-1
  MRL 122mm: 185 BM-21; **140mm**: BM-14
  MOR 600 incl **81mm**; **82mm**; **120mm**; **160mm**
  SSM 12 FROG-7, 12 SS-21, 6 Scud-B
  ATGW 12 TOW, 24 *Dragon*, 35 AT-3 *Sagger*
  RL 66mm: M72 LAW
  RCL 75mm: M-20; **82mm**: B-10; **107mm**: B-11
  ATK GUNS 85mm: D-44; **100mm**
  AD GUNS 20mm: 52 M-167, 20 M-163 *Vulcan* SP;
    23mm: 100 ZSU-23-4; **37mm**: 150 M-1939; **57mm**:
    120 S-60; **85mm**: KS-12
  SAM SA-7/-9/-13/-14

Navy 1,800

BASES Aden, Hodeida
FACILITIES Al Mukalla, Perim Island, Socotra (these
have naval support equipment)
PATROL AND COASTAL COMBATANTS 13
  MISSILE CRAFT 5
  3 *Huangfen* with C-801 SSM (only 4 C-801 between
    the 3 craft)
  2 *Tarantul* 1 PFM with 4 SS-N-2C *Styx* SSM (1 non-op)
  plus 6 boats
  PATROL, INSHORE 8
  3 *Sana'a* (US *Broadsword* 32m) (1 non-op) PFI, 5 Sov
  Zhuk PFI< (3 non-op)
MINE COUNTERMEASURES 6
  1 Sov *Natya* MSO
  5 Sov *Yevgenya* MHC
AMPHIBIOUS 1
  1 *Ropucha* LST, capacity 190tps/10 tks
  plus craft: 2 Sov *Ondatra* LCM
AUXILIARIES 2
  2 *Toplivo* AOT

Air Force 3,500

49 cbt ac (plus some 40 in store), 8 attack hel
FGA 10 F-5E, 17 Su-20/-22
FTR 11 MiG-21, 5 MiG-29
TPT 2 An-12, 4 An-26, 3 C-130H, 4 IL-14, 3 IL-76
HEL 2 AB-212, 14 Mi-8, 1 AB-47, 8 Mi-35 (attack)
TRG 2* F-5B, 4* MiG-21U, 14 YAK-11

AIR DEFENCE 2,000
SAM some SA-2, SA-3, SA-6
AAM AA-2 *Atoll*, AIM-9 *Sidewinder*

Paramilitary 70,000

MINISTRY OF THE INTERIOR FORCES 50,000

TRIBAL LEVIES at least 20,000

COAST GUARD
(slowly being established)
5 Fr *Interceptor* PCI<

MILITARY DEVELOPMENTS

Regional Trends

Central and South Asia continues to commit more government resources to defence than any other region apart from the Middle East. Seemingly endless civil wars persist in Sri Lanka and Afghanistan, and governments faced internal security challenges from armed groups in Tajikistan and, increasingly, in Uzbekistan during 1998–99. But the predominant military event in South Asia in 1999 was the ten weeks of fighting between India and Pakistan in Kashmir from May to July.

India and Pakistan

In early May 1999, a substantial infiltration from the Pakistani to the Indian side of the Line of Control in the Kargil area of Kashmir took the Indian government by surprise. It seems clear that the infiltrators included Pakistani regular forces and Islamic militants who were from both the Kashmir region and Afghanistan. Whatever Islamabad's political motives might have been, the military objectives were clear. The hope was to dominate the only land route from Srinagar to Leh along the Drass–Kargil road, which is essential to India for maintaining its forces in this part of Indian-controlled Kashmir, including its troops on the disputed Siachen border area. Pakistan's move to occupy key points on the Indian side of the Line of Control on a permanent basis was a departure from the usual pattern of sporadic raids using Islamic, mainly Kashmiri, militants to carry out bombings and other terrorist acts.

The Indian government placed strict constraints on its military commanders by forbidding them to conduct land or air operations on or over the Pakistani side of the Line of Control. The purpose of this restraint was to assure as much international political support as possible for the Indian case in the confrontation. This policy brought important political benefits, but Indian forces suffered greater casualties as a result. In particular, the conflict might have ended earlier if the Indian Air Force had been allowed to attack the infiltrators' supply bases, and there would have been less need for the Army to seize mountain heights at 13,000–15,000 feet. A large proportion of the casualties in these operations included the most highly trained men in the force. Official sources say that about 450 Indian troops were killed by the time the main fighting ended on 24 July 1999, although some estimates place the toll higher. These sources also indicated that there was an unusually high percentage of officers among the casualties. While the combatants' now explicit nuclear capabilities made no direct difference to the conduct of military operations, it may have encouraged Pakistani boldness in the expectation that the Indian military response would be tempered by a perceived need for restraint. What is certain, however, is that the nuclear factor exercised the international community. In particular, it prompted intervention by US President Clinton who put pressure on Pakistani Prime Minister Nawaz Sharif to withdraw the infiltrators from the Indian side of the Line of Control.

The after-effects of the conflict will no doubt put a strain on defence budgets. The Indians will feel compelled to maintain higher force-levels in the region than before and to increase the number of troops trained in high-altitude mountain warfare. The strain on personnel resources will be keenly felt, given the other pressures faced by the Indian military, not only in Kashmir but in other regions such as the north-east where the forces are supporting the effort to defeat Naga and Bodo terrorism. The direct effect on procurement plans is harder to determine. India may now want to improve its capabilities in air-delivered precision-guided weapons to improve its ability to pinpoint targets effectively when flight approaches are severely constrained. The Indian

Air Force carried out some 550 bombing missions during the Kargil conflict and tried upgrading some of its bombs by basic strap-on laser-guidance equipment. Both India and Pakistan will undoubtedly pursue their missile programmes more vigorously to advance their relative capabilities.

Central Asia

Two attempts to negotiate a cease-fire through direct talks between the main combatants in the Afghan civil war failed in January and July 1999. The talks in Tashkent on 18–19 July were chaired by the UN special representative to Afghanistan, Lakhdar Brahimi, and brought together senior officials of the six states bordering Afghanistan – Pakistan, Iran, China, Uzbekistan, Tajikistan and Turkmenistan. Russian and US representatives also attended. Following the failure of the negotiations, the *Taleban* movement, which controls about 90% of the country, launched an offensive on 28 July against the Northern Alliance led by Ahmad Shah Masood. This was the most significant military breakthrough in the past two years of fighting. In particular, it led to the capture of the air base at Bagram, 50 kilometres north of Kabul. While dislodging Masood's forces from their stronghold in the Panjshir valley in the far north-east remains a difficult proposition for the *Taleban*, at least the advances, if held, are likely to reduce the threat of rocket attacks on Kabul.

Uzbekistan, often seen as one of the more stable of the Central Asian states, experienced a series of bomb attacks in the capital, Tashkent, during February 1999, apparently targeting President Islam Karimov. Islamic fundamentalists were blamed for the bombings and the government carried out a series of arrests, trials and executions. Continuing pressure on the fundamentalists by the security forces, allegedly seeking more suspects, has resulted in a flow of refugees from Uzbekistan into Tajikistan, straining relations between the two countries. Russian Border Troops remain in Tajikistan, mainly conducting counter-drug operations along the Tajik–Afghan border with some success. Nevertheless, large-scale drug smuggling continues and will continue to destabilise Tajikistan, as competing factions struggle for control of the trade.

Sri Lanka

In Sri Lanka, an end to the civil war, waged since 1983 between the government and the Liberation Tigers of Tamil Eelam (LTTE), seems as remote as ever. Government offensives in January–March 1999 resulted in territorial gains, and three senior LTTE commanders were killed in a sea battle. However, a decisive military victory over the LTTE in their main bases in the north of the country remains elusive. The LTTE continue to combine their land and sea operations with terrorist bombings in the capital, Colombo. For example, moderate Tamil leader, Neelan Thiruchelvam of the Tamil United Liberation Front, was killed by a suicide bomber on 29 July 1999 in a bid to derail a peace plan involving devolution of power to the Tamil community, due to be put before the Sri Lankan parliament the following month. As long as the LTTE will not countenance proposals short of full independence, the government will be faced with the draining expense of seeking a military solution.

DEFENCE SPENDING

Regional defence spending grew by almost 5% in real terms to $21 billion in 1998 from $20bn in 1997 (measured in 1997 US dollars), according to *The Military Balance* estimates. The increase was most marked in South Asia where spending rose by some 5.6% compared to a 3% fall in Central Asia. There was an improvement in regional economic performance, with gross domestic product (GDP) higher by nearly 6% in real terms, which contrasted with the experience of much of the rest of Asia. The Kazakstan economy was the only one in the region to experience a set-back, with GDP down by 2.5%. Better economic performance overall meant that military expenditure as a proportion of GDP declined marginally from 5.7% in 1997 to 5.4% in 1998. Budgetary data for 1999 suggest that regional defence spending will grow by around 3% in real terms during 1999.

India accounts for two thirds of regional military spending, and India and Pakistan together account for nearly 85%. India's spending is mostly transparent, but not that of Pakistan, where an increasingly significant part of military funding is outside the defence budget as the country seeks to reconcile its economic difficulties with its military objectives. Lack of openness in defence accounting in the Central Asian Republics continues, and the military outlays are almost certainly understated in official figures.

The regional arms trade was worth $1.8bn in 1998, unchanged from 1997. Russia and China are the region's principal weapons suppliers, while India's indigenous programmes also provide a substantial market for US and Western European sub-systems and components.

India

In 1999, India increased its defence budget for the fifth time in six years to Rs457bn ($10.7bn). This was 11% higher in nominal terms than the 1998 budget of Rs412bn which itself was 16% above the previous year. In real terms, the 1999 budget, released in late February 1999, represents an increase of around 5%. The May–July escalation of armed conflict in Kashmir and the increased military commitments called for in the region will lead to increased costs, particularly for India.

Table 17 Indian defence expenditure by service/department, 1994–1999

(1998 US$m)	1994	%	1995	%	1996	%	1997	%	1998	%	1999	%
Army	4,273	52.9	4,673	53.0	4,630	53.4	5,663	57.2	5,218	52.2	5,496	52.3
Air Force	2,236	27.7	2,274	25.8	2,221	25.6	2,468	24.9	2,271	22.7	2,350	22.4
Navy	1,043	12.9	1,246	14.1	1,175	13.5	1,168	11.8	1,448	14.5	1,554	14.8
R&D	432	5.3	454	5.1	429	4.9	365	3.7	431	4.3	640	6.1
DP&S, other	99	1.2	165	1.9	221	2.6	237	2.4	618	6.2	458	4.4
Total	8,083	100	8,812	100	8,676	100	9,901	100	9,986	100	10,499	100
% Change			4.6		9.0		-1.6		14.1		0.9		5.1

Capital spending, covering Research and Development, Procurement and Construction, increased from to $2.5bn in 1998 to $2.9bn in 1999. There is also increased funding in 1999 for both Atomic Energy and Space, including, in both cases, dual-use or military-specific programmes. Together, these two areas are scheduled to receive 1999 funding of $1.1bn, up from $952 million in 1998.

Technical difficulties in the development stages continue to plague India's wide-ranging programme for major conventional weapon platforms, leading to lengthy delays and cost overruns. This has compelled the government to hedge against the prospect that its sizeable investment in pursuit of self-sufficiency in armaments will be slow to pay off. Much defence equipment for the armed forces and sub-systems for the defence industry are still imported. India is still Russia's second-largest defence market after China. Flight testing of the 2,000(+)km range *Agni* 2 medium-range ballistic missile (MRBM) took place in April 1999, while development of a 3,500 km-range *Agni* 3 variant is thought to be under way. Other indigenous missile programmes are reported to include two strategic missiles, the *Surya* intercontinental ballistic missile (ICBM) and the *Dhanush* submarine-launched ballistic missile (SLBM) and a submarine-launched cruise missile (SLCM) the *Sagarika*. Tactical missiles reportedly about to enter production include the *Akash* medium-range surface-to-air missile (SAM), the *Trishul* short-range SAM, and the *Nag* anti-tank guided weapon (ATGW), while development of the *Astra* air-to-air missile (AAM) is under way.

Table 18 Indian defence and military-related spending by function, 1997–1999

(US$m)	1997 outturn	1998 outturn	1999 budget
Personnel, Operations & Maintenance			
MoD	89	84	83
Defence Pensions	1,362	1,762	1,722
Army	5,056	5,351	5,606
Navy	671	761	788
Air Force	1,427	1,336	1,416
Defence ordnance factories	227	68	31
Recoveries and Receipts	-1,624	-1,846	-1,804
Sub-total	**7,208**	**7,517**	**7,841**
R&D, Procurement and Construction			
Tri-Service Defence R&D	192	138	167
Army	588	667	872
Navy	643	740	797
Air Force	1,088	882	982
Other	49	42	48
Recoveries and Receipts	-53		
Sub-total	2,507	2,469	2,865
Total Defence Budget	**9,715**	**9,986**	**10,706**
Other military-related funding			
Paramilitary forces	815	891	940
Department of Atomic Energy	625	586	694
Department of Space	287	366	411
Intelligence Bureau	59	57	67
Total	**1,786**	**1,901**	**2,112**

The Navy's search for a replacement for the *Viraat* aircraft carrier (now in refit until 2001) continues. Interest in the Russian carrier *Admiral Gorshkov* has not resulted in a commitment to purchase, and no contract has yet been placed for the 24,000-tonne air-defence carrier first mooted in 1997. The second of a planned six *Delhi*-class destroyers with area SAMs (DDG) was undergoing sea-trials in mid-1999. The start of construction of the third has been delayed. The Navy took delivery of the ninth *Kilo* 877-class submarine from Russia in January 1998. Two *Kilo* 636-class submarines are on order for 2000–01 delivery, and two more German-licenced Type 209s are on order for production in India and delivery in 2003–05. The Navy has also ordered three improved *Krivak* 3 frigates from Russia in May 1998 for delivery in 2002–03. Domestic production of the first batch of 12 light helicopters for the Navy has been delayed by engine problems experienced by the two prototypes, and first deliveries are not now expected before the end of 2000. Both the Army and Air Force are also expected to order the helicopter.

The failure of the domestically-produced *Arjun* main battle tank (MBT) to demonstrate acceptable reliability in user trials delayed full-scale production until early 1999, when an order for the first batch of 124 was placed for delivery from 2001. Pakistan's purchase of 320 T-80s from Ukraine and India's difficulties with the *Arjun* programme have reportedly led the Indian Army to consider a direct purchase, followed by licensed production, of the T-90 MBTs from Russia as a complement or an alternative. The Army has purchased 42 T-72VT armoured recovery vehicles (ARVs) from Slovakia in 1999, following a similar purchase of 43 from Poland. The Army has taken delivery of a further 12 2S6 *Tunguska* air-defence systems from Russia following delivery of 12 in 1996.

The Light Combat Aircraft development programme has been delayed by over a year by US export restrictions on key components. Russian suppliers have taken over technical support for the programme, including responsibility for the engine. The planned entry-into-service date has slipped to 2003. The Air Force received ten more Su-30 fighter, ground attack aircraft (FGAs) from Russia in 1998, following delivery of the first eight in 1997. The balance of the 40 ordered is due for delivery in 1999–2000. An additional ten were ordered in late 1998. The schedule of the MiG-21 upgrade programme for 125 aircraft has slipped, with completion now planned for 2003 instead of 2000.

Pakistan

The Pakistani government only provides an aggregate figure for defence spending, without any detailed breakdown. The official 1999 defence budget, released in June 1999, amounts to Rs142bn ($2.7bn), down from Rs145bn ($3.2bn) in 1998. Official outlays for 1998 were Rs128bn ($2.8bn), which excludes $327m received from the US in reimbursement for the F-16s embargoed in 1990 under the Pressler Amendment. By comparison, *The Military Balance* estimates that spending in 1998 was $4bn, which includes paramilitary and nuclear spending outside the defence budget. A growing proportion of Pakistan's military expenditure is off-budget, as the government attempts to reconcile the demands of its international creditors (particularly the International Monetary Fund) with those of the armed forces.

Pakistan tested the 2000km-plus-range *Ghauri* 2 MRBM (also known as *Hatf* 6 and reportedly based on the North Korean *Taepo-dong* 1) in April 1999. Development work is continuing on the 750km-range *Shaheen* surface-to-surface missile (SSM), also known as the *Hatf* 4, which is reportedly based on the Chinese M-9, and production reportedly began in mid-1999. Development work on the 3,000km *Ghauri* 3 has begun, again with reported North Korean assistance. Deliveries of 320 T-80UD MBTs to the Army from Ukraine were completed in early 1999, following the receipt of 110 in 1998. Delivery to the Navy of the first of three *Agosta* submarines has been delayed by a year, and is now expected by the end of 1999. The second boat has been laid down in France but will be fitted out in Pakistan, while the third in the series will be produced entirely in Pakistan. Deliveries are planned for 2002. The Pakistani Air Force had taken delivery of the first eight of 40 upgraded *Mirage* III fighters by April 1999, again after some delay which was reportedly due to Pakistan's financial constraints.

Sri Lanka

Sri Lankan official defence outlays in 1998 were Rs57.2bn ($886m), some Rs12.2bn ($189m) over budget. If outlays for paramilitary forces are added, the total is estimated at Rs63bn ($975m). Recent Army acquisitions include 36 Type 66 152mm towed artillery from China, while the Air Force is to acquire two modernised Mi-35 (the export variant of the Mi-24) armed helicopters from Russia in 1999.

Bangladesh

In Bangladesh, the 1999 defence budget is for T30bn ($618m), compared to T29bn ($619m) in 1998 when the outlay was T26bn ($593m). There is confirmation that the Air Force has contracted for eight MiG-29s from Russia, four of which were for delivery in 1999. Meanwhile deliveries of Chinese F-7 aircraft continue. The delivery schedule includes four FT-7 trainers in 1999–2000. Four more L-39 advanced trainers have been ordered from the Czech Republic. The Air Force also took delivery of three more Mi-17 helicopters in early 1999.

Central Asia

There is little information on defence budgets in Central Asia, because there is little or no public accounting of defence spending. There is also significant military funding and spending under internal security allocations outside defence budgets. Kazakstan's 1999 defence budget fell to T14.8bn ($115m) from T19.9bn ($259m) in 1998. The country's internal security funding in 1998 is higher than the defence allocation at T22.3bn ($173m), but it, too, was down from the 1997 level of T34.1bn ($443m). Following delivery of a batch of ten Su-27 FGAs from Russia in 1997, the Air Force is to receive a further 16 in 1999, together with the S-300 SAM system. Given the decline in the defence budget, it is not clear how these purchases are to be funded. Unusually, the Uzbekistan government reported 1996 military spending to the UN for the August 1998 *Report of the Secretary-General: Objective Information on Military Matters, including Transparency of Military Expenditures*. The armed forces took delivery of 120 armoured personnel carriers (APCs) (possibly BTR-80s) from Russia in 1997.

Table 19 Arms orders and deliveries, Central and South Asia, 1997–1999

Supplier	Classification	Designation	Units	Order Date	Delivery Date	Comment
Bangladesh						
UK	MSI	*River*	4	1993	1995	1 converted to AGOR April 1997
US	hel	B-206L	3	1995	1997	
PRC	MSO	T-43	4	1995	1997	
SK	OPV	*Madhumati*	1	1995	1998	
PRC	FGA	F-7	24	1996	1997	Deliveries continuing through 1999. 15 delivered previously
RF	radar	IL-117 3-D	2	1996	1999	Requirement for 3 more
RF	hel	Mi-17	3	1997	1999	Following delivery of 12 1992–96
PRC	trg	FT-7B	4	1997	1999	
US	tpt	C-130B	4	1997	1999	
RF	FGA	MiG-29B	8	1999	1999	Order placed 1999 after delay
ROK	FF		1	1998	2002	
Cz	trg	L-39ZA	4	1999	2000	Following delivery of 8 in 1995
India						
RF	PFM	*Tarantul 1*	11	1984	1987	Licence-built in Goa; 11th of class delivered 1997
dom	SSN	ATV	1	1982	2004	Possibly SLBM compatible
dom	SSBN	SSBN	1	1982	2004	Development
dom	ICBM	*Surya*		1983		Development
dom	SLBM	*Dhanush*		1983	2003	Reported in development for new SSBN
dom	SLCM	*Sagarika*		1983	2003	For new SSBN. 300km range. May be ballistic
dom	MRBM	*Agni*		1983	1998	Development completed 1998 after 3 tests. Production 1998
dom	MRBM	*Agni 2*		1983	2000	Development. Range 2,000–2,500km. Tested April 1999
dom	MRBM	*Agni 3*		1983		Development. Range 3,500km
dom	SSM	*Prithvi* 150	75	1983	1995	150km range. Low-volume production continues. 75 delivered late 1996
dom	SSM	*Prithvi*		1983	1999	Naval variant. Deployed Jan 1999
dom	SSM	*Prithvi* 250		1983	1995	Range 250km
dom	SSM	*Prithvi* 350		1983	1998	Land and naval variants in dev
dom	SAM	*Akash*		1983	1999	Development. High-altitude SAM. Entry into service planned 2000

Supplier	Classification Designation		Units	Order Date	Delivery Date	Comment
dom	SAM	*Trishul*		1983	1999	In dev. May enter service 1999
dom	ATGW	*Nag*		1983	1999	Ready for production mid-1999
dom	AAM	*Astra*		1999	2002	Development. 1st test planned July 1999
dom	FGA	LCA	7	1983	2005	In-service date may advance to 2003
RF	SSK	*Kilo*	1	1983	1998	Unit 10. 2 more to be licence built in Ind
dom	FFG	*Brahmaputra*	3	1989	1998	2nd in 1999, 3rd in 2003
dom	hel	ALH	12	1984	2000	Tri-service requirement for 300 Delivery may slip to 2001
dom	ELINT	HS-748		1990		Development
dom	UAV	*Nishant*	14	1991	1999	Development. 3 prototypes built. 14 pre-production units on order
dom	DD	*Delhi*	3	1986	1997	1st in 1997, 2nd delivered 1998. 6 req
dom	corvette	*Kukhri*	8	1983	1989	6th of class delivered 1997
dom	LST	*Magyar*	2	1991	1997	2nd of class. 1 building
dom	OPV	*Samar*	4	1991	1996	3 delivered 1996–99. 1 building
RF	AD	2S6	24	1994	1996	12 units in 1996, 12 1998–99
dom	sat	Ocean sat	1	1995	1999	Remote sensing
dom	AGHS	*Sandhayak*	2	1995	1999	Following delivery of 5 1981–93
dom	sat	IRS-1C	1	1995	1996	Launched 1995. Currently used for mil purposes
Ukr	FGA	MiG-21	5	1995	1997	
RF	TKR AC	IL-78	6	1996	1998	First 2 delivered early 1998
RF	FGA	MiG-21	125	1996	2003	Upgrade. Fr and Il avionics
RF	ASSM	SS-N-25	16	1996	1997	Deliveries continue
RF	FGA	Su-30MK	40	1996	1997	8 delivered 1997, 10 1998, 12 1999, 10 2000
RF	FGA	Su-30MKI	10	1998	2001	
Il	PFC	*Super Dvora MK3*	6	1996		First delivery 1998. Il designation T-81
RF	FF	*Krivak* III	3	1997	2002	2 for delivery by 2002, 3rd by 2003
RF	hel	KA-31	3	1997	2002	
Ge	SS	Type 209	2	1997	2003	To be built in Ind
dom	CV		1	1997		
US	MPA	P-3C	3	1997		Delayed due to sanctions
UK	FGA	*Harrier* TMk4	2	1997	1999	2 ex-RN ac for delivery 1999
dom	SAM	S-300	24	1998	2000	24–36 launchers
RSA	APC	*Casspir*	90	1998	1999	10 delivered. Remaining 80 to be delivered late 1999
RF	SLCM	SS-NX-27		1998	2004	For *Krivak* 3 frigate. First export
UK	FGA	*Jaguar*	18	1998	2001	Upgrade for up to 60
dom	MBT	*Arjun*	124	1974	2001	Ordered 1999
RF	MBT	T-90	300	1999	1999	Under negotiation
Fr	FGA	*Mirage* 2000	10	1999	2002	Approved but not contracted
dom	trg	HJT-36	200	1999	2004	
Pl	trg	TS-11	12	1999	2000	Option on 8 more
dom	CV	*Viraat*	1	1999	2001	Upgrade (formerly ex-UK *Hermes*)
RF	CV	*Admiral Gorshkov*	1	1999		Subject of negotiation
Slvk	ARV	T-72 VT	42	1999	2001	Original order for 85. 43 purchased from Pl
Pl	ARV	WZT-3	43	1999	2001	Original order for 85. 42 supplied from Slvk
Il	arty	M-46	35	1999	2000	Il upgrade of Sov arty supplied mid-1980s

Supplier	Classification	Designation	Units	Order Date	Delivery Date	Comment
Kazakstan						
US	PCI	*Dauntless*	1	1996	1997	
RF	FGA	Su-27	16	1997	1999	4 delivered early 1999, 10 in 1997
RF	SAM	S-300		1997	2000	
Maldives						
Tu	APC	*Cobra*	3	1995	1997	
Pakistan						
dom	sat	*Badar* 2				Development
dom	sat	*Badar* 1				Multi-purpose sat. In operation
col	trg	K-8	6	1987	1994	With PRC. Requirement for 100
US	APC	M113	775	1989	1990	Licensed production; deliveries to 1999
dom	MBT	*Al-Khalid*		1991	1998	In acceptance trials
Fr	MHC	*Munsif*	3	1992	1992	Second delivered 1996. Third 1998
PRC	FGA	FC-1		1993	2005	In co-development with PRC, requirement for up to 150
dom	MRBM	*Ghauri*		1993	1998	Range 1,500km. Test April 1998. aka *Hatf* 5
dom	MRBM	*Ghauri* 2		1993	1999	Development. Range 2,000–2,300km. April 1999 test. aka *Hatf* 6
dom	MRBM	*Ghauri* 3		1993		Development. Range 3,000km. Based on *Taepo-dong* 2
dom	SSM	*Hatf* 2		1994	1996	Development. Based on PRC M-11
dom	SSM	*Hatf* 3		1994		Development. Range 600–800km. Based on M-9
dom	SSM	*Shaheen* 1		1994	1999	In production mid-1999. Range 750km. Based on M-9. aka Hatf 4
Fr	SS	*Agosta* 90	3	1994	1999	Last 2 to be built in Pak
US	MPA	PC-3C	3	1995	1996	With 28 *Harpoon* SAM. Deliveries 1996–97
PRC	tpt	Y-12	4	1996	1997	2 for Air Force and 2 for Army
Fr	FGA	*Mirage* III	40	1996	1998	Upgrade. 8 delivered by April 1999
Ukr	MBT	T-80UD	320	1996	1996	105 delivered 1997; 110 delivered 1998
PRC	arty	130mm	27	1998		
dom	PFM	Mod. *Larkana*	1	1996	1997	Commissioned 14 August 1997. 2 more planned
PRC	PGG	*Shujat* 2	1	1997	1999	
PRC	FGA	F-7MG	50	1999	2001	Unconfirmed
Sri Lanka						
US	MPA	*Beech* 200	4	1995	1997	Used in MPA role
IL	UAV	*Super Scout*				
Ukr	tpt	AN-32	4	1995	1996	
PRC	PCO	*Haiqing*	3	1994	1996	1 in service 1996. 2 delivered 1997
Cz	MBT	T-55	3	1995	1997	
Col	FAC	*Super Dvora*	6	1995	1997	Built in Ska with Il assistance
Ukr	cbt hel	Mi-24	2	1995	1996	1 delivered 1998
Ukr	cbt hel	Mi-24	2	1998	1999	
RF	cbt hel	Mi-35	2	1997	1999	May be 4. 5 delivered previously
US	PCI	*Trinity*	6	1997	1997	
US	tpt	C-130	3	1997	1999	
PRC	arty	152mm	36	1999	2000	
UK	ACV	M10		1995	1999	Hovercraft
Uzbekistan						
RF	APC	BTR 80	120	1995	1997	APC type unconfirmed

Afghanistan — Afg

	1997	1998	1999	2000
GDP	ε$1.6bn	ε$1.7bn		
per capita	ε$700	ε$700		
Growth	ε6%	ε6%		
Inflation	ε14%	ε14%		
Debt	ε$6.0bn	ε$6.2bn		
Def exp	ε$200m	ε$250m		
$1 =afgani[a]	3,000	3,000	3,000	

[a] Market rate **1999** ε$1 = Afs4,700

Population[b]				ε23,800,000

(Pashtun 38%, Tajik 25%, Hazara 19%, Uzbek 12%, Aimaq 4%, Baluchi 0.5%)

Age	*13–17*	*18–22*	*23–32*
Men	1,402,000	1,162,000	1,974,000
Women	1,347,000	1,104,000	1,858,000

[b] Includes ε1,500,000 refugees in Pakistan, ε1,000,000 in Iran, ε150,000 in Russia and ε50,000 in Kyrgyzstan

Total Armed Forces

Taleban now controls two-thirds of Afghanistan, and continues to mount mil ops against an alliance of former President Burhanuddin Rabbani's government troops, led by former Defence Minister Ahmad Shah Masoud and the National Islamic Alliance (NIA) of General Abdul Rashid Dostam. The alliance appears to receive little support from Shi'a opposition groups.

EQUIPMENT

It is impossible to show the division of ground force equipment among the different factions. The list below represents weapons known to be in the country in April 1992. Individual weapons quantities are unknown.

MBT T-54/-55, T-62
LT TK PT-76
RECCE BRDM-1/-2
AIFV BMP-1/-2
APC BTR-40/-60/-70/-80/-152
TOWED ARTY 76mm: M-1938, M-1942; **85mm**: D-48; **100mm**: M-1944; **122mm**: M-30, D-30; **130mm**: M-46; **152mm**: D-1, D-20, M-1937 (ML-20)
MRL 122mm: BM-21; **140mm**: BM-14; **220mm**: 9P140 *Uragan*
MOR 82mm: M-37; **107mm**; **120mm**: M-43
SSM *Scud*, FROG-7
ATGW AT-1 *Snapper*, AT-3 *Sagger*
RCL 73mm: SPG-9; **82mm**: B-10
AD GUNS: 14.5mm; **23mm**: ZU-23, ZSU-23-4 SP; **37mm**: M-1939; **57mm**: S-60; **85mm**: KS-12; **100mm**: KS-19
SAM SA-7/-13

Air Force

Only the former government–NIM alliance and *Taleban*

have aircraft. These groups have a quantity of Su-17/22 and MiG-21s and both have some Mi-8/17. The inventory shows ac in service in April 1992. Since then, an unknown number of fixed-wing ac and hel have either been shot down or destroyed on the ground. It is believed that the *Taleban* have about 20 MiG-21 and Su-22, and 5 L-39, all being used in the FGA role. The NIM have about 30 Su-17/22, 30 MiG-21 and 10 L-39. The number of helicopters on each side is unknown.

FGA 30 MiG-23, 80 Su-7/-17/-22
FTR 80 MiG-21F
ARMED HEL 25 Mi-8, 35 Mi-17, 20 Mi-25
TPT ac 2 Il-18D; 50 An-2, An-12, An-26, An-32 **hel** 12 Mi-4
TRG 25 L-39*, 18 MiG-21*

AIR DEFENCE

SAM 115 SA-2, 110 SA-3, *Stinger*, SAM-7, SAM-14, **37mm**, **85mm** and **100mm** guns
AD Guns some 200–300

Opposition Groups

Afghan insurgency was a broad national movement, united only against the Najibullah government.

GROUPS ORIGINALLY BASED IN PESHAWAR

Islamic Fundamentalist

TALEBAN ε25,000 **Leaders** Maulewi Mohamed Omar, Maulewi Mohamed Rabbi **Area** southern Afghanistan **Ethnic group** Pashtun. Formed originally from religious students in Madrassahs (both Pashtun and non-Pashtun)

Traditionalist Moderate

ISLAMIC REVOLUTIONARY MOVEMENT (*Haraka't-Inqila'b-Isla'mi*) ε25,000 **Leader** Mohammed Nabi Mohammed **Area** Farah, Zabol, Paktia, southern Ghazni, eastern Lowgar, western Paktia, northern Nimruz, northern Helmand, northern Kandahar **Ethnic group** Pashtun. Has backed *Taleban*

NATIONAL ISLAMIC FRONT (*Mahaz-Millin Isla'mi*) ε15,000 **Leader** Sayyed Amhad Gailani **Area** eastern Paktia (Vardak–Lowgar border) **Ethnic group** Pashtun

NATIONAL LIBERATION FRONT[a] (*Jabha't-Nija't-Milli'*) ε15,000 **Leader** Sibghatullah Modjaddi **Area** enclaves in Kandahar, Zabol provinces, eastern Konar **Ethnic group** Pashtun

ISLAMIC SOCIETY (*Jamia't Isla'mi*) ε60,000 **Leader** Burhanuddin Rabbani **Area** eastern and northern Farah, Herat, Ghowr, Badghis, Faryab, northern Jowzjan, northern Balkh, northern Kondoz, Takhar, Baghlan, Kapisa, northern Laghman, Badakhshan **Ethnic groups** Turkoman, Uzbek, Tajik

ISLAMIC PARTY (*Hizbi-Isla'mi-Gulbuddin*)[a] ε50,000 **Leader** Gulbuddin Hekmatyar **Area** northern and southern Kabul, Parvan, eastern Laghman, northern Nangarhar, south-eastern Konar; large enclave at

Badghis–Ghowr–Jowzjan junction, western Baghlan; enclaves in Farah, Nimruz, Kandahar, Oruzgan and Zabol **Ethnic groups** Pashtun, Turkoman, Tajik

ISLAMIC PARTY (*Hizbi-Isla'mi-Kha'lis*) ε40,000
  Leader Yu'nis Kha'lis **Area** central Paktia, Nangarhar, south-east Kabul **Ethnic group** Pashtun

ISLAMIC UNION (*Ittiha'd-Isla'mi Barai Azadi*) ε18,000
  Leader Abdul Rasul Sayyaf **Area** east of Kabul
  Ethnic group Pashtun

GROUPS ORIGINALLY BASED IN IRAN

HEZBI-WAHDAT (Unity Party)[a] umbrella party of Shi'a groups

  Sazman-e-Nasr some 50,000 **Area** Bamian, northern Oruzgan, eastern Ghowr, southern Balkh, southern Samangan, south-western Baghlan, south-eastern Parvan, northern Vardak **Ethnic group** Hazara

  Shura-Itifaq-Islami some 30,000+ **Area** Vardak, eastern Bamian **Ethnic group** Hazara

  Haraka't-e-Islami 20,000 **Area** west of Kabul; enclaves in Kandahar, Ghazni, Vardak, Samangan, Balkh **Ethnic groups** Pashtun, Tajik, Uzbek

  Pasdaran-e-Jehad 8,000

  Hizbollah 4,000

  Nehzat 4,000

NATIONAL ISLAMIC MOVEMENT (NIM)[a]
Formed in March 1992, mainly from troops of former Afghan Army Northern Comd. Predominantly Uzbek, Tajik, Turkoman, Ismaeli and Hazara Shi'a. Str ε65,000 (120–150,000 in crisis). 2 Corps HQ, 5–7 inf div, some indep bde

[a] Form the Supreme Coordination Council

Bangladesh				**Bng**
	1997	**1998**	**1999**	**2000**
GDP	Tk1.4tr	Tk1.5tr		
	($32bn)	($33bn)		
per capita	$1,600	$1,700		
Growth	5.9%	5.6%		
Inflation	5.7%	7.4%		
Debt	$18.7bn	$20.6bn		
Def exp	Tk26bn	Tk29bn		
	($593m)	($619m)		
Def bdgt			Tk30bn	
			($618m)	
FMA (US)	$0.3m	$0.3m	$0.4m	$0.4m
$1 = taka	43.9	46.9	48.5	
Population			130,156,000 (Hindu 12%)	
Age	*13–17*	*18–22*	*23–32*	
Men	7,969,000	7,390,000	11,636,000	
Women	7,607,000	6,950,000	11,018,000	

Total Armed Forces

ACTIVE 137,000

Army 120,000

7 inf div HQ • 17 inf bde (some 26 bn) • 1 armd bde (2 armd regt) • 2 armd regt • 1 arty div (6 arty regt) • 1 engr bde • 1 AD bde

EQUIPMENT†

  MBT some 100 PRC Type-59/-69, 100 T-54/-55
  LT TK some 40 PRC Type-62
  APC 60 BTR-70, 20 BTR-80, some MT-LB, ε50 YW531
  TOWED ARTY 105mm: 30 Model 56 pack, 50 M-101; **122mm**: 20 PRC Type-54; **130mm**: 40+ PRC Type-59
  MRL 122mm: reported
  MOR 81mm; **82mm**: PRC Type-53; **120mm**: 50 PRC Type-53
  RCL 106mm: 30 M-40A1
  ATK GUNS 57mm: 18 6-pdr; **76mm**: 50 PRC Type-54
  AD GUNS 37mm: 16 PRC Type-55; **57mm**: PRC Type-59
  SAM some HN-5A

Navy† 10,500

BASES Chittagong (HQ), Dhaka, Khulna, Kaptai
FRIGATES 4
  FFG 1 *Osman* (PRC *Jianghu* I) with 2 x 5 ASW mor, plus 2 x 2 CSS-N-2 *Hai Ying* 2 (*HY* 2) SSM, 2 x 2 100mm guns
  FF 3
    1 *Umar Farooq* (UK *Salisbury*) with 1 x 3 *Squid* ASW mor, 1 x 2 115mm guns
    2 *Abu Bakr* (UK *Leopard*) with 2 x 2 115mm guns
PATROL AND COASTAL COMBATANTS 45
MISSILE CRAFT 10
  5 *Durdarsha* (PRC *Huangfeng*) with 4 *HY* 2 SSM
  5 *Durbar* (PRC *Hegu*) PFM< with 2 SY-1 SSM
TORPEDO CRAFT 8 PRC *Huchuan* PFT< with 2 533mm TT
PATROL, OFFSHORE 1 *Madhumati* (J *Sea Dragon*) with 1 x 76mm gun
PATROL, COASTAL 3
  1 *Durjoy* (PRC *Hainan*) with 4 x 5 ASW RL
  2 *Meghna* fishery protection
PATROL, INSHORE 18
  8 *Shahead Daulat* (PRC *Shanghai* II) PFI, 2 *Karnaphuli*, 1 *Bishkali* PCI, 1 *Bakarat* PCI, 4 Type 123K PFT, 2 *Akshay* PCI
PATROL, RIVERINE 5 *Pabna*<
MINE COUNTERMEASURES 4
  3 *Shapla* (UK *River*) MSI, 1 *Sagar* MSO
AMPHIBIOUS craft only
  7 LCU, 4 LCM, 3 LCVP

SUPPORT AND MISCELLANEOUS 8

1 coastal AOT, 1 AR, 1 AT/F, 1 AT, 2 *Yuch'in* AGHS, 1 *Shaibal* AGOR (UK *River*) (MCM capable), 1 *Shaheed Ruhul Amin* (trg)

Air Force† 6,500

65 cbt ac, no armed hel **Flying hours** 100–120
FGA/FTR 4 sqn with 18 A-5, 16 F-6, 16 F-7M, 7 FT-7B
TPT 3 An-32
HEL 3 sqn with 11 Bell 212, 7 Mi-8, 11 Mi-17
TRG 20 PT-6, 12 T-37B, 8 CM-170, 8* L-39ZA, 2 Bell 206L
AAM AA-2 *Atoll*

Forces Abroad

UN AND PEACEKEEPING

CROATIA (UNMOP): 1 obs **GEORGIA** (UNOMIG): 9 obs **IRAQ/KUWAIT** (UNIKOM): 807 incl 5 obs **TAJIKISTAN** (UNMOT): 3 obs **WESTERN SAHARA** (MINURSO): 6 obs

Paramilitary 55,200

BANGLADESH RIFLES 30,000

border guard; 41 bn

ARMED POLICE 5,000

rapid action force (forming)

ANSARS (Security Guards) 20,000+ in bn

A further 180,000 unembodied

COAST GUARD 200

(HQ Chittagong and Khulma)
1 *Bishkhali* PCI
(force in its infancy and expected to expand)

India				Ind
	1997	**1998**	**1999**	**2000**
GDP	Rs15.6tr	Rs19.0tr		
	($431bn)	($469bn)		
per capita	$1,600	$1,700		
Growth	5.0%	6.7%		
Inflation	7.2%	13.2%		
Debt	$94bn	$101bn		
Def exp[a]	Rs465bn	Rs580bn		
	($12.8bn)	($14.1bn)		
Def bdgt			Rs412bn	Rs457bn
			($10.0bn)	($10.7bn)
FMA[b] (US)	$0.4m	$0.2m	$0.5m	$0.5m
FMA (Aus)	$0.2m	$0.2m	$0.2m	
$1 = rupee	36.3	41.3	42.7	

[a] Incl exp on paramil org
[b] UNMOGIP **1997** $7m **1998** $8m

Population			999,839,000
(Hindu 80%, Muslim 14%, Christian 2%, Sikh 2%)			
Age	*13–17*	*18–22*	*23–32*
Men	52,985,000	48,592,000	85,587,000
Women	49,572,000	45,011,000	78,187,000

Total Armed Forces

ACTIVE 1,173,000

RESERVES 528,400

Army 300,000 (first-line reserves within 5 years' full-time service, a further 500,000 have commitment until age 50) **Territorial Army** (volunteers) 33,400 **Air Force** 140,000 **Navy** 55,000

Army 980,000

HQ: 5 Regional Comd, 4 Fd Army, 11 Corps
3 armd div (each 2–3 armed, 1 SP arty (2 SP fd, 1 med regt) bde) • 4 RAPID div (each 2 inf, 1 mech bde) • 18 inf div (each 2–5 inf, 1 arty bde; some have armd regt) • 9 mtn div (each 3–4 bde, 1 or more arty regt) • 1 arty div (3 bde) • 15 indep bde: 7 armd, 5 inf, 2 mtn, 1 AB/cdo • 1 SSM regt (*Prithvi*) • 4 AD bde (plus 14 cadre) • 3 engr bde
These formations comprise
    59 tk regt (bn) • 355 inf bn (incl 25 mech, 8 AB, 3 cdo) • 190 arty regt (bn) reported: incl 1 SSM, 2 MRL, 50 med (11 SP), 69 fd (3 SP), 39 mtn, 29 AD arty regt; perhaps 2 SAM gp (3–5 bty each) plus 15 SAM regt • 14 hel sqn: 6 atk, 8 air obs

EQUIPMENT

MBT ε3,414 (ε1,100 in store): some 700 T-55 (450 op), ε1,500 T-72/M1, 1,200 *Vijayanta*, ε14 *Arjun*
LT TK ε90 PT-76
RECCE ε100 BRDM-2
AIFV 350 BMP-1, 1,000 BMP-2 (*Sarath*)
APC 157 OT-62/-64 (in store), some *Casspir*
TOWED ARTY 4,175 (perhaps 600 in store) incl: **75mm**: 900 75/24 mtn, 215 FRY M-48; **105mm**: some 1,300 IFG Mk I/II, 50 M-56; **122mm**: some 550 D-30; **130mm**: 750 M-46; **155mm**: 410 FH-77B
SP ARTY 105mm: 80 *Abbot* (ε30 in store); **130mm**: 100 mod M-46 (ε70 in store); **152mm**: some 2S19
MRL 122mm: 150 incl BM-21, LRAR; **214mm**: *Pinacha* (being deployed)
MOR 81mm: L16A1, E1; **120mm**: 500 Brandt AM-50, E1; **160mm**: 500 M-1943, 200 Tampella M-58 (all in store)
SSM *Prithvi* (3–5 launchers)
ATGW *Milan*, AT-3 *Sagger*, AT-4 *Spigot* (some SP), AT-5 *Spandrel* (some SP)
RCL 84mm: *Carl Gustav*; **106mm**: 1,000+ M-40A1
AD GUNS some 2,400: **20mm**: Oerlikon (reported); **23mm**: 300 ZU 23-2, 100 ZSU-23-4 SP; **30mm**: 24 2S6 SP; **40mm**: 1,200 L40/60, 800 L40/70

SAM 180 SA-6, 620 SA-7, 50 SA-8B, 400 SA-9, 45
SA-3, SA-13, 500 SA-16
SURV MUFAR, *Green Archer* (mor)
UAV *Searcher* (reported), *Nishant*
HEL 199 *Chetak*, *Cheetah*
LC 2 LCVP

RESERVES

Territorial Army 25 inf bn, plus 29 'departmental' units
DEPLOYMENT
North 2 Corps with 8 inf, 2 mtn div **West** 3 Corps
with 1 armd, 5 inf div, 3 RAPID **Central** 1 Corps
with 1 armd, 1 inf, 1 RAPID **East** 3 Corps with 1 inf,
7 mtn div **South** 2 Corps with 1 armd, 3 inf div

Navy 53,000

(incl 5,000 Naval Aviation and ε1,200 Marines, ε2,000
women)
PRINCIPAL COMMAND Western, Eastern, South-
ern, Far Eastern
SUB-COMMAND Submarine, Naval Air
BASES Mumbai (Bombay) (HQ Western Comd), Goa
(HQ Naval Air), Karwar (under construction), Kochi
(Cochin) (HQ Southern Comd), Vishakhapatnam (HQ
Eastern and submarines), Calcutta, Madras, Port Blair
(Andaman Is) (HQ Far Eastern Comd), Arakonam
(Naval Air)
FLEETS Western base Bombay **Eastern base**
Visakhapatnam
SUBMARINES 16
SSK 16
9 *Sindhughosh* (Sov *Kilo*) with 533mm TT
4 *Shishumar* (Ge T-209/1500) with 533mm TT
3 *Kursura* (Sov *Foxtrot*)† with 533mm TT (plus 3 in
reserve)
PRINCIPAL SURFACE COMBATANTS 26
CARRIERS 1 *Viraat* (UK *Hermes*) (29,000t) CVV
Air group typically **ac** 6 *Sea Harrier* ftr/attack **hel** 6
Sea King ASW/ASUW (*Sea Eagle* ASM) (in refit until
April 2001)
DESTROYERS 7
DDG 7
5 *Rajput* (Sov *Kashin*) with 2 x 2 SA-N-1 *Goa* SAM, 4
SS-N-2C *Styx* SSM, 5 533mm TT, 2 ASW RL, 1 Ka-
25 or 28 hel (ASW)
2 *Delhi* with 16 SS-N-25 *Sapless* SSM, 2 x SA-N-7
Gadfly SAM, 1 100mm gun, 5 533mm TT, 2 hel
FRIGATES 13
FFG 4
1 *Brahmaputra* with 20 SA-N-4 *Gecko* SAM, 8 x SS-N-
25 *Sapless* SSM, 1 x 76mm gun
3 *Godavari* with 1 *Sea King* hel, 2 x 3 324mm ASTT, 4
SS-N-2C *Styx* SSM and 1 x 2 SA-N-4 *Gecko* SAM
FF 9
5 *Nilgiri* (UK *Leander*) with 2 x 3 ASTT, 4 with 1 x 3
Limbo ASW mor, 1 *Chetak* hel, 2 with 1 *Sea King*, 1 x

2 ASW RL, 2 114mm guns (plus 1 in reserve)
1 *Krishna* (UK *Leander*) (trg role)
3 *Arnala* (Sov *Petya*) with 4 ASW RL, 3 533mm TT
CORVETES 5
4 *Khukri* with 2 or 4 SS-N-2C *Styx* SSM, hel deck
1 mod *Khukri* with 8 x SS-N-25 *Sapless* SSM
PATROL AND COASTAL COMBATANTS 40
CORVETTES 19
3 *Vijay Durg* (Sov *Nanuchka* II) with 4 SS-N-2B *Styx*
SSM
6 *Veer* (Sov *Tarantul*) with 4 *Styx* SSM
6 *Vibhuti* (similar to *Tarantul*) with 4 *Styx* SSM
4 *Abhay* (Sov *Pauk* II) (ASW) with 4 ASTT, 2 ASW mor
MISSILE CRAFT 6 *Vidyut* (Sov *Osa* II) with 4 *Styx* (all
non-op) (plus 6 *Osa* 1 reserve and 2 *Osa* 1 for special
forces penetration)
PATROL, OFFSHORE 7 *Sukanya* PCO
PATROL, INSHORE 8
6 SDB Mk 3 (1 SDB Mk 2 may be op)
2 *Super Dvora*
MINE WARFARE 18
MINELAYERS 0
none, but *Kamorta* FF and *Pondicherry* MSO have
minelaying capability
MINE COUNTERMEASURES 18
12 *Pondicherry* (Sov *Natya*) MSO, 6 *Mahé* (Sov
Yevgenya) MSI<
AMPHIBIOUS 9
2 *Magar* LST, capacity 500 tps, 18 tk, 1 hel (plus 1
fitting out)
7 *Ghorpad* (Sov *Polnocny* C) LSM, capacity 140 tps, 6 tk
Plus craft: 10 *Vasco da Gama* LCU
SUPPORT AND MISCELLANEOUS 31
1 *Jyoti* AO, 6 small AO, 1 *Amba* (Sov *Ugra*) AS, 1 div
spt , 2 AT/F, 6 *Sandhayak* and 4 *Makar* AGHS, 1 *Tir*
trg, 1 *Sagardhwani* AGOR, 3 torpedo recovery
vessels, 1 AH, 2 *Osa* 1 (special forces insertion), 1
Deepak plus 1 mod *Deepak* AOR

NAVAL AVIATION (5,000)
79 cbt ac, 83 armed hel **Flying hours** some 180
ATTACK 2 sqn with 20 *Sea Harrier* FRS Mk-51, 1 T-60
trg plus 2 T-4 (on order)
ASW 6 hel sqn with 26 *Chetak*, 7 Ka-25, 18 Ka-28, 31
Sea King Mk 42A/B
MR 3 sqn with 8 Il-38, 11 Tu-142M *Bear* F, 19 Do-228,
18 BN-2 *Defender*
COMMS 1 sqn with **ac** 10 Do-228 **hel** 3 *Chetak*
SAR 1 **hel** sqn with 6 *Sea King* Mk 42C
TRG 2 sqn with **ac** 6 HJT-16, 8 HPT-32 **hel** 2 *Chetak*, 4
Hughes 300
MISSILES
AAM R-550 *Magic* I and II
ASM *Sea Eagle*, *Sea Skua*

MARINES (1,200)
1 regt (3 gp)

Air Force 140,000

774 cbt ac, 34 armed hel. 5 Air Comd **Flying hours** 150
Five regional commands
FGA 18 sqn
   1 with 8 Su-30K, 3 with 53 MiG-23 BN/UM, 4 with
     88 *Jaguar* S(I), 6 with 147 MiG-27, 4 with 69 MiG-
     21 MF/PFMA
FTR 20 sqn
   4 with 66 MiG-21 FL/U, 10 with 169 MiG-21 bis/U,
     1 with 26 MiG-23 MF/UM, 3 with 64 MiG-29, 2
     with 35 *Mirage* 2000H/TH (believed to have
     secondary GA capability), 8 Su-30MK
ECM 4 *Canberra* B(I) 58 (ECM/target towing, plus 2
   Canberra TT-18 target towing)
ELINT 2 Boeing 707, 2 Boeing 737
AEW 4 HS-748
TANKER 6 IL-78
MARITIME ATTACK 6 *Jaguar* S(I) with *Sea Eagle*
ATTACK HEL 3 sqn with 32 Mi-25
RECCE 2 sqn
   1 with 8 *Canberra* (6 PR-57, 2 PR-67)
   1 with 6* MiG-25R, 2* MiG-25U
MR/SURVEY 2 *Gulfstream* IV SRA, 2 *Learjet* 29
TRANSPORT
   ac 12 sqn
     6 with 105 An-32 *Sutlej*, 2 with 45 Do-228, 2 with
     28 BAe-748, 2 with 25 Il-76 *Gajraj*
   hel 11 sqn with 73 Mi-8, 50 Mi-17, 10 Mi-26 (hy tpt)
VIP 1 HQ sqn with 2 Boeing 737-200, 7 BAe-748, 6 Mi-8
TRG ac 28 BAe-748 (trg/tpt), 120 *Kiran* I, 56 *Kiran* II,
   88 HPT-32, 38 *Hunter* (20 F-56, 18 T-66), 14* *Jaguar*
   B(1), 9* MiG-29UB, 44 TS-11 *Iskara* hel 20 *Chetak*, 2
   Mi-24, 2* Mi-35
MISSILES
   ASM AS-7 *Kerry*, AS-11B (ATGW), AS-12, AS-30, *Sea
    Eagle*, AM 39 *Exocet*, AS-17 *Krypton*
   AAM AA-7 *Apex*, AA-8 *Aphid*, AA-10 *Alamo*, AA-11
    Archer, R-550 *Magic*, Super 530D
   SAM 38 sqn with 280 *Divina* V75SM/VK (SA-2),
    Pechora (SA-3), SA-5, SA-10

Forces Abroad

UN AND PEACEKEEPING
IRAQ/KUWAIT (UNIKOM): 5 obs SIERRA LEONE
(UNOMSIL): 6 obs WESTERN SAHARA
(MINURSO): 10 obs

Paramilitary 1,090,000 active

NATIONAL SECURITY GUARDS 7,400
(Cabinet Secretariat)
Anti-terrorism contingency deployment force,
comprising elements of the armed forces, CRPF and
Border Security Force

SPECIAL PROTECTION GROUP 3,000
Protection of VVIP
SPECIAL FRONTIER FORCE 9,000
(Cabinet Secretariat)
mainly ethnic Tibetans
RASHTRIYA RIFLES 40,000 (Ministry of Defence)
36 bn in 12 Sector HQ
DEFENCE SECURITY CORPS 31,000
provides security at Defence Ministry sites
INDO-TIBETAN BORDER POLICE 32,200 (Ministry of
Home Affairs)
28 bn, Tibetan border security
ASSAM RIFLES 52,500 (Ministry of Home Affairs)
7 HQ, 31 bn, security within north-eastern states,
mainly Army-officered; better trained than BSF
RAILWAY PROTECTION FORCES 70,000
CENTRAL INDUSTRIAL SECURITY FORCE 88,600
(Ministry of Home Affairs)[a]
guards public-sector locations
CENTRAL RESERVE POLICE FORCE (CRPF) 165,300
(Ministry of Home Affairs)
130–135 bn incl 10 rapid action, 2 *Mahila* (women);
internal security duties, only lightly armed,
deployable throughout the country
BORDER SECURITY FORCE (BSF) 185,000 (Ministry
of Home Affairs)
some 150 bn, small arms, some lt arty, tpt/liaison air spt
HOME GUARD (R) 472,000
authorised, actual str 416,000 in all states except
Arunachal Pradesh and Kerala; men on lists, no trg
STATE ARMED POLICE 400,000
For duty primarily in home state only, but can be
moved to other states, incl 24 bn India Reserve Police
(commando-trained)
CIVIL DEFENCE 394,000 (R)
in 135 towns in 32 states
COAST GUARD over 5,500
   PATROL CRAFT 36
    3 *Samar* OPV, 9 *Vikram* OPV, 21 *Jija Bai*, 3 SDB-2 plus
    16 boats
   AVIATION
    3 sqn with ac 14 Do-228, hel 15 *Chetak*

[a] Lightly armed security guards only

Opposition

HOLY ISLAMIC ARMY: str n.k. Operates in Kashmir

Foreign Forces

UN (UNMOGIP): 46 mil obs from 8 countries

Kazakstan   Kaz

	1997	1998	1999	2000
GDP	t1.7tr	t1.8tr		
	($22bn)	($22bn)		
per capita	$3,600	$3,700		
Growth	1.7%	-2.5%		
Inflation	17.4%	7%		
Debt	$4.3bn	$7.9bn		
Def exp[a]	t38bn	t39bn		
	($503m)	($498m)		
Def bdgt		t19.9bn	t17.0bn	
		($259m)	($132m)	
FMA[b] (US)	$0.4m	$0.6m	$0.6m	$0.6m
$1=tenge	75.4	78.3	128.9	

[a] Incl exp on paramilitary forces
[b] Excl US Cooperative Threat Reduction Programme funds for nuclear dismantlement and demilitarisation. Bdgt 1993–99 ε$300m. Programme continues through 2000

Population			14,952,000

(Kazak 51%, Russian 32%, Ukrainian 5%, German 2%, Tatar 2%, Uzbek 2%)

Age	*13–17*	*18–22*	*23–32*
Men	890,000	799,000	1,337,000
Women	869,000	787,000	1,309,000

Total Armed Forces

ACTIVE 65,800

Terms of service 31 months

Army 46,800

2 Army Corps HQ (third to form) • 1 TD • 2 MRD (1 trg) • 1 MR, 1 AB • 1 arty, 1 SSM bde • 1 indep MRR • 2 arty regt

EQUIPMENT
MBT 630 T-72 (plus some 300+ in store)
RECCE 140 BRDM
ACV 1,000 incl BMP-1/-2, BRM AIFV, BTR-70/-80, MT-LB APC (plus some 1,000 in store)
TOWED ARTY 550: **122mm**: D-30; **152mm**: D-20, 2A65, 2A36
SP ARTY 150: **122mm**: 2S1; **152mm**: 2S3
MRL 170: **122mm**: BM-21; **220mm**: 9P140 *Uragan*
MOR 130: **120mm**: 2B11, M-120
SSM 10 SS-21
ATK GUNS **100mm**: 125 T-12

(In 1991, the former Soviet Union transferred some 2,680 T-64/-72s, 2,428 ACVs and 6,900 arty to storage bases in Kazakstan. This eqpt is under Kazak control, but has deteriorated considerably).

Air Force 19,000

(incl Air Defence)
1 Air Force div, 131 cbt ac **Flying hours** 25
FTR 1 regt with 40 MiG-29
FGA 3 regt
  1 with 14 Su-25
  1 with 16 Su-24
  1 with 14 Su-27
RECCE 1 regt with 12 Su-24*
TRG 12 L-39, 4 Yak-18
HEL numerous Mi-8, Mi-29
STORAGE some 75 MiG-27/MiG-23/MiG-23UB/ MiG-25/MiG-29/SU-27
AIR DEFENCE
  FTR 1 regt with 32 MiG-31, 3 MiG-25
  SAM 100 SA-2, SA-3, SA-5
MISSILES
  ASM AS-7 *Kerry*, AS-9 *Kyle*, S-10 *Karen*, AS-11 *Killer*
  AAM AA-6 *Acrid*, AA-7 *Apex*, AA *Aphid*

Forces Abroad

TAJIKISTAN 300: 1 border gd bn

Paramilitary 34,500

STATE BORDER PROTECTION FORCES ε12,000
(Ministry of Defence) incl
  MARITIME BORDER GUARD (3,000)
  BASES Aktau
  PATROL AND COASTAL COMBATANTS 10
  5 *Guardian* PCI, 1 *Dauntless* PCI, 4 *Almaty* PCI, plus 2 boats
INTERNAL SECURITY TROOPS ε20,000 (Ministry of Interior)
PRESIDENTIAL GUARD 2,000
GOVERNMENT GUARD 500

Kyrgyzstan   Kgz

	1997	1998	1999	2000
GDP	s30bn	s34bn		
	($1.8bn)	($1.8bn)		
per capita	$2,000	$2,100		
Growth	9.9%	2.0%		
Inflation	26.3%	13.6%		
Debt	$934m	$1,700m		
Def exp[a]	s1,175m	s1,350m		
	($68m)	($65m)		
Def bdgt		s573m	s950m	
		($28m)	($24m)	
FMA (US)	$0.3m	$0.3m	$0.3m	$0.4m
$1=som	17.4	20.8	39.0	

[a] Incl exp on paramilitary forces

Population				4,600,000

(Kyrgyz 56%, Russian 17%, Uzbek 13%, Ukrainian 3%)

Age	13–17	18–22	23–32
Men	278,000	234,000	358,000
Women	273,000	232,000	354,000

Total Armed Forces

ACTIVE 9,200

Terms of service 18 months

RESERVES 57,000

Army 6,800

1 MRD (3 MR, 1 tk, 1 arty, 1 AA regt)
1 indep MR bde (mtn)
EQUIPMENT
  MBT 210 T-72
  RECCE 34 BRDM-2
  AIFV 98 BMP-1, 101 BMP-2, 20 BRM-1K
  APC 45 BTR-70
  TOWED ARTY 161: **100mm**: 18 M-1944 (BS-3);
    122mm: 72 D-30, 37 M-30; **152mm**: 34 D-1
  COMBINED GUN/MOR 120mm: 12 2S9
  MOR 120mm: 6 2S12, 48 M-120
  ATGW 26 AT-3 *Sagger*
  AD GUNS 57mm: 24 S-60
  SAM SA-7

Air Force 2,400

ac and hel assets inherited from Sov Air Force trg school;
Kgz failed to maintain pilot trg for foreign students
AC 28 L-39, 26 MiG-21, 2 An-12, 2 An-26
HEL 11 Mi-24, 19 Mi-8
AIR DEFENCE
  SAM SA-2, SA-3, SA-7

Paramilitary ε3,000

BORDER GUARDS ε3,000 (Kyrgyz conscripts, Russian officers)

Nepal N

	1997	1998	1999	2000
GDP	NR281bn	NR315bn		
	($4.9bn)	($5.1bn)		
per capita	$1,400	$1,400		
Growth	4.5%	3.9%		
Inflation	4.0%	10.0%		
Debt	$2.5bn	$2.7bn		
contd	1997	1998	1999	2000
Def exp	NR2.4bn	NR2.5bn		
	($42m)	($38m)		
Def bdgt			NR3.5bn	
			($52m)	
FMA (US)	$0.2m	$0.2m	$0.2m	$0.3m
$1=rupee	58.0	66.0	67.4	
Population				23,602,000

(Hindu 90%, Buddhist 5%, Muslim 3%)

Age	13–17	18–22	23–32
Men	1,434,000	1,186,000	1,788,000
Women	1,354,000	1,103,000	1,634,000

Total Armed Forces

ACTIVE 46,000 (to be 50,000)

Army 46,000

1 Royal Guard bde (incl 1 MP bn) • 7 inf bde (16 inf
bn) • 44 indep inf coy • 1 SF bde (incl 1 AB bn, 2 indep
SF coy, 1 cav sqn (*Ferret*)) • 1 arty bde (1 arty, 1 AD
regt) • 1 engr bde (4 bn)
EQUIPMENT
  RECCE 40 *Ferret*
  TOWED ARTY† 75mm: 6 pack; **94mm**: 5 3.7in mtn
    (trg); **105mm**: 14 pack (ε6 op)
  MOR 81mm; 120mm: 70 M-43 (ε12 op)
  AD GUNS 14.5mm: 30 PRC Type 56; 37mm: PRC
    40mm: 2 L/60

AIR WING (215)
no cbt ac, or armed hel
TPT ac 1 BAe-748, 2 *Skyvan* hel 2 SA-316B *Chetak*, 1
  SA-316B, 1 AS-332L (*Puma*), 2 AS-332L-1 (*Super
  Puma*), 1 Bell 206, 2 Bell 206L, 2 AS-350 (*Ecureuil*)

Forces Abroad

UN AND PEACEKEEPING
CROATIA (UNMOP): 1 obs **LEBANON** (UNIFIL)
601: 1 inf bn **TAJIKISTAN** (UNMOT): 5 obs

Paramilitary 40,000

POLICE FORCE 40,000

Opposition

COMMUNIST PARTY OF NEPAL (United Marxist and
Leninist): armed wing ε1–1,500

Pakistan   Pak

	1997	1998	1999	2000
GDP	Rs2.4tr	Rs2.8tr		
	($58bn)	($61bn)		
per capita	$2,300	$2,400		
Growth	-0.4%	5.3%		
Inflation	11.4%	6.2%		
Debt	$30bn	$31bn		
Def exp	Rs161bn	Rs180bn		
	($3.9bn)	($4.0bn)		
Def bdgt		Rs145bn	Rs142bn	
		($3.2bn)	($2.7bn)	
FMA*a* (US)	$2.5m	$1.5m	$2.9m	$0.4m
FMA (Aus)	$0.02m	$0.02m	$0.02m	
$1=rupee	41.1	45.0	51.7	
a UNMOGIP **1997** $7m **1998** $8m				

Population	144,350,000 (less than 3% Hindu)		
Age	*13–17*	*18–22*	*23–32*
Men	8,520,000	7,317,000	11,814,000
Women	8,051,000	6,622,000	10,485,000

Total Armed Forces

ACTIVE 587,000

RESERVES 513,000

Army ε500,000; obligation to age 45 (men) or 50 (officers); active liability for 8 years after service **Navy** 5,000 **Air Force** 8,000

Army 520,000

9 Corps HQ • 2 armd div • 9 Corps arty bde • 19 inf div • 7 engr bde • 1 area comd (div) • 3 armd recce regt • 7 indep armd bde • 1 SF gp (3 bn) • 9 indep inf bde • 1 AD comd (3 AD gp: 8 bde)
AVN 17 sqn
  7 ac, 8 hel, 1 VIP, 1 obs flt
EQUIPMENT
  MBT 2,320+: 15 M-47, 250 M-48A5, 50 T-54/-55, 1,200 PRC Type-59, 250 PRC Type-69, 200+ PRC Type-85, ε300 T-80UD
  APC 850 M-113
  TOWED ARTY 1,590: **85mm**: 200 PRC Type-56; **105mm**: 300 M-101, 50 M-56 pack; **122mm**: 200 PRC Type-60, 400 PRC Type-54; **130mm**: 200 PRC Type-59-1; **155mm**: 30 M-59, 60 M-114, 124 M-198; **203mm**: 26 M-115
  SP ARTY 240: **105mm**: 50 M-7; **155mm**: 150 M-109A2; **203mm**: 40 M-110A2
  MRL **122mm**: 45 *Azar* (PRC Type-83)
  MOR **81mm**: 500; **120mm**: 225 AM-50, M-61
  SSM 18 *Hatf* 1, *Hatf* 2, *Shaheen* 1
  ATGW 800 incl: *Cobra*, 200 TOW (incl 24 on M-901 SP), *Green Arrow* (PRC *Red Arrow*)
  RL **89mm**: M-20 3.5in

RCL **75mm**: Type-52; **106mm**: M-40A1
  AD GUNS 2,000+ incl: **14.5mm; 35mm**: 200 GDF-002; **37mm**: PRC Type-55/-65; **40mm**: M1, 100 L/60; **57mm**: PRC Type-59
  SAM 350 *Stinger, Redeye*, RBS-70, 500 *Anza* Mk-1/-2
  SURV RASIT (veh, arty), AN/TPQ-36 (arty, mor)
AIRCRAFT
  SURVEY 1 *Commander* 840
  LIAISON 1 Cessna 421, 2 *Commander* 690, 80 *Mashshaq*, 1 F-27
  OBS 40 O-1E, 50 *Mashshaq*
HELICOPTERS
  ATTACK 20 AH-1F (TOW)
  TPT 12 Bell 47G, 7 -205, 10 -206B, 16 Mi-8, 6 IAR/SA-315B, 23 IAR/SA-316, 35 SA-330, 5 UH-1H

Navy 22,000

(incl Naval Air, ε1,200 Marines and ε2,000 Maritime Security Agency (see *Paramilitary*))
BASE Karachi (Fleet HQ)
SUBMARINES 10
SSK 7
  1 *Khalid* (Fr *Agosta* 90B) with 533mm TT, *Exocet* SM39 USGW
  2 *Hashmat* (Fr *Agosta*) with 533mm TT (F-17 HWT), *Harpoon* USGW
  4 *Hangor* (Fr *Daphné*) with 533mm TT (L-5 HWT), *Harpoon* USGW
SSI 3 MG110 (SF delivery)
PRINCIPAL SURFACE COMBATANTS 8
FRIGATES 8
  FFG 6 *Tariq* (UK *Amazon*) with 4 x *Harpoon* SSM (in 3 of class), 1 x LY-60N SAM (in 3 of class), 2 x 3 324mm ASTT (in 2 of class); 1 114mm gun (2 *Lynx* hel delivered)
  FF 2 *Shamsher* (UK *Leander*) with SA-319B hel, 1 x 3 ASW mor, plus 2 114mm guns
PATROL AND COASTAL COMBATANTS 10
MISSILE CRAFT 5
  4 PRC *Huangfeng* with 4 *HY* 2 SSM
  1 x *Jalat* II with 4 C-802 SSM
PATROL, COASTAL 1 *Larkana* PCC
PATROL, INSHORE 3
  2 *Quetta* (PRC *Shanghai*) PFI
  1 *Rajshahi* PCI
MINE COUNTERMEASURES 3
  3 *Munsif* (Fr *Eridan*) MHC
SUPPORT AND MISCELLANEOUS 10
  1 *Behr Paima* AGHS, 2 *Gwadar* AOT, 1 *Attack* AOT, 1 *Nasr* AO, 1 *Moawin* AOR, 3 AT, 1 *Fuqing* AOR

NAVAL AIR
7 cbt ac, 12 armed hel
ASW/MR 1 sqn with 4 *Atlantic* plus 2 in store, 3 P-3C (operated by Air Force)
ASW/SAR 2 hel sqn with 4 SA-319B (ASW), 6 *Sea King*

Mk 45 (ASW), 2 *Lynx* HAS Mk-3 (ASW)
COMMS 3 Fokker F-27 **ac** (Air Force)
ASM *Exocet* AM-39

MARINES (ε1,200)
1 cdo/SF gp

Air Force 45,000

389 cbt ac, no armed hel **Flying hours** some 210
FGA 7 sqn
  1 with 16 *Mirage* (13 IIIEP (some with AM-39 ASM),
    3 IIIDP (trg))
  3 (1 OCU) with 52 *Mirage* 5 (40 -5PA/PA2, 10 5PA3
    (ASuW), 2 5DPA/DPA2)
  3 with 42 Q-5 (A-5 *Fantan*)
FTR 10 sqn
  4 with 50 J-6/JJ-6, (F-6/FT-6), 3 (1 OCU) with 25 F-
    16A/B, 2 (1 OCU) with 77 J-7 (F-7P), 1 with 43
    Mirage IIIO
RECCE 1 sqn with 11* *Mirage* IIIRP
SAR 1 hel sqn with 15 SA-319
TPT ac 12 C-130 (11 B/E, 1 L-100), 2 Boeing 707, 1
  Boeing 737, 1 *Falcon* 20, 2 F-27-200 (1 with Navy), 1
  Beech *Super King Air* 200, **hel** 15 SA 316/319, 4
  Cessna 172, 1 Cessna 560 *Citation*, 1 *Piper* PA-34
  Seneca, 4 MFI-17B *Mashshaq*, 2 *Falcon* 20F (ELINT/
  ECM)
TRG 30 JJ-5 (FT-5), 30 JJ-6 (FT-6), 13 FT-7, 40* MFI-17B
  Mashshaq, 10 T-33A, 30 T-37B/C, 12 K-8, 11* F-16B,
  7* *Mirage* IIIOD
AD 7 SAM bty
  6 each with 24 *Crotale*, 1 with 6 CSA-1 (SA-2)
MISSILES
  ASM AM-39 *Exocet*, AGM-65 *Maverick*, AS 30,
    AGM-84 *Harpoon*
  AAM AIM-7 *Sparrow*, AIM-9 *Sidewinder*, R-530
  ARM AGM-88 *Harm*

Forces Abroad

UN AND PEACEKEEPING
CROATIA (UNMOP): 1 obs **GEORGIA** (UNOMIG): 6
obs **IRAQ/KUWAIT** (UNIKOM): 6 obs **WESTERN
SAHARA** (MINURSO): 64 incl 5 obs

Paramilitary ε247,000 active

NATIONAL GUARD 185,000
incl *Janbaz* Force, *Mujahid* Force, National Cadet Corps,
Women Guards
FRONTIER CORPS 35,000 (Ministry of Interior)
11 regt (40 bn), 1 indep armd car sqn; 45 UR-416 APC
PAKISTAN RANGERS ε25,000 (Ministry of Interior)
MARITIME SECURITY AGENCY ε2,000
1 *Alamgir* (US *Gearing* DD) (no ASROC or TT), 4

Barakat OPV, 4 (PRC *Shanghai*) PFI
COAST GUARD
some 33 PFI, plus boats

Foreign Forces

UN (UNMOGIP): 46 mil obs from 8 countries

Sri Lanka — Ska

	1997	1998	1999	2000
GDP	Rs891bn	Rs1,029bn		
	($14.8bn)	($15.9bn)		
per capita	$3,800	$4,100		
Growth	6.0%	5.6%		
Inflation	9.6%	9.4%		
Debt	$9.2bn	$9.6bn		
Def exp	Rs56bn	Rs63bn		
	($949m)	($975m)		
Def bdgt		Rs45bn	Rs57bn	
		($694m)	($807m)	
FMA (US)	$0.2m	$0.2m	$0.2m	$0.2m
$1 = rupee	59.0	64.6	70.9	
Population				18,844,000

(Sinhalese 74%, Tamil 18%, Moor 7%; Buddhist 69%,
Hindu 15%, Christian 8%, Muslim 8%)

Age	*13–17*	*18–22*	*23–32*
Men	927,000	901,000	1,578,000
Women	890,000	867,000	1,548,000

Total Armed Forces

ACTIVE some 110–115,000
(incl recalled reservists)

RESERVES 4,200
Army 1,100 **Navy** 1,100 **Air Force** 2,000
Obligation 7 years, post regular service

Army ε90–95,000

(incl 42,000 recalled reservists; ε1,000 women)
10 div • 1 mech inf bde • 1 air mobile bde • 23 inf bde
• 1 indep SF bde (1 cde bde) • 1 armd regt • 3 armd
recce regt (bn) • 4 fd arty (1 reserve) • 4 fd engr regt (1
reserve)
EQUIPMENT
  MBT ε25 T-55 (perhaps 18 op)
  RECCE 26 *Saladin*, 15 *Ferret*, 12 Daimler *Dingo*
  AIFV 16 BMP (12 -1, 4 -2) (trg)
  APC 35 PRC Type-85, 10 BTR-152, 31 *Buffel*, 30
    Unicorn, 10 Shorland, 6 *Hotspur*, 30 *Saracen*
  TOWED ARTY 76mm: 12 FRY M-48; **85mm**: 12
    PRC Type-56; **88mm**: 12 25-pdr; **130mm**: 12 PRC

Type-59-1; **152mm:** PRC Type-66 (reported)
MRL 107mm: 1
MOR 81mm: 276; **82mm:** 19; **107mm:** 12; **120mm:** 36
  M-43
RCL 105mm: 15 M-65; **106mm:** 34 M-40
AD GUNS 40mm: 24 L-40; **94mm:** 3 3.7in
SURV AN/TPQ-36 (arty)
UAV 1 *Seeker*

Navy 10,000

(incl 1,100 recalled reservists)
BASES Colombo (HQ), Trincomalee (main base),
Karainagar, Tangalle, Kalpitiya, Galle, Welisara
PATROL AND COASTAL COMBATANTS 54
PATROL, COASTAL 1 *Jayesagara* PCC
PATROL, INSHORE 53
  3 *Sooraya*, 2 *Rana* (PRC MOD *Shanghai* II) PFI
  1 *Parakrambahu* (PRC *Houxin*) PFC
  3 Il *Dvora* PFI<
  8 Il *Super Dvora* PFI<
  3 ROK *Killer* PFI<
  6 *Trinity Marine* PCF
  2 *Shaldag* PCF
  4 *Colombo* PCF
  1 *Ranarisi* PFI
  22 PCI<
  some 36 boats
AMPHIBIOUS 1
  1 *Wuhu* LSM
  plus 7 craft: 2 LCM, 2 LCU, 1 ACV, 2 fast personnel
  carrier

Air Force 10,000

22 cbt ac, 15 armed hel **Flying hours** 420
FGA 4 F-7M, 1 FT-7, 2 FT-5, 4 *Kfir*-C2, 1 *Kfir*-TC2
ARM AC 8 SF-260TP, 2 FMA IA58A *Pucara*
ATTACK HEL 11 Bell 212, 2 Mi-24V, 2 Mi-35
TPT 1 sqn with **ac** 3 BAe 748, 1 Cessna 421C, 1 *Super
  King Air*, 1 Y-8, 7 Y-12, 4 An-24, 4 An-32B, 1 Cessna
  150 **hel** 3 Bell 412 (VIP)
HEL 9 Bell 206, 5 Mi-17 (plus 6 in store)
TRG incl 4 DHC-1, 4 SF-260 W, 3 Bell 206
RESERVES Air Force Regt, 3 sqn; Airfield
  Construction, 1 sqn
UAV 5 *Superhawk*

Paramilitary ε100,300

POLICE FORCE (Ministry of Defence) 70,100
incl reserves, 1,000 women and Special Task Force:
3,000-strong anti-guerrilla unit
NATIONAL GUARD ε15,000
HOME GUARD 15,200

Opposition

LIBERATION TIGERS OF TAMIL EELAM (LTTE)
ε6,000
Leader Velupillai Prabhakaran

Tajikistan   Tjk

	1997	1998	1999	2000
GDPᵃ	Tr443bn	Tr1,025bn		
	($1.1bn)	($1.2bn)		
per capita	$900	$900		
Growth	1.7%	5.3%		
Inflation	164%	103%		
Debt	$893m	$1,271m		
Def expᵃ	ε$132m	ε$100m		
Def bdgtᵃ			$18m	
$1=rouble	600	850	1,035	

ᵃ UNMOT **1997** $8m **1998** $8m

Population				6,620,000

(Tajik 67%, Uzbek 25%, Russian 2%, Tatar 2%)

Age	*13–17*	*18–22*	*23–32*
Men	406,000	322,000	472,000
Women	393,000	313,000	463,000

Total Armed Forces

ACTIVE some 7–9,000
Terms of service 24 months
A number of potential officers are being trained at the
Higher Army Officers and Engineers College, Dushanbe.
It is planned to form an Air Force sqn and to acquire Su-25
from Belarus, 5 Mi-24 and 10 Mi-8 have been procured.

Army some 7,000

2 MR bde (incl 1 trg), 1 mtn bde
1 SF bde, 1 SF det (εbn+)
1 SAM regt

EQUIPMENT
  MBT 40 T-72
  AIFV 85 BMP-1/-2
  APC 40 BTR-60/-70/-80
  TOWED ARTY 122mm: 12 D-30
  MOR 122mm: 12
  SAM 20 SA-2/-3

Paramilitary ε1,200

BORDER GUARDS ε1,200 (Ministry of Interior)

Opposition

ISLAMIC MOVEMENT OF TAJIKISTAN some 5,000
Signed peace accord with government on 27 June
1997. Integration with govt forces slowly proceeding

Foreign Forces

UN (UNMOT): 71 mil obs from 14 countries
RUSSIA Frontier Forces ε14,500 (Tajik conscripts,
Russian officers) **Army** 8,200; 1 MRD
  EQUIPMENT
    MBT 190 T-72
    AIFV/APC 313 BMP-2, BRM-1K, BTR-80
    SP ARTY 122mm: 66 2S1; **152mm**: 54 2S3
    MRL 122mm: 12 BM-21; **220mm**: 12 9P140
    MOR 120mm: 36 PM-38
    AIR DEFENCE
      SAM 20 SA-8
KAZAKSTAN ε300: 1 border gd bn

Turkmenistan — Tkm

	1997	1998	1999	2000
GDP	ε$3.9bn	ε$4.2bn		
per capita	$1,800	$2,000		
Growth	-25.9%	4.5%		
Inflation	84%	16.8%		
Debt	$1,771m	$1,665m		
Def exp	ε$138m	ε$117m		
Def bdgt			$242m	
FMA (US)	$0.3m	$0.3m	$0.3m	$0.3m
$1 = manat	4,165	7,000	14,000	
Population				5,000,000
(Turkmen 77%, Uzbek 9%, Russian 7%, Kazak 2%)				
Age	*13–17*	*18–22*	*23–32*	
Men	258,000	216,000	346,000	
Women	252,000	213,000	342,000	

Total Armed Forces

ACTIVE 17–19,000
Terms of service 24 months

Army 14–16,000

4 MRD (1 trg) • 1 arty bde • 1 MRL regt • 1 ATK regt
• 1 SSM bde • 1 engr bde • 2 SAM bde • 1 indep air
aslt bn
EQUIPMENT
  MBT 570 T-72
  RECCE 14 BRDM-2
  AIFV 156 BMP-1, 405 BMP-2, 51 BRM
  APC 728 BTR (-60/-70/-80)

TOWED ARTY 122mm: 197 D-30; **152mm**: 76 D-1,
  72 2A65
SP ARTY 152mm: 16 2S3
COMBINED GUN/MOR 120mm: 12 2S9
MRL 122mm: 60 BM-21; **220mm**: 54 9P140
MOR 82mm: 31; **120mm**: 42 PM-38
SSM 12 *Scud*
ATGW AT-2 *Swatter*, AT-3 *Sagger*, AT-4 *Spigot*, AT-5
  Spandrel
ATK GUNS 85mm: 6 D-44; **100mm**: 48 MT-12
AD GUNS 23mm: 28 ZSU-23-4 SP; **57mm**: 22 S-60
SAM 27 SA-4

Navy none

Has announced intention to form a Navy/Coast Guard.
Caspian Sea Flotilla (see **Russia**) is operating as a joint RF,
Kaz and Tkm flotilla under RF comd based at Astrakhan.

Air Force 3,000

(incl Air Defence)
89 cbt ac (plus 218 in store)
FGA/FTR 1 composite regt with 22 MiG-29, 2 MiG-
  29U, 65 Su-17
TRG 1 unit with 3 Su-7B, 2 L-39
TPT/GENERAL PURPOSE 1 composite sqn with 3
  An-12, 1 An-26, 10 Mi-24, 8 Mi-8
AIR DEFENCE
  FTR 2 regt with 48 MiG-23, 10 MiG-23U 24 MiG-25
    (both regt non-operational)
  SAM 50 SA-2/-3/-5
  IN STORE 172 MiG-23, 46 Su-25

Uzbekistan — Uz

	1997	1998	1999	2000
GDP	s936bn	s1,344bn		
	($11.5bn)	($12.2bn)		
per capita	$2,500	$2,700		
Growth	2.4%	4.4%		
Inflation	45%	23%		
Debt	$2.8bn	$2.3bn		
Def exp[a]	$610m	$657m		
Def bdgt			$330m	
FMA (US)	$0.3m	$0.4m	$0.5m	$0.5m
$1 = som[b]	73.8	91.4	122	

[a] Incl exp on paramilitary forces
[b] Market rate **1999** $1 = εs570

Population				23,500,000
(Uzbek 73%, Russian 6%, Tajik 5%, Kazak 4%, Kara-				
kalpak 2%, Tatar 2%, Korean <1%, Ukrainian <1%)				
Age	*13–17*	*18–22*	*23–32*	
Men	1,462,000	1,219,000	1,881,000	
Women	1,432,000	1,203,000	1,880,000	

Total Armed Forces

ACTIVE ε74,000
(incl MoD staff and centrally controlled units)
Terms of service conscription, 18 months

Army 50,000

3 Corps HQ • 2 tk, 4 MR, 1 lt mtn, 1 mot bde • 2 air
aslt, 1 air-mobile, 1 *Spetsnaz* bde • 4 arty, 1 MRL bde •
1 National Guard bde

EQUIPMENT
  MBT 370 incl T-54, T-62, T-64 plus some T-72
  RECCE 35 BRDM-2
  AIFV 273 BMP-2, 130 BMD-1
  APC 36 BTR-70, 290 BTR-80, 145 BTR-D
  TOWED ARTY 122mm: 90 D-30; **152mm:** 28 D-1, 49
    D-20, 32 2A36
  SP ARTY 122mm: 18 2S1; **152mm:** 17 2S3, 2S5
    (reported); **203mm:** 48 2S7
  COMBINED GUN/MOR 120mm: 69 2S9
  MRL 122mm: 33 BM-21; **220mm:** 48 9P140
  MOR 120mm: 18 PM-120, 19 2S12, 5 2B11
  ATK GUNS 100mm: 39 MT-12
(In 1991 the former Soviet Union transferred some 2,000 tanks
(T-64), 1,200 ACV and 750 arty to storage bases in Uzbekistan.
This eqpt is under Uzbek control, but has deteriorated
considerably.)

Air Force some 4,000

150 cbt ac, 42 attack hel
FGA 26 Su-17/Su-17UB, 23 Su-24, 20 Su-25
FTR 39 MiG-29/MiG-29UB, 31 Su-27/Su-27UB
RECCE 11* Su-24
TPT 28 An-12 plus 9 other tpt ac
TRG 14 L-39
HELICOPTERS
  ATTACK 42 Mi-24
  ASLT 58 Mi-8T
  TPT 26 Mi-6, 1 Mi-26
SAM 45 SA-2/-3/-5

Paramilitary ε18–20,000

INTERNAL SECURITY TROOPS (Ministry of Interior)
ε17–19,000

NATIONAL GUARD (Ministry of Defence) 1,000
1 bde

MILITARY DEVELOPMENTS

Regional Trends

Despite a decline in defence spending between 1996 and 1998, the region remains the second largest arms market after the Middle East. There is little prospect of change in the underlying regional security concerns, which means that, as economies recover, military spending is likely to increase in 1999 and 2000. In international terms, the dominant security issues are the North Korean missile and weapons of mass destruction (WMD) programmes and tensions over China and Taiwan. The troubled domestic politics of the second most populous country in the region, Indonesia, could also have international repercussions. Secessionist movements challenge the state's integrity and the Indonesian security forces are fully stretched in attempting to contain conflict in a number of provinces – in some instances they even contribute to it.

China

While China's military capabilities continue to advance they have not developed in a manner that alters the regional balance. For example, while China can undoubtedly cause serious disruption to Taiwan by targeting the shipping lanes and firing missiles at the island itself, it does not have the capability to make an opposed landing with amphibious or other forces. Since 1996, the deployment of DF-15 (CSS-6, M-9), DF-11 (CSS-7, M-11) and modernised DF-21(CSS-5) medium-range ballistic missiles (MRBMs) in the coastal area opposite Taiwan has increased to some 150–200. On 9 July 1999, tensions were once again exacerbated when the Taiwanese President Lee Teng-hui said diplomacy between China and Taiwan should be conducted on a 'state-to-state' basis. This caused China to reiterate its longstanding position that it did not rule out the use of force to bring about the re-unification of China. There was an increase in military activity in July along the coast opposite Taiwan, which was billed as 'mobilisation' exercises, as well as incursions into Taiwanese airspace, but it was mainly a war of words. Nevertheless, these tensions increase the demand from Taiwan for more advanced military equipment, including a missile-defence capability. Equally, Japan's interest in a missile-defence capability, driven by a possible North Korean threat, but also inspired by China, is unsettling for the Beijing leadership. Theatre missile defence (TMD) is a particularly sensitive issue for China, not only because such a development will degrade its medium-range missile capability in the region, but also because its strategic capabilities are limited compared with those in the US and Russia. The systems being considered for theatre defence may also become part of a US limited national missile defence (NMD) capability. China's strategic capability is composed of less than 200 nuclear warheads, of which only perhaps 20–30 would be operational at any given time. To be sure of overcoming even a limited missile-defence capability, China would have to spend resources on increasing its strategic weapons and enhancing countermeasures (including using multiple warheads). China is also vulnerable to counter-force attack as it has no mobile land-based strategic missiles in service yet and only one ballistic-missile submarine (SSBN), which is not always operational.

The development of missile-defence systems will no doubt reinforce China's determination to continue with its strategic-weapon modernisation programme. This was indicated by the flight test on 3 August 1999 of the *Dong-Feng*-31 (DF-31) land-based mobile missile, which is assessed to have a range of up to 8,000km (minimum range 2,000km), and is generally considered to be a replacement for the DF-4. It could begin to enter service between 2002 and 2005. A submarine-launched version of the DF-31 (designated JL-2) is also under development. Tensions between China and the US were also raised following a January 1999 US Congressional report that accused

China of espionage at US nuclear laboratories. While it is possible that China's nuclear capabilities might have been advanced through information gleaned from this source, there is no direct evidence to suggest that its nuclear programmes have made more progress than might otherwise have been expected.

North-east Asia

While North Korea's conventional force capabilities must have degraded due to economic stringency, they still represent a serious and direct threat to South Korea. Wider international security concerns have been aroused by Pyongyang's determination to pursue its missile programmes. Following the surprise launch of a *Taepo-dong*-1 missile over the Sea of Japan in August 1998, North Korea has pressed ahead with the development of the longer-range *Taepo-dong*-2, which some analysts assess to have the capability to reach the western fringes of the US. While *Taepo-dong*-2's designed range is thought to be 3,500km, this can be extended significantly by lessening the weight of the missile by, for example, using a lighter warhead. These developments have repercussions in increasing demands in the US and Japan for resources to be committed to developing missile defences, leading in turn to antagonisms with China. They have also prompted Japan to press ahead with programmes to acquire reconnaissance satellites. There is now South Korean pressure to acquire surface-to-surface missiles (SSMs) with a range of out to 500km, covering the whole of North Korea, thus enhancing the South's counter-force capability. Until now, under an agreement with the US, South Korea has limited its SSM capability to a maximum range of 180km. Other repercussions of North Korea's missile programmes could include a negative effect on support from the US, Japan and South Korea for funding the Korean Peninsula Energy Development Organisation (KEDO), which is building two light-water nuclear-power stations in North Korea in return for Pyongyang relinquishing its nuclear-weapon programme. However, both South Korea and Japan have now committed themselves to the financing agreement for KEDO. Following approval by its National Assembly on 12 August 1999, South Korea will provide $3.22bn under the arrangement, while the Japanese Diet approved the provision of $1bn in July 1999. Other contributors are the EU with $80m; and the US, which is providing $55m specifically for oil supplies to North Korea (while construction of the power stations is in progress) and for KEDO's administration. Thus, despite the tensions over the missiles issue, by August 1999 KEDO was nearer than before to achieving its full funding-target of nearly $5.2bn.

At sea, tensions between North Korea and its neighbours have arisen on three counts. First, Japanese vessels used their weapons in anger for the first time since 1945 when they opened fire on North Korean fishing vessels entering Japanese territorial waters in March 1999. Second, in June 1999, North Korean fishing boats violating South Korean waters were accompanied by naval vessels. In the resulting clashes, a North Korean patrol boat was sunk and a number of vessels on both sides were damaged. Third, Pyongyang protested strongly against the first full-scale joint naval exercises between South Korea and Japan that were held in August 1999.

South-east Asia

While they remain on a minor scale, tensions have arisen over competing territorial claims on the Spratley Islands and surrounding waters. At their July 1999 summit meeting, member countries of the Association of South-East Asian Nations (ASEAN), now numbering ten following Cambodia's entry in May 1999, were unable to make progress in resolving their differences over the islands. This made it all the more difficult for them to resist China's claims. For example, China has undertaken construction work on Mischief Reef, a thousand miles from the nearest Chinese territory, prompting diplomatic protests from the Philippines. This is among the concerns which have prompted Manila to agree to the return of US naval forces to the Philippines on a regular basis, seven years after US bases there closed. Under a new visiting-forces agreement, approved by the Philippines Senate in May 1999, the US has permission to use ports in the Philippines and to participate in annual joint exercises with up to 2,000 troops on each side.

Indonesia is by far the worst affected in South-east Asia by internal armed conflict. In particular, progress towards the UN-supervised referendum on the future of East Timor, planned for 30 August, has led to violence between the pro- and anti-separatist factions. The Indonesian military have been implicated in attacks on supporters of secession by militia groups attempting to disrupt the process. Violence continues in other provinces where there are strong separatist movements, such as Aceh and Irian Jaya. In Aceh in particular, the armed forces and police have engaged in vigorous offensives against separatists, resulting in many civilian deaths. For example, there is strong evidence that up to 50 villagers were killed by security forces in the Betung Ateuh valley in western Aceh in a single incident in July 1999. Such draconian actions only serve to increase hostility to the central government. If the East Timor referendum results in a vote for secession, Jakarta may well be faced with increased secessionist pressure from other provinces. Whatever government takes power after the November 1999 presidential election, it will have to embark on radical political and economic reform to avoid a widening of domestic conflict and increasing disintegration of the country. Ethnic and religious (Muslim–Christian) conflicts, such as that in Ambon in August 1999, further complicate the situation.

DEFENCE SPENDING

Defence expenditure in East Asia and Australasia is estimated to have fallen from $140bn in 1997 to $131bn in 1998 (measured in 1997 dollars), or around 6% in real terms. 1998 was the third successive year of decline in regional spending after outlays peaked at $144bn in 1995. Even so, the region remains the second-largest importer of arms after the Middle East. Regional defence spending in 1999 is expected to rise by some 6% in real US dollar terms. This is due partly to increased budgetary allocations and partly to recovery in the major regional currencies.

The economic crisis in East Asia from mid-1997 resulted in a decline of over 7% in regional gross domestic product (GDP) in 1998, when measured in US dollars at average annual exchange rates, following a 4% fall in 1997. Japan's economy declined by 2.6% in 1998, while there were steeper GDP falls in South Korea (-5.8%), Thailand (-8%), Indonesia (-13.7%), and Malaysia (-6.8%). China, Taiwan and Singapore managed some economic growth, although at below previous levels. Most regional governments, with the important exceptions of China and Taiwan, reacted to the crisis either by cutting defence budgets or by holding them around existing levels. At the same time, many regional currencies experienced significant depreciation in the course of 1998, which reduced the dollar purchasing power of defence budgets. Both factors hit the regional arms market. However, while the value of regional arms orders was lower in 1998 than in previous years, existing contracts were largely completed to schedule, with the result that the value of regional arms deliveries remained at a high level by global standards. Regional defence industries are also increasingly drawn into the process of globalisation, with the result that the regional market for intermediate defence-related systems and components (mainly firm-to-firm) is the second only to NATO's internal market in its scale. Resumed growth seems certain as the economic crisis recedes.

Domestic procurement in Japan, China, and South Korea (after some rescheduling in 1997 and 1998) has maintained its momentum, and is accompanied by high-value imports of military sub-systems and components. Taiwan's procurement, mainly from foreign suppliers, includes a new round of requirements. Procurement in ASEAN countries, again mainly from foreign sources, was subject to some rescheduling during 1997 and 1998, but only Indonesia made significant outright programme cancellations.

Japan

Japan's defence budget fell in yen terms in 1998 for the first time since the Japanese Defence Agency (JDA) was established in 1954. This has been followed by a further fall in 1999 from ¥4,929bn to ¥4,920bn. However, the nominal US dollar value of the 1999 budget shows an increase, with $40.7bn comparing with $37.6bn in 1998, owing to the yen's appreciation against the dollar. The budget excludes ¥12.1bn ($100m) for the Special Action Committee on Okinawa (SACO) fund towards the costs of vacating US military bases. The JDA contribution towards the costs of US forces in Japan is ¥276bn ($2.3bn) in 1999.

Around 22% of Japan's defence budget goes on procurement, approaching half the proportion spent by the US and countries with comparable defence industrial capabilities, such as the UK and France. In 1999, the JDA is planning to spend some $7.6bn on new equipment and $1.1bn on Research and Development. Japan's major production programme is the F-2 Close Air Support aircraft (a derivative of the F-16). The first operational squadron is due to be formed in early 2000. Of the total requirement of 120, 45 aircraft were planned for delivery under the FY1996–2000 Five Year Mid-Term Defence Programme (MTDP). Eight F-2s have been ordered in 1999 for some $868m – an indication of the high unit cost.

Table 20 Japan: defence budget by function and selected other budgets, 1993–1999

(1998 $bn)		1993	1994	1995	1996	1997	1998	1999
Personnel		19.4	21.3	23.4	19.9	17.9	16.6	17.6
Supplies		27.1	28.7	30.0	26.5	23.7	21.0	22.3
of which	Procurement	10.8	10.7	9.8	8.8	7.9	7.2	7.6
	R&D	1.2	1.3	1.6	1.4	1.3	1.0	1.1
	Maintenance	7.6	8.5	9.4	8.4	7.5	6.9	7.2
	Other including Infrastructure	7.5	8.2	9.2	8.0	7.0	6.1	6.4
Total defence budget		46.5	50.0	53.4	46.4	41.7	37.6	39.9
SACO						0.1	0.1	0.1
Maritime Safety Agency		1.5	1.7	1.8	1.5	1.4	1.3	1.4
Veterans (Imperial Japanese Army)		15.5	16.4	17.1	14.0	11.8	10.3	10.6
Space		1.7	1.9	2.1	2.3	2.5	2.7	3.1

Table 21 Japan: defence budget by armed service, 1993–1999

(1998 $bn)		1993	1994	1995	1996	1997	1998	1999
Japanese Defense Agency		41.3	44.2	47.0	40.9	36.8	33.4	35.2
of which	Ground Self-Defense Force	16.7	18.2	20.2	17.2	15.3	14.2	14.9
	Maritime Self-Defense Force	10.9	11.9	12.0	10.9	9.6	8.6	9.2
	Air Self-Defense Force	11.8	12.1	12.5	10.7	9.8	8.8	9.1
	Other	1.9	2.1	2.4	2.2	2.1	1.8	2.0
Defense Facility Administration Agency		5.2	5.8	6.4	5.5	4.9	4.3	4.7
Total defence budget		46.5	50.0	53.4	46.4	41.7	37.6	39.9

Japan has committed some ¥557m ($5m) to TMD feasibility studies since 1995. The 1999 research allocation is ¥960m ($8m). Under the joint TMD programme with the US, Japan's research and development (R&D) costs are expected to be around $250m over five years. The reconnaissance satellite programme is expected to cost at least $1.3bn, for which funding is contained in supplementary appropriations to the FY1998 and 1999 budgets.

China and Taiwan

Military expenditures continue to rise in mainland China and Taiwan, which are both less affected by the economic difficulties experienced by regional neighbours. China's GDP in 1998, measured using purchasing power parity (see page 11) rather than market exchange rates, was some $166bn higher than in 1997 if Hong Kong is included. The country's official defence budget increased from Y91bn ($11bn) in 1998 to Y105bn ($12.6bn) in 1999. The 13% increase in real terms reflects some compensation for the military following the government's July 1998 decision to put an end to the commercial activities of the People's Liberation Army (PLA). Chinese defence spending remains non-transparent, and official accounts substantially understate the real level of military expenditure, estimated at more than $37bn in 1998, or about three times official figures.

China has a large range of conventional weapons in production or in development, and also continues to order high-value weapon systems from Russia. Delivery of the last of four *Kilo* submarines was completed in early 1999. Licensed production of the Su-27 aircraft is gearing up with the first flight of two prototypes in January 1999. China is expected to produce about 15 in 1999–2000 out of the 200 planned. China is reported to have reached agreement with Russia in June 1999 on the purchase of 50 Su-30 fighter, ground attack aircraft (FGAs) for delivery from 2002. China's domestic procurement programmes continue to provide a substantial market for Russia and for US and West European sub-systems.

Taiwan's 1999 defence budget of NT$357bn ($10.9bn) covers an 18-month period from July 1999 to December 2000. By comparison, the 1998 budget was NT$269bn ($9.8bn), while the plan for calendar year 1999 is NT$286bn ($8.3bn). These figures exclude the special budget covering the purchase of 150 F-16s (mostly delivered by August 1999) and 60 *Mirage* 2000s, deliveries of which were completed in late 1998, more than a year ahead of schedule. These purchases amount to an expenditure of NT$301bn ($11–12bn) over the period 1993–2001, of which NTS289bn had been spent by 1998.

In response to growing numbers of deployed Chinese missiles, Taiwan is seeking to improve its air-defence and airborne-reconnaissance capabilities. In 1999, the armed forces have ordered an early warning radar similar to the USAF *Pave Paws* radar and upgrades of their *Patriot* SAMs to PAC-3 standard. There are also reports in 1999 that the Navy is to purchase *Aegis* destroyers from the US, which can be equipped with a TMD system.

The Koreas

South Korea's defence spending has fallen considerably in dollar terms owing to the depreciation of the won. The 1999 defence allocation is won13.7tr ($11.6bn) rising to a requested won15.4tr ($12.8bn) for 2000. By comparison the revised 1998 budget was won13.8tr ($9.8bn) after the initial 14.2tr won ($10.2bn) allocation was cut. Supplementary allocations in the course of the year boosted outlays to won18.5tr ($13.2bn), around 15% less in real terms than 1997 outlays. The 2000–04 defence plan amounts to won81.5tr ($68bn), of which won27tr (over $22bn) is for procurement.

The currency depreciation had an impact on the foreign-exchange component of the defence budget. Direct support for US forces in South Korea cost some $333m in 1999, an increase of 6% over 1998. (The US had requested $440m.) South Korean orders of US equipment in the pipeline were worth over $8bn in 1998. None of these have been cancelled, but there has been some rescheduling. New orders from the US amounted to $270m in 1998. The 1999 foreign currency procurement allocation amounts to $450m, compared to $1bn in 1998. Current programmes include the outstanding 32 licence-built F-16C/Ds of the original order of 120 for delivery by the end of 1999. Another 20 F-16s have been ordered in 1999. The Air Force requirement for 4 B-767 (AWACS) aircraft, announced in September 1997, has slipped, as has the schedule for the KTX-2 advanced training aircraft, whose full development was approved in late 1997 after prolonged uncertainty.

First deliveries will be in 2005. Licensed production of nine German Type 209 submarines continues, with six delivered by the end of 1998. New programmes under the 2000–04 defence plan include: US *Aegis*-class destroyers under the KDX-3 programme; a new FGA programme; attack helicopters; a continuing reconnaissance satellite programme; a new submarine programme (for which Russian *Kilo* derivatives are under consideration); and the long-standing area air-defence requirement. South Korean defence exports increased sharply in 1998 to $157m from $60m in 1997.

Table 22 South Korea: defence budget by function, 1996–1998

(US$bn)	1996	%	1997	%	1998	%
Personnel	7.2	44.1	6.7	43.4	4.5	42.4
O&M	2.5	15.3	2.4	15.6	1.8	17.1
Procurement incl R&D	4.3	26.3	4.2	27.3	2.9	27.6
Construction and Pensions	2.3	14.3	2.1	13.6	1.4	12.9
Total	**16.2**	*100.0*	**15.3**	*100.0*	**10.5**	*100.0*

Note   Figures exclude funds for the Defence and Aerospace industry estimated at more than $1bn a year

North Korea published its budget in 1999 for the first time since 1994. Defence is allocated won3bn ($1.3bn) – 15% of the budget – slightly up on 1998 when defence allocations were won2.9bn. Official figures suggest that government spending, including that on defence, has declined by nearly 40% since 1994. National income, which has been in decline since the beginning of the decade, may have grown by up to 4% in 1998.

ASEAN

The ten ASEAN members account for around 15% of regional spending. Based on official figures, the biggest ASEAN defence budget is now that of Singapore, whose 1999 budget of S$7.3bn ($4.2bn) is the same in nominal terms as it was in 1998. Orders in 1999 include eight AH-64D *Apache* attack helicopters from the US. Brunei's defence budget and outlays have increased since 1995 because of an extensive modernisation programme. Outlays in 1996 were $268m. In 1997, the defence operating budget was B$820m ($552m) falling to B$548m ($357m) in 1998. Outlays including capital spending were B$562m ($378m) in 1997, and B$632m ($378m) in 1998. The 1996–2000 capital-equipment budget for defence is B$466m ($300m). Brunei's defence spending as a proportion of GDP was over 7% in 1998. Elsewhere in ASEAN the purchasing power of defence budgets has fallen in line with currency depreciation. Malaysia's 1999 defence budget, including procurement, is RM8.6bn ($2.3bn). Several planned procurements have been put on hold, but the first three of a planned 27 offshore patrol vessels (OPVs) have been ordered from Germany. The Navy is to commission two *Lekiu*-class frigates from the UK, whose delivery has been delayed for technical reasons. Indonesia's declared defence-operating budget in 1999 is Rp12.2tr ($1.5bn). This figure excludes capital spending of Rp2.3tr ($280m), and also understates real spending by some margin. The Philippines has delayed the initial phase of its modernisation programme, scheduled to cost P50bn ($2.9bn) between 1996 and 2000, because of the reduced purchasing power of the defence budget (amounting to P52bn ($1.4bn) in 1999). Thailand's 1998 defence outlay was b86bn ($2.1bn), while the 1999 budget is b77bn ($2.1bn), with the same planned for 2000. There has been another large nominal increase in Myanmar's 1999 defence budget to K32.6bn from K24.5bn in 1998. Vietnam released its government budget for the first time in June 1999, but no details of defence spending were provided. The most recent details of defence spending date back to 1997, when the defence budget was d8tr ($685m). Cambodia, the newest ASEAN member, is planning to reduce defence spending, which accounted for over 4% of its GDP in 1998, to 3% of GDP in 2000.

Table 23 Arms orders and deliveries, East Asia and Australasia, 1997–1999

Supplier	Classification	Designation	Units	Order Date	Delivery Date	Comment
Australia						
dom	FGA	F-111	71	1990	1999	Upgrade of F/RF-111C
dom	SS	*Collins*	6	1987	1996	Swe license. Deliveries to 2001; 4 delivered
dom	FF	*Anzac*	6	1989	1996	Ge design, four delivered to date
Ca	LACV	*ASLAV*	276	1992	1996	Second batch of 150 for delivery 2001
dom	MHC	*Huon*	6	1994	1999	1st of 6. Deliveries continuing to 2002
dom	FGA	F-111	36	1995	1996	Upgrade continuing
US	MPA	P-3C	17	1996	1999	Upgrade to AP-3C
US	tpt	C-130J	12	1996	1999	Deliveries to 2000. Two-year slippage
US	hel	SH-2G	11	1997	2000	Deliveries to 2002. *Penguin* ASSM from No
UK	trg	*Hawk*-100	33	1997	1999	Final delivery 2006
US	hel	CH-47D	2	1997	1999	Follow-on; 4 D models delivered 1994
UK	FGA	F/A-18	71	1998	2005	Upgrade. AMRAAM (US), ASRAAM (UK)
US	PFC	045		1999	1999	Under two-year lease
dom	FFG	*Adelaide*	6	1999	2001	Upgrade to 2006
dom	LACV	*Bushmaster*	370	1999	2001	
US	AEW	B-737	7	1999	2004	
Brunei						
CH	trg	PC-7	4	1996	1997	
UK	trg	*Hawk 100/20*	10	1996	1999	
Indo	MPA	CN-235	3	1996	1999	Requirement for up to 12
US	hel	UH-60L	4	1996	1997	
Fr	SAM	*Mistral*	16	1997	1999	Launchers
Fr	ASSM	*Exocet*	59	1997	1999	
UK	FAC	*Waspada*	3	1997	1998	Upgrade
UK	OPV	OPV	3	1995	2000	Believed scaled-down version of Mal *Leiku* FF
Fr	SAM	*Mistral*	16	1998	1999	16 launchers
Cambodia						
Cz	MBT	T-55	40	1994	1994	Ex-Cz, deliveries continuing 1995
Cz	APC	OT-64	30	1994	1995	
Il	trg	L-39	8	1994	1996	Second-hand. Only 2 delivered by Jan 1998
Ge	PCR	*Koh Chhlam*	2	1995	1997	Built in Mal
Il	FGA	MiG-21	19	1995	1997	Upgrade
RF	FAC	*Stenka*	2	1996	1997	Upgrade
China						
dom	ICBM	DF-41		1985	2005	Development. DF-41 range 12,000km
dom	ICBM	DF-31		1985	2005	Dev. DF-31 range 8,000km. Tested Aug 1999
dom	SLBM	JL-2		1985	2008	Development. Range 8,000km
dom	IRBM	DF-21X		1999		Modernised DF-15
dom	SSGN	Type 093	1	1985	2002	Similar to RF *Victor* 3. Launch expected 2000
dom	SSBN	Type 094	4	1985	2008	Development programme
dom	ASSM	C701			1999	Development completed
dom	SRBM	DF-11	100	1988	1996	Production continuing
dom	SRBM	DF-15	300	1988	1996	Production continuing
RF	SAM	S-300	30	1990	1992	Continued in 1998
RF	SAM	SA-15	35	1995	1997	Orders: 15 (1995), 20 (1999). Deliveries to 2000
dom	SLCM	C-801(mod)		1997		Development (also known as YJ-82)
Col	ASM	KR-1		1997		In dev with RF. Kh-31P variant
RF	SAM	FT-2000		1998		
dom	bbr	H-6			1998	Still in production
col	trg	K-8	15	1987	1994	Development with Pak
dom	FGA	JH-7	20	1988	1993	Upgrade to FBC-2 standard has begun

Supplier	Classification	Designation	Units	Order Date	Delivery Date	Comment
RF	FGA	SU-27	200	1996	1998	15 units for production 1998–2000
RF	FGA	SU-30	50	1999	2002	
dom	FGA	FC-1		1990	2005	With Pak (150 units). First flight in 2000
dom	FGA	F-8IIM		1993	1996	Modernisation completed 1999
dom	FGA	F-10		1993		Development continues
UK	MPA	*Jetstream*	2	1997	1998	For Hong Kong Government
Il	AEW	Il-76	4	1997		
RF	tkr	Il-78	4	1998		
dom	MBT	Type-85-III	400	1985	1990	Development complete 1997
dom	MBT	Type-90		1987		For export only. No production by 1997
RF	AIFV	BMD-3		1997		Could be BMD-1
dom	ATGW	*Red Arrow 8E*		1996	1998	Modernised *Red Arrow* ATGW
Fr	hel	AS-365	50	1986	1989	Local production continues
Fr	hel	AS-350	8	1988	1996	Locally assembled. Designated Z-11
RF	hel	Mi-17	35	1995	1996	Delivered 30 1997. Order for 5 more 1997
RF	AO	*Nanchang*	1	1988	1996	Stern RAS only
dom	FF	*Luhu*	3	1991	1996	Second of class commissioned 1996
RF	SS	*Kilo*	4	1993	1995	Deliveries to 1999. 2 Type 877, 2 Type 636
dom	SS	*Song*	2	1994	2002	Two *Song* under construction at Wuhan
dom	SS	*Ming*	6	1994	1997	All six units under construction
dom	AGI	*Shiyan 970*	1	1995	1999	Sea trials in 1999
dom	DDG	*Shenzhen*	2	1996	1999	*Luhai*-class. Second for delivery in 2000
dom	DMS		1	1996	1997	Defence Mobilisation Ship
RF	DDG	*Sovremennyy*	2	1996	2000	
RF	hel	Ka-28	12	1998	2000	For DDG operation
RF	SSM	SS-N-22		1998	2002	Might be *Yakhont*
dom	FF	*Jiangwei 2*	2	1998	1999	One doing sea trials, one building
col	hel	EC-120		1990		In development with Fr and Sgp

Taiwan

Supplier	Classification	Designation	Units	Order Date	Delivery Date	Comment
dom	FGA	IDF	130	1982	1994	Deliveries completed 1999
US	FF	*Perry*	7	1989	1993	Final delivery in 1998
US	hel	CH-47	7	1990	1993	3 in 1993, 4 in 1997
Fr	FF	*LaFayette*	6	1992	1996	Deliveries to 1998
US	hel	AH-1W	63	1992	1993	Delivering to 1997
US	FGA	F-16A/B	150	1992	1997	60 delivered in 1997
Fr	FGA	*Mirage* 2000	60	1992	1997	Deliveries completed in 1999
Fr	AAM	*Magic*	480	1992	1997	
Fr	AAM	*MICA*	960	1992	1997	
dom	PGG	*Jin Chiang*	13	1992	1994	First of class delivered 1994
US	SAM	*Patriot*	6	1993	1997	Completed 1998. Upgrade to PAC-3 standard
US	tpt	C-130	12	1993	1995	Deliveries continue
US	SAR hel	S-70C	4	1994	1998	
US	LST	*Newport*	2	1994	1997	Rented from US
US	recce	S-2T	32	1995	1997	
dom	XFPB		6	1995	1997	National Police Administration
US	MBT	M-60A3	300	1995	1996	Ex-US. Deliveries through 1997
US	arty	M-109A5	28	1995	1998	
Fr	SAM	*Mistral*	550	1995	1997	
US	SAM	*Avenger*	74	1996	1998	
US	MPA	P-3		1996		With *Harpoon* SAM
US	hel	TH-67	30	1996	1998	
dom	OPV	*Chin Chiang*	11	1996	2000	Deliveries from 2000

Supplier Classification		Designation Units		Order Date	Delivery Date	Comment
Sgp	recce	RF-5E		1996	1998	Unspecified number of F-5E entered service as RF-5E
US	SAM	*Stinger*	1299	1996	1998	
dom	trg	AT-3	40	1997		Order resheduled
US	hel	OH-58D	13	1998	2001	Following deliveries of 26 1994–95
US	FFG	*Knox*	5	1997	1998	Delivery of 6 1992–96. Deliveries to 1999
US	ASSM	*Harpoon*	58	1998		
dom	PFM	*Kwang Hua*	50	1999	2003	New generation, high-speed stealth craft – postponed in 1999
US	hel	CH-47SD	9	1999	2002	Following deliveries of 7 1993–97
US	radar	*Pave Paws*		1999	2002	
US	LSD	*Anchorage*	1	1999		USS *Pensacola* to replace existing 2 LSDs
dom	FF	*Chengkung*	1	1999	2001	Eighth of class ordered. *Perry*-class
US	AEW	E-2T	4	1999	2002	Following delivery of 4 in 1995
US	DDG	*Aegis*	4	1999	2003	TMD-capable
Indonesia						
Aus	tpt	*Nomad*	20	1996	1997	
UK	APC	*Tactica*	19	1994	1996	Deliveries 1996–97
UK	lt tk	*Scorpion*	50	1995	1997	In addition to previous 50. 39 delivered 1998 incl 9 *Stormers*
Fr	APC	VBL	36	1995	1997	
Slvk	APC	BVP-2	9	1996	1998	Includes 2 BVP-2K, originally from Ukr
UK	trg	*Hawk* 109	24	1993	1996	Deliveries to 1997
UK	FGA	*Hawk* 209	16	1996	1999	12 were to be delivered in 1999
Nl	tpt	F-28	8	1996	1998	For Armed Forces Headquarters Foundation
dom	MPA	CN-235MP	3	1996	1999	
US	hel	NB-412	1	1996	1998	Licence-produced
Ge	hel	BO-105	3	1996	1998	40 delivered between 1980–93
Fr	SAM	*Mistral*		1996	1998	
Japan						
US	SAM	*Patriot*	160	1991	1994	PAC-2
dom	mor	L16	42	1999	2000	
dom	mor	120mm	27	1999	2000	
dom	SP arty	Type-96	3	1999	2000	
dom	SP arty	155 mm	4	1999	2000	Replacing Type-75. Entered prod in 1999
Col	arty	FH70		1999	2000	40 required under 1996–2000 MTDP
dom	MRL	MLRS	9	1999	2000	45 required under 1996–2000 MTDP
dom	AAA	Type-87	1	1999	2000	1 delivered 1998
dom	MBT	Type 90	17	1999	2000	90 required under 1996–2000 MTDP
dom	AIFV	Type-89	2	1999	2000	2 delivered 1998
dom	APC	Type-96	28	1999	2000	157 required under 1996–2000 MTDP
dom	APC	Type-82	1	1999	2000	1 delivered 1998
dom	lt tk	Type-87	1	1999	2000	1 delivered 1998
dom	hel	AH-1S		1999	2000	3 required under 1996–2000 MTDP
dom	hel	OH-1	3	1999	2000	Cost $66 million
dom	hel	UH-60JA	3	1999	2000	Cost $84 million
dom	hel	CH-47JA	2	1999	2000	9 required under 1996–2000 MTDP
dom	recce ac	LR-2	1	1999	2000	Cost $24 million
dom	SAM	*Hawk*		1999	2000	
dom	ASSM	Type-88	4	1999	2000	24 required under 1996–2000 MTDP
dom		Type-96	6	1999	2000	
dom	FF	*Murasame*	1	1999	2000	7 required under 1996–2000 MTDP
dom	SS	*Oyasio Class*	1	1999	2000	5 required under 1996–2000 MTDP

Supplier	Classification	Designation	Units	Order Date	Delivery Date	Comment
dom	MCMV	*Sugashima*	2	1999	2000	
dom	FAC	2		1999	2000	
dom	LST	*Oosumi Class*	1	1999	2000	
dom	AK	1		1999	2000	
dom	hel	SH-60J	9	1999	2000	37 required under 1996–2000 MTDP
dom	FGA	F-2	8	1999	2000	45 required under 1996–2000 MTDP
dom	hel	CH-47J	2	1999	2000	4 required under 1996–2000 MTDP
dom	SAR	U-125A	2	1999	2000	Cost $76 million
dom	hel	UH-60J	2	1999	2000	Cost $59 million
dom	trg	T-4	10	1999	2000	54 required under 1996–2000 MTDP
dom	trg	T-400		1999	2000	
dom	tpt	U-4		1999	2000	
US	AEW	B-767	4	1991	1998	
dom	BMD	TMD		1997		Development. Joint with US from late 1998
dom	recce	sat	4	1998	2002	Development Prog. 2 optical, 2 radar
dom	trg	T-X	50	2000		Dev Prog. Replacing Fuji T-3s. Delayed
dom	SAR			1996		US-1 replacement in development
dom	AAM	XAAM-5		1994	2001	Development
dom	SP arty	155mm		1994	2000	Entered production 1999. Replacing Type-75

North Korea

Supplier	Classification	Designation	Units	Order Date	Delivery Date	Comment
dom	SSM	*No-dong*		1988	1997	Dev complete by end 1996. Deployed 1997
dom	MRBM	*Taepo-dong 1*				Tested October 1998
dom	MRBM	*Taepo-dong 2*				Test was expected August 1999
RF	hel	Mi-17	5	1998	1998	
Kaz	FGA	Mig-21	40	1999	1999	Also spare parts for existing fleet

South Korea

Supplier	Classification	Designation	Units	Order Date	Delivery Date	Comment
dom	MBT	K1		1995	1996	Upgrade programme began in 1996
dom	sat	*KITSAT-3*		1995	1999	
Ge	SS	Type 209	9	1987	1993	Deliveries to 2000
US	hel	UH-60P	138	1988	1990	Deliveries to 1999
US	FGA	F-16C/D	120	1992	1995	Licence. Deliveries to 1999.
US	FGA	F-16C/D	20	1999	2003	Follow on order after orders for 120
US	AAM	AMRAAM	190	1996	1998	
US	AAM	*Sidewinder*	284	1996	1998	
Il	AAM	*Popeye*	100	1996	1999	
dom	AIFV	M-113	175	1993	1994	Deliveries to 1998
US	hel	CH-47E	6	1993	1997	
RF	APC	BTR-80	20	1995	1996	Deliveries to 1998
RF	AIFV	BMP-3	23	1995	1996	Deliveries to 1999
RF	MBT	T-80	33	1995	1996	Deliveries to 1999
US	trg	T-38	30	1996	1997	Ex-US, lease
US	SIGINT	*Hawker 800*	10	1996	1999	
dom	APC	KIFV	2,000	1981	1985	Still producing in 1998, includes exports
dom	DDG	KDX	6	1996	1998	3 delivered by end of 1999
US	MRL	MLRS	29	1997	1999	10 delivered in 1998
Il	UAV	*Harpy*	100	1997	1999	
dom	trg	KTX-2	94	1997	2005	Development
Fr	utl	F-406	5	1997	1999	
dom	SAM	*Pegasus*		1997	1999	Development
Fr	SAM	*Mistral*	1,294	1997	1998	Missiles
IL	UAV	*Searcher*	3	1997	1998	
RF	SAM	*Igla*		1997	1999	
RF	ATGW	*Metis*		1997	1999	

Supplier	Classification	Designation	Units	Order Date	Delivery Date	Comment
US	AEW	B-767	4	1998		Delivery delayed
UK	hel	*Lynx*	13	1997	1999	
Indo	tpt	CN-235	8	1997	1999	Delivery delayed
dom	SAM	M-SAM		1998	2008	Development
Ge	hel	BO-105	12	1998	1999	
US	AAV	AAV7A1	57	1998	2001	Licence. Following delivery of 103 from US
dom	SPA	XK9	68	1998	1999	
RF	tpt	Be-200	1	1998	2000	
dom	SAM	*P-SAM*		1998	2003	Development
dom	SSM	*Hyonmu*		1999		300km and 500km variants
Malaysia						
UK	FF	*Lekiu-class*	2	1992	1999	Acceptance delayed for technical reasons
dom	trg	MD3-160	20	1993	1995	Deliveries to 1997
ROK	APC	KIFV	111	1993	1994	Deliveries completed 1997
US	FGA	F/A-18	8	1993	1997	All delivered 1997
It	corvette	*Assad*	4	1995	1997	Originally for Irq. Deliveries 1997–99
It	ASSM	*Otomat*	4	1996	1998	
Fr	ASSM	*Exocet*	4	1996	1998	
Indo	tpt	CN-235	6	1995	1999	
US	hel	S-70A	2	1996	1998	
Ge	OPV	*Meko A 100*	6	1997	2002	Licence built. Req for 27 over 20 years
US	LST	*Newport*	1	1997	2000	
RF	FGA	Mig-29	18	1997	1999	Upgrade
It	trg	MB-339	2	1998	1999	
RF	hel	Mi-17	2	1998	1999	
Myanmar						
PRC	FF	Mod *Jianghu*	2	1994	1998	
RF	hel	M-17	6	1995	1996	
PRC	FGA	F-7	21	1996	1998	Following deliveries of 36 1991–96
PRC	trg	K-8	4	1998	2000	
New Zealand						
US	tpt	C-130J	5	1999		Lease of 5 to 7. Delayed
Aus	FFG	*Anzac*	2	1989	1997	With Aus. 2nd delivered 1999
US	ASW	P3-K	6	1995	1998	Upgrade. 1 delivered
US	TAGOS	*Stalwart*	1	1996	1997	Towed array ship
Fr	SAM	*Mistral*	12	1996	1997	Delvery of 2 launchers in late 1997
US	trg	CT-4E	13	1997	1998	11 delivered. Lease programme
US	hel	SH-2F	4	1997	1997	Leased until arrival of SH-2G
US	hel	SH-2G	5	1997	2000	
US	FGA	F-16A/B	28	1998	2002	Leased for 10 years
Papua New Guinea						
Sgp	mor	120 mm	3	1995	1996	
	cbt hel	Mi-24	6	1994	1997	
Aus	PCC	*Pacific Forum*	4	1995	1997	
Indo	hel	BO-105	1	1998	1999	
Philippines						
ROC	OPV	*PoHang*	3			Requirement delayed 1998
US	tpt	C-130B	2	1995	1998	
US	hel	B-412	4	1995	1997	
UK	APC		38	1995	1997	Type unknown
UK	corvette	*Jacinto*	3	1996	1997	Ex-UK
US	trg	T-41	5	1997	1998	
ROC	FGA	F-5A	5	1997	1998	Ex-ROK
ROC	FGA	F-5E	40	1999		

Supplier	Classification	Designation	Units	Order Date	Delivery Date	Comment
Singapore						
dom	AIFV	IFV	500	1991	1999	Two batches: 300 then 200
Fr	hel	AS-532	20	1992	1994	Deliveries over 1994–97
dom	OPV	*Fearless*	12	1993	1996	Deliveries to 1999
US	hel	CH-47D	6	1994	1997	Based in US for pilot training
US	FGA	F-16C/D	42	1995	1998	First order for 18, follow-on for 24
Swe	SS	*Sjoormen Clas*	4	1995	1997	Deliveries through 1999
Indo	arty	155mm	5	1996	1997	Surplus equipment
dom	LST	*Endurance*	4	1997	1999	Deliveries to 2000
RF	SAM	SA-16/SA-18		1997	1998	
IL	UAV	*Searcher*	40	1997	1997	
US	tkr ac	KC-135	4	1997	2000	
US	hel	CH-47D	8	1997	2000	Follow-on order after 1994 order for 6
dom	construction	*Naval Base*	1	1998	2000	At Changi
US	cbt hel	AH-64D	8	1999	2003	
Thailand						
PRC	FF	Type 26-T	2	1991	1995	Second for delivery late 1996/early 1997
Sp	CV	CV 911	1	1992	1997	
US	hel	S-70B	6	1993	1996	Deliveries to 1997
Cz	trg	L-39	36	1994	1995	Deliveries to 1997
US	FGA	A-7	18	1994	1995	Deliveries to 1997
US	ASW	S-70B	6	1994	1997	First of six delivered March 97
Swe	SAM	RBS NS-70		1995	1997	
Sp	FGA	AV-8S	9	1995	1997	
Fr	hel	AS-532	3	1995	1996	Two delivered 1996, third 1997
A	arty	155mm	36	1995	1996	18 delivered 1996, 18 1998
US	MBT	M-60	125	1995	1996	24 delivered 1996, 101 1997
Ukr	trg	L-39	4	1995	1997	Used
US	LACV	AAV-7	3	1995	1997	
US	APC	M113	82	1995	1997	63 delivered 1997
US	APC	M113	155	1996	1998	130 APCs from US, 25 from Ge.
US	FGA	F/A-18C/D	8	1996		Cancelled
Indo	tpt	CN-235	2	1996		Delayed
Fr	APC	VAB NG		1997		Selected to replace 300 M-113. Order delayed
Fr	sat			1997		Order for recce sat delayed in late 1997
Il	UAV	*Searcher*	4	1997		
It	MHC	*Lat Ya*	2	1996	1998	Deliveries to December 1999
dom	corvette		3	1996		Programme cancelled in 1997
It	MCMV	*Gaeta*	2	1996	1998	
US	LST	*Newport*	1	1997	1999	
Aus	LCU		3	1997		
US	FF		1	1996	1998	
Vietnam						
DPRK	SS	*Sang-o*	2	1996	1997	May be *Yugo* midget submarines
RF	FGA	Su-27	6	1995	1997	Deliveries to 1998
Il	FGA	MiG-21		1996		Upgrade
RF	corvette	*Taruntul 2*	2	1997	1999	Following delivery of 2 *Taruntul* 1995
DPRK	SSM	*Scud*		1999	1999	Probably *Scud*-Cs; quantity unknown

Australia   Aus

	1997	1998	1999	2000
GDP	A$529bn	A$578bn		
	($380bn)	($390bn)		
per capita	$21,000	$22,000		
Growth	3.1%	4.9%		
Inflation	0.3%	0.8%		
Publ Debt	40.9%	37.0%		
Def exp	A$11.6bn	A$12.0bn		
	($8.6bn)	($8.1bn)		
Def bdgt		A$10.4bn	A$11.1bn	A$11.2bn
		($7.0bn)	($7.2bn)	($7.3bn)
US$1=A$	1.34	1.59	1.53	
Population				19,082,000
(Asian 4%, Aborigines <1%)				
Age	*13–17*		*18–22*	*23–32*
Men	686,000		685,000	1,508,000
Women	648,000		652,000	1,459,000

Total Armed Forces

ACTIVE 55,200
(incl 7,400 women)

RESERVES 27,730
GENERAL RESERVE
Army 23,330 **Navy** 1,800 **Air Force** 2,060

Army 25,200

integrated = formation/unit comprising active and reserve personnel
(incl 2,600 women)
1 Land HQ, 1 Joint Force HQ, 1 Task Force HQ (integrated), 1 bde HQ
1 armd regt (integrated), 2 recce regt (1 integrated), 1 SF (SAS) regt, 6 inf bn (2 integrated), 1 cdo bn (integrated), 2 indep APC sqn (1 integrated), 1 med arty regt, 2 fol arty regt (1 integrated), 1 AD regt (integrated), 3 cbt engr regt (1 integrated), 2 avn regt

RESERVES

GENERAL RESERVE 23,330
1 div HQ, 7 bde HQ, 1 cdo, 1 recce, 1 APC, 1 med arty, 3 fd arty, 3 cbt engr, 2 engr construction regt, 13 inf bn; 1 indep fd arty bty; 1 recce, 3 fd engr sqn; 3 regional force surveillance units

EQUIPMENT

MBT 71 *Leopard* 1A3 (excl variants)
AIFV 46 M-113 with **76mm** gun
LAV 111 ASLAV-25
APC 463 M-113 (excl variants, 364 being upgraded, 119 in store)
TOWED ARTY 105mm: 246 M2A2/L5, 104 *Hamel*; **155mm**: 35 M-198

MOR 81mm: 296
RCL 84mm: 577 *Carl Gustav*; **106mm**: 74 M-40A1
SAM 19 *Rapier*, 17 RBS-70
AC 4 *King Air* 200, 2 DHC-6 (all on lease)
HEL 36 S-70 A-9, 43 Bell 206 B-1 *Kiowa* (to be upgraded), 25 UH-1H (armed), 17 AS-350B, 4 CH-47D
MARINES 15 LCM
SURV 14 RASIT (veh, arty), AN-TPQ-36 (arty, mor)

Navy 14,200

(incl 990 Fleet Air Arm; 2,100 women)
Maritime Comd, Support Comd, Training Comd
BASES Sydney, NSW (Maritime Comd HQ) 3 DDG, 3 FFG, 2 PFI, 1 LSH, 1 AO, 2 LCH, 2 MSI, 5 MSA
Garden Island, WA 3 SS, 3 FFG, 1 DD, 1 FFH, 1 AO, 2 PFC, 1 AGS, 1 ASR **Cairns, Qld** 5 PFC, 5 AGS, 2 LCH **Darwin, NT** 6 PFC, 1 LCH

SUBMARINES 4†

SSK 4 *Collins* with sub-*Harpoon* SSM and MK48 HWT
PRINCIPAL SURFACE COMBATANTS 11
DESTROYERS DDG 3 *Perth* (US *Adams*) with 1 SM-1 MR SAM/*Harpoon* SSM launcher; plus 2 x 3 ASTT (Mk 46 LWT), 2 127mm guns
FRIGATES 8
FFG 8
6 *Adelaide* (US *Perry*), with S-70B-2 *Sea Hawk* hel, 2 x 3 ASTT, *Harpoon* SSM, SM MRI SAM
2 *Anzac* with *Sea Sparrow* VLS SAM, 1 127mm gun, 6 324mm TT, plus hel

PATROL AND COASTAL COMBATANTS 16
PATROL, INSHORE 16 *Freemantle* PFI
MINE COUNTERMEASURES 8
2 *Rushcutter* MHI, 2 *Bandicoot*, 2 *Kooraaga* MSA, 1 *Brolga* MSI, 1 *Huon* MHC
AMPHIBIOUS 9
5 *Balikpapan* LCH, capacity 3 tk (plus 3 in store)
1 *Tobruk* LST
2 *Kanimbla* (US *Newport*) LST, capacity 450 tps, 2 LCM **hel** 4 Army *Blackhawk* or 3 *Sea King*, no beach landing capability
1 *Jervis Bay* (high speed catamaran), capacity 500 trp (on 2 yr lease)
SUPPORT AND MISCELLANEOUS 11
1 *Success* (mod Fr *Durance*), 1 *Westralia* AO, 1*Protector* sub trials and safety, 1 AGS, 4 small AGHS, 3 *Fish* (TRV)
FLEET AIR ARM (990)
no cbt ac, 16 armed hel
ASW 1 hel sqn with 16 S-70B-2 *Sea Hawk*
UTL/SAR 1 sqn with 6 AS-350B, 3 Bell 206B and 2 BAe-748 (EW trg), 1 hel sqn with 7 *Sea King* Mk 50/50A

Air Force 15,800

(incl 2,700 women); 126 cbt ac incl MR, no armed hel

Flying hours F-111, 200; F/A-18, 175

FGA/RECCE 2 sqn with 17 F-111C, 15 F-111G, 4 RF-111C

FTR/FGA 3 sqn with 52 F/A-18 (50 -A, 2 -B)

OCU 1 with 17* F/A-18B

TAC TRG 1 sqn with 16 MB-326H, 3 PC-9A

AIRCRAFT R&D 2* F/A-18, 4 C-47

MR 2 sqn with 19* P-3C, 3 TAP-3B

FAC 1 flt with 3 PC-9

TKR 4 Boeing 707

TPT 7 sqn

  2 with 24 C-130 (12 -E, 12 -H); C-130E to be replaced one-for-one by C-130J, starting Sep 1999

  1 with 5 Boeing 707 (4 fitted for AAR)

  2 with 14 DHC-4 (*Caribou*)

  1 VIP with 5 *Falcon* 900

  1 with 10 HS-748 (8 for navigation trg, 2 for VIP tpt)

TRG 59 PC-9, 14 MB-326, 2 Beech-200 *Super King Air*

AD *Jindalee* OTH radar: 1 experimental, 3 planned, 3 control and reporting units (1 mobile)

MISSILES

  ASM AGM-84A, AGM-142

  AAM AIM-7 *Sparrow*, AIM-9M *Sidewinder*

Forces Abroad

Advisers in **Fji, Indo, Solomon Islands, Th, Vanuatu, Tonga, Western Samoa, Kiribati**

MALAYSIA Army ε115; 1 inf coy (on 3-month rotational tours) **Air Force** 33; det with 2 P-3C **ac**

PAPUA NEW GUINEA 38; trg unit

UN AND PEACEKEEPING

EGYPT (MFO): 26 obs **MIDDLE EAST** (UNTSO): 12 obs **PAPUA NEW GUINEA**: 150 (Bougainville Peace Monitoring Group)

Paramilitary

AUSTRALIAN CUSTOMS SERVICE

  ac 3 DHC-8, 3 *Reims* F406, 6 BN-2B-20, 1 *Strike Aerocommander* 500 **hel** 1 Bell 206L-4; about 6 boats

Foreign Forces

US Air Force 260; **Navy** 40; joint facilities at NW Cape, Pine Gap and Nurrungar

NEW ZEALAND Air Force 47; 6 A-4K/TA-4K, (trg for Australian Navy); 9 navigation trg

SINGAPORE 230; Flying Training School with 27 S-211 **ac**

Brunei   Bru

	1997	1998	1999	2000
GDP	B$8.1bn	B$8.1bn		
	($5.4bn)	($5.5bn)		
per capita	$7,300	$7,300		
Growth	4.1%	1.0%		
Inflation	1.7%	0.0%		
Debt	$1.4bn	$1.5bn		
Def exp	B$562m	B$632m		
	($378m)	($378m)		
Def bdgt		B$596m	εB$620m	
		($357m)	($365m)	
US$1 = B$	1.43	1.6	1.7	
Population				325,000

(Muslim 71%; Malay 67%, Chinese 16%, non-Malay indigenous 6%)

Age	13–17	18–22	23–32
Men	16,000	14,000	28,000
Women	15,000	14,000	25,000

Total Armed Forces

ACTIVE 5,000

(incl 600 women)

RESERVES 700

Army 700

Army 3,900

(incl 250 women)

3 inf bn • 1 armd recce sqn • 1 SAM bty: 2 tps with *Rapier* • 1 engr sqn

EQUIPMENT

  LT TK 16 *Scorpion*

  APC 26 VAB, 2 *Sultan*, 24 AT-104 (in store)

  MOR 81mm: 24

  RL *Armbrust* (reported)

  SAM 12 *Rapier* (with *Blindfire*), *Mistral* (being delivered)

RESERVES

1 bn

Navy 700

BASE Muara

PATROL AND COASTAL COMBATANTS 6†

MISSILE CRAFT 3 *Waspada* PFM with 2 MM-38 *Exocet* SSM

PATROL, INSHORE 3 *Perwira* PFI

PATROL, RIVERINE boats

AMPHIBIOUS craft only

  2 LCU; 1 SF sqn plus boats

Air Force 400

no cbt ac, 6 armed hel
HEL 2 sqn
  1 with 10 Bell 212, 1 Bell 214 (SAR), 4 UH-60L, 4 S-70
  1 with 6 Bo-105 armed hel (**81mm** rockets)
VIP TPT 2 S-70 hel, 2 Bell 412ST
TRG ac 2 SF-260W, 4 PC-7, 1 CN235 **hel** 2 Bell 206B

Paramilitary ε3,750

GURKHA RESERVE UNIT ε2,000+
2 bn
ROYAL BRUNEI POLICE 1,750
7 PCI<

Foreign Forces

UK Army some 1,050; 1 Gurkha inf bn, 1 hel flt, trg
school
SINGAPORE 500; trg school incl hel det (5 UH-1)

Cambodia   Cam

	1997	1998	1999	2000
GDP	εr10.2tr	εr13.6tr		
	($3.4bn)	($3.6bn)		
per capita	$700	$700		
Growth	1.0%	5.0%		
Inflation	3.2%	14.7%		
Debt	$2.1bn	$2.2bn		
Def exp	εr425bn	εr570bn		
	($144m)	($152m)		
Def bdgt			εr500bn	εr400bn
			($129m)	($100m)
FMA (US)	$1.5m			
FMA (Aus)	$0.1m	$0.2m	$0.1m	
FMA (PRC)	$3.0m			
$1=riel	2,946	3,744	3,870	
Population				10,654,000
(Khmer 90%, Vietnamese 5%, Chinese 1%)				
Age	*13–17*	*18–22*		*23–32*
Men	597,000	478,000		876,000
Women	584,000	470,000		868,000

Total Armed Forces

ACTIVE ε149,000 (to reduce)
(incl Provincial Forces, perhaps only 19,000 cbt capable)
Terms of service conscription authorised but not
implemented since 1993

Army ε99,000

6 Mil Regions (incl 1 special zone for capital) • 12 inf

div[a] • 3 indep inf bde • 1 protection bde (4 bn) • 9
indep inf regt • 3 armd bn • 1 AB/SF regt • 4 engr
regt (3 fd, 1 construction) • some indep recce, arty, AD
bn

EQUIPMENT
  MBT 100+ T-54/-55, plus PRC Type-59
  LT TK 10 PT-76
  APC 210 BTR-60/-152, M-113, 30 OT-64 (SKOT)
  TOWED ARTY some 400: **76mm:** M-1942; **122mm:**
    M-1938, D-30; **130mm:** Type 59
  MRL 107mm: Type-63; **122mm:** 8 BM-21; **132mm:**
    BM-13-16; **140mm:** 20 BM-14-16
  MOR 82mm: M-37; **120mm:** M-43; **160mm:** M-160
  RCL 82mm: B-10; **107mm:** B-11
  AD GUNS 14.5mm: ZPU 1/-2/-4; **37mm:** M-1939;
    57mm: S-60
  SAM SA-7

[a] Inf div established str 3,500, actual str some 1,500

Navy ε3,000

(incl 1,500 Naval Infantry)
PATROL AND COASTAL COMBATANTS 10
PATROL, INSHORE 4
  4 Sov *Stenka* PFI, 1 x 2 23mm gun
RIVERINE 6
  2 Sov *Zhuk* PCI<, 2 Koh *Chhlam*, 2 PCF, plus 8 LCVP

NAVAL INFANTRY (1,500)
  7 inf, 1 arty bn

Air Force 2,000

24 cbt ac†; no armed hel
FTR 19† MiG-21 (only 8 serviceable)
TPT 2 An-24, 1 An-26, Tu-134, 2 Y-12, 1 BN-2
HEL 1 Mi-8, 7 Mi-17, 2 Mi-26
TRG 5* L-39, 5 *Tecnam* P-92

Provincial Forces some 45,000

Reports of at least 1 inf regt per province, with varying
numbers of inf bn with lt wpn

Paramilitary

MILITIA
org at village level for local defence: ε10–20 per village;
not all armed

Opposition

***FUNCINPEC*/KHMER PEOPLE'S LIBERATION
FRONT (KPNLF)** ε1–2,000
alliance between Prince Ranariddh's party and the
KPNLF

China, People's Republic of   PRC

	1997	1998	1999	2000
GDP[ab]	Y7.5tr	Y8.0tr		
	($639bn)	($703bn)		
per capita	$3,400	$3,700		
Growth	8.8%	7.8%		
Inflation	2.8%	0.8%		
Debt	$148bn	$156bn		
Def exp[a]	ε$36.6bn	ε$37.5bn		
Def bdgt[c]		Y90.9bn	Y104.7bn	
		($11.0bn)	($12.6bn)	
$1 =yuan	8.29	8.28	8.28	

[a] PPP est incl extra-budgetary mil exp
[b] Excl Hong Kong: GDP 1998 HK$1,289bn ($166bn)
[c] Def bdgt shows official figures at market rates

Population			1,244,000,000

(Tibetan, Uighur and other non-Han 8% **Xinjiang**
Muslim ε60% of which Uighur ε44% **Tibet** Chinese
ε60%, Tibetan ε40%)

Age	13–17	18–22	23–32
Men	51,283,000	49,954,000	120,861,000
Women	48,432,000	46,723,000	113,286,000

Total Armed Forces

ACTIVE some ε2,480,000 (being reduced)
(incl perhaps 1,275,000 conscripts, some 136,000
women)
Terms of service selective conscription; all services 2 years

RESERVES 1,200,000+
militia reserves being formed on a province-wide basis

Strategic Missile Forces

OFFENSIVE (100,000)+
org in 6 bases (army level) plus 1 testing base, with
bde/regt incl 1 msl testing and trg regt; org varies by
msl type but may incl up to 5 base spt regt per msl base
ICBM 15–20
  15–20 DF-5 (CSS-4); mod tested with MIRV
IRBM ε66
  20+ DF-4 (CSS-3)
  38+ DF-3 (CSS-2)
  ε8 DF-21 (CSS-5)
SLBM 1 *Xia* SSBN with 12 CSS-N-3 (JL-1)
SRBM about 150 DF-15 (CSS-6/M-9) (range 600km),
  DF-11 (CSS-7/M-11) (range 120–300+km)
DEFENSIVE
Tracking stations Xinjiang (covers Central Asia) and
  Shanxi (northern border)
Phased-array radar complex ballistic-missile early-
  warning

Army ε1,830,000

(perhaps 1,075,000 conscripts) (reductions continue)
7 Mil Regions, 27 Mil Districts, 3 Garrison Comd
21 Integrated Group Armies (GA: about 60,000,
  equivalent to Western corps), org varies, normally
  with 3 inf div, 1 tk, 1 arty, 1 AAA bde or 3 inf, 1 tk
  div, 1 arty, 1 AAA bde, cbt readiness category varies
  (reorg reported)
Summary of cbt units
Group Army 44 inf div (ε 3 mech inf) incl 3 with
  national level rapid-reaction role and at least 9 with
  regional rapid-reaction role ready to mobilise in 24-
  48 hours; 10 tk div, 12 tk bde, 5 arty div, 20 arty bde,
  7 hel regt, 13 inf bde
Independent 5 inf div, 1 tk, 2 inf bde, 1 arty div, 3 arty
  bde, 4 AAA bde
Local Forces (Garrison, Border, Coastal) 12 inf div, 1
  mtn bde, 4 inf bde, 87 inf regt/bn
AB (manned by Air Force) 1 corps of 3 div
Support Troops incl 50 engr, 50 sigs regt
EQUIPMENT
MBT some 8,300: incl 6,000 Type-59-I/-II, 200 Type-69-
  I/-II (mod Type-59), 800 Type-69III/-79, 500 Type-80,
  800 Type-85-IIM
LT TK 1,200 Type-63 amph, 800 Type-62/62I
AIFV/APC 5,500 incl 2,000 Type-63, some Type-77
  (BTR-50PK), Type-90, WZ-523, WZ-551, Type-86
  (WZ-501), 100 BMD-3
TOWED ARTY 14,500: **100mm**: Type-59 (fd/ATK);
  122mm: Type-54-1, Type-60, Type-83, D-30;
  130mm: Type-59/-59-1; **152mm**: Type-54, Type-66,
  Type-83; **155mm**: WAC-21
SP ARTY 122mm: Type-70/-70I, Type-85, Type-89
  (reported); **152mm**: Type-83
COMBINED GUN/MOR 100 2S23 *Nona-SVK*
MRL 122mm: Type-81, Type-89 SP, Type-90/-90A;
  130mm: Type-70 SP, Type-82, Type-85 SP; **273mm**:
  Type-83
MOR 82mm: Type-53/-67/-W87/-82 (incl SP);
  100mm: Type-71 reported; **120mm**: Type-55 (incl
  SP); **160mm**: Type-56
ATGW HJ-73 (*Sagger*-type), HJ-8 (TOW/*Milan*-type)
RL 62mm: Type-70-1
RCL 75mm: Type-56; **82mm**: Type-65, Type-78;
  105mm: Type-75
ATK GUNS 100mm: Type-73, Type-86; **120mm**:
  Type-89 SP
AD GUNS 23mm: Type-80; **37mm**: Type-55/-65/-
  74; **57mm**: Type-59, -80 SP; **85mm**: Type-56;
  100mm: Type-59
SAM HN-5A/-B/-C (SA-7 type), QW-1/-2, HQ-
  61A, HQ-7, PL-9C
SURV *Cheetah* (arty), Type-378 (veh), RASIT (veh, arty)
HEL 60+ Mi-17, 25 Mi-8, Mi-6, 30 Z-9/-WZ-9, 8 SA-
  342 (with HOT), 20 S-70, Z-11
UAV ASN-104/-105

RESERVES

(undergoing major re-org on provincial basis): perhaps 1,000,000; 50 inf, arty and AD div, 100 indep inf, arty regt

DEPLOYMENT

(GA units only)

North-east Shenyang MR (Heilongjiang, Jilin, Liaoning MD): ε300,000: 4 GA, 3 tk, 13 inf, 1 arty div

North Beijing MR (Beijing, Tianjin Garrison, Nei Mongol, Hebei, Shanxi MD): ε410,000: 5 GA, 3 tk, 13 inf, 1 arty div

West Lanzhou MR (incl Ningxia, Shaanxi, Gansu, Qing-hai, Xinjiang MD): ε220,000: 2 GA, 1 tk, 4 inf div plus 1 tk bde

South-west Chengdu MR (incl Sichuan, Guizhou, Yunnan, Xizang MD): ε180,000: 2 GA, 4 inf, 1 arty div plus 2 tk bde

South Guangzhou MR (Hubei, Hunan, Guangdong, Guangxi, Hainan MD): ε180,000: 2 GA, 4 inf plus 2 tk bde (Air Force) div. Hong Kong: ε4,500: 1 inf bde (3 inf, 1 mech inf, 1 arty regt, 1 engr bn), 1 hel unit

Centre Jinan MR (Shandong, Henan MD): ε240,000: 3 GA, 2 tk, 7 inf, 1 AB (Air Force), 1 arty div

East Nanjing MR (Shanghai Garrison, Jiangsu, Zhejiang, Fujian, Jiangxi, Anhui MD): ε300,000: 3 GA, 2 tk, 8 inf, 1 arty div

Navy ε230,000

(incl 26,000 Coastal Regional Defence Forces, 26,000 Naval Air Force, some 5,000 Marines and some 40,000 conscripts)

SUBMARINES 71

(some may be armed with Russian wake-homing torp)

STRATEGIC 1 SSBN

TACTICAL 69

SSN 5 *Han* (Type 091) with 533mm TT. 3 can carry YJ 8-2 (C-801 derivative) SLCM (submerged launch)

SSG 1 mod *Romeo* (Type S5G), with 6 C-801 (YJ-6, *Exocet* derivative) SSM; plus 533mm TT (test platform)

SS 63

1 *Song* with YJ 8-2 SLCM (C-802 derivative) SLCM (submerged launch), 6 533mm TT (not fully op)

2 *Kilo*-class (Type EKM 877) with 533mm TT, prob wake-homing torp

2 *Kilo*-class (Type EKM 636) with 533mm TT, prob wake-homing torp

2 *Ming* (Type ES5C/D) with 533mm TT

15 imp *Ming* (Type ES5E) with 533mm TT

41 *Romeo* (Type ES3B)† with 533mm TT (some 32 additional *Romeo*-class mothballed)

OTHER ROLES 1 *Golf* (SLBM trials)

PRINCIPAL SURFACE COMBATANTS 53

DESTROYERS 18

DDG 18

2 *Luhu* with 4 x 2 YJ-8/CSS-N-4 SSM, 1 x 2 100mm gun, 2 Z-9A (Fr *Panther*) hel, plus 2 x 3 ASTT, 1 x 8

Crotale SAM

1 *Luda* III with 4 x 2 YJ-8/CSS-N-4 SSM, 2 x 2 130mm gun, 2 x 3 ASTT

2 mod *Luda* with 1 x 2 130mm guns, 2 Z-9C (Fr *Panther*) hel (OTHT), 2 x 3 ASTT, 2 x 3 HY-1/CSS-N-2 SSM

13 *Luda* (Type-051) (ASUW) with 2 x 3 CSS-N-2/C-201/HY 2, 2 x 2 130mm guns; plus 2 x 12 ASW RL, (2 also with 1 x 8 *Crotale* SAM)

FRIGATES about 35 FFG

4 *Jiangwei* with 2 x 3 C-801 SSM, 1 x 6 XHQ-61/CSA-N-1 SAM, 2 x 6 ASW mortar, 1 x 2 100mm gun, 1 Z-9C (Fr *Panther*) hel

About 31 *Jianghu*; 3 variants:

About 26 Type I, with 4 x 5 ASW RL, plus 2 x 2 SY-1/CSS-N-1 SSM, 2 100mm guns

About 1 Type II, with 2 x 5 ASW RL, plus 1 x 2 SY-1/CSS-N-1 SSM, 1 x 2 100mm guns, 1 Z-9C (Fr *Panther*) hel

About 4 Type III, with 8 C-801/CSS-N-4 SSM, 2 x 2 100mm guns; plus 4 x 5 ASW RL

PATROL AND COASTAL COMBATANTS about 676

MISSILE CRAFT 92

4 *Huang* with 6 C-801 SSM

20 *Houxin* with 4 C-801 SSM

Some 38 *Huangfeng/Hola* (Sov *Osa* I-Type) with 4 SY-1 SSM

30 *Houku* (*Komar*-Type) with 2 SY-1 SSM

TORPEDO CRAFT about 125

100 *Huchuan* PHT

some 25 P-6, all < with 2 533mm TT

PATROL CRAFT about 459

COASTAL about 103

2 *Haijui* with 3 x 5 ASW RL

About 96 *Hainan* with 4 ASW RL

5 *Haiqing* with 2 x 6 ASW mor

INSHORE about 311

300 *Shanghai*, 11 *Haizhui*

RIVERINE about 45<

(Some minor combatants have reportedly been assigned to paramilitary forces (People's Armed Police, border guards, the militia) to the Customs Service, broken up or put into store. Totals, therefore, may be high.)

MINE WARFARE about 119

MINELAYERS 1

1 *Wolei*

In addition, *Luda* class DDG, *Hainan*, *Shanghai* PC and T-43 MSO have minelaying capability

MINE COUNTERMEASURES about 118

27 Sov T-43 MSO

7 *Wosao* MSC

About 80 *Lienyun* aux MSC

3 *Wochang* and 1 *Shanghai* II MSI; (plus about 4 drone MSI and 42 reserve)

AMPHIBIOUS 70

8 *Yukan* LST, capacity about 200 tps, 10 tk

3 *Shan* (US LST-1) LST, capacity about 150 tps, 16 tk

6 *Yuting* LST, capacity 4 *Jingsah* ACV, 2 hel plus tps

31 *Yuliang*, 1 *Yuling*, 1 *Yudeng* LSM, capacity about

100 tps, 3 tk
12 *Yuhai* LSM capacity 250 tps 2tk
1 *Yudao* LSM
7 *Quonsha* tpt capacity 400 tps, 350 tons cargo
Plus about 140 craft: 90 LCU, 40 LCP, 10 LCT

SUPPORT AND MISCELLANEOUS about 160

1 *Nanchang* AOR
2 *Fuqing* AO, 33 AOT, 14 AF, 10 AS, 1 ASR, 2 AR, 2 *Qiongsha* AH, 30 tpt, 33 AGOR/AGOS, 4 ice-breakers, 1 DMS, 25 AT/F, 1 hel trg, 1 trg

COASTAL REGIONAL DEFENCE FORCES (25,000)

ε80 indep arty and SSM regt deployed in 25 coastal defence regions to protect naval bases, offshore islands and other vulnerable points
  GUNS 85mm, 100mm, 130mm
  SSM HY-2/C-201/CSS-C-3, HY-4/C-401/CSS-C-7
  AD GUNS 37mm, 57mm

MARINES (some 5,000)

2 bde (3 marine, 1 mech inf, 1 lt tk, 1 arty bn); special recce units
RESERVES on mob to total 8 div (24 inf, 8 tk, 8 arty regt), 2 indep tk regt. 3 Army div also have amph role

EQUIPMENT

LT TK Type-63 amph
APC Type-77-II
ARTY 122mm: Type-54, Type-70 SP
MRL 107mm: Type-63
ATGW HJ-8
SAM HN-5

NAVAL AIR FORCE (25,000)

541 shore-based cbt ac, 25 armed hel
BBR 7 H-6, 15 H-6D reported with 2 YJ-6/6I anti-ship ALCM; about 60 H-5 torpedo-carrying lt bbr
FGA some 40 Q-5
FTR some 295 J-6, 66 J-7, 18 J-8/8I, 12 J-8II, 24 J-8III
RECCE 7 HZ-5
MR/ASW 4* ex-Sov Be-6 *Madge*, 4* PS-5 (SH-5)
HEL
  ASW 9 SA-321, 12 Z-8, 12 Z-9
  TPT 50 Y-5, 4 Y-7, 6 Y-8, 2 YAK-42, 6 An-26, 10 Mi-8
TRG 53 PT-6, 16* JJ-6, 4* JJ-7
MISSILES
  ALCM YJ-6/C-601, YJ-8K/C-801K, YJ-8IK/C-802K
(Naval ftr integrated into national AD system)

DEPLOYMENT AND BASES
NORTH SEA FLEET

coastal defence from Korean border (Yalu River) to south of Lianyungang (approx 35°10'N); equates to Shenyang, Beijing and Jinan MR, and to seaward
BASES Qingdao (HQ), Dalian (Luda), Huludao, Weihai, Chengshan, Yuchi; 9 coastal defence districts
FORCES 2 SS, 3 escort, 1 MCM, 1 amph sqn; plus Bohai Gulf trg flotillas; about 300 patrol and coastal combatants

EAST SEA FLEET

coastal defence from south of Lianyungang to Dongshan (approx 35°10'N to 23°30'N); equates to Nanjing Military Region, and to seaward
BASES HQ Dongqian Lake (Ninbo), Shanghai Naval base, Dinghai, Hangzhou, Xiangshan; 7 coastal defence districts
FORCES 2 SS, 2 escort, 1 MCM, 1 amph sqn; about 250 patrol and coastal combatants
  Naval Infantry 1 cadre div
  Coastal Regional Defence Forces Nanjing Coastal District

SOUTH SEA FLEET

coastal defence from Dongshan (approx 23°30'N) to Vietnamese border; equates to Guangzhou MR, and to seaward (including Paracel and Spratly Islands)
BASE Hong Kong
  PATROL AND COASTAL COMBATANTS 8
    4 *Houjian* PGG with 6 C-801 SSM, 4 PCI
  SUPPORT AND MISCELLANEOUS 5
    2 *Wuhu* LSM capacity 250 tps 2 tk; 3 *Catamaran*
OTHER BASES Zhanjiang (HQ), Shantou, Guangzhou, Haikou, Dongguan City, Yulin, Beihai, Huangpu; plus outposts on Paracel and Spratly Islands; 9 coastal defence districts
FORCES 2 SS, 2 escort, 1 MCM, 1 amph sqn; about 300 patrol and coastal combatants
  Naval Infantry 1 bde

Air Force 420,000

(incl strategic forces, 220,000 AD personnel and 160,000 conscripts); some 3,520 cbt ac, few armed hel
Flying hours H-6: 80; J-7 and J-8: <100; Su-27: <100
7 Mil Air Regions, HQ Beijing
Combat elm org in 7 armies of varying numbers of air div (each with 3 regt of 3 sqn of 3 flt of 3–4 ac, 1 maint unit, some tpt and trg ac); tpt ac in regt only
BBR med 3 regt with 120 H-6 (some may be nuclear-capable), some 200+ H-5 (some with YJ-8 ASM)
FGA <400 Q-5
FTR 3,000, some 60 regt with about 1,500 J-6/B/D/E, 700 J-7II/III/M/E, 50 Su-27SK/UBK, 2 J-11, 250 J-8/8I/8II
RECCE ε290: ε40 HZ-5, 150 JZ-5, 100 JZ-6 ac
TPT ε425: incl 18 BAe *Trident* 1E/2E, 10 Il-18, 10 Il-76, 300 Y-5, 25 Y-7, 45 Y-8 (some tkr), 15 Y-11, 2 Y-12
HEL some 210: incl 6 AS-332 (VIP), 4 Bell 214, 30 Mi-8, 100 Z-5, 70 Z-9
TRG ε200: incl HJ-5, JJ-6, JJ-7
MISSILES
  AAM PL-2/-2A, PL-5B/5C/5E, PL-7, PL-8, PL-9, 50+ AA-8, 250+ AA-10, 250+ AA-11
  ASM YJ-6/C-601, YJ-6I/C-611, HY-2/HY-4; YJ-8 K/C-801K, YJ-8IK/C-802K
  AD ARTY ε8,000: 16 div: 16,000 **37mm, 57mm, 85mm** and **100mm** guns; 28 indep AD regts (100+ SAM units with 500+ HQ-2/2A/2B, 100 SA-10, SA-12, FT-2000)

Forces Abroad

UN AND PEACEKEEPING
MIDDLE EAST (UNTSO): 5 obs **IRAQ/KUWAIT**
(UNIKOM): 11 obs **WESTERN SAHARA**
(MINURSO): 16 obs

Paramilitary ε1,100,000 active

PEOPLE'S ARMED POLICE (Ministry of Defence)
ε1,100,000 (to increase)

45 div (14 each with 4 regt, remainder no standard
org) incl **Internal security** ε730,000 **Border defence**
200,000 **Guards, Comms** ε69,000

Fiji				Fji
	1997	**1998**	**1999**	**2000**
GDP	F$3.1bn	F$3.4bn		
	($1.9bn)	($2.0bn)		
per capita	$5,800	$6,100		
Growth	3.6%	4.0%		
Inflation	3.3%	5.7%		
Debt	$210m	$241m		
Def exp	F$70m	F$65m		
	($48m)	($33m)		
Def bdgt		F$45m	F$54m	
		($23m)	($27m)	
FMA (US)				$0.2m
FMA (Aus)	$2m	$3m	$3m	
US$1=F$	1.44	1.99	1.98	
Population				805,000
(Fijian 51%, Indian 44%, European/other 5%)				
Age	*13–17*	*18–22*	*23–32*	
Men	46,000	44,000	65,000	
Women	44,000	40,000	63,000	

Total Armed Forces

ACTIVE some 3,500
(incl recalled reserves)
RESERVES some 6,000
(to age 45)

Army 3,200

(incl 300 recalled reserves)
7 inf bn (incl 4 cadre) • 1 engr bn • 1 arty bty • 1
special ops coy
EQUIPMENT
TOWED ARTY 88mm: 4 25-pdr (ceremonial)
MOR 81mm: 12

Navy 300

BASES Walu Bay, Viti (trg)
PATROL AND COASTAL COMBATANTS 9
PATROL, INSHORE 9
3 *Kula* (*Pacific Forum*) PCI, 4 *Vai* (*Il Dabur*) PCI<, 2
Levuka PCI<
SUPPORT AND MISCELLANEOUS 1
1 *Cagi Donu* presidential yacht (trg)

Forces Abroad

UN AND PEACEKEEPING
EGYPT (MFO): 339; 1 inf bn(-) **IRAQ/KUWAIT**
(UNIKOM): 5 obs **LEBANON** (UNIFIL): 596; 1 inf bn
PAPUA NEW GUINEA: Bougainville Peace Monitor-
ing Group

Indonesia				Indo
	1997	**1998**	**1999**	**2000**
GDP	Rp626tr	Rp951tr		
	($215bn)	($189bn)		
per capita	$4,500	$4,400		
Growth	4.6%	-13.7%		
Inflation	6.7%	57.7%		
Debt	$136bn	$147bn		
Def exp[a]	εRp14tr	εRp50tr		
	($4.8bn)	($5.0bn)		
Def bdgt		Rp9.4tr	Rp12.2tr	
		($939m)	($1,498m)	
FMA (US)	$0.1m	$0.5m	$0.6m	$0.4m
FMA (Aus)	$4.5m	$4.0m	$5.2m	
$1=rupiah	2,909	10,014	8,138	
[a] Incl mil exp on procurement and def industry				
Population				203,479,000
(Muslim 87%; Javanese 45%, Sundanese 14%,				
Madurese 8%, Malay 8%, Chinese 3%, other 22%)				
Age	*13–17*	*18–22*	*23–32*	
Men	11,069,000	10,780,000	17,353,000	
Women	10,586,000	10,356,000	17,772,000	

Total Armed Forces

ACTIVE 298,000
Terms of service 2 years selective conscription authorised

RESERVES 400,000
Army cadre units; numbers, str n.k., obligation to age
45 for officers

Army ε230,000

Strategic Reserve (KOSTRAD) (30,000)

2 inf div HQ • 3 inf bde (9 bn) • 3 AB bde (9 bn) • 2 fd arty regt (6 bn) • 1 AD arty regt (2 bn) • 2 armd bn • 2 engr bn

11 Mil Area Comd (to be 17) (KODAM) (150,000) (Provincial (KOREM) and District (KODIM) comd)
2 inf bde (6 bn) • 67 inf bn (incl 4 AB) • 8 cav bn • 11 fd arty, 10 AD bn • 8 engr bn • 1 composite avn sqn, 1 hel sqn

Special Forces (KOPASSUS) (ε6,200 incl 4,800 cbt); to be 5 SF gp (incl 2 cbt, 1 counter-terrorist, 1 int, 1 trg)

EQUIPMENT
LT TK some 275 AMX-13 (to be upgraded), 30 PT-76, 60 *Scorpion*
RECCE 69 *Saladin* (16 upgraded), 55 *Ferret* (13 upgraded), 18 VBL
APC 200 AMX-VCI, 45 *Saracen* (14 upgraded), 60 V-150 *Commando*, 22 *Commando Ranger*, 80 BTR-40, 14 BTR-50PK, 40 *Stormer* (incl variants)
TOWED ARTY 76mm: 100 M-48; **105mm**: 170 M-101, 10 M-56; **155mm**: 5 FH 2000
MOR 81mm: 800; **120mm**: 75 Brandt
RCL 90mm: 90 M-67; **106mm**: 45 M-40A1
RL 89mm: 700 LRAC
AD GUNS 20mm: 125; **40mm**: 90 L/70; **57mm**: 200 S-60
SAM 51 *Rapier*, 42 RBS-70
AC 1 BN-2 *Islander*, 2 C-47, 4 NC-212, 2 Cessna 310, 2 *Commander* 680, 18 *Gelatik* (trg), 3 DHC-5
HEL 9 Bell 205, 14 Bo-105, 7 NB-412, 10 Hughes 300C (trg)

Navy 47,000

(incl ε1,000 Naval Air and 12,000 Marines)

PRINCIPAL COMMAND
WESTERN FLEET HQ Teluk Ratai (Jakarta)
BASES Primary Teluk Ratai, Belawan **Other** 10 plus minor facilities
EASTERN FLEET HQ Surabaya
BASES Primary Surabaya, Ujung Pandang, Jayapura **Other** 13 plus minor facilities

MILITARY SEALIFT COMMAND (KOLINLAMIL)
controls some amph and tpt ships used for inter-island comms and log spt for Navy and Army (assets incl in Navy and Army listings)

SUBMARINES 2
SSK 2 *Cakra* (Ge T-209/1300) with 533mm TT (Ge HWT)

FRIGATES 17
FFG 10
6 *Ahmad Yani* (Nl *Van Speijk*) with 1 *Wasp* hel (Mk 44 LWT), 2 x 3 ASTT SAM, 2 x 4 *Harpoon* SSM, 1 76mm gun, *Mistral* SAM
3 *Fatahillah* with 2 x 3 ASTT (not *Nala*), 1 x 2 ASW mor, 1 *Wasp* hel (*Nala* only), 2 x 2 MM-38 *Exocet* SSM, 1 120mm gun
1 *Hajar Dewantara* (FRY) (trg) with 2 533mm TT, 1

ASW mor, 2 x 2 MM-38 *Exocet* SSM, 1 57mm gun
FF 7
4 *Samadikun* (US *Claud Jones*) with 2 x 3 ASTT, 1 76mm gun
3 *M. K. Tiyahahu* (UK *Tribal*) with 1 *Wasp* hel, 1 x 3 *Limbo* ASW mor, 2 114mm guns, *Mistral* SAM

PATROL AND COASTAL COMBATANTS 58
CORVETTES 16 *Kapitan Patimura* (GDR *Parchim*)
MISSILE CRAFT 4 *Mandau* (Ko *Dagger*) PFM with 4 MM-38 *Exocet* SSM, 1 57mm gun
TORPEDO CRAFT 4 *Singa* (Ge Lürssen 57m (NAV I)) with 2 533mm TT and 1 57mm gun
PATROL CRAFT 34
COASTAL 5
4 *Kakap* (Ge Lürssen 57m (NAV III)) PFC, with 40mm gun and hel deck
1 *Barakuda* PCI
INSHORE 29
8 *Sibarau* (Aust *Attack*) PCI
2 *Bima Samudera* PHT
1 *Barabzuda* PCI
18<

MINE COUNTERMEASURES 13
2 *Pulau Rengat* (mod Nl *Tripartite*) MCC (sometimes used for coastal patrol)
2 *Pulau Rani* (Sov T-43) MCC (mainly used for coastal patrol)
9 *Palau Rote* (Ge *Kondor* II)† MSC (mainly used for coastal patrol, 7 non-op)

AMPHIBIOUS 28
6 *Teluk Semangka* LST, capacity about 200 tps, 17 tk, 2 with 3 hel (1 fitted as hospital ship)
1 *Teluk Amboina* LST, capacity about 200 tps, 16 tk
7 *Teluk Langsa* (US LST-512) and 2 *Teluk Banten* (mod US LST-512) LST, capacity 200 tps, 16 tks
14 *Teluk Gilimanuk* (Ge *Frosch* I/II) LST)
Plus about 65 LCM and LCVP

SUPPORT AND MISCELLANEOUS 15
1 *Sorong* AO, 1 *Arun* AOR (UK *Rover*), 2 Sov *Khobi* AOT, 1 cmd/spt/replenish, 1 AR, 2 AT/F, 6 AGOR/AGOS, 1 *Barakuda* (Ge *Lürsson Nav* IV) presidental yacht

NAVAL AIR (ε1,000)
49 cbt ac, 21 armed hel
ASW 6 *Wasp* HAS-1 (3 non-op)
MR 9 N-22 *Searchmaster* B, 6 *Searchmaster* L, 10 NC-212 (MR/ELINT), 14 N-22B, 6 N-24, 3 CN-235 MP
TPT 4 *Commander*, 10 NC-212, 2 DHC-5, 20 *Nomad* (6 VIP)
TRG 2 *Bonanza* F33, 6 PA-38
HEL 3* NAS-332F (2 non-op), 5* NBo-105, 4* Bell-412

MARINES (12,000)
2 inf bde (6 bn) • 1 SF bn(-) • 1 cbt spt regt (arty, AD)
EQUIPMENT
LT TK 100 PT-76†
RECCE 14 BRDM

AIFV 10 AMX-10 PAC 90
APC 24 AMX-10P, 60 BTR-50P
TOWED ARTY 48: **105mm**: 20 LG-1 Mk II; **122mm**: 28 M-38
MOR 81mm
MRL 140mm: 15 BM-14
AD GUNS 40mm: 5 L60/70; **57mm**

Air Force 21,000

91 cbt ac, no armed hel; 2 Air Operations Areas
FGA 5 sqn
  1 with 19 A-4 (18 -E, 1 TA-4H)
  1 with 10 F-16 (6 -A, 4 -B)
  2 with 8 *Hawk* Mk 109 and 16 *Hawk* Mk 209 (FGA/ftr)
  1 with 14 *Hawk* Mk 53 (FGA/trg)
FTR 1 sqn with 12 F-5 (8 -E, 4 -F)
RECCE 1 sqn with 12* OV-10F
MR 1 sqn with 3 Boeing 737-200
TKR 2 KC-130B
TPT 19 C-130 (9 -B, 3 -H, 7 -H-30), 3 L100-30, 1 Boeing 707, 4 Cessna 207, 5 Cessna 401, 2 C-402, 6 F-27-400M, 1 F-28-1000, 2 F-28-3000, 10 NC-212, 1 *Skyvan* (survey), 23 CN-235-110
HEL 10 S-58T, 10 Hughes 500, 11 NAS-330, 2 NAS-332L (VIP), 4 NBO-105CD, 2 Bell 204B
TRG 3 sqn with 39 AS-202, 2 Cessna 172, 22 T-34C, 6 T-41D

Deployment

ARMY
EAST TIMOR ε5,000

Forces Abroad

UN AND PEACEKEEPING
CROATIA (UNMOP): 1 obs **GEORGIA** (UNOMIG): 4 obs **IRAQ/KUWAIT** (UNIKOM): 5 obs **TAJIKISTAN** (UNMOT): 4 obs

Paramilitary

POLICE (*POLRI*) some 194,000
incl 6,000 police 'mobile bde' (BRIMOB) org in 56 coy, incl counter-terrorism unit (*Gegana*)
  EQPT APC 34 *Tactica*; **ac** 1 *Commander*, 2 Beech 18, 1 PA-31T, 1 Cessna-U206, 2 NC- 212 **hel** 19 NBO-105, 3 Bell 206
MARINE POLICE (12,000)
  about 10 PCC, 9 PCI and 6 PCI< (all armed)
KAMRA (People's Security) (R) 1,500,000
some 300,000 undergo 3 weeks' basic trg each year; part-time police auxiliary
WANRA (People's Resistance) (R)
part-time local military auxiliary force under Regional

Military Comd (KOREM)
CUSTOMS
  about 72 PFI<, armed
SEA COMMUNICATIONS AGENCY (responsible to Department of Communications)
  5 Kujang PCI, 4 Golok PCI (SAR), plus boats

Opposition

FRETILIN (Revolutionary Front for an Independent East Timor) some 70 incl spt
FALINTIL mil wing; small arms
FREE PAPUA ORGANISATION (OPM) ε150 (100 armed)
FREE ACEH MOVEMENT (*Gerakan Aceh Merdeka*) 50 armed reported

Japan				**J**
	1997	**1998**	**1999**	**2000**
GDP	¥507tr	¥495tr		
	($4.2tr)	($3.8tr)		
per capita	$23,900	$23,700		
Growth	0.9%	-2.6%		
Inflation	1.7%	0.7%		
Publ Debt	87.4%	99.9%		
Def exp	¥4.9tr	¥4.9tr		
	($40.9bn)	($37.7bn)		
Def bdgt			¥5.0tr	
			($41.1bn)	
$1=yen	121	131	121	
Population		126,515,000 (Korean <1%)		
Age	*13–17*	*18–22*		*23–32*
Men	3,770,000	4,266,000		9,458,000
Women	3,590,000	4,059,000		9,037,000

Total Armed Forces

ACTIVE some 236,300
(incl 1,400 Central Staffs; some 9,100 women)

RESERVES some 49,900

READY RESERVE Army (GSDF) some 2,000
GENERAL RESERVE Army (GSDF) some 46,000 **Navy** (MSDF) some 1,100 **Air Force** (ASDF) some 800

Army (Ground Self-Defense Force) some 145,900

5 Army HQ (Regional Comds) • 1 armd div • 11 inf div (6 at 7,000, 5 at 9,000 each); 1 inf bde • 2 composite bde • 1 AB bde • 1 arty bde; 2 arty gp • 2 AD bde; 3 AD gp • 4 trg bde (incl 1 spt); 2 trg regt • 5 engr bde •1 hel bde • 5 ATK hel sqn

EQUIPMENT

MBT some 40 Type-61 (retiring), some 870 Type-74, some 170 Type-90
RECCE some 90 Type-87
AIFV some 60 Type-89
APC some 270 Type-60, some 340 Type-73, some 230 Type-82
TOWED ARTY 155mm: some 460 FH-70
SP ARTY 105mm: some 20 Type-74; **155mm:** some 200 Type-75; **203mm:** some 90 M-110A2
MRL 130mm: some 60 Type-75 SP; **227mm:** some 50 MLRS
MOR incl **81mm:** some 680; **107mm:** some 270; **120mm:** some 300 (some SP)
SSM some 80 Type-88 coastal
ATGW some 170 Type-64, some 240 Type-79, some 260 Type-87
RL 89mm: some 1,430
RCL 84mm: some 2,720 *Carl Gustav*; **106mm:** some 270 (incl Type 60 SP)
AD GUNS 35mm: some 30 twin, some 50 Type-87 SP
SAM some 320 *Stinger*, some 60 Type 81, some 110 Type 91, some 40 Type 93, some 200 I HAWK
AC some 10 LR-1, some LR-2
ATTACK HEL some 90 AH-1S
TPT HEL 3 AS-332L (VIP), some 40 CH-47J/JA, some 170 OH-6D, some 150 UH-1H/J, some UH-60JA
SURV Type-92 (mor), J/MPQ-P7 (arty)

Maritime Self-Defence Force some 43,800

(incl some 12,000 Air Arm; and some 1,800 women)
BASES Yokosuka, Kure, Sasebo, Maizuru, Ominato
FLEET Surface units org into 4 escort flotillas of 8 DD/FF each **Bases** Yokosuka, Kure, Sasebo, Maizuru
SS org into 2 flotillas **Bases** Kure, Yokosuka
Remainder assigned to 5 regional districts

SUBMARINES 16

SSK 16
7 *Harushio* with 6 x 533mm TT (J Type-89 HWT) with *Harpoon* USGW
7 *Yuushio* with 533mm TT (J Type-89 HWT), *Harpoon* USGW
2 *Oyashio* with 6 x 533mm TT, Sub *Harpoon* USGW

PRINCIPAL SURFACE COMBATANTS some 55

DESTROYERS some 9
DDG 9
4 *Kongo* with 2 VLS for *Standard* SAM and ASROC SUGW (32 cells forward, 64 cells aft), 2 x 4 *Harpoon* SSM, 1 127mm gun, 2 x 3 ASTT and hel deck
2 *Hatakaze* with 1 SM-1-MR Mk 13 SAM, 2 x 4 *Harpoon* SSM, 1 x 8 ASROC SUGW (Mk 46 LWT) 2 x 3 ASTT, 2 127mm guns
3 *Tachikaze* with 1 SM-1-MR, 1 x 8 ASROC SUGW, 2 x 3 ASTT, 2 127mm guns, *Harpoon* SSM
FRIGATES some 46
FFG 34

2 *Shirane* with 3 SH-60J ASW hel, 1 x 8 ASROC SUGW, 2 x 3 ASTT, 2 127mm guns, *Sea Sparrow* SAM
8 *Asagiri* with 1 SH-60J hel, 1 x 8 ASROC SUGW, 2 x 3 ASTT, 2 x 4 *Harpoon* SSM
11 *Hatsuyuki* with 1 SH-60J, 1 x 8 ASROC SUGW, 2 x 3 ASTT, 2 x 4 *Harpoon* SSM
4 *Murasame* with 1 SH-60J hel, 1 VLS *Sea Sparrow* SAM, 1 VLS ASROC SUGW, 2 x 3 ASTT, 8 *Harpoon* SSM
6 *Abukuma* with 1 x 8 ASROC SUGW, 2 x 3 ASTT, 2 x 4 *Harpoon* SSM
2 *Yubari* with 2 x 3 ASTT, 1 x 4 ASW RL, 2 x 4 *Harpoon* SSM
1 *Ishikari* with 2 x 3 ASTT, 1 x 4 ASW RL, 2 x 4 *Harpoon* SSM
FF 12
6 *Chikugo* with 1 x 8 ASROC SUGW, 2 x 3 ASTT
2 *Haruna* with 3 SH-60J hel, 1 x 8 ASROC SUGW, 2 x 3 ASTT, 2 127mm guns
2 *Takatsuki* with 1 x 8 ASROC SUGW, 2 x 3 ASTT, 1 x 4 ASW RL, 2 127mm gun
2 *Yamagumo* with 1 x 8 ASROC SUGW, 2 x 3 ASTT, 1 x 4 ASW RL

PATROL AND COASTAL COMBATANTS 3

MISSILE CRAFT 3 *Sparviero* Type PHM with 4 SSM-1B

MINE COUNTERMEASURES 34

2 *Uraga* MCM spt with hel deck; can lay mines
16 *Hatsushima* MCC
9 *Uwajima* MCC
3 *Yaeyama* MSO
1 *Fukue* coastal MCM spt
1 *Nijima* coastal MCM spt
2 *Sugashima* MSC

AMPHIBIOUS 6

1 *Osumi* LST, capacity 330 tps, 10 tk, 2 LCAC (large flight deck)
3 *Miura* LST, capacity 200 tps, 10 tk
2 *Atsumi* LST, capacity 130 tps, 5 tk
Plus craft: 2 *Yura* and 2 *Ichi-Go* LCM, 2 LCAC, 11 LCM

SUPPORT AND MISCELLANEOUS 19

3 *Towada* AOE, 1 *Sagami* AOE (all with hel deck), 2 AS/ARS, 1 *Minegumo* trg, 1 *Kashima* (trg), 2 trg spt, 8 AGOR/AGOS, 1 icebreaker

AIR ARM (ε12,000)

some 90 cbt ac, some 90 armed hel
Flying hours P-3: 500
7 Air Groups
MR 10 sqn (1 trg) with some 90 P-3C
ASW 6 land-based hel sqn (1 trg) with some 30 HSS-2B, 4 shipboard sqn with some 60 SH-60J
MCM 1 hel sqn with some 10 MH-53E
EW 1 sqn with several EP-3
TPT 1 sqn with several YS-11M
SAR some 10 US-1A, some 10 S-61 hel, some 10 UH-60J
TRG 4 sqn with **ac** some 40 T-5, some 30 TC-90, some 10 YS-11T/M **hel** some 10 OH-6D, some 30 DA

Air Self-Defence Force some 45,200

some 330 cbt ac, no armed hel, 7 cbt air wings
Flying hours 150
FGA 2 sqn with some 40 F-I, 1 sqn with some 20 F-4EJ
FTR 10 sqn
  8 with some 160 F-15J/DJ
  2 with some 50 F-4EJ
RECCE 1 sqn with some 20* RF-4E/EJ
AEW 1 sqn with some 10 E-2C, 4 Boeing E-767
(AWACS)
EW 2 sqn with 1 EC-1, some 10 YS-11 E
AGGRESSOR TRG 1 sqn with some 10 F-15DJ
TPT 4 sqn, 4 flt
  3 with some 20 C-1, some 10 C-130H, a few YS-11
  1 with a few 747-400 (VIP)
  4 flt heavy-lift hel with some 10 CH-47J
SAR 1 wg (10 det) with **ac** some 10 MU-2, some 10 U-
125 **hel** some 20 KV-107, some 10 UH-60J
CAL 1 sqn with a few YS-11, a few U-125-800
TRG 5 wg, 12 sqn with some 30 T-1A/B, some 40* T-2,
some 40 T-3, some 50 T-4, some 10 T-400
LIAISON some 10 T-33, some 90 T-4, several U-4
TEST 1 wg with a few F-15J, some 10 T-4

AIR DEFENCE

ac control and warning: 4 wg, 28 radar sites
6 SAM gp (24 sqn) with some 120 *Patriot*
Air Base Defence Gp with **20mm** *Vulcan* AA guns,
Type 81, Type 91, *Stinger* SAM
ASM ASM-1, ASM-2
AAM AAM-1, AAM-3, AIM-7 *Sparrow*, AIM-9 *Sidewinder*

Forces Abroad

UN AND PEACEKEEPING
SYRIA/ISRAEL (UNDOF): 45

Paramilitary 12,000

MARITIME SAFETY AGENCY (Coast Guard) 12,000
(Ministry of Transport, no cbt role)
  PATROL VESSELS some 328
  Offshore (over 1,000 tons) 42, incl 1 *Shikishima* with
  2 *Super Puma* hel, 2 *Mizuho* with 2 Bell 212, 8 *Soya*
  with 1 Bell 212 hel, 2 *Izu*, 28 *Shiretok* and 1 Kojima
  (trg) **Coastal** (under 1,000 tons) 36 **Inshore** some 250
  patrol craft most<
  MISC about 90 service, 80 tender/trg vessels
  AC 5 NAMC YS-11A, 2 Short *Skyvan*, 16 *King Air*, 1
  Cessna U-206G
  HEL 32 Bell 212, 4 Bell 206, 2 Hughes 369

Foreign Forces

US 40,100: **Army** 1,800; 1 Corps HQ **Navy** 5,200; bases
at Yokosuka (HQ 7th Fleet) and Sasebo **Marines**
19,200; 1 MEF in Okinawa **Air Force** 13,900; 1 Air

Force HQ (5th Air Force), 90 cbt ac, 1 ftr wg, 2 sqn with
36 F-16, 1 wg, 3 sqn with 54 F-15C/D, 1 sqn with 15
KC-135, 1 SAR sqn with 8 HH-60, 1 sqn with 2 E-3
AWACS; 1 airlift wg with 16 C-130E/H, 4 C-21, 3 C-9;
1 special ops gp with 4 MC-130P, 4 MC-130E

Korea, Democratic People's Republic Of (North) DPRK

	1997	1998	1999	2000
GNP[a]	ε$14bn	ε$14bn		
per capita	$900	$900		
Growth	-6.8%	5.0%		
Inflation	ε5%	ε5%		
Debt	$12bn	$12bn		
Def exp	ε$2.3bn	ε$2.0bn		
Def bdgt		won2.92bn	won2.96bn	
		($1.3bn)	($1.3bn)	
$1=won[b]	2.2	2.2	2.2	

[a] PPP est. GNP is larger than GDP because of remitted
earnings of DPRK expatriates in Japan and ROK
[b] Market rate **1997** $1=won70–100

Population				21,500,000
Age	*13–17*	*18–22*	*23–32*	
Men	1,035,000	994,000	2,515,000	
Women	1,066,000	1,062,000	2,221,000	

Total Armed Forces

ACTIVE ε1,082,000

Terms of service **Army** 5–8 years **Navy** 5–10 years **Air
Force** 3–4 years, followed by compulsory part-time
service to age 40. Thereafter service in the Worker/
Peasant Red Guard to age 60

RESERVES 4,700,000

Army 600,000 **Navy** 65,000 are assigned to units (see
Paramilitary)

Army ε950,000

20 Corps (1 armd, 4 mech, 12 inf, 2 arty, 1 capital
defence) • 27 inf div • 15 armd bde • 14 inf • 21 arty •
9 MRL bde
Special Purpose Forces Comd (88,000): 10 *Sniper* bde
(incl 2 amph, 2 AB), 12 lt inf bde (incl 3 AB), 17 recce,
1 AB bn, 'Bureau of Reconnaissance SF' (8 bn)
Army tps: 6 hy arty bde (incl MRL), 1 *Scud* SSM bde, 1
FROG SSM regt
Corps tps: 14 arty bde incl 122mm, 152mm SP, MRL

RESERVES
40 inf div, 18 inf bde
EQUIPMENT
  MBT some 3,500: T-34, T-54/-55, T-62, Type-59

LT TK 500 PT-76, M-1985
APC 2,500 BTR-40/-50/-60/-152, PRC Type-531, VTT-323 (M-1973)
TOTAL ARTY (excl mor) 10,300
TOWED ARTY 3,500: **122mm**: M-1931/-37, D-74, D-30; **130mm**: M-46; **152mm**: M-1937, M-1938, M-1943
SP ARTY 4,700: **122mm**: M-1977, M-1981, M-1985, M-1991; **130mm**: M-1975, M-1981, M-1991; **152mm**: M-1974, M-1977; **170mm**: M-1978, M-1989
COMBINED GUN/MOR: 120mm (reported)
MRL 2,300: **107mm**: Type-63; **122mm**: BM-21, BM-11, M-1977/-1985/-1992/-1993; **240mm**: M-1985/-1989/-1991
MOR 7,500: **82mm**: M-37; **120mm**: M-43 (some SP); **160mm**: M-43
SSM 24 FROG-3/-5/-7; some 30 *Scud-C*, *No-dong*
ATGW: AT-1 *Snapper*, AT-3 *Sagger* (some SP), AT-4 *Spigot*, AT-5 *Spandrel*
RCL 82mm: 1,700 B-10
AD GUNS 11,000: **14.5mm**: ZPU-1/-2/-4 SP, M-1984 SP; **23mm**: ZU-23, M-1992 SP; **37mm**: M-1939, M-1992; **57mm**: S-60, M-1985 SP; **85mm**: KS-12; **100mm**: KS-19
SAM ε10,000+ SA-7/-16

Navy ε46,000

BASES East Coast Toejo (HQ), Changjon, Munchon, Songjon-pardo, Mugye-po, Mayang-do, Chaho Nodongjagu, Puam-Dong, Najin **West Coast** Nampo (HQ), Pipa Got, Sagon-ni, Chodo-ri, Koampo, Tasa-ri 2 Fleet HQ
SUBMARINES 26
SSK 26
   22 PRC Type-031/Sov *Romeo* with 533mm TT
   4 Sov *Whiskey*† with 533mm and 406mm TT
   (Plus some 45 SSI and 21 *Sang-O* SSC mainly used for SF ops, but some with 2 TT, all +)
FRIGATES 3
FFG 3
   1 *Soho* with 4 ASW RL, plus 4 SS-N-2 *Styx* SSM, 1 100mm gun and hel deck
   2 *Najin* with 2 x 5 ASW RL, plus 2 SS-N-2 *Styx* SSM, 2 100mm guns
PATROL AND COASTAL COMBATANTS some 309
CORVETTES 5
   3 *Sariwon* with 1 85mm gun
   2 *Tral* with 1 85mm gun
MISSILE CRAFT 43
   15 *Soju*, 8 Sov *Osa*, 4 PRC *Huangfeng* PFM with 4 SS-N-2 *Styx*, 6 *Sohung*, 10 Sov *Komar* PFM with 2 SS-N-2
TORPEDO CRAFT some 103
   3 Sov *Shershen* with 4 533mm TT
   60 *Ku Song* PHT
   40 *Sin Hung* PHT
PATROL CRAFT 158

COASTAL 25
   6 *Hainan* PFC with 4 ASW RL, 13 *Taechong* PFC with 2 ASW RL, 6 *Chong-Ju* with 1 85mm gun, (2 ASW mor)
INSHORE some 133
   18 SO-1, 12 *Shanghai* II, 3 *Chodo*, some 100<
MINE COUNTERMEASURES about 23 MSI<
AMPHIBIOUS 10
   10 *Hantae* LSM, capacity 350 tps, 3 tk
   plus craft 15 LCM, 15 LCU, about 100 Nampo LCVP, plus about 130 hovercraft
SUPPORT AND MISCELLANEOUS 7
   2 AT/F, 1 AS, 1 ocean and 3 inshore AGHS
COASTAL DEFENCE
   2 SSM regt: *Silkworm* in 6 sites, and probably some mobile launchers
   GUNS 122mm: M-1931/-37; **130mm**: SM-4-1, M-1992; **152mm**: M-1937

Air Force 86,000

593 cbt ac, armed hel
Flying hours 30 or less
BBR 3 lt regt with 82 H-5 (Il-28)
FGA/FTR 15 regt
   3 with 107 J-5 (MiG-17), 4 with 159 J-6 (MiG-19), 4 with 130 J-7 (MiG-21), 1 with 46 MiG-23, 1 with 16 MiG-29, 1 with 18 Su-7, 1 with 35 Su-25. (34 MiG-21s reportedly purchased to start replacing J-5/J-6)
TPT ac ε300 An-2/Y-5, 6 An-24, 2 Il-18, 4 Il-62M, 2 Tu-134, 4 Tu-154 **hel** 80 Hughes 500D, 139 Mi-2, 15 Mi-8/-17, 48 Z-5
TRG incl 10 CJ-5, 7 CJ-6, 6 MiG-21, 170 Yak-18, 35 FT-2 (MiG-15UTI)
MISSILES
   AAM AA-2 *Atoll*, AA-7 *Apex*
   SAM ε45 SA-2 bty, 7 SA-3, 2 SA-5, many thousands of SA-7/14/16

Forces Abroad

advisers in some 12 African countries

Paramilitary 189,000 active

SECURITY TROOPS (Ministry of Public Security) 189,000
incl border guards, public safety personnel
WORKER/PEASANT RED GUARD some 3,500,000
Org on a provincial/town/village basis; comd structure is bde – bn – coy – pl; small arms with some mor and AD guns (but many units unarmed)

Korea, Republic Of (South)   ROK

	1997	1998	1999	2000
GDP	won421tr	won450tr		
	($443bn)	($426bn)		
per capita	$13,000	$12,400		
Growth	5.5%	-5.8%		
Inflation	4.5%	7.5%		
Debt	$158bn	$152bn		
Def exp	won14.0tr	won18.5tr		
	($14.8bn)	($13.2bn)		
Def bdgt			won13.7tr	won15.4tr
			($11.6bn)	($12.8bn)
$1=won	951	1,401	1,186	
Population				47,000,000
Age	*13–17*	*18–22*		*23–32*
Men	1,849,000	2,010,000		4,371,000
Women	1,730,000	1,873,000		4,094,000

Total Armed Forces

ACTIVE 672,000

(incl ε159,000 conscripts)
Terms of service conscription **Army** 26 months **Navy**
and **Air Force** 30 months; First Combat Forces
(Mobilisation Reserve Forces) or Regional Combat
Forces (Homeland Defence Forces) to age 33

RESERVES 4,500,000

being re-org

Army 560,000

(incl 140,000 conscripts)
HQ: 3 Army (1st and 3rd to merge), 11 Corps (two to
be disbanded)
3 mech inf div (each 3 bde: 3 mech inf, 3 tk, 1 recce, 1
engr bn; 1 fd arty bde) • 19 inf div (each 3 inf regt, 1
recce, 1 tk, 1 engr bn; 1 arty regt (4 bn)) • 2 indep inf
bde • 7 SF bde • 3 counter-infiltration bde • 3 SSM bn
with NHK-I/-II (*Honest John*) • 3 AD arty bde • 3 I
HAWK bn (24 sites), 2 *Nike Hercules* bn (10 sites) • 1
avn comd

RESERVES
1 Army HQ, 23 inf div
EQUIPMENT
  MBT 800 Type 88, 80 T-80U, 400 M-47, 850 M-48
  AIFV 40 BMP-3
  APC incl 1,700 KIFV, 420 M-113, 140 M-577, 200 Fiat
  6614/KM-900/-901, 40 BMP-3
  TOWED ARTY some 3,500: **105mm**: 1,700 M-101,
  KH-178; **155mm**: M-53, M-114, KH-179; **203mm**:
  M-115
  SP ARTY 155mm: 1,040 M-109A2; **175mm**: M-107;
  203mm: M-110

  MRL 130mm: 156 *Kooryong* (36-tube)
  MOR 6,000: **81mm**: KM-29; **107mm**: M-30
  SSM 12 NHK-I/-II
  ATGW TOW-2A, *Panzerfaust*, AT-7
  RCL 57mm, 75mm, 90mm: M67; **106mm**: M40A2
  ATK GUNS 58: **76mm**: 8 M-18; **90mm**: 50 M-36 SP
  AD GUNS 600: **20mm**: incl KIFV (AD variant), 60
  M-167 *Vulcan*; **30mm**: 20 B1 HO SP; **35mm**: 20
  GDF-003; **40mm**: 80 L60/70, M-1
  SAM 350 *Javelin*, 60 *Redeye*, 130 *Stinger*, 170 *Mistral*,
  SA-16, 110 I HAWK, 200 *Nike Hercules*, *Chun Ma*
  (reported)
  SURV RASIT (veh, arty), AN/TPQ-36 (arty, mor),
  AN/TPQ-37 (arty)
  AC 5 O-1A
  HEL
    ATTACK 75 AH-1F/-J, 68 Hughes 500 MD, BO-
    105 (being delivered)
    TPT 15 CH-47D
    UTL 170 Hughes 500, 130 UH-1H, 98 UH-60P

Navy 60,000

(incl 25,000 Marines and ε19,000 conscripts)
BASES Chinhae (HQ), Cheju, Inchon, Mokpo, Mukho,
Pukpyong, Pohang, Pusan
FLEET COMMANDS 3
SUBMARINES 19
SSK 8 *Chang Bogo* (Ge T-209/1200) with 8 533 TT
SSI 11
  3 KSS-1 *Dolgorae* (175t) with 2 406mm TT
  8 *Dolphin* (175t) with 2 406mm TT
PRINCIPAL SURFACE COMBATANTS 39
DESTROYERS 6
  DDG 6
    3 *King Kwanggaeto* with 8 *Harpoon* SSM, 1 *Sea
    Sparrow* SAM, 1 127mm gun, 1 *Super Lynx* hel
    3 *Kwang Ju* (US *Gearing*) with 2 or 3 x 2 127mm guns,
    2 x 3 ASTT; 5 with 2 x 4 *Harpoon* SSM, 2 with 1 x 8
    ASROC SUGW, 1 *Alouette* III hel
FRIGATES 9
  FFG 9 *Ulsan* with 2 x 3 ASTT (Mk 46 LWT), 2 x 4
  Harpoon SSM
CORVETTES 24
  24 *Po Hang* with 2 x 3 ASTT; some with 2 x 1 MM-38
  Exocet SSM
PATROL AND COASTAL COMBATANTS 84
CORVETTES 4 *Dong Hae* (ASW) with 2 x 3 ASTT
MISSILE CRAFT 5
  5 *Pae Ku*-52 (US *Asheville*) 2 x 2 *Harpoon* SSM, 1 x
  76mm gun
PATROL, COASTAL 75
  75 *Kilurki*-11 (*Sea Dolphin*) 37m PFI
MINE WARFARE 15
MINELAYERS 1
  1 *Won San* ML

MINE COUNTERMEASURES 14

6 *Kan Keong* (mod It *Lerici*) MHC
8 *Kum San* (US MSC-268/289) MSC

AMPHIBIOUS 14

4 *Alligator* (RF) LST, capacity 700 tons vehicles
7 *Un Bong* (US LST-511) LST, capacity 200 tps, 16 tk
3 *Ko Mun* (US LSM-1) LSM, capacity 50 tps, 4 tk
Plus about 36 craft; 6 LCT, 10 LCM, about 20 LCVP

SUPPORT AND MISCELLANEOUS 13

2 AOE, 2 spt AK, 2 AT/F, 2 salv/div spt, 1 ASR,
about 4 AGHS (civil-manned, Ministry of
Transport-funded)

NAVAL AIR

23 cbt ac; 47 armed hel
ASW 3 sqn
  2 **ac** 1 with 15 S-2E, 1 with 8 P-3C
  1 **hel** with 25 Hughes 500MD
1 flt with 8 SA-316 hel, 12 *Lynx* (ASW)

MARINES (25,000)

2 div, 1 bde • spt units
  EQUIPMENT
  MBT 60 M-47
  AAV 60 LVTP-7, 3 AAV-7
  TOWED ARTY 105mm, 155mm
  SSM *Harpoon* (truck-mounted)

Air Force 52,000

488 cbt ac, no armed hel. 8 cbt, 2 tpt wg
FGA 10 sqn
  4 with 88 F-16C/D (a further 72 for delivery)
  6 with 195 F-5E/F
FTR 4 sqn with 130 F-4D/E
CCT 1 sqn with 22* A-37B
FAC 10 O-2A
RECCE 1 sqn with 18* RF-4C, 10* RF-5A
SAR 1 hel sqn, 15 UH-60
TPT ac 2 BAe 748 (VIP), 1 Boeing 737-300 (VIP), 1 C-
  118, 10 C-130H, 15 CN-235M **hel** 16 UH-1H/N, 6
  CH-47, 3 Bell-412, 3 AS-332, 3 VH-60
TRG 25* F-5B, 50 T-37, 30 T-38, 25 T-41B, 18 *Hawk* Mk-67
UAV 3 *Searcher*
MISSILES
  ASM AGM-65A *Maverick*, AGM-88 HARM, AGM-
  130, AGM-142
  AAM AIM-7 *Sparrow*, AIM-9 *Sidewinder*, AIM-120B
  AMRAAM
  SAM *Nike-Hercules*, I HAWK, *Javelin*, *Mistral*

Forces Abroad

UN AND PEACEKEEPING

GEORGIA (UNOMIG) 3 obs **INDIA/PAKISTAN**
(UNMOGIP): 9 obs **WESTERN SAHARA**
(MINURSO): 20

Paramilitary ε4,500 active

CIVILIAN DEFENCE CORPS (to age 50) 3,500,000
MARITIME POLICE ε4,500
  PATROL CRAFT 81
    OFFSHORE 10
    3 *Mazinger* (HDP-1000) (1 CG flagship), 1 *Han
    Kang* (HDC-1150), 6 *Sea Dragon/Whale* (HDP-600)
    COASTAL 33
    22 *Sea Wolf/Shark*, 2 *Bukhansan*, 7 *Hyundai*-type, 2
    Bukhansan
    INSHORE 38
    18 *Seagull*, about 20<, plus numerous boats
  SUPPORT AND MISCELLANEOUS 3 salvage
  HEL 9 Hughes 500

Foreign Forces

US 36,530: **Army** 27,500: 1 Army HQ, 1 inf div **Navy**
300 **Air Force** 8,600: 1 HQ (7th Air Force): 90 cbt ac, 2
ftr wg; 3 sqn with 72 F-16, 1 sqn with 6 A-10, 12 OA-10,
1 special ops sqn with 5MH -53J **USMC** 130

Laos   Lao

	1997	1998	1999	2000
GDP	kip2.2tr	n.k.		
	($1.8bn)	($1.9bn)		
per capita	$2,600	$2,700		
Growth	7.2%	5.0%		
Inflation	14.2%	91.0%		
Debt	$2.3bn	$2.5bn		
Def exp	εkip90bn	εkip230bn		
	($72m)	($70m)		
Def bdgt			εkip300bn	
			($70m)	
FMA (US)	$2.5m	$3.5m	$4.0m	
$1 = kip	1,257	3,298	4,274	
Population				5,355,000

(**lowland** Lao Loum 68% **upland** Lao Theung 22%
highland Lao Soung incl Hmong and Yao 9%,
Chinese and Vietnamese 1%)

Age	*13–17*	*18–22*	*23–32*
Men	301,000	240,000	372,000
Women	296,000	237,000	371,000

Total Armed Forces

ACTIVE ε29,100

Terms of service conscription, 18 months minimum

Army 25,000

4 Mil Regions • 5 inf div • 7 indep inf regt • 5 arty, 9
AD arty bn • 3 engr (2 construction) regt • 65 indep

inf coy • 1 lt ac liaison flt

EQUIPMENT

MBT 30 T-54/-55, T-34/85

LT TK 25 PT-76

APC 70 BTR-40/-60/-152

TOWED ARTY **75mm**: M-116 pack; **105mm**: 25 M-101; **122mm**: 40 M-1938 and D-30; **130mm**: 10 M-46; **155mm**: M-114

MOR **81mm**; **82mm**; **107mm**: M-2A1, M-1938; **120mm**: M-43

RCL **57mm**: M-18/A1; **75mm**: M-20; **106mm**: M-40; **107mm**: B-11

AD GUNS **14.5mm**: ZPU-1/-4; **23mm**: ZU-23, ZSU-23-4 SP; **37mm**: M-1939; **57mm**: S-60

SAM SA-3, SA-7

Navy (Army Marine Section) ε600

PATROL AND COASTAL COMBATANTS some 16

PATROL, RIVERINE some 16
some 12 PCI<, 4 LCM, plus about 40 boats

Air Force 3,500

26 cbt ac; no armed hel

FGA 2 sqn with some 20 MiG-21

TPT 1 sqn with 4 An-2, 5 An-24, 4 An-26, 4 Yak-12, 2 Yak-40

HEL 1 sqn with 2 Mi-6, 10 Mi-8, 12 Mi-17, 3 SA-360

TRG *6 MiG-21UB, 8 Yak-18

AAM AA-2 *Atoll*

Paramilitary

MILITIA SELF-DEFENCE FORCES 100,000+

village 'home-guard' org for local defence

Opposition

Numerous factions/groups; total armed str: ε2,000
United Lao National Liberation Front (ULNLF) largest group

Malaysia   Mal

	1997	1998	1999	2000
GDP	RM275bn	RM290bn		
	($93bn)	($88bn)		
per capita	$10,800	$11,200		
Growth	7.7%	-8.8%		
Inflation	2.6%	5.3%		
Debt	$47bn	$49bn		
Def exp[a]	RM9.5bn	RM12.9bn		
	($3.4bn)	($3.3bn)		
Def bdgt[b]		RM5.8bn	RM5.9bn	
		($1.5bn)	($1.6bn)	

contd	1997	1998	1999	2000
FMA (US)	$0.6m	$0.9m	$0.7m	$0.7m
FMA (Aus)	$4.3m	$3.5m	$4.2m	
$1=ringgit	2.81	3.9	3.8	

[a] Incl procurement and def industry exp
[b] Excl procurement allocation in 1998 and 1999

Population			22,094,000

(Muslim 54%; Malay and other indigenous 64%, Chinese 27%, Indian 9%; in **Sabah** and **Sarawak** non-Muslim Bumiputras form the majority of the population; 1,000,000+ Indonesian and Filipino illegal immigrants in 1997)

Age	13–17	18–22	23–32
Men	1,209,000	1,011,000	1,743,000
Women	1,151,000	966,000	1,693,000

Total Armed Forces

ACTIVE 105,000

RESERVES 40,600
Army 37,800 Navy 2,200 Air Force 600

Army 80,000

2 Mil Regions • 1 HQ fd comd, 4 area comd (div) • 1 mech inf, 10 inf bde • 1 AB bde (3 AB bn, 1 lt arty regt, 1 lt tk sqn – forms Rapid Deployment Force)

Summary of combat units
5 armd regt • 31 inf bn • 3 AB bn • 5 fd arty, 1 AD arty, 5 engr regt
1 SF regt (3 bn)
AVN 1 hel sqn

RESERVES

Territorial Army 1 bde HQ; 12 inf regt, 4 highway sy bn

EQUIPMENT

LT TK 26 *Scorpion* (**90mm**)

RECCE 162 SIBMAS, 140 AML-60/-90, 92 *Ferret* (60 mod)

APC 111 KIFV (incl variants), 184 V-100/-150 *Commando*, 25 *Stormer*, 459 *Condor* (150 to be upgraded), 37 M-3 Panhard

TOWED ARTY **105mm**: 75 Model 56 pack, 40 M-102A1 († in store); **155mm**: 12 FH-70

MOR **81mm**: 300

ATGW SS-11, *Eryx*

RL **89mm**: M-20; **92mm**: FT5

RCL **84mm**: *Carl Gustav*; **106mm**: 150 M-40

AD GUNS **35mm**: 24 GDF-005; **40mm**: 36 L40/70

SAM 48 *Javelin*, *Starburst*, 12 *Rapier*

HEL 10 SA-316B

ASLT CRAFT 165 *Damen*

Navy 12,500

(incl 160 Naval Air)

Fleet Operations Comd (HQ Lumut)
Naval Area 1 Kuantan **Naval Area 2** Labuan
BASES Naval Area 1 Kuantan **Naval Area 2** Labuan,
Sandakan (Sabah) **Naval Area 3** Lumut **Naval Area 4**
Sungei Antu (Sarawak) plus trg base at Penerang
SUBMARINES 0
but personnel training in India, Italy and Turkey
PRINCIPAL SURFACE COMBATANTS 4
FRIGATES 4
 FFG 2 *Leiku* with 8 x MM-40 *Exocet* SSM, 1 x VLS
 Seawolf SAM, 6 x 324mm TT
 FF 2
 1 *Hang Tuah* (UK *Mermaid*) with 1 x 3 *Limbo* ASW
 mor, hel deck for *Wasp*; plus 1 x 2 102mm gun (trg)
 1 *Rahmat* with 1 x 3 ASW mor, 1 114mm gun hel
 deck (trg)
PATROL AND COASTAL COMBATANTS 41
CORVETTES 6
 4 *Laksamana* (It *Assad*) with 6 OTO *Melara* SSM, 1
 Selenia SAM 1 76mm gun 6 324mm TT
 2 *Kasturi* (FS 1500) with 2 x 2 ASW mor, deck for
 WASP hel, 4 MM-38 *Exocet* SSM, 1 100mm gun
MISSILE CRAFT 8
 4 *Handalan* (Swe *Spica*) with 4 MM-38 *Exocet* SSM
 4 *Perdana* (Fr *Combattante* II) with 2 *Exocet* SSM
PATROL CRAFT 27
 OFFSHORE 2 *Musytari* with 1 100mm gun, hel deck
 INSHORE 25
 6 *Jerong* PFI, 1 *Kedah*, 4 *Sabah*, 14 *Kris* PCI
MINE COUNTERMEASURES 5
 4 *Mahamiru* (mod It *Lerici*) MCO
 1 diving tender (inshore)
AMPHIBIOUS 3
 2 *Sri Banggi* (US LST-511) LST, capacity 200 tps, 16 tk
 (but usually employed as tenders to patrol craft)
 1 *Sri Inderapura* (US *Newport*) LST, capacity 400 tps,
 10 tk
 Plus 115 craft: LCM/LCP/LCU
SUPPORT AND MISCELLANEOUS 3
 2 log/fuel spt, 1 AGHS

NAVAL AIR (160)
no cbt ac, 17 armed hel
 HEL 17 *Wasp* HAS-1

Air Force 12,500

87 cbt ac, no armed hel; 4 Air Div
Flying hours 60
FGA 4 sqn
 3 with 8 *Hawk* 108, 17 *Hawk* 208, 10 MB-339
 1 with 8 F/A-18D
FTR 3 sqn
 1 with 13 F-5E, 2 RF-5E
 2 with 15 MiG-29, 2 MiG-29U
MR 1 sqn with 4 Beech-200T
TKR 2 KC-130H

TRANSPORT 4 sqn
 1 with 6 DHC-4
 1 with 5 C-130H
 1 with 6 C-130H-30, 3 C-130H-MP, 2 KC-130, 10
 Cessna 402B
 1 with **ac** 1 *Falcon*-900 (VIP), 2 BAC-125, 1 F-28 **hel** 2
 AS-61N, 3 Agusta-109, 2 S-70A
 HEL 3 sqn with 30 S-61A, 12 SA-316A/B
TRAINING
 AC 37 PC-7 (12* wpn trg), 20 MD3-160, 3 F-SF
 HEL 12 SA-316
MISSILES
 AAM AIM-9 *Sidewinder*, AA-8 *Aphid*, AA-10 *Alamo*,
 AA-11 *Archer*
 ASM AGM-65 *Maverick*, *Harpoon*

AIRFIELD DEFENCE
1 field sqn
SAM 1 sqn with *Starburst*

Forces Abroad

UN AND PEACEKEEPING
IRAQ/KUWAIT (UNIKOM): 6 obs **WESTERN**
SAHARA (MINURSO): 13 obs

Paramilitary ε20,100

POLICE-GENERAL OPS FORCE 18,000
5 bde HQ: 21 bn (incl 2 Aboriginal, 1 Special Ops
 Force), 4 indep coy
 EQPT ε100 Shorland armd cars, 140 AT-105 *Saxon*,
 ε30 SB-301 APC
MARINE POLICE about 2,100
 BASES Kuala, Kemaman, Penang, Tampoi,
 Kuching, Sandakan
 PATROL CRAFT, INSHORE 30
 15 *Lang Hitam* (38m) PFI, 6 *Sangitan* (29m), 9
 improved PX PFI, plus 6 tpt, 2 tugs, 120 boats
POLICE AIR UNIT
 ac 6 Cessna *Caravan* I, 4 Cessna 206, 7 PC-6 **hel** 1 Bell
 206L, 2 AS-355F
AREA SECURITY UNITS (aux General Ops Force) 3,500
89 units
BORDER SCOUTS (in Sabah, Sarawak) 1,200
PEOPLE'S VOLUNTEER CORPS (RELA) 240,000
some 17,500 armed
CUSTOMS SERVICE
 PATROL CRAFT, INSHORE 56
 6 *Perak* (Vosper 32m) armed PFI, about 50 craft<

Foreign Forces

AUSTRALIA 148: **Army** 115; 1 inf coy **Air Force** 33;
det with 2 P-3C **ac**

Mongolia — Mgl

	1997	1998	1999	2000
GDP	t737bn	t811bn		
	($933m)	($965m)		
per capita	$2,100	$2,200		
Growth	4.0%	3.5%		
Inflation	36.7%	9.5%		
Debt	$718m	$670m		
Def exp	t18.2bn	t17.0bn		
	($23m)	($20m)		
Def bdgt		t18.7bn	t19.7bn	
		($24m)	($21m)	
FMA (US)	$0.4m	$0.4m	$0.4m	$0.5m
$1=tugrik	790	841	950	
Population				2,438,000

(Kazak 4%, Russian 2%, Chinese 2%)

	13–17	18–22	23–32
Age			
Men	155,000	137,000	225,000
Women	148,000	131,000	217,000

Total Armed Forces

ACTIVE 9,100

(incl 4,000 conscripts, 300 construction tps and 500 Civil Defence – see *Paramilitary*)

Terms of service conscription: males 18–28 years, 1 year

RESERVES 140,000

Army 140,000

Army 7,500 (4,000 conscripts)

7 MR bde (all under str) • 1 arty bde • 1 lt inf bn (rapid-deployment) • 1 AB bn

EQUIPMENT

MBT 580 T-54/-55/-62
RECCE 120 BRDM-2
AIFV 400 BMP-1
APC 250 BTR-60
TOWED ARTY 300: **122mm**: M-1938/D-30; **130mm**: M-46; **152mm**: ML-20
MRL **122mm**: 130+ BM-21
MOR 140: **82mm, 120mm, 160mm**
ATK GUNS 200 incl: **85mm**: D-44/D-48; **100mm**: BS-3, MT-12

Air Defence 800

9 cbt ac; 12 armed hel
Flying hours 22
2 AD regt
FTR 1 sqn with 8 MiG-21, 1 Mig-21U
ATTACK HEL 11 Mi-24
TPT (Civil Registration) 15 An-2, 12 An-24, 3 An-26, 1 An-30, 2 Boeing 727, 1 Airbus A310-300

AD GUNS: 150: **14.5mm**: ZPU-4; **23mm**: ZU-23, ZSU-23-4; **57mm**: S-60
SAM 250 SA-7

Paramilitary 7,200 active

BORDER GUARD 6,000 (incl 4,700 conscripts)

INTERNAL SECURITY TROOPS 1,200 (incl 800 conscripts) 4 gd units

CIVIL DEFENCE TROOPS (500)

CONSTRUCTION TROOPS (300)

Myanmar — My

	1997	1998	1999	2000
GDP[a]	K1,068bn	K1,144bn		
	($28bn)	($31bn)		
per capita	$1,000	$1,100		
Growth	7.0%	6.2%		
Inflation	29.7%	51.5%		
Debt	$5.1bn	$5.2bn		
Def exp[a]	K28bn	K33bn		
	($2.2bn)	($2.1bn)		
Def bdgt[a]		K24.5bn	K32.6bn	
		($1.7bn)	($1.7bn)	
$1=kyat[b]	6.24	6.34	6.35	

[a] PPP est
[b] Market rate **1998** $1=K250–300

Population			50,887,000

(Burmese 68%, Shan 9%, Karen 7%, Rakhine 4%, Chinese 3+%, Other: Chin, Kachin, Kayan, Lahu, Mon, Palaung, Pao, Wa, 9%)

	13–17	18–22	23–32
Age			
Men	2,654,000	2,393,000	4,228,000
Women	2,587,000	2,343,000	4,206,000

Total Armed Forces

ACTIVE some 429,000 reported (incl People's Police Force and People's Militia – see *Paramilitary*)

Army 325,000

10 lt inf div (each 3 tac op comd (TOC))
12 Regional Comd (each with 10 regt)
32 TOC with 145 garrison inf bn
Summary of cbt units
245 inf bn • 7 arty bn • 4 armd bn • 2 AA arty bn
EQUIPMENT†

MBT 100 PRC Type-69II
LT TK 105 Type-63 (ε60 serviceable)
RECCE 45 *Ferret*, 40 *Humber*, 30 *Mazda* (local manufacture)

APC 20 *Hino* (local manufacture), 250 Type-85
TOWED ARTY 76mm: 100 M-1948; **88mm**: 50 25-pdr; **105mm**: 96 M-101; **140mm**: 5.5in
MRL 107mm: 30 Type-63
MOR 81mm; **82mm**: Type-53; **120mm**: Type-53, 80 Soltam
RCL 84mm: 500 *Carl Gustav*; **106mm**: M40A1
ATK GUNS 60: **57mm**: 6-pdr; **76.2mm**: 17-pdr
AD GUNS 37mm: 24 Type-74; **40mm**: 10 M-1; **57mm**: 12 Type-80
SAM HN-5A (reported)

Navy† 10,000

(incl 800 Naval Infantry)
BASES Bassein, Mergui, Moulmein, Seikyi, Yangon (Monkey Point), Sittwe
PATROL AND COASTAL COMBATANTS 68
CORVETTES 2
1 *Yan Taing Aung* (US PCE-827)†
1 *Yan Gyi Aung* (US *Admirable* MSF)†
MISSILE CRAFT 6 *Houxin* with 4 C-801 SSM
PATROL, OFFSHORE 3 *In Daw* (UK *Osprey*)
PATROL, COASTAL 10 *Yan Sit Aung* (PRC *Hainan*)
PATROL, INSHORE 18
12 US PGM-401/412, 3 FRY PB-90 PFI<, 3 *Swift* PGM 421
PATROL, RIVERINE about 29
2 *Nawarat*, 2 imp FRY Y-301 and 10 FRY Y-301, about 15<, plus some 25 boats
AMPHIBIOUS craft only
1 LCU, 10 LCM
SUPPORT 9
6 coastal tpt, 1 AOT, 1 diving spt, 1 buoy tender, plus 6 boats

NAVAL INFANTRY (800) 1 bn

Air Force 9,000

83 cbt ac, 29 armed hel
FTR 3 sqn with 25 F-7, 5 FT-7
FGA 2 sqn with 22 A-5M
CCT 2 sqn with 12 PC-7, 9 PC-9, 10 *Super Galeb* G4
TPT 3 F-27, 4 FH-227, 5 PC-6A/-B, 2 Y-8D
LIAISON/TRG 4 Cessna 180, 1 Cessna *Citation* II, 4 K-8
HEL 4 sqn with 12 Bell 205, 6 Bell 206, 9 SA-316, 18* Mi-2, 11* Mi-17, 10 PZL W-3 *Sokol*

Paramilitary ε85,250

PEOPLE'S POLICE FORCE 50,000

PEOPLE'S MILITIA 35,000

PEOPLE'S PEARL AND FISHERY MINISTRY ε250

11 patrol boats (3 *Indaw* (Dk *Osprey*) PCC, 3 US *Swift* PGM PCI, 5 Aus *Carpentaria* PCI<)

Opposition and Former Opposition

GROUPS WITH CEASE-FIRE AGREEMENTS
UNITED WA STATE ARMY (UWSA) ε12,000 **Area** Wa hills between Salween river and Chinese border; formerly part of CPB
KACHIN INDEPENDENCE ARMY (KIA) some 8,000 **Area** northern Myanmar, incl Kuman range, the Triangle. Reached cease-fire agreement with government in October 1993
MONG TAI ARMY (MTA) (formerly Shan United Army) ε3,000+ **Area** along Thai border and between Lashio and Chinese border
SHAN STATE ARMY (SSA) ε3,000 **Area** Shan state
MYANMAR NATIONAL DEMOCRATIC ALLIANCE ARMY (MNDAA) 2,000 **Area** northeast Shan state
MON NATIONAL LIBERATION ARMY (MNLA) ε1,000 **Area** on Thai border in Mon state
NATIONAL DEMOCRATIC ALLIANCE ARMY (NDAA) ε1,000 **Area** eastern corner of Shan state on China–Laos border; formerly part of CPB
PALAUNG STATE LIBERATION ARMY (PSLA) ε700 **Area** hill tribesmen north of Hsipaw
NEW DEMOCRATIC ARMY (NDA) ε500 **Area** along Chinese border in Kachin state; former Communist Party of Burma (CPB)
DEMOCRATIC KAREN BUDDHIST ORGANISATION (DKBO) ε100–500 armed

GROUPS STILL IN OPPOSITION
MONG TAI ε8,000
KAREN NATIONAL LIBERATION ARMY (KNLA) ε4,000 **Area** based in Thai border area; political wg is Karen National Union (KNU)
ALL BURMA STUDENTS DEMOCRATIC FRONT ε2,000
KARENNI ARMY (KA) >1,000 **Area** Kayah state, Thai border

New Zealand NZ

	1997	1998	1999	2000
GDP	NZ$99bn	NZ$98bn		
	($58bn)	($58bn)		
per capita	$17,300	$18,100		
Growth	3.3%	0.2%		
Inflation	1.2%	1.3%		
Publ debt	37.5%	38.7%		
Def exp	NZ$1.4bn	NZ$1.6bn		
	($904m)	($881m)		
Def bdgt			NZ$1.6bn	
			($846m)	
US$1 = NZ$	1.56	1.86	1.87	
Population				3,835,000

(Maori 15%, Pacific Islander 6%)

Age	13–17	18–22	23–32
Men	141,000	137,000	277,000
Women	132,000	131,000	289,000

Total Armed Forces

ACTIVE 9,530

(incl some 1,370 women)

RESERVES some 6,300

Regular some 2,400 **Army** 1,500 **Navy** 850 **Air Force** 10
Territorial 3,890 **Army** 3,900 **Navy** 500 **Air Force** 350

Army 4,400

(incl 520 women)
1 Land Force Comd HQ • 2 Land Force Gp HQ • 1
APC/Recce regt (-) • 2 inf bn • 1 arty regt (2 fd bty, 1
AD tp) • 1 engr regt (-) • 2 SF sqn (incl 1 reserve)

RESERVES
Territorial Army 6 inf bn, 4 fd arty bty, 2 armd sqn
(incl 1 lt recce)
EQUIPMENT
  LT TK 8 *Scorpion*
  APC 72 M-113 (incl variants)
  TOWED ARTY 105mm: 24 *Hamel*
  MOR 81mm: 50
  RL 94mm: LAW
  RCL 84mm: 63 *Carl Gustav*
  SAM 12 *Mistral*
  SURV *Cymbeline* (mor)

Navy 2,080

(incl 350 women)
BASE Auckland (Fleet HQ)
FRIGATES 3
  FFG 2 *Anzac* with 8 *Sea Sparrow* VLS SAM, 1 127mm
  gun, 6 324mm TT, *Seasprite* hel
  FF 1 *Waikato* (UK *Leander*) with 1 SH-2F hel, 2 x 3
  ASTT and 3 with 2 114mm guns
PATROL AND COASTAL COMBATANTS 4
  4 *Moa* PCI (reserve trg)
SUPPORT AND MISCELLANEOUS 6
  1 *Resolution* AGS (US *Stalwart*), 1 *Endeavour* AOR, 2
  coastal AGHS, 1 trg, 1 sail trg

NAVAL AIR
no cbt ac, 4 armed hel
HEL 4 SH-2F *Sea Sprite* (see Air Force)

Air Force 3,050

(incl 500 women); 42 cbt ac, no armed hel
Flying hours A-4: 180

AIR COMMAND
FGA 2 sqn with 14 A-4K, 5 TA-4K
MR 1 sqn with 6* P-3K *Orion*
LIGHT ATTACK/TRG 1 sqn for *ab initio* and ftr lead-
in trg with 17* MB-339C
ASW 4 SH-2F (Navy-assigned)
TPT 2 sqn
  ac 1 with 5 C-130H, 2 Boeing 727
  hel 1 with 13 UH-1H, 5 Bell 47G (trg)
TRG 1 sqn with 13 CT-4E
MISSILES
  ASM AGM-65B/G *Maverick*
  AAM AIM-9L *Sidewinder*

Forces Abroad

AUSTRALIA 47; 3 A-4K, 3 TA-4K, 9 navigation trg
SINGAPORE 11; spt unit
UN AND PEACEKEEPING
BOSNIA (SFOR II): 27 **CAMBODIA** (CMAC): 2
CROATIA (UNMOP): 2 obs **EGYPT** (MFO): 26
KUWAIT (CJTF-K): 1 **LAOS** (UXOL): 2 **MIDDLE
EAST** (UNTSO): 7 obs **MOZAMBIQUE** (MADP): 2
PAPUA NEW GUINEA: 30 (Bougainville Peace
Monitoring Group) **UN NEW YORK** (UNSCOM): 3

Papua New Guinea				PNG
	1997	1998	1999	2000
GDP	K10.7bn	K11.3bn		
	($5.2bn)	($5.5bn)		
per capita	$2,500	$2,600		
Growth	-5.4%	3.8%		
Inflation	3.5%	13.5%		
Debt	$2.3bn	$2.3bn		
Def exp	K93m	K115m		
	($65m)	($56m)		
Def bdgt		K86m	K80m	
		($42m)	($29m)	
FMA (US)	$0.1m	$0.2m	$0.2m	$0.2m
FMA (Aus)	$13.8m	$9.6m	$6.7m	
$1=kina	1.43	2.06	2.73	
Population				4,759,000
Age	13–17	18–22		23–32
Men	269,000	241,000		410,000
Women	255,000	225,000		373,000

Total Armed Forces

ACTIVE ε4,300

Army ε3,800

2 inf bn • 1 engr bn

EQUIPMENT

MOR 81mm; 120mm: 3

Maritime Element 400

BASES Port Moresby (HQ), Lombrum (Manus Island) (patrol boat sqn); forward bases at Kieta and Alotau

PATROL AND COASTAL COMBATANTS 7

PATROL, INSHORE 4 *Tarangau* (Aust *Pacific Forum* 32-m) PCI, 3 Vosper type PCI

AMPHIBIOUS 2

2 *Salamaua* (Aust *Balikpapan*) LSM, plus 4 other landing craft, manned and operated by the civil administration

Air Force 100

no cbt ac, no armed hel
TPT 2 CN-235, 3 IAI-201 *Arava*, 1 CN-212
HEL †4 UH-1H

Foreign Forces

AUSTRALIA 38; trg unit
BOUGAINVILLE PEACE MONITORING GROUP some 300 tps from Aus (ε150), NZ (130), Fiji, Tonga, Vanuatu

Philippines   Pi

	1997	1998	1999	2000
GDP	P2.4tr	P2.7tr		
	($73bn)	($65bn)		
per capita	$3,200	$3,200		
Growth	5.2%	-0.5%		
Inflation	5.0%	9.0%		
Debt	$45bn	$51bn		
Def exp[a]	P42bn	P61bn		
	($1.4bn)	($1.5bn)		
Def bdgt[b]		P41bn	P52bn	
		($1.0bn)	($1.4bn)	
FMA (US)	$1.3m	$1.3m	$1.4m	$1.4m
FMA (Aus)	$2.9m	$3.0m	$3.8m	
$1=peso	27.5	40.1	38.1	

[a] Incl paramil exp
[b] A five-year supplementary procurement budget of P50bn ($1.9bn) for 1996–2000 was approved in Dec 1996

Population			75,656,000

(Muslim 5–8%; **Mindanao provinces** Muslim 40–90%; Chinese 2%)

Age	*13–17*	*18–22*	*23–32*
Men	4,191,000	3,717,000	6,176,000
Women	4,047,000	3,585,000	5,977,000

Total Armed Forces

ACTIVE 110,000

RESERVES 131,000
Army 100,000 (some 75,000 more have commitments)
Navy 15,000 **Air Force** 16,000 (to age 49)

Army 73,000

5 Area Unified Comd (joint service) • 8 inf div (each with 3 inf bde, 1 arty bn) • 1 special ops comd with 1 lt armd bde ('regt'), 1 scout ranger, 1 SF regt • 5 engr bn • 1 arty regt HQ • 1 Presidential Security Group

EQUIPMENT

LT TK 65 *Scorpion*
AIFV 85 YPR-765 PRI
APC 100 M-113, 20 *Chaimite*, 100 V-150, some 128 *Simba*
TOWED ARTY 105mm: 230 M-101, M-102, M-26 and M-56; 155mm: 12 M-114 and M-68
MOR 81mm: M-29; 107mm: 40 M-30
RCL 75mm: M-20; 90mm: M-67; 106mm: M-40 A1
AC 4 Cessna (-170, -172, P-206, U-206), 1 Beech 65

Navy† ε20,500

(incl 8,500 Marines)
6 Naval Districts
BASES Sangley Point/Cavite, Zamboanga, Cebu
FRIGATES FF 1 *Rajah Humabon* (US *Cannon*) with ASW mor, 76mm gun

PATROL AND COASTAL COMBATANTS 67
PATROL, OFFSHORE 14
3 *Emilio Jacinto* (ex-UK *Peacock*) with 1 76mm gun
2 *Rizal* (US *Auk*) with hel deck, 2 76mm gun, 3 x 2 ASTT
8 *Miguel Malvar* (US PCE-827)
1 *Magat Salamat* (US-MSF)
PATROL, INSHORE 53
2 *Aguinaldo*, 3 *Kagitingan*, 22 *José Andrada* PCI<, 5 *Thomas Batilo* (ROK *Sea Dolphin*), and about 21 other PCI<

AMPHIBIOUS some 9
2 US *F. S. Beeson*-class LST, capacity 32 tk plus 150 tps, hel deck
Some 7 *Zamboanga del Sur* (US LST-1/511/542) LST, capacity either 16tk or 10tk plus 200 tps
Plus about 39 craft: 30 LCM, 3 LCU, some 6 LCVP

SUPPORT AND MISCELLANEOUS 11
2 AOT (small), 1 AR, 3 AGOR/AGOS, 3 spt, 2 water tkr

NAVAL AVIATION

2 cbt ac, no armed hel
MR/SAR ac 2 BN-2A *Defender*, 1 *Islander* **hel** 4 Bo-105 (SAR)

MARINES (8,500)

3 bde (10 bn) to be 2 bde (6 bn)

EQUIPMENT
AAV 30 LVTP-5, 55 LVTP-7
LAV 24 LAV-300 (reported)
TOWED ARTY 105mm: 150 M-101
MOR 4.2in (107mm): M-30

Air Force 16,500

42 cbt ac, some 97 armed hel
FTR 1 sqn with 6 F-5A/B
ARMED HEL 3 sqn with 60 Bell UH-1H/M, 16 AUH-76 (S-76 gunship conversion), 21 Hughes 500/520MD
MR 1 F-27M
RECCE 4 RT-33A, 21* OV-10 *Broncos*
SAR ac 4 HU-16 hel 10 Bo-105C
PRESIDENTIAL AC WG ac 1 F-27, 1 F-28 hel 2 Bell 212, 4 Bell-412, 2 S-70A, 2 SA-330
TPT 3 sqn
    1 with 2 C-130B, 3 C-130H, 3 L-100-20, 5 C-47, 7 F-27
    2 with 2 BN-2 *Islander*, 14 N-22B *Nomad Missionmaster*
HEL 2 sqn with 55 Bell 205, 16 UH-1H
LIAISON 10 Cessna (7 -180, 2 -210, 1 -310), 5 DHC-2, 12 U-17A/B
TRG 4 sqn
    1 with 4 T-33A, 1 with 14 T-41D, 1 with 15 SF-260TP, 1 with 15* S-211
AAM AIM-9B *Sidewinder*

Paramilitary 42,500 active

PHILIPPINE NATIONAL POLICE 40,500 (Department of Interior and Local Government)
62,000 active aux; 15 Regional, 73 Provincial Comd
COAST GUARD 3,500
Command devolving initially to the President before settling under the Department of Transport and Communications
    EQPT 3 *De Haviland* PCI, 4 *Basilan* (US PGM-39/42) PCI, plus some 35 *Swift* PCI, 3 SAR hel (by 2000)
CITIZEN ARMED FORCE GEOGRAPHICAL UNITS (CAFGU) 60,000
Militia, 56 bn; part-time units which can be called up for extended periods

Opposition and Former Opposition

Groups with Cease-fire Agreements
    BANGSA MORO ARMY (armed wing of Moro National Liberation Front (MNLF); Muslim) ε5,000
Groups Still in Opposition
    NEW PEOPLE'S ARMY (NPA; communist) ε8,000
    MORO ISLAMIC LIBERATION FRONT (breakaway from MNLF; Muslim) ε8,000 (up to 13,000 reported)

MORO ISLAMIC REFORMIST GROUP (breakaway from MNLF; Muslim) 900
ABU SAYAF GROUP ε500

Singapore   Sgp

	1997	1998	1999	2000
GDP	S$143bn	S$161bn		
	($96bn)	($96bn)		
per capita	$25,400	$25,900		
Growth	6.7%	1.5%		
Inflation	2.0%	-0.3%		
Debt	$9.9bn	$10.5bn		
Def exp	S$6.9bn	S$8.1bn		
	($4.6bn)	($4.8bn)		
Def bdgt		S$7.3bn	S$7.3bn	
		($4.4bn)	($4.2bn)	
FMA (Aus)	$0.7m	$0.5m	$0.5m	
US$1=S$	1.48	1.67	1.72	
Population				3,200,000
(Chinese 76%, Malay 15%, Indian 6%)				
Age	*13–17*	*18–22*		*23–32*
Men	116,000	108,000		248,000
Women	110,000	103,000		241,000

Total Armed Forces

ACTIVE ε73,000
(incl 39,800 conscripts)
Terms of service conscription 24–30 months

RESERVES ε275,000
Army ε261,200; annual trg to age 40 for men, 50 for officers Navy ε6,300 Air Force ε7,500

Army 50,000

(35,000 conscripts)
3 combined arms div (mixed active/reserve formations) each with 2 inf bde (each 3 inf bn), 1 mech bde, 1 recce, 2 arty, 1 AD, 1 engr bn
1 Rapid Deployment div (mixed active/reserve formations) with 3 inf bde (incl 1 air mob, 1 amph)
1 mech bde
Summary of active units
    9 inf bn • 4 lt armd/recce bn • 4 arty bn • 1 cdo (SF) bn • 4 engr bn

RESERVES
9 inf bde incl in mixed active/reserve formations listed above. 1 op reserve div with additional inf bde. 2 People's Defence Force cmd with 7+ bde gp. Total cbt units ε60 inf, ε8 lt armd/recce, ε8 arty, 1 cdo (SF), ε8 engr bn

EQUIPMENT

MBT some 60 *Centurion* (reported)
LT TK ε350 AMX-13SM1
RECCE 22 AMX-10 PAC 90
AIFV 22 AMX-10P, some IFV-25
APC 750+ M-113A1/A2 (some with 40mm AGL, some with 25mm gun), 30 V-100, 250 V-150/-200 *Commando*, some IFV-40/50
TOWED ARTY 105mm: 60 LG1; **155mm:** 38 Soltam M-71S, 16 M-114A1 (may be in store), 45 M-68 (may be in store), 52 FH-88, 18 FH-2000
MOR 81mm (some SP); **120mm:** 50 (some SP in M-113); **160mm:** 12 Tampella
ATGW 30+ *Milan*
RL *Armbrust*; **89mm:** 3.5in M-20
RCL 84mm: ε200 *Carl Gustav*; **106mm:** 90 M-40A1 (in store)
AD GUNS 20mm: 30 GAI-CO1 (some SP)
SAM 60: RBS-70 (some SP in V-200) (Air Force), *Mistral* (Air Force)
SURV AN/TPQ-36/-37 (arty, mor)

Navy ε9,500

incl 4,500 full time (2,700 regular and 1,800 national service) plus 5,000 op ready reserve
COMMANDS Fleet (1st and 3rd Flotillas) **Coastal** and **Naval Logistic, Training Command**
BASES Pulau Brani, Tuas (Jurong)
SUBMARINES 3
SSK 3 *Challenger* (Swe *Sjoormen*) with 4 533mm TT
PATROL AND COASTAL COMBATANTS 24
CORVETTES 6 *Victory* (Ge Lürssen 62m) with 8 *Harpoon* SSM, 2 x 3 ASTT (1 x 2 *Barak* SAM being fitted)
MISSILE CRAFT 18
6 *Sea Wolf* (Ge Lürssen 45m) PFM with 2 x 2 *Harpoon* SSM, 4 x 2 *Gabriel* SSM, 1 x 2 *Mistral/Simbad* SAM
12 *Fearless* OPV with 2 *Mistral/Sadral* SAM, 1 76mm gun, 6 with 6 324mm TT
MINE COUNTERMEASURES 4
4 *Bedok* (SW *Landsort*) MHC (*Jupiter* diving spt has mine-hunting capability)
AMPHIBIOUS 3
1 *Perseverance* (UK *Sir Lancelot*) LSL with 1 x 2 *Mistral/Simbad* SAM, capacity 340 tps, 16 tk, hel deck
2 *Endurance* LST with 2 x 2 *Mistral/Simbad* SAM, capacity 350 tps, 18 tk, 4 LCVP
Plus craft: 6 LCM, 30 LCU, and boats
SUPPORT AND MISCELLANEOUS 2
1 *Jupiter* diving spt and salvage, 1 trg

Air Force 13,500

(incl 3,000 conscripts; 7,500 op ready reserve); 174 cbt ac, 20 armed hel
FGA 8 sqn
3 with 51 A-4SU, 24 TA-4SU

1 with 7 F-16 (3 -A, 4 -B) (with a further 18 F-16C/D in US)
2 sqns of 24 F-16C/D being delivered
2 with 28 F-5S, 9 F-5F (secondary GA role)
RECCE 1 sqn with 8 RF-5S
AEW 1 sqn with 4 E-2C
ARMED HEL 2 sqn with 20 AS 550A2/C2
TRANSPORT 5 sqn
AC 3 sqn
1 with 4 KC-130B (tkr/tpt), 5 C-130H (1 ELINT), 1 KC-130H (tkr)
1 with 5 F-50 *Enforcer* (tpt/MR)
HEL 4 sqn
1 with 19 UH-1H, 2 with 22 AS-332M (incl 5 SAR), 6 AS-532UL
1 with 3 CH-47D (plus 3 in USA)
TRG 2 sqn
1 with 27 SIAI S-211
1 with 26 SF-260
UAV 1 sqn with 40 *Searcher*, 24 *Chukar* III

AIR DEFENCE SYSTEMS DIVISION

4 field def sqn
Air Defence Bde 1 sqn with **35mm** Oerlikon, 1 sqn with I HAWK, 1 sqn with Blind Fire *Rapier*
Air Force Systems Bde 1 sqn mobile radar, 1 sqn LORADS
Divisional Air Def Arty Bde (attached to Army divs) 1 bn with *Mistral* (SAM), 3 sqn RBS 70 (SAM), SA-18 *Igla*
MISSILES
AAM AIM-7P *Sparrow*, AIM-9 N/P *Sidewinder*
ASM AGM-65B *Maverick*, AGM-65G *Maverick*

Forces Abroad

AUSTRALIA 230; flying trg school with 27 S-211
BRUNEI 500; trg school, incl hel det (with 5 UH-1H)
FRANCE 200: trg 18, mostly TA-4SU (Cazaux AFB)
SOUTH AFRICA *Searcher* UAV trg det Hoedspruit AFB
TAIWAN 3 trg camps (incl inf and arty)
THAILAND 1 trg camp (arty)
US 3 CH-47D (ANG facility Grand Prairie, TX); 12 F-16C/D (leased from USAF at Luke AFB, AZ); 12 F-16C/D (at Cannon AFB, NM); KC-135 trg det at McConnell AFB, KS (no Singaporean ac yet)

UN AND PEACEKEEPING
IRAQ/KUWAIT (UNIKOM): 6 obs

Paramilitary ε108,000+ active

SINGAPORE POLICE FORCE
incl Police Coast Guard
12 *Swift* PCI< and about 60 boats
Singapore Gurkha Contingent (750)
CIVIL DEFENCE FORCE 120,000
(incl 1,500 regulars, 3,600 conscripts, ε60,000 former Army reservists, 60,000+ volunteers); 1 construction bde (2,500 conscripts)

Foreign Forces

NEW ZEALAND 11; spt unit
US 150: **Air Force** 40 **Navy** 90 **USMC** 20

Taiwan (Republic Of China) ROC

	1997	1998	1999	2000
GNP	NT$8.1tr	NT$9.3tr		
	($296bn)	($310bn)		
per capita	$13,800	$14,700		
Growth	6.8%	4.8%		
Inflation	0.9%	3.2%		
Debt	$24.6bn	$26bn		
Def exp[a]	NT$375bn	NT$425bn		
	($13.6bn)	($14.2bn)		
Def bdgt[b]			NT$275bn	NT$357bn
			($8.3bn)	($10.9bn)
US$1=NT$ (new Taiwan dollar)				
		27.5	30.0	32.7

[a] Incl special appropriations for procurement and infra-structure amounting to NT$301bn ($11bn) 1993–2001. Between 1993–98, NT$208bn ($8bn) was spent out of NT$289bn ($11bn) appropriated for these years.
[b] 1999 def bdgt covers 18 month period Jul 1999–Dec 2000.

Population				21,795,000
(Taiwanese 84%, mainland Chinese 14%)				
Age		*13–17*	*18–22*	*23–32*
Men		983,000	991,000	1,836,000
Women		939,000	937,000	1,736,000

Total Armed Forces

ACTIVE ε376,000
Terms of service 2 years

RESERVES 1,657,500
Army 1,500,000 with some obligation to age 30 **Navy** 32,500 **Marines** 35,000 **Air Force** 90,000

Army ε240,000

(incl mil police)
3 Army, 1 AB Special Ops HQ • 10 inf div • 2 mech inf div • 2 AB bde • 6 indep armd bde • 1 tk gp • 2 AD SAM gp with 6 SAM bn: 2 with *Nike Hercules*, 4 with I HAWK • 2 avn gp, 6 avn sqn

RESERVES
7 lt inf div
EQUIPMENT
MBT 100 M-48A5, 450+ M-48H, 169 M-60A3
LT TK 230 M-24 (**90mm** gun), 675 M-41/Type 64
AIFV 225 M-113 with **20–30mm** cannon
APC 650 M-113, 300 V-150 *Commando*
TOWED ARTY 105mm: 650 M-101 (T-64); **155mm**:

M-44, 90 M-59, 250 M-114 (T-65); **203mm**: 70 M-115
SP ARTY 105mm: 100 M-108; **155mm**: 45 T-69, 110 M-109A2/A5; **203mm**: 60 M-110
COASTAL ARTY 127mm: US Mk 32 (reported)
MRL 117mm: KF VI; **126mm**: KF III/IV towed and SP
MOR 81mm: M-29 (some SP); **107mm**
SSM *Ching Feng*
ATGW 1,000 TOW (some SP)
RCL 90mm: M-67; **106mm**: 500 M-40A1, Type 51
AD GUNS 40mm: 400 (incl M-42 SP, Bofors)
SAM 40 Nike *Hercules* (to be retired), 100 HAWK, *Tien Kung* (*Sky Bow*) -1/-2, 30 *Avenger*, 2 *Chaparral*, ε6 *Patriot*
AC 20 O-1
HEL 110 UH-1H, 53 AH-1S, 30 TH-67, 26 OH-58D, 12 KH-4, 7 CH-47, 5 Hughes 500
UAV *Mastiff* III

DEPLOYMENT
Quemoy 35–40,000; 4 inf div **Matsu** 8–10,000; 1 inf div

Navy 68,000

(incl 30,000 Marines)
3 Naval Districts
BASES Tsoying (HQ), Makung (Pescadores), Keelung, Hualien (ASW HQ) (New East Coast fleet set up and based at Suo; 6 *Chin Yang*-class FF)
SUBMARINES 4
SSK 4
2 *Hai Lung* (Nl mod *Zwaardvis*) with 533mm TT
2 *Hai Shih* (US *Guppy* II) with 533mm TT (trg only)
PRINCIPAL SURFACE COMBATANTS 37
DESTROYERS 16
DDG 16
7 *Chien Yang* (US *Gearing*) (*Wu Chin* III conversion) with 10 SM-1 MR SAM (boxed), 1 x 8 ASROC SUGW, 2 x 3 ASTT, plus 1 *Hughes* MD-500 hel
4 *Fu Yang* (US *Gearing*); 5 with 1 *Hughes* MD 500 hel, 1 with 1 x 8 ASROC SUGW, all with 2 x 3 ASTT, 1 or 2 x 2 127mm guns, 3 or 5 *Hsiung Feng* I (*HF* 1) (Il *Gabriel*) SSM
2 *Po Yang* (US *Sumner*)† with 1 or 2 x 2 127mm guns, 2 x 3 ASTT; 5 or 6 *HF* 1 SSM, 1 with 1 *Hughes* MD-500 hel
3 *Kun Yang* (US *Fletcher*) with 2 or 3 127mm guns; 1 76mm gun, 2 x 3 ASTT with 5 *HF* 1 SSM†
FRIGATES 21
FFG 21
7 *Cheng Kung* with 8 HF2 SSM, 1 SM-1 MR SAM, 2 x 3 ASTT, 2 S-70C hel
6 *Kang Ding* (Fr *La Fayette*) with 8 HF2 SSM, 4 *Sea Chaparral* SAM, 1 76mm gun, 6 324mm TT, 1 S-70C hel
8 *Chin Yang* (US *Knox*) with 1 x 8 ASROC SUGW, 1 SH-2F hel, 4 ASTT, *Harpoon* SSM (from ASROC launchers), 1 127mm gun

PATROL AND COASTAL COMBATANTS 104

MISSILE CRAFT 59
2 *Lung Chiang*† PFM with 2 *HF* 1 SSM
7 *Jinn Chiang* PFM with 4 *HF* 1 SSM
50 *Hai Ou* (mod Il *Dvora*)< with 2 *HF* 1 SSM
PATROL, INSHORE 45 (op by Maritime Police)
22 Vosper-type 32m PFI, 7 PCI, about 16 PCI<

MINE COUNTERMEASURES 12

4 *Yung Chou* (US *Adjutant*) MSC
4 (ex-US) *Aggressive* MSO
4 *Yung Feng* MSC converted from oil-rig spt ships

AMPHIBIOUS 18

1 *Pensacola* (US *Anchorage*) LSD
2 *Chung Ho* (US *Newport*) LST capacity 400 troops,
    500 tons vehicles, 4 LCVP
1 *Kao Hsiung* (US LST 511) LCC
10 *Chung Hai* (US LST 511) LST, capacity 16 tk, 200 tps
4 *Mei Lo* (US LSM-1) LSM, capacity about 4 tk
Plus about 325 craft; some 20 LCU, 205 LCM, 100
    LCVP and assault LCVP

SUPPORT AND MISCELLANEOUS 20

3 AO, 2 AR, 1 *Wu Yi* combat spt with hel deck, 2
    Yuen Feng and 2 *Wu Kang* attack tpt with hel deck,
    2 tpt, 7 AT/F, 1 *Te Kuan* AGOR

COASTAL DEFENCE 1

1 SSM coastal def bn with *Hsiung Feng* (*Gabriel*-type)

NAVAL AIR

31 cbt ac; 21 armed hel
    MR 1 sqn with 31 S-2 (24 -E, 7 -G)
    HEL 12* Hughes 500MD, 9* S-70C ASW *Defender*, 9
    S-70C(M)-1

MARINES (30,000)

2 div, spt elm
EQUIPMENT
    AAV LVTP-4/-5
    TOWED ARTY 105mm, 155mm
    RCL 106mm

Air Force 68,000

598 cbt ac, no armed hel
Flying hours 180
FGA/FTR 23 sqn
    6 with 200 F-5 (7 -B, 213 -E, 52 -F) (ε70 in store)
    6 with 130 *Ching-Kuo*
3 with 60 *Mirage* 2000-5
7 with 150 F-16A/B (incl one sqn recce capable)
1 with 22 AT-3
RECCE 2 with 8 RF-5E, 16 ACH-1
AEW 4 E-2T
EW 1 with 2 C-130HE, 2 CC-47
SAR 1 sqn with 17 S-70C
TPT 3 ac sqn
    2 with 19 C-130H (1 EW)
    1 VIP with 4 -727-100, 11 Beech 1900, 3 *Fokker* F-50, 1
        Boeing 727

HEL 5 CH-34, 1 S-62A (VIP), 14 S-70
TRG ac incl 36* AT-3A/B, 40 T-38A, 42 T-34C
MISSILES
    ASM AGM-65A *Maverick*
    AAM AIM-4D *Falcon*, AIM-9J/P *Sidewinder*, *Shafrir*,
        Sky Sword I and II, MATRA *Mica*, MATRA R550
        Magic 2

Forces Abroad

US F-16 conversion unit at Luke AFB

Paramilitary ε26,650

SECURITY GROUPS 25,000

National Police Administration (Ministry of Interior);
Bureau of Investigation (Ministry of Justice); **Military
Police** (Ministry of Defence)
MARITIME POLICE ε1,000
about 38 armed patrol boats; also man many of the
patrol craft listed under Navy
CUSTOMS SERVICE (Ministry of Finance) 650
5 PCO, 2 PCC, 1 PCI, 5 PCI<; most armed

Foreign Forces

SINGAPORE 3 trg camps

Thailand   Th

	1997	1998	1999	2000
GDP	b4.8tr	b5.1tr		
	($154bn)	($137bn)		
per capita	$8,400	$8,200		
Growth	-0.4%	-8.0%		
Inflation	5.6%	8.1%		
Debt	$93bn	$99bn		
Def exp	b104bn	b86bn		
	($3.3bn)	($2.1bn)		
Def bdgt		b81.0bn	b77.4bn	b77.3bn
		($2.0bn)	($2.1bn)	($2.0bn)
FMA (US)	$4.8m	$3.9m	$4.6m	$1.6m
FMA (Aus)	$2.5m	$2.5m	$3.0m	
$1=baht	31.4	41.4	37.2	
Population				63,726,000
(Thai 75%, Chinese 14%, Muslim 4%)				
Age	*13–17*	*18–22*		*23–32*
Men	3,158,000	3,171,000		6,084,000
Women	3,052,000	3,078,000		5,922,000

Total Armed Forces

ACTIVE 306,000

RESERVES 200,000

Army 190,000

4 Regional Army HQ, 2 Corps HQ • 2 cav div • 3 armd inf div • 2 mech inf div • 1 lt inf div • 2 SF div • 1 arty div, 1 AD arty div (6 AD arty bn) • 1 engr div • 4 economic development div • 1 indep cav regt • 8 indep inf bn • 4 recce coy • armd air cav regt with 3 air-mobile coy • Some hel flt • Rapid Reaction Force (1 bn per region forming)

RESERVES

4 inf div HQ

EQUIPMENT

MBT 12 PRC Type-69 (trg/in store), 150+ M-48A5, 127 M-60 (74 A3, 53 A1)
LT TK 154 *Scorpion*, 250 M-41, 106 *Stingray*
RECCE 32 Shorland Mk 3
APC 340 M-113A1/A3, 162 V-150 *Commando*, 18 *Condor*, 450 PRC Type-85 (YW-531H)
TOWED ARTY 105mm: 24 LG1 Mk 2, 285 M-101/-101 mod, 12 M-102, 32 M-618A2 (local manufacture); **130mm:** 15 PRC Type-59; **155mm:** 56 M-114, 62 M-198, 32 M-71, 42 GHN-45/A1
SP ARTY 155mm: 20 M-109A2
MOR 81mm (incl 21 M-125A3 SP), **107mm** incl M-106A1 SP; **120mm:** 12 M-1064A3 SP
ATGW TOW (incl 18 M-901A5), 300 *Dragon*
RL M-72 LAW
RCL 75mm: M-20; **106mm:** 150 M-40
AD GUNS 20mm: 24 M-163 *Vulcan*, 24 M-167 *Vulcan*; **37mm:** 122 Type-74; **40mm:** 80 M-1/M-42 SP, 48 L/70; **57mm:** 24+ PRC Type-59
SAM *Redeye*, some *Aspide*, HN-5A
AIRCRAFT
    TPT 2 C-212, 2 Beech 1900C-1, 4 C-47, 10 Cessna 208, 2 Short 330UTT, 2 *Beech King Air*, 2 *Jetstream* 41
    LIAISON 60 O-1A, 5 T-41A, 5 U-17A
    TRG 17 T-41D, 20+ MX-7-235
HELICOPTERS
    ATTACK 4 AH-1F
    TPT 8 CH-47, 40 Bell (incl -206, -212, -214), 69 UH-1H
    TRG 36 Hughes 300C, 3 OH-13, 7 TH-55
SURV RASIT (veh, arty), AN-TPQ-36 (arty, mor)

Navy 73,000

(incl 1,700 Naval Air, 20,000 Marines, 7,000 Coastal Defence)
FLEETS 1st North Thai Gulf **2nd** South Thai Gulf
1 Naval Air Division
BASES Bangkok, Sattahip (Fleet HQ), Songkhla, Phang Nga, Nakhon Phanom (HQ Mekong River Operating Unit)

PRINCIPAL SURFACE COMBATANTS 15

AIRCRAFT CARRIER 1 *Chakri Naruebet* with 8 AV-8S *Matador* (*Harrier*), 6 S-70B *Seahawk* hel, 3 x 6 *Sadral* SAM, 8 VLS *Sea Sparrow* SAM
FRIGATES 14

FFG 8
2 *Naresuan* with 2 x 4 *Harpoon* SSM, 8 cell *Sea Sparrow* SAM, 1 127mm gun, 6 324mm TT, 1 SH-2G hel
2 *Chao Phraya* (PRC *Jianghu* III) with 8 C-801 SSM, 2 x 2 100mm guns, 2 x 5 ASW RL (plus 1 undergoing weapons fit), Bell 212 hel
2 *Kraburi* (PRC *Jianghu* IV type) with 8 C-801 SSM, 1 x 2 100mm guns, 2 x 5 ASW RL and Bell 212 hel
2 *Phutthayotfa Chulalok* (US *Knox*) (leased from US) with 8 *Harpoon* SSM, 8 ASROC ASTT, 1 127mm gun, 1 Bell 212 hel
FF 6
1 *Makut Rajakumarn* with 2 x 3 ASTT (*Sting Ray* LWT); plus 2 114mm guns (training)
2 *Tapi* (US PF-103) with 2 x 3 ASTT (Mk 46 LWT)
2 *Tachin* (US *Tacoma*) with 2 x 3 ASTT (trg)
1 *Pin Klao* (US *Cannon*) with 1 76mm gun, 6 324mm TT

PATROL AND COASTAL COMBATANTS 88

CORVETTES 5
2 *Rattanakosin* with 2 x 3 ASTT (*Sting Ray* LWT); plus 2 x 4 *Harpoon* SSM, 8 *Aspide* SAM
3 *Khamronsin* with 2 x 3 ASTT; plus 1 76mm gun
MISSILE CRAFT 6
3 *Ratcharit* (It Breda 50m) with 4 MM-38 *Exocet* SSM
3 *Prabparapak* (Ge Lürssen 45m) with 5 *Gabriel* SSM
PATROL CRAFT 77
    COASTAL 13
    1 PC30 PCC
    3 *Chon Buri* PFC, 6 *Sattahip*, 3 PCD
    INSHORE 64
    7 T-11 (US PGM-71), 9 T-91, about 33 PCF and 15 PCR plus boats

MINE COUNTERMEASURES 7

2 *Lat Ya* (It *Gaeta*) MCMV
2 *Bang Rachan* (Ge Lürssen T-48) MCC
2 *Bangkeo* (US *Bluebird*) MSC
1 *Thalang* MCM spt with minesweeping capability (Plus some 12 MSB)

AMPHIBIOUS 9

2 *Sichang* (Fr PS-700) LST, capacity 14 tk, 300 tps with hel deck (trg)
5 *Angthong* (US LST-511) LST, capacity 16 tk, 200 tps
2 *Kut* (US LSM-1) LSM, capacity about 4 tk
Plus about 51 craft: 9 LCU, about 24 LCM, 1 LCG, 2 LSIL, 3 hovercraft, 12 LCVP

SUPPORT AND MISCELLANEOUS 16

1 *Similan* AO (1 hel) , 1 *Chula* AO, 5 AO, 3 AGHS, 6 trg

NAVAL AIR (1,700)

(incl 300 conscripts); 67 cbt ac; 5 armed hel
FTR 9 *Harrier* (7 AV-8, 2 TAV-8)
MR/ATTACK 5 Cessna T-337 *Skymasters*, 14 A-7E, 4 TA-7C, 5 O-1G, 4 U-17B
MR/ASW 3 P-3T *Orion* (plus 2 P-3A in store), 1 UP-3T, 6 Do-228, 3 F-27 MPA, 8 S-2F, 5 N-24A *Nomad*
ASW HEL 5 S-70B
SAR/UTILITY 2 CL-215, 8 Bell 212, 5 Bell 214, 4 UH-

1H, 5 S-76N

ASM AGM-84 *Harpoon* (for F-27MPA, P-3T)

MARINES (20,000)

1 div HQ, 2 inf regt, 1 arty regt (3 fd, 1 AA bn); 1 amph aslt bn; recce bn

EQUIPMENT

AAV 33 LVTP-7

TOWED ARTY 155mm: 12 GC-45

ATGW TOW, *Dragon*

Air Force 43,000

162 cbt ac, no armed hel

Flying hours 100

FGA 3 sqn

1 with 14 F-5A/B • 2 with 36 F-16 (26 -A, 10 -B)

FTR 2 sqn with 33 F-5E, 6 -F

ARMED AC 5 sqn

1 with 4 AC-47 • 3 with 22 AU-23A • 1 with 19* N-22B *Missionmaster* (tpt/armed)

ELINT 1 sqn with 3 IAI-201

RECCE 2 sqn with 25* OV-10C, 3* RF-5A

SURVEY 2 *Learjet* 35A, 3 *Merlin* IVA, 3 GAF N-22B *Nomads*

TPT 3 sqn

1 with 6 C-130H, 6 C-130H-30, 3 DC-8-62F

1 with 3 C-123-K, 4 BAe-748

1 with 6 G-222

VIP Royal flight **ac** 1 Airbus A-310-324, 1 Boeing 737-200, 3 *King Air* 200, 2 BAe-748, 3 *Merlin* IV **hel** 2 Bell 412, 3 AS-532A2

TRG 24 CT-4, 29 *Fantrainer*-400, 13 *Fantrainer*-600, 10 SF-260, 15 T-33A/RT-33A, 22 PC-9, 6 -C, 12 T-37, 34 L-39ZA/MP

LIAISON 3 *Commander*, 1 *King Air* E90, 2 O-1 *Bird Dog*, 2 *Queen Air*, 3 *Basler Turbo*-67

HEL 2 sqn

1 with 17 S-58T • 1 with 25 UH-1H

AAM AIM-9B/J *Sidewinder*, AIM-120 AMRAAM, *Python* 3

AIR DEFENCE

1 AA arty bty: 4 *Skyguard*, 1 *Flycatcher* radars, each with 4 fire units of 2 30mm Mauser/Kuka guns

SAM *Blowpipe*, *Aspide*, RBS NS-70, *Starburst*

Forces Abroad

UN AND PEACEKEEPING

IRAQ/KUWAIT (UNIKOM): 5 obs

Paramilitary ε71,000 active

THAHAN PHRAN (Hunter Soldiers) 18,500

volunteer irregular force; 27 regt of some 200 coy

NATIONAL SECURITY VOLUNTEER CORPS 50,000

MARINE POLICE 2,500

3 PCO, 3 PCC, 8 PFI, some 110 PCI<

POLICE AVIATION 500

ac 1 *Airtourer*, 6 AU-23, 2 Cessna 310, 1 Fokker 50, 1 CT-4, 2 CN 235, 8 PC-6, 2 Short 330 **hel** 27 Bell 205A, 14 Bell 206, 3 Bell 212, 6 UH-12, 5 KH-4

BORDER PATROL POLICE 18,000

PROVINCIAL POLICE ε50,000

incl ε500 Special Action Force

Foreign Forces

SINGAPORE 1 trg camp (arty)

US Army 40 **Air Force** 30 **Navy** 10 **USMC** 40

Vietnam   Vn

	1997	1998	1999	2000
GDP	d296tr	d340tr		
	($25bn)	($27bn)		
per capita	$1,100	$1,200		
Growth	8.8%	5.0%		
Inflation	3.2%	7.7%		
Debt	$22bn	$22bn		
Def exp	ε$1,004m	ε$925m		
Def bdgt			ε$891m	
$1=dong	11,659	12,980	13,893	
Population		80,433,000 (Chinese 3%)		
Age	*13–17*	*18–22*	*23–32*	
Men	4,401,000	3,988,000	6,906,000	
Women	4,250,000	3,861,000	6,763,000	

Total Armed Forces

ACTIVE ε484,000

(referred to as 'Main Force')

Terms of service 2 years Army and Air Defence, 3 years Air Force and Navy, specialists 3 years, some ethnic minorities 2 years

RESERVES some 3–4,000,000

'**Strategic Rear Force**' (see also *Paramilitary*)

Army ε412,000

8 Mil Regions, 2 special areas • 14 Corps HQ • 58 inf div[a] • 3 mech inf div • 10 armd bde • 15 indep inf regt • SF incl AB bde, demolition engr regt • Some 10 fd arty bde • 8 engr div • 10–16 economic construction div • 20 indep engr bde

EQUIPMENT

MBT 45 T-34, 850 T-54/-55, 70 T-62, 350 PRC Type-59

LT TK 300 PT-76, 320 PRC Type-62/63

RECCE 100 BRDM-1/-2

AIFV 300 BMP
APC 1,100 BTR-40/-50/-60/-152, YW-531, M-113
TOWED ARTY 2,300: **76mm; 85mm; 100mm**: M-1944, T-12; **105mm**: M-101/-102; **122mm**: Type-54, Type-60, M-1938, D-30, D-74; **130mm**: M-46; **152mm**: D-20; **155mm**: M-114
SP ARTY 152mm: 30 2S3; **175mm**: M-107
COMBINED GUN/MOR 120mm: 2S9 reported
ASLT GUNS 100mm: SU-100; **122mm**: ISU-122
MRL 107mm: 360 Type 63; **122mm**: 350 BM-21; 140mm: BM-14-16
MOR 82mm, 120mm: M-43; **160mm**: M-43
SSM Scud B (reported)
ATGW AT-3 Sagger
RCL 75mm: PRC Type-56; **82mm**: PRC Type-65, B-10; **87mm**: PRC Type-51
AD GUNS 12,000: **14.5mm; 23mm**: incl ZSU-23-4 SP; **30mm; 37mm; 57mm; 85mm; 100mm**
SAM SA-7/-16

[a] Inf div str varies from 5,000 to 12,500

Navy ε42,000

(incl 27,000 Naval Infantry)
Four Naval Regions
BASES Hanoi (HQ), Cam Ranh Bay, Da Nang, Haiphong, Ha Tou, Ho Chi Minh City, Can Tho, plus several smaller bases
SUBMARINES 2
SSI 2 DPRK Yugo
FRIGATES 6
FFG 1 Barnegat (US Cutter) with 2 SS-N-2A Styx SSM, 1 127mm gun
FF 5
  3 Sov Petya II with 2 ASW RL, 10 406mm TT, 4 76mm gun
  2 Sov Petya III with 2 ASW RL, 3 533mm TT, 4 76mm gun
PATROL AND COASTAL COMBATANTS 40
CORVETTES 1 HO-A (Type 124A) with 8 SS-N-25 Zvezda SSM, SA-N-5 SAM
MISSILE CRAFT 10
  8 Sov Osa II with 4 SS-N-2 Styx SSM
  2 Sov Tarantul with 4 SS-N-2D Styx SSM
TORPEDO CRAFT 10
  5 Sov Turya PHT with 4 533mm TT (2 without TT)
  5 Sov Shershen PFT with 4 533mm TT
PATROL, INSHORE 19
  4 Sov SO-1, 3 US PGM-59/71, 10 Zhuk<, 2 Sov Poluchat PCI; plus large numbers of river patrol boats
MINE COUNTERMEASURES 11
  2 Yurka MSC, 4 Sonya MSC, 2 PRC Lienyun MSC, 1 Vanya MSI, 2 Yevgenya MSI, plus 5 K-8 boats
AMPHIBIOUS 6
  3 US LST-510-511 LST, capacity 200 tps, 16 tk
  3 Sov Polnocny LSM, capacity 180 tps, 6 tk

Plus about 30 craft: 12 LCM, 18 LCU
SUPPORT AND MISCELLANEOUS 30+
incl 1 trg, 1 AGHS, 4 AO, about 12 small tpt, 2 ex-Sov floating docks and 3 div spt. Significant numbers of small merchant ships and trawlers are taken into naval service for patrol and resupply duties. Some of these may be lightly armed

NAVAL INFANTRY (27,000)
(amph, cdo)

Air Force 15,000

189 cbt ac, 43 armed hel (plus many in store). 3 Air Div
FGA 2 regt with 53 Su-22, 12 Su-27
FTR 5 regt with 124 MiG-21bis/PF
ATTACK HEL 26 Mi-24
MR 4 Be-12
ASW HEL 8 Ka-25, 5 Ka-28, 6 Ka-32
SURVEY 2 An-30
TPT 3 regt incl 12 An-2, 4 An-24, 30 An-26, 8 Tu-134, 13 Yak-40
HEL some 70 incl Mi-6, Mi-8/-17
TRG 3 regt with 52 **ac**, incl L-39, MiG-21U, Yak-18
AAM AA-2 Atoll, AA-8 Aphid, AA-10 Allamo
ASM AS-9 Kyle

Air Defence Force 15,000

Being merged with the Air Force
14 AD div
SAM some 66 sites with SA-2/-3/-6/-7/-16
AD 4 arty bde: **37mm, 57mm, 85mm, 100mm, 130mm**
People's Regional Force: ε1,000 units, 6 radar bde: 100 sites

Paramilitary 40,000 active

LOCAL FORCES some 4–5,000,000
incl **People's Self-Defence Force** (urban units), **People's Militia** (rural units); these comprise static and mobile cbt units, log spt and village protection pl; some arty, mor and AD guns; acts as reserve
BORDER DEFENCE CORPS ε40,000
COAST GUARD
being established; came into effect on 1 Sept 1998

Foreign Forces

RUSSIA 700: naval facilities; ELINT station

MILITARY DEVELOPMENTS

Intra-regional relations continued to improve in 1999, particularly between those countries with long-standing disputes over borders or territory. The Brasilia Agreements, signed in October 1998, ended the boundary dispute between Peru and Ecuador. While there is no recent history of conflict, the last remaining border issue between Argentina and Chile, in the Andean region known as *Campos de Hielo*, was also settled by a treaty signed in Buenos Aires in December 1998. For most governments in the region, with the exception of Colombia and Mexico, the challenge from armed insurgency is steadily diminishing. However, destabilising cross-border activities, mainly smuggling and other illegal actions conducted by remaining guerrilla forces and criminal groups, continue to cause concern. Colombia's borders with Panama and Venezuela are particularly troublesome. While the acquisition of major weapon systems by states in the region has declined during 1998 and 1999, some programmes for combat aircraft, warships (in particular submarines) and main battle tanks (MBTs) continue, although some of these more expensive weapon systems have little relevance to the immediate security challenges facing the region's armed forces. Argentina is, for the second year running, the largest contributor to peacekeeping operations outside the region, with contingents in UN missions in Cyprus and Kuwait.

Insurgency and Terrorism

The most active guerrilla campaigns are in Colombia and the Chiapas region of Mexico. The Colombian government attempted to engage both the *Fuerzas Armadas Revolucionarias de Colombia* (FARC) and the *Ejército de Liberación Nacional de Colombia* (ELN) in a peace process beginning in late 1998. FARC's participation was conditional on government forces withdrawing from areas in the south for a 90-day period, but right-wing militias of the *Autodefensas Unidas de Colombia* (AUC) remained active in the 'demilitarised' zones. Despite this, sporadic peace talks between the government and FARC leaders followed, but they had not, by August 1999, brought a respite in the fighting. According to government reports in April 1999, FARC and the ELN controlled some 12% of Colombia. This left around 140 municipalities without a government, police or military presence. Some independent reports, however, attribute control of 40% of the country to the guerrillas. While it is unlikely that the guerrillas have been able to maintain continuous control over this amount of territory, they undoubtedly exploited the opportunity to regroup and retrain in those areas from which government forces withdrew. Fighting resurged in June and July 1999, ahead of a planned reopening of government–FARC talks on 19 July, when FARC, supported by the smaller ELN, launched one of their largest offensives for some years in at least 20 different areas of the country. They bombed banks, blew up bridges and energy installations, blocked roads and attacked police barracks. The talks were postponed and government forces responded with a counter-offensive in which they claimed to have killed at least 280 guerrillas. Some 60 soldiers and police were reported killed and 40 or more taken hostage. The government is counting the cost of conceding safe havens to the insurgents and entering into negotiations without commitment by both sides to a cease-fire.

In Mexico, military operations against the *Ejército Zapatista de Liberación Nacional* (EZLN) and the smaller *Ejército Popular Revolucionario* (EPR) in the state of Chiapas continue to require more than 20,000 personnel. The EZLN campaign is now in its sixth year and, while conflict is generally low-level, there have been no direct talks between the guerrilla group and the government since 1996. The rebels appear to be willing to negotiate only via sympathetic non-government groups or the Internet, where their leader, self-styled *Subcommandante* Marcos, posts statements.

Guerrilla and terrorist activities continue to decline in Peru. The leader of the *Sendero Luminoso* (Shining Path) Maoist group, Oscar Ramirez Durand, was finally captured in July 1999, in an operation which involved some 1,500 government troops. The arrest, in a mountainous region in the east of the country near Jauja, has probably ended a guerrilla campaign that began in 1980 and is thought to have cost the lives of some 30,000 military and civilian personnel. The number of active members of the *Sendero Luminoso* declined sharply after the capture of its founder, Abimael Guzman, in 1992, after which the group ceased to have the capability to overthrow the government. There will now be mounting pressure on President Alberto Fujimori to ease the draconian anti-terrorist legislation ahead of the 2000 presidential election.

La Mission de Observadores Militares Ecuador–Peru (MOMEP) ended in June 1999 following the full implementation of the October 1998 Brasilia Agreements. The mission, which lasted three years, comprised military personnel from Argentina, Brazil, Chile and US.

Organised Crime and Insecurity

The primary security preoccupation of many armed forces in the region on a day-to-day basis is helping to combat organised crime and contain the destabilising violence induced by the drug trade and related crime in poor urban and rural areas. However, the armed forces frequently appear to be reluctant to equip and train effectively for internal security roles involving both international criminal groups and state-level, rural and urban law-enforcement bodies. Law-enforcement failures have led to the increasing 'privatisation' of violence, as individuals and militia groups take the law and their protection into their own hands. The public's feeling of insecurity has also been reflected in a tendency to elect to political office former generals campaigning on a public-order platform, as in Bolivia in 1997, Paraguay in 1998 and, most recently, Venezuela in late-1998. In Venezuela, public concern at the deterioration in public order contributed directly to the victory of President Hugo Chavez, leader of one of the country's two failed military coups in 1992. However, in other major states in the region, such as Argentina, Brazil and Chile, civil–military relations continue to improve. For example, the appointment of Élicio Álvarez as Brazil's Defence Minister on 10 June 1999 brought the country's armed forces under direct civilian control for the first time since the return to civilian government in 1985.

DEFENCE SPENDING

Regional defence expenditure declined by almost 3% in 1998 to $37bn, measured in constant 1997 US dollars, according to *The Military Balance* estimates. The general level of annual defence budgets set for 1998 had suggested that spending for the year would show a small increase over 1997. In the event, a combination of factors, including weakness in international markets for some of the region's major commodities, currency depreciation and apprehension that an economic crisis of East Asian dimensions was imminent in Latin America, persuaded governments, particularly those of countries with the largest economies, to cut back their spending. Defence budgets were not spared, although the cuts were generally less than in other areas.

Evidence from current-year defence budgets suggests that while defence spending in the region has generally increased in nominal terms in 1999, it may be static in real terms as a result both of pre-emptive austerity measures taken by many governments and of currency depreciation against the US dollar. In mid-1999, there are indications that commodity prices, notably of oil, are recovering and with them government revenues, which should strengthen local currencies. The combination of increases in pay, in spending on operations and maintenance, and, in particular, in procurement, makes it unlikely that defence spending can be contained at the reduced 1998 levels for long.

Defence-spending cuts in 1998 particularly affected equipment orders. The value of arms deliveries declined to £1.7bn from an estimated $2bn in 1997, in line with expectations. However, there should be a renewed rise from 1999 as current commitments are realised and new orders materialise.

Economics and Regional Security

In 1998, natural disasters, the impact of external economic shocks and unfavourable global prices for oil and other Latin American commodities helped to halve the rate of growth in gross domestic product (GDP) to around 2.3% and to constrain government spending, including that on defence and security. The *El Niño* climate upheaval which began in 1997 caused drought and floods throughout the region in 1998, with Peru and Ecuador worst hit. Hurricane *Georges* caused widespread damage in Caribbean countries in September 1998 and Central America was hit by Hurricane *Mitch*, one of the century's most destructive hurricanes, in late October and December. These natural disasters forced supplementary expenditures on several governments. In addition, government revenues were hit by the impact of lower world prices for the some of the region's staple exports, particularly oil, and this triggered budget cuts early in the 1999 fiscal year. However, prospects for the regional economy were recovering by mid-1999, which could eventually allow government spending, including on defence, to increase again.

Selected Budgets and Expenditure

Mexico Mexico's defence budget rose to P23.4bn ($2.4bn) in 1999, from P20bn ($2.2bn) in 1998. The Navy took delivery of two *Knox*-class frigates from the US in 1998, with delivery of a third now approved by the US Congress.

Cuba Cuban spending on defence and security is officially P630m ($27m) in 1999, representing just 5% of the government budget for the year.

Brazil Brazil's initial defence budget for 1998 of R16.1bn was subsequently reduced to R15.9bn. The 1999 budget rose in nominal terms to R17.5bn, but exchange-rate devaluation has reduced the dollar value from $13.7bn in 1998 to $10.2bn in 1999. The government has announced its intention to combine the individual ministries for the armed forces under a single Ministry of Defence established in April 1999.

Table 24 Brazil: defence spending, 1995–1999

(US$m)	1995 Budget	1995 Outlay	1996 Budget	1996 Outlay	1997 Budget	1997 Revised	1997 Outlay	1998 Budget	1998 Revised	1999 Budget
Army	7,920	6,444	7,060	6,595	6,906	7,001	6,606	6,493	6321	5,083
Navy	5,420	3,914	4,273	3,749	4,032	4,088	3,769	3,755	3,755	2,611
Air Force	4,609	3,759	4,212	3,604	3,697	3,774	3,439	3,354	3,353	2,347
MOD	95	252	101	101	132	132	132	250	250	205
Total	18,045	14,369	15,646	14,050	14,767	14,995	13,945	13,851	13,678	10,245

Table 25 Brazil: defence budget by service and function, 1999

(US$m)	Army	%	Navy	%	Air Force	%	Other	%	Total
Personnel, Pensions and O&M	3,976	83.2	1,779	73.9	1,414	64.9	n.a.	n.a.	7,170
Procurement & Construction	805	16.8	628	26.1	764	35.1	n.a.	n.a.	2,197
Other or Undistributed									878
Total	4,781	100	2,408	100	2,178	100	878	–	10,245

In this year's edition of *The Military Balance,* estimates for Brazil's defence spending back to 1985 have been revised to include state-level spending on the Military Police, a paramilitary organisation whose funding would be counted as military spending under definitions used by the IISS, but is not included in the Brazilian defence budget. The largest and richest of Brazil's 27 states, Sao Paulo, budgeted $891m for the Military Police in 1998 and its civilian police budget was $623m.

Brazilian orders for eight EMB-145 airborne early warning (AEW) and electronic surveillance aircraft have been confirmed, with deliveries in 2001, as part of the *Sistema de Viligencia de Amazonia* (SIVAM) programme. The first 33 of 99 AL-X trainers and light attack aircraft, also part of SIVAM, are to be delivered in 1999. An order for the third batch of 13 AMX light fighter, ground-attack (FGA) aircraft was made in 1998, following delivery of 54 aircraft in two batches under the collaborative project with Venezuela and Italy. The Air Force has chosen an Israeli-led consortium to upgrade 45 F-5 FGAs. Twenty A4-KU *Skyhawks* have been delivered along with at least three TA-4KU trainers. These were due to be operational by the end of 1999 and to be flown from the carrier *Minas Gerais* once its refit is complete. The last of three Type 209 *Tupi* submarines built under licence was launched in June 1998 for commissioning in mid-1999, while the first of two improved *Tupi* (*Tikuna*) submarines was laid down in June 1998. A project for the first indigenously designed and built submarine is in hand with a planned completion date of 2010. Of a total order of 87 *Leopard* 1 tanks from Belgium, 27 were delivered in 1998. Deliveries continued in 1999.

Argentina Defence accounts for 7.4% of Argentinian government spending, while the Ministry of the Interior, whose budget has included funding for the paramilitary forces (National Guard and Coast Guard) since 1998, accounts for 5.4%. The Presidential Budget (which may include discretionary procurement spending, including on military items) accounts for a further 5.9%. As well as excluding funding for the paramilitary forces, the defence budget also appears to exclude some procurement spending. Among the country's more significant procurement orders are the refit of two *Espora* (*Meko* 140) frigates, due to be completed by the end of 2000, and the delivery of six (out of an order of eight) P-3 maritime patrol aircraft from the US. The Argentinian government released the first *Libro Blanco de la Defensa Nacional* in 1999, following the example of Chile in 1997.

Table 26 **Argentina: defence expenditure by function, 1998**

(US$m)	Central Organisation	State-level Organisation	Pensions	Total
Personnel	1,863	4	5	1,872
Operations & Maintenance	539	7	15	561
Equipment	128	2	0	130
Other	10	1	0	11
Pensions			1,186	1,186
Total Defence	**2,540**	**15**	**1,206**	**3,760**
Parishment Forces				690
R&D (1997)				15
Total				**4,465**

Chile The government of Chile released its first *Libro de la Defensa Nacional de Chile* in August 1997 and an English-language version in September 1998. These publications include details of funding for procurement (from the Codelco copper fund) and for military pensions (from the Social Security budget) which are excluded from the official defence budget released in Chile and figures provided to UN organisations. This year, *The Military Balance* estimates for Chile back to 1985 have been revised to include spending on the paramilitary *Carabiñeros*.

Table 27 Chile: defence-related expenditure, 1996–1999

(US$m)	1996	1997	1998	1999
Defence budget	1,057	1,158	1,325	1,257
Codelco Copper Fund (for equipment)	285	280	250	215
Pensions for retired military personnel	545	591	560	648
Other	108	119	77	97
Defence-related expenditure	1,995	2,148	2,212	2,217
Paramilitary *Carabiñeros*	748	775	800	820

Table 28 Chile: defence and security funding by service, 1998–1999

(US$m)	1998	%	1999	%
Army	553	16.5	521	17.2
Navy	496	14.8	478	15.7
Air Force	266	7.9	249	8.2
Military Pensions	560	16.7	648	21.3
Other	337	10.1	321	10.6
Sub-total	2,212	66.1	2,217	73.0
Paramilitary	800	23.9	820	27.0
Armed Forces Commercial Revenue	335	10.0	n.k.	n.k.
Total	3,347	100.0	3037	100.0

Chile's requirement for F-5 and *Mirage* 5 replacements, for which the competition was suspended in July 1998, was formally postponed in November 1998. The Navy's programme for a new class of six frigates has also been delayed by the budget cuts announced in mid-1998. The order for two *Scorpene* submarines from a Franco-Spanish consortium has been confirmed, with commissioning expected in 2003 and 2005. In January 1999, the Army took delivery of the first 14 of 200 used *Leopard*-1V tanks from the Netherlands, following deliveries in 1998 of 21 used AMX-30B tanks from France out of a total order of up to 60.

Table 29 Bolivia: defence expenditure, 1995–1999

(US$m)	1995	%	1996	%	1997	%	1998	%	1999	%
Personnel	100.8	79.1	106.5	79.3	113.0	78.1	122.3	81.4	111.1	82.7
O&M	23.7	18.6	26.3	19.5	30.1	20.8	26.8	17.8	23.0	17.1
Procurement	1.1	0.8	0.4	0.3	0.2	0.2	1.2	0.8	0.3	0.2
R&D	1.2	0.9	1.0	0.8	1.1	0.8	–		–	
Construction	0.7	0.6	0.2	0.1	0.2	0.2	–		–	
Total	127.4	100.0	134.4	100.0	144.7	100.0	150.4	100.0	134.4	100.0

Bolivia, Colombia and Venezuela Bolivia's 1999 defence budget was down 11% in US dollar terms from $150m in 1998 to $134m. The fall in nominal terms was a larger 8%. Over 80% of the budget goes to pay manpower costs and pensions. Most of the balance is spent on Operations and Maintenance (O&M), with very little left for procurement.

Colombia's defence budget for 1999 is at similar levels to 1998. The armed forces plan to allocate some $1.3bn, including grant aid, to procurement over the next four years. The National

Police are to take delivery of 6 UH-60 *Black Hawk* helicopters between September 1999 and January 2000, together with some 25 UH-1 improved *Huey* helicopters, as grant aid under the US counter-drugs programme.

Table 30 **Colombia: defence and security budget, 1998–1999**		
(US$m)	1998	1999
Ministry of National Defence	439	346
Army	700	784
Navy	196	210
Air Force	177	222
Sub-total MND	**1,513**	**1,562**
National Police	1,116	1,181
State funding for security	971	944
Total Security Budget	**3,600**	**3,687**

Table 31 **Venezuela: official defence budgets by service, 1997–1999**			
(1997 US$m)	1997	1998	1999
Army	278	249	276
Navy	139	124	126
Air Force	138	130	132
National Guard	222	195	201
Sub-total	**777**	**699**	**736**
Procurement and other	764	581	598
Total	**1,541**	**1,280**	**1,334**

Table 32 **Venezuela: official defence budgets by function, 1997–1999**			
(1997 US$m)	1997	1998	1999
Personnel	1,213	1,009	1,027
Operations & Maintenance	236	212	278
Procurement	91	60	30
Total	**1,540**	**1,281**	**1,334**

The outgoing *Caldera* initially set Venezuela's 1999 defence budget at B859bn ($1.5bn), and then cut it to B805bn ($1.4bn). However, the new government headed by President Chavez is committed to the 20% public sector pay increase approved by the *Caldera* in April 1999, so 1999 defence spending is likely to stay at the level originally planned. The Air Force ordered eight AMX training aircraft and light FGAs from collaborative partners Italy and Brazil in late 1998, following orders earlier in the year for 12 SF-260 primary trainers and 10 MB-339FD advanced trainers from Italy. Air defence modernisation is under way with the *Guardian* upgrade involving the integration of new *Flycatcher* radars from the Netherlands and the *Barak*-1 SAM from Israel. Six AS-532 *Cougar* helicopters are due for delivery from France in 2000. Modernisation in the US of two of the 6 *Lupo*-class frigates was funded in 1998.

Table 33 Arms orders and deliveries, Caribbean and Latin America, 1997–1999

Supplier	Classification	Designation	Units	Order Date	Delivery Date	Comment
Argentina						
Fr	hel	AS-555	4	1991	1997	
US	ac	OV-1D	11	1995	1996	
US	FGA	A-4AR	36	1995	1997	Upgrade
UK	APC	Tactica	9	1995	1997	
dom	arty	155mm		1995	1996	Development
US	hel	UH-1H	8	1996	1998	Acquired ex US
US	MPA	P-3B	8	1996	1997	Deliveries to 1999
US	hel	H-300C	2	1996	1997	
US	tpt	C-130B	5	1996	1997	
US	LAW	M72	900	1997	1999	
US	FGA	A-4M	8	1997	1999	Further 11 for cannibalisation
US	hel	UH-1H	8	1997	1998	
US	tkr ac	KC-135	1	1998	2000	
Fr	AO	Durance	1	1998	1999	
Bahamas						
US	tpt	C-26	2	1997	1998	
US	OPV	Bahamas	2	1997	1999	Contract options for 4 more
Bolivia						
dom	PFC	PFC	23	1997	1999	
US	FGA	TA-4J	18	1997	1998	12 for op and 6 for spare parts. Ex-USN ac
Brazil						
dom	AAM	MAA-1	40	1976	1998	Under test since mid-1998
Col	FGA	AM-X	54	1980	1989	Deliveries continue. 2 delivered 1997
Fr	hel	AS-350	77	1985	1988	Prod under licence continues at low rate
Ge	SSK	Type 209	5	1985	1994	First 1989. 2 1994–96. 2 launched 1998
Ge	PCI	Grauna	10	1986	1993	Last 2 delivered 1997–98
UK	hel	Lynx	9	1993	1996	Deliveries 1996–97
dom	MRL	ASTROS 2	20	1994	1998	4 ordered 1996, 16 1998
Be	MBT	Leopard 1	87	1995	1997	55 delivered 1998–99
US	APC	AAV-7	14	1995	1997	
US	hel	UH-1H	20	1995	1997	
UK	MSC	River	4	1995	1998	Ex-UK RN. Deliveries delayed from 1995
US	MBT	M-60A3	91	1995	1997	
US	hel	S-70A	4	1995	1997	Formerly based in Ec for MOMEP duties
dom	FF	Niteroi	6	1995	1999	Upgrade
It	arty	105mm	10	1995	1997	
It	arty	155mm	15	1996	1997	
dom	AEW	EMB-145	8	1997	2001	5 AEW, 3 Remote Sensing
Fr	tpt	F-406	5	1997	1999	For delivery 1999–2001
dom	ATGW	MSS-1.2	40	1997	2001	Development
Col	FGA	AM-X	13	1998	2001	3rd batch
Kwt	FGA	A-4	23	1998	1998	Ex-Kwt Air Force. Includes 3 TA-4
It	PCI	Grajau	16	1998		Based on Meatini (G-11) class
Il	FGA	F-5	45	1998	2000	Upgrade
dom	trg	AL-X	99	1995	1999	First 33 to be delivered 1999
UK	arty	105mm	18	1999	2001	
Swe	torp	Tp-62	50	1999	2000	For Tupi SS
US	MPA	P-3A/B	12	1999	2002	
Chile						
Il	ASSM	Gabriel	10	1995	1997	
Il	FAC	Saar 4.5	2	1995	1997	

Supplier	Classification	Designation	Units	Order Date	Delivery Date	Comment
dom	FGA	A-36	3	1995	1997	Upgrade
Fr	SAM	*Mistral*	12	1995	1997	
Ge	FAC	Type 148	4	1995	1997	Ex-Ge Navy; built in Fr
Be	APC	M-113	128	1995	1998	
Swe	MCMV	Minelayer	1	1995	1997	
Sp	tpt	C-212	3	1995	1997	Deliveries to 1997 for a total of 9
Fr	trg	C-101	2	1995	1997	1st upgrade to *Halcon* II delivered
UK	ASSM	MM-38 *Exocet*	4	1996	1998	*Excalibur* ASSM; refurbished in Fr
Fr	MBT	AMX-30B	60	1996	1998	Ex-Fr Army
US	recce	*Caravan 1*	3	1996	1998	
US	tpt	C-130B	4	1996	1997	
UK	arty	M101	100	1996	1998	Upgrade
Col	MRL	*Rayo*		1996	1999	Development Programme
US	tpt	R-182	8	1997	1998	
RSA	arty	M71	24	1997	1998	
Ge	PGG	*Tiger*	2	1997	1998	
Fr	SS	*Scorpene*	2	1997	2003	1st to be commissioned 2003, 2nd 2005
US	hel	UH-60	12	1998	1998	First delivery Jul 1998
dom	MPA	P-3	2	1998	1999	Upgrade for up to 8
Nl	MBT	*Leopard 1*	200	1998	1999	First batch of 14 delivered Jan 1999

Colombia

US	hel	UH-1H	20	1994	1996	Deliveries 1996 and 1997
US	tpt	C-130B	7	1995	1997	
Sp	tpt	CN-235	3	1996	1998	
RF	hel	Mi-17	10	1997	1997	
dom	utl	*Gavilan*	12	1997	1998	
US	hel	B-212	6	1998	1998	First 3 to arrive in Jul/Aug 1998
US	hel	UH-60L	6	1998	1999	For delivery Sep 1999–Jan 2000
US	hel	UH-1	25	1998	1999	For delivery 1999
US	hel	MD-530F	2	1998	1999	National Police

Ecuador

Nic	AAA	ZU-23	34	1996	1997	
Nic	MBT	T-55	3	1996	1997	
Il	AAM	*Python 3*	100	1996	1999	
US	ASW hel	Bell 412EP	2	1996	1998	1st delivered late 1998, 2nd early 1999
RF	SAM	SA-8		1996	1997	
RF	hel	Mi-17	7	1997	1998	
Il	FGA	*Kfir*	11	1998	1999	Upgrade.
Il	FGA	*Kfir*	2	1998	1999	Ex-IAF; also upgrade of 11

El Salvador

US	ACV	*Hummer*	2			
US	hel	MD-520N	2	1997	1998	

Guatemala

dom	APC	*Danto*		1994	1998	For internal security duties
Chl	trg	T-35B	10	1997	1998	Ex-Chl Air Force

Honduras

US	FGA	*Super Mystere*	11	1997	1998	

Jamaica

Fr	hel	AS-555	4	1997	1999	

Mexico

RF	tpt	An-32	2			
dom	PCO		1	1993	1997	First indigenously built warship
US	hel	UH-1H	73	1993	1996	For counter-drug op and disaster relief
Be	lt tk	AMX 13	136	1994	1995	97 delivered 1995, 5 1996 and 34 1998

Supplier	Classification	Designation	Units	Order Date	Delivery Date	Comment
US	hel	B-206	18	1995	1996	
Ukr	hel	Mi-17	12	1995	1997	*Erint* delivered 1998
US	FF	*Knox*	3	1996	1998	Third for delivery 1999
US	recce	C-26	4	1996	1997	For counter-drug surveillance
US	LST	*Newport*	1	1998	1999	Excess Defense Articles (EDA)
US	hel	MD-520N	8	1998	1999	
Nicaragua						
US	PFC	IMT	6			
US	OPV	*Protector*	2			
Panama						
ROC	hel	UH-1H	5	1997	1997	Free transfer
Paraguay						
ROC	tpt hel	UH-1H	2	1997	1997	
ROC	FGA	F-5E	4	1997	1998	Total of 12 in all
ROC	PCI		2	1998	1999	Free transfer
Peru						
Bel	FGA	Su-25	18	1995	1998	
Bel	FGA	MiG-29	18	1995	1996	Deliveries 1996–97
RF	FGA	MiG-29	3	1998	1998	Plus spares
Fr	ASSM	*Exocet*	8	1995	1997	Deliveries to 1998
It	ASSM	*Otomat*	12	1995	1997	Deliveries to 1998
RF	tpt	Il-103	6	1999	1999	
Cz	arty	D-30	6	1998	1998	
Cz	trg	ZLIN-242L	18	1998	1998	
Suriname						
Sp	MPA	C-212-400	2	1997	1998	Second delivered 1999
Uruguay						
UK	tac hel	*Wessex*	6	1996	1997	Free transfer
Il	MBT	T-55	11	1996	1997	Deliveries to 1998
Cz	MRL	RM-70	1	1998	1998	
Cz	SP arty	2S1	6	1998	1998	
Venezuela						
US	PCI	*Integridad*	10	1991	1997	
RF	hel	Mi-17	18	1995	1996	Deliveries into 1997, refurbished in Pl
Pl	tpt	M-28	12	1996	1996	Deliveries 1996–98
Sp	MPA	C-212	3	1997	1998	Plus modernisation of existing C-212-200
US	FGA	F-16B	2	1997	1999	
US	hel	B-212	2	1997	1999	US grant aid for counter-drug op
Fr	hel	AS-532	6	1997	2000	
US	hel	UH-1H	5	1997	1999	
Swe	ATGW	AT-4		1997	1999	
US	FF	*Lupo*	2	1998	2001	Upgrade and modernisation
Swe	radar	*Giraffe*	4	1998	1999	4 truck-mounted systems
It	trg	SF-260E	12	1998	1999	Requirement for 12 more
US	PCI	PCI	12	1998	1999	Aluminium 80 foot craft
US	PCI	PCI	10	1998	1999	Aluminium 54 foot craft
It	trg	MB-339FD	10	1998	2000	Req for up to 24. Deliveries to 2001
It	FGA	AMX	8	1998	2001	In cooperation with Br. Up to 24 req
US	SAR hel	AB-412EP	4	1998	1999	Option for a further 2
Il	SAM	*Barak-1*	3	1999	2000	Part of *Guardian* Air Defence modernisation
Swe	SAM	RBS-70	500	1999	2000	Includes AT-4 ATGW
Fr	radar	*Flycatcher*	3	1999	2000	Deliveries to early 2002. Part of *Guardian*

Dollar GDP figures for several countries in Latin America are based on Inter-American Development Bank estimates. In some cases, the dollar conversion rates are different from the average exchange rate values shown under the country entry. Dollar GDP figures may vary from those cited in *The Military Balance* in previous years. Defence budgets and expenditures have been converted at the dollar exchange rate used to calculate GDP.

Antigua and Barbuda   AB

	1997	1998	1999	2000
GDP	EC$1.6bn	EC$1.7bn		
	($580m)	($610m)		
per capita	$5,500	$5,700		
Growth	5.3%	2.8%		
Inflation	2.0%	2.0%		
Ext Debt	$365m	$357m		
Def exp	EC$7m	EC$11m		
	($3m)	($4m)		
Def bdgt		EC$11m	EC$11m	
		($4m)	($4m)	
FMA		$0.1m	$0.1m	$0.1m
US$1=EC$ (East Caribbean dollar)				
	2.7	2.7	2.7	
Population				71,000
Age	*13–17*	*18–22*	*23–32*	
Men	5,000	5,000	6,000	
Women	5,000	5,000	8,000	

Total Armed Forces

ACTIVE 150

(all services form combined Antigua and Barbuda Defence Force)

RESERVES 75

Army 125

Navy 25

BASE St Johns
PATROL CRAFT 2
  PATROL, INSHORE 3
  1 *Swift* PCI with 1 12.7mm, 2 7.62mm gun
  1 *Dauntless* PCI with 1 7.62mm gun
  1 *Point* PCI

Argentina   Arg

	1997	1998	1999	2000
GDP	P323bn	P342bn		
	($273bn)	($289bn)		
per capita	$9,700	$10,200		
Growth	7.8%	4.0%		
Inflation	0.5%	1.0%		
Debt	$111bn	$138bn		
Def exp	P5.0bn	P5.3bn		
	($5.0bn)	($5.3bn)		
Def bdgt		P3.7bn	P3.9bn	P4.0bn
		($3.7bn)	($3.9bn)	($4.0bn)
FMA (US)	$0.6m	$0.6m	$0.6m	$0.8m
$1=peso	1.0	1.0	1.0	
Population				35,467,000
Age	*13–17*	*18–22*	*23–32*	
Men	1,631,000	1,598,000	2,710,000	
Women	1,578,000	1,551,000	2,645,000	

Total Armed Forces

ACTIVE 70,500

RESERVES 375,000

Army 250,000 (incl **National Guard** 200,000 **Territorial Guard** 50,000) **Navy** 75,000 **Air Force** 50,000

Army 40,000

3 Corps
  1 with 1 armd, 1 mech bde, 1 trg bde
  1 with 1 inf, 1 mtn bde
  1 with 1 armd, 3 mech, 1 mtn bde
Corps tps: 1 lt armd cav regt (recce), 1 arty, 1 AD arty, 1 engr bn in each Corps

STRATEGIC RESERVE

1 AB bde
1 mech bde (4 mech, 1 armd cav, 2 SP arty bn)
Army tps
  1 mot inf bn (Army HQ Escort Regt) • 1 mot cav regt (Presidential Escort) • 1 SF coy, 3 avn bn • 1 AD arty bn, 2 engr bn

EQUIPMENT
  MBT 200 TAM
  LT TK 56 AMX-13, 106 SK-105 *Kuerassier*
  RECCE 48 AML-90
  AIFV 165 AMX-VCI, 100 VCTP
  APC 129 M-5 half-track, 300 M-113, 70 MOWAG *Grenadier* (mod *Roland*)
  TOWED ARTY 105mm: 184 M56 *Oto Melara*; **155mm:** 109 CITEFA Models 77/-81
  SP ARTY 155mm: 24 Mk F3, 10 VCA (*Palmaria*)
  MRL 105mm: <10 SLAM *Pampero*; **127mm:** <10 SLAM SAPBA-1
  MOR 81mm: 1,100; **120mm:** 309 Brandt (37 SP in

VCTM AIFV)
ATGW 600 SS-11/-12, *Cobra (Mamba)*, 2,100 *Mathogo*
RL 66mm: M-72
RCL 75mm: 75 M-20; **90mm:** 100 M-67; **105mm:** 930
M-1968
AD GUNS 30mm: 120; **35mm:** 100 GDF-001; **40mm:**
250 L/60/-70 (in store); **90mm:** 20
SAM <40† *Tigercat*, <40† *Blowpipe*, 6 *Roland*
SURV RASIT also RATRAS (veh, arty), *Green Archer*
(mor), *Skyguard*
AC 1 C212-200, 5 Cessna 207, 5 *Commander* 690, 3
DHC-6, 3 G-222, 1 *Merlin IIIA*, 5 *Merlin IV*, 1
Queen Air, 1 *Sabreliner*, 5 T-41, 23 OV-1D
HEL 6 A-109, 3 AS-332B, 1 Bell 212, 4 FH-1100, 5 SA-
315B, 1 SA-330, 10 UH-1H, 8 UH-12

Navy 20,000

(incl 2,000 Naval Aviation and 2,800 Marines)
NAVAL AREAS Centre from River Plate to 42° 45' S
South from 42° 45' S to Cape Horn **Antarctica**
BASES Buenos Aires, Espora (Naval Air), Treleur, Rio
Santiago (shipbuilding), Puerto Belgrano (HQ Centre),
Punta Indio (Naval Air training), Mar del Plata
(submarine base), Ushuaia (HQ South), Caleta Paula
(fisheries protection)
SERVICEABILITY very poor throughout Navy

SUBMARINES 3
SSK 3
2 *Santa Cruz* (Ge TR-1700) with 533mm TT (SST-4
HWT)
1 *Salta* (Ge T-209/1200) with 533mm TT (SST-4 HWT)

PRINCIPAL SURFACE COMBATANTS 13
DESTROYERS
DDG 6
2 *Hercules* (UK Type 42) with 1 x 2 *Sea Dart* SAM; plus
1 SA-319 hel (ASW), 2 x 3 ASTT, 4 MM-38 *Exocet*
SSM, 1 114mm gun (incl 1 in reserve)
4 *Almirante Brown* (Ge MEKO 360) with 2 SA-316 hel,
2 x 3 ASTT, 8 MM-40 *Exocet* SSM, 1 127mm gun
FRIGATES
FFG 7
4 *Espora* (Ge MEKO 140) with 2 x 3 ASTT, hel deck, 4
MM-38 *Exocet* SSM
3 *Drummond* (Fr A-69) with 2 x 3 ASTT, 4 MM-38
Exocet SSM, 1 100mm gun

PATROL AND COASTAL COMBATANTS 14
TORPEDO CRAFT 2 *Intrepida* (Ge Lürssen 45m) PFT
with 2 533mm TT (SST-4 HWT) (one poss with 2
MM-38 SSM)
PATROL, OFFSHORE 8
1 *Teniente Olivieri* (ex-US oilfield tug)
3 *Irigoyen* (US *Cherokee* AT)
2 *King* (trg) with 3 105mm guns
2 *Sobral* (US *Sotoyomo* AT)
PATROL, INSHORE 4 *Baradero* (*Dabur*) PCI<

AMPHIBIOUS craft only
4 LCM, 16 LCVP
SUPPORT AND MISCELLANEOUS 10
1 AGOR, 3 tpt, 1 AT/F, 1 icebreaker, 2 trg, 1 AGOR,
1 Fr *Durance* AO/T (in refit)

NAVAL AVIATION (2,000)
31 cbt ac, 8† armed hel
Carrier air crew training on Brazilian CV *Minas Gerais*
ATTACK 1 sqn with 6 *Super Etendard*
MR/ASW 1 sqn with 5 S-2E/T, 5 P-3B, 4 *Super King Air*
200, 10 Cessna-337
EW 1 L-188E
HEL 2 sqn
1 ASW/tpt with 4 ASH-3H (ASW) and 2 AS-61D
(tpt), 4 AS-555
1 spt with 6 SA-316
TPT 1 sqn with 3 F-28-3000, 3 L-188, 4 *Queen Air* 80, 9
Super King Air
SURVEY 3 PC-6B (Antarctic flt)
TRG 2 sqn with 7* EMB-326, 9* MB-326 *Xavante*, 5*
MB-339A, 10 T-34C
MISSILES
ASM AM-39 *Exocet*, AS-12, *Martín Pescador*
AAM R-550 *Magic*

MARINES (2,800)
FLEET FORCES 2 (being reorg into 7 coy gp), each with
2 bn, 1 amph recce coy, 1 fd arty bn, 1 atk, 1 engr coy
AMPH SPT FORCE 1 marine inf bn
1 AD arty regt (bn)
2 SF bn
EQUIPMENT
RECCE 12 ERC-90 *Lynx*
AAV 21 LVTP-7
APC 6 MOWAG *Grenadier*, 35 Panhard VCR
TOWED ARTY 105mm: 15 M-101/Model 56;
155mm: 6 M-114
MOR 81mm: 70
ATGW 50 *Bantam*, *Cobra (Mamba)*
RL 89mm: 60 M-20
RCL 105mm: 30 1974 FMK1
AD GUNS 30mm: 10 HS-816; **35mm:** GDF-001
SAM *Blowpipe*, *Tigercat*
HEL 8 UH-1H (reported)

Air Force 10,500

125 cbt ac, 27 armed hel, 9 air bde, 10 AD arty bty, 1 SF
(AB) coy
AIR OPERATIONS COMMAND (9 bde)
FGA/FTR 7 sqn
3 with 4 *Mirage* 5P, 14 Mirage IIIEA, 19 *Dagger Nesher*
(17 -A, 2 -B)
2 with 20 A-4AR, 5 TA-4AR (31 A-4AR by end 2000)
2 with 39 IA-58A
TKR 2 KC-130H

SAR 3 SA-315 hel
TPT 5 sqn: **ac** 1 Boeing 757 (VIP), 3 Boeing 707, 5 C-130B, 6 -H, 1 L-100-30, 6 DHC-6, 10 F-27, 4 F-28, 5 IA-50, 2 *Merlin* IVA, 1 S-70A (VIP); Antarctic spt unit with 1 DHC-6 **hel** 4 Bell 212, 1 CH-47C, 17 MD-500 (armed), 10 UH-1H (armed)
SURVEY/RECCE/CAL 1 sqn with 2 Boeing 707, 2 IA-50, 3 *Learjet* 35, 1 PA-31
LIAISON 1 sqn with 20 Cessna 182, 1 C-320, 7 *Commander*, 1 *Sabreliner*
AIR TRAINING COMMAND
  AC 27 EMB-312, 14* IA-63, 10* MS-760, 30 T-34B, 8 Su-29AR
  HEL 3 Hughes 500D
MISSILES
  ASM ASM-2 *Martín Pescador*
  AAM AIM-9B *Sidewinder*, R-530, R-550, *Shafrir*

Forces Abroad

UN AND PEACEKEEPING
CROATIA (UNMOP): 1 obs CYPRUS (UNFICYP) 412: 1 inf bn IRAQ/KUWAIT (UNIKOM): 84 engr KOSOVO 500 troops offered MIDDLE EAST (UNTSO): 3 obs WESTERN SAHARA (MINURSO): 1 obs

Paramilitary 31,240

GENDARMERIE (Ministry of Interior) 18,000
5 Regional Comd, 16 bn
  EQPT Shorland recce, 40 UR-416; **81mm** mor; **ac** 3 *Piper*, 5 PC-6 **hel** 5 SA-315
PREFECTURA NAVAL (Coast Guard) 13,240
7 comd
  SERVICEABILITY better than Navy
  EQPT 5 *Mantilla*, 1 *Delfin* PCO, 1 *Mandubi* PCO; 4 PCI, 21 PCI< plus boats; **ac** 5 C-212 **hel** 2 AS-330L, 1 AS-365, 3 AS-565MA, 2 Bell-47, 2 Schweizer-300C

Bahamas

	1997	1998	1999	2000
				Bs
GDP	B$3.4bn	B$3.6bn		
	($3.4bn)	($3.6bn)		
per capita	$13,500	$13,900		
Growth	3.5%	2.5%		
Inflation	0.5%	1.4%		
Debt	$362m	$325m		
Def exp	B$22m	B$22m		
	($22m)	($22m)		
Def bdgt		B$22m	B$23m	
		($22m)	($23m)	
FMA (US)	$1.1m	$1.1m	$1.1m	$1.1m
US$1=B$	1.0	1.0	1.0	

Population			293,000
Age	13–17	18–22	23–32
Men	14,000	15,000	31,000
Women	13,000	14,000	29,000

Total Armed Forces

ACTIVE 860

Navy (Royal Bahamian Defence Force) 860

(incl 70 women)
BASE Coral Harbour, New Providence Island
MILITARY OPERATIONS PLATOON 1
  ε120; Marines with internal and base sy duties
PATROL AND COASTAL COMBATANTS 7
PATROL, INSHORE 7
  3 *Protector* PFI, 1 *Marlin*, 2 *Cape* PFI, 1 *Kieth Nelson* PFI
SUPPORT AND MISCELLANEOUS 8
  1 *Fort Montague* (AG), 2 *Dauntless* (AG), 2 converted fishing vessels, 1 diving boat, 1 LCM, 1 AG
HARBOUR PATROL UNITS 4
  2 *Boston* whaler, 2 *Wahoo*
AIRCRAFT 4
  1 Cessna 404, 1 Cessna 421C, 2 C-26

Barbados

	1997	1998	1999	2000
				Bds
GDP	B$4.4bn	B$4.7bn		
	($2.2bn)	($2.3bn)		
per capita	$6,300	$6,600		
Growth	0.9%	3.3%		
Inflation	7.7%	1.5%		
Debt	$507m	$499m		
Def exp	B$23m	B$23m		
	($12m)	($12m)		
Def bdgt		B$22m	B$23m	
		($11m)	($12m)	
FMA		$0.1m	$0.1m	$0.1m
US$1=B$	2.0	2.0	2.0	

Population			265,000
Age	13–17	18–22	23–32
Men	11,000	11,000	23,000
Women	11,000	11,000	22,000

Total Armed Forces

ACTIVE 610

RESERVES 430

Army 500

Navy 110

BASES St Ann's Fort Garrison (HQ), Bridgetown
PATROL AND COASTAL COMBATANTS 3
PATROL, OFFSHORE 2
  1 *Kebir* PCO with 2 12.7mm gun
  1 *Dauntless* PCI
PATROL, INSHORE 3 *Guardian* II PCI< plus boats

Belize   Bze

	1997	1998	1999	2000
GDP	BZ$1.2bn	BZ$1.3bn		
	($610m)	($640m)		
per capita	$2,700	$2,700		
Growth	4.4%	3.4%		
Inflation	1.0%	-0.7%		
Debt	$233m	$252m		
Def exp	εBZ$31m	εBZ$33m		
	($16m)	($17m)		
Def bdgt		BZ$17m	BZ$17m	
		($8m)	($9m)	
FMA (US)	$0.2m	$0.3m	$0.3m	$0.3m
US$1=BZ$	2.0	2.0	2.0	
Population				237,000
Age	*13–17*	*18–22*	*23–32*	
Men	14,000	12,000	19,000	
Women	14,000	12,000	19,000	

Total Armed Forces

ACTIVE ε1,050

RESERVES 700

Army ε1,050

3 inf bn (each 3 inf coy), 1 spt gp, 3 Reserve coy
EQUIPMENT
  MOR 81mm: 6
  RCL 84mm: 8 *Carl Gustav*

MARITIME WING
  PATROL CRAFT 2 *Wasp* PCI, plus some 9 armed
  boats and 3 LCU

AIR WING
No cbt ac or armed hel
  MR/TPT 2 BN-2B *Defender*
  TRG 1 T 67-200 *Firefly*

Bolivia   Bol

	1997	1998	1999	2000
GDP	B41.1bn	B47.3bn		
	($7.8bn)	($8.3bn)		
per capita	$2,700	$2,800		
Growth	4.3%	4.5%		
Inflation	4.7%	7.6%		
Debt	$5.5bn	$5.5bn		
Def exp	B786m	B828m		
	($155m)	($150m)		
Def bdgt			B828m	B762m
			($150m)	($134m)
FMA (US)	$46m	$36m	$41m	$49m
$1=boliviano	5.3	5.5	5.7	
Population				8,137,000
Age	*13–17*		*18–22*	*23–32*
Men	418,000		337,000	546,000
Women	424,000		360,000	581,000

Total Armed Forces

ACTIVE 32,500 (to be 35,000)
(incl some 22,800 conscripts)
Terms of service 12 months, selective

Army 25,000

(incl some 18,000 conscripts)
HQ: 6 Mil Regions
Army HQ direct control
  2 armd bn • 1 mech cav regt • 1 Presidential Guard
  inf regt
10 'div'; org, composition varies; comprise
  8 cav gp (5 horsed, 2 mot, 1 aslt) • 1 mot inf 'regt'
  with 2 bn • 22 inf bn (incl 5 inf aslt bn) • 10 arty
  'regt' (bn) • 1 AB 'regt' (bn) • 6 engr bn
EQUIPMENT
  LT TK 36 SK-105 *Kuerassier*
  RECCE 24 EE-9 *Cascavel*
  APC 18 M-113, 10 V-100 *Commando*, 20 MOWAG
  Roland, 24 EE-11 *Urutu*
  TOWED ARTY 75mm: 70 incl M-116 pack, ε10
  Bofors M-1935; **105mm**: 30 incl M-101, FH-18;
  122mm: 18 PRC Type-54
  MOR 81mm: 50; **107mm**: M-30
  AC 1 C-212, 1 *King Air* B90, 1 *Cheyenne* II, 1 *Seneca*
  III, 5 Cessna (4 -206, 1 -421B)

Navy 4,500

(incl 1,700 Marines and 1,800 conscripts)
NAVAL AREAS 3 (Strategic Logistic Support)
NAVAL DISTRICTS 6, covering Lake Titicaca and the
rivers; each 1 flotilla
BASES Riberalta (HQ), Tiquina (HQ), Puerto Busch,

Puerto Guayaramerín (HQ), Puerto Villaroel, Trinidad (HQ), Puerto Suárez (HQ), Cobija (HQ), Santa Cruz (HQ), Bermejo (HQ), Cochabamba (HQ), Puerto Villarroel

PATROL CRAFT, RIVERINE some 67 riverine craft/boats (42 *Zodiac*, 1 *Rayder*, 14 *Guardian*, 10 *Nav Sea*), plus 8 US *Boston* whalers and 27 *Rodman* small PC

SUPPORT AND MISCELLANEOUS some 18 logistic support and patrol craft

MARINES (1,700)

6 bn (1 in each District)

Air Force 3,000

(incl perhaps 2,000 conscripts); 50 cbt ac, 10 armed hel
FGA 18 AT-33AN
ARMED HEL 1 sqn with 10 Hughes 500M hel
SAR 1 hel sqn with 4 HB-315B, 2 SA-315B, 1 UH-1
SURVEY 1 sqn with 5 Cessna 206, 1 C-210, 1 C-402, 3 *Learjet* 25/35
TPT 3 sqn
    1 VIP tpt with 1 L-188, 1 *Sabreliner*, 2 *Super King Air*
    2 tpt with 14 C-130A/B/H, 4 F-27-400, 1 IAI-201, 2 *King Air*, 2 C-47, 4 *Convair* 580
LIAISON ac 9 Cessna 152, 1 C-185, 13 C-206, 1 C-208, 2 C-402, 2 Beech *Bonanza*, 2 Beech *Barons*, PA-31, 4 PA-34 **hel** 2 Bell 212, 22 UH-1H
TRG 1 Cessna 152, 2 C-172, 20* PC-7, 4 SF-260CB, 15 T-23, 12* T-33A, 1 *Lancair* 320
AD 1 air-base def regt (Oerlikon twin **20mm**, 18 PRC Type-65 **37mm**, some truck-mounted guns)

Paramilitary 37,100

NATIONAL POLICE some 31,100

9 bde, 2 rapid action regt, 27 frontier units

NARCOTICS POLICE some 6,000

Brazil
Br

	1997	1998	1999	2000
GDP	R867bn	R901bn		
	($570bn)	($583bn)		
per capita	$5,900	$6,200		
Growth	3.6%	0.2%		
Inflation	7.5%	3.2%		
Debt	$193bn	$235bn		
Def exp	R20.0bn	R21.4bn		
	($18.5bn)	($18.4bn)		
Def bdgt		R16.1bn	R17.5bn	
		($13.8bn)	($10.3bn)	
FMA (US)	$0.9m	$0.7m	$1.4m	$1.7m
$1=real	1.1	1.2	1.7	

Population			170,057,000
Age	*13–17*	*18–22*	*23–32*
Men	8,722,000	8,216,000	14,381,000
Women	8,641,000	8,213,000	14,499,000

Total Armed Forces

ACTIVE 291,000

(incl 48,200 conscripts)
Terms of service 12 months (can be extended to 18)

RESERVES

Trained first-line 1,115,000; 400,000 subject to immediate recall **Second-line** 225,000

Army 189,000

(incl 40,000 conscripts)
HQ: 7 Mil Comd, 11 Mil Regions; 8 div (3 with Regional HQ)
    1 armd cav bde (2 armd cav, 1 armd, 1 arty bn), 3 armd inf bde (each 2 armd inf, 1 armd cav, 1 arty bn), 4 mech cav bde (each 2 mech cav, 1 armd cav, 1 arty bn) • 10 motor inf bde (26 bn) • 1 lt inf bde (3 bn) • 4 jungle bde • 1 frontier bde (6 bn) • 1 AB bde (3 AB, 1 arty bn) • 1 coast and AD arty bde (6 bn) • 3 cav guard regt • 10 arty gp (4 SP, 6 med) • 2 engr gp (9 bn) • 10 engr bn (incl 2 railway) (to be increased to 34 bn)
AVN 1 hel bde (1 bn of 4 sqn)
EQUIPMENT
    MBT 87 *Leopard* 1, 91 M-60A3
    LT TK 286 M-41B/C
    RECCE 409 EE-9 *Cascavel*
    APC 219 EE-11 *Urutu*, 584 M-113
    TOWED ARTY 105mm: 319 M-101/-102, 56 pack, 22 L118; **155mm**: 92 M-114
    SP ARTY 105mm: 72 M-7/-108
    MRL 108mm: SS-06; 16 ASTROS II
    MOR 81mm: 707; **107mm**: 236 M-30; **120mm**: 77 K6A3
    ATGW 4 *Milan*, 18 *Eryx*
    RL 84mm: 115 AT-4
    RCL 84mm: 127 *Carl Gustav*; **106mm**: 163 M-40A1
    AD GUNS 134 incl **35mm**: GDF-001; **40mm**: L-60/-70 (some with BOFI)
    SAM 4 *Roland* II, 40 SA-18
    HEL 3 S-70A, 35 SA-365, 19 AS-550 *Fennec*, 16 AS-350 (armed)

Navy 52,000

(incl 1,150 Naval Aviation, 13,900 Marines and 3,200 conscripts)
OCEANIC NAVAL DISTRICTS 5 plus 1 Riverine; 1 Comd
BASES Ocean Rio de Janeiro (*HQ I Naval District*), Salvador (*HQ II District*), Recife (*HQ III District*), Belém

(*HQ IV District*), Floriancholis (*HQ V District*) **River**
Ladario (*HQ VI District*), Manaus
SUBMARINES 4
SSK 4
  3 *Tupi* (Ge T-209/1400) with 533mm TT (UK *Tigerfish*
  HWT)
  1 *Humaitá* (UK *Oberon*) with 533mm TT (UK *Tigerfish*
  HWT)
PRINCIPAL SURFACE COMBATANTS 19
CARRIERS 1 *Minas Gerais* (UK *Colossus*) CV (ASW),
typically ASW **hel** 4–6 ASH-3H, 3 AS-332 and 2 AS-
355; has been used by Argentina for embarked
aircraft training
FRIGATES 14
FFG 6
  4 *Greenhaigh* (ex-UK *Broadsword*) with 4 MM-38
  Exocet SSM, *Seawolf* MOD 4 SAM
  2 *Constitução* with 1 *Lynx* hel, 2 x 3 ASTT, *Ikara*
  SUGW, 1 x 2 ASW mor, 2 MM-40 *Exocet* SSM, 1
  114mm gun
FF 8
  4 *Niteroi*; 2 114mm guns, 1 x 2 ASW mor, 2 x 3 ASTT,
  1 *Lynx* hel
  4 *Para* (US *Garcia*) with 1 x 8 ASROC ASW, 2 x 3
  ASTT, 1 *Lynx* hel; plus 2 127mm guns
CORVETTES 4
  4 *Inhauma*, with 1 *Lynx* hel, 2 x 3 ASTT, 4 MM-40
  Exocet SSM, 1 114mm gun
PATROL AND COASTAL COMBATANTS 37
PATROL, OFFSHORE 17
  7 *Imperial Marinheiro* PCO, 10 *Grajaü* PCC
PATROL, INSHORE 15
  6 *Piratini* (US PGM) PCI, 3 *Aspirante Nascimento* PCI
  (trg), 6 *Tracker* PCI<
PATROL, RIVERINE 5
  3 *Roraima* and 2 *Pedro Teixeira*
MINE COUNTERMEASURES 6
  6 *Aratü* (Ge *Schütze*) MSI
AMPHIBIOUS 4
  2 *Ceara* (US *Thomaston*) LSD capacity 350 tps, 38 tk
  1 *Duque de Caxais* (US *de Soto County* LST), capacity
  600 tps, 18 tk
  1 *Mattoso Maia* (US *Newport* LST) capacity 400 tps,
  500 tons veh, 3 LCVP, 1 LCPL
  Plus some 48 craft: 3 LCU, 10 LCM, 35 LCVP
SUPPORT AND MISCELLANEOUS 25
  2 polar research, 1 AGOR, 5 AGS, 16 buoy tenders, 1
  Mod *Niteroi* (tng)

NAVAL AVIATION (1,400)
22 cbt ac, 54 armed hel
FGA 22 A-4/TA-4 (being delivered)
ASW 6 SH-3B, 7 SH-3D, 6 SH-3G/H
ATTACK 14 *Lynx* MK-21A
UTL 2 sqn with 5 AS-332, 12 AS-350 (armed), 9 AS-355
  (armed)
TRG 1 hel sqn with 13 TH-57

ASM AS-11, AS-12, *Sea Skua*

MARINES (13,900)
FLEET FORCE 1 amph div (1 comd, 3 inf bn, 1 arty gp)
REINFORCEMENT COMD 5 bn incl 1 engr, 1 SF
INTERNAL SECURITY FORCE 8+ regional gp
EQUIPMENT
  RECCE 6 EE-9 Mk IV *Cascavel*
  AAV 11 LVTP-7A1, 13 AAV-7A1
  APC 28 M-113, 5 EE-11 *Urutu*
  TOWED ARTY 105mm: 15 M-101, 18 L-118;
    155mm: 6 M-114
  MOR 81mm; 120mm: 8 K 6A3
  ATGW RB-56 *Bill*
  RL 89mm: 3.5in M-20
  RCL 106mm: 8 M-40A1
  AD GUNS 40mm: 6 L/70 with BOFI

Air Force 50,000

(incl 5,000 conscripts); 274 cbt ac, 29 armed hel
AIR DEFENCE COMMAND 1 gp
  FTR 2 sqn with 18 *Mirage* F-103E/D (14 *Mirage* IIIE/
    4 DBR)
TACTICAL COMMAND 10 gp
  FGA 3 sqn with 48 F-5E/-B/-F, 37 AMX
  CCT 2 sqn with 58 AT-26 (EMB-326)
  RECCE 2 sqn with 4 RC-95, 10 RT-26, 12 *Learjet* 35
    recce/VIP, 3 RC-130E
  LIAISON/OBS 7 sqn
    1 with **ac** 8 T-27
    5 with **ac** 31 U-7
    1 with **hel** 29 UH-1H (armed)
MARITIME COMMAND 4 gp
  MR/SAR 3 sqn with 10 EMB-110B, 20 EMB-111
TRANSPORT COMMAND
  6 gp (6 sqn)
    1 with 9 C-130H, 2 KC-130H • 1 with 4 KC-137
    (tpt/tkr) • 1 with 12 C-91 • 1 with 17 C-95A/B/C
    • 1 with 17 C-115 • 1 (VIP) with **ac** 1 VC-91, 12
    VC/VU-93, 2 VC-96, 5 VC-97, 5 VU-9, 2 Boeing
    737-200 **hel** 3 VH-4
  7 regional sqn with 7 C-115, 86 C-95A/B/C, 6 EC-9
    (VU-9)
  HEL 6 AS-332, 8 AS-355, 4 Bell 206, 27 HB-350B
  LIAISON 50 C-42, 3 Cessna 208, 30 U-42
TRAINING COMMAND
  AC 38* AT-26, 97 C-95 A/B/C, 25 T-23, 98 T-25, 61*
    T-27 (*Tucano*), 14* AMX-T
  HEL 4 OH-6A, 25 OH-13
  CAL 1 unit with 2 C-95, 1 EC-93, 4 EC-95, 1 U-93
MISSILES
  AAM AIM-9B *Sidewinder*, R-530, *Magic* 2,
    MAA-1 *Piranha*

Forces Abroad

UN AND PEACEKEEPING
CROATIA (UNMOP): 1 Obs

Paramilitary

PUBLIC SECURITY FORCES (R) some 385,600
in state mil pol org (state militias) under Army control
and considered Army Reserve

Chile   Chl

	1997	1998	1999	2000
GDP	pCh32.3tr	pCh36.0tr		
	($77.1bn)	($81.2bn)		
per capita	$11,300	$11,700		
Growth	5.5%	3.3%		
Inflation	6.3%	5.0%		
Debt	$28.6bn	$35.4bn		
Def exp	pCh1,225bn	pCh1,386bn		
	($2.9bn)	($3.0bn)		
Def bdgt		pCh969bn	pCh1,033bn	
		($2.1bn)	($2.1bn)	
FMA (US)	$0.4m	$0.5m	$0.5m	$0.5m
$1 =pCh (Chilean peso)				
	419	460	483	
Population				14,919,000
Age	*13–17*	*18–22*	*23–32*	
Men	697,000	632,000	1,223,000	
Women	671,000	610,000	1,195,000	

Total Armed Forces

ACTIVE 93,000
(incl 30,600 conscripts)
Terms of service **Army** 1 year **Navy** and **Air Force** 22
months

RESERVES 50,000
Army 50,000

Army 51,000
(incl 27,000 conscripts)
7 Mil Regions, 2 Corps HQ
8 div; org, composition varies; comprise
   14 mot inf, 9 mtn inf, 10 armd cav, 8 arty, 7 engr regt
Army tps: 1 avn bde, 1 engr, 1 AB regt (1 AB, 1 SF bn)
EQUIPMENT
MBT 100 M-4A3 (in store), 60 AMX-30, 67 *Leopard* 1
   (being delivered)
LT TK 21 M-24 (in store), 60 M-41 (being replaced
   by *Leopard* 1)

RECCE 50 EE-9 *Cascavel*
AIFV 20 MOWAG *Piranha* with **90mm** gun
APC 355 M-113, 180 Cardoen/MOWAG *Piranha*, 30
   EE-11 *Urutu*
TOWED ARTY 105mm: 66 M-101, 54 Model 56;
   155mm: 12 M-71
SP ARTY 155mm: 12 Mk F3
MOR 81mm: 300 M-29; **107mm**: 15 M-30; **120mm**:
   125 FAMAE (incl 50 SP)
ATGW *Milan/Mamba, Mapats*
RL 89mm: 3.5in M-20
RCL 150 incl: **57mm**: M-18; **106mm**: M-40A1
AD GUNS 20mm: 60 incl some SP (*Cardoen*/MOWAG)
SAM 50 *Blowpipe, Javelin*, 12 *Mistral*
AIRCRAFT
TPT 9 C-212, 1 *Citation* (VIP), 5 CN-235, 4 DHC-6, 3
   PA-31, 8 PA-28 Piper *Dakota*, 3 Cessna-208 *Caravan*
TRG 16 Cessna R-172, 8 Cessna R-182
HEL 2 AB-206, 3 AS-332, 15 Enstrom 280 FX, 21
   Hughes MD-530F (armed trg), 10 SA-315, 9 SA-330

Navy 29,000
(incl 600 Naval Aviation, 2,700 Marines, 1,300 Coast
Guard and 2,100 conscripts)
DEPLOYMENT AND BASES
MAIN COMMAND Fleet (includes DD and FF),
submarine flotilla, tpt. Remaining forces allocated to 4
Naval Zones **1st** 26ºS–36ºS approx: Valparaiso (HQ)
2nd 36ºS–43ºS approx: Talcahuano (HQ), Puerto Montt
3rd 43ºS to Antarctica: Punta Arenas (HQ), Puerto
Williams **4th** north of 26ºS approx: Iquique (HQ)
SUBMARINES 4
SSK 4
  2 *O'Brien* (UK *Oberon*) with 8 533mm TT (Ge HWT)
  2 *Thompson* (Ge T-209/1300) with 8 533mm TT (HWT)
PRINCIPAL SURFACE COMBATANTS 6
DESTROYERS
  DDG 3
   2 *Prat* (UK *Norfolk*) with 1 x 2 *Seaslug* 2 SAM, 4 MM-
    38 *Exocet* SSM, 1 x 2 114mm guns, 1 AB-206B hel, 2
    x 3 ASTT (Mk 44)
    (1 unit retains *Seaslug*, both have *Barak* SAM)
   1 *Blanco Encalada* (UK *Norfolk*) with 4 MM-38, *Exocet*
    SSM, 1 x 2 114mm guns, 2 AS-332F hel, 2 x 3 ASTT
    (Mk 44), 2 x 8 *Barak* 1 SAM, 1 with 1 x 2 *Seaslug*
    SAM in addition
FRIGATES
  FFG 3 *Condell* (mod UK *Leander*), 2 with 2 x 3 ASTT
   (Mk 44), 1 hel; plus 1 with 2 x 2 MM-40 *Exocet* SSM,
   1 with 2 MM-38 *Exocet* SSM, 1 x 2 114mm guns
PATROL AND COASTAL COMBATANTS 29
MISSILE CRAFT 8
  3 *Casma* (Il *Sa'ar* 4) PFM with 4 *Gabriel* SSM, 2 76mm gun
  1 *Iquique* (Il *Sa'ar* 3) with 6 *Gabriel* SSM, 1 76mm gun
  4 *Tiger* (Ge Type 148) PFM with 4 *Exocet* SSM, 1
   76mm gun

PATROL, OFFSHORE 4
3 *Taito* OPV, 1 *Vidal Gormaz* AGOR
PATROL, INSHORE 17
3 *Micalvi* PCC, 10 *Grumete Diaz* (Il *Dabur*) PCI<, 4
Guacolda (Ge Lürssen 36-m)

AMPHIBIOUS 3
2 *Maipo* (Fr *Batral*) LSM, capacity 140 tps, 7 tk
1 *Valdivia*† (US *Newport*) LST, capacity 400 tps, 500t
vehicles (non-op)
Plus craft: 2 *Elicura* LCT, 1 *Pisagua* LCU

SUPPORT AND MISCELLANEOUS 9
1 *Araucano* AO, 1 tpt, 1 ARS, 1 AS with mine-laying
capability, *Viel* antarctic patrol, 1 trg, 3 AT

NAVAL AVIATION (600)
8 cbt ac, 20 armed hel
MR 1 sqn with 4* EMB-111N, 4* P-3A *Orion*, 8
Cessna *Skymaster* (plus 2 in store)
ASW HEL 1 sqn with 6 AS-532 (4 with AM-39 *Exocet*,
2 with torp)
LIAISON 1 sqn with 3 C-212A
HEL 1 sqn with 8 BO-105, 6 UH-57
TRG 1 sqn with 6 PC-7
ASM AM-39 *Exocet*

MARINES (2,700)
4 gp: 4 inf, 2 trg bn, 4 cdo coy, 4 fd arty, 1 SSM bty, 4
AD arty bty • 1 amph bn
EQUIPMENT
LT TK 30 *Scorpion*
APC 40 MOWAG *Roland*
TOWED ARTY 105mm: 16 KH-178, **155mm**: 28 G-5
COASTAL GUNS 155mm: 16 GPFM-3
MOR 81mm: 50
SSM *Excalibur*
RCL 106mm: ε30 M-40A1
SAM *Blowpipe*

COAST GUARD (1,300)
(integral part of the Navy)
PATROL CRAFT 21
2 *Alacalufe*, 15 *Rodman* PCI, 4 *Pillan* PCI, plus about
30 boats

Air Force 13,000

(incl 1,500 conscripts); 90 cbt ac, no armed hel
Flying hours: 100
5 Air Bde, 5 wg
FGA 2 sqn
1 with 15 *Mirage* 5BA (MRIS), 6 *Mirage* BD (MRIS)
1 with 16 F-5 (13 -E, 3 -F)
CCT 2 sqn with 24 A-37B, 10 A-36
FTR/RECCE 1 sqn with 15 *Mirage* 50 (8 -FCH, 6 -CH, 1
-DCH), 4 *Mirage* 5-BR
RECCE 2 photo units with 1 *King Air* A-100, 2 *Learjet* 35A
AEW 1 IAI-707 *Phalcon*
TPT ac 3 Boeing 707(tkr), 1 Boeing 737-500 (VIP), 2 C-

130H, 4 C-130B, 4 C-212, 9 Beech 99 (ELINT, tpt,
trg), 14 DHC-6 (5 -100, 9 -300), 1 *Gulfstream* III (VIP),
1 *Beechcraft* 200 (VIP), 1 Cessna 206 (amph)
HEL 1 S-70A, 9 UH-1H (being replaced by S-70A at
rate of 1/yr), 12 UH-60, 8 Bo-105, 5 SA-315B
TRG 1 wg, 3 flying schools **ac** 16 PA-28, 19 T-35A/B, 13
T-36, 15 T-37B/C, 6 *Extra* 300 **hel** 3 Bell 206A
MISSILES
ASM AS-11/-12
AAM AIM-9B *Sidewinder*, *Shafrir*, *Python* III
AD 1 regt (5 gp) with **20mm**: S-639/-665, GAI-CO1
twin; **35mm**: Oerlikon GDF-005, MATRA *Mistral*,
Mygalle

Forces Abroad

UN AND PEACEKEEPING
INDIA/PAKISTAN (UNMOGIP): 4 obs **MIDDLE
EAST** (UNTSO): 3 obs

Paramilitary 29,500

CARABINEROS (Ministry of Defence) 29,500
8 zones, 38 districts
APC 20 MOWAG *Roland*
MOR 60mm, 81mm
AC 22 Cessna (6 C-150, 10 C-182, 6 C-206), 1 *Metro*
HEL 2 Bell 206, 12 Bo-105

Opposition

**FRENTE PATRIOTICO MANUEL RODRIGUEZ –
AUTONOMOUS FACTION** (FPMR-A) ε800
leftist

Colombia				Co
	1997	**1998**	**1999**	**2000**
GDP	pC104tr	pC126tr		
	($76bn)	($79bn)		
per capita	$6,100	$6,200		
Growth	3.2%	1.8%		
Inflation	18.5%	19.0%		
Debt	$31bn	$34bn		
Def exp	pC2.9tr	pC3.6tr		
	($2.5bn)	($2.5bn)		
Def bdgt		pC3.6tr	pC3.7tr	
		($2.5bn)	($2.3bn)	
FMA (US)	$33m	$44m	$39m	$41m
$1=pC (Colombian peso)				
	1,141	1,426	1,596	
Population				36,999,000
Age	*13–17*	*18–22*	*23–32*	
Men	1,946,000	1,848,000	3,301,000	
Women	1,857,000	1,778,000	3,251,000	

Total Armed Forces

ACTIVE 144,000

(incl some 74,700 conscripts)
Terms of service 12–18 months, varies (all services)

RESERVES 60,700

(incl 2,000 first-line) **Army** 54,700 **Navy** 4,800 **Air Force** 1,200

Army 121,000

(incl 63,800 conscripts)
5 div HQ
17 bde
  6 mech each with 3 inf, 1 mech cav, 1 arty, 1 engr bn
  2 air-portable each with 2 inf bn
  9 inf (8 with 2 inf bn, 1 with 4 inf bn)
2 arty bn
Army tps
  3 Mobile Counter Guerrilla Force (bde) (each with 1 cdo unit, 4 bn) – 2 more forming
  2 trg bde with 1 Presidential Guard, 1 SF, 1 AB, 1 mech, 1 arty, 1 engr bn
  1 AD arty bn
  1 army avn unit
EQUIPMENT
LT TK 30 M-3A1 (in store)
RECCE 12 M-8, 8 M-20, 120 EE-9 *Cascavel*
APC 80 M-113, 76 EE-11 *Urutu*, 4 RG-31 *Nyala*
TOWED ARTY 75mm: 50 M-116; **105mm:** 130 M-101
MOR 81mm: 125 M-1; **120mm:** 120 Brandt
ATGW TOW
RCL 106mm: M-40A1
AD GUNS 40mm: 30 Bofors
HEL 20: incl 10 Mi-17, OH-6A (reported)

Navy (incl Coast Guard) 15,000

(incl 8,500 Marines, 100 Naval Aviation and 7,000 conscripts)
BASES Ocean Cartagena (main), Buenaventura, Málaga (Pacific) **River** Puerto Leguízamo, Barranca-bermeja, Puerto Carreño (tri-Service Unified Eastern Command HQ), Leticia, Puerto Orocue, Puerto Inirida
SUBMARINES 4
SSK 2 *Pijao* (Ge T-209/1200) with 8 533mm TT (Ge HWT)
SSI 2 *Intrepido* (It SX-506) (SF delivery)
CORVETTES 4
  4 *Almirante Padilla* with 1 Bo-105 hel (ASW), 2 x 3 ASTT, 8 MM-40 *Exocet* SSM
PATROL AND COASTAL COMBATANTS 104
PATROL, OFFSHORE 6
  3 *Pedro de Heredia* (ex-US tugs), 1 *Esperanta* (Sp *Cormoran*) PCO, 2 *Lazaga* PCF

PATROL, INSHORE 9
  1 *Quito Sueno* (US *Asheville*) PFI, 2 *Castillo Y Rada* (*Swiftship* 32m) PCI, 2 *José Palas* PCI<, 2 *José Garcia* PCI<, 2 *Jaime Gomez* PCI
PATROL, RIVERINE 89
  3 *Arauca*, 10 *Diligente*, 9 *Tenerife*, 5 *Rio Magdalena*, 20 *Delfin*, 42 *Pirana*
SUPPORT AND MISCELLANEOUS 42
  3 AGOS, 21 AG, 17 AT, 1 trg

MARINES (8,500)

2 bde (each of 2 bn), 1 amph aslt, 1 river ops (15 amph patrol units), 1 SF, 1 sy bn
No hy eqpt (to get EE-9 *Cascavel* recce, EE-11 *Urutu* APC)

NAVAL AVIATION (100)

  AC 2 *Commander*, 2 PA-28, 2 PA-31
  HEL 2 Bo-105

Air Force 8,000

(some 3,900 conscripts); 72 cbt ac, 72 armed hel
AIR COMBAT COMMAND
FGA 2 sqn
  1 with 12 *Mirage* 5, 1 with 13 *Kfir* (11 -C2, 2 -TC2)
TACTICAL AIR SUPPORT COMMAND
CBT ac 1 AC-47, 2 AC-47T, 3 IA-58A, 22 A-37B, 6 AT-27
ARMED HEL 12 Bell 205, 5 Bell 212, 2 Bell 412, 2 UH-1B, 25 UH-60, 11 MD-500ME, 2 MD-500D, 3 MD-530F, 10 Mi-17
RECCE 8 *Schweizer* SA 2-37A, 13* OV-10, 3 C-26
MILITARY AIR TRANSPORT COMMAND
  AC 1 Boeing 707, 2 Boeing 727, 14 C-130B, 2 C-130H, 1 C-117, 2 C-47, 2 CASA 212, 2 *Bandeirante*, 1 F-28, 3 CN-235
  HEL 17 UH-1H
AIR TRAINING COMMAND
  AC 14 T-27 (*Tucano*), 3 T-34M, 13 T-37, 8 T-41
  HEL 2 UH-1B, 4 UH-1H, 12 F-28F
MISSILES
AAM AIM-9 *Sidewinder*, R-530

Forces Abroad

UN AND PEACEKEEPING
EGYPT (MFO) 358: 1 inf bn

Paramilitary 87,000

NATIONAL POLICE FORCE 87,000
  ac 5 OV-10A, 12 Gavilan, 11 *Turbo Thrush* hel 11 Bell-206L, 7 Bell-212, 2 Hughes 500D, 49 UH-1H, 3 UH-60L

COAST GUARD
integral part of Navy

Opposition

COORDINADORA NACIONAL GUERRILLERA SIMON BOLIVAR **(CNGSB)** loose coalition of guerrilla gp incl **Revolutionary Armed Forces of Colombia (FARC)** ε10,000 active; **National Liberation Army (ELN)** ε5,000, pro-Cuban; **People's Liberation Army (EPL)** ε500 **UNITED SELF DEFENCE FORCE OF COLOMBIA (AUC):** ε5,000 right-wing paramilitary group

Costa Rica CR

	1997	1998	1999	2000
GDP	C2.2tr	C2.6tr		
	($8.8bn)	($9.5bn)		
per capita	$6,600	$7,000		
Growth	3.2%	6.2%		
Inflation	13.2%	11.6%		
Debt	$3.4bn	$3.6bn		
Sy exp[a]	C13.6bn	C17.6bn		
	($59m)	($71m)		
Sy bdgt		C17.6bn	C19.8bn	
		($71m)	($72m)	
FMA (US)	$0.2m	$0.2m	$0.2m	$0.2m
$1=colon	233	249	274	

[a] No defence forces. Budgetary data are for border and maritime policing and internal security.

Population			3,659,000
Age	*13–17*	*18–22*	*23–32*
Men	191,000	172,000	299,000
Women	184,000	166,000	289,000

Total Armed Forces

ACTIVE Nil

Paramilitary 8,400

CIVIL GUARD 4,400
7 urban *comisaria*[a] • 1 tac police *comisaria* • 1 special ops unit • 6 provincial *comisaria*

BORDER SECURITY POLICE 2,000
2 Border Sy Comd (8 *comisaria*)
MARITIME SURVEILLANCE UNIT (300)
  BASES Pacific Golfito, Punta Arenas, Cuajiniquil, Quepos **Atlantic** Limon, Moin, Barra del Colorado
  PATROL CRAFT, INSHORE 8†
    1 *Isla del Coco* (US *Swift* 32m) PFI
    1 *Astronauta Franklin Chang* (US *Cape Higgon*) PCI
    6 PCI<; plus about 10 boats
AIR SURVEILLANCE UNIT (300)
  No cbt ac
  ac 1 Cessna O-2A, 1 DHC-4, 1 PA-31, 1 PA-34, 4 U206G **hel** 2 MD-500E, 1 Mi-17

RURAL GUARD (Ministry of Government and Police) 2,000
8 comd; small arms only

[a] *comisaria* = reinforced coy

Cuba C

	1997	1998	1999	2000
GDP	ε$14bn	ε$14bn		
per capita	$2,200	$2,300		
Growth	2.5%	1.2%		
Inflation	1.9%	2.7%		
Debt	$12bn	$12bn		
Def exp	ε$720m	ε$750m		
Def bdgt			P630m	
			($27m)	
$1=peso	22	23	23	

Population			11,254,000
Age	*13–17*	*18–22*	*23–32*
Men	408,000	402,000	1,064,000
Women	383,000	377,000	1,004,000

Total Armed Forces

ACTIVE ε65,000
Terms of service 2 years

RESERVES
Army 39,000 **Ready Reserves** (serve 45 days per year) to fill out Active and Reserve units; see also *Paramilitary*

Army ε45,000

(incl conscripts and Ready Reserves)
HQ: 3 Regional Comd, 3 Army
  4–5 armd bde • 9 mech inf bde (3 mech inf, 1 armd, 1 arty, 1 AD arty regt) • 1 AB bde • 14 reserve bde • 1 frontier bde
AD arty regt and SAM bde
EQUIPMENT † (some 75% in store)
  MBT ε1,500 incl: T-34, T-54/-55, T-62
  LT TK some PT-76
  RECCE some BRDM-1/-2
  AIFV some BMP-1
  APC ε700 BTR-40/-50/-60/-152
  TOWED ARTY 700: **76mm:** ZIS-3; **122mm:** M-1938, D-30; **130mm:** M-46; **152mm:** M-1937, D-1
  SP ARTY 40: **122mm:** 2S1; **152mm:** 2S3
  MRL 300: **122mm:** BM-21; **140mm:** BM-14
  MOR 1,000: **82mm:** M-41/-43; **120mm:** M-38/-43
  STATIC DEF ARTY JS-2 (**122mm**) hy tk, T-34 (**85mm**)
  ATGW AT-1 *Snapper*, AT-3 *Sagger*
  ATK GUNS 85mm: D-44; **100mm:** SU-100 SP, T-12

AD GUNS 400 incl: **23mm**: ZU-23, ZSU-23-4 SP; **30mm**: M-53 (twin)/BTR-60P SP; **37mm**: M-1939; **57mm**: S-60 towed, ZSU-57-2 SP; **85mm**: KS-12; **100mm**: KS-19
SAM SA-6/-7/-8/-9/-13/-14/-16

Navy ε5,000

(incl 550+ Naval Infantry, ε3,000 conscripts); 4 op flotillas
NAVAL DISTRICTS Western HQ Cabanas **Eastern** HQ Holquin
BASES Cienfuegos, Cabanas, Havana, Mariel, Punta Movida, Nicaro
SUBMARINES 1
SSK 1 Sov *Foxtrot* with 533mm and 406mm TT (non-op)
FRIGATES 2
FF 2 Sov *Koni* with 2 ASW RL (non-op)
PATROL AND COASTAL COMBATANTS 5
MISSILE CRAFT 4 Sov *Osa* I/II†
PATROL, COASTAL 1 Sov *Pauk* II PFC with 2 ASW RL, 4 ASTT
MINE COUNTERMEASURES 6
2 Sov *Sonya* MSC, 4 Sov *Yevgenya* MHC
SUPPORT AND MISCELLANEOUS 2
1 AGI, 1 AGHS
NAVAL INFANTRY (550+)
2 amph aslt bn
COASTAL DEFENCE
ARTY **122mm**: M-1931/37; **130mm**: M-46; **152mm**: M-1937
SSM 2 SS-C-3 systems, some mobile *Bandera* IV (reported)

Air Force ε10,000

(incl AD and conscripts); 130† cbt ac of which only some 25 are operational, 45 armed hel
Flying hours less than 50
FGA 2 sqn with 10 MiG-23BN
FTR 4 sqn
    2 with 30 MiG-21F, 1 with 50 MiG-21bis, 1 with 20 MiG-23MF, 6 MiG-29
    (Probably only some 3 MiG-29, 10 MiG-23, 5 MiG-21bis in operation)
ATTACK HEL 45 Mi-8/-17, Mi-25/35
ASW 5 Mi-14 hel
TPT 4 sqn with 8 An-2, 1 An-24, 15 An-26, 1 An-30, 2 An-32, 4 Yak-40, 2 Il-76 (Air Force ac in civilian markings)
HEL 40 Mi-8/-17
TRG 25 L-39, 8* MiG-21U, 4* MiG-23U, 2* MiG-29UB, 20 Z-326
MISSILES
ASM AS-7

AAM AA-2, AA-7, AA-8, AA-10, AA-11
SAM 13 active SA-2, SA-3 sites
CIVIL AIRLINE
10 Il-62, 7 Tu-154, 12 Yak-42, 1 An-30 used as troop tpt

Paramilitary 26,500 active

YOUTH LABOUR ARMY 65,000

CIVIL DEFENCE FORCE 50,000

TERRITORIAL MILITIA (R) ε1,000,000

STATE SECURITY (Ministry of Interior) 20,000

BORDER GUARDS (Ministry of Interior) 6,500
    about 20 Sov *Zhuk* and 3 Sov *Stenka* PFI<, plus boats

Foreign Forces

US 1,080: **Navy** 590 **Marines** 490
RUSSIA 810: 800 SIGINT, ε10 mil advisers

Dominican Republic				**DR**
	1997	**1998**	**1999**	**2000**
GDP	pRD215bn	pRD242bn		
	($10bn)	($11bn)		
per capita	$4,700	$5,100		
Growth	8.2%	7.3%		
Inflation	6.7%	4.8%		
Debt	$3.9bn	$3.8bn		
Def exp	pRD2.4bn	pRD2.4bn		
	($120m)	($120m)		
Def bdgt		εpRD1.1bn	εpRD1.2bn	
		($72m)	($76m)	
FMA (US)	$0.6m	$0.6m	$0.5m	$0.5m
$1 = pRD (peso República Dominicana)				
	14.3	14.7	15.9	
Population				8,155,000
Age	*13–17*	*18–22*	*23–32*	
Men	451,000	408,000	713,000	
Women	440,000	399,000	702,000	

Total Armed Forces

ACTIVE 24,500

Army 15,000

3 Defence Zones • 4 inf bde (with 8 inf, 1 arty bn, 2 recce sqn) • 1 armd, 1 Presidential Guard, 1 SF, 1 arty, 1 engr bn
EQUIPMENT
LT TK 12 AMX-13 (**75mm**), 12 M-41A1 (**76mm**)

RECCE 8 V-150 *Commando*
APC 20 M-2/M-3 half-track
TOWED ARTY 105mm: 22 M-101
MOR 81mm: M-1; **120mm:** 24 ECIA

Navy 4,000

(incl marine security unit and 1 SEAL unit)
BASES Santo Domingo (HQ), Las Calderas

PATROL AND COASTAL COMBATANTS 15
PATROL, OFFSHORE 6
  1 *Mella* (Ca *River*) (comd/trg), 2 *Cambiaso* (US
  Cohoes), 2 *Canopus* PCO, 1 *Prestol* (US *Admirable*)
PATROL, INSHORE 9
  1 *Betelgeuse* (US PGM-71), 1 *Capitan Alsina* (trg), 1
  Balsam PCI, some 6 PCI<
AMPHIBIOUS craft only
  2 LCU
SUPPORT AND MISCELLANEOUS 4
  1 AOT (small harbour), 3 AT/F

Air Force 5,500

10 cbt ac, no armed hel
Flying hours probably less than 60
CCT 1 sqn with 8 A-37B
TPT 1 sqn with 3 C-47, 1 *Commander* 680
LIAISON 1 Cessna 210, 2 PA-31, 3 *Queen Air* 80, 1
  King Air
HEL 8 Bell 205, 2 SA-318C, 1 SA-365 (VIP)
TRG 2* AT-6, 6 T-34B, 3 T-41D
AB 1 SF (AB) bn
AD 1 bn with 4 **20mm** guns

Paramilitary 15,000

NATIONAL POLICE 15,000

Ecuador   Ec

	1997	1998	1999	2000
GDP	ES79tr	n.k.		
	($20bn)	($20bn)		
per capita	$4,600	$4,600		
Growth	3.3%	1.0%		
Inflation	30.7%	36.1%		
Debt	$15bn	$15bn		
Def exp[a]	εES2.4tr	εES2.9tr		
	($692m)	($532m)		
Def bdgt[a]		εES2.0tr	εES4.0tr	
		($571m)	($407m)	
FMA[b] (US)	$1m	$1m	$1.7m	$1.7m
$1=ES (Ecuadorean sucre)				
	3,998	5,447	9,835	

[a] incl extra-budgetary funding
[b] MOMEP 1996ε $15m 1997ε $15m 1998ε $15m

Population			12,651,000
Age	13–17	18–22	23–32
Men	702,000	645,000	1,097,000
Women	682,000	629,000	1,075,000

Total Armed Forces

ACTIVE 57,100
Terms of service conscription 1 year, selective

RESERVES 100,000
Ages 18–55

Army 50,000

4 Defence Zones
  1 div with 2 inf bde (each 3 inf, 1 armd, 1 arty bn) •
  1 armd bde (3 armd, 1 mech inf, 1 SP arty bn) • 2 inf
  bde (5 inf, 3 mech inf, 2 arty bn) • 3 jungle bde (2
  with 3, 1 with 4 jungle bn)
Army tps: 1 SF (AB) bde (4 bn), 1 AD arty gp, 1 avn gp
  (4 bn), 3 engr bn
EQUIPMENT
MBT 3 T-55
LT TK 108 AMX-13
RECCE 27 AML-60/-90, 30 EE-9 *Cascavel*, 10 EE-3
  Jararaca
APC 20 M-113, 80 AMX-VCI, 30 EE-11 *Urutu*
TOWED ARTY 105mm: 50 M2A2, 30 M-101, 24
  Model 56; **155mm:** 12 M-198, 12 M-114
SP ARTY 155mm: 10 Mk F3
MRL 122mm: 6 RM-70
MOR 81mm: M-29; **107mm:** 4.2in M-30; **160mm:** 12
  Soltam
RCL 90mm: 380 M-67; **106mm:** 24 M-40A1
AD GUNS 14.5mm: 128 ZPU-1/-2; **20mm:** 20 M-
  1935; **23mm:** 34 ZU-23; **35mm:** 30 GDF-002 twin;
  37mm: 18 Ch; **40mm:** 30 L/70
SAM 75 *Blowpipe*, 90 SA-18 (reported), SA-8
AIRCRAFT
SURVEY 1 Cessna 206, 1 *Learjet* 24D
TPT 1 CN-235, 1 DHC-5, 3 IAI-201, 1 *King Air* 200, 2
  PC-6
LIAISON/TRG/OBS 1 Cessna 172, 1 -182
HELICOPTERS
SURVEY 3 SA-315B
TPT/LIAISON 9 AS-332, 4 AS-350B, 1 Bell 214B, 3
  SA-315B, 3 SA-330, 30 SA-342

Navy 4,100

(incl 250 Naval Aviation and 1,500 Marines)
BASES Guayaquil (main base), Jaramijo, Galápagos
Islands

SUBMARINES 2

SSK 2 *Shyri* (Ge T-209/1300) with 533mm TT (Ge SUT HWT)

FRIGATES 2

FF 2 *Presidente Eloy Alfaro* (ex-UK *Leander Batch* II) with 1 206B hel

PATROL AND COASTAL COMBATANTS 11

CORVETTES 6 *Esmeraldas* with 2 x 3 ASTT, hel deck, 2 x 3 MM-40 *Exocet* SSM

MISSILE CRAFT 5

3 *Quito* (Ge Lürssen 45m) with 4 MM-38 *Exocet* SSM
2 *Manta†* (Ge Lürssen 36m) with 4 *Gabriel* II SSM

AMPHIBIOUS 1

1 *Hualcopo* (US LST-512-1152) LST, capacity 200 tps, 16 tk

SUPPORT AND MISCELLANEOUS 8

1 AGHS, 1 ex-GDR depot ship, 1 AOT (small), 1 *Calicuchima* (ex-UK *Throsk*) AE, 1 water carrier, 2 armed AT/F, 1 trg

NAVAL AVIATION (250)

LIAISON 1 *Super King Air* 200, 1 *Super King Air* 300, 1 CN-235

TRG 3 T-34C

HEL 2 Bell 230, 4 Bell 206, 4 TH-57, 2 Bell 412 EP

MARINES (1,500)

3 bn: 2 on garrison duties, 1 cdo (no hy weapons/veh)

Air Force 3,000

78 cbt ac, no armed hel

OPERATIONAL COMMAND

2 wg, 5 sqn

FGA 3 sqn
1 with 8 *Jaguar* S (6 -S(E), 2 -B(E))
1 with 10 *Kfir* C-2, 2 TC-2
1 with 20 A-37B
FTR 1 sqn with 13 *Mirage* F-1JE, 1 F-1JB
CCT 4 *Strikemaster* Mk 89A

MILITARY AIR TRANSPORT GROUP

2 civil/military airlines:
TAME 6 Boeing 727, 2 BAe-748, 4 C-130B, 2 C-130H, 3 DHC-6, 1 F-28, 1 L-100-30
ECUATORIANA 3 Boeing 707-320, 1 DC-10-30, 2 Airbus A-310
LIAISON 1 *King Air* E90, 1 *Sabreliner*
LIAISON/SAR hel 2 AS-332, 1 Bell 212, 6 Bell-206B, 5 SA-316B, 1 SA-330, 2 UH-1B, 24 UH-1H
TRG incl 22 AT-33*, 20 Cessna 150, 5 C-172, 17 T-34C, 1 T-41

MISSILES

AAM R-550 *Magic, Super* 530, *Shafrir, Python* 3 (possibly)

AB 1 AB sqn

Paramilitary 270

COAST GUARD 270

PATROL, INSHORE 7
1 25 *De Julio* PCI, 2 5 *De Agosto* PCI, 2 10 *De Agosto* PCI<, 1 *Point* PCI, 1 PGM-71 PCI, plus some 6 boats

El Salvador — EIS

	1997	1998	1999	2000
GDP	C98bn	C104bn		
	($9.0bn)	($9.6bn)		
per capita	$2,800	$2,900		
Growth	4.0%	3.5%		
Inflation	4.5%	2.5%		
Debt	$2.7bn	$2.6bn		
Def exp	εC1.5bn	εC1.4bn		
	($176m)	($160m)		
Def bdgt		C986m	C983m	
		($113m)	($112m)	
FMA (US)	$0.5m	$0.5m	$0.5m	$0.5m
$1 = colon	8.8	8.8	8.8	
Population				6,077,000
Age	*13–17*	*18–22*		*23–32*
Men	369,000	347,000		512,000
Women	356,000	338,000		533,000

Total Armed Forces

ACTIVE 24,600

Terms of service selective conscription, 1 year

RESERVES

Ex-soldiers registered

Army ε22,300

(incl 4,000 conscripts)
6 Mil Zones • 6 inf bde (each of 2 inf bn, 1 inf det) • 1 special sy bde (2 MP, 2 border gd bn) • 8 inf det (bn) • 1 engr comd (3 engr bn) • 1 arty bde (3 fd, 1 AD bn) • 1 mech cav regt (2 bn) • 2 indep bn (1 Presidential Guard, 1 sy) • 1 special ops gp (1 para bn, 1 naval inf, 1 SF coy)

EQUIPMENT

RECCE 10 AML-90
APC 40 M-37B1 (mod), 8 UR-416
TOWED ARTY 105mm: 24 M-101, 36 M-102, 18 M-56 (in store)
MOR 81mm: incl 300 M-29; 120mm: 60 UB-M52, M-74
RL 94mm: LAW; 82mm: B-300
RCL 90mm: 400 M-67; 106mm: 20+ M-40A1 (in store)
AD GUNS 20mm: 36 FRY M-55, 4 TCM-20

Navy 700

(incl some 90 Naval Infantry and spt forces)
BASES La Uníon, La Libertad, Acajutla, El Triunfo, Guija Lake
PATROL AND COASTAL COMBATANTS 5
PATROL, INSHORE 5
  3 *Camcraft* 30m, 2 PCI<, plus 22 river boats
AMPHIBIOUS craft only
  2 LCM

NAVAL INFANTRY (Marines) (some 90)
1 sy coy

Air Force 1,600

(incl AD and ε200 conscripts); 31 cbt ac, 17 armed hel
Flying hours A-37: 90
CBT AC 1 sqn with 10 A-37B, 2 AC-47, 6 CM-170, 2 *Ouragan*
ARMED HEL 1 sqn with 8 Hughes 500D/E, 9 UH-1M
RECCE 8* O-2A
TPT 1 sqn with ac 1 C-47, 5 Basler Turbo-67, 1 C-123K, 1 *Commander*, 1 DC-6B, 1 *Merlin* IIIB, 9 *Rallye* **hel** 1 sqn with 12 UH-1H tpt hel (incl 4 SAR)
LIAISON 2 Cessna-210
TRG 3 T-41C/D, 6 TH-300, 3* O-2A, 5 T-35

Forces Abroad

UN AND PEACEKEEPING
WESTERN SAHARA (MINURSO): 2 Obs

Paramilitary 12,000

NATIONAL CIVILIAN POLICE (Ministry of Public Security) some 12,000 (to be 16,000)
  small arms; ac 1 Cessna O-2A **hel** 1 UH-1H, 2 Hughes-520N, 1 MD-500D
  10 river boats

Guatemala				Gua
	1997	**1998**	**1999**	**2000**
GDP	q108bn	q122bn		
	($12.3bn)	($13.3bn)		
per capita	$3,800	$3,900		
Growth	4.1%	4.9%		
Inflation	9.2%	7.0%		
Debt	$3.7bn	$4.0bn		
Def exp	εq1.1bn	εq1.0bn		
	($182m)	($156m)		
Def bdgt		q874m	q845m	
		($137m)	($120m)	
FMA[a] (US)	$2m	$2.2m	$3.7m	$3.2m
$1=quetzal	6.0	6.4	7.0	

[a] MINUGUA **1997** $5m

Population			11,900,000
Age	*13–17*	*18–22*	*23–32*
Men	713,000	609,000	910,000
Women	692,000	594,000	899,000

Total Armed Forces

(National Armed Forces are combined; the Army provides log spt for Navy and Air Force)

ACTIVE ε31,400
(ε23,000 conscripts)
Terms of service conscription; selective, 30 months
RESERVES
Army ε35,000 (trained) **Navy** (some) **Air Force** 200

Army 29,200

(incl ε23,000 conscripts)
15 Mil Zones (22 inf, 1 trg bn, 6 armd sqn) • 2 strategic bde (4 inf, 1 lt armd bn, 1 recce sqn, 2 arty bty) • 1 SF gp (3 coy incl 1 trg) • 2 AB bn • 5 inf bn gp (each 1 inf bn, 1 recce sqn, 1 arty bty) • 1 Presidential Guard bn • 1 engr bn
RESERVES ε19 inf bn
EQUIPMENT
  LT TK 10 M-41A3
  RECCE 7 M-8, 9 RBY-1
  APC 10 M-113, 7 V-100 *Commando*, 30 *Armadillo*
  TOWED ARTY 75mm: 8 M-116; **105mm**: 12 M-101, 8 M-102, 56 M-56
  MOR 81mm: 55 M-1; **107mm**: 12 M-30; **120mm**: 18 ECIA
  RL 89mm: 3.5in M-20
  RCL 57mm: M-20; **105mm**: 64 Arg M-1974 FMK-1; **106mm**: 56 M-40A1
  AD GUNS 20mm: 16 M-55, 16 GAI-DO1

Navy ε1,500

(incl some 650 Marines)
BASES Atlantic Santo Tomás de Castilla **Pacific** Puerto Quetzal
PATROL CRAFT, INSHORE 15
  1 *Kukulkan* (US *Broadsword* 32m) PFI, 2 *Stewart* PCI, 6 *Cutlas* PCI, 6 *Vigilante* boats (plus 20 river patrol craft and 2 LCP)

MARINES (some 650)
2 under-str bn

Air Force 700

10† cbt ac, 12 armed hel. Serviceability of ac is less than 50%

CBT AC 1 sqn with 4 Cessna A-37B, 1 sqn with 6 PC-7
TPT 1 sqn with 4 T-67 (mod C-47 *Turbo*), 2 F-27, 1
Super King Air (VIP), 1 PA 301 *Navajo*, 4 Arava 201
LIAISON 1 sqn with 2 Cessna 206, 1 Cessna 310
HEL 1 sqn with 12 armed hel (9 Bell 212, 3 Bell 412), 9
Bell 206, 3 UH-1H, 3 S-76
TRG 6 T-41, 5 T-35B, 5 Cessna R172K

TACTICAL SECURITY GROUP
3 CCT coy, 1 armd sqn, 1 AD bty (Army units for
air-base sy)

Paramilitary 7,000 active

NATIONAL POLICE 7,000
21 departments, 1 SF bn, 1 integrated task force (incl
mil and treasury police)
TREASURY POLICE (2,500)

Guyana   Guy

	1997	1998	1999	2000
GDP	G$115bn	G$119bn		
	($748m)	($740m)		
per capita	$3,200	$3,200		
Growth	6.2%	-3.0%		
Inflation	4.2%	5.0%		
Debt	$1.6bn	$1.5bn		
Def exp	G$1.1bn	G$1.2bn		
	($7m)	($8m)		
Def bdgt		G$850m	G$900m	
		($6m)	($6m)	
FMA (US)	$0.2m	$0.2m	$0.2m	$0.2m
US$1=G$	142	151	161	
Population				842,000
Age	*13–17*	*18–22*	*23–32*	
Men	43,000	40,000	78,000	
Women	41,000	38,000	75,000	

Total Armed Forces

ACTIVE (combined Guyana Defence Force) some 1,600

RESERVES some 1,500
People's Militia (see *Paramilitary*)

Army 1,400

(incl 500 Reserves)
1 inf bn, 1 SF, 1 spt wpn, 1 engr coy
EQUIPMENT
RECCE 3 Shorland, 6 EE-9 *Cascavel* (reported)
TOWED ARTY 130mm: 6 M-46
MOR 81mm: 12 L16A1; 82mm: 18 M-43; 120mm: 18
M-43

Navy 100

(plus 170 reserves)
BASES Georgetown, New Amsterdam
2 boats

Air Force 100

no cbt ac, no armed hel
TPT ac 1 BN-2A, 1 *Skyvan* 3M **hel** 1 Bell 206, 1 Bell 412

Paramilitary

GUYANA PEOPLE'S MILITIA (GPM) some 1,500

Haiti   RH

	1997	1998	1999	2000
GDP	G52bn	G60bn		
	($1.9bn)	($2.0bn)		
per capita	$1,000	$1,100		
Growth	1.1%	3.1%		
Inflation	20.6%	12.7%		
Debt	$1,028m	$1,086m		
Sy exp	G768m	G800m		
	($46m)	($48m)		
Sy bdgt		G800m	G850m	
		($48m)	($51m)	
FMA[a] (US)	$0.3m	$0.3m	$0.3m	$6.3m
$1=gourde	16.7	16.8	16.8	

[a] UN **1996** $243m **1997** $57m **1998** $18m

Population				7,564,000
Age	*13–17*	*18–22*	*23–32*	
Men	417,000	370,000	604,000	
Women	408,000	364,000	604,000	

Total Armed Forces

ACTIVE Nil

Paramilitary

In 1994, the military government of Haiti was replaced by
a civilian administration. The former armed forces and
police were disbanded and an Interim Public Security
Force (IPSF) of 3,000 formed. A National Police Force of
ε5,300 personnel has now been formed. All Army
equipment has been destroyed.
The United Nations Civilian Police Mission in Haiti
(MIPONUH) maintains some 285 civ pol to assist the
government of Haiti by supporting and contributing to the
professionalisation of the National Police Force.

NAVY (Coast Guard) 30 (being developed)
BASE Port-au-Prince
PATROL CRAFT boats only

AIR FORCE (disbanded in 1995)

Foreign Forces

US USMC 230

Honduras   Hr

	1997	1998	1999	2000
GDP	L61bn	L71bn		
	($4.7bn)	($5.0bn)		
per capita	$2,200	$2,200		
Growth	4.9%	3.0%		
Inflation	20.2%	13.7%		
Debt	$4.1bn	$4.0bn		
Def exp	εL1,310m	εL1,300m		
	($101m)	($97m)		
Def bdgt		L479m	L500m	
		($36m)	($36m)	
FMA (US)	$0.4m	$0.5m	$0.5m	$0.5m
$1=lempira	13.0	13.4	14.1	
Population				6,621,000
Age	13–17	18–22	23–32	
Men	391,000	337,000	538,000	
Women	378,000	328,000	528,000	

Total Armed Forces

ACTIVE 8,300

RESERVES 60,000
Ex-servicemen registered

Army 5,500

6 Mil Zones
4 inf bde
   3 with 3 inf, 1 arty bn • 1 with 3 inf bn
1 special tac gp with 1 inf (AB), 1 SF bn
1 armd cav regt (2 mech bn, 1 lt tk, 1 recce
   sqn, 1 arty, 1 AD arty bty)
1 engr bn
1 Presidential Guard coy
RESERVES
1 inf bde
EQUIPMENT
   LT TK 12 *Scorpion*
   RECCE 3 *Scimitar*, 1 *Sultan*, 50 *Saladin*, 13 RBY-1
   TOWED ARTY 105mm: 24 M-102; **155mm:** 4 M-198
   MOR 60mm; 81mm; 120mm: 60 FMK; **160mm:** 30
   Soltam
   RL 84mm: 120 *Carl Gustav*
   RCL 106mm: 80 M-40A1
   AD Guns 20mm: 24 M-55A2, 24 TCM-20

Navy 1,000

(incl 400 Marines)
BASES Atlantic Puerto Cortés, Puerto Castilla **Pacific**
Amapala
PATROL CRAFT, INSHORE 10
   3 *Guaymuras* (US *Swiftship* 31m) PFI
   2 *Copan* (US *Lantana* 32m) PFI<
   5 PCI<, plus 28 riverine boats
AMPHIBIOUS craft only
   1 *Punta Caxinas* LCT; plus some 3 ex-US LCM
MARINES (400)
3 indep coy (-)

Air Force 1,800

49 cbt ac, no armed hel
FGA 2 sqn
   1 with 13 A-37B, 4 A-36 *Halcon*
   1 with 5 F-5E, 1 -F
FTR 11 *Super Mystère* B2
TPT 5 C-47, 3 C-130A, 1 IAI-201, 2 IAI-1123
LIAISON 1 sqn with 3 Cessna 172, 2 C-180, 2 C-185, 3
   Commander, 1 PA-31, 1 PA-34
HEL 9 Bell 412, 4 Hughes 500, 6 UH-1B/H, 1 S-76
TRG 4* C-101CC, 6 U-17A, 11* EMB-312, 5 T-41A
AAM *Shafrir*

Forces Abroad

UN AND PEACEKEEPING
WESTERN SAHARA (MINURSO): 12 Obs

Paramilitary 6,000

PUBLIC SECURITY FORCES (Ministry of Public
Security and Defence) 6,000
11 regional comd

Foreign Forces

US 400: **Army** 160 **Marines** 70 **Air Force** 170

Jamaica   Ja

	1997	1998	1999	2000
GDP	J$230bn	n.k.		
	($5bn)	($5bn)		
per capita	$3,400	$3,500		
Growth	-1.4%	-1.9%		
Inflation	9.2%	8.6%		
Debt	$4.0bn	$4.1bn		
Def exp	J$1.5bn	J$1.6bn		
	($42m)	($44m)		

contd	1997	1998	1999	2000
Def bdgt		J$1.6bn	J$2.0bn	
		($44m)	($52m)	
FMA (US)	$1.2m	$1.1m	$1.3m	$1.3m
US$1=J$	35.4	36.6	38.3	
Population				2,500,000
Age	*13–17*	*18–22*	*23–32*	
Men	122,000	121,000	227,000	
Women	121,000	118,000	228,000	

Total Armed Forces

ACTIVE (combined Jamaican Defence Force) some 2,830

RESERVES some 950
Army 877 **Coast Guard** 60 **Air Wing** 16

Army 2,500

2 inf, 1 spt bn, 1 engr regt (4 sqn)
EQUIPMENT
APC 13 V-150 *Commando* (all reported non-op)
MOR 81mm: 12 L16A1

RESERVES 877
1 inf bn

Coast Guard 190

BASE Port Royal, out stations at Discovery Bay and Pedro Cays
PATROL CRAFT, INSHORE 7
1 *Fort Charles* PFI (US 34m), 1 *Paul Bogle* (US-31m), 1 *Holland Bay* PCI, 4 *Dauntless* PCI, plus 5 boats

Air Wing 140

no cbt ac, no armed hel
AC 2 BN-2A, 1 Cessna 210, 1 *King Air*
HEL 4 Bell 206, 3 Bell 212, 3 UH-1H, 4 AS-355

Mexico Mex

	1997	1998	1999	2000
GDP	NP3.1tr	NP3.8tr		
	($372bn)	($400bn)		
per capita	$7,500	$7,900		
Growth	7.0%	4.8%		
Inflation	20.6%	15.9%		
Debt	$150bn	$156bn		
Def exp	NP29bn	NP35bn		
	($3.7bn)	($3.8bn)		
Def bdgt			NP20.1bn	NP23.2bn
			($2.2bn)	($2.4bn)

contd	1997	1998	1999	2000
FMA (US)	$6m	$6m	$9m	$11m
$1=new peso	7.9	9.1	9.6	
Population		97,122,000 (Chiapas region 4%)		
Age	*13–17*	*18–22*	*23–32*	
Men	5,226,000	4,883,000	8,771,000	
Women	5,080,000	4,786,000	8,783,000	

Total Armed Forces

ACTIVE 178,770
(60,000 conscripts)
Terms of service 1 year conscription (4 hours per week) by lottery

RESERVES 300,000

Army 130,000

(incl ε60,000 conscripts)
12 Mil Regions
41 Zonal Garrisons incl 1 armd, 19 mot cav, 1 mech inf, 7 arty regt, plus 3 arty, 8 inf bn • 4 armd bde (each 2 armd recce, 1 arty regt, 1 ATK gp, 1 mech inf bn) • 1 Presidential Guard bde (3 inf, 1 SF, 1 arty bn) • 1 mot inf bde (3 mot inf regt) • 2 inf bde (each 3 inf bn, 1 arty bn) • 1 AB bde (3 bn) • 1 MP, 1 engr bde • 1 SF 'corps' with 64 airmobile SF gp • AD, engr and spt units
EQUIPMENT
RECCE 40 M-8, 119 ERC-90F *Lynx*, 40 VBL, 25 MOWAG, 40 MAC-1
APC 40 HWK-11, 32 M-2A1 half-track, 40 VCR/TT, 24 DN-3, 40 DN-4 *Caballo*, 70 DN-5 *Toro*, 495 AMX-VCI, 95 BDX, 26 LAV-150 ST, some BTR-60 (reported)
TOWED ARTY 75mm: 18 M-116 pack; 105mm: 16 M-2A1/M-3, 80 M-101, 80 M-56
SP ARTY 75mm: 5 DN-5 *Bufalo*
MOR 81mm: 1,500; 120mm: 75 Brandt
ATGW *Milan* (incl 8 VBL)
RL 82mm: B-300
ATK GUNS 37mm: 30 M-3
AD GUNS 12.7mm: 40 M-55; 20mm: 40 Oerlikon
SAM RBS-70

Navy 37,000

(incl 1,100 Naval Aviation and 10,000 Marines)
NAVAL REGIONS Gulf 6 **Pacific** 11
BASES Gulf Vera Cruz (HQ), Tampico, Chetumal, Ciudad del Carmen, Yukalpetén, Lerna, Frontera, Coatzacoalcos, Isla Mujéres **Pacific** Acapulco (HQ), Ensenada, La Paz, San Blas, Guaymas, Mazatlán, Manzanillo, Salina Cruz, Puerto Madero, Lázaro Cárdenas, Puerto Vallarta

PRINCIPAL AND SURFACE COMBATANTS 9

DESTROYERS 3

DD 3

2 *Ilhuicamina* (ex-*Quetzalcoatl*) (US *Gearing*) with 1 x 8 ASROC SUGW, 2 x 3 ASTT, 2 x 2 127mm guns and 1 Bo-105 hel

1 *Cuitlahuac* (US *Fletcher*) with 5 533mm TT, 5 127mm guns

FRIGATES 6

FF 6

2 *Knox* with 1 x 8 ASROC SUGW, 4 x 324mm TT, 1 x 127mm gun, 1 x BO 105 hel

2 *H. Galeana* (US *Bronstein*) with 1 x 8 ASROC SUGW, 2 x 3 ASTT, 1 x 2 76mm guns

1 *Comodoro Manuel Azueta* (US *Edsall*) (trg)

1 *Zacatecas* (US *Lawrence/Crosley*) with 1 127mm gun

PATROL AND COASTAL COMBATANTS 105

PATROL, OFFSHORE 40

4 *S. J. Holzinger* (ex-*Uxmal*) (imp *Uribe*) with Bo-105 hel

6 *Cadete Virgilio Uribe* (Sp '*Halcon*') with Bo-105 hel

17 *Leandro Valle* (US *Auk* MSF)

1 *Guanajuato* with 2 102mm gun

11 D-01 (US *Admirable* MSF), 3 with hel deck

1 *Centenario* OPV with 2 40mm gun

PATROL, INSHORE 47

4 *Isla* (US *Halter*) XFPB

31 *Quintana Roo* (UK *Azteca*) PCI

3 *Cabo* (US *Cape Higgon*) PCI

2 *Punta* (US *Point*) PCI

7 *Tamiahua* (US *Polimar*)

PATROL, RIVERINE 18<, plus boats

AMPHIBIOUS 3

2 *Panuco* (US-511) LST

1 *Grijalva* (US-511) LST

SUPPORT AND MISCELLANEOUS 21

3 AOT, 1 PCI spt, 3 log spt, 6 AT/F, 5 AGHS, 1 *Durango* tpt, plus 2 other tpt

NAVAL AVIATION (1,100)

9 cbt ac, no armed hel

MR 1 sqn with 9* C-212-200M

MR HEL 12 Bo-105 (8 afloat)

TPT 1 C-212, 2 C-180, 3 C-310, 1 DHC-5, 1 FH-227, 1 *King Air* 90, 1 *Learjet* 24, 1 *Commander*, 2 C-337, 2 C-402, 2 An-32

HEL 3 Bell 47, 4 SA-319, 20 UH-1H, 20 Mi-8/17, 4 AS-355

TRG ac 8 Cessna 152, 10 F-33C *Bonanza*, 10 L-90 *Redigo* **hel** 4 MD-500E

MARINES (10,000)

3 marine bde (each 3 bn), 1 AB bde (3 bn) • 1 Presidential Guard bn • 14 regional bn • 1 Coast def gp: 2 coast arty bn • 1 indep sy coy

EQUIPMENT

AAV 25 VAP-3550

TOWED ARTY 105mm: 16 M-56

MRL 51mm: 6 *Firos*

MOR 100 incl 60mm, 81mm

RCL 106mm: M-40A1

AD GUNS 20mm: Mk 38; **40mm**: Bofors

Air Force 11,770

125 cbt ac, 95 armed hel

FTR 1 sqn with 8 F-5E, 2 -F

CCT 9 sqn

7 with 74 PC-7

2 with 27 AT-33

ARMED HEL 1 sqn with 1 Bell 205, 27 Bell 206, 25 Bell 212, 20 UH-1H

RECCE 1 photo sqn with 14* *Commander* 500S, 1 SA 2-37A, 4 C-26

TPT 5 sqn with 2 BN-2, 12 C-47, 1 C-54, 10 C-118, 9 C-130A, 5 *Commander* 500, 5 DC-6 *Skytrain*, 2 F-27, 5 Boeing 727, 1 sqn with 12 IAI-201 (tpt/SAR)

HEL 4 Bell 205, 3 SA-332, 2 UH-60, 6 S-70A, 73 UH-1H, 12 Mi-8, 17 Mi-17

PRESIDENTIAL TPT ac 1 Boeing 757, 3 Boeing 737, 1 L-188, 3 FH-227, 2 *Merlin*, 4 *Sabreliners* **hel** 1 AS-332, 2 SA-330, 2 UH-60, 2 Bell-412

LIAISON/UTL 2 *King Air*, 1 *Musketeer*, 40 Beech *Bonanza* F-33A, 10 Beech *Musketeer*

TRG ac 20 CAP-10, 20 L-90 *Redigo*, 5 T-39 *Sabreliner* **hel** 22* MD 530F (SAR/paramilitary/trg)

Paramilitary

RURAL DEFENCE MILITIA (R) 14,000

COAST GUARD

4 *Mako* 295 PCI

Nicaragua   Nic

	1997	1998	1999	2000
GDP	Co19bn	n.k.		
	($2.5bn)	($2.7bn)		
per capita	$2,000	$2,100		
Growth	5.0%	4.0%		
Inflation	7.3%	17.0%		
Debt	$6.0bn	$6.3bn		
Def exp	Co258m	Co314m		
	($36m)	($30m)		
Def bdgt		Co314m	Co300m	
		($30m)	($26m)	
FMA (US)	$0.1m	$0.1m	$0.2m	$0.2m
$1=Co (Cordoba oro)				
	9.5	10.6	11.5	
Population				4,695,000
Age	*13–17*	*18–22*		*23–32*
Men	319,000	261,000		334,000
Women	283,000	240,000		374,000

Total Armed Forces

ACTIVE ε16,000

Terms of service voluntary, 18–36 months

Army 14,000

Reorganisation in progress
5 Regional Comd (10 inf, 1 tk coy) • 2 mil det (2 inf bn)
• 1 lt mech bde (1 mech inf, 1 tk, 1 recce bn, 1 fd arty
gp (2 bn), 1 atk gp) • 1 comd regt (1 inf, 1 sy bn) • 1 SF
bde (3 SF bn) • 1 tpt regt (incl 1 APC bn) • 1 engr bn

EQUIPMENT
MBT some 127 T-55 (42 op remainder in store)
LT TK 10 PT-76 (in store)
RECCE 20 BRDM-2
APC 102 BTR-152 (in store), 64 BTR-60
TOWED ARTY 122mm: 12 D-30, 100 *Grad* 1P (single-
tube rocket launcher); **152mm**: 30 D-20 (in store)
MRL 107mm: 33 Type-63; **122mm**: 18 BM-21
MOR 82mm: 579; **120mm**: 24 M-43; **160mm**: 4 M-
160 (in store)
ATGW AT-3 *Sagger* (12 on BRDM-2)
RCL 82mm: B-10
ATK GUNS 57mm: 354 ZIS-2 (90 in store); **76mm**:
83 Z1S-3; **100mm**: 24 M-1944
SAM 200+ SA-7/-14/-16

Navy ε800

BASES Corinto, Puerto Cabezzas, El Bluff

PATROL AND COASTAL COMBATANTS 5
PATROL, INSHORE 5
2 Sov *Zhuk* PFI<, 3 *Dabur* PCI, plus boats

MINE COUNTERMEASURES 2
2 *Yevgenya* MCI

Air Force 1,200

no cbt ac, 15 armed hel
TPT 2 An-2, 5 An-26
HEL 15 Mi-17 (tpt/armed) (5 serviceable), 1 Mi-17 (VIP)
UTL/TRG ac 1 Cessna 180, 1 Cessna T-41D, 2 Cessna U-17
ASM AT-2 *Swatter* ATGW
AD GUNS 1 air def gp, 18 ZU-23, 18 C3-*Morigla* M1

Panama · Pan

	1997	1998	1999	2000
GDP	B9bn	B9bn		
	($8.7bn)	($9.2bn)		
per capita	$6,400	$6,600		
Growth	4.2%	3.9%		
Inflation	1.2%	0.6%		

contd	1997	1998	1999	2000
Debt	$5.1bn	$5.4bn		
Sy bdgt	B112m	B120m	B124m	
	($112m)	($120m)	($124m)	
FMA (US)			$0.1m	$0.1m
$1=balboa	1.0	1.0	1.0	
Population				2,836,000
Age	*13–17*	*18–22*	*23–32*	
Men	144,000	137,000	253,000	
Women	137,000	131,000	246,000	

Total Armed Forces

ACTIVE Nil

Paramilitary ε11,800

NATIONAL POLICE FORCE 11,000
Presidential Guard bn (-), 1 MP bn plus 8 coys, 18
Police coy, 1 SF unit (reported); no hy mil eqpt, small
arms only

NATIONAL MARITIME SERVICE ε400
BASES Amador (HQ), Balboa, Colón
PATROL CRAFT, INSHORE 7
2 *Panquiaco* (UK *Vosper* 31.5m), 1 *President* HI
Remeliik PCI, 1 *General Esteban Huertas* PCI, 1 *Tres
de Noviembre* (ex-USCG *Cape Higgon*), 2 ex-US
MSB 5-class (plus about 10 other ex-US patrol/spt
craft and boats)

NATIONAL AIR SERVICE 400
TPT 1 CN-235-2A, 1 BN-2B, 1 PA-34, 3 CASA-212M
Aviocar
TRG 6 T-35D
HEL 2 Bell 205, 6 Bell 212, 13 UH-1H

Paraguay · Py

	1997	1998	1999	2000
GDP	Pg21tr	Pg26tr		
	($8.9bn)	($9.0bn)		
per capita	$3,800	$3,700		
Growth	2.5%	-0.5%		
Inflation	7.0%	11.5%		
Debt	$2.2bn	$2.2bn		
Def exp	Pg310bn	Pg360bn		
	($134m)	($131m)		
Def bdgt		Pg280bn	Pg262bn	
		($102m)	($90m)	
FMA (US)	$0.2m	$0.2m	$0.2m	$0.2m
$1=Pg (Paraguayan guarani)				
	2,191	2,756	2,912	

Population			5,499,000
Age	*13–17*	*18–22*	*23–32*
Men	299,000	259,000	431,000
Women	288,000	250,000	416,000

Total Armed Forces

ACTIVE 20,200 (to reduce)

(12,900 conscripts)

Terms of service 12 months **Navy** 2 years

RESERVES some 164,500

Army 14,900

(10,400 conscripts)
3 corps HQ • 9 div HQ (6 inf, 3 cav) • 9 inf regt (bn) •
3 cav regt (horse) • 3 mech cav regt • Presidential
Guard (1 inf, 1 MP bn, 1 arty bty) • 20 frontier det • 3
arty gp (bn) • 1 AD arty gp • 4 engr bn

EQUIPMENT
MBT 5 M-4A3
RECCE 8 M-8, 5 M-3, 30 EE-9 *Cascavel*
APC 10 EE-11 *Urutu*
TOWED ARTY 75mm: 20 Model 1927/1934;
   105mm: 15 M-101; **152mm**: 6 Vickers 6in (coast)
MOR 81mm: 80
RCL 75mm: M-20
AD GUNS 30: **20mm**: 20 Bofors; **40mm**: 10 M-1A1

Navy 3,600

(incl 900 Marines, 800 Naval Aviation, Harbour and
River Guard, and ε1,900 conscripts)
BASES Asunción (Puerto Sajonia), Bahía Negra,
Ciudad Del Este

PATROL AND COASTAL COMBATANTS 17
PATROL, COASTAL 17
  2 *Paraguais* with 4 120mm guns
  2 *Nanawa* PCO with 4 40mm and 2 12.7mm guns
  1 *Itapu* PCR with 1 40mm, 6 12.7mm guns, 2 81mm
    mor
  1 *Capitan Cabral* PCR with 1 40mm, 2 20mm, 2
    12.7mm guns
  2 *Capitan Ortiz* PFC
  7 *Rodman* SS/101 PCI (plus 15 riverine boats)
  2 ROC PFC

SUPPORT AND MISCELLANEOUS 5
  1 tpt, 1 trg/tpt, 1 AGHS<, 2 LCT

MARINES (900)
(incl 200 conscripts); 2 bn

NAVAL AVIATION (800)
2 cbt ac, no armed hel
  CCT 2 AT-6G

LIAISON 2 Cessna 150, 2 C-206, 1 C-210
HEL 2 HB-350, 1 OH-13

Air Force 1,700

(incl 600 conscripts); 28 cbt ac, no armed hel
  FTR/FGA 8 F-5E, 4 F-5F
  CCT 6 AT-33, 6 EMB-326, 4 T-27
  LIAISON 1 Cessna 185, 4 C-206, 2 C-402, 2 T-41
  HEL 3 HB-350, 1 UH-1B, 2 UH-1H, 4 UH-12, 4 Bell
    47G
  TPT 1 sqn with 5 C-47, 4 C-212, 3 DC-6B, 1 DHC-6
    (VIP), 1 C-131D
  TRG 6 T-6, 10 T-23, 5 T-25, 10 T-35, 1 T-41

Paramilitary 14,800

SPECIAL POLICE SERVICE 14,800
(incl 4,000 conscripts)

Peru				Pe
	1997	**1998**	**1999**	**2000**
GDP	NS174bn	NS188bn		
	($59bn)	($61bn)		
per capita	$4,300	$4,400		
Growth	7.4%	1.0%		
Inflation	8.6%	7.3%		
Debt	$28bn	$30bn		
Def exp	εNS3.4bn	εNS2.9bn		
	($1.3bn)	($990m)		
Def bdgt		εNS2.3bn	εNS2.5bn	
		($792m)	($744m)	
FMA[a] (US)	$26m	$32m	$45m	$48m
$1=new sol	2.7	2.9	3.4	
[a] MOMEP **1996** ε$15m **1997** ε$15m **1998** ε$15m				
Population				25,469,000
Age	*13–17*	*18–22*		*23–32*
Men	1,347,000	1,276,000		2,220,000
Women	1,335,000	1,267,000		2,211,000

Total Armed Forces

ACTIVE 115,000
(incl 64,000 conscripts)
Terms of service 2 years, selective

RESERVES 188,000
Army only

Army 75,000

(incl 52,000 conscripts)
6 Mil Regions

Army tps

1 AB div (3 cdo, 1 para bn, 1 arty gp) • 1 Presidential Escort regt • 1 AD arty gp

Regional tps

3 armd div (each 2 tk, 1 armd inf bn, 1 arty gp, 1 engr bn) • 1 armd gp (3 indep armd cav, 1 fd arty, 1 AD arty, 1 engr bn) • 1 cav div (3 mech regt, 1 arty gp) • 7 inf div (each 3 inf bn, 1 arty gp) • 1 jungle div • 2 med arty gp • 2 fd arty gp • 1 indep inf bn • 1 indep engr bn • 3 hel sqn

EQUIPMENT

MBT 300 T-54/-55 (ε50 serviceable)

LT TK 110 AMX-13 (ε30 serviceable)

RECCE 60 M-8/-20, 10 M-3A1, 50 M-9A1, 15 Fiat 6616, 30 BRDM-2

APC 130 M-113, 12 BTR-60, 130 UR-416, Fiat 6614, *Casspir*, 4 Repontec

TOWED ARTY 105mm: 20 Model 56 pack, 130 M-101; **122mm**: 36 D-30; **130mm**: 36 M-46; **155mm**: 36 M-114

SP ARTY 155mm: 12 M-109A2, 12 Mk F3

MRL 122mm: 14 BM-21

MOR 81mm: incl some SP; **107mm**: incl some SP; **120mm**: 300 Brandt, ECIA

ATGW 400 SS-11

RCL 106mm: M40A1

AD GUNS 23mm: 80 ZSU-23-2, 35 ZSU-23-4 SP; **30mm**: 10 2S6 SP; **40mm**: 45 M-1, 80 L60/70

SAM SA-7, 236 SA-16, *Javelin*

AC 13 Cessna incl 1 C-337, 1 *Queen Air* 65, 5 U-10, 3 U-17, 1 U-150, 2 U-206, 4 AN-32B

HEL 2 Bell 47G, 2 Mi-6, 26 Mi-8, 13 Mi-17, 6 SA-315, 5 SA-316, 3 SA-318, 2 *Agusta* A-109

Navy 25,000

(incl some 800 Naval Aviation, 3,000 Marines, 1,000 Coast Guard and 10,000 conscripts)

NAVAL AREAS Pacific, Lake Titicaca, Amazon River

BASES Ocean Callao, San Lorenzo Island, Paita, Talara **Lake** Puno **River** Iquitos, Puerto Maldonado

SUBMARINES 8

SSK 6 *Casma* (Ge T-209/1200) with 533mm TT (It A184 HWT) (2 in refit)

SSC 2 *Abato* with 533mm TT, 1 127mm gun (Plus 1 *Pedrera* (US *Guppy* I) with 533mm TT (Mk 37 HWT) alongside trg only)

PRINCIPAL SURFACE COMBATANTS 7

CRUISERS 2

1 *Almirante Grau* (Nl *De Ruyter*) with 4 x 2 152mm guns, 8 *Otomat* SSM

1 *Aguirre* (Nl *De 7 Provincien*) with 3 SH-3D *Sea King* hel (ASW/ASUW) (Mk 46 LWT/AM-39 *Exocet*), 2 x 2 152mm guns

DESTROYERS

DDG 1 *Ferre* (UK *Daring*) with 4 x 2 MM-38 *Exocet* SSM, 3 x 2 114mm guns, hel deck

FRIGATES

FFG 4 *Carvajal* (mod It *Lupo*) with 1 AB-212 hel (ASW OTHT), 2 x 3 ASTT; plus 8 *Otomat* Mk 2 SSM, 1 127mm gun (2 non-op)

PATROL AND COASTAL COMBATANTS 11

MISSILE CRAFT 6 *Velarde* PFM (Fr PR-72 64m) with 4 MM-38 *Exocet* SSM

PATROL CRAFT 1 *Unanue* (ex-US *Sotoyomo*) PCC (Antarctic ops)

RIVERINE 4

2 *Marañon*

2 *Amazonas*

AMPHIBIOUS 3

3 *Paita* (US *Terrebonne Parish*) LST, capacity 395 tps, 16 tk

SUPPORT AND MISCELLANEOUS 9

3 AO, 1 AGOR, 1 AOT, 1 tpt, 2 AGHS, 1 AT/F (SAR)

LAKE PATROL

4 craft

NAVAL AVIATION (some 800)

7 cbt ac, 9 armed hel

ASW/MR 4 sqn with **ac** 5 *Super King Air* B 200T, 3 EMB-111A, 1 F-27 **hel** 5 AB-212 ASW, 4 ASH-3D (ASW)

TPT 2 An-32B, 1 Y-12

LIAISON 4 Bell 206B, 6 UH-1D hel, 3 Mi-8

TRG 1 Cessna 150, 5 T-34C

ASM *Exocet* AM-39 (on SH-3 hel)

MARINES (3,000)

1 Marine bde (5 bn, 1 recce, 1 cdo coy)

EQUIPMENT

RECCE V-100

APC 15 V-200 *Chaimite*, 20 BMR-600

MOR 81mm; **120mm** ε18

RCL 84mm: *Carl Gustav*; **106mm**: M-40A1

AD GUNS twin 20mm SP

COASTAL DEFENCE 3 bty with 18 **155mm** how

Air Force 15,000

(incl 2,000 conscripts); 114 cbt ac†, 23 armed hel

BBR 8 *Canberra*

FGA 2 gp, 6 sqn

3 with 28 Su-22 (incl 4* Su-22U), 18 Su-25 (incl 8* Su-25UB)

3 with 23 Cessna A-37B

FTR 3 sqn

1 with 10 *Mirage* 2000P, 2 -DP

2 with 9 *Mirage* 5P, 2 -DP

1 with 14 MiG-29 (incl 2 MiG-29UB)

ATTACK HEL 1 sqn with 23 Mi-24/-25

RECCE 1 photo-survey unit with 2 *Learjet* 25B, 2 -36A

TKR 1 Boeing KC 707-323C

TPT 3 gp, 7 sqn

  ac 17 An-32, 3 AN-72, 4 C-130A, 6 -D, 5 L-100-20, 2 DC-8-62F, 12 DHC-5, 8 DHC-6, 1 FH-227, 9 PC-6, 6 Y-12, 1 Boeing 737 **hel** 3 sqn with 8 Bell 206, 14 B-212, 5 B-214, 1 B-412, 10 Bo-105C, 5 Mi-6, 3 Mi-8, 35 Mi-17, 5 SA-316

PRESIDENTIAL FLT 1 F-28, 1 *Falcon* 20F

LIAISON ac 2 Beech 99, 3 Cessna 185, 1 Cessna 320, 15 *Queen Air* 80, 3 *King Air* 90, 1 PA-31T **hel** 8 UH-1D

TRG ac 2 Cessna 150, 25 EMB-312, 13 MB-339A, 20 T-37B/C, 15 T-41A/-D **hel** 12 Bell 47G

MISSILES

  ASM AS-30

  AAM AA-2 *Atoll*, AA-8 *Aphid*, AA-10 *Alemo*, R-550 *Magic*

  AD 3 SA-2, 6 SA-3 bn with 18 SA-2, 24 SA-3 launchers

Paramilitary 77,000

NATIONAL POLICE 77,000

General Police 43,000 **Security Police** 21,000 **Technical Police** 13,000

  100+ MOWAG *Roland* APC

COAST GUARD (1,000)

  5 *Rio Nepena* PCC, 3 PCI, 10 riverine PCI<

RONDAS CAMPESINAS (peasant self-defence force) perhaps 2,000 *rondas* 'gp', up to pl strength, some with small arms. Deployed mainly in emergency zone.

Opposition

SENDERO LUMINOSO (Shining Path) ε1,500–2,000 Maoist

MOVIMIENTO REVOLUCIONARIO TUPAC AMARU (MRTA) ε600

mainly urban gp

Suriname   Sme

	1997	1998	1999	2000
GDP	gld n.k.	gld n.k.		
	($338m)	($356m)		
per capita	$4,300	$4,600		
Growth	4.7%	3.4%		
Inflation	7.2%	21.1%		
Debt	$180m	$158m		
Def exp	εgld n.k.	εgld n.k.		
	($15m)	($15m)		
Def bdgt		εgld n.k.	εgld n.k.	
		($15m)	($15m)	
FMA (US)	$0.1m	$0.1m	$0.1m	$0.1m
$1=guilder	401	401	401	

Population			416,000
Age	*13–17*	*18–22*	*23–32*
Men	22,000	18,000	35,000
Women	21,000	18,000	35,000

Total Armed Forces

ACTIVE ε1,800

(all services form part of the Army)

Army 1,400

1 inf bn (4 inf coy) • 1 mech cav sqn • 1 MP 'bde' (bn)

EQUIPMENT

  RECCE 6 EE-9 *Cascavel*

  APC 9 YP-408, 15 EE-11 *Urutu*

  MOR 81mm: 6

  RCL 106mm: M-40A1

Navy 240

BASE Paramaribo

PATROL CRAFT, INSHORE 3

  3 *Rodman* 100 PCI, plus 5 boats

Air Force ε160

4 cbt ac, no armed hel

TPT/TRG 2 C-212-400 (configured for MPA), 1* BN-2 *Defender*, 1* PC-7

LIAISON 1 Cessna U206

HEL 2 SA-316, 1 AB-205

Trinidad and Tobago   TT

	1997	1998	1999	2000
GDP	TT$37bn	TT$39bn		
	($5.9bn)	($6.3bn)		
per capita	$9,900	$10,500		
Growth	3.9%	4.5%		
Inflation	3.7%	4.0%		
Debt	$2.7bn	$3.2bn		
Def exp	εTT$520m	εTT$550m		
	($83m)	($88m)		
Def bdgt		εTT$550m	εTT$580m	
		($88m)	($94m)	
FMA (US)	$0.1m	$0.1m	$0.1m	$0.1m
US$1=TT$	6.3	6.3	6.2	
Population			1,348,000
Age	*13–17*	*18–22*	*23–32*
Men	71,000	63,000	104,000
Women	70,000	63,000	108,000

Total Armed Forces

ACTIVE ε2,700

(all services form part of the Trinidad and Tobago Defence Force)

Army ε2,000

2 inf bn • 1 spt bn
EQUIPMENT
  MOR 60mm: ε40; **81mm:** 6 L16A1
  RL 82mm: 13 B-300
  RCL 82mm: B-300

Coast Guard 700

(incl 50 Air Wing)
BASE Staubles Bay (HQ), Hart's Cut, Point Fortin, Tobago, Galeota
PATROL CRAFT, INSHORE 10 (some non-op)
  2 *Wasp* PCC
  2 *Barracuda* PFI (Sw *Karlskrona* 40m) (non-op)
  4 *Plymouth* PCI< (plus 10 boats and 2 auxiliary vessels)
  2 *Point* PCC (not armed)
AIR WING
  2 C-26, 1 Cessna 310, 1 C-402, 1 C-172

Uruguay — Ury

	1997	1998	1999	2000
GDP	pU189bn	pU218bn		
	($13bn)	($14bn)		
per capita	$8,800	$9,200		
Growth	6.0%	2.5%		
Inflation	19.8%	10.8%		
Debt	$6.4bn	$6.9bn		
Def exp	εpU2.9bn	εpU3.3bn		
	($307m)	($315m)		
Def bdgt		pU2.9bn	pU2.6bn	
		($273m)	($238m)	
FMA (US)	$0.3m	$0.3m	$0.3m	$0.3m
$1 =pU (Uruguayan peso)				
	9.4	10.5	11.1	
Population				3,247,000
Age	*13–17*	*18–22*	*23–32*	
Men	132,000	136,000	246,000	
Women	127,000	131,000	241,000	

Total Armed Forces

ACTIVE 25,600

Army 17,600

4 Mil Regions/div HQ • 5 inf bde (4 of 3 inf bn, 1 of 1 mech, 1 mot, 1 para bn) • 3 cav bde (10 cav bn (4 horsed, 3 mech, 2 mot, 1 armd)) • 1 arty bde (2 arty, 1 AD arty bn) • 1 engr bde (3 bn) • 3 arty, 4 cbt engr bn
EQUIPMENT
  MBT 15 T-55
  LT TK 17 M-24, 29 M-3A1, 22 M-41A1
  RECCE 18 EE-3 *Jararaca*, 15 EE-9 *Cascavel*
  AIFV 10 BMP-1
  APC 18 M-113, 50 *Condor*, 60 OT-64 SKOT
  TOWED ARTY 75mm: 12 Bofors M-1902; **105mm:** 48 M-101A/M-102; **155mm:** 5 M-114A1
  MRL 122mm: 2 RM-70
  MOR 81mm: 97; **107mm:** 8 M-30; **120mm:** 44
  ATGW 5 *Milan*
  RCL 57mm: 30 M-18; **106mm:** 30 M-40A1
  AD GUNS 20mm: 6 M-167 *Vulcan*; **40mm:** 8 L/60

Navy 5,000

(incl 280 Naval Aviation, 400 Naval Infantry, 1,600 *Prefectura Naval* (Coast Guard))
BASES Montevideo (HQ), La Paloma, Fray Bentos
FRIGATES 3
FF 3 *General Artigas* (Fr *Cdt Rivière*) with 2 x 3 ASTT, 1 x 2 ASW mor, 2 100mm guns
PATROL AND COASTAL COMBATANTS 10
PATROL, INSHORE 10
  2 *Colonia* PCI (US *Cape*), 3 *15 de Noviembre* PFI (Fr *Vigilante* 42m), 1 *Salto* PCI, 1 *Paysandu* PCI, 3 other PCI
MINE COUNTERMEASURES 4
  4 *Temerario* MSC (Ge *Kondor* II)
AMPHIBIOUS craft only
  3 LCM, 2 LCVP
SUPPORT AND MISCELLANEOUS 6
  1 *Presidente Rivera* AOT, 1 *Vanguardia* ARS, 1 *Campbell* (US *Auk* MSF) PCO (Antarctic patrol/research), 1 AT (ex-GDR *Elbe*-Class), 1 trg, 1 AGHS
NAVAL AVIATION (280)
1 cbt ac, no armed hel
  ASW 1 *Super King Air* 200T
  TRG/LIAISON 2 T-28, 2 T-34B, 2 T-34C, 2 PA-34-200T, 3 C-182
  HEL 3 Wessex Mk60, 5 Wessex HC2, 2 Bell 47G, 2 SH-34J
NAVAL INFANTRY (400)
1 bn

Air Force 3,000

27 cbt ac, no armed hel
Flying hours 120

CBT AC 2 sqn
  1 with 10 A-37B, 1 with 5 IA-58B
SURVEY 1 EMB-110B1
HEL 1 sqn with 2 Bell 212, 6 UH-1H, 6 *Wessex* HC2
TPT 3 sqn with 3 C-212 (tpt/SAR), 3 EMB-110C, 1 F-27, 3 C-130B, 1 Cessna 310 (VIP), 1 Cessna 206
LIAISON 2 Cessna 182, 2 *Queen Air* 80, 5 U-17, 1 T-34A
TRG 12* T-34A/B, 5 T-41D, 5 PC-7U

Forces Abroad

UN AND PEACEKEEPING
EGYPT (MFO): 60 **GEORGIA** (UNOMIG): 3 obs **INDIA/PAKISTAN** (UNMOGIP): 3 obs **IRAQ/KUWAIT** (UNIKOM): 5 Obs **TAJIKISTAN** (UNMOT): 2 obs **WESTERN SAHARA** (MINURSO): 13 obs

Paramilitary 920

GUARDIA DE GRANADEROS 450

GUARDIA DE CORACEROS 470

COAST GUARD (1,600)
Prefectura Naval (PNN) is part of the Navy

Venezuela   Ve

	1997	1998	1999	2000
GDP	Bs43bn	Bs52bn		
	($88bn)	($89bn)		
per capita	$8,500	$8,500		
Growth	5.1%	-0.7%		
Inflation	50.0%	35.8%		
Debt	$32bn	$40bn		
Def exp	Bs752bn	Bs716bn		
	($1,540m)	($1,307m)		
Def bdgt		Bs716bn	Bs805bn	
		($1,307m)	($1,388m)	
FMA (US)	$1m	$1m	$1.1m	$1.1m
$1=bolivar	489	548	580	
Population				23,767,000
Age	*13–17*	*18–22*	*23–32*	
Men	1,231,000	1,157,000	1,996,000	
Women	1,185,000	1,118,000	1,943,000	

Total Armed Forces

ACTIVE 79,000
(incl National Guard and ε31,000 conscripts)
Terms of service 30 months selective, varies by region for all services

RESERVES ε8,000
Army

Army 34,000
(incl 27,000 conscripts)
6 inf div • 1 armd bde • 1 cav bde • 7 inf bde (18 inf, 1 mech inf, 4 fd arty bn) • 1 AB bde • 2 Ranger bde (1 with 4 bn, 1 with 2 bn) • 1 avn regt
RESERVES ε6 inf, 1 armd, 1 arty bn
EQUIPMENT
  MBT 81 AMX-30
  LT TK 75 M-18, 36 AMX-13, 80 *Scorpion* 90
  RECCE 30 M-8
  APC 25 AMX-VCI, 100 V-100, 30 V-150, 100 *Dragoon* (some with 90mm gun), 35 EE-11 *Urutu*
  TOWED ARTY 105mm: 40 Model 56, 40 M-101; 155mm: 12 M-114
  SP ARTY 155mm: 10 Mk F3
  MRL 160mm: 20 LAR SP
  MOR 81mm: 165; 120mm: 60 Brandt
  ATGW AS-11, 24 *Mapats*
  RL 84mm: AT-4
  RCL 84mm: *Carl Gustav*; 106mm: 175 M-40A1
  SURV RASIT (veh, arty)
  AC 3 IAI-202, 2 Cessna 182, 2 C-206, 2 C-207
  ATTACK HEL 5 A-109 (ATK)
  TPT HEL 4 AS-61A, 3 Bell 205, 6 UH-1H
  LIAISON 2 Bell 206

Navy 15,000
(incl 1,000 Naval Aviation, 5,000 Marines, 1,000 Coast Guard and ε4,000 conscripts)
NAVAL COMMANDS Fleet, Marines, Naval Avn, Coast Guard, Fluvial (River Forces)
NAVAL FLEET SQN submarine, frigate, patrol, amph, service
BASES Main bases Caracas (HQ), Puerto Cabello (submarine, frigate, amph and service sqn), Punto Fijo (patrol sqn) Minor bases Puerto de Hierro, Puerto La Cruz, El Amparo (HQ Arauca River), Maracaibo, La Guaira, Ciudad Bolivar (HQ Fluvial Forces)
SUBMARINES 2
SSK 2 *Sabalo* (Ge T-209/1300) with 533mm TT (SST-4 HWT)
FRIGATES 6
FFG 6 *Mariscal Sucre* (It *Lupo*) with 1 AB-212 hel (ASW/OTHT), 2 x 3 ASTT (A-244S LWT); 8 *Teseo* SSM, 1 127mm gun, 1 x 8 *Aspide* SAM (2 in refit)
PATROL AND COASTAL COMBATANTS 6
MISSILE CRAFT 6
  3 *Constitución* PFM (UK Vosper 37m), with 2 *Teseo* SSM
  3 *Constitución* PFI with 4 *Harpoon* SSM

AMPHIBIOUS 4

4 *Capana* LST (Sov *Alligator*), capacity 200 tps, 12 tk
Plus craft: 2 LCU (river comd), 12 LCVP

SUPPORT AND MISCELLANEOUS 5

1 log spt, 1 trg, 1 *Punta Brava* AGHS, 2 AGHS

NAVAL AVIATION (1,000)

7 cbt ac, 8 armed hel
ASW 1 hel sqn (afloat) with 8 AB-212
MR 1 sqn with 4 C-212-200 MPA, 3 C-212-400
TPT 2 C-212, 1 DHC-7, 1 *Rockwell Commander* 680
LIAISON 1 Cessna 310, 1 C-402, 1 *King Air* 90, 3 C-212-400
HEL 2 Bell 412

MARINES (5,000)

4 inf bn • 1 arty bn (3 fd, 1 AD bty) • 1 amph veh bn •
1 river patrol, 1 engr, 2 para/cdo unit
EQUIPMENT
AAV 11 LVTP-7 (to be mod to -7A1)
APC 25 EE-11 *Urutu*, 10 *Fuchs/Transportpanzer* 1
TOWED ARTY 105mm: 18 Model 56
AD GUNS 40mm: 6 M-42 twin SP

COAST GUARD (1,000)

BASE La Guaira; operates under Naval Command
and Control, but organisationally separate
PATROL, OFFSHORE 2
2 *Almirante Clemente* (It FF type)
PATROL, INSHORE 4
4 *Petrel* (USCG *Point*-class) PCI
plus 27 river patrol craft and boats
plus 1 support ship

Air Force 7,000

(some conscripts); 124 cbt ac, 31 armed hel
Flying hours 155
FTR/FGA 6 air gp
1 with 16 CF-5A/B (12 A, 4 B), 7 NF-5A/B
1 with 16 *Mirage* 50EV/DV
2 with 21 F-16A/B (14 A, 7 B)
2 with 20 EMB-312

RECCE 15* OV-10A
ECM 3 *Falcon* 20DC
ARMED HEL 1 air gp with 10 SA-316, 12 UH-1D, 5 UH-1H, 4 AS-532
TPT ac 7 C-123, 5 C-130H, 8 G-222, 2 HS-748, 2 B-707 (tkr) **hel** 2 Bell 214, 4 Bell 412, 8 AS-332B, 2 UH-1N, 18 Mi-8/17
PRESIDENTIAL FLT 1 Boeing 737, 1 *Gulfstream* III, 1 *Gulfstream* IV, 1 *Learjet* 24D **hel** 1 Bell 412
LIAISON 9 Cessna 182, 1 *Citation* I, 1 *Citation* II, 2 *Queen Air* 65, 5 *Queen Air* 80, 5 *Super King Air* 200, 9 SA-316B *Alouette* III
TRG 1 air gp: 12* EMB-312, 20 T-34, 17* T-2D, 12 SF-260E
MISSILES
AAM R-530 *Magic*, AIM-9L *Sidewinder*, AIM-9P *Sidewinder*
ASM *Exocet*
AD GUNS 20mm: some IAI TC-20; 35mm; 40mm: 114: Bofors L/70 towed, Otobreda 40L70 towed
SAM 10 *Roland*, RBS-70

National Guard (*Fuerzas Armadas de Cooperación*) 23,000

(internal sy, customs)
8 regional comd
EQUIPMENT
20 UR-416 AIFV, 24 Fiat-6614 APC, 100 **60mm** mor, 50 **81mm** mor ac 1 *Baron*, 1 BN-2A, 2 Cessna 185, 5 -U206, 4 IAI-201, 1 *King Air* 90, 1 *King Air* 200C, 2 *Queen Air* 80, 6 M-28 *Skytruck* **hel** 4 A-109, 20 Bell 206, 2 Bell 212
PATROL CRAFT, INSHORE 52 boats

Forces Abroad

UN AND PEACEKEEPING
IRAQ/KUWAIT (UNIKOM): 2 obs WESTERN
SAHARA (MINURSO): 3 obs

Sub-Saharan Africa

MILITARY DEVELOPMENTS

Sub-Saharan Africa accounted for over half of all the armed conflicts taking place around the world in 1999, and some of the most costly in terms of human life. Three-quarters of the countries in the region are engaged in armed conflict, or confronted by a significant threat from armed groups with a mixture of political and economic motives. Among those countries which have managed to avoid domestic armed conflict, several are intervening in wars elsewhere in the region or are involved in multilateral peacekeeping. Conflict is particularly concentrated in the swathe of territory stretching from the Horn of Africa in the east through Central Africa into Angola in the west. The civil wars in the Horn, the Democratic Republic of Congo (DROC), and, to some extent, that in Angola, have become international conflicts involving several regional neighbours. The border conflict between Ethiopia and Eritrea has developed into a costly war of attrition which threatens to draw in the warring parties in Sudan and Somalia. An important feature of domestic conflicts continues to be the rising number of private militias supporting political and ethnic groups and often engaged in criminal activities.

Horn of Africa

A peace plan to end the war between Eritrea and Ethiopia, sponsored by the Organisation for African Unity (OAU) and supported by the UN, has been agreed in principle by the two governments, but implementation is delayed. The plan calls for Eritrea to pull back its forces from territory it occupied after 6 May 1998, while Ethiopia is required to withdraw from positions taken after 7 February 1999. Both countries would be required to accept OAU and UN observers to oversee the troop redeployments. The fighting continues sporadically despite efforts by OAU, UN and US envoys to persuade the two governments to call a halt. Accurate data is difficult to obtain, but the war could have resulted in as many as 16,000 deaths and nearly half a million people displaced by mid-1999. The conflict began to take on an international aspect during 1999, with both antagonists seeking to open another front by increasing their contacts and military activities with the warring factions in Somalia, and engaging in cross-border military operations in Sudan in support of opposition groups there. However, by mid-1999 both Addis Ababa and Asmara were seeking to improve diplomatic relations with Khartoum because their cross-border activities were generating support for their own domestic armed opposition groups. Despite Eritrea's earlier backing of the *Front pour la Restoration de l'Unité et la Démocratie* (FRUD), a former Djibouti insurgent group, Djibouti's involvement in the current conflict has so far been confined to allowing Ethiopia, which is now deprived of its rights of access to the Eritrean port of Assab, to use Djibouti port facilities.

The Sudanese government has taken steps to improve its relations with Western countries. In particular, it acceded to the 1993 Chemical Weapons Convention in May 1999. Sudan's history of chemical-weapon programmes was brought to the fore by the 20 August 1998 US cruise missile attack on the al-Shifa pharmaceutical plant, which was alleged to be involved in chemical-weapon activities in support of Osama bin Laden's terrorist group. The 16-year old civil war continues between the Sudan Peoples' Liberation Army (SPLA), based in Sudan's mainly Christian and Animist south, and the Muslim-dominated Khartoum government. The year-long partial cease-fire, to allow aid agencies to operate in the south-western province of Bahr al-Ghazal, ended in July 1999, but peace talks continued.

Central Africa

The civil war in DROC escalated into an international conflict during the second half of 1998.

President Laurent Kabila's Alliance of Democratic Forces for the Liberation of Congo-Zaire (ADFL) coalition fell apart when Rwanda and Uganda withdrew their support and began offensive operations, mainly in eastern DROC, in support of the *Rassemblement Congolais pour la Démocratie* (RCD) against former *Forces Armées de Rwanda* (FAR) Hutu insurgents and *Interahamwe* rebels. Zimbabwe, Namibia, Angola, Chad and Sudan have sent troops to support Kabila. Most heavily involved is Zimbabwe, which could have had as many as 10,000 troops as well as combat aircraft engaged in the conflict by mid-1999, and has also, along with Libya, provided war materiel and funding. This operation has overstretched Harare's resources and, in an attempt to damp down domestic disquiet, the government has sought to play down the number of casualties. It claims that well below 100 have been killed, but, while reliable casualty estimates are scarce, independent sources have placed the toll nearer 700, along with losses of aircraft and other major equipment.

DROC and the six foreign governments most directly involved in the conflict signed a UN-backed cease-fire agreement in Lusaka on 10 July 1999. None of the rebel groups fighting in eastern DROC were signatories and the fighting continued, but the OAU and the UN went ahead with setting up the Joint Military Commission of military observers, provided for in the agreement to oversee implementation of the cease-fire. Under its commander, General Lalli Rachid of Algeria, it had established its headquarters in Zambia by the end of July 1999.

The resurgence of the Angolan civil war in late 1998 continued into 1999, and there were reports that the forces of *União Nacional para a Independência Total de Angola* (UNITA) were again engaged over the border with DROC. By mid-1999, the rebels had expanded their area of operations and were putting considerable pressure on the Angolan government's *Forças Armadas Angolanas* (FAA). UNITA has shown the capability to attack towns and villages less than 100 kilometres from the Angolan capital Luanda, and has won back the diamond-rich Lunda Sul and Lunda Norte provinces, which generate the finance, estimated at $500m in 1998, for its war effort. The rebel forces pose a threat to oil-producing areas around Soyo and in the Cabinda enclave, which provide the Angolan government with revenues of some $1.5 billion a year. Partly in response to military set backs, Luanda has set out to garner international support for its campaign against UNITA and to isolate its leader, Jonas Savimbi. On 23 July 1999, the Angolan government issued a warrant for Savimbi's arrest on charges of war crimes, and lobbied for the UN to set up an international court and to issue an international arrest warrant for Savimbi.

In neighbouring Congo, internal armed conflict between the private militias supporting various political factions flared up again in December 1998 and continued in 1999. With both FAA and UNITA forces involved, the war is effectively an extension of Angola's domestic conflict and part of the struggle for control of mineral resources in the adjacent Angolan province of Cabinda.

West Africa

In Sierra Leone, forces of the Nigerian-led Economic Community of West African States (ECOWAS) Military Observer Group (ECOMOG) continued operations in the north and around the capital Freetown until the May 1999 cease-fire. They had been operating in Sierra Leone since March 1998 against the Revolutionary United Front (RUF) and the Armed Council Revolutionary Force (ACRF). Nigeria had already given notice that it intended to withdraw its forces, numbering some 11,000, from Sierra Leone by the end of 1999, mainly because of the drain on its resources caused by the protracted military operations and the change in Nigerian domestic politics. In Guinea-Bissau, the military rebellion led by General Ansumane Mané against the government of President João Bernardo Vieira achieved victory in May. Senegalese and Guinean troops, sent to support Vieira soon after the rebellion broke out in June 1998, had been replaced by ECOMOG forces under the November 1998 Abuja Agreement (financial constraints delayed their arrival until February 1999). These forces in turn were mainly withdrawn in June 1999, following the government's defeat, but

General Mané and his transitional prime minister Francisco Fadul requested ECOMOG to retain a presence in the country until the elections planned for 28 November 1999.

While Senegal was sending its troops abroad on peacekeeping missions, its own civil war with separatist rebels in the Casamance region grew more intense, particularly in June 1999. The principal rebel leader, Augustin Diamacoune Senghor, while engaged in peace negotiations with the government, has difficulty in dealing with the more hard-line groups supporting the independence movement. In Nigeria, military government formally ended in May 1999 when an elected government, headed by former general and president, Olusegun Obasanjo, took over from General Abdulsalam Abubakar's regime. Despite the great strides taken in democratic development and military reform, the security forces are challenged by large-scale ethnic violence. For example, the conflict between Hausas and Yorubas in July 1999 in Kano in the north and Sagama in the south led to at least 70 deaths. The violence is not always purely ethnic in character. In the Warri region of the Niger Delta, for example, inequities in sharing oil wealth are at the heart of the problem, and the issue is further complicated by the local population's sufferings from environmental damage caused directly and indirectly by the oil companies.

On a more optimistic note, millions of rounds of ammunition and at least 10,000 small arms and light weapons in Liberia were collected in July 1999 and destroyed under a UN monitored plan as part of the peace settlement at the end of the civil war. All foreign forces have been withdrawn apart from some UN military observers and a small ECOMOG training mission. However, there is evidence that President Charles Taylor has been supporting RUF activities in Sierra Leone, fuelling the conflict there.

Southern Africa

By the end of 1999, foreign forces had largely been withdrawn from Lesotho. These forces had been invited into the country by Prime Minister Pakalitha Mosisili to help him deal with the civil disturbances, involving at least half of the 3,000-strong Royal Lesotho Defence Force, in the wake of elections in May 1998. In response to Mosisili's request, some 3,400 personnel from the South African National Defence Force (SANDF) and 400 from the Botswana Defence Force had launched *Operation Boleas* in September 1998. The military operation continued until late October 1998.

Apart from *Operation Boleas*, the SANDF has not embarked on any operations abroad, although there has been pressure on the South African government for the force to play a direct role in regional peacekeeping efforts. The SANDF is much absorbed with internal reorganisation and reform and would have difficulty deploying a force of any significant size abroad. In the course of reorganisation, SANDF operations are now integrated under a Chief of Joint Operations. The force's personnel strength will continue to decline from the present 85,000 to about 70,000 – half the level of four years ago. The land-force element has a demanding task in supporting the South African Police Service, particularly in border areas, which means that only very limited numbers would be available for overseas deployment. The Air Force continues to suffer a severe shortage of air-crew and has only 52% of the pilots required, according to reports. The Navy's capabilities have continued to decline due to lack of resources. For example, only one of its three submarines is operational, although there are plans to buy Type 209s from Germany as replacements. While an equipment modernisation plan worth $5bn has had parliamentary approval, it is questionable whether it will be fully implemented given the pressures on government spending overall.

DEFENCE SPENDING

Escalation of armed conflict in Africa has resulted in a significant increase in the region's military spending. Expenditure rose in 1998 for the second successive year, to reach $9.7bn (in 1997 US dollars) compared with $9.2bn in 1997, according to estimates by *The Military Balance*. This represents real growth of 5%, but the figure is much higher if South Africa, with the continuing steep decline in its defence spending, is removed from the calculation. Underlying growth in the rest of the region is 14%, and military expenditure would be still higher, by up to $1bn, if extra-regional military assistance and funding of armed opposition groups and militias were included. Regional gross domestic product (GDP) grew by less than 1% in real terms in 1998, while government spending on defence as a proportion of GDP increased to 3.8% from 3.4% in 1997. While regional consumer-price inflation dipped from 13.7% in 1997 to 12% in 1998, external debt remains high. The deterioration of public finances in several countries has been partly due to weak prices for Africa's principal mineral and commodity exports. The steep decline in gold prices from June 1999 seriously affected the foreign earnings of a number of countries, particularly Ghana and South Africa. However, the most important factor in many cases has been the onerous and unbudgeted costs of military conflict.

Regional Arms Trade

The escalation of Africa's wars led to a large increase in the regional arms market. *The Military Balance* estimates that the market's value, including both equipment and services like private militia companies, grew to some $1.7bn in 1998 from $1bn in 1997. The structure of the sub-Saharan arms trade is the most diverse in the world, and covers everything from advanced modern weaponry and second-hand major conventional weapons systems to large quantities of light weapons, small arms and ammunition. A larger number of major weapons covered by the UN Register of Conventional Arms was exported to the region in 1998, with leading suppliers including Russia, China and a number of East European countries. Bulgaria and Ukraine were particularly active. Modern fighters (Russian Su-27s to Ethiopia and MiG-29s to Eritrea) were exported to belligerents in the region for the first time since the end of the Cold War. In 1998, the major conflicts also attracted private military companies, which included a strong presence of personnel from Eastern Europe and South Africa.

War Financing

The major conflicts in the Horn of Africa, Central Africa and Angola are financed, directly or indirectly, from external sources. Some foreign governments are contributing. For example, Iran is supporting the Sudanese regime and Libya is backing the governments of DROC and its allies Zimbabwe and Chad; Zimbabwe itself is lending to DROC, reportedly in return for mineral rights. Taxes raised by warring governments to fund the fighting are mostly derived from export levies on oil, diamonds and other mineral commodities; and war loans are raised from the external private sector in return for property rights or concessions on oil and mineral assets. Contributions from, or what amounts in some cases to confiscations from, national diasporas are also contributing to the war efforts. In addition, many governments in the region have access to structural adjustment funding from the International Monetary Fund (IMF) and development assistance, including for demobilisation programmes, from the World Bank. This is raising questions about the multilateral banks' inadvertent role as financiers to Africa's wars. Their equivocal position has been all the more noticeable in a period when the UN itself has been increasingly unable or unwilling to commit to peacekeeping operations, and the US and Europe have been preoccupied by military commitments in the Balkans and elsewhere.

The Horn of Africa

The mismatch between official spending figures and actual outlays is nowhere more apparent than in the Horn of Africa. The civil war in Sudan is estimated to be costing the government around $400m a year – a half of all government spending – while the opposition groups increasingly target economic assets in the south of the country, such as oil and diamonds, to fund their military needs. Ethiopia, engaged in its increasingly costly border war with Eritrea since May 1998, declared a defence budget of B995m ($140m) for 1998, rising to B3,500m ($467m) in 1999. Outlays in 1998 were an estimated B2,700m ($379m). Eritrea has not released its defence budget since 1997 when it was N1.4bn ($196m). Its defence spending is estimated to have been $208m in 1998 and to be $236m in 1999. The expensive weapon purchases by both belligerents, starting in late 1998 and continuing in 1999, suggest that military spending will be significantly higher than budgeted for. Reports suggest that Ethiopia took delivery from Russia in late 1998 of four Su-27 fighters (of a total order of eight) and a mixture of Mi-17 utility and Mi-24 attack helicopters, amounting to 12 in all. Ethiopia also purchased some 140 T-55 main battle tanks (MBTs) from Bulgaria during 1998, of which 50 were delivered during the year. Light weapons and ammunition have been supplied by China. Orders in 1999 include ten 2S19 152mm howitzers from Russia. In the same period, Russia sold six MiG-29 fighters to Eritrea and four Mi-17 helicopters, while Eritrean orders from Russia in 1999 include 200 SA-18 surface-to-air (SAM) missiles. These arms transfers appear contrary to the commitments under the Wassenaar Arrangement which both Russia and Bulgaria signed in July 1996.

East and Central Africa

Military spending by all the warring parties in the region, and particularly by DROC, Zimbabwe and Uganda, is well above budgeted figures and Libya has been reported as contributing $60–100m in finance to Chad and Zimbabwe and fuel supplies on credit to DROC. Uganda's official defence budget for 1998 was S165bn ($133m) rising to S170bn ($120m) in 1999, whereas official outlays for 1998 were $39m higher at S213bn ($172m). The real outlay is estimated at $226m. Uganda took delivery of some 90 T-54/55 MBTs from Bulgaria in late 1998.

Table 34 Ghana: defence spending in 1997 and 1998

(cedim/(US$m))	1997 Budget		1997 Outlay		1998 Budget	
General Administration	314	0.2	314	0.2	394	0.2
General Headquarters	36,272	17.7	36,599	17.9	49,625	21.4
Army	27,926	13.6	27,926	13.6	30,264	13.1
Navy	5,713	2.8	5,520	2.7	6,735	2.9
Air Force	7,933	3.9	7,806	3.8	8,996	3.9
Sub-Total	78,157	38.1	78,164	38.1	96,013	41.5
Procurement & Construction	16,853	8.2	9,994	4.9	36,800	15.9
ECOMOG	10,000	4.9	9,892.1	4.8	12,000	5.2
Total	105,010	51.2	98,050	47.8	144,813	62.6

West Africa

Nigeria's defence budget for 1999 is N25.7bn ($278m at the new 1999 exchange rate), compared to N21bn ($228m) budgeted for internal security. These figures understate real military spending (estimated at $2.1bn) in 1998, as they exclude procurement and military construction funding, military pensions, state-level funding for military governors, and funding for paramilitary forces under the Ministry of the Interior. In January 1999, the military lost their privileged access to foreign currency at the subsidised official rate of US$1=N22. Ghana's defence budget increased from $51m in 1997 (outlays $48m) to $63m in 1998. Ghana's ECOMOG contribution cost some $5m in both 1997 and 1998. These figures may exclude some military funding under other budget headings. By comparison, Cameroon's defence budget in 1998 was CFA fr86bn ($146m), a figure which again understates the real military outlay.

Southern Africa

South Africa's defence budget in 1999 rose in nominal terms to R10.7bn ($1.7bn) from R10.3bn ($1.9bn) in 1998, but its purchasing power declined in terms of the US dollar and other hard currencies. By comparison, the police budget is R14.5bn ($2.3bn) in 1999 compared with $13.9bn ($2.5bn) in 1998.

Table 35 South Africa's defence budget, 1995–2000

(Rm/US$m)	1995		1996		1997		1998		1999		2000		2001	
Administration	378	104	478	111	4,72.6	103	452	82	678	109	657	106	662	107
Army	3,980	1,097	4,214	980	4,288	931	3,924	710	3,619	584	3,361	542	3,378	545
Air Force	1,753	483	2,104	489	2,083	452	1,903	344	1,944	314	1,884	304	1,906	307
Navy	778	215	781	182	802	174	833	151	842	136	808	130	842	136
Medical Support	739	204	873	203	887	193	910	165	939	151	909	147	937	151
General Support and other	367	101	617	143	633	n.k.	637	115	778	125	752	121	757	122
Special Defence Account and other	3,525	9,72	1,854	431	1,942	421	1,591	288	1,829	295	2,529	408	2,849	459
Total Defence Budget	11,521	3,176	10,921	2,540	11,107	2,410	10,250	1,853	10,628	1,714	10,899	1,758	11,329	1,827
Estimated Total Budget including Provinces, Intelligence and Capital Works	12,517	3,451	12,185	2,834	11,598	2,517	11,844	2,142	11,970	1,931	12,287	1,982	12,581	2,029

The first of 12 *Rooivalk* attack helicopters for the South African Air Force was delivered in January 1999. In November 1998, the government announced its choice of preferred bidders for the SANDF modernisation programmes, valued at $5bn over 15 years, for which the competitions had run since October 1997. Procurement plans (for initial delivery dates stretching from 2002 to 2009) include: 28 JAS-39 *Grippens* from Sweden; 24 *Hawk* trainers and light attack aircraft from the UK; 40 A-119 light helicopters from Italy; four naval *Lynx* helicopters from the UK; and four *Meek* A-200 corvettes and three modernised Type 209 submarines from Germany. Pretoria is seeking a substantial countertrade package from the successful suppliers, including some $4bn in direct and indirect offsets, $10bn in exports arising from industrial participation, and $4bn in local sales, as well as the creation of 65,000 new jobs. South Africa's exports of defence equipment declined in 1998 to R646m ($118m) compared to R1,320m ($294m) in 1997. These figures exclude revenues from defence services provided by private military and security organisations.

Operation Boleas in Lesotho cost the SANDF some $7m, while the operation's cost to the Botswana Defence Force over the September 1998–April 1999 period was given as $4m. Namibia's defence budget rises from N$443m ($80m) in 1998 to N$559m ($90m) in 1999.

The Angolan government is estimated to have spent nearly $1bn on defence in 1998, accounting for over half of its spending overall.

Table 36 Arms orders and deliveries, Sub-Saharan Africa, 1997–1999

Supplier	Classification	Designation	Units	Order Date	Delivery Date	Comment
Angola						
US	tpt	C-130	6	1996	1997	
RF	MBT	T-72		1997	1999	
RF	hel	Mi-17	6	1997	1997	
RF	FGA	MiG-23	18	1997	1997	Deliveries into 1998
Kaz	MRL	BM-21	4	1997	1998	RF state of origin
Bel	APC	BMP-1	7	1998	1999	
Bel	MRL	BM-21		1998	1999	RF state of origin
Ukr	cbt hel	Mi-24	6	1998	1998	For UNITA
Ukr	FGA	MiG-23	6	1998	1998	For UNITA
Botswana						
US	tpt	C-130B	2	1996	1997	Ex-USAF
Ca	FGA	F-5	13	1996	1996	Ex-CAF. 3 delivered 1996, rest 1997
A	lt tk	SK-105	20	1997	1998	Option on further 20
Burundi						
RSA	APC	RG-31	12	1997	1998	
Cameroon						
RSA	FGA	MB-326	6	1995	1997	
Il	arty	155mm	8	1996	1997	4 in 1997, 4 in 1998
Congo						
RSA	APC	Mamba	18	1995	1997	
Côte d'Ivoire						
PRC	AF	Atchan	1	1994	1998	Logistic support ship
RSA	APC	RG-31	2	1995	1997	
Fr	trg	Alphajet	2	1996	1997	Repair and overhaul
Democratic Republic of Congo						
Bel	MRL	BM-21	6	1996	1997	
Pl	mor	120mm	18	1997	1998	With 1,000 rounds of ammunition
Eritrea						
It	trg	MB-339C	6	1996	1997	
Il	tpt	IAI-1125	1	1997	1998	
RF	FGA	MiG-29	6	1998	1998	
SF	trg	Rodrigo	8	1998	1999	
RF	hel	Mi-17	4	1998	1999	
RF	SAM	SA-18	200	1999	1999	
Mol	FGA	MiG-21	6	1999	1999	
Ga	FGA	Su-25	8	1999	1999	
Ethiopia						
US	tpt	C-130B	4	1995	1998	Ex-USAF
RF	cbt hel	Mi-24	4	1998	1998	
RF	hel	Mi-17	8	1998	1998	
Bg	MBT	T-55	140	1998	1995	50 delivered 1998. Deliveries to 1999
R	FGA	Mig-21/23	10	1998	1999	
RF	FGA	Su-27	8	1998	1998	
RF	SP arty	152mm	10	1999	1999	
Kenya						
UK	PCI		4	1995	1996	
Fr	LACV		4	1997	1998	Riot control armoured cars
Mauritius						
Chl	OPV	Vigilant	1	1993	1996	Ca design, for Coast Guard
Fr	hel	AS-555	1	1996	1997	
Namibia						
Br	PCI			1996	1999	

Supplier	Classification	Designation	Units	Order Date	Delivery Date	Comment
RSA	arty	140mm	24	1997	1998	Free transfer
Ge	APC	MK2	30	1998	1999	
Niger						
LAR	tpt	An-26	1	1996	1997	
Rwanda						
RSA	APC	RG-31 *Nyala*	6	1995	1996	
RSA	APC	RG-31	14	1995	1997	4 in 1997, 10 in 1998
R	lt wpns			1996	1997	116 tonnes of Kalashnikovs Feb/Apr 1997
Slvk	MRL	122mm	5	1996	1997	
Bel	cbt hel	Mi-24	2	1997	1997	Via Uga
Senegal						
Fr	LACV		10	1997	1998	Fr donated to MISAB
Sierra Leone						
PRC	PFI	*Shanghai* 2	2	1995	1997	
Ukr	cbt hel	Mi-24	2	1996	1999	
Bel	cbt hel	Mi-24B	2	1996	1997	
Ukr	FGA	*Alphajet*	3	1997	1997	
South Africa						
dom	AAM	R-*Darter*		1988	1998	Dev prog continuing, user trials 1998
dom	FGA	*Cheetah*-C	38	1988	1991	Upgrade with Il assistance through 1994
dom	hel	SA-332	50	1989	1991	SA-330 upgrade to AS-332 standard continuing to 1996
dom	APC	*Mamba*	586	1993	1995	Production ended in 1998. Mk 2 in dev
CH	trg	PC-7	60	1993	1995	Deliveries to 1996
US	tpt	C-130	5	1995	1997	5 C-130 from US, upgrades for 12 C-130s through 2002
dom	cbt hel	*Rooivalk*	12	1996	1999	Deliveries to 2000
Ge	SS	Type 209	3	1996	1999	Upgrade through 2004 for 3 *Daphne*-class SS
dom	arty	155mm		1997	2006	Development
Ge	SS	Type 209	3	1998	2004	Deliveries 2004–6
Ge	corvette	*Meek* A-200	4	1998	2002	Deliveries through 2004
dom	arty	LIW 35 DPG		1998		Development. Twin 35mm gun completed first trials
It	hel	A-119	40	1998	2002	
Swe	FGA	JAS-39	28	1998	2009	Deliveries 2009–14
UK	FGA	*Hawk*	24	1998	2004	
UK	cbt hel	*Lynx*	4	1998	2002	
dom	SS	*Daphne*	3	1998	1999	Upgrade 1999–2004
Tanzania						
RSA	hel	SA-316	4	1998	1998	Free transfer
Togo						
Bg	SP arty	122mm	6	1996	1997	
Pl	AIFV	BWP-2	20	1996	1997	
Uganda						
Ukr	MBT	T-54/T-55	60	1994	1995	Second-hand
Bel	cbt hel	Mi-24	2	1997	1997	4 contracted
RF	FGA	MiG-21/23	28	1998	1998	
Bg	MBT	T-54	90	1998	1998	All delivered in 1998
RSA	APC	*Chubby*		1998		Mine Clearing veh
Zimbabwe						
Fr	ACV	ACMAT	23	1992	1999	
US	tpt	C-130	2	1995	1996	
It	trg	SF-260F	6	1997	1999	
RF	cbt hel	Mi-24	10	1999	1999	

Dollar GDP figures in Sub-Saharan Africa are usually based on African Development Bank estimates. In several cases, the dollar GDP values do not reflect the exchange rates shown in the country entry.

Angola   Ang

	1997	1998	1999	2000
GDP	ε$8.2bn	ε$8.1bn		
per capita	$1,600	$1,500		
Growth	7.6%	-1.1%		
Inflation	111.2%	82.3%		
Debt	$11.0bn	$12.0bn		
Def exp	ε$764m	ε$955m		
Def bdgt		$458m	$574m	
FMA[a] (Fr)	$0.01m	$0.03m	$0.5m	
FMA (US)	$0.2m	$0.0m	$0.1m	$0.1m
$1 =kwanza[b]				
	229,000	392,000	696,500	

[a] UNOMA **1997** $135m **1998** $46m
[b] Market rate **1999** $1=εk1.5m

Population			12,055,000

(Ovimbundu 37%, Kimbundu 25%, Bakongo 13%)

	13–17	18–22	23–32
Men	654,000	553,000	840,000
Women	656,000	557,000	857,000

Total Armed Forces

ACTIVE ε112,500

A unified national army, including UNITA troops, was to have been formed with a str of ε90,000. The integration process has been abandoned and civil war between government and UNITA forces resumed in December 1998.

Army ε100,000

35 regts (armd and inf – str vary)

EQUIPMENT†
  MBT 100 T-54/-55, ε230 T-62, ε30 T-72
  RECCE some 40+ BRDM-2
  AIFV ε350 BMP-1/-2
  APC 100 BTR-60/-152
  TOWED ARTY 300: incl **76mm**: M-1942 (ZIS-3);
    85mm: D-44; **122mm**: D-30; **130mm**: M-46
  ASLT GUNS **100mm**: SU-100
  MRL **122mm**: 50 BM-21, 40 RM-70; **240mm**: some
    BM-24
  MOR **82mm**: 250; **120mm**: 40+ M-43
  ATGW AT-3 *Sagger*
  RCL 500: **82mm**: B-10; **107mm**: B-11
  AD GUNS 200+: **14.5mm**: ZPU-4; **23mm**: ZU-23-2,
    20 ZSU-23-4 SP; **37mm**: M-1939; **57mm**: S-60
    towed, 40 ZSU-57-2 SP
  SAM SA-7/-14

Navy ε1,500

BASE Luanda (HQ)
PATROL, INSHORE 7†
  4 *Mandume* Type 31.6m PCI, 3 *Patrulheiro* PCI (all
  non-op)
MINE COUNTERMEASURES 1†
  1 Sov *Yevgenya* MHC (non-op)
AMPHIBIOUS 1†
  1 Sov *Polnochny* LSM, capacity 100 tps, 6 tk (non-op)
  Plus craft

COASTAL DEFENCE
  SS-C-1 *Sepal* at Luanda (non-op)

Air Force/Air Defence 11,000

85 cbt ac, 28 armed hel
FGA 30 MiG-23, 9 Su-22, 16 Su-25
FTR 20 MiG-21 MF/bis
CCT/RECCE 10* PC-7/9
MR 2 EMB-111, 1 F-27MPA, 1 *King Air* B-200B
ATTACK HEL 15 Mi-25/35, 5 SA-365M (guns), 6 SA-
  342 (HOT), 2 Mi-24B
TPT 2 An-2, 9 An-26, 6 BN-2, 2 C-212, 4 PC-6B, 2 L-100-
  20, 2 C-130
HEL 8 AS-565, 30 IAR-316, 6 Mi-8/17
TRG 3 Cessna 172, 6 Yak-11
AD 5 SAM bn, 10 bty with 40 SA-2, 12 SA-3, 25 SA-6,
  15 SA-8, 20 SA-9, 10 SA-13 (mostly unserviceable)
MISSILES
  ASM HOT, AT-2 *Swatter*
  AAM AA-2 *Atoll*

Forces Abroad

DROC: ε600; **CONGO**: 800–1,000

Paramilitary 15,000

RAPID-REACTION POLICE 15,000

Opposition

UNITA (Union for the Total Independence of Angola)
ε25–35,000 fully equipped tps plus 30,000 spt militia reported
  EQPT BMP-1, BMP-2 AIFV, T-34/-85, T-55, T-62
    MBT, misc APC; **75mm, 76mm, 100mm, 122mm,
    130mm, 155mm** fd guns; BM-21 **122mm** MRL;
    81mm, 82mm, 120mm mor; **85mm** RPG-7 RL;
    75mm RCL; **12.7mm** hy machine guns; **14.5mm,
    20mm**, ZU-23-2 **23mm** AA guns; SAM-7

FLEC (Front for the Liberation of the Cabinda Enclave)
ε600 (claims 5,000)
Small arms only

Benin   Bn

	1997	1998	1999	2000
GDP	fr1.2tr	fr1.3tr		
	($2.1bn)	($2.2bn)		
per capita	$1,900	$1,900		
Growth	5.8%	4.4%		
Inflation	3.5%	5.7%		
Debt	$1.6bn	$1.7bn		
Def exp	εfr16bn	εfr19bn		
	($27m)	($32m)		
Def bdgt		εfr17bn	εfr21bn	
		($29m)	($35m)	
FMA (Fr)	$1.0m	$1.0m	$1.0m	
FMA (US)	$0.4m	$0.4m	$0.4m	$0.4m
$1=CFA fr	584	590	609	
Population				6,130,000
Age	*13–17*	*18–22*	*23–32*	
Men	363,000	297,000	421,000	
Women	372,000	311,000	458,000	

Total Armed Forces

ACTIVE ε4,800

Terms of service conscription (selective), 18 months

Army 4,500

3 inf, 1 AB/cdo, 1 engr bn, 1 armd sqn, 1 arty bty
EQUIPMENT
    LT TK 20 PT-76 (op status uncertain)
    RECCE 9 M-8, 14 BRDM-2, 10 VBL
    TOWED ARTY 105mm: 4 M-101, 12 L-118
    MOR 81mm
    RL 89mm: LRAC

Navy† ε150

BASE Cotonou
PATROL, INSHORE 1
    1 *Patriote* PFI (Fr 38m)<, plus 4 Sov *Zhuk*< PFI (non-op)

Air Force† 150

no cbt ac
AC 2 An-26, 2 C-47, 1 *Commander* 500B, 2 Do-128, 1 Boeing 707-320 (VIP), 1 F-28 (VIP), 1 DHC-6
HEL 2 AS-350B, 1 SE-3130

Paramilitary 2,500

GENDARMERIE 2,500

4 mobile coy

Botswana   Btwa

	1997	1998	1999	2000
GDP	P18.0bn	P20.4bn		
	($3.7bn)	($4.0bn)		
per capita	$5,700	$6,000		
Growth	6.9%	4.5%		
Inflation	8.5%	6.8%		
Debt	$550m	$500m		
Def exp	P879m	P1,080m		
	($241m)	($256m)		
Def bdgt		P868m	P990m	
		($205m)	($212m)	
FMA (US)	$0.4m	$0.5m	$0.5m	$0.5m
$1=pula	3.65	4.23	4.67	
Population				1,657,000
Age	*13–17*	*18–22*	*23–32*	
Men	101,000	85,000	130,000	
Women	103,000	87,000	134,000	

Total Armed Forces

ACTIVE 9,000

Army 8,500 (to be 10,000)

2 inf bde: 4 inf bn, 1 armd recce, 2 AD arty, 1 engr regt, 1 cdo unit • 1 arty bde
EQUIPMENT
    LT TK 36 *Scorpion* (incl variants), 30 SK-105 *Kuerassier*
    RECCE 12 V-150 *Commando* (some with **90mm** gun), RAM-V
    APC 30 BTR-60
    TOWED ARTY 105mm: 12 lt, 6 Model 56 pack; **155mm**: Soltam (reported)
    MOR 81mm: 12; **120mm**: 6 M-43
    ATGW 6 TOW (some SP on V-150)
    RCL 84mm: 50 *Carl Gustav*
    AD GUNS 20mm: 7 M-167
    SAM 12 SA-7, 10 SA-16, 5 *Javelin*

Air Wing 500

32 cbt ac, no armed hel
FTR/FGA 10 F-5A, 3 F-5B
TPT 2 CN-235, 2 *Skyvan* 3M, 1 BAe 125-800, 2 CN-212 (VIP), 1 *Gulfstream* IV, 12* BN-2 *Defender*
TRG 2 sqn 2 Cessna 152, 7* PC-7
HEL 5 AS-350B, 5 Bell 412

Paramilitary 1,000

POLICE MOBILE UNIT 1,000

(org in territorial coy)

Burkina Faso   BF

	1997	1998	1999	2000
GDP	fr1.8tr	fr1.9tr		
	($3.0bn)	($3.2bn)		
per capita	$900	$1,000		
Growth	5.5%	6.0%		
Inflation	2.1%	5.7%		
Debt	$1.3bn	$1.4bn		
Def exp	εfr39bn	εfr47bn		
	($67m)	($80m)		
Def bdgt		εfr45bn	εfr46bn	
		($76m)	($76m)	
FMA (Fr)	$1.0m	$1.0m	$1.0m	
$1=CFA fr	584	590	609	
Population				11,809,000
Age	*13–17*	*18–22*	*23–32*	
Men	684,000	557,000	824,000	
Women	660,000	543,000	848,000	

Total Armed Forces

ACTIVE 10,000

(incl *Gendarmerie*)

Army 5,600

6 Mil Regions • 5 inf 'regt': HQ, 3 'bn' (each 1 coy of 5 pl) • 1 AB 'regt': HQ, 1 'bn', 2 coy • 1 tk 'bn': 2 pl • 1 arty 'bn': 2 tp • 1 engr 'bn'
EQUIPMENT
    RECCE 15 AML-60/-90, 24 EE-9 *Cascavel*, 10 M-8, 4 M-20, 30 *Ferret*
    APC 13 M-3
    TOWED ARTY 105mm: 8 M-101; **122mm**: 6
    MRL 107mm: PRC Type-63
    MOR 81mm: Brandt
    RL 89mm: LRAC, M-20
    RCL 75mm: PRC Type-52
    AD GUNS 14.5mm: 30 ZPU
    SAM SA-7

Air Force 200

5 cbt ac, no armed hel
TPT 1 *Beech Super King*, 1 *Commander* 500B, 2 HS-748, 2 N-262, 1 Boeing 727 (VIP)
LIAISON 2 Cessna 150/172, 1 SA-316B, 1 AS-350, 3 Mi-8/17
TRG 5* SF-260W/WL

Forces Abroad

UN AND PEACEKEEPING
CAR (MINURCA): 126 tps

Paramilitary

GENDARMERIE 4,200
SECURITY COMPANY (CRG) 250
PEOPLE'S MILITIA (R) 45,000 trained

Burundi   Bu

	1997	1998	1999	2000
GDP	fr322bn			
	($1.1bn)	($1.1bn)		
per capita	$600	$600		
Growth	0.3%	4.6%		
Inflation	31.2%	11.9%		
Debt	$1.1bn	$1.1bn		
Def exp	εfr30bn	εfr36bn		
	($85m)	($80m)		
Def bdgt		fr27bn	fr35bn	
		($60m)	($65m)	
FMA (US)	$0.1m	$0.1m		
$1=franc	352	448	537	
Population	ε7,046,000 (Hutu 85%, Tutsi 14%)			
Age	*13–17*	*18–22*	*23–32*	
Men	426,000	343,000	523,000	
Women	388,000	315,000	486,000	

Total Armed Forces

ACTIVE 45,500

(incl *Gendarmerie*)

Army ε40,000

7 inf bn • 2 lt armd 'bn' (sqn), 1 arty bn • 1 engr bn • some indep inf coy • 1 AD bty
RESERVES
    10 bn (reported)
EQUIPMENT
    RECCE 85 incl 18 AML (6-60, 12-90), 7 Shorland, 30 BRDM-2
    APC 9 Panhard M-3, 20 BTR-40
    TOWED ARTY 122mm: 18 D-30
    MRL 122mm: 12 BM-21
    MOR 100+ incl 82mm: M-43; **120mm**
    RL 83mm: *Blindicide*
    RCL 75mm: 15 PRC Type-52
    AD GUNS 375: **14.5mm**: 15 ZPU-4; **23mm**: ZU-23; **37mm**: Type-54
    SAM SA-7
AIR WING (200)
4 cbt ac, no armed hel
TRG 4* SF-260W/TP
TP 2 DC-3
HEL 3 SA-316B, 2 Mi-8

Paramilitary

GENDARMERIE ε5,500 (incl ε50 Marine Police): 16
territorial districts
BASE Bujumbura
3 *Huchan* (PRC Type 026) PHT† plus 1 LCT, 1 spt, 4
boats

**GENERAL ADMINISTRATION OF STATE
SECURITY** ε1,000

Opposition

FORCES FOR THE DEFENCE OF DEMOCRACY
(FDD) ε3–4,000
HUTU PEOPLE'S LIBERATION PARTY
(PALIPEHUTU) armed wing (**FNL**) ε2–3,000

Cameroon — Crn

	1997	1998	1999	2000
GDP	fr5.0bn	fr5.2bn		
	($8.6bn)	($8.8bn)		
per capita	$2,200	$2,300		
Growth	5.2%	5.0%		
Inflation	2.0%	2.1%		
Debt	$9.2bn	$9.3bn		
Def exp	εfr140bn	εfr150bn		
	($240m)	($250m)		
Def bdgt		fr86bn	fr95bn	
		($146m)	($156m)	
FMA (US)	$0.1m	$0.1m	$0.2m	$0.2m
FMA (Fr)	$1.6m	$1.5m	$2m	
$1=CFA fr	584	590	609	
Population				15,113,000
Age	*13–17*	*18–22*	*23–32*	
Men	845,000	723,000	1,085,000	
Women	843,000	725,000	1,103,000	

Total Armed Forces

ACTIVE ε22,100
(incl *Gendarmerie*)

Army 11,500

8 Mil Regions each 1 inf bn under comd • Presidential
Guard: 1 guard, 1 armd recce bn, 3 inf coy • 1 AB/cdo
bn • 1 arty bn (5 bty) • 5 inf bn (1 trg) • 1 AA bn (6
bty) • 1 engr bn
EQUIPMENT
  RECCE 8 M-8, *Ferret*, 8 V-150 *Commando* (**20mm**
  gun), 5 VBL

AIFV 14 V-150 *Commando* (**90mm** gun)
APC 21 V-150 *Commando*, 12 M-3 half-track
TOWED ARTY 75mm: 6 M-116 pack; **105mm:** 16
  M-101; **130mm:** 12 Type-59; **155mm:** 4 I1
MRL 122mm: 20 BM-21
MOR 81mm (some SP); **120mm:** 16 Brandt
ATGW *Milan*
RL 89mm: LRAC
RCL 57mm: 13 PRC Type-52; **106mm:** 40 M-40A2
AD GUNS 14.5mm: 18 PRC Type-58; **35mm:** 18
  GDF-002; **37mm:** 18 PRC Type-63

Navy ε1,300

BASES Douala (HQ), Limbe, Kribi
PATROL AND COASTAL COMBATANTS 17
MISSILE CRAFT 1 *Bakassi* (Fr P-48) PFM with 2 x 4
  MM-40 *Exocet* SSM
PATROL, INSHORE 2
  1 *L'Audacieux* (Fr P-48) PFI, 1 *Quartier* PCI
PATROL, RIVERINE 14
  8 US *Swift*-38†, 6 *Simonneau*†

Air Force 300

15 cbt ac, 4 armed hel
1 composite sqn, 1 Presidential Fleet
FGA 4† *Alpha Jet*, 5 CM-170, 6 MB-326
MR 2 Do-128D-6
ATTACK HEL 4 SA-342L (with HOT)
TPT ac 3 C-130H/-H-30, 1 DHC-4, 4 DHC-5D, 1 IAI-
  201, 2 PA-23, 1 *Gulfstream* III, 1 Do-128, 1 Boeing 707
  hel 3 Bell 206, 3 SE-3130, 1 SA-318, 3 SA-319, 2 AS-
  332, 1 SA-365

Paramilitary

GENDARMERIE 9,000
10 regional groups; about 10 US *Swift*-38 (see Navy)

Cape Verde — CV

	1997	1998	1999	2000
GDP	E21bn	E23bn		
	($224m)	($237m)		
per capita	$2,100	$2,200		
Growth	3.0%	4.1%		
Inflation	8.5%	4.5%		
Debt	$200m	$225m		
Def exp	εE350m	εE380m		
	($4m)	($4m)		
Def bdgt		εE380m	εE400m	
		($4m)	($4m)	
FMA (US)	$0.1m	$0.1m	$0.1m	$0.1m
FMA (Fr)	$0.1m	$0.1m		
$1=escudo	93	98	95	

Population			459,000
Age	*13–17*	*18–22*	*23–32*
Men	27,000	23,000	36,000
Women	27,000	24,000	40,000

Total Armed Forces

ACTIVE ε1,100

Terms of service conscription (selective)

Army 1,000

2 inf bn gp
EQUIPMENT
  RECCE 10 BRDM-2
  TOWED ARTY **75mm**: 12; **76mm**: 12
  MOR **82mm**: 12; **120mm**: 6 M-1943
  RL **89mm**: 3.5in
  AD GUNS **14.5mm**: 18 ZPU-1; **23mm**: 12 ZU-23
  SAM 50 SA-7

Coast Guard ε50

1 *Kondor* I PCC
1 *Zhuk* PCI<, 1 *Espadarte* PCI<

Air Force under 100

no cbt ac
MR 1 Do-228

<table>
<tr><th colspan="6">Central African Republic   CAR</th></tr>
<tr><td></td><td>**1997**</td><td>**1998**</td><td>**1999**</td><td>**2000**</td></tr>
<tr><td>**GDP**</td><td>fr572bn</td><td>fr619bn</td><td></td><td></td></tr>
<tr><td></td><td>($1.0bn)</td><td>($1.1bn)</td><td></td><td></td></tr>
<tr><td>*per capita*</td><td>$1,200</td><td>$1,300</td><td></td><td></td></tr>
<tr><td>**Growth**</td><td>4.6%</td><td>5.6%</td><td></td><td></td></tr>
<tr><td>**Inflation**</td><td>0.6%</td><td>2.2%</td><td></td><td></td></tr>
<tr><td>**Debt**</td><td>$919m</td><td>$930m</td><td></td><td></td></tr>
<tr><td>**Def exp**</td><td>εfr23bn</td><td>εfr29bn</td><td></td><td></td></tr>
<tr><td></td><td>($39m)</td><td>($49m)</td><td></td><td></td></tr>
<tr><td>**Def bdgt**</td><td></td><td>εfr23bn</td><td>εfr28bn</td><td></td></tr>
<tr><td></td><td></td><td>($39m)</td><td>($46m)</td><td></td></tr>
<tr><td>**FMA**[a] (US)</td><td>$0.2m</td><td>$0.2m</td><td>$0.1m</td><td></td></tr>
<tr><td>**FMA** (Fr)</td><td>$2.0m</td><td>$2.0m</td><td>$1.0m</td><td></td></tr>
<tr><td>**$1=CFA fr**</td><td>584</td><td>590</td><td>609</td><td></td></tr>
<tr><td colspan="5">[a] MISAB **1997–98** $102m; MINURCA **1998** $47m</td></tr>
</table>

Population			3,774,000
Age	*13–17*	*18–22*	*23–32*
Men	203,000	169,000	287,000
Women	203,000	174,000	284,000

Total Armed Forces

ACTIVE 4,950
(incl *Gendarmerie*)
Terms of service conscription (selective), 2 years; reserve obligation thereafter, term n.k.

Army 2,500

1 Republican Guard regt (2 bn) • 1 territorial defence regt (bn) • 1 combined arms regt (1 mech, 1 inf bn) • 1 spt/HQ regt • 1 Presidential Guard bn
EQUIPMENT†
  MBT 4 T-55
  RECCE 10 *Ferret*
  APC 4 BTR-152, some 10 VAB, 25+ ACMAT
  MOR **81mm**; **120mm**: 12 M-1943
  RL **89mm**: LRAC
  RCL **106mm**: 14 M-40
  RIVER PATROL CRAFT 9<

Air Force 150

no cbt ac, no armed hel
TPT 1 Cessna 337, 1 *Mystère Falcon* 20, 1 *Caravelle*
LIAISON 6 AL-60, 6 MH-1521
HEL 1 AS-350, 1 SE-3130

Paramilitary

GENDARMERIE 2,300
3 regional legions, 8 'bde'

Foreign Forces

UN (MINURCA): 1,230 tps from 10 countries

<table>
<tr><th colspan="5">Chad   Cha</th></tr>
<tr><td></td><td>**1997**</td><td>**1998**</td><td>**1999**</td><td>**2000**</td></tr>
<tr><td>**GDP**</td><td>fr609bn</td><td>fr664bn</td><td></td><td></td></tr>
<tr><td></td><td>($1.0bn)</td><td>($1.1bn)</td><td></td><td></td></tr>
<tr><td>*per capita*</td><td>$800</td><td>$900</td><td></td><td></td></tr>
<tr><td>**Growth**</td><td>8.6%</td><td>6.4%</td><td></td><td></td></tr>
<tr><td>**Inflation**</td><td>5.6%</td><td>4.5%</td><td></td><td></td></tr>
<tr><td>**Debt**</td><td>$1,011m</td><td>$1,070m</td><td></td><td></td></tr>
<tr><td>**Def exp**</td><td>εfr25bn</td><td>εfr37bn</td><td></td><td></td></tr>
<tr><td></td><td>($43m)</td><td>($63m)</td><td></td><td></td></tr>
<tr><td>**Def bdgt**</td><td></td><td>εfr27bn</td><td>εfr29bn</td><td></td></tr>
<tr><td></td><td></td><td>($44m)</td><td>($48m)</td><td></td></tr>
<tr><td>**FMA** (Fr)</td><td>$2.0m</td><td>$2.0m</td><td>$2.1m</td><td></td></tr>
<tr><td>**FMA** (US)</td><td>$0.03m</td><td>$0.1m</td><td>$0.1m</td><td>$0.1m</td></tr>
<tr><td>**$1=CFA fr**</td><td>584</td><td>590</td><td>609</td><td></td></tr>
</table>

Population			7,172,000
Age	*13–17*	*18–22*	*23–32*
Men	383,000	316,000	497,000
Women	383,000	317,000	506,000

Total Armed Forces

ACTIVE ε30,350

(incl Republican Guard)
Terms of service conscription authorised

Army ε25,000

(being re-organised)
7 Mil Regions
EQUIPMENT
  MBT 60 T-55
  AFV 4 ERC-90, some 50 AML-60/-90, 9 V-150 with
    90mm, some EE-9 *Cascavel*
  TOWED ARTY 105mm: 5 M-2
  MOR 81mm; 120mm: AM-50
  ATGW *Milan*
  RL 89mm: LRAC
  RCL 106mm: M-40A1; **112mm**: APILAS
  AD GUNS 20mm, 30mm

Air Force 350

4 cbt ac, no armed hel
TPT ac 3 C-130, 1 C-212, 1 An-26 **hel** 2 SA-316
LIAISON 2 PC-6B, 5 Reims-Cessna FTB 337
TRG 2* PC-7, 2* SF-260W

Forces Abroad

UN AND PEACEKEEPING
CAR (MINURCA): 126 tps

Paramilitary 4,500 active

REPUBLICAN GUARD 5,000
GENDARMERIE 4,500

Opposition

WESTERN ARMED FORCES str n.k.

Foreign Forces

FRANCE 900: 2 inf coy; 1 AML sqn(-); 2 C-160, 1 C-130, 3 F-ICT, 2 F-ICR

Congo   RC

	1997	1998	1999	2000
GDP	fr1.3tr	fr1.2tr		
	($2.9bn)	($2.1bn)		
per capita	$2,000	$1,800		
Growth	0.3%	-8.0%		
Inflation	13.1%	5.5%		
Debt	$4.7bn	$4.8bn		
Def exp	εfr43bn	εfr48bn		
	($74m)	($81m)		
Def bdgt		εfr37bn	εfr45bn	
		($63m)	($74m)	
FMA (US)	$0.1m			
FMA (Fr)	$2.0m	$2.0m	$1.0m	
$1=CFA fr	584	590	609	
Population				3,045,000

(Kongo 48%, Sangha 20%, M'Bochi 12%, Teke 17%,
European mostly French 3%)

Age	*13–17*	*18–22*	*23–32*
Men	175,000	141,000	223,000
Women	165,000	134,000	215,000

Total Armed Forces

ACTIVE ε10,000

Army 8,000

2 armd bn • 2 inf bn gp (each with lt tk tp, 76mm gun bty) • 1 inf bn • 1 arty gp (how, MRL) • 1 engr bn • 1 AB/cdo bn
EQUIPMENT†
  MBT 25 T-54/-55, 15 PRC Type-59 (some T-34 in store)
  LT TK 10 PRC Type-62, 3 PT-76
  RECCE 25 BRDM-1/-2
  APC M-3, 50 BTR (30 -60, 20 -152), 18 Mamba
  TOWED ARTY 76mm: M-1942; **100mm**: 10 M-1944;
    122mm: 10 D-30; **130mm**: 5 M-46; **152mm**: some D-20
  MRL 122mm: 8 BM-21; **140mm**: BM-14-16
  MOR 82mm; 120mm: 10 M-43
  RCL 57mm: M-18
  ATK GUNS 57mm: 5 M-1943
  AD GUNS 14.5mm: ZPU-2/-4; **23mm**: ZSU-23-4 SP;
    37mm: 28 M-1939; **57mm**: S-60; **100mm**: KS-19

Navy† ε800

BASE Pointe Noire
PATROL AND COASTAL COMBATANTS ε3†
PATROL, INSHORE 3†
  3 Sov *Zhuk* PFI<†
PATROL, RIVERINE n.k.
  boats only

Air Force† 1,200

12 cbt ac, no armed hel
FGA 12 MiG-21
TPT 5 An-24, 1 An-26, 1 Boeing 727, 1 N-2501
TRG 4 L-39
HEL 2 SA-316, 2 SA-318, 1 SA-365, 2 Mi-8
MISSILES
AAM AA-2 *Atoll*

Paramilitary 2,000 active

GENDARMERIE 2,000
20 coy
PEOPLE'S MILITIA 3,000
being absorbed into national Army
PRESIDENTIAL GUARD
(forming)

Côte D'Ivoire   CI

	1997	1998	1999	2000
GDP	fr60.tr	fr6.6tr		
	($11.7bn)	($12.6bn)		
per capita	$1,600	$1,700		
Growth	7.0%	6.0%		
Inflation	5.2%	4.7%		
Debt	$21bn	$21bn		
Def exp	εfr59bn	εfr70bn		
	($101m)	($119m)		
Def bdgt		εfr70bn	εfr109bn	
		($119m)	($179m)	
FMA (US)	$0.2m	$0.2m	$0.2m	$0.2m
FMA (Fr)	$2.1m	$2.0m	$2.0m	
$1=CFA fr	584	590	609	
Population				16,508,000
Age	*13–17*	*18–22*	*23–32*	
Men	984,000	778,000	1,133,000	
Women	982,000	781,000	1,125,000	

Total Armed Forces

ACTIVE ε13,900
(incl Presidential Guard, *Gendarmerie*)
Terms of service conscription (selective), 6 months
RESERVES 12,000

Army 6,800

4 Mil Regions • 1 armd, 3 inf bn, 1 arty gp • 1 AB, 1
AA, 1 engr coy
EQUIPMENT
 LT TK 5 AMX-13
 RECCE 7 ERC-90 *Sagaie*, 16 AML-60/-90, 10 *Mamba*

APC 16 M-3, 13 VAB
TOWED ARTY 105mm: 4 M-1950
MOR 81mm; 120mm: 16 AM-50
RL 89mm: LRAC
RCL 106mm: M-40A1
AD GUNS 20mm: 16, incl 6 M-3 VDA SP; **40mm**: 5
 L/60

Navy ε900

BASE Locodjo (Abidjan)
PATROL AND COASTAL COMBATANTS 3
PATROL, COASTAL 1 *Le Vigilant* (Fr SFCN 47m) PCC
PATROL, INSHORE 2 *L'Ardent* (Fr *Patra*) PCI†
AMPHIBIOUS 1
 1 *L'Eléphant* (Fr *Batral*) LST, capacity 140 tps, 7 tk, hel
 deck, plus some 8 craft†

Air Force 700

5† cbt ac, no armed hel
FGA 1 sqn with 5† *Alpha Jet*
TPT 1 hel sqn with 1 SA-318, 1 SA-319, 1 SA-330, 4 SA 365C
PRESIDENTIAL FLT ac 1 F-28, 1 *Gulfstream* IV, 3
 Fokker 100 **hel** 1 SA-330
TRG 3 Beech F-33C, 2 Reims Cessna 150H
LIAISON 1 Cessna 421, 1 *Super King Air* 200

Forces Abroad

UN AND PEACEKEEPING
CAR (MINURCA): 233 tps

Paramilitary

PRESIDENTIAL GUARD 1,100
GENDARMERIE 4,400
VAB APC, 4 patrol boats
MILITIA 1,500

Foreign Forces

FRANCE 570: 1 marine inf bn (18 AML 60/90); 1 AS-
555 hel

Democratic Republic of Congo   DROC

	1997	1998	1999	2000
GDP	$5.8bn	$5.5bn		
per capita	$500	$400		
Growth	-5.7%	-6.0%		
Inflation	176%	5.0%		
Debt	$15bn	$16bn		

contd	1997	1998	1999	2000
Def exp	ε$308m	ε$364m		
Def bdgt		ε$250m	ε$400m	
FMA (US)			$0.1m	$0.1m
$1 = congolese franc [a]				
	ε94,000	ε138,000	ε1.38	

[a] Congolese franc became sole legal tender in July 1999

Population				ε48,000,000

(Bantu and Hamitic 45%; minority groups include Hutus and Tutsis)

Age	13–17	18–22	23–32
Men	2,932,000	2,344,000	3,411,000
Women	2,901,000	2,338,000	3,442,000

Total Armed Forces

ACTIVE ε55,900

Army ε55,000

10 inf, 1 Presidential Guard bde
1 mech inf bde

EQUIPMENT†

MBT 20 PRC Type-59 (being refurbished), some 40 PRC Type-62

RECCE† 60 AML (30 -60, 30 -90)

APC 12 M-113, 12 YW-531, 60 Panhard M-3, some *Casspir*, *Wolf* Turbo 2

TOWED ARTY 75mm: 30 M-116 pack; **85mm**: 20 Type-56; **122mm**: 20 M-1938/D-30, 15 Type-60; **130mm**: 8 Type-59

MRL 107mm: 20 Type 63; **122mm**: 16 BM-21

MOR 81mm; **107mm**: M-30; **120mm**: 50 Brandt

RCL 57mm: M-18; **75mm**: M-20; **106mm**: M-40A1

AD GUNS 14.5mm: ZPU-4; **37mm**: 40 M-1939/ Type 63; **40mm**: L/60

SAM SA-7

Navy ε900

BASES Coast Banana **River** Boma, Matadi, Kinshasa **Lake Tanganyika** (4 boats)

PATROL AND COASTAL COMBATANTS 7†

PATROL, INSHORE 7†

5 PRC *Shanghai* II PFI (most non-op)

2 *Swiftships*<, plus about 6 armed boats (most non-op)

Paramilitary

NATIONAL POLICE incl Rapid Intervention Police (National and Provincial forces)

Opposition

CONGOLESE DEMOCRATIC OPPOSITION str n.k.

MOVEMENT FOR THE LIBERATION OF THE CONGO str n.k.

Foreign Forces

In support of government:
  NAMIBIA: ε2,000 **SUDAN**: ε1,500 reported
  ZIMBABWE: up to 10,000 reported
In support of opposition:
  RWANDA: up to 4,000 reported **UGANDA**: ε5,000

Djibouti   Dj

	1997	1998	1999	2000
GDP	fr71bn	fr74bn		
	($402m)	($416m)		
per capita	$900	$900		
Growth	1.0%	1.9%		
Inflation	3.7%	2.0%		
Debt	$248m	$270m		
Def exp	εfr3.6bn	εfr3.8bn		
	($20m)	($21m)		
Def bdgt		εfr3.5bn	εfr3.9bn	
		($20m)	($23m)	
FMA (US)	$0.2m	$0.1m	$0.1m	$0.1m
FMA (Fr)	$1.2m	$1.1m	$1.4m	
$1 = franc	178	178	178	

Population				733,000

(Somali 60%, Afar 35%)

Age	13–17	18–22	23–32
Men	40,000	33,000	53,000
Women	39,000	34,000	58,000

Total Armed Forces

ACTIVE ε9,600
(incl *Gendarmerie*)

Army ε8,000

3 Comd (North, Central, South) • 1 inf bn, incl mor, ATK pl • 1 arty bty • 1 armd sqn • 1 border cdo bn • 1 AB coy • 1 spt bn

EQUIPMENT

RECCE 15 VBL, 4 AML-60†

APC 12 BTR-60 (op status uncertain)

TOWED ARTY 122mm: 6 D-30

MOR 81mm: 25; **120mm**: 20 Brandt

RL 73mm; **89mm**: LRAC

RCL 106mm: 16 M-40A1

AD GUNS 20mm: 5 M-693 SP; **23mm**: 5 ZU-23; **40mm**: 5 L/70

Navy ε200

BASE Djibouti
PATROL CRAFT, INSHORE 7
  5 *Sawari* PCI<, 2 *Moussa Ali* PCI<, plus boats

Air Force 200

no cbt ac or armed hel
TPT 2 C-212, 2 N-2501F, 2 Cessna U206G, 1 *Socata* 235GT
HEL 3 AS-355, 1 AS-350; Mi-8, Mi-24 hel from **Eth**

Paramilitary ε3,000 active

GENDARMERIE (Ministry of Defence) 1,200
1 bn, 1 patrol boat
NATIONAL SECURITY FORCE (Ministry of Interior)
ε3,000

Foreign Forces

FRANCE ε2,600: incl 1 marine inf (-); 1 Foreign Legion
regt (-), 26 ERC90 recce, 6 155mm arty, 16 AA arty, 3
amph craft: 1 sqn: **ac** 6 *Mirage* F-1C (plus 4 in store), 1
C-160 **hel** 1 SA-319, 2 SA-330

Opposition

FRONT FOR THE RESTORATION OF UNITY
AND DEMOCRACY: str n.k.

Equatorial Guinea   EG

	1997	1998	1999	2000
GDP	fr225bn	fr264bn		
	($385m)	($447m)		
per capita	$2,400	$2,700		
Growth	76%	14.5%		
Inflation	4.9%	3.0%		
Debt	$291m	$300m		
Def exp	εfr3bn	εfr5bn		
	($5.1m)	($8.0m)		
Def bdgt		εfr3.0bn	εfr4.0bn	
		($5.0m)	($6.6m)	
FMA (Fr)	$0.1m	$0.1m	$0.1m	
$1=CFA fr	584	590	609	
Population				513,000
Age	*13–17*	*18–22*	*23–32*	
Men	27,000	22,000	36,000	
Women	27,000	22,000	36,000	

Total Armed Forces

ACTIVE 1,320

Army 1,100

3 inf bn
EQUIPMENT
  RECCE 6 BRDM-2
  APC 10 BTR-152

Navy† 120

BASES Malabo (Santa Isabel), Bata
PATROL CRAFT, INSHORE 2 PCI<†

Air Force 100

no cbt ac or armed hel
TPT ac 1 Yak-40, 3 C-212, 1 Cessna-337 **hel** 2 SA-316

Paramilitary

GUARDIA CIVIL
2 coy
COAST GUARD
1 PCI<

Eritrea   Er

	1997	1998	1999	2000
GDP	ε$780m	ε$820m		
per capita	$400	$400		
Growth	7.0%	3.0%		
Inflation	3.2%	6.0%		
Debt	$250m	$450m		
Def exp	ε$196m	ε$292m		
Def bdgt		ε$196m	ε$236m	
FMA (US)	$0.4m	$0.4m	$0.4m	$0.4m
$=nakfa	7.2	7.2	7.2	
Population				ε3,994,000
(Tigrinya 50%, Tigre and Kunama 40%, Afar 4%, Saho 3%)				
Age	*13–17*	*18–22*	*23–32*	
Men	238,000	199,000	303,000	
Women	236,000	198,000	301,000	

Total Armed Forces

ACTIVE ε180–200,000 (incl ε130–150,000 conscripts)
Terms of service 18 months (6 month mil trg)
RESERVES ε120,000 (reported)
Total holdings of army assets n.k.

Army ε180,000

5 div (4 inf 1 cdo)

EQUIPMENT

MBT T-54/-55
RECCE BRDM-2
AIFV/APC BMP-1, BTR-60
TOWED ARTY 85mm: D-44; 122mm: D-30; 130mm: M-46
MRL 122mm: BM-21
MOR 120mm; 160mm
RL 73mm: RPG-7
ATGW AT-3 *Sagger*
SAM SA-18 (reported)

Navy 1,100

BASES Massawa (HQ), Assab, Dahlak
PATROL AND COASTAL COMBATANTS 10
PATROL, INSHORE 10
2 Sov Zhuk<, 4 *Super Dvora* PCF<, 1 *Osa* II PFM, 3 *Swiftships* PCI
AMPHIBIOUS 4
2 *Edic* LCT
2 *Chamo* LST (Ministry of Transport)
plus 2 *Soviet* LCU

Air Force ε1,000

19† cbt ac
There are reports that the air force has acquired MiG-29s in response to the conflict with Ethiopia. Current types and numbers are assessed as follows:
FTR/FGA 2† MiG-23, 8† MiG-21, 4 MiG-29
TPT 3 Y-12, 1 IAI-1125
TRG 6 L-90 *Redigo*, 5* MB-339CE
HEL 4 Mi-17

Opposition

ALLIANCE OF ERITREAN NATIONAL FORCES: str ε3,000 incl **Eritrean Liberation Front of Abdullah Idris (ELF-AI)** and **Eritrean Liberation Front – National Congress (ELF-NC)**: str n.k.

Ethiopia				Eth
	1997	1998	1999	2000
GDP	EB42bn ($6.3bn)	EB45bn ($6.4bn)		
per capita	$500	$500		
Growth	5.3%	0.5%		
Inflation	-6.4%	6.2%		
Debt	$10bn			
Def exp	EB900m ($134m)	εEB2,700m ($379m)		
Def bdgt			EB995m ($140m)	EB3,500m ($467m)

contd	1997	1998	1999	2000
FMA (US)	$0.3m	$0.3m	$0.5m	$0.5m
FMA (Fr)			$0.1m	
$1 =birr	6.47	6.71	7.12	
Population			ε57,000,000	

(Oromo 40%, Amhara and Tigrean 32%, Sidamo 9%, Shankella 6%, Somali 6%, Afar 4%)

Age	13–17	18–22	23–32
Men	3,706,000	2,993,000	4,513,000
Women	3,580,000	2,856,000	4,346,000

Total Armed Forces

ACTIVE ε325,500
The Ethiopian armed forces were formed following Eritrea's declaration of independence in April 1993. Extensive demobilisation of former members of the Tigray People's Liberation Front (TPLF) has taken place, while efforts to introduce a 'national balance' are being made involving recruitment from other ethnic groups. The armed forces are still in transition. Ethiopia auctioned off its naval assets in Sep 1996. Reports indicate that large quantities of eqpt are in preservation. Numbers in service should be treated with caution. Large increase in numbers due to war with Eritrea.

Army ε350,000

Being re-org to consist of 3 Mil Regions each with corps HQ (each corps 2 divs, 1 reinforced mech bde); strategic reserve div of 6 bde will be located at Addis Ababa
MBT ε500 T-54/-55, T-62
RECCE/AIFV/APC ε200, incl BRDM, BMP, BTR-60/-152
TOWED ARTY 76mm: ZIS-3; 85mm: D-44; 122mm: D-30/M-30; 130mm: M-46
MRL BM-21
MOR 81mm: M-1/M-29; 82mm: M-1937; 120mm: M-1938
ATGW AT-3 *Sagger*
RCL 82mm: B-10; 107mm: B-11
AD GUNS 23mm: ZU-23, ZSU-23-4 SP; 37mm: M-1939; 57mm: S-60
SAM 65: SA-2, SA-3, SA-7

Air Force ε2,500

† 71 cbt ac, 24 armed hel
Air Force operability improved as it played an active role in the war with Eritrea. Russia has agreed to supply Su-27s and several armed and support hels. Types and numbers of ac are assessed as follows:
FGA 40 MiG-21MF, 18 MiG-23BN, 5 MiG-27, 8 Su-27
TPT 4 C-130B, 6 An-12, 2 DH-6, 1 Yak-40 (VIP), 2 Y-12
TRG 10 L-39, 10 SF-260
ATTACK HEL 24 Mi-24
TPT HEL 22 Mi-8

Opposition

THE OROMO LIBERATION FRONT: str several hundred
OGADEN NATIONAL LIBERATION FRONT: str n.k.

Gabon   Gbn

	1997	1998	1999	2000
GDP	fr3.5tr	fr3.6tr		
	($6.0bn)	($6.1bn)		
per capita	$5,300	$5,500		
Growth	4.5%	1.7%		
Inflation	3.5%	1.7%		
Debt	$3.9bn	$3.8bn		
Def exp	εfr67bn	εfr78bn		
	($115)	($132m)		
Def bdgt		εfr73bn	εfr77bn	
		($124m)	($127m)	
FMA (Fr)	$1.0m	$1.0m	$1.0m	
FMA (US)			$0.05m	$0.1m
$1=CFA fr	584	590	609	
Population				1,473,000
Age	13–17	18–22	23–32	
Men	72,000	58,000	94,000	
Women	72,000	59,000	99,000	

Total Armed Forces

ACTIVE ε4,700

Army 3,200

Presidential Guard bn gp (1 recce/armd, 3 inf coy, arty, AA bty), under direct presidential control
8 inf, 1 AB/cdo, 1 engr coy
EQUIPMENT
  RECCE 14 EE-9 *Cascavel*, 24 AML-60/-90, 6 ERC-90 *Sagaie*, 12 EE-3 *Jararaca*, 14 VBL
  AIFV 12 EE-11 *Urutu* with **20mm** gun
  APC 9 V-150 *Commando*, Panhard M-3, 12 VXB-170
  TOWED ARTY 105mm: 4 M-101
  MRL 140mm: 8 *Teruel*
  MORS 81mm: 35; 120mm: 4 Brandt
  ATGW 4 *Milan*
  RL 89mm: LRAC
  RCL 106mm: M40A1
  AD GUNS 20mm: 4 ERC-20 SP; 23mm: 24 ZU-23-2; 37mm: 10 M-1939; 40mm: 3 L/70

Navy ε500

BASE Port Gentil (HQ)
PATROL AND COASTAL COMBATANTS 3
MISSILE CRAFT 1 *General Nazaire Boulingu* PFM (Fr 42m) with 4 SS 12M SSM
PATROL, COASTAL 2 *General Ba'Oumar* (Fr P-400 55m)
AMPHIBIOUS 2
  1 *President Omar Bongo* (Fr *Batral*) LST, capacity 140 tps, 7 tk; plus craft 1 LCM

Air Force 1,000

16 cbt ac, 5 armed hel
FGA 9 *Mirage* 5 (2 -G, 4 -GII, 3 -DG)
MR 1 EMB-111
TPT 1 C-130H, 3 L-100-30, 1 EMB-110, 2 YS-11A, 1 CN-235
HELICOPTERS
  ATTACK 5 SA-342
  TPT 3 SA-330C/-H
  LIAISON 3 SA-316/-319
PRESIDENTIAL GUARD
  CCT 4 CM-170, 3 T-34
  TPT ac 1 ATR-42F, 1 EMB-110, 1 *Falcon* 900 hel 1 AS-332

Forces Abroad

UN AND PEACEKEEPING
CAR (MINURCA): 125 tps

Paramilitary 4,800

COAST GUARD ε2,800
boats only
GENDARMERIE 2,000
3 'bde', 11 coy, 2 armd sqn, air unit with 1 AS-355, 2 AS-350

Foreign Forces

FRANCE 700: 1 marine inf bn (4 AML 60) ac 1 C-160 hel 1 AS-555

The Gambia   Gam

	1997	1998	1999	2000
GDP	D4.0bn	D4.4bn		
	($396m)	($417m)		
per capita	$1,100	$1,200		
Growth	3.8%	3.9%		
Inflation	2.9%	1.0%		
Debt	$470m	$480m		
Def exp	εD150m	εD160m		
	($15m)	($15m)		
Def bdgt		εD156m	εD180m	
		($15m)	($16m)	
$1=dalasi	10.2	10.6	11.2	

Population			1,200,000
Age	*13–17*	*18–22*	*23–32*
Men	64,000	54,000	81,000
Women	65,000	52,000	81,000

Total Armed Forces

ACTIVE 800

Gambian National Army 800

Presidential Guard (reported) • 2 inf bn • engr sqn

MARINE UNIT (about 70)
BASE Banjul
PATROL CRAFT, INSHORE 3
  3 PFI<, boats

Ghana Gha

	1997	1998	1999	2000
GDP	C14.0tr	C14.0tr		
	($8.9bn)	($8.9bn)		
per capita	$2,200	$2,200		
Growth	3.0%	3.0%		
Inflation	27.9%	27.9%		
Debt	$6.4bn	$6.4bn		
Def exp[a]	εC275bn	εC310bn		
	($134m)	($135m)		
Def bdgt	C95bn	C133bn	C150bn	
	($46m)	($58m)	($64m)	
FMA (US)	$0.2m	$0.3m	$0.4m	$0.4m
$1=cedi	2,050	2,300	2,340	

[a] Defence and security budget including police

Population			19,454,000
Age	*13–17*	*18–22*	*23–32*
Men	1,153,000	952,000	1,419,000
Women	1,147,000	950,000	1,431,000

Total Armed Forces

ACTIVE 7,000

Army 5,000

2 Comd HQ • 2 bde (6 inf bn (incl 1 UNIFIL, 1 ECOMOG), spt unit) • 1 Presidential Guard, 1 trg bn • 1 recce regt (3 sqn) • 1 arty 'regt' (1 arty, 2 mor bty) • 1 AB force (incl 1 para coy) • 1 SF bn • 1 fd engr regt (bn)
EQUIPMENT
  RECCE 3 EE-9 *Cascavel*
  AIFV 50 MOWAG *Piranha*
  TOWED ARTY 122mm: 6 D-30

MOR 81mm: 50; **120mm**: 28 Tampella
RCL 84mm: 50 *Carl Gustav*
AD GUNS 14.5mm: 4 ZPU-2, ZPU-4; **23mm**: 4 ZU-23-2
SAM SA-7

Navy 1,000

COMMANDS Western and Eastern
BASES HQ Western Sekondi **HQ Eastern** Tema
PATROL AND COASTAL COMBATANTS 4
PATROL, COASTAL 2 *Achimota* (Ge *Lürssen* 57m) PFC
PATROL, INSHORE 2 *Dzata* (Ge *Lürssen* 45m) PCI

Air Force 1,000

19 cbt ac, no armed hel
TPT 5 Fokker (4 F-27, 1 F-28 (VIP)); 1 C-212, 6 *Skyvan*
HEL 4 AB-212 (1 VIP, 3 utl), 2 Mi-2, 4 SA-319
TRG 12* L-29, 2* L-39, 2* MB 339F, 3* MB-326K

Forces Abroad

UN AND PEACEKEEPING
CROATIA (UNMOP): 2 obs **LEBANON** (UNIFIL): 644; 1 inf bn **IRAQ/KUWAIT** (UNIKOM): 6 obs **SIERRA LEONE** (ECOMOG): 500+ **TAJIKISTAN** (UNMOT): 4 obs **WESTERN SAHARA** (MINURSO): 13 incl 6 obs

Guinea Gui

	1997	1998	1999	2000
GDP	fr3.7tr	fr4.0tr		
	($3.2bn)	($3.4bn)		
per capita	$900	$900		
Growth	4.7%	4.9%		
Inflation	5.2%	4.0%		
Debt	$3.2bn	$3.3bn		
Def exp	εfr59bn	εfr72bn		
	($54m)	($61m)		
Def bdg		εfr65bn	εfr75bn	
		($55m)	($57m)	
FMA (US)	$0.2m	$0.2m	$0.2m	$0.2m
FMA (Fr)	$1.1m	$1.1m	$1.4m	
$1=franc	1,100	1,185	1,312	

Population			7,426,000
Age	*13–17*	*18–22*	*23–32*
Men	423,000	350,000	524,000
Women	431,000	354,000	530,000

Total Armed Forces

ACTIVE 9,700
(perhaps 7,500 conscripts)
Terms of service conscription, 2 years

Army 8,500

1 armd bn • 1 arty bn • 1 cdo bn • 1 engr bn • 5 inf bn
• 1 AD bn • 1 SF bn

EQUIPMENT†

MBT 30 T-34, 8 T-54
LT TK 20 PT-76
RECCE 25 BRDM-1/-2, 2 AML-90
APC 40 BTR (16 -40, 10 -50, 8 -60, 6 -152)
TOWED ARTY **76mm**: 8 M-1942; **85mm**: 6 D-44;
    122mm: 12 M-1931/37
MOR **82mm**: M-43; **120mm**: 20 M-1938/43
RCL **82mm**: B-10
ATK GUNS **57mm**: M-1943
AD GUNS **30mm**: twin M-53; **37mm**: 8 M-1939;
    57mm: 12 S-60, PRC Type-59; **100mm**: 4 KS-19
SAM SA-7

Navy 400

BASES Conakry, Kakanda
PATROL AND COASTAL COMBATANTS 4
PATROL, INSHORE 4
    2 US *Swiftships* 77, 2 other PCI<

Air Force† 800

8 cbt ac, no armed hel
FGA 4 MiG-17F, 4 MiG-21
TPT 4 An-14, 1 An-24
TRG 2 MiG-15UTI
HEL 1 IAR-330, 1 Mi-8, 1 SA-316B, 1 SA-330, 1 SA-342K
MISSILES
    AAM AA-2 *Atoll*

Forces Abroad

SIERRA LEONE (ECOMOG): 1,000–2,000
UN AND PEACEKEEPING
WESTERN SAHARA (MINURSO): 3 obs

Paramilitary 2,600 active

PEOPLE'S MILITIA 7,000
GENDARMERIE 1,000
REPUBLICAN GUARD 1,600

Guinea-Bissau				GuB
	1997	1998	1999	2000
GDP	fr159bn	fr164bn		
	($272m)	($278m)		
per capita	$900	$1,000		
Growth	5.1%	0.6%		
Inflation	49.1%	13.9%		

contd	1997	1998	1999	2000
Debt	$921m	$940m		
Def exp	ε$8m	ε$15m		
Def bdgt		ε$8m	ε$10m	
FMA (Fr)	$0.1m	$0.1m		
FMA (US)	$0.1m	$0.1m	$0.1m	$0.1m
$1 = CFA fr		590	609	
Population				1,174,000
Age	*13–17*	*18–22*	*23–32*	
Men	66,000	58,000	92,000	
Women	65,000	54,000	85,000	

Total Armed Forces

ACTIVE ε9,250 (all services, incl *Gendarmerie*, form part
of the armed forces)

Terms of service conscription (selective)
Following a revolt by dissident army tps, quelled by
forces from Senegal and Guinea, a peace agreement
was made which included the deployment of ε1,500
ECOMOG tps from Benin, The Gambia and Togo. Tps
from Senegal and Guinea were to withdraw on
completion of ECOMOG deployment. Manpower and
equipment totals should be treated with caution.

Army 6,800

1 armd 'bn' (sqn) • 5 inf, 1 arty bn • 1 recce, 1 engr coy

EQUIPMENT

MBT 10 T-34
LT TK 20 PT-76
RECCE 10 BRDM-2
APC 35 BTR-40/-60/-152, 20 PRC Type-56
TOWED ARTY **85mm**: 8 D-44; **122mm**: 18 M-1938/
    D-30
MOR **82mm**: M-43; **120mm**: 8 M-1943
RL **89mm**: M-20
RCL **75mm**: PRC Type-52; **82mm**: B-10
AD GUNS **23mm**: 18 ZU-23; **37mm**: 6 M-1939;
    57mm: 10 S-60
SAM SA-7

Navy ε350

BASE Bissau
PATROL AND COASTAL COMBATANTS 3
PATROL, INSHORE 3
    2 *Alfeite* PCC<, 1 PCI<
AMPHIBIOUS craft only
    1 LCM

Air Force 100

3 cbt ac, no armed hel
FTR/FGA 3 MiG-17
HEL 1 SA-318, 2 SA-319

Paramilitary

GENDARMERIE 2,000

Kenya				Kya
	1997	**1998**	**1999**	**2000**
GDP	sh601bn	sh645bn		
	($9.8bn)	($10.0bn)		
per capita	$1,400	$1,400		
Growth	1.3%	1.3%		
Inflation	12.0%	7.1%		
Debt	$6.8bn	$6.8bn		
Def exp	εsh16bn	εsh19bn		
	($269m)	($315m)		
Def bdgt		εsh13.0bn	εsh16bn	
		($216m)	($245m)	
FMA (US)[a]	$0.3m	$0.4m	$0.4m	$0.4m
$1 =shilling	59	60	65	

[a] Excl ACRI and East Africa Regional funding

Population		30,677,000 (Kikuyu ε22–32%)	
Age	*13–17*	*18–22*	*23–32*
Men	1,971,000	1,673,000	2,400,000
Women	1,964,000	1,676,000	2,424,000

Total Armed Forces

ACTIVE 24,200

Army ε20,500

1 armd bde (3 armd bn) • 2 inf bde (1 with 2, 1 with 3 inf bn) • 1 indep inf bn • 1 arty. bde (2 bn) • 1 AD arty bn • 1 engr bde • 2 engr bn • 1 AB bn • 1 indep air cav bn

EQUIPMENT
MBT 76 Vickers Mk 3
RECCE 72 AML-60/-90, 12 *Ferret*, 8 Shorland
APC 52 UR-416, 10 Panhard M-3 (in store)
TOWED ARTY 105mm: 40 lt, 8 pack
MOR 81mm: 50; **120mm**: 12 Brandt
ATGW 40 *Milan*, 14 *Swingfire*
RCL 84mm: 80 *Carl Gustav*
AD GUNS 20mm: 50 TCM-20, 11 Oerlikon; **40mm**: 13 L/70

Navy 1,200

BASE Mombasa
PATROL AND COASTAL COMBATANTS 7
MISSILE CRAFT 6
2 *Nyayo* (UK Vosper 57m) PFM with 4 *Ottomat* SSM, 1 *Mamba*, 3 *Madaraka* (UK *Brooke Marine* 37m/ 32m), PFM with 4 *Gabriel* II SSM

PATROL, INSHORE 1 *Simba* with 2 40mm gun
AMPHIBIOUS craft only
2 *Galana* LCM
SUPPORT AND MISCELLANEOUS I
1 AT

Air Force 2,500

30 cbt ac, 34 armed hel
FGA 10 F-5 (8 -E, 2 -F)
TPT 7 DHC-5D, 6 Do-28D-2, 1 PA-31, 3 DHC-8, 1 Fokker 70 (VIP)
ATTACK HEL 11 Hughes 500MD (with TOW), 8 Hughes 500ME, 15 Hughes 500M
TPT HEL 9 IAR-330, 3 SA-330, 1 SA-342
TRG 12 *Bulldog* 103/127, 8* *Hawk* Mk 52, 12* *Tucano*, **hel** 2 Hughes 500D
MISSILES
ASM AGM-65 *Maverick*, TOW
AAM AIM-9 *Sidewinder*

Forces Abroad

UN AND PEACEKEEPING
CROATIA (UNMOP): 1 obs **IRAQ/KUWAIT** (UNIKOM): 4 obs **SIERRA LEONE** (UNOMSIL): 2 obs **WESTERN SAHARA** (MINURSO): 8 obs

Paramilitary 5,000

POLICE GENERAL SERVICE UNIT 5,000 (may have increased to 9,000)
AIR WING ac 7 Cessna lt **hel** 3 Bell (1 206L, 2 47G)
POLICE NAVAL SQN/CUSTOMS about 5 PCI< (2 Lake Victoria), some 12 boats

Lesotho				Ls
	1997	**1998**	**1999**	**2000**
GDP	M5.3bn	M6.6bn		
	($1.2bn)	($1.2bn)		
per capita	$2,300	$2,300		
Growth	7.2%	1.5%		
Inflation	8.9%	8.4%		
Debt	$600m	$530m		
Def exp	M148m	M230m		
	($32m)	($42m)		
Def bdgt		M170m	M210m	
		($31m)	($34m)	
FMA (US)	$0.1m	$0.1m	$0.1m	$0.1m
$1 =maloti	4.6	5.5	6.2	

Population			2,180,000
Age	*13–17*	*18–22*	*23–32*
Men	126,000	108,000	163,000
Women	124,000	108,000	164,000

Total Armed Forces

ACTIVE 2,000

A mutiny on 22 September 1998 was quelled by military intervention by South Africa and Botswana. Tps from these countries withdrew on 15 May 1999. Manpower and equipment str should be treated with caution.

Army 2,000

7 inf coy • 1 spt coy (incl recce/AB, 81mm mor) • 1 air sqn

EQUIPMENT
RECCE 10 Il *Ramta*, 8 Shorland, AML-90
MOR 81mm: some
RCL 106mm: M-40
AC 3 C-212 *Aviocar* 300, 1 Cessna 182Q
HEL 2 Bo-105 CBS, 1 Bell 47G, 1 Bell 412 SP, 1 Bell 412EP

Liberia   Lb

	1997	1998	1999	2000
GDP	ε$1.1bn	ε$1.2bn		
per capita	$1,100	$1,000		
Growth	ε4.0%	n.k.		
Inflation	ε11%	n.k.		
Debt	$2.0bn	$2.5bn		
Def exp	ε$45m	ε$45m		
Def bdgt			L$330m	
			($8m)	
FMA[a]				
US$1=L$[b]	1.0	1.0	1.0	

[a] UNOMIL **1997** $19m; ECOMOG **1990–98** ε$525m
[b] Market rate **1999** $1=L$41

Population				ε3,500,000
(Americo-Liberians 5%)				
Age	*13–17*	*18–22*	*23–32*	
Men	166,000	136,000	188,000	
Women	162,000	131,000	176,000	

Total Armed Forces

ACTIVE

Plans for the new unified armed forces provide for:
Army 4,000 • **Navy** 1,000 • **Air Force** 300

Madagascar   Mdg

	1997	1998	1999	2000
GDP	fr18tr	fr19tr		
	($4.6bn)	($4.8bn)		
per capita	$700	$700		
Growth	3.7%	3.5%		
Inflation	4.5%	6.3%		
Debt	$4.1bn	$3.5bn		
Def exp	εfr190bn	εfr240bn		
	($37m)	($44m)		
Def bdgt		εfr220bn	εfr273bn	
		($40m)	($52m)	
FMA (US)	$0.1m	$0.1m	$0.1m	$0.1m
FMA (Fr)	$1.2m	$1.2m	$1.4m	
$1=franc	5,091	5,441	5,220	
Population				15,097,000
Age	*13–17*	*18–22*	*23–32*	
Men	874,000	724,000	1,092,000	
Women	852,000	708,000	1,083,000	

Total Armed Forces

ACTIVE some 21,000

Terms of service conscription (incl for civil purposes), 18 months

Army some 20,000

2 bn gp • 1 engr regt

EQUIPMENT
LT TK 12 PT-76
RECCE 8 M-8, ε20 M-3A1, 10 *Ferret*, ε35 BRDM-2
APC ε30 M-3A1 half-track
TOWED ARTY 76mm: 12 ZIS-3; 105mm: some M-101; 122mm: 12 D-30
MOR 82mm: M-37; 120mm: 8 M-43
RL 89mm: LRAC
RCL 106mm: M-40A1
AD GUNS 14.5mm: 50 ZPU-4; 37mm: 20 Type-55

Navy† 500

(incl some 100 Marines)
BASES Diégo-Suarez, Tamatave, Fort Dauphin, Tuléar, Majunga
PATROL CRAFT 1
   1 *Malaika* (Fr PR48m) PCI†
AMPHIBIOUS 2
   1 *Toky* (Fr *Batram*) LSM, capacity 30 tps, 4 tk
   plus craft: 1 LCT (Fr *Edic*)
SUPPORT AND MISCELLANEOUS 1
   1 tpt/trg

Air Force 500

12 cbt ac, no armed hel
FGA 1 sqn with 4 MiG-17F, 8 MiG-21FL
TPT 4 An-26, 1 BN-2, 2 C-212, 2 Yak-40 (VIP)
HEL 1 sqn with 6 Mi-8
LIAISON 1 Cessna 310, 2 Cessna 337, 1 PA-23
TRG 4 Cessna 172

Paramilitary 7,500

GENDARMERIE 7,500
incl maritime police with some 5 PCI<

Malawi				Mlw
	1997	1998	1999	2000
GDP	K42bn	K52bn		
	($2.1bn)	($2.2bn)		
per capita	$800	$900		
Growth	6.6%	3.6%		
Inflation	7.2%	17.5%		
Debt	$2.3bn	$2.5bn		
Def exp	εK420m	εK800m		
	($23m)	($26m)		
Def bdgt		εK650m	εK1,170m	
		($21m)	($27m)	
FMA (US)	$0.2m	$0.3m	$0.3m	$0.3m
FMA (ROC)	$2.0m			
$1=kwacha	18.0	31.1	44.1	
Population				10,819,000
Age	*13–17*	*18–22*	*23–32*	
Men	634,000	508,000	759,000	
Women	628,000	506,000	792,000	

Total Armed Forces

ACTIVE 5,000 (all services form part of the Army)

Army 5,000

2 inf bde each with 3 inf bn
1 indep para bn
1 general spt bn (incl arty, engr)
EQUIPMENT (less than 50% serviceability)
  RECCE 20 *Fox*, 8 *Ferret*, 12 *Eland*
  TOWED ARTY 105mm: 9 lt
  MOR 81mm: 8 L16
  SAM 15 *Blowpipe*

MARITIME WING (220)
BASE Monkey Bay (Lake Nyasa)
  PATROL CRAFT 2
  1 *Kasungu* PCI†, 1 *Namacurra* PCI<, some boats

AMPHIBIOUS craft only
  1 LCU

AIR WING (80)
no cbt ac, no armed hel
  TPT AC 1 sqn with 3 Do-228, 1 Do-28D, 1 *King Air*
  C90, 1 HS-125-800
  TPT HEL 2 SA-330F, 1 AS-365N

Paramilitary 1,000

MOBILE POLICE FORCE (MPF) 1,000
8 Shorland armd car **ac** 3 BN-2T *Defender* (border
patrol), 1 *Skyvan* 3M, 4 Cessna **hel** 2 AS-365

Mali				RMM
	1997	1998	1999	2000
GDP	fr1.4tr	fr1.6tr		
	($2.5bn)	($2.7bn)		
per capita	$600	$600		
Growth	6.7%	5.4%		
Inflation	2.8%	3.5%		
Debt	$3.0bn	$3.2bn		
Def exp	εfr25bn	εfr31bn		
	($43m)	($53m)		
Def bdgt		εfr27bn	εfr29bn	
		($46m)	($48m)	
FMA (US)	$0.2m	$0.3m	$0.3m	$0.3m
FMA (Fr)	$1.0m	$1.0m	$1.2m	
$1=CFA fr	584	590	609	
Population		11,200,000 (Tuareg 6–10%)		
Age	*13–17*	*18–22*	*23–32*	
Men	621,000	504,000	753,000	
Women	645,000	526,000	794,000	

Total Armed Forces

ACTIVE about 7,350 (all services form part of the Army)
Terms of service conscription (incl for civil purposes), 2
years (selective)

Army about 7,350

2 tk • 4 inf • 1 AB, 2 arty, 1 engr, 1 SF bn • 2 AD, 1
SAM bty
EQUIPMENT†
  MBT 21 T-34, T-54/-55 reported
  LT TK 18 Type-62
  RECCE 20 BRDM-2
  APC 30 BTR-40, 10 BTR-60, 10 BTR-152
  TOWED ARTY 85mm: 6 D-44; **100mm**: 6 M-1944;
    122mm: 8 D-30; **130mm**: M-46 reported
  MRL 122mm: 2 BM-21

MOR 82mm: M-43; **120mm**: 30 M-43
AD GUNS 37mm: 6 M-1939; **57mm**: 6 S-60
SAM 12 SA-3

NAVY† (about 50)
BASES Bamako, Mopti, Segou, Timbuktu
PATROL CRAFT, RIVERINE 3<

AIR FORCE (400)
16† cbt ac, no armed hel
FGA 5 MiG-17F
FTR 11 MiG-21
TPT 2 An-24, 1 An-26
TRG 6 L-29, 1 MiG-15UTI, 4 Yak-11, 2 Yak-18
HEL 1 Mi-8, 1 AS-350

Forces Abroad

UN AND PEACEKEEPING
CAR (MINURCA): 125 tps
SIERRA LEONE (ECOMOG): 500+

Paramilitary 4,800

GENDARMERIE 1,800
8 coy
REPUBLICAN GUARD 2,000
MILITIA 3,000
NATIONAL POLICE 1,000

Mauritius | | | | Ms

	1997	1998	1999	2000
GDP	R86bn	R96bn		
	($4.2bn)	($4.5bn)		
per capita	$15,100	$16,000		
Growth	5.6%	5.3%		
Inflation	6.9%	6.1%		
Debt	$1.8bn	$2.0bn		
Def exp	εR1.9bn	εR2.1bn		
	($92m)	($87m)		
Def bdgt		R351m	R400m	
		($16m)	($16m)	
FMA (US)	$0.02	$0.1m	$0.1m	$0.1m
$1=rupee	20.6	22.8	25.2	
Population				1,180,000
Age	13–17	18–22	23–32	
Men	52,000	54,000	101,000	
Women	51,000	53,000	102,000	

Total Armed Forces

ACTIVE Nil

Paramilitary ε1,500

SPECIAL MOBILE FORCE ε1,000
6 rifle, 2 mob, 1 engr coy, spt tp
APC 10 VAB
MOR 81mm: 2
RL 89mm: 4 LRAC

COAST GUARD ε500
PATROL CRAFT 13
1 *Vigilant* (Ca *Guardian* design) OPV, capability for 1 hel
9 *Marlin* (Ind *Mandovi*) PCI
1 SDB-3 PFI
2 Sov *Zhuk* PCI<, plus 26 boats
MR 1 Do-228-101, 1 BN-2T *Defender*, 3 SA-316B

POLICE AIR WING
2 *Alouette* III

Mozambique | | | Moz

	1997	1998	1999	2000
GDP	M17tr	M24tr		
	($1.9bn)	($2.0bn)		
per capita	$1,000	$1,100		
Growth	8.0%	8.0%		
Inflation	16.5%	2.2%		
Debt	$7.0bn	$7.2bn		
Def exp	M830bn	M950bn		
	($72m)	($80m)		
Def bdgt			M1,200bn	
			($97m)	
FMA (US)	$0.2m	$0.2m	$0.2m	$0.2m
$1=metical	11,544	11,875	12,436	
Population				16,300,000
Age	13–17	18–22	23–32	
Men	1,118,000	932,000	1,416,000	
Women	1,130,000	948,000	1,453,000	

Total Armed Forces

ACTIVE ε5,100–6,100
Terms of service conscription, 2–3 years

Army ε4–5,000 (to be 12–15,000)

5 inf, 3 SF, 1 log bn • 1 engr coy
EQUIPMENT† (ε10% or less serviceability)
MBT some 80 T-54/-55 (300+ T-34, T-54/-55 non-op)
RECCE 30 BRDM-1/-2
AIFV 40 BMP-1
APC 150+ BTR-60, 100 BTR-152
TOWED ARTY 100+: **76mm**: M-1942; **85mm**: 150+: D-44, D-48, Type-56; **100mm**: 24 M-1944; **105mm**: M-101; **122mm**: M-1938, D-30; **130mm**: 24 M-46;

152mm: 20 D-1
MRL **122mm**: 30 BM-21
MOR **82mm**: M-43; **120mm**: M-43
RCL **75mm**; **82mm**: B-10; **107mm**: B-11
AD GUNS 400: **20mm**: M-55; **23mm**: 90 ZU-23-2;
  37mm: 100 M-1939; **57mm**: 90: S-60 towed, ZSU-57-2 SP
SAM SA-7

Navy 100

BASES Maputo (HQ), Beira, Nacala, Pemba, Inhambane **Ocean** Quelimane **Lake Nyasa** Metangula
PATROL AND COASTAL COMBATANTS 3
  PATROL, INSHORE 3 PCI< (non-op) Lake Malawi

Air Force 1,000

(incl AD units); no cbt ac, 4† armed hel
TPT 1 sqn with 5 An-26, 2 C-212, 4 PA-32 *Cherokee*
TRG 1 Cessna 182, 7 ZLIN-326
HEL
  ATTACK 4† Mi-24
  TPT 5 Mi-8
  AD SAM †SA-2, 10 SA-3

<table>
<tr><th colspan="2">Namibia</th><th></th><th>Nba</th></tr>
<tr><th></th><th>1997</th><th>1998</th><th>1999</th><th>2000</th></tr>
<tr><td>GDP</td><td>N$15bn
($2.5bn)</td><td>N$17bn
($2.6bn)</td><td></td><td></td></tr>
<tr><td>per capita</td><td>$4,700</td><td>$4,700</td><td></td><td></td></tr>
<tr><td>Growth</td><td>1.8%</td><td>1.5%</td><td></td><td></td></tr>
<tr><td>Inflation</td><td>8.9%</td><td>5.0%</td><td></td><td></td></tr>
<tr><td>Debt</td><td>$107m</td><td>$137m</td><td></td><td></td></tr>
<tr><td>Def exp</td><td>N$416m
($90m)</td><td>N$510m
($92m)</td><td></td><td></td></tr>
<tr><td>Def bdgt</td><td></td><td>N$443m
($89m)</td><td>N$559m
($90m)</td><td></td></tr>
<tr><td>FMA (US)</td><td>$0.2m</td><td>$0.2m</td><td>$0.2m</td><td>$0.2m</td></tr>
<tr><td>US$1=N$</td><td>4.6</td><td>5.5</td><td>6.2</td><td></td></tr>
<tr><td>Population</td><td></td><td></td><td></td><td>1,834,000</td></tr>
<tr><td>Age</td><td>13–17</td><td>18–22</td><td>23–32</td><td></td></tr>
<tr><td>Men</td><td>108,000</td><td>89,000</td><td>136,000</td><td></td></tr>
<tr><td>Women</td><td>107,000</td><td>88,000</td><td>135,000</td><td></td></tr>
</table>

Total Armed Forces

ACTIVE 9,000

Army 9,000

5 inf bn • 1 cbt spt bde with 1 arty, 1 AD, 1 ATK regt

EQUIPMENT
MBT some T-34, T-54/-55 (serviceability doubtful)
RECCE BRDM-2
APC some *Casspir*, ε50 *Wolf*, BTR-152
TOWED ARTY **140mm**: 24 G2
MRL **122mm**: 5 BM-21
MOR **81mm**; **82mm**
RCL **82mm**: B-10
ATK GUNS **57mm**; **76mm**: M-1942 (ZIS-3)
AD GUNS **14.5mm**: 50 ZPU-4; **23mm**: 15 *Zumlac* (ZU-23-2) SP
SAM SA-7

AIR WING
ac 1 *Falcon* 900, 1 *Learjet* 36, 6 Cessna 337/02-A, 2 Y-12 **hel** 2 SA-319 *Alouette*

Coast Guard ε100

(fishery protection, part of the Ministry of Fisheries)
BASE Walvis Bay
PATROL CRAFT 2
  1 *Osprey*, 1 *Oryx*
  1 Cessna a/c, 1 hel

Forces Abroad

DROC: ε2,000

<table>
<tr><th colspan="2">Niger</th><th></th><th>Ngr</th></tr>
<tr><th></th><th>1997</th><th>1998</th><th>1999</th><th>2000</th></tr>
<tr><td>GDP</td><td>fr922bn
($1.6bn)</td><td>fr971bn
($1.7bn)</td><td></td><td></td></tr>
<tr><td>per capita</td><td>$800</td><td>$800</td><td></td><td></td></tr>
<tr><td>Growth</td><td>3.5%</td><td>2.7%</td><td></td><td></td></tr>
<tr><td>Inflation</td><td>2.9%</td><td>4 6%</td><td></td><td></td></tr>
<tr><td>Debt</td><td>$1.6bn</td><td>$1.7bn</td><td></td><td></td></tr>
<tr><td>Def exp</td><td>εfr13bn
($22m)</td><td>εfr15bn
($25m)</td><td></td><td></td></tr>
<tr><td>Def bdgt</td><td></td><td>εfr13bn
($22m)</td><td>εfr17bn
($28m)</td><td></td></tr>
<tr><td>FMA (US)</td><td></td><td></td><td></td><td></td></tr>
<tr><td>FMA (Fr)</td><td>$1.1m</td><td>$1.1m</td><td>$1.2m</td><td></td></tr>
<tr><td>FMA (LAR)</td><td>$4.0m</td><td></td><td></td><td></td></tr>
<tr><td>$1=CFA fr</td><td>584</td><td>590</td><td>609</td><td></td></tr>
<tr><td>Population</td><td colspan="4">10,337,000 (Tuareg 8–10%)</td></tr>
<tr><td>Age</td><td>13–17</td><td>18–22</td><td>23–32</td><td></td></tr>
<tr><td>Men</td><td>578,000</td><td>466,000</td><td>680,000</td><td></td></tr>
<tr><td>Women</td><td>582,000</td><td>474,000</td><td>705,000</td><td></td></tr>
</table>

Total Armed Forces

ACTIVE 5,300
Terms of service selective conscription (2 years)

Army 5,200

3 Mil Districts • 4 armd recce sqn • 7 inf, 2 AB, 1 engr coy

EQUIPMENT
RECCE 90 AML-90, 35 AML-60/20, 7 VBL
APC 22 M-3
MOR 81mm: 19 Brandt; **82mm**: 17; **120mm**: 4 Brandt
RL 89mm: 36 LRAC
RCL 75mm: 6 M-20; **106mm**: 8 M-40
ATK GUNS 85mm; 90mm
AD GUNS 20mm: 39 incl 10 M-3 VDA SP

Air Force 100

no cbt ac or armed hel
TPT 1 C-130H, 1 Do-28, 1 Do-228, 1 Boeing 737-200
(VIP), 1 An-26
LIAISON 2 Cessna 337D

Paramilitary 5,400

GENDARMERIE 1,400

REPUBLICAN GUARD 2,500

NATIONAL POLICE 1,500

Nigeria   Nga

	1997	1998	1999	2000
GDP	ε$48bn	ε$49bn		
per capita	$1,300	$1,300		
Growth	5.1%	1.5%		
Inflation	8.6%	10.0%		
Debt	$35bn	$29bn		
Def exp	ε$2.0bn	ε$2.1bn		
Def bdgt		N22bn	N26bn	
		($1,005m)	($1,080m)	
$1 = naira	21.9	21.9	92.6	
Population				ε113,000,000

(*North* Hausa and Fulani *South-west* Yoruba *South-east* Ibo; these tribes make up ε65% of population)

Age	13–17	18–22	23–32
Men	7,306,000	6,290,000	9,410,000
Women	7,305,000	6,369,000	9,783,000

Total Armed Forces

ACTIVE 94,000

RESERVES
planned, none org

Army 79,000

1 armd div (2 armd bde) • 1 composite div (1 mot inf,
1 amph bde, 1 AB bn) • 2 mech div (each 1 mech, 1
mot inf bde) • 1 Presidential Guard bde (2 bn) • 1 AD
bde • each div 1 arty, 1 engr bde, 1 recce bn

EQUIPMENT
MBT 50 T-55†, 150 Vickers Mk 3
LT TK 140 *Scorpion*
RECCE ε120 AML-60, 60 AML-90, 55 *Fox*, 75 EE-9
Cascavel, 72 VBL (reported)
APC 10 *Saracen*, 300 Steyr 4K-7FA, 70 MOWAG
Piranha, EE-11 *Urutu* (reported)
TOWED ARTY 105mm: 200 M-56; **122mm**: 200 D-
30/-74; **130mm**: 7 M-46; **155mm**: 24 FH-77B (in
store)
SP ARTY 155mm: 27 *Palmaria*
MRL 122mm: 11 APR-21
MOR 81mm: 200; **82mm**: 100; **120mm**: 30+
RCL 84mm: *Carl Gustav*; **106mm**: M-40A1
AD GUNS 20mm: some 60; **23mm**: ZU-23, 30 ZSU-
23-4 SP; **40mm**: L/60
SAM 48 *Blowpipe*, 16 *Roland*
SURV RASIT (veh, arty)

Navy 5,500

(incl Coast Guard)
BASES Lagos, HQ Western Comd Apapa **HQ
Eastern Comd** Calabar **Akwa Ibom state** Warri, Port
Harcourt, Ibaka

FRIGATES 1
FF 1 *Aradu* (Ge MEKO 360)† with 1 *Lynx* hel, 2 x 3
ASTT; 8 *Otomat* SSM, 1 127mm gun

PATROL AND COASTAL COMBATANTS 26
CORVETTES 1† *Erinomi* (UK Vosper Mk 9) with 1 x 3
Seacat, 1 76mm gun, 1 x 2 ASW mor† (plus 1 non-op)
MISSILE CRAFT 5
2 *Ekpe* (Ge Lürssen 57m) PFM with 4 *Otomat* SSM
(non-op)
3† *Ayam* (Fr *Combattante*) PFM with 2 x 2 MM-38
Exocet SSM
PATROL, INSHORE 20
4 *Makurdi* (UK *Brooke Marine* 33m) (non-op)
6 *Simmoneau* 500
some 10 PCI<

MINE COUNTERMEASURES 2
2 *Ohue* (mod It *Lerici*) MCC (non-op)

AMPHIBIOUS 1
1 *Ambe* (Ge) LST (1 non-op), capacity 220 tps 5 tk

SUPPORT AND MISCELLANEOUS 5
1 *Lana* AGHS, 3 AT, 1 nav trg

NAVAL AVIATION
HEL 2† *Lynx* Mk 89 MR/SAR

Air Force 9,500

91† cbt ac, 15† armed hel

FGA/FTR 3 sqn
   1 with 19 *Alpha Jet* (FGA/trg)
   1 with 6† MiG-21MF, 4† MiG-21U, 12† MiG-21B/FR
   1 with 15† *Jaguar* (12 -SN, 3 -BN)
ARMED HEL †15 Bo-105D
TPT 2 sqn with 5 C-130H, 3 -H-30, 17 Do-128-6, 2 Do-228 (VIP), 5 G-222 **hel** 4 AS-332, 2 SA-330
PRESIDENTIAL FLT ac 1 Boeing 727, 2 *Gulfstream*, 2 *Falcon* 900, 1 BAe 125-1000
TRG ac† 23* L-39MS, 12* MB-339AN, 59 Air *Beetle* **hel** 14 Hughes 300
AAM AA-2 *Atoll*

Forces Abroad

UN AND PEACEKEEPING
CROATIA (UNMOP): 1 obs **IRAQ/KUWAIT** (UNIKOM): 5 obs **SIERRA LEONE**: ε10–12,000 **TAJIKISTAN** (UNMOT): 8 obs **WESTERN SAHARA** (MINURSO): 5 obs

Paramilitary

COAST GUARD
incl in Navy
PORT SECURITY POLICE ε2,000
about 60 boats and some 5 hovercraft
SECURITY AND CIVIL DEFENCE CORPS (Ministry of Internal Affairs)
   POLICE UR-416, 70 AT-105 *Saxon*† APC **ac** 1 Cessna 500, 3 Piper (2 *Navajo*, 1 *Chieftain*) **hel** 4 Bell (2 -212, 2 -222)

Total Armed Forces

ACTIVE ε37–47,000 (all services, incl *Gendarmerie*, form part of the Army)

Army ε30–40,000

6 inf bde, 1 mech inf regt
EQUIPMENT
   MBT 12 T-54/-55
   RECCE AML-245, 15 AML-60, AML-90, 16 VBL
   APC some BTR, Panhard, 6 RG-31 *Nyala*
   TOWED ARTY 105mm†; 122mm: 6
   MRL 122mm: 5 RM-70
   MOR 81mm: 8; 120mm
   AD GUNS 14.5mm; 23mm; 37mm
   SAM SA-7
   HEL 2 Mi-24 (reported)

Forces Abroad

DROC: up to 4,000 reported

Paramilitary 7,000

GENDARMERIE 7,000

Opposition

ε7,000 former govt tps dispersed in DROC. Some have returned to Rwanda with associated *Interahamwe* militia. Equipped with small arms and lt mor only.

Rwanda				Rwa
	1997	**1998**	**1999**	**2000**
GDP	fr562bn	fr636bn		
	($1.9bn)	($2.0bn)		
per capita	$500	$600		
Growth	10.9%	10.5%		
Inflation	11.0%	8.1%		
Debt	$1.1bn	$1.2bn		
Def exp	εfr31bn	εfr44bn		
	($103m)	($141m)		
Def bdgt		εfr39bn	εfr45bn	
		($112m)	($134m)	
FMA (US)	$0.4m	$0.5m	$0.3m	$0.3m
$1 = franc	302	312	335	
Population	ε8,480,000 (Hutu 80%, Tutsi 19%)			
Age	*13–17*	*18–22*		*23–32*
Men	545,000	439,000		632,000
Women	560,000	455,000		661,000

Senegal				Sen
	1997	**1998**	**1999**	**2000**
GDP	fr2.7tr	fr2.8tr		
	($4.5bn)	($4.8bn)		
per capita	$1,800	$1,900		
Growth	5.2%	4.8%		
Inflation	1.8%	1.1%		
Debt	$3.6bn	$3.8bn		
Def exp	fr41bn	fr48bn		
	($71m)	($81m)		
Def bdgt		fr40bn	fr43bn	
		($68m)	($71m)	
FMA (US)	$0.7m	$0.8m	$0.7m	$0.7m
FMA (Fr)	$2.1m	$1.8m	$2.1m	
$1 = CFA fr	584	590	609	
Population				9,442,000

(Wolof 36%, Fulani 17%, Serer 17%, Toucouleur 9%, Mandingo 9%, Diola 9%, of which 30–60% in Casamance)

Age	13–17	18–22	23–32
Men	578,000	470,000	686,000
Women	572,000	466,000	692,000

Total Armed Forces

ACTIVE 11,000

Terms of service conscription, 2 years selective

RESERVES n.k.

Army 10,000 (3,500 conscripts)

7 Mil Zone HQ • 4 armd bn • 1 engr bn • 6 inf bn • 1 Presidential Guard (horsed) • 1 arty bn • 3 construction coy • 1 cdo bn • 1 AB bn • 1 engr bn
EQUIPMENT
  RECCE 10 M-8, 4 M-20, 30 AML-60, 27 AML-90
  APC some 16 Panhard M-3, 12 M-3 half-track
  TOWED ARTY 18: **75mm**: 6 M-116 pack; **105mm**: 6 M-101/HM-2; **155mm**: ε6 Fr Model-50
  MOR 81mm: 8 Brandt; **120mm**: 8 Brandt
  ATGW 4 *Milan*
  RL 89mm: 31 LRAC
  AD GUNS 20mm: 21 M-693; **40mm**: 12 L/60

Navy 600

BASES Dakar, Casamance
PATROL AND COASTAL COMBATANTS 10
PATROL, COASTAL 2
  1 *Fouta* (Dk *Osprey*) PCC
  1 *Njambuur* (Fr SFCN 59m) PFC
PATROL, INSHORE 8
  3 *Saint Louis* (Fr 48m) PCI, 3 *Senegal* II PFI<, 2 *Alioune Samb* PCI<
AMPHIBIOUS craft only
  1 *Edic* 700 LCT

Air Force 400

8 cbt ac, no armed hel
MR/SAR 1 EMB-111
TPT 1 sqn with 6 F-27-400M, 1 Boeing 727-200 (VIP), 1 DHC-6 *Twin Otter*
HEL 2 SA-318C, 2 SA-330, 1 SA-341H
TRG 4* CM-170, 4* R-235 *Guerrier*, 2 *Rallye* 160, 2 R-235A

Forces Abroad

UN AND PEACEKEEPING
CAR (MINURCA): 129 tps **IRAQ/KUWAIT** (UNIKOM): 5 obs

Paramilitary ε5,800

GENDARMERIE ε5,800
12 VXB-170 APC
CUSTOMS
2 PCI<, boats

Opposition

CASAMANCE MOVEMENT OF DEMOCRATIC FORCES 2–3,000 eqpt with lt wpns

Foreign Forces

FRANCE 1,200: 1 marine inf bn (14 AML 60/90); **ac** 1 *Atlantic*, 1 C-160 **hel** 1 SA-319

Seychelles				**Sey**
	1997	**1998**	**1999**	**2000**
GDP	SR2.7bn	SR2.9bn		
	($355m)	($367m)		
per capita	$4,600	$4,700		
Growth	8.2%	2.0%		
Inflation	0.6%	2.6%		
Debt	$147m	$147m		
Def exp	SR51m	SR55m		
	($10m)	($11m)		
Def bdgt		SR54m	SR56m	
		($10m)	($11m)	
FMA (US)	$0.1m	$0.1m	$0.1m	$0.1m
$1 = rupee	5.0	5.3	5.3	
Population				73,000
Age	13–17		18–22	23–32
Men	4,000		4,000	7,000
Women	4,000		4,000	7,000

Total Armed Forces

ACTIVE 450 (all services, incl Coast Guard, form part of the Army)

Army 200

1 inf coy
1 sy unit
EQUIPMENT†
  RECCE 6 BRDM-2
  MOR 82mm: 6 M-43
  RL RPG-7
  AD GUNS 14.5mm: ZPU-2/-4; **37mm**: M-1939
  SAM 10 SA-7

Paramilitary 250 active

NATIONAL GUARD 250

COAST GUARD (200)

(incl 20 Air Wing and ε80 Marines)
BASE Port Victoria
PATROL, INSHORE 2
1 *Andromache* (It *Pichiotti* 42m) PFI, 1 *Zhuk* PFI<
plus 1 *Cinq Juin* LCT (govt owned but civilian
operated)

AIR WING (20)

No cbt ac, no armed hel
MR 1 BN-2 *Defender*
TPT 1 Reims-Cessna F-406/*Caravan* 11
TRG 1 Cessna 152

Sierra Leone   SL

	1997	1998	1999	2000
GDP	ε$752m	ε$769m		
per capita	$700	$700		
Growth	-5.0%	0.7%		
Inflation	7.4%	14.5%		
Debt	$1.2bn	$1.2bn		
Def exp	ε$51m	ε$26m		
Def bdgt		$5m	$5m	
FMA (US)			$0.1m	
FMA (UK)			$7.3m	
ECOMOG **1997–98** ε$79m				
$1 =leone	981	1,564	1,635	
Population				ε5,237,000
Age	*13–17*	*18–22*		*23–32*
Men	282,000	236,000		365,000
Women	281,000	235,000		369,000

Total Armed Forces

ACTIVE ε3,000

Following the civil war of May–June 1997, restoration of the
legitimate government of President Kabbah was achieved
on 10 March 1998 by ECOWAS forces. A ceasefire between
government and opposition forces is in place. A new national army is to form with a strength of some 5,000.

EQUIPMENT

MOR 81mm: 3; **82mm**: 2; **120mm**: 2
RCL 84mm: *Carl Gustav*
AD GUNS 12.7mm: 4; **14.5mm**: 3
SAM SA-7
HEL 2 Mi-24

Navy ε200

BASE Freetown

PATROL AND COASTAL COMBATANTS 3†

1 PRC *Shanghai* II PFI, 1 *Swiftship* 32m† PFI, 1 *Fairy
Marine Tracker* II

Foreign Forces

UN AND PEACEKEEPING

UN (UNOMSIL): 14 mil obs from 5 countries.
ECOMOG: tps from **Gha** 500+, **Gui** 1,000–2,000,
RMM 500+, **Nga** 10–12,000 reported

Somali Republic   SR

	1997	1998	1999	2000
GDP	ε$840m	ε$853m		
per capita	$1,200	$1,200		
Growth	0.0%	0.0%		
Inflation	ε16%	ε16%		
Debt	$2.5bn	$2.5bn		
Def exp	ε$40m	ε$40m		
Def bdgt			$13m	
$1 =shillingᵃ	2,620	2,620	2,620	

ᵃ Market rate June **1997** $1=8,000 shillings

Population		ε6,300,000 (Somali 85%)	
Age	*13–17*	*18–22*	*23–32*
Men	587,000	477,000	687,000
Women	585,000	474,000	691,000

Total Armed Forces

ACTIVE Nil

Following the 1991 revolution, no national armed forces have
yet been formed. The Somali National Movement has
declared northern Somalia the independent 'Republic of
Somaliland', while insurgent groups compete for local
supremacy in the south. Heavy military equipment is in poor
repair or inoperable.

Clan/Movement Groupings

'SOMALILAND' (northern Somalia) Total armed forces
reported as some 12,900
UNITED SOMALI FRONT clan Issa **leader**
   Abdurahman Dualeh Ali
SOMALI DEMOCRATIC ALLIANCE clan Gadabursi
SOMALI NATIONAL MOVEMENT 5–6,000 **clan**
   Issaq, 3 factions (Tur, Dhegaweyne, Kahin)
UNITED SOMALI PARTY clan Midigan/Tumaal
   leader Ahmed Guure Adan

SOMALIA

SOMALI SALVATION DEMOCRATIC FRONT
   3,000 **clan** Darod **leader** Abdullah Yusuf Ahmed
UNITED SOMALI CONGRESS clan Hawiye **sub-
clan** Habr Gidir **leaders** Hussein Mohamed

Aideed/Osman Atto
Ali Mahdi Faction 10,000(-) **clan** Abgal **leader**
Mohammed Ali Mahdi
SOMALI NATIONAL FRONT 2–3,000 **clan** Darod
sub-clan Marehan **leader** General Omar Hagi
Mohammed Hersi
SOMALI DEMOCRATIC MOVEMENT clan
Rahenwein/Dighil
SOMALI PATRIOTIC MOVEMENT 2–3,000 **clan**
Darod **leader** Ahmed Omar Jess

South Africa · RSA

	1997	1998	1999	2000
GDP	R595bn	R645bn		
	($129bn)	($131bn)		
per capita	$5,700	$5,700		
Growth	1.7%	0.1%		
Inflation	8.5%	6.9%		
Debt	$67bn	$66bn		
Def exp	R11.6bn	R11.8bn		
	($2.5bn)	($2.1bn)		
Def bdgt		R10.3bn	R10.6bn	R10.9bn
		($1.9bn)	($1.7bn)	($1.8bn)
FMA (US)	$0.7m	$0.8m	$0.9m	$0.8m
$1 = rand	4.6	5.5	6.2	
Population				39,700,000
Age	*13–17*	*18–22*	*23–32*	
Men	2,484,000	2,241,000	3,674,000	
Women	2,451,000	2,224,000	3,679,000	

Total Armed Forces

ACTIVE 69,950

(incl 11,930 MoD staff, 5,500 South African Military
Health Service; 16,998 women; 18,791 civilians)
Terms of service voluntary service in 4 categories (full
career, up to 10 yrs, up to 6 yrs, 1 yr voluntary military
service)
Racial breakdown 49,908 black, 23,714 white, 10,306
coloured, 979 Asian

RESERVES 88,045

Army 85,338 **Navy** 834 **Air Force** 377 **Medical Service**
(SAMHS) 402

Army 37,970

REGULAR COMPONENT

9 'type' formations
5 regional joint task forces (each consists of HQ and a
number of group HQ, but no tps which are provided when necessary by FTF and PTF units from
'type' formations)
18 group HQ

1 mech inf bde HQ (designated units 1 tk, 1 armd car,
2 mech inf bn, 4 inf, 1 arty, 1 AD, 1 engr bn)
1 AB bde (FTF: 1 AB bn, AB trg school; PTF: 2 AB bn, 1
arty, 1 AD, 1 engr regt)
1 SF bde (2 bn)
18 inf bn (incl 1 mech, 4 mot), 1 armd car, 1 AD regt

RESERVE FORCE

3 tk, 3 armd car, 6 mech inf, 6 mot inf, 3 SP arty, 3 AD,
3 engr bn
some 183 inf 'bn' home-defence units

EQUIPMENT

MBT some 124 *Olifant* 1A/-B (plus 100 in store)
RECCE 235 *Eland*-90 (in store), 188 *Rooikat*-76
AIFV 1,240 *Ratel*-20
APC 429 *Casspir*, 545 *Mamba*
TOWED ARTY 140mm: 75 G-2; **155mm:** 72 G-5
SP ARTY 155mm: 43 G-6
MRL 127mm: 25 *Bateleur* (40 tube), 72 *Valkiri* (24 tube)
MOR 81mm: 1,190 (incl some SP); **120mm:** 36
ATGW ZT-3 *Swift* (52 SP), *Milan*
RL 92mm: FT-5
RCL 106mm: 100 M-40A1 (some SP)
AD GUNS 20mm: 84 *Ystervark* SP; **23mm:** 36
Zumlac (ZU-23-2) SP; **35mm:** 99 GDF Mk1/3 (in
store), 48 GDF Mk5
SURV *Green Archer* (mor), *Cymbeline* (mor)

Navy 5,150

NAVAL HQ Pretoria, Flag Officer, Fleet Simon's Town
FLOTILLAS submarine, strike, MCM
BASES Simon's Town, Durban (Salisbury Island)

SUBMARINES 3

SSK 3 *Spear* (Mod Fr *Daphné*) with 550mm TT (2
non-op)

PATROL AND COASTAL COMBATANTS 9

MISSILE CRAFT 6 *Warrior* (Il *Reshef*) with 6–8
Skerpioen (Il *Gabriel*) SSM (incl 2 in refit) plus 2 in
reserve

PATROL, INSHORE 3

3 T craft PCI

MINE COUNTERMEASURES 8

4 *Kimberley* (UK *Ton*) MSC (incl 1 in refit) plus 2 in
reserve
4 *River* (Ge *Navors*) MHC (incl 2 in refit)

SUPPORT AND MISCELLANEOUS 36

1 *Drakensberg* AO with 2 hel and extempore amph
capability (perhaps 60 tps and 2 small LCU)
1 *Outeniqua* AO with similar capability as *Drakensberg*
1 AGHS (Hecla)
1 diving spt
1 Antarctic tpt with 2 hel (operated by Ministry of
Environmental Affairs)
3 AT
28 harbour patrol
plus craft: 8 LCU

Air Force 9,400

(incl 800 women); 116 cbt ac, ε3 attack and several extempore armed hel
Air Force Command Post, Pretoria, and 6 type formations
Flying hours 160
FTR/FGA 2 sqn
  1 sqn with 33 *Cheetah* C
  1 sqn with 30 *Impala* Mk2
TPT/TKR/EW 1 sqn with 5 Boeing 707-320 (EW/tkr)
TPT 5 sqn
  1 with 4 *Super King Air* 300, 11 Cessna-208 *Caravan*, 1 PC-12
  1 (VIP) with 5 HS-125, 4 *Super King Air* 200, 1 *King Air* 300, 2 *Citation* II, 2 *Falcon* 50, 1 *Falcon* 900
  1 with 11 C-47 TP
  1 with 12 C-130
  1 with 4 CASA-212, 1 CASA-235
LIAISON/FAC 14 Cessna 185A/D/E, 1 PC-12
HEL 5 sqn: 4 with 56 SA-316/-319 *Alouette* III (some armed), 41 *Oryx* (some armed), 9 BK-117, 1 SA-365 (VIP); 1 with 2 *Rooivalk* (12 entering service)
TRG COMD 5 schools
  12* *Cheetah* D, 35* *Impala* Mk1, 58 PC-7
UAV *Seeker, Scout*
MISSILES
  ASM AS-11/-20/-30
  AAM R-530, R-550 *Magic*, AIM-9 *Sidewinder*, V-3A/B *Kukri*, *Python* 3
GROUND DEFENCE
RADAR 2 Air Control Sectors, 3 fixed and some mob radars
SAAF Regt: 9 security sqn

South African Military Health Service (SAMHS) 5,500

(incl 2,500 women); a separate service within the SANDF. 9 regional med comd

Foreign Forces

Singapore: *Searcher* UAV trg det

Sudan				Sdn
	1997	1998	1999	2000
GDP	ε$7.5bn	ε$7.9bn		
per capita	$1,300	$1,400		
Growth	5.5%	3.5%		
Inflation	32%	19.3%		
Debt	$18bn	$18bn		
Def exp	ε$413m	ε$385m		
Def bdgt		ε$248m	ε$430m	
$1 = pound	1,578	1,950	2,487	

Population	ε32,194,000

(Muslim 70%, *mainly in North;* Christian 10%, *mainly in South;* African 52%, *mainly in South;* Arab 39%, *mainly in North*)

Age	13–17	18–22	23–32
Men	1,888,000	1,596,000	2,399,000
Women	1,805,000	1,526,000	2,306,000

Total Armed Forces

ACTIVE 94,700

(incl ε20,000 conscripts)
Terms of service conscription (males 18–30), 3 years

Army ε90,000

(incl ε20,000 conscripts)
1 armd div • 1 recce bde • 6 inf div (regional comd) • 10+ arty bde (incl AD) • 1 AB div (incl 1 SF bde) • 3 arty regt • 1 mech inf bde • 1 engr div • 1 border gd div • 24 inf bde
EQUIPMENT
  MBT 200 T-54/-55, 20 M-60A3, 10+ PRC Type-59
  LT TK 20 PRC Type-62
  RECCE 6 AML-90, 30 *Saladin*, 80 *Ferret*, 60 BRDM-1/-2
  AIFV 6 BMP-2
  APC 90 BTR-50/-152, 80 OT-62/-64, 36 M-113, 100 V-100/-150, 120 *Walid*
  TOWED ARTY 600 incl: **85mm**: D-44; **105mm**: M-101 pack, Model 56 pack; **122mm**: D-74, M-1938, Type-54/D-30; **130mm**: M-46/PRC Type 59-1
  SP ARTY 155mm: 6 AMX Mk F-3
  MRL 107mm: 200 Type-63; **122mm**: 50 BM-21
  MOR 81mm: 120; **82mm**; **120mm**: 12 M-43, 24 AM-49
  ATGW 4 *Swingfire*
  RCL 106mm: 40 M-40A1
  ATK GUNS 40 incl: **76mm**: M-1942; **100mm**: M-1944
  AD GUNS 425 incl: **14.5mm**; **20mm**: M-167 towed, M-163 SP; **23mm**: ZU-23-2; **37mm**: M-1939/Type-63, Type-55; **57mm**: Type-59
  SAM SA-7
  SURV RASIT (veh, arty)

Navy ε1,700

BASES Port Sudan (HQ), Flamingo Bay (Red Sea), Khartoum (Nile)
PATROL AND COASTAL COMBATANTS 6
  PATROL, INSHORE 2 *Kadir* PCI<
  PATROL, RIVERINE 4 PCI<, about 12 armed boats
AMPHIBIOUS craft only
  some 2 *Sobat* (FRY DTK-221) LCT (used for transporting stores)

Air Force 3,000

(incl Air Defence); 51† cbt ac, 9 armed hel
6 fighter sqn • 1 trg sqn • 1 hel bde • 1 air transport bde • 2 spt bde
FGA 9 F-5 (7 -E, 2 -F), 9 PRC J-5 (MiG-17), 9 PRC J-6 (MiG-19), 6 F-7 (MiG-21)
FTR 6 MiG-23, PRC J-6 (MiG-19)
TPT 4 An-24, 4 C-130H, 4 C-212, 3 DHC-5D, 6 EMB-110P, 1 F-27, 2 *Falcon* 20/50
HEL 11 AB-412, 8 IAR/SA-330, 4 Mi-4, 8 Mi-8, 4* Mi-24B, 5* Mi-35
TRG incl 4* MiG-15UTI, 4* MiG-21U, 2* JJ-5, 2* JJ-6, 10 PT-6A
AD 5 bty SA-2 SAM (18 launchers)
AAM AA-2 *Atoll*

Forces Abroad

DROC ε1,500 reported

Paramilitary 15,000

POPULAR DEFENCE FORCE 15,000 active

85,000 reserve; mil wg of National Islamic Front; org in bn of 1,000

Opposition

NATIONAL DEMOCRATIC ALLIANCE

coalition of many groups, of which the main forces are:

SUDANESE PEOPLE'S LIBERATION ARMY

(SPLA) 20–30,000

four factions, each org in bn, operating mainly in southern Sudan; some captured T-54/-55 tks, BM-21 MRL and arty pieces, but mainly small arms plus **60mm** and **120mm** mor, **14.5mm** AA, SA-7 SAM

SUDAN ALLIANCE FORCES ε500

based in Eritrea, operate in border area

BEJA CONGRESS FORCES ε500

operates on Eritrean border

NEW SUDAN BRIGADE ε2,000

operates on Ethiopian and Eritrean borders

Foreign Forces

IRAN: some mil advisers

Tanzania   Tz

	1997	1998	1999	2000
GDP	sh4.7tr	sh5.6tr		
	($3.6bn)	($3.8bn)		
per capita	$700	$700		
Growth	3.3%	4.0%		
Inflation	16.1%	12.8%		
Debt	$7.3bn	$7.4bn		
Def exp	εsh75bn	εsh95bn		
	($123m)	($143m)		
Def bdgt		sh71bn	sh102bn	
		($106m)	($148m)	
FMA (US)[a]		$0.2m	$0.2m	$0.2m
$1 =shilling	612	665	691	

[a] Excl ACRI and East Africa Regional funding

Population			31,977,000
Age	*13–17*	*18–22*	*23–32*
Men	1,859,000	1,499,000	2,237,000
Women	1,918,000	1,581,000	2,389,000

Total Armed Forces

ACTIVE ε34,000

Terms of service incl civil duties, 2 years

RESERVES 80,000

Army 30,000+

5 inf bde • 1 tk bde • 2 arty bn • 2 AD arty bn • 2 mor bn • 2 ATK bn • 1 engr regt (bn)
EQUIPMENT†
MBT 30 PRC Type-59 (15 op), 35 T-54 (all non-op)
LT TK 30 PRC Type-62, 40 *Scorpion*
RECCE 40 BRDM-2
APC 66 BTR-40/-152, 30 PRC Type-56
TOWED ARTY 76mm: 45 ZIS-3; **85mm**: 80 PRC Type-56; **122mm**: 20 D-30, 100 PRC Type-54-1; **130mm**: 40 PRC Type-59-1
MRL 122mm: 58 BM-21
MOR 82mm: 350 M-43; **120mm**: 50 M-43
RCL 75mm: 540 PRC Type-52

Navy† ε1,000

BASES Dar es Salaam, Zanzibar, Mwanza (Lake Victoria – 4 boats)
PATROL AND COASTAL COMBATANTS 7
TORPEDO CRAFT 2 PRC *Huchuan* PHT< with 2 533mm TT
PATROL, INSHORE 5
  2 PRC *Shanghai* II PFI
  3 *Thornycroft* PC<
AMPHIBIOUS craft only
  2 *Yunnan* LCU

Air Defence Command 3,000

(incl ε2,000 AD tps); 19 cbt ac†, no armed hel
FTR 3 sqn with 3 PRC J-5 (MiG-17), 10 J-6 (MiG-19), 6 J-7 (MiG-21)
TPT 1 sqn with 3 DHC-5D, 1 PRC Y-5, 2 CH Y-12, 3 HS-748, 2 F-28, 1 HS-125-700
HEL 4 AB-205
LIAISON ac 5 Cessna 310, 2 Cessna 404, 1 Cessna 206 **hel** 6 Bell 206B
TRG 2 MiG-15UTI, 5 PA-28
AD GUNS 14.5mm: 40† ZPU-2/-4; **23mm:** 40 ZU-23; **37mm:** 120 PRC Type-55
SAM† 20 SA-3, 20 SA-6, 120 SA-7

Paramilitary 1,400 active

POLICE FIELD FORCE 1,400

18 sub-units incl Police Marine Unit
  MARINE UNIT (100)
    boats only
  AIR WING
    ac 1 Cessna U-206 **hel** 2 AB-206A, 2 Bell 206L, 2 Bell 47G

Togo				**Tg**
	1997	**1998**	**1999**	**2000**
GDP	fr817bn	fr860bn		
	($1.4bn)	($1.4bn)		
per capita	$1,300	$1,300		
Growth	4.8%	0.1%		
Inflation	7.0%	6.1%		
Debt	$1.4bn	$1.7bn		
Def exp	εfr17bn	εfr20bn		
	($29m)	($34m)		
Def bdgt		εfr19bn	εfr21bn	
		($32m)	($35m)	
FMA (Fr)	$1.0m	$1.0m	$0.8m	
FMA (US)	$0.03m			
$1=CFA fr	584	590	609	
Population				4,854,000
Age	*13–17*	*18–22*		*23–32*
Men	290,000	222,000		326,000
Women	291,000	234,000		353,000

Total Armed Forces

ACTIVE some 6,950 (up to 10,000 reported)
Terms of service conscription, 2 years (selective)

Army 6,500

2 inf regt
  1 with 1 mech bn, 1 mot bn
1 with 2 armd sqn, 3 inf coy; spt units (trg)
1 Presidential Guard regt: 2 bn (1 cdo), 2 coy
1 para cdo regt: 3 coy
1 spt regt: 1 fd arty, 2 AD arty bty; 1 log/tpt/engr bn

EQUIPMENT

  MBT 2 T-54/-55
  LT TK 9 *Scorpion*
  RECCE 6 M-8, 3 M-20, 10 AML (3 -60, 7 -90), 36 EE-9 *Cascavel*, 2 VBL
  AIFV 20 BMP-2 (reported)
  APC 4 M-3A1 half-track, 30 UR-416
  TOWED ARTY 105mm: 4 HM-2
  SP ARTY 122mm: 6 reported
  MOR 82mm: 20 M-43
  RCL 57mm: 5 ZIS-2; **75mm:** 12 PRC Type-52/-56; **82mm:** 10 PRC Type-65
  AD GUNS 14.5mm: 38 ZPU-4; **37mm:** 5 M-39

Navy ε200

(incl Marine Infantry unit)
BASE Lomé
PATROL CRAFT, INSHORE 2
  2 *Kara* (Fr *Esterel*) PFI<

Air Force †250

16 cbt ac, no armed hel
FGA 5 *Alpha Jet*, 4 EMB-326G
TPT 2 *Baron*, 2 DHC-5D, 1 Do-27, 1 F-28-1000 (VIP), 1 Boeing 707 (VIP), 2 Reims-Cessna 337
HEL 1 AS-332, 2 SA-315, 1 SA-319, 1 SA-330
TRG 4* CM-170, 3* TB-30

Forces Abroad

UN AND PEACEKEEPING

CAR (MINURCA): 126 tps

Paramilitary 750

GENDARMERIE (Ministry of Interior) 750
1 trg school, 2 reg sections, 1 mob sqn

Uganda				**Uga**
	1997	**1998**	**1999**	**2000**
GDP	Ush7.4tr	Ush8.1tr		
	($6.8bn)	($7.3bn)		
per capita	$1,700	$1,800		
Growth	5.0%	5.5%		
Inflation	7.2%	0.0%		
Debt	$3.6bn	$3.7bn		
Def exp	Ush180bn	Ush280bn		
	($166m)	($226m)		

contd	1997	1998	1999	2000
Def bdgt		Ush165bn	Ush170bn	
		($133m)	($120m)	
FMA (US)[a]	$0.3m	$0.4m	$0.4m	$0.4m
$1=shilling	1,083	1,240	1,423	
[a] Excl ACRI and East Africa Regional funding				
Population				21,640,000
Age	*13–17*	*18–22*	*23–32*	
Men	1,203,000	1,046,000	1,499,000	
Women	1,218,000	1,039,000	1,633,000	

Total Armed Forces

ACTIVE ε30–40,000

Ugandan People's Defence Force
ε30–40,000

4 div (1 with 5, 1 with 3, 2 with 2 bde)
EQUIPMENT†
  MBT ε140 T-54/-55
  LT TK ε20 PT-76
  RECCE 40 *Eland*, 60 *Ferret* (reported)
  APC 20 BTR-60, 4 OT-64 SKOT, 10(+) *Mamba*, some *Buffel*
  TOWED ARTY 76mm: 60 M-1942; **122mm**: 20 M-1938; **130mm**: ε12; **155mm** (reported)
  MRL 122mm: BM-21
  MOR 81mm: L 16; **82mm**: M-43; **120mm**: 60 Soltam
  ATGW 40 AT-3 *Sagger*
  AD GUNS 14.5mm: ZPU-1/-2/-4; **23mm**: 20 ZU-23; **37mm**: 20 M-1939
  SAM SA-7
  AVN 4 cbt act, 2 armed hel
  TRG 3†* L-39, 1 SF*-260
  TPT HEL 1 Bell 206, 1 Bell 412, 4 Mi-17, 2* Mi-24
  TPT/LIAISON HEL 1 AS-202 *Bravo*, 1 *Gulfstream* III

Forces Abroad

DROC: ε5,000

Paramilitary ε600 active

BORDER DEFENCE UNIT ε600
  small arms
LOCAL DEFENCE UNITS ε5–10,000
POLICE AIR WING
  hel 2 Bell 206, 2 Bell 212
MARINES (ε400)
  8 riverine patrol craft<, plus boats

Opposition

LORD'S RESISTANCE ARMY ε2,000
(ε1,000 in Uganda, remainder in Sudan)
ALLIED DEMOCRATIC FORCES ε500–1,000
UGANDA NATIONAL SALVATION FRONT: str n.k.
UGANDA FEDERAL DEMOCRATIC FORCES: (an amalgamation of groups): str n.k.

Zambia   Z

	1997	1998	1999	2000
GDP	K5.2tr	K6.3tr		
	($3.4bn)	($3.4bn)		
per capita	$900	$900		
Growth	4.6%	-2.1%		
Inflation	24.8%	30.6%		
Debt	$7.2bn	$6.5bn		
Def exp	εK83bn	εK120bn		
	($59m)	($64m)		
Def bdgt		K99bn	K186bn	
		($53m)	($79m)	
FMA (US)	$0.2m	$0.1m	$0.2m	$0.2m
FMA (PRC)	$2.0m			
$1=kwacha	1,400	1,862	2,370	
Population				10,076,000
Age	*13–17*	*18–22*	*23–32*	
Men	613,000	499,000	732,000	
Women	603,000	495,000	759,000	

Total Armed Forces

ACTIVE 21,600

Army 20,000

(incl 3,000 reserves)
3 bde HQ • 1 arty regt • 9 inf bn (3 reserve) • 1 engr bn • 1 armd regt (incl 1 armd recce bn)
EQUIPMENT
  MBT 10 T-54/-55, 20 PRC Type-59
  LT TK 30 PT-76
  RECCE ε60 BRDM-1/-2 (ε12 serviceable)
  APC 13 BTR-60
  TOWED ARTY 76mm: 35 M-1942; **105mm**: 18 Model 56 pack; **122mm**: 25 D-30; **130mm**: 18 M-46
  MRL 122mm: 50 BM-21
  MOR 81mm: 55; **82mm**: 24; **120mm**: 14
  ATGW AT-3 *Sagger*
  RCL 57mm: 12 M-18; **75mm**: M-20; **84mm**: *Carl Gustav*
  AD GUNS 20mm: 50 M-55 triple; **37mm**: 40 M-1939; **57mm**: 55 S-60; **85mm**: 16 KS-12
  SAM SA-7

Air Force 1,600

63+ cbt ac, some armed hel
FGA 1 sqn with 12 J-6 (MiG-19)+
FTR 1 sqn with 12 MiG-21 MF+ (8 undergoing
refurbishment)
TPT 1 sqn with 4 An-26, 4 C-47, 3 DHC-4, 4 DHC-5D
VIP 1 fleet with 1 HS-748, 3 Yak-40
LIAISON 7 Do-28, 2 Y-12
TRG 2*-F5T, 2* MiG-21U+, 12* *Galeb* G-2, 15* MB-
326GB, 8* SF-260MZ
HEL 1 sqn with 4 AB-205A, 5 AB-212, 12 Mi-8
LIAISON HEL 12 AB-47G
MISSILES
    ASM AT-3 *Sagger*
    SAM 1 bn; 3 bty: SA-3 *Goa*

Forces Abroad

UN AND PEACEKEEPING
SIERRA LEONE (UNOMSIL): 2 obs

Paramilitary 1,400

POLICE MOBILE UNIT (PMU) 700
1 bn of 4 coy
POLICE PARAMILITARY UNIT (PPMU) 700
1 bn of 3 coy

Zimbabwe   Zw

	1997	1998	1999	2000
GDP	Z$104bn	Z$140bn		
	($6.4bn)	($6.6bn)		
per capita	$2,300	$2,300		
Growth	4.2%	0.8%		
Inflation	18.8%	27.0%		
Debt	$5.0bn	$5.2bn		
Def exp	Z$3.6bn	Z$7bn		
	($304m)	($327m)		
Def bdgt		Z$4.2bn	Z$6.4bn	
		($196m)	($168m)	
FMA (US)	$0.3m	$0.3m	$0.3m	$0.3m
US$1=Z$	11.9	21.4	38.3	
Population				12,050,000
Age	*13–17*	*18–22*	*23–32*	
Men	781,000	634,000	974,000	
Women	773,000	631,000	974,000	

Total Armed Forces

ACTIVE ε39,000

Army ε35,000

5 bde HQ • 1 Mech bde, 1 arty bde, 1 Presidential
Guard gp • 1 armd sqn • 15 inf bn (incl 2 guard, 1
mech, 1 cdo, 1 para) • 1 fd arty regt • 1 AD regt • 1
engr regt
EQUIPMENT
    MBT 22 PRC Type-59, 10 PRC Type-69
    RECCE 80 EE-9 *Cascavel* (**90mm** gun)
    APC 30 PRC Type-63 (YW-531), UR-416, 40 *Crocodile*
    TOWED ARTY 122mm: 12 PRC Type-60, 4 PRC
    Type-54
    MRL 107mm: 18 PRC Type-63; **122mm**: 52 RM-70
    MOR 81mm/82mm 502; **120mm**: 14 M-43
    AD GUNS 215 incl **14.5mm**: ZPU-1/-2/-4; **23mm**:
    ZU-23; **37mm**: M-1939
    SAM 17 SA-7

Air Force 4,000

58 cbt ac, 24 armed hel
Flying hours 100
FGA 2 sqn
    1 with 11 *Hunters* (9 FGA-90, 1 -F80, 1 T-81)
    1 with 8 *Hawk* Mk 60/60A
FTR 1 sqn with 12 PRC F-7 (MiG-21)
RECCE 1 sqn with 14* Reims-Cessna 337 *Lynx*
TRG/RECCE/LIAISON 1 sqn with 22 SF-260 *Genet* (9
    -C, 6* -F, 5* -W, 2* TP)
TPT 1 sqn with 6 BN-2, 8 C-212-200 (1 VIP)
HEL 1 sqn with 24 SA-319 (armed/liaison), 1 sqn with
    8 AB-412, 2 AS-532UL (VIP)

Forces Abroad

DROC: up to 10,000 reported

Paramilitary 21,800

ZIMBABWE REPUBLIC POLICE FORCE 19,500
(incl Air Wg)
POLICE SUPPORT UNIT 2,300

The International Arms Trade

The international arms trade was worth an estimated $56.9bn in 1998 compared with $56bn in 1997. While this was an increase in nominal terms, there was a marginal decline in real terms to $55.8bn measured in 1997 constant dollars. The relatively stable global figure masked considerable variation at regional level. Arms deliveries to East Asia and Australasia increased marginally, and they almost doubled to Sub-Saharan Africa. There was a small decline in deliveries to NATO members and European countries outside NATO, as well as to the Middle East and North Africa region, which remains by far the largest market for complete weapon systems. Deliveries to the Caribbean and Latin America fell 16%, while those to the Central and South Asia region were at similar levels to 1997.

Arms deliveries in 1998 were hardly affected by the cumulative impact of the 1997–98 Asian economic crisis and the oil-price weakness which adversely affected the economies of all producing countries and particularly of those in the Gulf. The value of new contracted orders did, however, decline in 1998, by some 6% on 1997. The level of committed orders between 1996 and 1998 suggests that the value of deliveries will decline in 1999 and 2000 by around 5% from peak 1997–1998 levels.

Saudi Arabia remained by far the largest national market for arms in 1998, taking delivery of equipment valued at some $10.4bn compared to $11bn in 1997. In the Middle East, the value of arms deliveries to Israel ($1bn), Egypt ($1bn) and the United Arab Emirates (over $900m) also reached high levels in 1998. The second-largest arms purchaser in 1998 was Taiwan, where arms deliveries were valued at $6.3bn (1997 $6.8bn). Deliveries to Japan (worth $2.1bn) and South Korea (worth $1.4bn) remained at high levels, while those to Singapore rose to some $900m.

The US delivered arms and military services worth some $27bn in 1998, little changed from the 1997 level in nominal terms, but slightly down in real terms at around $26.5bn, measured in constant 1997 dollars, from the 1997 figure of $27.1bn. The US share of the global arms market increased slightly to 49%. Of the other leading suppliers, France increased arms deliveries to $9.8bn in 1998 from $7.4bn in 1997, and Russia to $2.8bn compared to $2.5bn. By comparison, UK arms deliveries fell to $9bn compared with their peak of $10.9bn in 1997. Israel's arms exports also declined to some $1.3bn from $1.5bn in 1997. The value of Chinese exports halved from $1bn to $500m during the year under the pressure of increasing competition from Russia, Ukraine, Belarus and Bulgaria.

Sources Where possible, arms-trade statistics given in *The Military Balance* are obtained directly from governments, but numerous other sources are also used. This edition's figures for both the US and Italy have been revised upwards substantially. The primary source for US government figures is *World Military Expenditures and Arms Transfers 1997*, released by the US Arms Control and Disarmament Agency (ACDA) in January 1999. The ACDA was incorporated into the State Department Bureau of Arms Control as of April 1999. Its figures have been revised to include higher estimates of US direct commercial sales, including firm-to-firm export trade. Another source for 1998 data on US foreign military sales (excluding US direct commercial sales) and markets in individual countries is *Conventional Arms Transfers to Developing Nations 1991–1998* (Richard F. Grimmett, Congressional Research Service (CRS), Washington DC, August 1999). Historical arms trade data are also taken from *World Military Expenditures and Arms Transfers 1997*. The UN Register of Conventional Arms is an invaluable source of information on annual equipment deliveries. The UK Ministry of Defence is the source for the table on global orders. Figures from the Aerospace Industries Association of America (AIAA), the Society of British Aerospace Companies (SBAC), and the European Association of Aerospace Industries (AECMA) are also used to support the analysis.

Table 37 Country suppliers to the international arms trade, 1992–1998

Market share %	$10m–$50m	$50m–$100m	$100m–$200m	$200m–$1bn	$1bn–$2obn	$2obn+
45–55%						US
35–45%					China, France, Germany, Israel, Italy, Russia, UK	
5–10%				Belarus, Belgium, Canada, Czech Rep, Netherlands, North Korea, Spain, South Africa, Sweden, Switzerland, Ukraine		
2–4%			Argentina, Austria, Brazil, Bulgaria, FRY, Indonesia, Portugal, South Korea			
1–2%		Australia, India, Iran, Norway, Poland, Romania, Singapore, Slovakia, Turkey, Zimbabwe				
0–1%	Chile, Denmark, Egypt, Finland, Greece, Hungary, Japan, Jordan, Kazakstan, Kyrgyzstan, Malaysia, Mexico, Pakistan, Saudi Arabia, Taiwan, Uzbekistan					

Market share (%)

Table 38 Value of arms deliveries and market share, 1987, 1992–1998

(constant 1997 US$m / % in italics)

	Total	USSR/ Russia		Warsaw Pact excl. USSR		US		UK		France		Germany		Total Western Europe		China		Israel		Others	
1987	88,907	31,186	*35.1*	5,507	*6.2*	23,989	*27.0*	7,359	*8.3*	7,969	*9.0*	2,159	*2.4*	22,099	*24.9*	2,566	*2.9*	1,460	*1.6*	2,101	*2.4*
1992	51,539	2,806	*5.4*	n.a.	*n.a.*	28,161	*54.6*	5,532	*10.7*	4,610	*8.9*	1,877	*3.6*	15,683	*30.4*	1,231	*2.4*	1,648	*3.2*	2,010	*3.9*
1993	46,890	3,390	*7.2*	n.a.	*n.a.*	26,075	*55.6*	5,106	*10.9*	3,199	*6.8*	1,629	*3.5*	12,417	*26.5*	1,199	*2.6*	1,606	*3.4*	2,202	*4.7*
1994	42,790	2,906	*6.8*	n.a.	*n.a.*	22,946	*53.6*	4,960	*11.6*	3,580	*8.4*	1,502	*3.5*	12,530	*29.3*	772	*1.8*	1,481	*3.5*	2,156	*5.0*
1995	46,891	3,687	*7.9*	n.a.	*n.a.*	23,989	*51.2*	7,776	*16.6*	3,970	*8.5*	1,442	*3.1*	15,212	*32.4*	657	*1.4*	1,293	*2.8*	2,053	*4.4*
1996	51,061	3,583	*7.0*	n.a.	*n.a.*	25,032	*49.0*	9,854	*19.3*	5,871	*11.5*	685	*1.3*	18,984	*37.2*	609	*1.2*	1,356	*2.7*	1,498	*2.9*
1997	55,996	2,500	*4.5*	n.a.	*n.a.*	27,118	*48.4*	10,948	*19.6*	7,419	*13.2*	751	*1.3*	21,820	*39.0*	1,000	*1.8*	1,521	*2.7*	2,037	*3.6*
1998	55,756	2,854	*5.1*	n.a.	*n.a.*	26,514	*48.6*	8,971	*16.2*	9,804	*17.6*	834	*1.5*	22,394	*40.2*	501	*0.9*	1,252	*2.2*	1,671	*3.0*

Table 39 Deliveries by other major arms suppliers, 1987, 1992–1998

(constant 1997 US$m)

	Italy	Sweden	Canada	Brazil	South Africa	Ukraine	Czech Republic	Belarus
1987	978	1013	978	877	209	n.a.	906	n.a.
1992	1,150	942	1,347	202	169	n.a.	167	n.a.
1993	749	540	820	110	238	313	183	n.k.
1994	610	573	782	203	246	200	209	n.k.
1995	789	514	305	209	284	200	161	177
1996	795	653	466	52	190	200	120	204
1997	1,213	481	339	52	294	500	183	388
1998	1,147	574	313	104	120	511	179	104

Table 40 Arms deliveries to South Asia, 1987, 1992–1998

(constant 1997 US$m)

	India	Pakistan	Afghanistan	Bangladesh	Sri Lanka
1987	4,050	459	1890	68	68
1992	782	699	n.k.	45	5
1993	295	602	5	32	22
1994	334	310	22	32	107
1995	365	522	21	63	167
1996	417	428	63	73	209
1997	500	469	104	83	261
1998	469	542	73	73	250

Table 41 Arms imports by NATO and Western Europe, 1987, 1992–1998

(constant 1997 US$m)

	US	Canada	Western Europe	Inter-firm trade between US and Western Europe[1]	Turkey	Total
1987	2,842	491	8,557	3,413	1,627	16,931
1992	1,610	536	11,000	5,433	1,919	20,498
1993	1,464	272	7,984	4,967	1,877	16,564
1994	1,123	296	7,054	4,506	1,669	14,648
1995	1,099	220	5,491	6,616	1,784	15,208
1996	1,078	255	7,445	6,369	1,460	16,607
1997	1,049	245	7,356	8,487	1,565	18,701
1998	1,098	225	7,562	7,900	1,554	18,340

Note [1] Inter-firm figures show firm-to-firm imports in intermediate markets for weapon subsystems and components for equipment purchased by NATO and Western European governments.
[2] Western Europe comprises NATO Europe, non-NATO EU countries and Switzerland.

Table 42 Identified arms orders, 1992–1998

(US$bn)

	Total	US		UK		France		Russia		Israel		Top 5		Other	
			%		%		%		%		%		%		%
1992	50.6	23.4	46.2	9.3	18.4	8.6	17.0	1.6	3.2	1.4	2.8	44.3	87.5	6.3	12.5
1993	59.4	33.0	55.6	10.8	18.2	6.9	11.6	1.8	3.0	1.8	3.0	54.3	91.4	5.1	8.6
1994	42.5	17.0	40.0	7.0	16.5	7.0	16.5	4.4	10.4	1.0	2.4	36.4	85.6	6.1	14.4
1995	45.2	19.1	42.3	7.8	17.3	7.4	16.4	2.4	5.3	1.0	2.2	37.7	83.4	7.5	16.6
1996	36.0	10.8	30.0	8.1	22.5	3.7	10.3	3.4	9.4	1.2	3.3	27.2	75.6	8.8	24.4
1997	41.6	16.4	39.4	8.9	21.4	4.1	9.9	3.2	7.7	1.9	4.6	34.5	82.9	7.1	17.1
1998	39.0	14.5	37.2	10.0	25.6	5.7	14.6	1.7	4.4	1.6	4.1	33.5	85.9	5.5	14.1

Table 43 Regional distribution of international arms deliveries, 1987, 1992–1998

(constant 1997 US$m)

	NATO and Western Europe	%	Eastern Europe	%	USSR/CIS	%	Middle East & North Africa	%	East Asia	%	South Asia	%	Latin America	%	Sub-Saharan Africa	%	Austra-lasia	%
1987	16,931	19.0	7,162	8.1	1,890	2.1	33,029	37.1	9,926	11.2	6,534	7.3	5,319	6.0	6,791	7.6	1,325	1.5
1992	20,498	39.8	261	0.5	100	0.2	18,120	35.2	7,444	14.4	1,557	3.0	1,400	2.4	887	1.7	1,416	2.7
1993	16,564	35.3	1,476	3.1	100	0.2	17,210	36.7	7,528	16.1	961	2.0	789	1.7	960	2.0	1,300	2.8
1994	14,648	34.2	1,356	3.2	90	0.2	14,111	33.0	8,167	19.1	805	1.9	808	1.9	1,387	3.2	1,411	3.3
1995	15,208	32.4	871	1.9	365	0.8	16,469	35.1	9,267	19.8	1,137	2.4	1,606	3.4	636	1.4	1,331	2.8
1996	16,607	32.5	1,252	2.5	313	0.6	16,490	32.3	11,212	22.0	1,189	2.3	1,773	3.5	766	1.5	1,460	2.9
1997	18,701	33.4	834	1.5	417	0.7	16,917	30.2	13,220	23.6	1,417	2.5	1,982	3.5	991	1.8	1,515	2.7
1998	18,340	32.9	782	1.4	391	0.7	16,745	30.0	13,236	23.7	1,408	2.5	1,658	3.0	1,690	3.0	1,554	2.8

Table 44 Arms deliveries to the Middle East and North Africa, 1987, 1992–1998

(constant 1997 US$m)

	Saudi Arabia	Iraq	Iran	Egypt	Israel	Syria	UAE	Kuwait	Libya	Algeria
1987	9,909	7,301	2,295	2,430	3,105	2,700	261	270	810	945
1992	10,815	n.k.	953	1,815	1,804	427	522	1,116	90	156
1993	9,283	n.k.	1,203	2,086	1,752	295	626	1,085	80	146
1994	8,459	n.k.	417	1,252	1,283	147	553	864	80	150
1995	9,387	n.k.	522	1,982	803	177	991	1,356	80	240
1996	9,596	n.k.	417	1,669	949	94	782	1,721	80	261
1997	11,001	n.k.	800	1,100	834	104	834	700	104	469
1998	10,409	n.k.	626	1,017	1,043	115	939	522	100	522

Table 45 Arms deliveries to East Asia, 1987, 1992–1998

(constant 1997 US$m)

	Japan	Taiwan	ROK	DPRK	Vietnam	China	Thailand	Malaysia	Singapore	Indonesia	Myanmar	Philippines
1987	1,512	1,408	1,012	567	2,565	877	581	95	418	351	27	95
1992	2,263	924	1,345	33	21	1,458	415	146	247	56	168	157
1993	2,809	1,093	1,867	5	21	629	153	295	142	98	142	66
1994	2,338	1,069	2,263	96	86	278	417	908	246	53	107	96
1995	2,399	1,252	1,784	100	209	756	1,147	782	209	177	146	94
1996	2,451	1,773	1,669	100	261	1,565	730	469	522	834	261	104
1997	2,242	6,780	1,356	100	156	417	495	313	469	417	313	156
1998	2,086	6,258	1,366	90	177	469	313	334	887	365	302	115

Analyses *and* **Tables**

TRANSATLANTIC MERGERS AND ACQUISITIONS GATHER PACE

There was a clear shift in the pattern of defence industry consolidation in NATO countries in 1999. As the scope for national consolidation has declined, there has been a relative increase in the number of European transnational mergers and acquisitions (M&A) and particularly in transatlantic transactions. The results of consolidation in the 1990s are becoming evident. There are now a small number of large, vertically-integrated defence firms in the US, France and the UK with a dominant presence in domestic, NATO and global markets. These firms are supported throughout the vertical chain by a transnational and increasingly transatlantic supply base. Further consolidation among the top-tier companies is inevitable, despite the competition concerns of some NATO governments. Under prevailing conditions of, at best, static defence spending, the major top-tier defence firms in Germany, Italy, Sweden, Netherlands and Spain are increasingly vulnerable to hostile acquisition or relegation to sub-contractor status unless they are willing to negotiate friendly mergers.

Mergers and Acquisitions in 1999

In 1999, defence firms in NATO countries continued to see the pursuit of specialisation and large-scale production as the key to profits in markets where business generally remains well below Cold War levels. This strategy led them to look increasingly beyond national borders for equity partners. Among prime contractors, there were further moves towards national consolidation, notably the merger of British Aerospace (BAe) and GEC Marconi Electronic Systems (MES). The sizeable US-located assets of the combined BAe entity make it the first transatlantic defence firm among top-tier producers. In France, Aerospatiale and Matra Hautes Technologies (MHT) merged in 1999, with MHT's parent, Lagardere taking 33% of the combined entity. The French government further reduced its equity in both Aerospatiale (to 47% after floating 17% on the stock market and reserving 3% for employee equity participation) and Thomson–CSF (from 44% to 34% after selling a 10% stake to the private sector company Alcatel). The merger of Aerospatiale–MHT and Thomson–CSF looks increasingly probable. In 1999, the first European transnational acquisition at prime-contractor level took place when Daimler–Chrysler Aerospace (DASA) acquired the Spanish aerospace firm Construcciones Aeronauticas SA (CASA). This was followed by the first transatlantic acquisition in the top-tier armoured fighting vehicle sector, when the US company General Motors bought the Swiss firm Motorwagenfabrik AG (MOWAG). In the US, the Department of Defense (DoD) blocked, on competition grounds, attempts by first General Dynamics and then Litton Industries to acquire the US shipbuilder Newport News. However, the DoD did approve the Litton acquisition of another shipbuilder, Avondale. At sub-contractor levels, the pace of consolidation quickened below the top-tier producers, and M&A transactions reflected both trans-European and transatlantic trends. The largest deals involved the US firm TRW, which acquired the US–UK merged entity Lucas Varity, while AlliedSignal, another US firm which has extensive European assets, acquired Honeywell, also of the US. While, for the present at least, national top-tier producers in both the US and Europe retain their market power with the help of continuing national protection from open competition, this applies less and less to smaller firms. The market power of national-only sub-contractors continues to erode in the face of a growing transatlantic sub-contractor base.

Merger of British Aerospace and GEC Marconi Electronic Systems

Assuming it goes ahead, the merger between BAe and MES in 1999 will represent a watershed in several respects. First it breaks the stalemate in European consolidation that arose because some governments have been slow to privatise state-owned defence firms and to lift restrictions on foreign ownership of their national champions. The development is also a blow to private-sector firms like Daimler–Chrysler, which were prolonging merger negotiations with BAe in the hope of securing higher prices for their defence and aerospace business. Second, the merger serves notice to European prime contractors, notably DASA in Germany, Finmeccannica Alenia in Italy, and CASA in Spain, that participation in European collaborative projects under uncompetitive conditions of *juste retour* (workshare allocations) was no longer sufficient to justify a place among NATO's top-tier of arms producers. The merger with MES transforms the new BAe into a vertically-integrated company, capable of competing with the top US contractors for NATO's major equipment programmes of the future. It does not compromise existing joint-venture arrangements with European firms. In the European context, the BAe–MES merger helps to dispel myths about the defence industries of NATO countries being divided into 'fortress America' and 'fortress Europe'. Initial reactions from NATO governments were unfavourable for varying reasons. European governments took the view that the merger effectively blocked the formation of a European defence and aerospace company, although there was already a stalemate on that front for other reasons. The US government envisaged competition problems arising from the merger, despite the fact that both companies were already national monopolies in their different sectors. In reality, the two firms' merger strategy has reflected their view of the future NATO defence market. They are joining forces to consolidate and build on their market strengths in both Europe and the US in the face of increasing competition from US majors, not only in NATO but also in the global market. As a result of this merger, a leading European company is set to become the third-largest defence company in the world. European governments will benefit as customers of a global player which can price competitively on the back of economies of scale. European economies at large will benefit in terms of employment and of securing a place as leading sources of defence technology. The merger will undoubtedly lead other European and US firms in the same direction.

Obstacles to Transatlantic Defence Industry Integration

Government resistance to the BAe–MES merger was not surprising. All NATO governments remain locked into symbiotic relationships with their national defence industries. What is still lacking is appreciation of why and how a competitive transatlantic defence industry can result in improved procurement. Since governments are customers of defence companies as well as the long-term custodians of the national defence industrial base, this sector of industry has been the slowest to adapt to the current developments in the global market. In other industrial sectors, fears of lost national competence in leading technologies and protection of domestic employment have been more easily assuaged by the obvious benefits of privatisation, competition and globalisation. In Europe, the defence industry is the last bastion of industrial policies designed to build and sustain national champions. European governments, as primary customers as well as financial sponsors and regulators, remain inclined to intervene, more often for domestic industrial reasons than on grounds of national security.

US policy on transatlantic defence firms illustrates different points. Over the past year there has been declining resistance to the idea of M&A between US and European prime contractors, influenced by the growing number of US sub-contractors buying in Europe and vice versa. US opposition to a competitive transatlantic top-tier of prime contractors is focused on two related areas. First, a belief that the US enjoys such a technological lead over Europe that it reaps no advantage from collaboration; second, concerns about the potential compromise of long-term US security through systematic technology transfer to Europe. The underlying perception of a blanket technology differential is flawed as there are many technologies and weapon sectors where European performance is at least as good as in the US. More transatlantic links in precisely

Analyses and Tables

these areas would reduce over-capacity in both the US and Europe, improve competition and drive down costs, much as is happening already at sub-contractor level. The bulk of the weapon sector does not present long-term security sensitivities. Such sensitivities only apply to the advanced technologies in which the US is most specialised. These are precisely the technologies which Europe lacks, and it is in these areas where controls on technology transfer will be the most stringent, and where the US will, in any event, determine the conditions of partnership.

Policy Options: harnessing industrial specialisation and scale in NATO procurement

As programmes originating in the Cold War run down or are quietly scrapped, there is an opportunity for a fresh approach to the institutional arrangements for cooperative equipment procurement. Current multilateral procurement bodies in NATO and Europe are trapped by past programmes and practices. One model for future NATO cooperation across the range of conventional-weapon systems might be the US Joint Strike Fighter (JSF) programme. The UK is a full partner with the US in this project alongside NATO partners Canada, Denmark, Italy, Netherlands, Norway and Turkey. The project reaches beyond NATO; Singapore is also a partner and Israel is likely to join.

Only those firms with a transatlantic structure are likely to flourish under contemporary procurement conditions, where a rapid rate of technology advance continues in the face of government fiscal constraints. Conversely, firms with primarily national orientation, cosseted by protectionist government purchasing are likely to find themselves relegated to minor sub-contractor or niche status. At present, M&A policies of those NATO governments most exercised by defence industrial consolidation appear to undervalue the benefits in terms of technology, cost savings and efficiency generated by industrial focus on specialisation and scale.

NATO governments can only take full advantage of the emerging transatlantic defence industrial supply base if they reform the way they procure equipment for their armed forces. It became clear during 1999 that NATO's surviving defence firms are opting for a transatlantic structure. If NATO governments do not follow suit with their procurement, the purchasing power of their defence equipment budgets will continue its decline at a time when governments need to advance rather than retard their military technologies.

Table 46 Selected mergers and acquisitions by NATO countries, 1999

T/N[1] Partner		Firm	Partner Firm	Estimated Value ($m)	Principal sector
Canada					
T	Fr, CH	Alcan	Pechiney, Alusuisse Lonza	12,900	materials
France					
N	Fr	Sagem	Framatome Sfim	21	avionics
T	US	Thomson-CSF	AlliedSignal Electro-Optics		optronics
N	Fr	Aerospatiale	Matra Hautes Technologies	8,350	aircraft
Germany					
T	Sp	DASA	CASA	1,570	aircraft
N	Ge	Rheinmetall	Buck Werke		electronics
N	Ge	Liebherr	ZF Luftfahrttechnikwerke		flight systems
Netherlands					
T	US	Granaria	Eagle-Picher	700	components
T	US	Getronics	Wang Global	1,850	information technology
Sweden					
T	UK	Investor Saab	Alvis Barracuda	9	materials
UK					
N	UK	UMECO	TI Group ASED	19	components

T/N[1] Partner		Firm	Partner Firm	Estimated Value ($m)	Principal sector
T	US	Meggitt	Whittaker Corporation	380	components
T	US	Smiths Industries	Environmental Technologies Group	14	NBC
T	US	Smiths Industries	Signal Processing Systems	15	electronics
T	US	BT	Control Data Systems	360	telecommunications
N	No	GEC	Kvaerner Shipbuiding	1	shipbuilding
N	UK	BAe	GEC Marconi	13,400	naval systems
T	US	TI Group	Walbro Corporation	635	fuel systems
T	US	TI Group	GE Tri-Manufacturing	58	aero-engines
T	No	Vickers	Ulstein	550	naval systems
T	Ge	TI Group	Busak and Shamban	450	materials
N	UK	Senior Engineering	Thornskill Willcox Hose	8	components
T	US	GKN	Interlake Chemtronics	553	components
T	US	GEC	Tracor	1,400	electronics
N	UK	Vosper Thorneycroft	Hunting Halmatic	20	patrol boats
US					
T	UK	Textron	David Brown	326	components
N	US	Rockwell	Kaiser Flight Dynamics		avionics
N	US	Northrop Grumman	California Microwave	93	information technology
N	US	General Dynamics	Gulfstream Aerospace	5,300	aircraft
T	US	TRW	Lucas Varity	7,000	aerospace
N	US	Precision Parts	Wyman-Gordon	825	aero-engines
N	US	Anteon	Analysis and Technology	104	naval systems
N	US	L-3	Scott Technologies Interstate	60	electronics
N	US	Woodward Governor	Textron Fuel Systems	160	utilities
N	US	L-3	Aydin Corporation	100	electronics
N	US	Veridian	Trident Data Systems	300	information technology
N	US	Barco	Metheus		C4I
N	US	Cordant Technologies	Howmet International	1,500	utilities
T	It	Kollmorgen	Calzoni	20	naval systems
N	US	Veridian	MRJ Technology Solutions		information technology
N	US	Alcoa	Reynolds	5,600	materials
T	CH	General Motors	MOWAG		light armoured vehicles
T	UK	Marmon	Bridport	48	components
N	UK	Fairchild	General Electric Kaynar	370	components
N	UK	Northrop Grumman	Allegheny Teledyne Ryan	140	UAV
N	UK	General Dynamics	GTE Communications	1,050	radio communications
N	US	Northrop Grumman	Data Procurement Corporation	35	information technology
N	US	Eaton Corporation	Aeroquip-Vickers	1,700	utilities
N	US	PPG Industries	Akzo Nobel PRC-Desoto	512	components
N	US	Litton Industries	Avondale	500	warships
N	US	AlliedSignal	Honeywell	15,500	electronics
N	US	Northrop Grumman	International Research Institute	55	information technology
N	US	Ametek	Gulton-Statham Transducers	23	components
N	US	Veridian	ERIM International		information technology
N	US	General Dynamics	NASSCO	415	warships
T	Fr	TRW	Peugeot Citroen SAAM	200	utilities
N	US	United Technologies	Sunstrand	4,300	electronics
N	US	BFGoodrich	Coltec	2,200	utilities

Notes   [1] T = Transnational; N = National

[2] The countries cited indicate where the companies involved are incorporated.

[3] The list includes M&A transactions announced in 1999 or incorporated in 1999. It excludes most transactions announced in 1998, whose incorporation began in 1998 and continued in 1999.

Analyses and Tables

Lessons From Kosovo: Military Operational Capabilities

The NATO air campaign against Yugoslavia from 24 March to 10 June 1999, and subsequent deployment of the NATO-led multinational land force (KFOR), underscored a number of lessons about weapons and equipment capabilities that require urgent attention from NATO and its partner countries. While in strictly military terms, NATO forces achieved their overall mission – forcing the withdrawal of Yugoslav forces from Kosovo and introducing a ground force to create more secure conditions for the return of displaced people – certain operational weaknesses were exposed which need to be remedied. The more important lessons centre on: command, control and communications systems; intelligence (including associated data handling); surveillance and target acquisition; precision-guided weapons; combat-support aircraft; and land-force deployment capabilities.

Surveillance, Target Acquisition and Intelligence

In the Kosovo campaign, the technical means of gathering information for target acquisition was a vital factor, given the shortage of reliable human intelligence sources. Unmanned aerial vehicles (UAV) played a more prominent role than in any previous military campaign, in gathering timely data for the target-acquisition and assessment process. Among the most frequently used UAVs were the US *Predator* and *Hunter*, and the CL-289, operated over Yugoslavia by French and German forces. The *Predator* is the most capable of these aircraft as it can operate at altitudes of up to 7,600 metres, with a typical endurance of up to 24 hours, compared to 600m and just 30 minutes for the CL-289. Endurance will vary depending on the weight of the payload. Both aircraft can carry a range of sensors, including: electro-optical cameras which send video pictures; infrared to pick up heat concentrations; and, in the case of the *Predator*, synthetic aperture radar (SAR), which makes out images through cloud cover. The *Predator* has full data-link capabilities and can operate in a signals-intelligence role by picking up an adversary's radio transmissions. It proved its worth as a reliable asset in operations over Bosnia-Herzegovina from 1995 to 1998, during which the deployed vehicles flew over 3,800 hours in approximately 600 sorties. Losses were few during that period, amounting to around four out of a total US holding (by the end of 1998) of just over 50. In their much more intensive use during *Operation Allied Force*, about 25 NATO UAVs were reported lost (of which 13 were US types). Some were shot down and others lost due to technical failure. Even the more limited-range CL-289 UAV was reported to be highly valuable to its French operators with its near real-time (1.5 seconds' lapse) video and infrared transmissions. This experience will doubtless encourage the French and other Europeans to improve their UAV capabilities substantially, in particular to acquire longer endurance, a SAR capability and improved data links. Improved data links are particularly important to enable the data from UAV sorties to be integrated with those from other sources, such as manned reconnaissance aircraft. The *Predator* data link, for example, can be fully integrated into the communications and command-and-control system, not only with its ground-station but also with E-8C Joint Surveillance and Target Acquisition System (JSTARS) aircraft. An increased demand for enhanced UAV capabilities will undoubtedly be a direct result of the NATO campaign in Kosovo. The relatively low cost compared to manned reconnaissance aircraft, and the bonus of not putting aircrew at risk, adds to the attractions of its technical capabilities. The advance in the technology of miniaturising sensors and in improved data transmission will widen the range of possibilities for this type of system. All the fielded European systems, in addition to the CL-289, such as the French *Crecerelle*, the UK *Phoenix*, the Belgian *Epervier* and the Italian *Meteor Mirach* 150, need upgrading. Some programmes are already in hand. The next generation of UAVs would be an excellent project for European collaboration.

Precision Weapons

The political constraints on military planners increased the importance of precision-guided weapons during the campaign. The disparity in capability between the US and European NATO members was particularly marked. While many more US aircraft were involved than of any other NATO member, quality as well as quantity resulted in the US delivering well over 80% of the munitions used during the 79-day campaign. As NATO wanted to minimise the risk of losing aircraft and aircrew, it was decided that the majority of attacking aircraft should operate above 5,000m. These tactics ensured that only two allied aircraft were lost to Yugoslav air-defence fire in nearly 10,000 bombing missions. But operating from a height of nearly three miles had a major drawback. All the precision-guided weapons delivered by the UK, for example, use laser, television or infrared guidance systems, which require line-of-sight with the target throughout the delivery process. In conditions of low cloud cover and thick mist, many aircraft operating from medium-level were either unable to fire their weapons because their targets were obscured, or lost contact with the weapon after launch. In the first 21 days of the campaign, NATO air forces enjoyed only seven days of favourable weather, and there were ten days when more than 50% of sorties had to be cancelled. The US was dominant in having the ability to deliver weapons with guidance systems that were not degraded by poor visibility. The weapons comprised, among others, the air-delivered Joint Direct Attack Munition (JDAM), and air- and sea-launched cruise missiles. These weapons use inertial navigation systems (INS) and receive navigational data from the satellite-based global positioning system (GPS). Of the Europeans, only the UK operated a cruise-missile capability during *Operation Allied Force*, firing the *Tomahawk* Land Attack Missile (TLAM) from a submarine. The UK fired 20 of the 240 TLAM launched during the campaign. The UK and France are developing air-launched cruise missiles with similarly advanced capabilities through their collaborative APACHE *(Storm Shadow)* project. This missile is being designed to be delivered by an aircraft such as the *Eurofighter* over 200 kilometres from a target. One of the effects of the Kosovo campaign will be that programmes to develop and modernise such weapons are likely to be sustained despite their expense. A major lesson of the campaign was that all participants, particularly the Europeans, held insufficient stocks of all types of precision-guided munitions. For example, the UK's stock of TLAMs was only 65 at the start of the campaign. Finally, while they are not precision weapons, bombs (US CBU-94's) used to deliver specially treated wire filaments to shut down electric-power grids were a notable development. When these weapons were dropped on five transformer sites on 3 May 1999, it is estimated that the power supply to 70% of the country was cut off. Given that the use of these weapons caused virtually no direct civilian casualties, their potential will no doubt feature prominently in NATO countries' assessments of the campaign.

Combat Support

In the just under 37,500 missions of the air campaign, combat-support missions outnumbered bombing missions by nearly three to one. While some combat-support operations included protective air patrols against possible attacks by Yugoslav aircraft, a very large number involved missions such as electronic warfare, reconnaissance, air-space command-and-control and air-to-air refuelling. The US EA-6B *Prowler* aircraft was considered to be particularly important in the effort to suppress Yugoslav air defences with its electronic counter-measures capability. NATO European air forces do not have a comparable capability. The *Prowler* ends its service life in about five years and the US does not have a replacement in view. It remains to be seen if the lesson of this aircraft's value is properly taken into account. Another vital combat-support asset in short supply was air-to-air refuelling aircraft. Because of the shortage of tankers, significant numbers of combat aircraft had to be deployed nearer to the theatre of operations, placing extra demands on resources, particularly

Analyses and Tables

logistic support. For example, the UK's *Tornado* GR-1s, based at Brüggen in Germany, were moved to Corsica during the campaign to reduce the demand on tanker aircraft. The US provided the majority of the tanker support, with some 150 deployed. European air forces have only a small number of these aircraft. France and the UK each had 12 tankers available for the operation, and Italy and Turkey had two each. Germany had none. If they have any pretensions to an independent military capability, this deficiency is a clear lesson for the Europeans.

Force-Deployment Capabilities

NATO European countries have just over two million active duty service personnel. A significant proportion of them are still conscripted, and thus of limited use both in terms of their deployment outside home territories and being sufficiently trained to engage in a wide range of operations using modern weapons and equipment. This shortcoming is particularly marked in specialist personnel such as engineers and communications and medical staff. In addition, only a small proportion of European forces (mainly British and French) can deploy a combined-arms force with the necessary field command-and-control infrastructure. These shortcomings were evident as the build-up for the full deployment of KFOR got under way in June 1999, and there were delays as countries had difficulties in fielding the forces that they had offered. Two months after its initial deployment on 12 June, the force had still not reached its target of 52,000 NATO personnel. It is a startling reality that only perhaps 2–3% of the personnel under arms in Europe are available for deployment on missions such as KFOR and the NATO Stabilisation Force (SFOR) in Bosnia.

Operation Allied Force also highlighted shortcomings in transport support for the deployment of forces and for their logistic needs. There was heavy reliance on the US, particularly on its C-17 fleet. While shorter-range transport aircraft such as the C-130 are widely available in most forces there was a lack of longer-range transports. Plans for a future European aircraft in this category range from the *Airbus* A-400M to a German-led project for a transport based on the Russian AN-70 aircraft. One method of transport seemingly not given sufficient consideration is the enhancement of the existing military sealift capability. Rapid reinforcement by air was a necessary requirement in the Cold War era because of the very short warning times involved. Given the degree of warning time and build-up in likely missions in current conditions, transport by sea could be better exploited.

Conclusions

This analysis has focused on a selection of key capabilities, but has not dealt with their management. In particular, there are some important lessons from *Operation Allied Force* regarding command-and-control (in particular air-space management), secure data and voice communications, targeting procedures and the proper integration of the collection and analysis of intelligence. Even the best combat aircraft and precision weapons will not be effective unless these battle-management capabilities are working efficiently. The capabilities outlined above show where investment has to be made in either enhancing existing capabilities, such as the UAV, precision-guided weapons and electronic counter-measures; or where a capability is lacking, such as air-to-air refuelling and air transport. European countries have a particular problem in not having sufficient numbers of professionals, particularly specialists, in their armed forces to sustain a combined-arms offensive operation of a significant size. They also have limited means to transport and sustain those forces they deploy in operations beyond their borders. At the EU summit in Cologne in June 1999, European leaders declared that the EU requires 'a capacity for autonomous action backed by credible military forces'. If this is to become a reality, increases in defence spending, or at least a radical reallocation of resources, along with genuine collaboration in defence procurement, are necessary.

UNITED NATIONS

Troops deployed in UN operations have declined steadily in recent years from peak levels of over 70,000 in 1993–95. On 1 August 1999, there were 14 UN peacekeeping operations around the world involving 9,123 troops from 37 countries. The leading contributors are shown below. The UN peacekeeping budget for the year to 30 June 1999 was $1.4 billion, falling to $900 million in the latest budgetary projection for the year to 30 June 2000. Arrears in payments of contributions to the UN peacekeeping budget amounted to $1.7bn at 30 June 1999.

Table 47 Average strength and cost of UN peacekeeping forces, 1991–1999

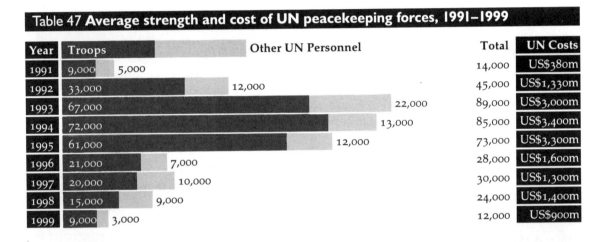

Year	Troops	Other UN Personnel	Total	UN Costs
1991	9,000	5,000	14,000	US$380m
1992	33,000	12,000	45,000	US$1,330m
1993	67,000	22,000	89,000	US$3,000m
1994	72,000	13,000	85,000	US$3,400m
1995	61,000	12,000	73,000	US$3,300m
1996	21,000	7,000	28,000	US$1,600m
1997	20,000	10,000	30,000	US$1,300m
1998	15,000	9,000	24,000	US$1,400m
1999	9,000	3,000	12,000	US$900m

Table 48 Leading troop contributors to UN operations (as at 30 June 1999)

Country	Strength	Country	Strength	Country	Strength
Poland	990	India	621	Egypt	328
Bangladesh	810	Nepal	601	UK	306
Austria	669	Fiji	596	France	247
Ghana	657	Finland	504	Côte d'Ivoire	235
Ireland	627	Argentina	496	Canada	219

Table 49 Leading financial contributors to UN operations, 1999[1]

(US$m)	Assessment	%	Arrears		Assessment	%	Arrears
US	284	31.5	966	Netherlands	14	1.6	—
Japan	158	17.6	19	Australia	12	1.5	—
Germany	86	9.5	10	Sweden	10	1.1	—
France	70	7.8	22	Belgium	10	1.1	—
UK	56	6.1	—	Brazil	3	0.3	14
Russia	32	3.6	129	Argentina	2	0.2	2
Italy	48	5.3	7	Sub-total	832	92.4	1,207
Canada	25	2.8	—	Other	68	7.6	340
Spain	23	2.5	—	Total	900	100.0	1,547

Note [1] Excluding voluntary contributions by member states

United Nations Truce Supervision Organisation (UNTSO)

Mission UNTSO was established in 1948 to assist the Mediator and Truce Commission supervise the truce in Palestine. Since then, its tasks have included supervising the 1949 General Armistice Agreements and the cease-fire in the Suez Canal area and the Golan Heights following the Arab–Israeli Six Day War of June 1967. UNTSO assists and cooperates with the UN Disengagement Observer Force (UNDOF) on the Golan Heights in the Israeli–Syrian sector, and with the UN Interim Force in Lebanon (UNIFIL) in the Israeli–Lebanese sector. UNTSO also has a presence in the Egyptian–Israeli sector in the Sinai, and maintains offices in Beirut and Damascus.
Headquarters Government House, Jerusalem.
Strength 141 military observers. **Contributors** Arg, Aus, A, Be, Ca, Chl, PRC, Da, Ea, SF, Fr, Irl, It, Nl, NZ, No, RF, Slvk, Slvn, Swe, CH, US.
Cost *1997* $27m *1998* $27m *1999* $47m. **Total cost to June 1999** $559m.

United Nations Disengagement Observer Force (UNDOF)

Mission UNDOF was established in 1974 after the 1973 Middle East war to maintain the cease-fire between Israel and Syria; supervise the disengagement of Israeli and Syrian forces; and supervise the areas of separation and limitation, as provided in the Agreement on Disengagement of 31 May 1974. The situation in the Israeli–Syrian sector has remained quiet and there have been no serious incidents.
Location Syrian Golan Heights **Headquarters** Damascus.
Strength 1,029 troops, assisted by 80 military observers from UNSTO's Observer Group Golan and supported by international and locally recruited civilian staff. **Contributors** A, Ca, J, Pl, Slvk.
Cost *1997* $38m *1998* $35m *1999* $35m. **Total cost to June 1999** $751m.

United Nations Interim Force in Lebanon (UNIFIL)

Mission UNIFIL was established in March 1978 to confirm the withdrawal of Israeli forces from southern Lebanon; restore international peace and security; and help the Lebanese government maintain effective authority in the area. UNIFIL has, however, been prevented from fully implementing its mandate. Israeli forces continue to occupy parts of southern Lebanon, where they and their local auxiliary in turn remain targets for attack by groups resisting the occupation.
Location Southern Lebanon **Headquarters** Naqoura.
Current Strength 4,496 troops assisted by 60 military observers from UNTSO's Observer Group Lebanon. **Contributors** Fji, SF, Fr, Gha, Ind, Irl, It, N, No, Pl.
Cost *1997* $121m *1998* $143m *1999* $149m. **Total cost to June 1999** $2,969m.

United Nations Iraq–Kuwait Observer Mission (UNIKOM)

Mission UNIKOM was established in April 1991 as part of the cease-fire arrangement at the end of the Gulf War to monitor the Iraq–Kuwait border area in the Khor Abdullah and demilitarised zones. The demilitarised zone extends 10 kilometres into Iraq and 5km into Kuwait from the agreed boundary between the two countries. UNIKOM's function is to deter violations of the inter-state boundary by direct action, and observe and report hostile or potentially hostile actions. Kuwait pays two-thirds of the costs.
Location Iraqi–Kuwaiti border area **Headquarters** Umm Qasr, Iraq.
Strength 909 troops, assisted by 149 military observers and supported by 200 international and locally recruited civilian staff. **Contributors** Units from Bng (infantry); Observers from Arg, A, Bng, Ca, PRC, Da, Fji, SF, Fr, Ge, Gha, Gr, Hu, Ind, Indo, Irl, It, Kya, Mal, Nga, Pak, Pl, R, RF, Sen,

Sgp, Swe, Th, Tu, UK, Ury, US, Ve.
Cost *1997* $50m *1998* $52m *1999* $54m. **Total cost to June 1999** $467m.

United Nations Peacekeeping Force in Cyprus (UNFICYP)

Mission UNFICYP was established in March 1964 to prevent a recurrence of fighting between the Greek Cypriot and Turkish Cypriot communities and to help restore and maintain law and order and peaceful conditions. Following a *de facto* cease-fire on 16 August 1974, UNFICYP's mandate was expanded to include supervising the cease-fire and maintaining a buffer zone between the lines of the Cyprus National Guard and the Turkish and Turkish Cypriot forces.
Location Cyprus **Headquarters** Nicosia.
Strength 1,228 troops, assisted by 35 civilian police and 330 international and locally recruited staff. **Contributors** Arg, Aus, A, Ca, SF, Hu, Irl, Nl, Slvn, UK.
Cost *1997* $46m *1998* $45m *1999* $46m (including voluntary contributions by Cyprus of one-third of the total cost and by Greece of $7m). **Total cost to June 1999** $973m.

United Nations Military Observer Group in India and Pakistan (UNMOGIP)

Mission UNMOGIP was established in January 1949 to supervise the cease-fire between India and Pakistan in the state of Jammu and Kashmir. Following the 1972 India–Pakistan agreement defining a Line of Control in Kashmir, India claimed that UNMOGIP's mandate had lapsed. Pakistan, however, did not agree. Consequently, the UN Secretary-General has declared that UNMOGIP's mission can only be terminated by the UN Security Council. In the absence of such a decision, UNMOGIP has been maintained with the same mandate and functions.
Location The cease-fire line between India and Pakistan in the state of Jammu and Kashmir.
Headquarters Rawalpindi (November–April); Srinagar (May–October).
Strength 46 military observers, supported by international and locally recruited police.
Contributors Be, Chl, Da, SF, It, ROK, Swe, Ury.
Cost *1997* $7m *1998* $8m *1999* $38m. **Total cost to June 1999** $153m.

United Nations Mission for the Referendum in Western Sahara (MINURSO)

Mission MINURSO was established in April 1991 in accordance with 'the settlement proposals', as accepted by Morocco and the *Frente Popular para la Liberación de Saguia el-Hamra y de Río de Oro* (POLISARIO) on 30 August 1988 to:
- monitor a cease-fire;
- verify the reduction of Moroccan troops in the territory;
- monitor the confinement of Moroccan and POLISARIO troops to designated locations, and ensure the release of all Western Saharan political prisoners or detainees;
- oversee the exchange of prisoners of war;
- implement the repatriation programme;
- identify and register qualified voters;
- organise and ensure a free referendum and proclaim the results.

In its limited deployment, MINURSO's primary function was restricted to complementing the identification process; verifying the cease-fire and cessation of hostilities; and monitoring local police and ensuring security and order at identification and registration sites. In May 1996, in the absence of any meaningful progress towards completing the settlement plan, the Security Council suspended the identification process, authorised the withdrawal of the civilian police component – except for a small number of officers to maintain contacts with the authorities on both sides – and decided to reduce the strength of MINURSO's military component by 20%.

Location Western Sahara **Headquarters** Laayoune.
Strength 27 troops, assisted by 32 civilian police monitors and 204 military observers, and supported by international and locally recruited staff. **Contributors** Arg, A, Bng, Ca, PRC, Et, ElS, Fr, Gha, Gr, Gui, Hr, Irl, It, Kya, Mal, Nga, Pak, Pl, Por, ROK, RF, Swe, Ury, US, Ve.
Civilian personnel provided by Ca, Et, Gha, Ind, Mal, Pak, Por, Swe.
Cost *1997* $29m *1998* $23m *1999* $52m. **Total cost to June 1999 $337m.**

United Nations Mission of Observers in Prevlaka (UNMOP)

Mission United Nations military observers have been deployed in the strategically important Prevlaka peninsula of Croatia since October 1992, when the Security Council authorised the UN Protection Force (UNPROFOR) to assume responsibility for monitoring the area's demilitarisation. Following UNPROFOR's restructuring in March 1995, those functions were carried out by United Nations Confidence Restoration Operation in Croatia (UNCRO). With the termination of UNCRO's mandate in January 1996, the Security Council authorised UN military observers as UNMOP to continue monitoring the demilitarisation of the peninsula for three months, to be extended for a further three months if the Secretary-General reported this would continue to help decrease tension. UNMOP is under the command and direction of a Chief Military Observer, who reports directly to the UN Secretariat in New York.
Location Prevlaka peninsula, Croatia **Headquarters** Dubrovnik.
Strength 27 military observers, supported by international and locally recruited staff.
Contributors Arg, Bng, Be, Br, Ca, Cz, Da, Et, SF, Gha, Indo, Irl, HKJ, Kya, N, NZ, Nga, No, Pak, Pl, Por, RF, Swe, CH, Ukr.
Cost *1997* $190m *1998* $190m *1999* $178m. **Total cost to June 1999 $498m.**

United Nations Observer Mission in Georgia (UNOMIG)

Mission UNOMIG was originally established to verify compliance with the 27 July 1993 cease-fire agreement between the government of Georgia and the Abkhaz authorities with special attention to the situation in the city of Sukhumi; to investigate reports of cease-fire violations; and to attempt to resolve such incidents with the parties involved. Following the signing in May 1994 of the Agreement on a Cease-fire and Separation of Forces by the Georgian and Abkhaz parties, UNOMIG's tasks are to:

*   monitor and verify the implementation of the Agreement;
*   observe the operation of the peacekeeping force of the Commonwealth of Independent States (CIS);
*   verify that troops do not remain in or re-enter the security zone and that heavy military equipment does not remain and is not re-introduced into the security zone or the restricted weapons zone;
*   monitor the storage areas for heavy military equipment withdrawn from the security zone and restricted weapons zone;
*   monitor the withdrawal of Georgian troops from the Kodori valley to locations beyond the frontiers of Abkhazia;
*   patrol the Kodori valley regularly;
*   investigate reported or alleged violations of the Agreement and attempt to resolve such incidents.

Location Georgia **Headquarters** Sukhumi.
Strength 100 military observers, supported by locally recruited staff. **Contributors** Alb, A, Bng, CH, Cz, Da, Et, Fr, Ge, Gr, Hu, Indo, HKJ, ROK, Pak, Pl, RF, Swe, Tu, UK, Ury, US.
Cost *1997* $18m *1998* $19m *1999* $31m. **Total cost to June 1999 $84m.**

United Nations Mission of Observers in Tajikistan (UNMOT)

Mission UNMOT was established in December 1994 to assist a Joint Commission – composed of representatives of the Tajik government and the Tajik opposition – to monitor the implementation of the Agreement on a Temporary Cease-fire and the Cessation of Other Hostile Acts on the Tajik–Afghan Border and within Tajikistan. Since the June 1997 peace accord its tasks are to:

- monitor the implementation of the Agreement of National Reconciliation and Peace Establishment of 27 June 1997 and the cessation of other hostile acts on the Tajik–Afghan border and within the country;
- investigate alleged violations of the agreement and report them;
- provide liaison with the mission of the Organisation for Security and Cooperation in Europe (OSCE), with the collective peacekeeping forces of the CIS in Tajikistan and with the border forces;
- provide support for the UN Secretary-General's Special Envoy;
- provide political liaison and coordination services to facilitate expeditious humanitarian assistance by the international community.

Location Tajikistan **Headquarters** Dushanbe.
Strength 31 military observers, 2 civilian police officers, supported by locally recruited staff.
Contributors A, Bng, Bg, Cz, Da, Gha, Indo, HKJ, N, Nga, Pl, Ukr, Ury.
Cost *1997* $8m *1998* $8m *1999* $19m. **Total cost to June 1999** $35m.

United Nations Mission in the Central African Republic (MINURCA)

Mission MINURCA was established on 15 April 1998 to:

- maintain security and stability in the area surrounding Bangui;
- supervise the final disposition of weapons;
- assist in efforts to train a national police force;
- provide advice and technical assistance for national elections;
- ensure the safety and freedom of movement of United Nations personnel and property.

MINURCA replaced the *Mission Interafricaine de Surveillance des Accords de Bangui* (MISAB).
Location Central African Republic **Headquarters** Bangui.
Strength 1,228 troops, 24 civilian police. **Contributors** Bn, BF, Ca, Cha, CI, Et, Fr, Gbn, Por, RMM, Sen, Tg, Tn.
Cost *1998* $52m *1999* $34m. **Total cost to June 1999** $70m.

United Nations Observer Mission in Sierra Leone (UNOMSIL)

Mission UNOMSIL was established in July 1998 to observe the disarmament, demobilisation and reintegration of ex-combatants, and to monitor the military and security situation within Sierra Leone. UNOMSIL's original mandate expired on 13 June 1999. The Security Council is considering a new resolution in the light of the peace accord agreed between the government and the armed groups.
Location Sierra Leone **Headquarters** Freetown.
Authorised Strength 2 military personnel, 25 military observers, accompanied by a medical unit and assisted by international and locally recruited civilian staff (as of 1 August, 15 and 5 civilian police).
Contributors PRC, Et, Ind, Kya, Kgz, Mal, NZ, Pak, RF, UK, Z.
Cost *1998* $18m *1999* $20m. **Total cost to June 1999** $38m.

Analyses and Tables

United Nations Mission in Bosnia and Herzegovina (UNMIBH)

Mission On 21 December 1995, the Security Council established the UN International Police Task Force (IPTF) and a United Nations civilian office for one year in accordance with the General Framework Agreement for Peace in Bosnia and Herzegovina (the Dayton Agreement) signed by the leaders of Bosnia and Herzegovina, Croatia and the Federal Republic of Yugoslavia on 14 December 1995. The operation has come to be known as UNMIBH. IPTF tasks include:

- monitoring, observing and inspecting law-enforcement activities and facilities, including associated judicial organisations, structures and proceedings;
- advising law-enforcement personnel and forces;
- training law-enforcement personnel;
- facilitating, within the IPTF mission of assistance, the parties' law enforcement activities;
- assessing threats to public order and advising on the capability of law-enforcement agencies to deal with such threats;
- advising government authorities in Bosnia-Herzegovina on organising effective civilian law-enforcement agencies;
- assisting the parties or law-enforcement agencies in Bosnia-Herzegovina, giving priority to ensuring conditions for free-and-fair elections.

Location Bosnia-Herzegovina **Headquarters** Sarajevo.

Strength 1,798 police monitors and 4 military personnel. **Contributors** Arg, A, Bng, Bg, Ca, Chl, Da, Et, Ea, SF, Fji, Fr, Ge, Gha, Gr, Hu, Icl, Ind, Indo, Irl, It, HKJ, Kya, L, Mal, N, Nl, Nga, No, Pak, Pl, Por, R, RF, Sen, Sp, Swe, CH, Th, Tn, Tu, Ukr, UK, US.

Cost *1997* $170m *1998* $190m *1999* $178m. **Total cost to June 1999** $498m.

OTHER MISSIONS

A number of peacekeeping missions are currently under way which are not under UN control. The major operations are shown below. Not shown are those of very brief duration or those that are covered under the regional text and country section concerned (for example the Economic Community of West African States (ECOWAS) Military Observer Group (ECOMOG) in Sierra Leone). The OSCE conducts a number of observer missions in areas of conflict – for example, Chechnya and Nagorno-Karabakh – which fluctuate in size and contributors. The Organisation also undertakes a number of important security-related non-military missions, such as supervising elections and conflict mediation (as in Tajikistan). There are 11 long-term missions deployed in Bosnia-Herzegovina, Croatia, Estonia, Georgia, Latvia, FRY (Kosovo Verification Mission and Kosovo, Sanjak and Vojvodina Mission of Long Duration), Moldova, FYROM (Skopje), Tajikistan and Ukraine. A small number of military observers are participating in these missions, but no armed forces formations are involved. While the OSCE describes these missions as long term, their mandates vary from three to six months (renewable).

Multinational Force and Observers (MFO)

Mission The MFO was established in August 1981, under the peace treaty between Israel and Egypt (the Camp David accords), to verify the withdrawal of Israeli forces from the Sinai peninsula and to monitor the force levels permitted in the zone covered by the treaty. The force is also required to help ensure freedom of navigation through the Strait of Tiran.

Location Sinai peninsula **Headquarters** Main headquarters in Rome with a forward headquarters in Sinai.

Strength 1,872. **Contributors** Aus, Ca, Co, Fji, Fr, Hu, It, NZ, No, Ury, US. The force includes a number of civilians on private contracts to fly air observation missions and for logistic-support duties.

Cost *1997* $51m *1998* $51m *1999* $51m. **Total cost to June 1999** $1,334m.

NATO Stabilisation Force (SFOR) II for Bosnia and Herzegovina

Mission SFOR II was established on 20 June 1998 to follow on from SFOR I. Its mission is to continue to support implementation of the 1995 General Framework Agreement for Peace in Bosnia and Herzegovina and respond to the resolutions of the Security Council. No date has been set for the end of the mandate. SFOR's principal tasks remain:

* to maintain the Zone of Separation (ZOS) and keep it free from armed groups, ensuring heavy weapons remain in approved storage areas, and ensure freedom of movement throughout the country for SFOR and civilian agencies. SFOR is to promote freedom of movement across the Inter-Entity Boundary Line (IEBL) for all citizens of Bosnia and Herzegovina, but cannot be expected to guarantee freedom of movement of individuals throughout Bosnia and Herzegovina or forcibly return refugees. By successfully accomplishing these principal military tasks, SFOR will contribute to a secure environment within which civilian agencies can continue to undertake economic development and reconstruction, establish political institutions, and create an overall climate of reconciliation for the people of Bosnia and Herzegovina;
* to maintain control of the airspace over Bosnia and Herzegovina and of the movement of military traffic over key ground routes;
* to continue to use Joint Military Commissions;
* to give selective support to international organisations in their humanitarian missions;
* to assist in observing and preventing interference with the movement of civilian populations, refugees and displaced persons, and to respond appropriately to deliberate violence;
* to assist in monitoring the clearance of minefields and obstacles.

Location Bosnia-Herzegovina with supporting elements in Croatia and bases in Italy and Hungary. A maritime component is at sea in the Adriatic with a naval unit based ashore at Split.

Headquarters

* The Commander of SFOR (COMSFOR) has a headquarters in Sarajevo and commands three divisions with their headquarters based in Mostar, Tuzla and Banja Luka.
* The Commander of the SFOR Air Component is the NATO Commander Allied Air Forces Southern Europe who exercises his operational control through his Combined Air Operations Centre (CAOC) at Vicenza, Italy.
* The SFOR Naval Component is commanded by NATO's Commander Allied Naval Forces Southern Europe. This component comprises ships from several nations which are formed into task forces and are available or can be called upon for support.
* NATO's Commander Allied Striking Forces Southern Europe commands carrier-based aviation and amphibious forces in the region. They are not an integral part of SFOR but are earmarked to support it if needed.

Strength up to 33,200 (up to 27,055 NATO forces and 6,110 from non-NATO countries). Being reduced in late 1999 to about 20,000. **Contributors NATO** Be, Ca, Cz, Fr, Ge, Gr, Hu, It, Lu, Nl, Pl, Por, Sp, Tu, UK, US. (Iceland, which has no armed forces, is contributing civilian medical personnel). **Non-NATO** A, Alb, Bg, Et, Ea, HKJ, Lat, L, Mal, Mor, R, RF, Slvk (civilian personnel only), Ukr.

Cost *1997* ε$5bn *1998* ε$4bn *1999* ε$4bn. **Total cost to June 1999** ε$9bn.

NATO Albania Force (AFOR)

Mission AFOR was established on 16 April 1999 to provide humanitarian assistance in support of and in close coordination with the UN High Commissioner for Refugees (UNHCR) and Albanian civil and military authorities, and to assist the refugees from Kosovo in Albania. AFOR's tasks at present include;

- the construction of refugee camps;
- engineering support to repair selected roads, airfields, or other appropriate infrastructure;
- providing transportation for refugee movements by both ground vehicles and by air (including medical evacuation);
- assisting in the transportation and distribution of food, water and supplies;
- assisting with electronic communication support as required;

Location Albania **Headquarters** Plepa, near Durres (Albania).
Strength 5,500. **Contributors NATO** Be, Ca, Cz, Da, Fr, Ge, Gr, Hu, It, Lu, Nl, No, Pl, Por, Sp, Tu, UK, US. **Non-NATO** A, Alb, L, UAE.
Cost *1999* ε$650m.

NATO Kosovo Force (KFOR)

Mission KFOR was established on 10 June 1999 to establish a security presence in Kosovo ensuring compliance with UN Security Council Resolution (UNSCR) 1244 and monitoring, verification and compliance with the terms of the 9 June 1999 Military Technical Agreement (MTA) signed by military authorities from the FRY and NATO. KFOR's principal tasks are:

- to verify the withdrawal of all FRY forces from Kosovo and beyond the Air Safety Zone/ Ground Safety Zone;
- to provide appropriate control of the borders of FRY in Kosovo with Albania and FYROM until the arrival of the UN's civilian mission;
- to maintain control of airspace;
- to assist the UNHCR with the safe return of refugees and displaced persons, as well as all other international entities involved in the implementation of the MTA or otherwise authorised by the UNSC;
- to establish liaison arrangements with local Kosovo authorities, and with FRY/Serbian civil and military authorities;

Location Kosovo with a small number of troops based in Greece to assist in the movement of goods and troops from Thessaloniki.
Headquarters Kosovo has been divided into five sectors with responsibilities allocated as follows:

- **North Sector** France with headquarters at Mitrovica
- **East Sector** UK with headquarters at Pristina
- **South East Sector** US with headquarters at Urosevac
- **South Sector** Germany with headquarters at Prizren
- **West Sector** Italy with headquarters at Pec
- ARRC headquarters at Pristina.

Strength up to 55,000 (up to 52,000 NATO forces and 3,000 from Non-NATO countries).
Contributors NATO Be, Ca, Da, Fr, Ge, Gr, Hu, It, Nl, No, Pl, Por, Sp, UK, US (small units from Cz, Icl, Lu, Tu). **Non-NATO** A, SF, R, RF, Ukr (smaller contingents provided by Bg, Ea, Lat, L, Slvk, Slvn, Swe).
Cost *1999* ε$10bn.

While the UN has no military force in Kosovo, it has deployed a police monitoring force and civil administration to the province, known as the United Nations Mission in Kososvo (UNMIK). UNMIK is projected to have a strength of 3,110 and a budget of $200m.

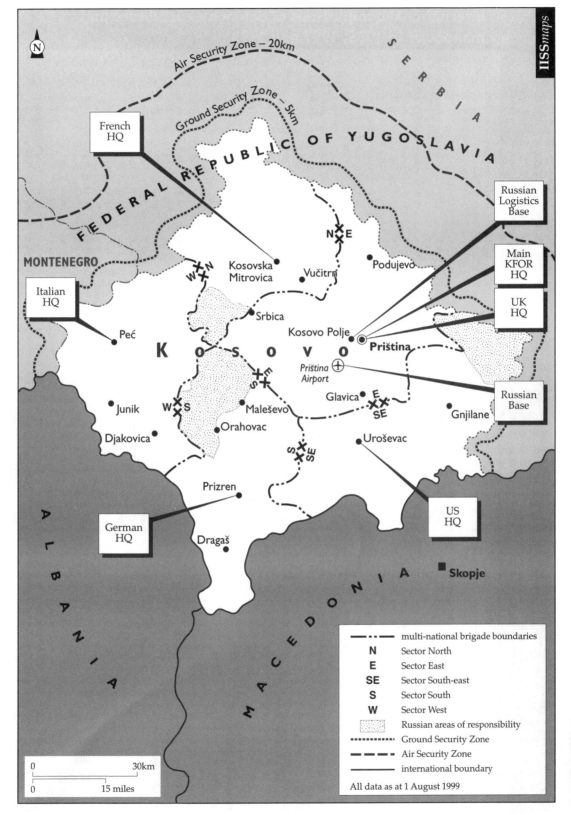

Air Security Zone – 20km

Ground Security Zone – 5km

S E R B I A

French HQ

Russian Logistics Base

Main KFOR HQ

UK HQ

FEDERAL REPUBLIC OF YUGOSLAVIA

MONTENEGRO

Italian HQ

N E

Kosovska Mitrovica

Vučitrn

Podujevo

W N

Peć

Srbica

K O S O V O

Kosovo Polje

Priština

Priština Airport

Russian Base

Junik

E S

W S

Maleševo

Glavica

E SE

Gnjilane

Djakovica

Orahovac

S SE

Uroševac

ALBANIA

Prizren

German HQ

Dragaš

US HQ

MACEDONIA

Skopje

multi-national brigade boundaries
N Sector North
E Sector East
SE Sector South-east
S Sector South
W Sector West
Russian areas of responsibility
Ground Security Zone
Air Security Zone
international boundary

All data as at 1 August 1999

0 — 30km

0 — 15 miles

Table 50 International comparisons of defence expenditure and military manpower in 1985, 1997 and 1998

(1997 constant prices)	Defence Expenditure US$m			US$ per capita			% of GDP			Numbers in Armed Forces (000)		Estimated Reservists (000)	Para-military (000)
	1985	1997	1998	1985	1997	1998	1985	1997	1998	1985	1998	1998	1998
Canada	11,147	7,801	6,637	439	272	229	2.2	1.2	1.1	83.0	60.6	28.6	9.4
US	367,711	276,324	265,890	1,537	1,031	982	6.5	3.4	3.2	2,151.6	1,401.6	1,796.7	89.0
NATO Europe													
Belgium	5,863	3,769	3,698	595	373	366	3.0	1.5	1.5	91.6	43.7	152.1	n.a.
Denmark	2,978	2,805	2,799	582	536	534	2.2	1.7	1.6	29.6	32.1	100.0	n.a.
France	46,522	41,523	39,807	843	708	676	4.0	3.0	2.8	464.3	358.8	292.5	93.4
Germany	50,220	33,217	32,387	662	405	395	3.2	1.6	1.5	478.0	333.5	315.0	n.a.
Greece	3,317	5,552	5,720	334	524	540	7.0	4.6	4.8	201.5	168.5	291.0	4.0
Iceland	n.a.	n.a.	n.a.	n.a.	n.a.	n.a.	n.a.	n.a.	n.a.	n.a.	n.a.	n.a.	0.1
Italy	24,471	22,724	22,633	428	393	391	2.3	2.0	2.0	385.1	298.4	304.0	255.7
Luxembourg	91	134	139	248	326	336	0.9	0.9	0.9	0.7	0.8	n.a	0.6
Netherlands	8,470	6,839	6,634	585	439	424	3.1	1.9	1.8	105.5	57.2	75.0	3.6
Norway	2,948	3,253	3,133	710	741	711	3.1	2.1	2.2	37.0	28.9	234.0	0.3
Portugal	1,746	2,388	2,334	171	242	236	3.1	2.3	2.3	73.0	53.6	210.9	40.9
Spain	10,731	7,671	7,272	278	196	186	2.4	1.4	1.3	320.0	194.0	447.9	75.8
Turkey	3,269	7,792	8,191	65	125	131	4.5	4.4	4.4	630.0	639.0	378.7	182.2
United Kingdom	45,408	35,736	36,613	803	611	624	5.2	2.8	2.8	327.1	210.9	319.6	n.a.
Subtotal NATO Europe	206,033	173,383	171,359	450	401	396	3.1	2.2	2.1	3,143.4	2,419.3	3,120.7	656.5
Total NATO	584,891	457,508	443,885	517	433	422	3.3	2.2	2.1	5,378.0	3,881.5	4,946.0	754.9
Non-NATO Europe													
Albania	269	94	98	91	26	26	5.3	6.7	6.6	40.4	54.0	155.0	13.5
Armenia	n.a.	138	146	n.a.	37	37	n.a.	9.2	8.4	n.a.	53.4	300.0	1.0
Austria	1,839	1,786	1,764	243	222	218	1.2	0.8	0.8	54.7	45.5	100.7	n.a.
Azerbaijan	n.a.	146	189	n.a.	20	26	n.a.	3.8	4.6	n.a.	72.2	575.7	15.0
Belarus	n.a.	451	452	n.a.	44	44	n.a.	3.4	3.2	n.a.	83.0	289.5	8.0
Bosnia-Herzegovina	n.a.	327	389	n.a.	74	87	n.a.	8.0	8.1	n.a.	40.0	100.0	46.0
Bulgaria	2,331	339	390	276	41	47	14.0	3.3	3.7	148.5	101.5	303.0	34.0
Croatia	n.a.	1,241	1,371	n.a.	264	286	n.a.	6.2	8.3	n.a.	56.2	220.0	40.0
Cyprus	124	505	489	186	594	569	3.6	6.0	5.5	10.0	10.0	88.0	0.6
Czech Republic	n.a.	987	1,132	n.a.	96	110	n.a.	1.9	2.1	n.a.	59.1	240.0	5.6
Czechoslovakia	3,338	n.a.	n.a.	214	n.a.	n.a.	8.2	n.a.	n.a.	203.3	n.a.	n.a.	n.a.
Estonia	n.a.	65	68	n.a.	44	47	n.a.	1.4	1.3	n.a.	4.3	14.0	2.8
Finland	2,139	1,956	1,855	436	381	360	2.8	1.6	1.5	36.5	31.7	500.0	3.4
FYROM	n.a.	132	136	n.a.	58	59	n.a.	10.2	9.9	n.a.	20.0	102.0	7.5
Georgia	n.a.	109	108	n.a.	20	20	n.a.	2.5	2.5	n.a.	33.2	250.0	n.k.
Hungary	3,380	666	647	317	66	64	7.2	1.4	1.4	106.0	43.3	90.3	14.1
Ireland	456	767	780	128	210	212	1.8	1.0	1.0	13.7	11.5	14.8	n.a.
Latvia	n.a.	156	157	n.a.	63	64	n.a.	2.8	2.5	n.a.	5.0	14.6	3.7
Lithuania	n.a.	135	134	n.a.	36	36	n.a.	1.4	1.3	n.a.	11.1	27.7	3.9

(1997 constant prices)	Defence Expenditure US$m			US$ per capita			% of GDP			Numbers in Armed Forces (000)		Estimated Reservists (000)	Para-military (000)
	1985	1997	1998	1985	1997	1998	1985	1997	1998	1985	1998	1998	1998
Malta	23	31	29	64	82	77	1.4	0.9	0.9	0.8	1.9	n.a.	n.a.
Moldova	n.a.	53	51	n.a.	12	12	n.a.	4.4	4.3	n.a.	11.1	66.0	3.4
Poland	8,202	3,073	3,356	220	79	87	8.1	2.3	2.2	319.0	240.7	406.0	23.4
Romania	1,987	793	870	87	35	39	4.5	2.3	2.3	189.5	219.7	470.0	75.9
Slovakia	n.a.	414	407	n.a.	77	75	n.a.	2.1	2.0	n.a.	45.5	20.0	2.6
Slovenia	n.a.	329	360	n.a.	163	179	n.a.	1.8	1.7	n.a.	9.6	53.0	4.5
Sweden	4,546	5,481	5,536	544	619	623	3.3	2.5	2.5	65.7	53.1	570.0	35.6
Switzerland	2,749	3,837	3,556	426	544	503	2.1	1.5	1.4	20.0	26.3	390.0	n.a.
Ukraine	n.a.	1,324	1,361	n.a.	26	27	n.a.	2.7	2.9	n.a.	346.4	1,000.0	71.0
FRY (Serbia-Montenegro)	4,759	1,489	1,523	204	140	144	3.8	9.2	9.1	241.0	114.2	400.0	38.0
Total	**36,142**	**26,821**	**27,353**	**246**	**146**	**146**	**4.8**	**3.6**	**3.6**	**1,449.1**	**1,803.2**	**6,760.3**	**453.5**
Russia	n.a.	64,000	53,912	n.a.	435	368	n.a.	5.8	5.2	n.a.	1,159.0	2,400.0	543.0
Soviet Union	343,616	n.a.	n.a.	1,232	n.a.	n.a.	16.1	n.a.	n.a.	5,300.0	n.a.	n.a.	n.a.
Middle East and North Africa													
Algeria	1,357	2,114	2,336	62	73	80	1.7	4.6	4.8	170.0	122.0	150.0	146.2
Bahrain	215	364	394	516	608	643	3.5	6.0	6.7	2.8	11.0	n.a.	9.9
Egypt	3,679	2,743	2,776	76	45	45	7.2	4.3	4.1	445.0	450.0	254.0	230.0
Gaza and Jericho	n.a.	n.a.	n.a.	n.a.	n.a.	n.a.	n.a.	n.a.	n.a.	n.a.	n.a.	n.a.	35.0
Iran	20,258	4,695	5,651	454	68	80	36.0	5.5	6.5	305.0	540.0	350.0	280.0
Iraq	18,328	1,250	1,372	1,153	56	59	25.9	7.4	7.3	520.0	429.0	650.0	50.0
Israel	7,196	11,321	11,040	1,700	1,947	1,844	21.2	11.9	11.6	142.0	175.0	430.0	6.1
Jordan	857	496	537	245	105	110	15.9	7.0	7.7	70.3	104.1	35.0	30.0
Kuwait	2,558	3,618	3,371	1,496	1,681	1,532	9.1	11.9	12.9	12.0	15.3	23.7	5.0
Lebanon	285	676	563	107	163	134	9.0	4.5	3.6	17.4	55.1	n.a.	13.0
Libya	1,923	1,250	1,431	511	215	238	6.2	4.7	5.3	73.0	65.0	40.0	0.5
Mauritania	74	24	25	44	10	10	6.5	2.2	2.2	8.5	15.7	n.a.	5.0
Morocco	913	1,386	1,630	42	48	56	5.4	4.1	4.6	149.0	196.3	150.0	42.0
Oman	3,072	1,976	1,887	1,920	965	886	20.8	12.2	13.6	29.2	43.5	n.a.	4.4
Qatar	427	1,346	1,320	1,357	2,037	1,967	6.0	13.7	12.0	6.0	11.8	n.a.	n.a.
Saudi Arabia	25,585	18,151	20,476	2,217	1,071	1,173	19.6	12.4	15.7	62.5	162.5	20.0	15.5
Syria	4,961	2,217	2,664	472	145	168	16.4	6.3	7.3	402.5	320.0	500.0	8.0
Tunisia	594	334	348	83	36	37	5.0	1.8	1.8	35.1	35.0	n.a.	12.0
UAE	2,910	2,424	2,937	2,078	978	1,138	7.6	5.1	6.5	43.0	64.5	n.a.	1.0
Yemen	696	411	388	69	25	22	9.9	7.2	6.6	64.1	66.3	40.0	80.0
Total	**95,890**	**56,798**	**61,147**	**768**	**541**	**538**	**12.3**	**7.0**	**7.4**	**2,557.4**	**2,882.0**	**2,642.7**	**963.5**
Central and Southern Asia													
Afghanistan	409	209	245	23	9	10	8.7	12.5	14.5	47.0	400.0	n.a.	n.a.
Bangladesh	356	593	607	4	5	5	1.4	1.9	1.9	91.3	121.0	n.a.	49.7
Bhutan	7	19	18	17	31	28	4.9	5.0	4.5	3.0	6.0	n.k.	1.0

Analyses and Tables

(1997 constant prices)

	Defence Expenditure US$m			US$ per capita			% of GDP			Numbers in Armed Forces (000)		Estimated Reservists (000)	Para-military (000)
	1985	1997	1998	1985	1997	1998	1985	1997	1998	1985	1998	1998	1998
India	8,921	12,805	13,780	12	13	14	3.0	3.0	3.0	1,260.0	1,175.0	528.4	1,090.0
Kazakhstan	n.a.	503	488	n.a.	31	31	n.a.	2.3	2.2	n.a.	55.1	n.a.	34.5
Kyrgyzstan	n.a.	68	64	n.a.	15	14	n.a.	3.9	3.6	n.a.	12.2	57.0	5.0
Maldives	5	34	37	26	128	138	3.9	10.6	11.1	n.k.	n.k.	n.k.	5.0
Nepal	51	42	37	3	2	2	1.5	0.9	0.7	25.0	50.0	n.a.	40.0
Pakistan	2,957	3,916	3,920	31	29	28	6.9	6.7	6.5	482.8	587.0	513.0	247.0
Sri Lanka	325	949	956	21	51	51	3.8	6.4	6.1	21.6	115.0	4.2	110.2
Tajikistan	n.a.	132	98	n.a.	22	16	n.a.	12.1	8.3	n.a.	9.0	n.a.	1.2
Turkmenistan	n.a.	138	114	n.a.	30	25	n.a.	3.6	2.8	n.a.	19.0	n.a.	n.k.
Uzbekistan	n.a.	610	644	n.a.	26	28	n.a.	5.3	5.4	n.a.	80.0	n.a.	20.0
Total	13,031	20,018	21,007	17	30	30	4.3	5.7	5.4	1,930.7	2,629.3	1,102.6	1,603.6
East Asia and Australasia													
Australia	7,755	8,625	7,384	492	462	391	3.4	2.3	1.9	70.4	57.4	33.7	1.0
Brunei	292	378	371	1,304	1,222	1,169	6.0	7.0	6.9	4.1	5.0	0.7	4.1
Cambodia	n.a.	144	149	n.a.	14	14	n.a.	4.2	4.2	35.0	139.0	n.a.	220.0
China	28,273	36,551	36,709	27	30	30	7.9	5.7	5.3	3,900.0	2,820.0	1,200.0	1,000.0
Fiji	20	48	32	29	61	40	1.2	2.6	1.6	2.7	3.5	6.0	n.a.
Indonesia	3,334	4,812	4,894	21	24	24	2.8	2.2	2.6	278.1	299.0	400.0	200.0
Japan	30,612	40,891	36,990	254	325	293	1.0	1.0	1.0	243.0	242.6	48.6	12.0
Korea, North	5,919	2,273	2,005	290	106	93	23.0	16.8	14.3	838.0	1,055.0	4,700.0	189.0
Korea, South	8,962	15,334	12,940	218	333	278	5.1	3.5	3.1	598.0	672.0	4,500.0	4.5
Laos	78	72	68	22	14	13	7.8	4.1	3.7	53.7	29.1	n.a.	100.0
Malaysia	2,513	3,377	3,222	161	157	146	5.6	3.6	3.7	110.0	110.0	40.6	20.1
Mongolia	49	23	20	26	10	8	9.0	2.5	2.1	33.0	9.8	137.0	7.2
Myanmar	1,252	2,167	2,058	34	45	42	5.1	7.7	6.8	186.0	349.6	n.a.	85.3
New Zealand	920	904	863	283	252	239	2.9	1.6	1.5	12.4	9.6	7.0	n.a.
Papua New Guinea	51	65	55	15	14	12	1.5	1.2	1.0	3.2	4.3	n.a.	n.a.
Philippines	675	1,422	1,462	12	20	20	1.4	1.9	2.3	114.8	117.8	131.0	42.5
Singapore	1,692	4,624	4,744	661	1,525	1,543	6.7	4.8	5.0	55.0	72.5	250.0	108.0
Taiwan	9,171	13,657	13,887	473	634	642	7.0	4.6	4.6	444.0	376.0	1,657.5	26.7
Thailand	2,669	3,326	2,041	52	54	32	5.0	2.2	1.5	235.3	306.0	200.0	71.0
Vietnam	3,418	1,004	907	55	13	11	19.4	4.0	3.4	1,027.0	484.0	3,000.0	40.0
Total	107,656	139,696	130,802	233	266	252	6.4	4.2	3.8	8,243.7	7,162.2	16,312.0	2,131.3

Caribbean, Central and Latin America

Caribbean

	Defence Expenditure US$m			US$ per capita			% of GDP			Numbers in Armed Forces (000)		Estimated Reservists (000)	Para-military (000)
	1985	1997	1998	1985	1997	1998	1985	1997	1998	1985	1998	1998	1998
Antigua and Barbuda	3	3	4	41	39	54	0.5	0.5	0.6	0.1	0.2	0.1	n.a.
Bahamas	14	22	22	59	82	75	0.5	0.6	0.6	0.5	0.9	n.a.	2.3
Barbados	16	12	11	74	41	43	0.9	0.5	0.5	1.0	0.6	0.4	n.a.
Cuba	2,275	720	735	225	65	66	9.6	5.2	5.3	161.5	60.0	39.0	19.0

(1997 constant prices)

	Defence Expenditure US$m			US$ per capita			% of GDP			Numbers in Armed Forces (000)		Estimated Reservists (000)	Para-military (000)
	1985	1997	1998	1985	1997	1998	1985	1997	1998	1985	1998	1998	1998
Dominican Republic	73	119	118	11	15	15	1.1	1.2	1.1	22.2	24.5	n.a.	15.0
Haiti	44	46	47	7	6	6	1.5	2.4	2.4	6.9	n.a.	n.a.	5.3
Jamaica	28	42	43	13	17	17	0.9	0.9	0.9	2.1	3.3	1.0	0.2
Trinidad and Tobago	104	40	42	88	30	31	1.4	0.7	0.7	2.1	2.6	n.a.	4.8
Central America													
Belize	6	16	16	34	69	70	1.4	2.6	2.6	0.6	1.1	0.7	n.a.
Costa Rica	41	59	69	16	17	19	0.7	0.7	0.7	n.a.	n.a.	n.a.	8.4
El Salvador	359	176	157	75	30	26	4.4	1.9	1.7	41.7	24.6	15.0	12.0
Guatemala	167	182	153	21	16	13	1.8	1.5	1.2	31.7	31.4	35.0	9.8
Honduras	103	101	95	23	16	15	2.1	2.1	2.0	16.6	8.3	60.0	6.0
Mexico	1,768	3,664	3,755	22	39	39	0.7	1.0	1.0	129.1	175.0	300.0	15.0
Nicaragua	314	36	29	96	8	6	17.4	1.4	1.1	62.9	17.0	n.a.	n.a.
Panama	128	114	118	59	41	42	2.0	1.3	1.3	12.0	n.a.	n.a.	11.8
South America													
Argentina	5,157	4,972	5,157	169	143	147	3.8	1.8	1.8	108.0	73.0	375.0	31.2
Bolivia	181	155	147	28	18	17	2.0	2.0	1.8	27.6	33.5	n.a.	37.1
Brazil	5,515	18,546	18,053	41	112	108	1.8	3.3	3.2	276.0	313.3	1,115.0	385.6
Chile	2,287	2,922	2,952	189	200	200	10.6	3.8	3.7	101.0	94.5	50.0	29.5
Colombia	604	2,542	2,474	21	71	68	1.6	3.3	3.2	66.2	146.3	60.7	87.0
Ecuador	405	692	522	43	57	42	1.8	3.5	2.6	42.5	57.1	100.0	0.3
Guyana	45	7	7	57	8	9	6.8	0.9	1.0	6.6	1.6	1.5	1.5
Paraguay	85	134	128	23	26	24	1.3	1.5	1.4	14.4	20.2	164.5	14.8
Peru	913	1,276	970	49	52	39	4.5	2.2	1.6	128.0	125.0	188.0	78.0
Suriname	12	15	15	30	36	35	2.4	4.4	4.2	2.0	1.8	n.a.	n.a.
Uruguay	340	307	309	113	96	96	3.5	2.3	2.3	31.9	25.6	n.a.	0.9
Venezuela	1,174	1,540	1,281	68	67	55	2.1	1.8	1.5	49.0	56.0	8.0	23.0
Total	22,160	38,458	37,429	61	51	49	3.2	2.0	1.9	1,344.2	1,297.2	2,513.9	798.5
Sub-Saharan Africa													
Horn Of Africa													
Djibouti	46	20	21	106	30	30	7.9	5.0	5.1	3.0	9.6	n.a.	3.0
Eritrea	n.a.	196	286	n.a.	52	74	n.a.	25.2	35.8	n.a.	47.1	120.0	n.a.
Ethiopia	636	134	372	15	3	7	17.9	2.1	6.0	217.0	120.0	n.a.	n.a.
Somali Republic	66	40	39	12	7	7	6.2	4.8	4.7	62.7	225.0	n.a.	n.a.
Sudan	152	413	377	7	14	12	3.2	5.5	4.8	56.6	94.7	n.a.	15.0
Central Africa													
Burundi	50	85	79	11	13	11	3.0	8.1	7.2	5.2	40.0	n.a.	3.5
Cameroon	226	240	249	22	17	17	1.4	2.8	2.9	7.3	13.1	n.a.	9.0
Cape Verde	5	4	4	16	9	8	0.9	1.7	1.6	7.7	1.1	n.a.	0.1

| (1997 constant prices) | Defence Expenditure | | | | | | | | | Numbers in Armed Forces (000) | | Estimated Reservists (000) | Para-military (000) |
| | US$m | | | US$ per capita | | | % of GDP | | | | | | |
	1985	1997	1998	1985	1997	1998	1985	1997	1998	1985	1998	1998	1998
Central African Republic	25	39	48	10	11	13	1.4	4.0	4.7	2.3	2.7	n.a.	2.3
Chad	53	43	61	11	6	9	2.9	4.1	5.6	12.2	25.4	n.a.	9.5
Congo	80	74	80	43	26	27	1.9	2.5	3.9	8.7	10.0	n.a.	5.0
DROC	115	308	356	4	7	8	1.5	5.3	6.6	48.0	50.0	n.a.	37.0
Equatorial Guinea	4	5	7	11	10	13	2.0	1.3	1.5	2.2	1.3	n.a.	0.3
Gabon	113	115	130	113	83	91	1.8	1.9	2.2	2.4	4.7	n.a.	4.8
Rwanda	47	103	138	8	13	17	1.9	5.5	6.9	5.2	47.0	n.a.	7.0
East Africa													
Kenya	365	269	309	18	9	10	3.1	2.7	3.1	13.7	24.2	n.a.	5.0
Madagascar	77	37	43	8	3	3	2.0	0.8	0.9	21.1	21.0	n.a.	7.5
Mauritius	3	87	90	4	75	77	0.3	2.1	2.1	1.0	n.a.	n.a.	1.8
Seychelles	11	10	10	175	141	142	2.1	2.9	2.9	1.2	0.2	n.a.	0.3
Tanzania	199	123	140	9	4	5	4.4	3.4	3.7	40.4	34.0	80.0	1.4
Uganda	75	166	221	5	8	11	1.8	2.4	3.1	20.0	40.0	n.a.	1.5
West Africa													
Benin	30	27	32	7	5	5	1.1	1.3	1.4	4.5	4.8	n.a.	2.5
Burkina Faso	48	67	78	6	6	7	1.1	2.2	2.5	4.0	5.8	n.a.	4.5
Côte d'Ivoire	108	101	116	11	7	7	0.8	0.9	0.9	13.2	8.4	12.0	7.0
Gambia, The	3	15	15	4	13	13	1.5	3.7	3.6	0.5	0.8	n.a.	n.a.
Ghana	90	134	132	7	7	7	1.0	1.5	1.4	15.1	7.0	n.a.	1.0
Guinea	74	51	60	12	7	8	1.8	1.6	1.8	9.9	9.7	n.a.	9.6
Guinea Bissau	16	8	15	18	7	13	5.7	3.1	5.5	8.6	7.3	n.a.	2.0
Liberia	40	45	44	18	14	13	2.4	3.9	3.9	6.8	14.0	n.a.	n.a.
Mali	43	43	52	6	4	5	1.4	1.7	2.0	4.9	7.4	n.a.	7.8
Niger	17	22	25	3	2	2	0.5	1.4	1.5	2.2	5.3	n.a.	5.4
Nigeria	1,069	1,965	2,060	11	18	19	3.4	4.1	4.3	94.0	77.0	n.a.	30.0
Senegal	90	71	80	14	8	9	1.1	1.6	1.7	10.1	11.0	n.k.	6.0
Sierra Leone	7	51	25	2	10	5	1.0	6.8	3.3	3.1	5.0	n.a.	0.8
Togo	27	29	33	9	6	7	1.3	2.1	2.4	3.6	7.0	n.a.	0.8
Southern Africa													
Angola	921	764	936	105	67	80	15.1	9.3	11.7	49.5	114.0	n.a.	15.0
Botswana	53	241	251	49	153	155	1.1	6.5	6.5	4.0	8.5	n.a.	1.0
Lesotho	66	32	41	42	15	19	4.6	2.8	3.5	2.0	2.0	n.a.	n.a.
Malawi	30	23	25	4	2	2	1.0	1.1	1.2	5.3	5.0	n.a.	1.0
Mozambique	340	72	78	25	5	5	8.5	3.9	3.9	15.8	6.1	n.a.	n.a.
Namibia	n.a.	89	90	n.a.	51	51	n.a.	3.6	3.6	n.a.	9.0	n.a.	0.1
South Africa	4,091	2,517	2,100	122	65	54	2.7	1.9	1.6	106.4	82.4	61.0	129.3
Zambia	57	59	63	8	6	6	1.1	1.7	1.9	16.2	21.6	n.a.	1.4
Zimbabwe	242	304	321	29	26	27	5.6	4.7	5.0	41.0	39.0	n.a.	21.8
Total	9,810	9,241	9,732	27	24	25	3.1	3.8	4.3	958.5	1,269.0	273.0	360.9

(1997 constant prices)

Global Totals

	Defence Expenditure						% of GDP			Numbers in Armed Forces (000)		Estimated Reservists (000)	Para-military (000)
	US$m			US$ per capita									
	1985	1997	1998	1985	1997	1998	1985	1997	1998	1985	1998	1998	1998
NATO	584,891	457,508	443,885	517 / 946	433 / 643	422 / 620	3.3 / 4.7	2.2 / 2.8	2.1 / 2.6	5,378.0	3,881.5	4,946.0	754.9
Non-NATO Europe	36,142	26,821	27,353	246 / n.a.	146 / 109	146 / 111	4.8 / n.a.	3.6 / 2.0	3.6 / 2.0	1,449.1	1,803.2	6,760.3	453.5
Russia	n.a.	64,000	53,912	n.a.	435	368	n.a.	5.8	5.2	n.a.	1,159.0	2,400.0	543.0
Soviet Union	343,616	n.a.	n.a.	1,232	n.a.	n.a.	16.1	n.a.	n.a.	5,300.0	n.a.	n.a.	n.a.
Middle East and North Africa	95,890	56,798	61,147	768 / 449	541 / 189	538 / 198	12.3 / 15.1	7.0 / 8.0	7.4 / 8.7	2,557.4	2,882.0	2,642.7	963.5
Central and South Asia	13,031	20,018	21,007	17 / 11	30 / 15	30 / 15	4.3 / n.a.	5.7 / 3.4	5.4 / 3.4	1,930.7	2,629.3	1,102.6	1,603.6
East Asia and Australasia	107,656	139,696	130,802	233 / 65	266 / 71	252 / 66	6.4 / 2.3	4.2 / 2.1	3.8 / 2.1	8,243.7	7,162.2	16,312.0	2,131.3
Caribbean, Central and Latin America	22,160	38,458	37,429	61 / 56	51 / 79	49 / 76	3.2 / 1.9	2.0 / 2.3	1.9 / 2.2	1,344.2	1,297.2	2,513.9	798.5
Sub-Saharan Africa	9,810	9,241	9,732	27 / 22	24 / 16	25 / 16	3.1 / 3.3	3.8 / 2.9	4.3 / 3.0	958.5	1,269.0	273.0	360.9
Global totals	1,213,197	812,539	785,269	388 / 287	240 / 140	229 / 134	6.7 / 5.2	4.3 / 2.7	4.2 / 2.6	27,161.6	22,083.4	36,950.5	7,609.1

Note

Under *Defence Expenditure per capita* and *Defence Expenditure as a proportion of GDP*, the top figure is the arithmetic mean of individual country values, and the bottom number is the arithmetic mean of the sum of regional and global totals.

Table 51 Conventional Armed Forces in Europe (CFE) Treaty

Manpower and Treaty Limited Equipment: current holdings and CFE limits on the forces of the Treaty members

Current holdings are derived from data declared as of 1 January 1999 and so may differ from *The Military Balance* listings

	Manpower		Tanks[1]		ACV[1]		Artillery[1]		Attack Helicopters		Combat Aircraft[2]	
	Holding	Limit	Holding	Limit	Holding	Limit	Holding	Limit	Holding	Limit	Holding	Limit
Budapest/Tashkent Group												
Armenia	60,000	60,000	102	220	204	220	225	285	7	50	6	100
Azerbaijan	69,920	70,000	262	220	331	220	303	285	15	50	48	100
Belarus	83,020	100,000	1,778	1,800	2,513	2,600	1,515	1,615	62	80	252	294
Bulgaria	80,779	104,000	1,475	1,475	1,986	2,000	1,744	1,750	43	67	233	235
Czech Republic[a]	58,193	93,333	938	957	1,219	1,367	754	767	34	50	114	230
Georgia	29,191	40,000	79	220	113	220	106	285	3	50	7	100
Hungary[a]	43,743	100,000	807	835	1,332	1,700	839	840	59	108	136	180
Moldova	10,677	20,000	0	210	209	210	153	250	0	50	0	50
Poland[a]	210,555	234,000	1,675	1,730	1,437	2,150	1,580	1,610	104	130	298	460
Romania	185,092	230,000	1,373	1,375	2,100	2,100	1,411	1,475	16	120	360	430
Russia[b]	605,171	1,450,000	5,510	6,400	10,064	11,480	6,299	6,415	761	875	2,870	3,431
Slovakia	44,880	46,667	478	478	683	683	383	383	19	40	94	100
Ukraine	320,000	450,000	4,014	4,080	4,902	5,050	3,739	4,040	265	330	964	1,090
North Atlantic Treaty Group												
Belgium	39,756	70,000	155	334	526	1,005	243	320	46	46	137	232
Canada[c]	0	10,660	0	77	0	263	0	32	0	13	0	90
Denmark	30,426	39,000	337	353	286	336	503	503	12	18	76	106
France	242,169	325,000	1,207	1,306	3,653	3,820	1,050	1,292	314	390	596	800
Germany	273,535	345,000	3,096	4,069	2,480	3,281	2,056	2,445	204	293	534	900
Greece	158,621	158,621	1,735	1,735	2,364	2,498	1,886	1,920	20	30	522	650
Italy	229,535	315,000	1,256	1,348	2,917	3,339	1,595	1,955	134	142	535	650
Netherlands	37,054	80,000	359	743	640	1,080	398	607	10	50	164	230
Norway	20,581	32,000	170	170	180	275	192	491	0	24	73	100
Portugal	35,178	75,000	187	300	355	430	359	450	0	26	101	160
Spain	160,372	300,000	676	891	1,181	2,047	1,150	1,370	28	90	201	310
Turkey[b]	512,922	530,000	2,554	2,795	2,515	3,120	2,811	3,523	26	103	346	750
UK[b]	217,525	260,000	542	1,015	2,396	3,176	429	636	249	371	533	900
US	101,724	250,000	846	4,006	1,704	5,152	558	2,742	136	404	223	784

Notes

[1] Includes TLE with land-based maritime forces (Marines, Naval Infantry etc.)

[2] Does not include land-based maritime aircraft for which a separate limit has been set.

[a] Czech Republic, Hungary and Poland became NATO members on 12 March 1999.

[b] Manpower and TLE is for that in the Atlantic to the Urals (ATTU) zone only

[c] Canada has now withdrawn all its TLE from the ATTU

Table 52 **Armoured Reconnaissance Vehicles** *key characteristics*

Definition An armoured combat vehicle fitted with an integral gun and fire control system, specifically designed and equipped for reconnaissance purposes. Reconnaissance vehicles which fall within the definition of a Heavy Armoured Combat Vehicle (HACV) are not shown in this table. Details of these vehicles were given in *The Military Balance 1996/97* p. 314. The entries are listed by country of origin (far-left column).

Original Producer[1]	Designation	In-service date[2]	Crew	W/T[3]	Max. road speed[4] (km/h)	Max. range[4,5] (km)	Armament (mm)	Ammo[6]	In service with[7]
Bg	EE-3 *Jararaca*	1990?–	5	T	61	500	23	600	Bg
Br	BRM-23	1980–?	3	W	100	700	12.7	n.k.	Cy, Ec, Gbn, Ury
Ca	LAV-25 *Coyote*	1996–98	4	W	100	660	25	420	Ca
CH	SPY	1980–	3	W	110	700	12.7	3,000	n.k.
	Eagle	1995–	4	W	125	450	7.62	400	Da, CH
Cz	*Snezka*	1998–	4	T	65	600	12.7	n.k.	Cz
Fr	VBL	1990–	2 or 3	W	95	600	7.62	3,000	Bn, Crm, Dj, Fr, Gbn, Gr, Indo, Kwt, Mex, Ngr, Nga, O, Por, Q, Rwa, Tg
Ge	SPz *Luchs* A2	1975–78	4	W	90	730	20	375	Ge
	Wiesel 1	1989–92	2	T	75	300	20	400	Ge
Hu	FUG D-944	1970–?	9	W	80	500	14.5	500	Hu
	OT-65	1965–66?	6	W	87	600	7.62	1,250	Cz, Hu, Slvk
It	Type-6616	1972–?	3	W	100	700	20	400	It, Pe, SR
J	Type-87	1988–	5	W	100	500	25	n.k.	J
R	ABI	n.k.	2 + 4	W	90	600	12.7	n.k.	Ag, R
RF	BMP-3K	1993–	6	T	70	600	30	600	RF
	BRM-1K	1976–?	3 + 8	T	65	600	73	40	RF, others n.k.
	BRDM-2	1966–?	4	W	100	750	14.5	500	Afg, Ag, Ang, Bn, Bg, Bu, CV, RC, Cr, C, Cz, Et, EG, Ea, Eth, Gui, GuB, Hu, Ind, Indo, Ir, Il, Kaz, Kgz, Lat, LAR, L, FYROM, Mdg, RMM, RIM, Mgl, Moz, Nba, Nic, Pe, Pl, R, RF, Sey, Slvk, Slvn, SR, Sdn, Syr, Tz, Tkm, Ukr, Uz, Vn, Ye, FRY, Z
	BRDM-1	1957–?	5	W	80	500	7.62	1,250	Afg, Alb, Bg, RC, C, Kaz, Gui, Moz, RF, Sdn, Z
Slvk	GAZ-39344 SIAM	1994–	2 + 4	W	95	700	14.5	500	RF
	Aligator	1998?	6	W	120	600	7.62	n.k.	n.k.
Sp	VEC	1978–?	3 + 2	W	103	800	25	170	Sp

Analyses *and* Tables

	Designation	In-service date	Crew	W/T	Max. road speed (km/h)	Max. range (km)	Armament (mm)	Ammo	In service with
Tu	*Akrep*	1994–	3	W	125	650	2 × 7.62	3,200	Tu
UK/Aus	Shorland S52	1988–	3	W	120	630	7.62	1,600	Arg, Brn, Btwa, Bu, Cy, Guy, Kya, Ls, LAR, Mal, RMM, Por, Syr, Th, UAE, UK
UK	*Fox*	1972–?	3	W	104	434	30	99	Mlw, Nga
	Ferret	1952–71	2 or 3	W	93	306	7.62	2,500	Brn, BF, Crn, CAR, Ind, Indo, HKJ, Kya, RL, Mdg, Mlw, Mal, My, N, Por, RSA, Ska, Sdn
	Hornet	1986–95	3	W	120	350	7.62	n.k.	n.k.
	Scimitar	1974–	3	T	80	644	30	165	Be, Hr, UK
	Sabre	1993–	3	T	80	644	30	165	UK
US	M-113 *Lynx*	1966–?	3	T	68	523	12.7	1,155	Ca
	M-113 C/-R	1966–?	3	T	68	523	12.7	1,155	Nl
	Cadillac Gage *Scout*	1983–	2 or 3	W	88	846	2 × 7.62	2,600	Et, Indo
	XM-1114 HMMWV	1994	4	W	125	443	12.7	n.k.	Lu, Q, US
	M-8	1943–45?	4	W	90	560	37	80	Bn, BF Crn, Gua, Mdg, Mex, Py, Pe, Sen, Tg, Ve
	M-20	1943–45?	6	W	90	560	12.7	1,000	Bn, BF, Pe, Sen, Tg
	M-3A1	1938	8	W	90	402	12.7	750	Mdg, Pe
	LAV-150	1984–	5	W	88	643	20	400	Btwa, Crn, DR, Q
	Staghound	1942–43	5	W	n.k.	n.k.	37	103	RL
	MAC-1	1963	4	W	104	480	20	n.k.	Mex

Notes

[1] The table shows only the original producer of each type of vehicle. Other licensed producer countries are not listed.

[2] In service date indicates the period during which equipment was brought into service. Where dates cannot be firmly established, '?' is used. Where equipment remains in production, an open date is given, i.e. 1979–

[3] W/T = Wheeled/Tracked

[4] Maximum speed and range assumes travel by road

[5] Maximum range does not include the fitting of long-range, additional, external or supplementary fuel tanks

[6] Ammo = Ammunition. Where available, figures are given for the maximum number of main armament rounds

[7] In service with – an index of country abbreviations can be found at pp. 320.

[8] n.k. = not known

Table 53 **Ballistic and cruise missiles**

Ballistic missiles

A ballistic missile is designed to deliver a warhead following a ballistic trajectory when the rocket engine thrust ends and does not rely on aerodynamic surfaces to produce lift. Payload data should be treated with care: a ballistic missile with a range of 200km carrying a 800kg payload could be modified to carry 500kg over 300km, or 200kg over 500km. Entries are grouped by country or countries of origin.

Name/ Designation	aka	Static/ Mobile (St/Mo)	Warhead design [1]	Range (km)	CEP [2] (m)	Countries operating • Remarks
ICBM *Range over 5,000km*: **MIRV**						
Fr						
M-45		SLBM	6	6,000	500	Fr •
RF						
SS-18 Mod 2	*Satan*	St	8	9,250	430	RF •
SS-18 Mod 4	*Satan*	St	10	16,000	430	RF •
SS-19	*Stiletto*	St	6	9,000	350	RF, Ukr •
SS-24	*Scalpel*	St/Mo	10	10,000	185	RF, Ukr •
SS-N-18	*Stingray*	SLBM	7	6,500	900	RF •
SS-N-20	*Sturgeon*	SLBM	10	8,300	500	RF •
SS-N-23	*Skiff*	SLBM	4	8,300	500	RF •
US						
LGM-30G	*Minuteman* III	St	3	13,000	120	US •
LGM-118	*Peacekeeper*	St	10	9,600	90	US •
C4	*Trident*	SLBM	8	7,400	450	US •
D5	*Trident*	SLBM	8	12,000	90	US, UK •
ICBM *Range over 5,000km*: **Single warhead**						
PRC						
CSS-4	DF-5	St	3,200kg	13,000	500	PRC •
CSS-NX-5	JL-2	SLBM	n.k.	8,000	n.k.	Development •
CSS-X-9	DF-31	Mo	700kg	8,000	n.k.	Development • To replace CSS-3
CSS-X-10	DF-41	Mo	800kg	12,000	n.k.	Development • To replace CSS-4
RF						
SS-18 Mod 1	*Satan*	St	n.k.	10,500	430	RF •
SS-18 Mod 3	*Satan*	St	n.k.	16,000	430	RF •
SS-25	*Sickle*	Mo	n.k.	10,500	350	RF •
SS-27	*Topol*-M	St/Mo	n.k.	10,500	350	RF •
SS-N-8	*Sawfly*	SLBM	n.k.	9,100	900	RF •
IRBM *Range 500–5,000km*: **MIRV**						
Fr						
M-4		SLBM	6	4,000	500	Fr •

Name/ Designation	aka	Static/ Mobile (St/Mo)	Warhead Design [1]	Range (km)	CEP [2] (m)	Countries operating • Remarks
IRBM *Range 500–5,000km*: **Single warhead**						
Ind						
Agni I		St	1,000kg	1,500	40	Ind • Prototype
Agni II		St	1,000kg	2,500	40	Development •
Ir						
Shahab		Mo	750kg	1,500	4,000	Development • Based on *No-dong*
Irq						
Al Hussein		Mo	500kg	600	1,000	Status unknown •
Il						
Jericho 1		Mo	1,000kg	500	1,000	Il •
Jericho 2		Mo	1,000kg	1,500	n.k.	Il •
DPRK						
No-dong 1		Mo	770kg	1,300	3,000	Status unknown • Based on *Scud-B*
No-dong 2		Mo	770kg	1,500	3,000	Status unknown •
Scud-C Variant		Mo	770kg	550	1,000	DPRK •
Taepo-dong 1		St	1,000kg	2,000	n.k.	Status unknown •
Taepo-dong 2		St	1,000kg	3,500	n.k.	Status unknown •
RF						
Scud-C		Mo	600kg	550	700	Ir, DPRK, RF, Syr •
Pak						
Hatf 3		Mo	500kg	600	n.k.	Development •
Shaheen	*Hatf* 4	Mo	n.k.	750	n.k.	Development •
Ghauri 1	*Hatf* 5	Mo	700kg	1,500	n.k.	Development • Based on *No-dong*
Ghauri II	*Hatf* 6	St	700kg	2,300	n.k.	Development •
PRC						
CSS-2	DF-3	Mo	2,150kg	2,800	1,000	PRC, Sau •
CSS-3	DF-4	St	2,200kg	4,750	1,500	PRC •
CSS-N-3	JL-1	SLBM	600kg	2,150	700	PRC •
CSS-5	DF-21	Mo	600kg	2,150	700	PRC •
CSS-6	DF-15/M-9	Mo	500kg	600	300	PRC •
SRBM *Range up to 500km*: **Single warhead**						
Arg						
Alacran		Mo	400kg	150	n.k.	Status unknown •
Et						
Project T	*Scud*	Mo	985kg	450	n.k.	Et • Improved *Scud*
Ind						
Prithvi SS-150		Mo	800kg	150	300	Ind •
Prithvi SS-250		Mo	500kg	250	400	Ind •
Prithvi SS-350		Mo	n.k.	350	n.k.	Development •
Pak						
Hatf 1		Mo	500kg	80	n.k.	Pak •
Hatf 2		Mo	500kg	300	n.k.	Pak •
PRC						
CSS-7	DF-11/M-11	Mo	800kg	280	600	
CSS-8		Mo	190kg	150	n.k.	Ir •

Name/ Designation	aka	Static/ Mobile (St/Mo)	Warhead Design [1]	Range (km)	CEP [2] (m)	Countries operating • Remarks
RF						
Frog-7		Mo	450kg	65	700	Afg, Bel, Et, LAR, DPRK, Pl, R, RF, Slvk, Syr, Ukr, Ye, FRY •
SS-1	*Scud*	Mo	950kg	180	3,000	Afg, Bel, Irq, Slvk, Ukr •
SS-1	*Scud*-B	Mo	985kg	300	450	Et, Ir, LAR, RF, Syr, Ye •
SS-21	*Scarab*	Mo	482kg	120	95	RF, Slvk, Syr, Ukr, Ye •
SS-23	*Spider*	Mo	450kg	500	30	Slvk •
SS-X-26		Mo	415kg	250	10	Development • Export-*Scud* replacement
ROK						
NHK-1/2		Mo	500kg	250	n.k.	ROK •
ROC						
Ching Feng		Mo	270kg	130	n.k.	ROC • Based on *Lance*
Tien Chi		Mo	500kg	300	n.k.	Development •
US						
MGM-52	*Lance*	Mo	n.k.	130	150	Il •
MGM-140	ATACMS, Block 1	Mo	560kg	165	n.k.	Gr, Tu, US •
MGM-140	ATACMS, Block 1A	Mo	160kg	300	n.k.	US •
MGM-140	ATACMS, Block 2	Mo	268kg	140	n.k.	US •

Notes

[1] The table shows designed warhead. Where there are multiple warheads, only the number of warheads are shown. Single design warhead weight is shown (kg) where known.

[2] As a measure of accuracy, Circular Error Probable (CEP) is the radius of a circle within which half of the warheads, from a given number of launched missiles, are expected to fall.

Cruise missiles

Cruise missiles are unmanned aerodynamic vehicles designed to deliver a warhead over a minimum range of 200km. They have their own propulsion systems operating throughout their flight and fly at approximately constant velocity. They have integral flight control and navigation systems. Entries are grouped by country or countries of origin.

Name/ Designation	aka	Platform	Warhead	Average warhead weight (kg)	Range (km)	Remarks
Fr						
APACHE	SCALP-EG	Air	HE	560	250	Development
ASMP		Air	Nuc	200	350	Development
Fr/UK						
APACHE	*Storm Shadow*	Air	HE	560	250	Development
Fr/Ge						
ANNG		Ship/Air	HE	n.k.	350	Development

Analyses and Tables

Name/ Designation	aka	Platform	Warhead	Average warhead weight (kg)	Range (km)	Remarks
Ge/Swe						
KEPD-350	*Taurus*	Air	HE	500	350	Development
Ind						
Lakshya		Land	HE	450	600	Development
Il						
Delilah-2		Land	HE	54	400	Development with PRC
Gabriel 4LR		Ship/Land/Air	HE	240	200	In service Il
It						
Teseo MK 3	*Ulisee*	Ship/Land	HE	160	250	Development
PRC						
CSSC-8, Upgrade	YJ-2/C-802	Ship/Land/Air	HE	165	600	In service PRC
RF						
AS-4	*Kitchen*	Air	Nuc/HE	1,000	400	In service RF
AS-6	*Kingfish*	Air	Nuc/HE	1,000	400	Possibly still in service
AS-15A	*Kent*	Air	Nuc	n.k.	2,400	In service RF
AS-15B	*Kent*	Air	Nuc	n.k.	3,000	In service RF, Ukr
AS-17	*Krypton*	Air	HE	90	200	In service RF, PRC
ASM-MS	*Alfa*	Ship/Land/Air	HE	300	300	Development
Kh-41	*Moskit*	Air	HE	320	250	Development
Kh-101		Air	HE	400	3,000	Development
SS-N-3B/C	*Shaddock/Sepal*	Land/Ship/SSN	Nuc/HE	1,000	300	In service RF
SS-N-12	*Sandbox*	Ship/SSN	Nuc/HE	1,000	550	In service RF
SS-N-19	*Shipwreck*	Ship/SSN	Nuc/HE	750	550	In service RF
SS-N-21	*Sampson*	SSN	Nuc/HE	410	2,400	In service RF
SS-N-25	SSC-6 *Stooge*	Land	HE	145	250	In service RF, Ind
3M51	*Biryuza*	Land/SSN	HE	200	200	Development
US						
AGM-84H	SLAM-ER	Air	HE	227	280	Development
AGM-86B	ALCM	Air	Nuc	450	2,500	Not deployed
AGM-86C	ALCM	Air	HE	450	650	In service US
RGM/UGM-109A	*Tomahawk* TLAM-N	Ship/SSN	Nuc	n.k.	2,500	Not deployed
RGM/UGM-109B	*Tomahawk* TASM	Ship/SSN	HE	454	450	In service US
UGM-109C	*Tomahawk* TLAM-C, Block 2	SSN	HE	454	900	Not deployed
RGM-109C	*Tomahawk* TLAM-C, Block 2	Ship	HE	454	1,300	Not deployed
UGM-109C	*Tomahawk* TLAM-C, Block 3	SSN	HE	318	1,150	In service US, UK
RGM-109C	*Tomahawk* TLAM-C, Block 3	Ship	HE	318	1,700	In service US
UGM-109D	*Tomahawk* TLAM-D	SSN	HE	n.k.	900	In service US
RGM-109D	*Tomahawk* TLAM-D	Ship	HE	n.k.	1,300	In service US
AGM-129	ACM	Air	Nuc	n.k.	3,000	In service US
AGM-158	JASSM	Air	HE	410	500	Development

Table 54 **Designations of aircraft and helicopters**

Notes

1 [Square brackets] indicate the type from which a variant was derived: 'Q-5 ... [MiG-19]' indicates that the design of the Q-5 was based on that of the MiG-19.

2 (Parentheses) indicate an alternative name by which an aircraft is known, sometimes in another version: 'L-188 ... *Electra* (P-3 *Orion*)' shows that in another version the Lockheed Type 188 *Electra* is known as the P-3 *Orion*.

3 Names given in 'quotation marks' are NATO reporting names, e.g., 'Su-27... "*Flanker*"'.

4 When no information is listed under 'Country of origin' or 'Maker', the primary reference given under 'Name/designation' should be looked up under 'Type'.

5 For country abbreviations, see 'Index of Countries and Territories' (pp. 319–20).

Type	Name/designation	Country of origin•Maker

Aircraft

Type	Name/designation	Country of origin•Maker
A-1	AMX	Br/It•AMX
A-1B	AMX	Br/It•AMX
A-3	*Skywarrior*	US•Douglas
A-4	*Skyhawk*	US•MD
A-5	*Fantan*	PRC•Nanchang
A-7	*Corsair* II	US•LTV
A-10	*Thunderbolt*	US•Fairchild
A-36	*Halcón* (C-101)	
A-37	*Dragonfly*	US•Cessna
A-50	'*Mainstay*' (Il-76)	RF•Beriev
A300		UK/Fr/Ge/Sp•Airbus Int
A310		UK/Fr/Ge/Sp•Airbus Int
A340		UK/Fr/Ge/Sp•Airbus Int
AC-47	(C-47)	
AC-130	(C-130)	
Air Beetle		Nga•AIEP
Airtourer		NZ•Victa
AJ-37	(J-37)	
Alizé		Fr•Breguet
Alpha Jet		Fr/Ge•Dassault–Breguet/Dornier
An-2	'*Colt*'	Ukr•Antonov
An-12	'*Cub*'	Ukr•Antonov
An-14	'*Clod*'	Ukr•Antonov
An-22	'*Cock*'	Ukr•Antonov
An-24	'*Coke*'	Ukr•Antonov
An-26	'*Curl*'	Ukr•Antonov
An-28	'*Cash*'	Ukr•Antonov
An-30	'*Clank*'	Ukr•Antonov
An-32	'*Cline*'	Ukr•Antonov
An-72	'*Coaler*'	Ukr•Antonov
An-74	'*Coaler-B*'	Ukr•Antonov
An-124	'*Condor*'	Ukr•Antonov
Andover	[HS-748]	
Arava		Il•IAI
AS-202	*Bravo*	CH•FFA
AT-3		ROC•AIDC
AT-6	(T-6)	
AT-11		US•Beech
AT-26	EMB-326	
AT-33	(T-33)	
Atlantic	(*Atlantique*)	Fr•Dassault–Breguet
AU-23	*Peacemaker* [PC-6B]	US•Fairchild
AV-8	*Harrier* II	US/UK•MD/BAe
Aztec	PA-23	US•Piper
B-1	*Lancer*	US•Rockwell
B-2	*Spirit*	US•Northrop Grumman
B-52	*Stratofortress*	US•Boeing
B-65	*Queen Air*	US•Beech
BAC-167	*Strikemaster*	UK•BAe

Type	Name/designation	Country of origin•Maker
BAe-125		UK•BAe
BAe-146		UK•BAe
BAe-748	(HS-748)	UK•BAe
Baron	(T-42)	
Be-6	'*Madge*'	RF•Beriev
Be-12	'*Mail*' (*Tchaika*)	RF•Beriev
Beech 50	*Twin Bonanza*	US•Beech
Beech 95	*Travel Air*	US•Beech
BN-2	*Islander, Defender, Trislander*	UK•Britten-Norman
Boeing 707		US•Boeing
Boeing 727		US•Boeing
Boeing 737		US•Boeing
Boeing 747		US•Boeing
Boeing 757		US•Boeing
Boeing 767		US•Boeing
Bonanza		US•Beech
Bronco	(OV-10)	
Bulldog		UK•BAe
C-1		J•Kawasaki
C-2	*Greyhound*	US•Grumman
C-5	*Galaxy*	US•Lockheed
C-7	DHC-7	
C-9	*Nightingale* (DC-9)	
C-12	*Super King Air* (*Huron*)	US•Beech
C-17	*Globemaster* III	US•McDonnell Douglas
C-18	[Boeing 707]	
C-20	(*Gulfstream* III)	
C-21	(*Learjet*)	
C-22	(Boeing 727)	
C-23	(*Sherpa*)	UK•Short
C-26	*Expediter/Merlin*	US•Fairchild
C-32		US•Boeing
C-37A		US•Gulfstream
C-38A	(*Astra*)	Il•IAI
C-42	(Neiva *Regente*)	Br•Embraer
C-46	*Commando*	US•Curtis
C-47	DC-3 (*Dakota*) (C-117 *Skytrain*)	US•Douglas
C-54	*Skymaster* (DC-4)	US•Douglas
C-91	HS-748	
C-93	HS-125	
C-95	EMB-110	
C-97	EMB-121	
C-101	*Aviojet*	Sp•CASA
C-115	DHC-5	Ca•De Havilland
C-117	(C-47)	
C-118	*Liftmaster* (DC-6)	
C-123	*Provider*	US•Fairchild
C-127	(Do-27)	Sp•CASA
C-130	*Hercules* (L-100)	US•Lockheed

Type	Name/designation	Country of origin•Maker
C-131	Convair 440	US•Convair
C-135	[Boeing 707]	
C-137	[Boeing 707]	
C-140	(Jetstar)	US•Lockheed
C-141	Starlifter	US•Lockheed
C-160		Fr/Ge•Transall
C-212	Aviocar	Sp•CASA
C-235		Sp•CASA
Canberra		UK•BAe
CAP-10		Fr•Mudry
CAP-20		Fr•Mudry
CAP-230		Fr•Mudry
Caravelle	SE-210	Fr•Aérospatiale
CC-115	DHC-5	
CC-117	(Falcon 20)	
CC-132	(DHC-7)	
CC-137	(Boeing 707)	
CC-138	(DHC-6)	
CC-144	CL-600/-601	Ca•Canadair
CF-5a		Ca•Canadair
CF-18	F/A-18	
Cheetah	[Mirage III]	RSA•Atlas
Cherokee	PA-28	US•Piper
Cheyenne	PA-31T [Navajo]	US•Piper
Chieftain	PA-31-350 [Navajo]	US•Piper
Ching-Kuo		ROC•AIDC
Citabria		US•Champion
Citation	(T-47)	US•Cessna
CJ-6	[Yak-18]	PRC•Nanchang
CL-215		Ca•Canadair
CL-415		Ca•Canadair
CL-600	Challenger	Ca•Canadair
CM-170	Magister [Tzukit]	Fr•Aérospatiale
CM-175	Zéphyr	Fr•Aérospatiale
CN-212		Sp/Indo•CASA/IPTN
CN-235		Sp/Indo•CASA/IPTN
Cochise	T-42	
Comanche	PA-24	US•Piper
Commander	Aero-/TurboCommander	US•Rockwell
Commodore	MS-893	Fr•Aérospatiale
CP-3	P-3 Orion	
CP-140	Aurora (P-3 Orion)	US•Lockheed
	Acturas	
CT-4	Airtrainer	NZ•Victa
CT-114	CL-41 Tutor	Ca•Canadair
CT-133	Silver Star [T-33]	Ca•Canadair
CT-134	Musketeer	
Dagger	(Nesher)	
Dakota		US•Piper
Dakota	(C-47)	
DC-3	(C-47)	US•Douglas
DC-4	(C-54)	US•Douglas
DC-6	(C-118)	US•Douglas
DC-7		US•Douglas
DC-8		US•Douglas
DC-9		US•MD
Deepak	(HPT-32)	
Defender	BN-2	
DHC-3	Otter	Ca•DHC
DHC-4	Caribou	Ca•DHC
DHC-5	Buffalo	Ca•DHC
DHC-6	Twin Otter, CC-138	Ca•DHC
DHC-7	Dash-7 (Ranger, CC-132)	Ca•DHC
DHC-8		Ca•DHC
Dimona	H-36	Ge•Hoffman
Do-27	(C-127)	Ge•Dornier
Do-28	Skyservant	Ge•Dornier
Do-128		Ge•Dornier
Do-228		Ge•Dornier
E-2	Hawkeye	US•Grumman
E-3	Sentry	US•Boeing
E-4	[Boeing 747]	US•Boeing
E-6	[Boeing 707]	
E-26	T-35A (Tamiz)	Chl•Enear
EA-3	[A-3]	
EA-6	Prowler [A-6]	
EC-130	[C-130]	
EC-135	[Boeing 707]	
EF-11	Raven	US•General Dynamic
Electra	(L-188)	
EMB-110	Bandeirante	
EMB-111	Maritime Bandeirante	Br•Embraer
EMB-120	Brasilia	Br•Embraer
EMB-121	Xingu	Br•Embraer
EMB-201	Ipanema	Br•Embraer
EMB-312	Tucano	Br•Embraer
EMB-326	Xavante (MB-326)	Br•Embraer
EMB-810	[Seneca]	Br•Embraer
EP-3	(P-3 Orion)	
Etendard/Super Etendard		Fr•Dassault
EV-1	(OV-1)	
F-1	[T-2]	J•Mitsubishi
F-4	Phantom	US•MD
F-5	-A/-B Freedom Fighter	
	-E/-F Tiger II	US•Northrop
F-5T	JJ-5	PRC•Shenyang
F-6	J-6	
F-7	J-7	
F-8	J-8	
F-14	Tomcat	US•Grumman
F-15	Eagle	US•MD
F-16	Fighting Falcon	US•GD
F-18	[F/A-18], Hornet	
F-21	Kfir	Il•IAI
F-27	Friendship	Nl•Fokker
F-28	Fellowship	Nl•Fokker
F-35	Draken	Swe•SAAB
F-104	Starfighter	US•Lockheed
F-111	EF-111	US•GD
F-117	Nighthawk	US•Lockheed
F-172	(Cessna 172)	Fr/US•Reims-Cessna
F/A-18	Hornet	US•MD
Falcon	Mystère-Falcon	
FB-111	(F-111)	
FH-227	(F-27)	US•Fairchild-Hiller
Firefly	(T-67M)	UK•Slingsby
Flamingo	MBB-233	Ge•MBB
FT-5	JJ-5	PRC•CAC
FT-6	JJ-6	
FT-7	JJ-7	
FTB-337	[Cessna 337]	
G-91		It•Aeritalia
G-115E	Tutor	Ge•Grob
G-222		It•Aeritalia
Galaxy	C-5	
Galeb		FRY•SOKO
Genet	SF-260W	
GU-25	(Falcon 20)	

Type	Name/ designation	Country of origin•Maker
Guerrier	R-235	
Gulfstream		US•Gulfstream Aviation
Gumhuria	(Bücker 181)	Et•Heliopolis
H-5	[Il-28]	PRC•Harbin
H-6	[Tu-16]	PRC•Xian
H-36	Dimona	
Halcón	[C-101]	
Harrier	(AV-8)	UK•BAe
Hawk		UK•BAe
HC-130	(C-130)	
HF-24	Marut	Ind•HAL
HFB-320	Hansajet	Ge•Hamburger FB
HJ-5	(H-5)	
HJT-16	Kiran	Ind•HAL
HPT-32	Deepak	Ind•HAL
HS-125	(Dominie)	UK•BAe
HS-748	[Andover]	UK•BAe
HT-2		Ind•HAL
HU-16	Albatross	US•Grumman
HU-25	(Falcon 20)	
Hunter		UK•BAe
HZ-5	(H-5)	
IA-50	Guaraní	Arg•FMA
IA-58	Pucará	Arg•FMA
IA-63	Pampa	Arg•FMA
IAI-201/-202	Arava	Il•IAI
IAI-1124	Westwind, Seascan	Il•IAI
IAI-1125	Astra	Il•IAI
Iak-52	(Yak-52)	R•Aerostar
IAR-28		R•IAR
IAR-93	Orao	FRY/R•SOKO/IAR
Il-14	'Crate'	RF•Ilyushin
Il-18	'Coot'	RF•Ilyushin
Il-20	(Il-18)	
Il-22	(Il-18)	
Il-28	'Beagle'	RF•Ilyushin
Il-38	'May'	RF•Ilyushin
Il-62	'Classic'	RF•Ilyushin
Il-76	'Candid' (tpt), 'Mainstay' (AEW)	RF•Ilyushin
Il-78	'Midas' (tkr)	RF•Ilyushin
Il-82	'Candid'	RF•Ilyushin
Il-87	'Maxdome'	RF•Ilyushin
Impala	[MB-326]	RSA•Atlas
Islander	BN-2	
J-2	[MiG-15]	PRC•
J-5	[MiG-17F]	PRC•Shenyang
J-6	[MiG-19]	PRC•Shenyang
J-7	[MiG-21]	PRC•Xian
J-8	[Sov Ye-142]	PRC•Shenyang
J-11	[Su-27]	PRC•Shenyang
J-32	Lansen	Swe•SAAB
J-35	Draken	Swe•SAAB
J-37	Viggen	Swe•SAAB
JA-37	(J-37)	
Jaguar		Fr/UK•SEPECAT
JAS-39	Gripen	Swe•SAAB
Jastreb		FRY•SOKO
Jetstream		UK•BAe
JJ-6	(J-6)	
JZ-6	(J-6)	
K-8		PRC/Pak•NAMC/PAC
KA-3	[A-3]	
KA-6	[A-6]	
KC-10	Extender [DC-10]	US•MD

Type	Name/ designation	Country of origin•Maker
KC-130	[C-130]	
KC-135	[Boeing 707]	
KE-3A	[Boeing 707]	
Kfir		Il•IAI
King Air		US•Beech
Kiran	HJT-16	
Kraguj		FRY•SOKO
Kudu	C-4M	
L-4	Cub	
L-18	Super Cub	US•Piper
L-19	O-1	
L-21	Super Cub	US•Piper
L-29	Delfin	Cz•Aero
L-39	Albatros	Cz•Aero
L-59	Albatros	Cz•Aero
L-70	Vinka	SF•Valmet
L-100	C-130 (civil version)	
L-188	Electra (P-3 Orion)	US•Lockheed
L-410	Turbolet	Cz•LET
L-1011	Tristar	US•Lockheed
Learjet	(C-21)	US•Gates
LR-1	(MU-2)	J•Mitsubishi
M-28	Skytruck	Pl•MIELEC
Magister	CM-170	
Marut	HF-24	
Mashshaq	MFI-17	Pak/Swe•PAC/SAAB
Matador	(AV-8)	
MB-326		It•Aermacchi
MB-339	(Veltro)	It•Aermacchi
MBB-233	Flamingo	
MC-130	(C-130)	
Mercurius	(HS-125)	
Merlin		US•Fairchild
Mescalero	T-41	
Metro		US•Fairchild
MFI-17	Supporter (T-17)	Swe•SAAB
MiG-15	'Midget' trg	RF•MiG
MiG-17	'Fresco'	RF•MiG
MiG-19	'Farmer'	RF•MiG
MiG-21	'Fishbed'	RF•MiG
MiG-23	'Flogger'	RF•MiG
MiG-25	'Foxbat'	RF•MiG
MiG-27	'Flogger D'	RF•MiG
MiG-29	'Fulcrum'	RF•MiG
MiG-31	'Foxhound'	RF•MiG
Mirage		Fr•Dassault
Missionmaster	N-22	
Mohawk	OV-1	
MS-760	Paris	Fr•Aérospatiale
MS-893	Commodore	
MU-2	LR-1	J•Mitsubishi
Musketeer	Beech 24	US•Beech
Mystère-Falcon		Fr•Dassault
N-22	Floatmaster, Missionmaster	Aus•GAF
N-24	Searchmaster B/L	Aus•GAF
N-262	Frégate	Fr•Aérospatiale
N-2501	Noratlas	Fr•Aérospatiale
Navajo	PA-31	US•Piper
NC-212	C-212	Sp/Indo•CASA/Nurtanio
NC-235	C-235	Sp/Indo•CASA/Nurtanio
Nesher	[Mirage III]	Il•IAI
NF-5	(F-5)	
Nightingale	(DC-9)	
Nimrod		UK•BAe

Type	Name/designation	Country of origin•Maker
Nomad		Aus•GAF
O-1	*Bird Dog*	US•Cessna
O-2	(Cessna 337 *Skymaster*)	US•Cessna
OA-4	(A-4)	
OA-37	*Dragonfly*	
Orao	IAR-93	
Ouragan		Fr•Dassault
OV-1	*Mohawk*	US•Rockwell
OV-10	*Bronco*	US•Rockwell
P-3	*Orion*	US•Lockheed
P-92		It•Teenam
P-95	EMB-110	
P-166		It•Piaggio
P-180	*Avanti*	It•Piaggio
PA-18	*Super Cub*	US•Piper
PA-23	*Aztec*	US•Piper
PA-28	*Cherokee*	US•Piper
PA-31	*Navajo*	US•Piper
PA-32	*Cherokee Six*	US•Piper
PA-34	*Seneca*	US•Piper
PA-36	*Pawnee Brave*	US•Piper
PA-38	*Tomahawk*	US•Piper
PA-42	*Cheyenne III*	US•Piper
PBY-5	*Catalina*	US•Consolidated
PC-6	*Porter*	CH•Pilatus
PC-6A/B	*Turbo Porter*	CH•Pilatus
PC-7	*Turbo Trainer*	CH•Pilatus
PC-9		CH•Pilatus
PC-12		CH•Pilatus
PD-808		It•Piaggio
Pillán	T-35	
PL-1	*Chien Shou*	ROC•AIDC
PLZ M-28	[An-28]	Pl•PZL
Porter	PC-6	
PS-5	[SH-5]	PRC•HAMC
PT-6	[CJ-6]	PRC•Nanchang
PZL M-28	M-28 [An-28]	Pl•PZL
PZL-104	*Wilga*	Pl•PZL
PZL-130	*Orlik*	Pl•PZL
Q-5	*'Fantan'* [MiG-19]	PRC•Nanchang
Queen Air	(U-8)	
R-160		Fr•Socata
R-235	*Guerrier*	Fr•Socata
RC-21	(C-21, *Learjet*)	
RC-47	(C-47)	
RC-95	(EMB-110)	
RC-135	[Boeing 707]	
RF-4	(F-4)	
RF-5	(F-5)	
RF-35	(F-35)	
RF-104	(F-104)	
RG-8A		US•Schweizer
RT-26	(EMB-326)	
RT-33	(T-33)	
RU-21	(*King Air*)	
RV-1	(OV-1)	
S-2	*Tracker*	US•Grumman
S-208		It•SIAI
S-211		It•SIAI
SA 2-37A		US•Schweizer
Sabreliner	(CT-39)	US•Rockwell
Safari	MFI-15	
Safir	SAAB-91 (SK-50)	Swe•SAAB
SC-7	*Skyvan*	UK•Short

Type	Name/designation	Country of origin•Maker
SE-210	*Caravelle*	
Sea Harrier	(*Harrier*)	
Seascan	IAI-1124	
Searchmaster	N-24 B/L	
Seneca	PA-34 (EMB-810)	US•Piper
Sentry	(O-2)	US•Summit
SF-37	(J-37)	
SF-260	(SF-260W *Warrior*)	It•SIAI
SH-37	(J-37)	
Sherpa	Short 330, C-23	UK•Short
Short 330	(*Sherpa*)	UK•Short
Sierra 200	(*Musketeer*)	
SK-35	(J-35)	Swe•SAAB
SK-37	(J-37)	
SK-60	(SAAB-105)	Swe•SAAB
SK-61	(*Bulldog*)	
Skyvan		UK•Short
SM-90		RF•Technoavia
SM-1019		It•SIAI
SP-2H	*Neptune*	US•Lockheed
SR-71	*Blackbird*	US•Lockheed
Su-7	*'Fitter A'*	RF•Sukhoi
Su-15	*'Flagon'*	RF•Sukhoi
Su-17/-20/-22	*'Fitter'*	RF•Sukhoi
Su-24	*'Fencer'*	RF•Sukhoi
Su-25	*'Frogfoot'*	RF•Sukhoi
Su-27	*'Flanker'*	RF•Sukhoi
Su-29		RF•Sukhoi
Su-30		RF•Sukhoi
Su-33		RF•Sukhoi
Su-34		RF•Sukhoi
Su-39		RF•Sukhoi
Super		Fr•Dassault
Shrike Aerocommander		US•Rockwell
Super Galeb		FRY•SOKO
T-1		J•Fuji
T-1A	*Jayhawk*	US•Beech
T-2	*Buckeye*	US•Rockwell
T-2		J•Mitsubishi
T-3		J•Fuji
T-17	(*Supporter*, MFI-17)	Swe•SAAB
T-23	*Uirapurú*	Br•Aerotec
T-25	*Neiva Universal*	Br•Embraer
T-26	EMB-326	
T-27	*Tucano*	Br•Embraer
T-28	*Trojan*	US•North American
T-33	*Shooting Star*	US•Lockheed
T-34	*Mentor*	US•Beech
T-35	*Pillán* [PA-28]	Chl•Enaer
T-36	(C-101)	
T-37	(A-37)	
T-38	*Talon*	US•Northrop
T-39	(*Sabreliner*)	US•Rockwell
T-41	*Mescalero* (Cessna 172)	US•Cessna
T-42	*Cochise* (*Baron*)	US•Beech
T-43	(Boeing 737)	
T-44	(*King Air*)	
T-47	(*Citation*)	
T-67M	(*Firefly*)	UK • Slingsby
T-400	(T-1A)	US•Beech
TB-20	*Trinidad*	Fr•Aérospatiale
TB-21	*Trinidad*	Fr•Socata
TB-30	*Epsilon*	Fr•Aérospatiale
TB-200	*Tobago*	Fr•Socata

Type	Name/ designation	Country of origin•Maker
TBM-700		Fr•Socata
TC-45	(C-45, trg)	
TCH-1		ROC•AIDC
Texan	T-6	
TL-1	(KM-2)	J•Fuji
Tornado		UK/Ge/It•Panavia
TR-1	[U-2]	US•Lockheed
Travel Air	Beech 95	
Trident		UK•BAe
Trislander	BN-2	
Tristar	L-1011	
TS-8	*Bies*	Pl•PZL
TS-11	*Iskra*	Pl•PZL
Tu-16	'Badger'	RF•Tupolev
Tu-22	'Blinder'	RF•Tupolev
Tu-26	'Backfire', (Tu-22M)	RF•Tupolev
Tu-95	'Bear'	RF•Tupolev
Tu-126	'Moss'	RF•Tupolev
Tu-134	'Crusty'	RF•Tupolev
Tu-142	'Bear F'	RF•Tupolev
Tu-154	'Careless'	RF•Tupolev
Tu-160	'Blackjack'	RF•Tupolev
Turbo Porter	PC-6A/B	
Twin Bonanza	Beech 50	
Twin Otter	DHC-6	
Tzukit	[CM-170]	Il•IAI
U-2		US•Lockheed
U-3	(Cessna 310)	US•Cessna
U-4	*Gulfstream* IV	US•Gulfstream Aviation
U-7	(L-18)	
U-8	(*Twin Bonanza/Queen Air*)	US•Beech
U-9	(EMB-121)	
U-10	*Super Courier*	US•Helio
U-17	(Cessna 180, 185)	US•Cessna
U-21	(*King Air*)	
U-36	(*Learjet*)	
U-42	(C-42)	
U-93	(HS-125)	
U-125	BAe 125-800	UK•BAe
U-206G	*Stationair*	US•Soloy
UC-12	(*King Air*)	
UP-2J	(P-2J)	
US-1		J•Shin Meiwa
US-2A	(S-2A, tpt)	
US-3	(S-3, tpt)	
UTVA-66		FRY•UTVA
UTVA-75		FRY•UTVA
UV-18	(DHC-6)	
V-400	*Fantrainer 400*	Ge•VFW
V-600	*Fantrainer 600*	Ge•VFW
Vampire	DH-100	
VC-4	*Gulfstream* I	
VC-10		UK•BAe
VC-11	*Gulfstream* II	
VC-91	(HS-748)	
VC-93	(HS-125)	
VC-97	(EMB-120)	
VC-130	(C-130)	
VFW-614		Ge•VFW
Vinka	L-70	
VU-9	(EMB-121)	
VU-93	(HS-125)	
WC-130	[C-130]	
WC-135	[Boeing 707]	US•Boeing

Type	Name/ designation	Country of origin•Maker
Westwind	IAI-1124	
Winjeel	CA-25	
Xavante	EMB-326	
Xingu	EMB-121	
Y-5	[An-2]	PRC•Hua Bei
Y-7	[An-24]	PRC•Xian
Y-8	[An-12]	PRC•Shaanxi
Y-12		PRC•Harbin
Yak-11	'Moose'	RF•Yakovlev
Yak-18	'Max'	RF•Yakovlev
Yak-28	'Firebar' ('Brewer')	RF•Yakovlev
Yak-38	'Forger'	RF•Yakovlev
Yak-40	'Codling'	RF•Yakovlev
Yak-42		RF•Yakovlev
Yak-55		RF•Yakovlev
YS-11		J•Nihon
Z-43		Cz•Zlin
Z-226		Cz•Zlin
Z-326		Cz•Zlin
Z-526		Cz•Zlin
Zéphyr	CM-175	

Helicopters

Type	Name/ designation	Country of origin•Maker
A-109	*Hirundo*	It•Agusta
A-129	*Mangusta*	It•Agusta
AB-...	(Bell 204/205/206/ 212/214, etc.)	It/US•Agusta/Bell
AH-1	*Cobra/Sea Cobra*	US•Bell
AH-2	*Rooivalk*	RSA•Denel
AH-6	(Hughes 500/530)	US•MD
AH-64	*Apache*	US•Hughes
Alouette II	SA-318, SE-3130	Fr•Aérospatiale
Alouette III	SA-316, SA-319	Fr•Aérospatiale
AS-61	(SH-3)	US/It•Sikorsky/Agusta
AS-332	*Super Puma*	Fr•Aérospatiale
AS-350	*Ecureuil*	Fr•Aérospatiale
AS-355	*Ecureuil* II	Fr•Aérospatiale
AS-365	*Dauphin*	Fr•Aérospatiale
AS-532	*Super Puma*	Fr•Aérospatiale
AS532 UL	*Cougar*	Fr•Eurocopter
AS-550	*Fennec*	Fr•Eurocopter
AS-565	*Panthar*	Fr•Eurocopter
ASH-3	(*Sea King*)	It/US•Agusta/Sikorsky
AUH-76	(S-76)	
Bell 47		US•Bell
Bell 205		US•Bell
Bell 206		US•Bell
Bell 212		US•Bell
Bell 214		US•Bell
Bell 222		US•Bell
Bell 406		US•Bell
Bell 412		US•Bell
Bo-105	(NBo-105)	Ge•MBB
CH-3	(SH-3)	
CH-34	*Choctaw*	US•Sikorsky
CH-46	*Sea Knight*	US•Boeing-Vertol
CH-47	*Chinook*	US•Boeing-Vertol
CH-53	*Stallion* (*Sea Stallion*)	US•Sikorsky
CH-54	*Tarhe*	US•Sikorsky
CH-113	(CH-46)	
CH-124	SH-3 (*Sea King*)	

Type	Name/designation	Country of origin•Maker
CH-139	Bell 206	
CH-146	Bell 412	Ca•Bell
CH-147	CH-47	
Cheetah	[SA-315]	Ind•HAL
Chetak	[SA-319]	Ind•HAL
Commando	(SH-3)	UK/US•Westland/Sikorsky
EH-60	(UH-60)	
EH-101		UK/It•Westland/Agusta
F-28F		US•Enstrom
FH-1100	(OH-5)	US•Fairchild-Hiller
Gazela	(SA-342)	Fr/FRY•Aérospatiale/SOKO
Gazelle	SA-341/-342	
H-34	(S-58)	
H-76	S-76	
HA-15	Bo-105	
HB-315	*Gavião* (SA-315)	Br/Fr•Helibras Aérospatiale
HB-350	*Esquilo* (AS-350)	Br/Fr•Helibras Aérospatiale
HD-16	SA-319	
HH-3	(SH-3)	
HH-34	(CH-34)	
HH-53	(CH-53)	
HH-65	(AS-365)	Fr•Eurocopter
Hkp-2	*Alouette* II/SE-3130	
Hkp-3	AB-204	
Hkp-4	KV-107	
Hkp-5	Hughes 300	
Hkp-6	AB-206	
Hkp-9	Bo-105	
Hkp-10	AS-332	
HR-12	OH-58	
HSS-1	(S-58)	
HSS-2	(SH-3)	
HT-17	CH-47	
HT-21	AS-332	
HU-1	(UH-1)	J/US•Fuji/Bell
HU-8	UH-1B	
HU-10	UH-1H	
HU-18	AB-212	
Hughes 300		US•MD
Hughes 500/520	*Defender*	US•MD
IAR-316/-330	(SA-316/-330)	R/Fr•IAR/Aérospatiale
Ka-25	'Hormone'	RF•Kamov
Ka-27	'Helix'	RF•Kamov
Ka-28	'Helix'	RF•Kamov
Ka-29	'Helix'	RF•Kamov
Ka-32	'Helix C'	RF•Kamov
Ka-50	*Hokum*	RF•Kamov
KH-4	(Bell 47)	J/US•Kawasaki/ Bell
KH-300	(Hughes 269)	J/US•Kawasaki/MD
KH-500	(Hughes 369)	J/US•Kawasaki/MD
Kiowa	OH-58	
KV-107	[CH-46]	J/US•Kawasaki/Vertol
Lynx		UK•Westland
MD-500/530	*Defender*	US•McDonnell Douglas
MH-6	(AH-6)	
MH-53	(CH-53)	
Mi-2	'Hoplite'	RF•Mil
Mi-4	'Hound'	RF•Mil
Mi-6	'Hook'	RF•Mil
Mi-8	'Hip'	RF•Mil
Mi-14	'Haze'	RF•Mil
Mi-17	'Hip'	RF•Mil
Mi-24	'Hind'	RF•Mil
Mi-25	'Hind'	RF•Mil
Mi-26	'Halo'	RF•Mil
Mi-28	'Havoc'	RF•Mil
NAS-332	AS-332	Indo/Fr•Nurtanio/Aérospatiale
NB-412	Bell 412	Indo/US•Nurtanio/Bell
NBo-105	Bo-105	Indo/Ge•Nurtanio/MBB
NH-300	(Hughes 300)	It/US•Nardi/MD
NSA-330	(SA-330)	Indo/Fr•Nurtanio/Aérospatiale
OH-6	*Cayuse* (Hughes 369)	US•MD
OH-13	(Bell 47G)	
OH-23	*Raven*	US•Hiller
OH-58	*Kiowa* (Bell 206)	
OH-58D	(Bell 406)	
Oryx	(SA-330)	
PAH-1	(Bo-105)	
Partizan	(*Gazela*, armed)	
PZL-W3	*Sokol*	Pl•Swidnik
RH-53	(CH-53)	
S-58	(*Wessex*)	US•Sikorsky
S-61	SH-3	
S-65	CH-53	
S-70	UH-60	US•Sikorsky
S-76		US•Sikorsky
S-80	CH-53	
SA-313	*Alouette* II	Fr•Aérospatiale
SA-315	*Lama* [*Alouette* II]	Fr•Aérospatiale
SA-316	*Alouette* III (SA-319)	Fr•Aérospatiale
SA-318	*Alouette* II (SE-3130)	Fr•Aérospatiale
SA-319	*Alouette* III (SA-316)	Fr•Aérospatiale
SA-321	*Super Frelon*	Fr•Aérospatiale
SA-330	*Puma*	Fr•Aérospatiale
SA-341/-342	*Gazelle*	Fr•Aérospatiale
SA-360	*Dauphin*	Fr•Aérospatiale
SA-365/-366	*Dauphin* II (SA-360)	
Scout	(*Wasp*)	UK•Westland
SE-316	(SA-316)	
SE-3130	(SA-318)	
Sea King	[SH-3]	UK•Westland
SH-2	*Sea Sprite*	US•Kaman
SH-3	(*Sea King*)	US•Sikorsky
SH-34	(S-58)	
SH-57	Bell 206	
SH-60	*Sea Hawk* (UH-60)	
Sioux	(Bell 47)	UK•Westland
TH-50	*Esquilo* (AS-550)	
TH-55	Hughes 269	
TH-57	*Sea Ranger* (Bell 206)	
TH-67	*Creek* (Bell 206B-3)	Ca•Bell
UH-1	*Iroquois* (Bell 204/205/212)	
UH-12	(OH-23)	US•Hiller
UH-13	(Bell 47J)	
UH-19	(S-55)	
UH-34T	(S-58T)	
UH-46	(CH-46)	
UH-60	*Black Hawk* (SH-60)	US•Sikorsky
VH-4	(Bell 206)	
VH-60	(S-70)	
Wasp	(*Scout*)	UK•Westland
Wessex	(S-58)	US/UK•Sikorsky/Westland
Z-5	[Mi-4]	PRC•Harbin
Z-6	[Z-5]	PRC•Harbin
Z-8	[SA-321]	PRC•Changhe
Z-9	[SA-365]	PRC•Harbin

Afghanistan Afg 159
Albania Alb 78
Algeria Ag 128
Angola Ang 252
Antigua and Barbuda AB 219
Argentina Arg 219
Armenia Arm 79
Australia Aus 183
Austria A 80
Azerbaijan Az 81

Bahamas Bs 221
Bahrain Brn 129
Bangladesh Bng 160
Barbados Bds 221
Belarus Bel 82
Belgium Be 48
Belize Bze 222
Benin Bn 253
Bolivia Bol 222
Bosnia-Herzegovina BiH 83
Botswana Btwa 253
Brazil Br 223
Brunei Bru 184
Bulgaria Bg 84
Burkina Faso BF 254
Burundi Bu 254

Cambodia Cam 185
Cameroon Crn 255
Canada Ca 49
Cape Verde CV 255
Central African Republic CAR 256
Chad Cha 256
Chile Chl 225
China, People's Republic of
  PRC 186
Colombia Co 226
Congo RC 257
Congo, Democratic Republic of
  DROC 258
Costa Rica CR 228
Côte d'Ivoire CI 258
Croatia Cr 85
Cuba C 228
Cyprus Cy 86
Czech Republic Cz 50

Denmark Da 51
Djibouti Dj 259
Dominican Republic DR 229

Ecuador Ec 230
Egypt Et 130
El Salvador ElS 231
Equatorial Guinea EG 260
Eritrea Er 260
Estonia Ea 87
Ethiopia Eth 261

Fiji Fji 189
Finland SF 88
France Fr 52

Gabon Gbn 262
Gambia, The Gam 262

Georgia Ga 90
Germany Ge 56
Ghana Gha 263
Greece Gr 58
Guatemala Gua 232
Guinea Gui 263
Guinea-Bissau GuB 264
Guyana Guy 233

Haiti RH 233
Honduras Hr 234
Hungary Hu 60

Iceland Icl 61
India Ind 161
Indonesia Indo 189
Iran Ir 132
Iraq Irq 133
Ireland Irl 90
Israel Il 135
Italy It 61

Jamaica Ja 234
Japan J 191
Jordan HKJ 136

Kazakstan Kaz 164
Kenya Kya 265
Korea, Democratic People's
  Republic of (North) DPRK ... 193
Korea, Republic of (South) ROK .. 195
Kuwait Kwt 137
Kyrgyzstan Kgz 164

Laos Lao 196
Latvia Lat 91
Lebanon RL 138
Lesotho Ls 265
Liberia Lb 266
Libya LAR 139
Lithuania L 92
Luxembourg Lu 64

Macedonia, Former Yugoslav
  Republic of FYROM 93
Madagascar Mdg 266
Malawi Mlw 267
Malaysia Mal 197
Mali RMM 267
Malta M 93
Mauritania RIM 140
Mauritius Ms 268
Mexico Mex 235
Moldova Mol 94
Mongolia Mgl 199
Morocco Mor 141
Mozambique Moz 268
Myanmar (Burma) My 199

Namibia Nba 269
Nepal N 165
Netherlands Nl 64
New Zealand NZ 200
Nicaragua Nic 236
Niger Ngr 269
Nigeria Nga 270

Norway No 66

Oman O 142

Pakistan Pak 166
Palestinian Autonomous Areas
  of Gaza and Jericho GzJ 144
Panama Pan 237
Papua New Guinea PNG 201
Paraguay Py 237
Peru Pe 238
Philippines Pi 202
Poland Pl 67
Portugal Por 69

Qatar Q 144

Romania R 94
Russia RF 112
Rwanda Rwa 271

Saudi Arabia Sau 145
Senegal Sen 271
Seychelles Sey 272
Sierra Leone SL 273
Singapore Sgp 203
Slovakia Slvk 96
Slovenia Slvn 97
Somali Republic SR 273
South Africa RSA 274
Spain Sp 70
Sri Lanka Ska 167
Sudan Sdn 275
Suriname Sme 240
Sweden Swe 97
Switzerland CH 99
Syria Syr 147

Taiwan (Republic of China)
  ROC 205
Tajikistan Tjk 168
Tanzania Tz 276
Thailand Th 206
Togo Tg 277
Trinidad and Tobago TT 240
Tunisia Tn 148
Turkey Tu 73
Turkmenistan Tkm 169

Uganda Uga 277
Ukraine Ukr 100
United Arab Emirates UAE 149
United Kingdom UK 75
United States US 20
Uruguay Ury 241
Uzbekistan Uz 169

Venezuela Ve 242
Vietnam Vn 208

Yemen, Republic of Ye 150
Yugoslavia, Federal Republic of
  (Serbia–Montenegro) FRY 102

Zambia Z 278
Zimbabwe Zw 279

Index of **Country Abbreviations**

A .... Austria
AB .... Antigua and Barbuda
Afg .... Afghanistan
Ag .... Algeria
Alb .... Albania
Ang .... Angola
Arg .... Argentina
Arm .... Armenia
Aus .... Australia
Az .... Azerbaijan

Bds .... Barbados
Be .... Belgium
Bel .... Belarus
BF .... Burkina Faso
Bg .... Bulgaria
BiH .... Bosnia-Herzegovina
Bn .... Benin
Bng .... Bangladesh
Bol .... Bolivia
Br .... Brazil
Brn .... Bahrain
Bru .... Brunei
Bs .... Bahamas
Btwa .... Botswana
Bu .... Burundi
Bze .... Belize

C .... Cuba
Ca .... Canada
Cam .... Cambodia
CAR .... Central African Republic
CH .... Switzerland
Cha .... Chad
Chl .... Chile
CI .... Côte d'Ivoire
Co .... Colombia
Cr .... Croatia
CR .... Costa Rica
Crn .... Cameroon
CV .... Cape Verde
Cy .... Cyprus
Cz .... Czech Republic

Da .... Denmark
Dj .... Djibouti
DPRK .... Korea, Democratic People's Republic of (North)
DR .... Dominican Republic
DROC .... Democratic Republic of Congo

Ea .... Estonia
Ec .... Ecuador
EG .... Equatorial Guinea
ElS .... El Salvador
Er .... Eritrea
Et .... Egypt
Eth .... Ethiopia

Fji .... Fiji
Fr .... France
FRY .... Federal Republic of Yugoslavia (Serbia–Montenegro)

FYROM .... Former Yugoslav Republic of Macedonia

Ga .... Georgia
Gam .... Gambia, The
Gbn .... Gabon
Ge .... Germany
Gha .... Ghana
Gr .... Greece
Gua .... Guatemala
GuB .... Guinea-Bissau
Gui .... Guinea
Guy .... Guyana
GzJ .... Palestinian Autonomous Areas of Gaza and Jericho

HKJ .... Jordan
Hr .... Honduras
Hu .... Hungary

Icl .... Iceland
Il .... Israel
Ind .... India
Indo .... Indonesia
Ir .... Iran
Irl .... Ireland
Irq .... Iraq
It .... Italy

J .... Japan
Ja .... Jamaica

Kaz .... Kazakstan
Kgz .... Kyrgyzstan
Kwt .... Kuwait
Kya .... Kenya

L .... Lithuania
Lao .... Laos
LAR .... Libya
Lat .... Latvia
Lb .... Liberia
Ls .... Lesotho
Lu .... Luxembourg

M .... Malta
Mal .... Malaysia
Mdg .... Madagascar
Mex .... Mexico
Mgl .... Mongolia
Mlw .... Malawi
Mol .... Moldova
Mor .... Morocco
Moz .... Mozambique
Ms .... Mauritius
My .... Myanmar (Burma)

N .... Nepal
Nba .... Namibia
Nga .... Nigeria
Ngr .... Niger
Nic .... Nicaragua
Nl .... Netherlands
No .... Norway
NZ .... New Zealand

O .... Oman

Pak .... Pakistan
Pan .... Panama
Pe .... Peru
Pi .... Philippines
Pl .... Poland
PNG .... Papua New Guinea
Por .... Portugal
PRC .... China, People's Republic of
Py .... Paraguay

Q .... Qatar

R .... Romania
RC .... Congo
RF .... Russia
RH .... Haiti
RIM .... Mauritania
RL .... Lebanon
RMM .... Mali
ROC .... Taiwan
ROK .... Korea, Republic of (South)
RSA .... South Africa
Rwa .... Rwanda

Sau .... Saudi Arabia
Sdn .... Sudan
Sen .... Senegal
Sey .... Seychelles
SF .... Finland
Sgp .... Singapore
Ska .... Sri Lanka
SL .... Sierra Leone
Slvk .... Slovakia
Slvn .... Slovenia
Sme .... Suriname
Sp .... Spain
SR .... Somali Republic
Swe .... Sweden
Syr .... Syria

Tg .... Togo
Th .... Thailand
Tjk .... Tajikistan
Tkm .... Turkmenistan
Tn .... Tunisia
TT .... Trinidad and Tobago
Tu .... Turkey
Tz .... Tanzania

UAE .... United Arab Emirates
Uga .... Uganda
UK .... United Kingdom
Ukr .... Ukraine
Ury .... Uruguay
US .... United States
Uz .... Uzbekistan

Ve .... Venezuela
Vn .... Vietnam

Ye .... Yemen, Republic of

Z .... Zambia
Zw .... Zimbabwe